City, County, Town and Township Index to the 1850 Federal Census Schedules

GALE GENEALOGY AND LOCAL HISTORY SERIES

Series Editor: J. Carlyle Parker, Head of Public Services and Assistant Library Director, California State College, Stanislaus; and Founder and Librarian Volunteer, Modesto California Branch Genealogical Library of the Genealogical Department of the Church of Jesus Christ of Latter-day Saints, Salt Lake City, Utah

General Editor: Paul Wasserman, Professor and former Dean, School of Library and Information Services, University of Maryland

Managing Editor: Denise Allard Adzigian, Gale Research Company

City, County, Town and Township Index to the 1850 Federal Census Schedules

Volume 6 in the Gale Genealogy and Local History Series

J. Carlyle Parker

Head of Public Services and Assistant Library Director
California State College, Stanislaus
and
Founder and Librarian Volunteer
Modesto California Branch Genealogical Library of the
Genealogical Department of the Church of Jesus Christ of
Latter-day Saints
Salt Lake City, Utah

Gale Research Company
Book Tower, Detroit, Michigan 48226

0493414   105668

Library of Congress Cataloging in Publication Data

Parker, J   Carlyle.
    City, county, town, and township index to the
1850 Federal census schedules.

    (Gale genealogy and local history series ; v. 6)
    1. United States—Genealogy—Indexes.   2. Cities
and towns—United States—Indexes.   3. United States
—Census, 1850—Indexes.   I. United States. Census
Office. 7th census, 1850. II. Title.
CS65.P37   929'.373   79-11644
ISBN 0-8103-1385-5

To

Janet

VITA

J. Carlyle Parker is head of public services and assistant library director at California State College, Stanislaus. He also founded and is the volunteer librarian of the Modesto California Branch Genealogical Library of the Genealogical Department of the Church of Jesus Christ of Latter-day Saints, Salt Lake City. He holds a B.A. in history from Brigham Young University and an M.L.S. from the University of California, Berkeley.

Parker has authored numerous articles and reviews for library and genealogical journals, and compiled and edited several bibliographies, indexes, and union catalogs. He also has conducted oral history interviews and is an instructor and lecturer on genealogical, historical, and oral history research.

CONTENTS

INTRODUCTION

For years many genealogists have been harassed by the lack of an index to the cities, towns, and townships of the 1850 U.S. federal population census schedules. The first problem that the lack of an index presents is the necessity of turning to road maps, atlases, gazetters, or place name literature to determine the county in which a town or city is located. This research step is essential, as all U.S. census schedules are arranged by county.

The second problem is that the schedules of many counties are to be found on more than one reel of microfilm. In most of these cases, it is necessary to consult more than one reel of microfilm to locate the desired town. The third problem is that communities and townships are not arranged in alphabetical order within county schedules.

Besides solving these three basic problems, this index also supplies the user with the National Archives microfilm order numbers and the microfilm call numbers used by the Genealogical Department Library of the Church of Jesus Christ of Latter-day Saints in Salt Lake City, Utah. These two numbers are important to researchers, as the most readily available sources for the use of the census schedules on microfilm are the National Archives, with its eleven branches throughout the United States which loan the schedules via the interlibrary loan services of any libraries, and the Genealogical Department which loans schedules for a small user fee for use in its over 273 branch libraries. When ordering on interlibrary loan any of the microfilms listed in this index from one of the branches of the National Archives, the microfilm publication number M432 must also be included. A call to any Church of Jesus Christ of Latter-day Saints, listed in the white pages or in the yellow pages under "Churches," should assist genealogists to determine the location of the nearest branch library of the genealogical department. The page numbers that relate to entries for each city, county, town, and township are also provided.

The pagination of the census schedules is confusing at best. Some of the schedules have been paged several times. For this index the latest handwritten pagination has been used. In most cases the older pagination, both printed and handwritten, has been crossed out. In addition, the microfilm copies of the schedules do not adhere to the organization of the bound schedules. There-fore, the pages of a city, county, town, or township taken from the last part of one bound schedule and continuing in the first part of another may appear on the same reel of microfilm and paged in two consecutive orders, the first being larger than the second, e.g., Ashland Co., OH, 761-1020, 1-332. There are also some towns with occasional pages that are completely out of sequence. Pagination for townships and counties include all of the communi-ties within their boundaries. Township pagination is also included in county pagination.

Besides cities, counties, towns, and townships, the index also includes boroughs, named census beats, districts, divisions, named election districts, grants, hun-dreds, parishes, plantations, named precincts, settlements, and villages. Most directional townships, e.g., east, north, south, and west, and all numerical census beats, census districts, election districts, precincts, and townships were not indexed. The names of post offices were not included in the 1850 census schedules and are, therefore, not included in this index.

The slave schedules have been excluded from this index because they include only the names of owners and the numbers of slaves. Also, none of the slave schedules include counties on more than one reel of microfilm.

The index is arranged in one alphabetical order. Mc and Mac are interfiled as Mac. St. and Ste. are filed as if spelled out. There are no cross refer-ences, but there are some double entries that serve the same purpose.

The National Archives created a manuscript index to their bound volumes of the 1850 census schedules: United States, National Archives, GEOGRAPHI-CAL SUBDIVISIONS IN THE FEDERAL POPULATION CENSUS SCHEDULES OF 1830, 1850, AND 1860, Washington, D.C., National Archives and Records Ser-vice, General Services Administration, 1963. This index is inadequate for use with the microfilm copies of the schedules. Nevertheless, it was used to prepare the working cards for the index of the microfilm. As the preparation of the microfilm index progressed, it was found that many communities had not been included in the bound volumes' index and that many place names had been misspelled.

Several gazetteers, volumes of place name literature, and an atlas were con-sulted in an attempt to verify the place names used in the census schedules. Spelling errors have been corrected when identified. There are undoubtedly numerous spelling errors that remain. The principle sources consulted are as follows:

Adams, James N., comp. "A List of Illinois Place Names." ILLINOIS LIBRARIES 50 (1968): 275-596. F539.A3 917.73'003 72-650037

Andriot, John L., comp. and ed. TOWNSHIP ATLAS OF THE UNITED STATES: NAMED TOWNSHIPS. McLean, Va.: Andriot Associates, 1977. G1201.F7A5 1977 912'73 76-151923

Blois, John T. GAZETTEER OF THE STATE OF MICHIGAN. Detroit: S.L. Rood, 1839. F564.B651 917.74'003 24-18627 897,469 Item 2 (Genealogical Department microfilm number)

Chamberlain, E., comp. THE INDIANA GAZETTEER, OR TOPOGRAPHI-CAL DICTIONARY OF THE STATE OF INDIANA. 3d ed. Indianapolis: E. Chamberlain, 1849. F524.C442 917.72'003 Rc-1620 873,978 Item 1

Charlton, Edwin Azro, comp. NEW HAMPSHIRE AS IT IS, IN THREE PARTS. . . . Claremont, N.H.: Tracy and Sanford, 1855. F34.C48 917.42 1-7939 823,666 Item 3

COLUMBIA LIPPINCOTT GAZETTEER OF THE WORLD. . . . Morning-side Heights, N.Y.: Columbia University Press, by arrangement with J.B. Lippincott Co., 1952. G103.L7 1952 910.3 52-9199

Espenshade, Abraham Howry. PENNSYLVANIA PLACE NAMES. The Pennsylvania State College Studies in History and Political Science, No. 1. State College: Pennsylvania State College, 1925. Reprint ed., Detroit: Gale Research, 1969. F147.E75 1969 917.48'003 68-30591

Fisher, Richard Swainson. GAZETTEER OF THE STATE OF MARYLAND. New York: J.H. Colton, 1852. F179.F6 917.52'003 Rc-3389 896,649

Gannett, Henry. A GAZETTEER OF TEXAS. 2d ed. U.S. Geological Survey, Bulletin No. 224, Series F, Geography, 36. Washington, D.C.: Government Printing Office, 1904. F384.Q20 917.64'003 4-19124 896,651 Item 2

Gudde, Erwin Gustav. CALIFORNIA PLACE NAMES; THE ORIGIN AND ETYMOLOGY OF CURRENT GEOGRAPHICAL NAMES. 3d ed. Rev. and enl. Berkeley: University of California Press, 1969. F859.G79 1969 917.94'003 68-26528

Gudde, Erwin Gustav, and Gudde, Elisabeth K., eds. CALIFORNIA GOLD CAMPS: A GEOGRAPHICAL AND HISTORICAL DICTIONARY OF CAMPS, TOWNS, AND LOCALITIES WHERE GOLD WAS FOUND AND MINED, WAYSIDE STATIONS AND TRADING CENTERS. Berkeley: University of California Press, 1975. F865.G82 1975 917.94'003 73-85788

Historical Records Survey, Arkansas. LIST OF POST OFFICES IN AR-KANSAS AS SHOWN BY EARLY NEWSPAPER FILES, 1817-1874. Pre-pared by Works Projects Administration, Project No. 5261-3. Arkansas History Commission, 1940. 830,165

Hunt, John Warren. WISCONSIN GAZETTEER. . . . Madison: B. Brown Printer, 1853. F579.H9 917.75'003 Rc-1727 897,468 Item 2

Kilbourn, John. THE OHIO GAZETTEER. . . . 8th ed. Columbus: J. Kilbourn, 1826. F489.K52 917.71'003 Rc-2121 Revised 476,928 Item 2

LIPPINCOTT'S NEW GAZETTEER; A COMPLETE PRONOUNCING GA-ZETTEER OR GEOGRAPHICAL DICTIONARY OF THE WORLD. Phila-delphia: J.B. Lippincott Co., 1913. G103.L7 1913 910.3

Nason, Elias. A GAZETTEER OF THE STATE OF MASSACHUSETTS. . . . Boston: B.B. Russell, 1874. F62.N26 917.44'003 1-12005 547,258 Item 1

Pearce, Thomas Matthews, Cassidy, Ina Sizer, and Pearce, Helen S., eds. NEW MEXICO PLACE NAMES; A GEOGRAPHICAL DICTIONARY. Albuquerque: University of New Mexico Press, 1965. F794.P4 917.89'003 64-17808

Rand McNally and Company. COMMERCIAL ATLAS & MARKETING GUIDE. 107th ed. New York: Rand McNally and Co., 1976. G1019.R22 912 Map 6-9

One problem that has not been resolved by this index is the difficulty of locating people in cities with wards. The easiest solution to this problem is to consult one of many census schedule indexes. Some of these indexes index all persons; others index only the heads of households and residents of households with surnames different from that of the head. Most of these indexes identify the ward and page of the names indexed. The majority of the census schedule indexes do not identify the National Archives or the Genealogical Department Library microfilm call numbers and require the use of this index to cities, counties, towns, and townships.

An alternative solution to finding people in cities is to consult a city directory for the name and address of persons of interest. After the address has been determined, then it is necessary to consult a ward atlas or map to determine in which ward a street address is located. City directories are listed and their locations are identified in Dorothea N. Spear's BIBLIOGRAPHY OF AMERICAN DIRECTORIES THROUGH 1860, Worcester, Mass., American Antiquarian Society, 1968. Most libraries will check a single directory for a single name. Nearly all of the directories listed in this bibliography are also available on microfiche and may be purchased from Research Publications Incorporated, Woodbridge, Connecticut. Some large public libraries and research libraries have purchased the entire microfiche collection and a few of them will lend them on interlibrary loan. Many cities with ward subdivisions in 1850 are included in E. Kay Kirkham's A HANDY GUIDE TO RECORD-SEARCHING IN THE LARGER CITIES OF THE UNITED STATES, INCLUDING A GUIDE TO THEIR VITAL RECORDS AND SOME MAPS WITH STREET INDEXES WITH OTHER INFORMATION OF VALUE, Logan, Utah, Everton Publishers, 1974. Additional ward maps are identified in WARD MAPS OF UNITED STATES CITIES; A SELECTIVE CHECKLIST OF PRE-1900 MAPS IN THE LIBRARY OF CONGRESS, a publication of the U.S. Library of Congress, Geography and Map Division, Washington, D.C., Government Printing Office, 1975. Reproductions of the maps in this list are also available for purchase from the photoduplication service of the Library of Congress.

A special thanks is due to the California State Library, Sutro Branch in San Francisco; the Genealogical Department of the Church of Jesus Christ of Latter-day Saints in Salt Lake City, Utah; The Oakland Genealogical Library; the Sacramento Genealogical Library; Jane Johnson, the interlibrary loan library assistant at California State College, Stanislaus; and the archivists and assistants of the San Bruno Federal Archives and Records Center for providing access to the 1,009 reels of microfilm that it was necessary to consult.

The majority of the microfilms consulted were borrowed by patrons of the Modesto California Stake Branch Genealogical Library from the Genealogical Department. Gratitude is extended to them for sharing their microfilms and for expressing their needs that led to the idea of preparing this index.

Dr. Theodore M. Burton, managing director, was gracious in permitting the call numbers of the Genealogical Department to be included in the index. Without the assistance of my spouse, Janet, and children, Denise, Nathan, and Bret, who periodically assisted as we visited other libraries, the index would still be in preparation. Janet also provided proofreading and helpful assistance throughout the entire three and one-half year project.

LIST OF ABBREVIATIONS

ACAD.	Academy
AL	Alabama
AM.	American
AR	Arkansas
BOR.	Borough
CA	California
CHAR.	Charleston
CO.	County
CORP.	Corporation
CT	Connecticut
DC	District of Columbia
DE	Delaware
DIST.	District
DIV.	Division
E.	East
EL.	Election
FL	Florida
GA	Georgia
GD	Genealogical Department
GT.	Grant
HUN.	Hundred
IA	Iowa
IL	Illinois
IN	Indiana

List of Abbreviations

KY	Kentucky
LA	Louisiana
LOU.	Louis
LOW.	Lower
MA	Massachusetts
MD	Maryland
ME	Maine
MI	Michigan
MID.	Middle
MISC.	Miscellaneous
MN	Minnesota
MO	Missouri
MS	Mississippi
MT.	Mount and Mountain
N.	North
NA	National Archives
NC	North Carolina
NH	New Hampshire
NJ	New Jersey
NM	New Mexico
NO.	Number
NY	New York
OH	Ohio
OR	Oregon
PA	Pennsylvania
PAR.	Parish
PHI.	Philadelphia
PHILA.	Philadelphia
PLANT.	Plantation
P.O.	Post Office
PREC.	Precinct
RD.	Road
REG.	Regiment
RI	Rhode Island

RUTHER.	Rutherford
SC	South Carolina
SET.	Settlement
SO.	South
ST.	Saint and Street
STE.	Saint
TN	Tennessee
TUR.	Turnpike
TWP.	Township
TX	Texas
UNINCORP.	Unincorporated
UP.	Upper
UT	Utah
VA	Virginia
VT	Vermont
W.	Ward and West
WI	Wisconsin

CITY, COUNTY, TOWN AND TOWNSHIP INDEX
TO THE 1850 FEDERAL CENSUS SCHEDULES

CITY, COUNTY, TOWN, OR TOWNSHIP	COUNTY	STATE	NA NO. M432	GD NO.	PAGES
ABBEVILLE CO.		SC	848	022,528	1-411
ABBOT	PISCATAQUIS	ME	267	443,504	453-70
ABBOTT	SHEBOYGAN	WI	1006	444,993	195-200
ABERDEEN	BROWN	OH	662	020,210	175-92
ABINGDON	WASHINGTON	VA	980	444,970	416-31
ABINGTON	KNOX	IL	113	007,686	765-66
ABINGTON	PLYMOUTH	MA	332	443,551	347-472
ABINGTON	LUZERNE	PA	794	444,762	185-253
ABINGTON TWP.	WAYNE	IN	180	442,958	409-434
ABINGTON TWP.	MONTGOMERY	PA	800	444,768	253-96
ABOITE TWP.	ALLEN	IN	135	007,748	491-503
ABRAHAM'S PLAINS DIST.	GRANVILLE	NC	631	444,644	399-412
ACCOMACK CO.		VA	932	029,707	1-311
ACCOMACK PARISH	ACCOMACK	VA	932	029,707	1-153
ACQUACKANONCK	PASSAIC	NJ	461	443,660	665-738
ACTON	YORK	ME	275	443,512	1-33
ACTON	MIDDLESEX	MA	323	443,542	259-97
ACUMA	VALENCIA	NM	470	443,668	494-503
ACWORTH	SULLIVAN	NH	441	443,645	433-62
ADA	KENT	MI	353	443,569	530-44
ADAIR CO.		KY	190	007,843	1-100
ADAIR CO.		MO	391	014,871	1-56
ADAMS	LA SALLE	IL	115	007,688	719-32
ADAMS	BERKSHIRE	MA	305	014,699	27-173
ADAMS	JEFFERSON	NY	516	017,092	493-569
ADAMS	GREEN	WI	999	444,986	589-95
ADAMS CO.		IL	97	007,670	1-655
ADAMS CO.		IN	135	007,748	1-157
ADAMS CO.		MS	368	014,847	1-104
ADAMS CO.		OH	657	020,205	1-465
ADAMS CO.		PA	743	020,593	1-652
ADAMS CO.		WI	994	034,508	1-8
ADAMS, JOHN Q. TWP.	WARREN	IN	178	442,956	111-24
ADAMS TWP.	ALLEN	IN	135	007,748	465-89
ADAMS TWP.	CARROLL	IN	137	007,750	677-92
ADAMS TWP.	CASS	IN	137	007,750	858-68
ADAMS TWP.	DECATUR	IN	142	007,755	207-244
ADAMS TWP.	HAMILTON	IN	148	442,926	287-310
ADAMS TWP.	MADISON	IN	158	442,936	269-300
ADAMS TWP.	MORGAN	IN	162	442,940	315-48
ADAMS TWP.	PARKE	IN	164	442,942	337-57
ADAMS TWP.	RIPLEY	IN	169	442,947	529-65
ADAMS TWP.	HILLSDALE	MI	351	443,567	915-42
ADAMS TWP.	CHAMPAIGN	OH	665	020,213	797-825
ADAMS TWP.	CLINTON	OH	668	020,216	377-400
ADAMS TWP.	COSHOCTON	OH	670	020,218	603-636
ADAMS TWP.	DARKE	OH	674	020,222	671-704
ADAMS TWP.	DEFIANCE	OH	674	020,222	62-72
ADAMS TWP.	GUERNSEY	OH	684	444,677	759-79
ADAMS TWP.	MONROE	OH	712	444,705	771-99
ADAMS TWP.	MUSKINGUM	OH	718	444,711	621-44
ADAMS TWP.	SENECA	OH	728	444,721	224-56
ADAMS TWP.	WASHINGTON	OH	738	444,731	507-537
ADAMS VILLAGE	SAUK	WI	1006	444,993	25-36
ADAMSBURG BOR.	WESTMORELAND	PA	837	444,805	327-23
ADAMSVILLE	CASS	MI	349	014,811	509-510
ADDISON	DU PAGE	IL	105	007,678	161-80
ADDISON	WASHINGTON	ME	272	443,509	291-318
ADDISON	STEUBEN	NY	598	444,314	383-471

Addison

CITY, COUNTY, TOWN, OR TOWNSHIP	COUNTY	STATE	NA NO. M432	GD NO.	PAGES
ALEXANDRIA	RAPIDES PAR.	LA	239	443,482	195-204
ALEXANDRIA	GRAFTON	NH	430	443,634	301-331
ALEXANDRIA	JEFFERSON	NY	515	017,091	1-76
ALEXANDRIA	LICKING	OH	702	444,695	333-38, 340
ALEXANDRIA	DE KALB	TN	876	444,832	1-6
ALEXANDRIA	ALEXANDRIA	VA	932	029,707	615-796
ALEXANDRIA BOR.	HUNTINGDON	PA	784	444,752	39-54
ALEXANDRIA CO.		VA	932	029,707	615-818
ALEXANDRIA TWP.	HUNTERDON	NJ	453	443,652	311-403
ALFORD	BERKSHIRE	MA	306	014,700	411-22
ALFRED	YORK	ME	276	443,513	377-408
ALFRED	ALLEGANY	NY	476	017,052	41-104
ALGANSEE TWP.	BRANCH	MI	347	014,809	753-67
ALGODONES	SANTA ANNA	NM	468	443,666	451-63
ALGOMA	KENT	MI	353	443,569	562-67
ALGOMA	WINNEBAGO	WI	1009	444,996	1042-58
ALGONQUIN	MC HENRY	IL	117	007,690	759-94
ALLAMAKEE CO.		IA	182	007,791	1-20
ALLEGAN	ALLEGAN	MI	346	014,808	43-60
ALLEGAN CO.		MI	346	014,808	1-126
ALLEGANY	POTTER	PA	825	444,793	252-63
ALLEGANY CO.		MD	277	013,194	1-528
ALLEGANY CO.		NY	475	017,051	1-400
ALLEGANY CO.		NY	476	017,052	401-736, 1-205
ALLEGHANY CO.		VA	933	029,708	1-68
ALLEGHENY CO.		PA	744	020,594	1-720
ALLEGHENY CO.		PA	745	020,595	1-518
ALLEGHENY CO.		PA	746	020,596	519-1126
ALLEGHENY CO.		PA	747	020,597	1-733
ALLEGHENY CO.		PA	748	020,598	1-687
ALLEGHENY TWP.	ARMSTRONG	PA	749	020,599	255-314
ALLEGHENY TWP.	BLAIR	PA	755	020,605	471-526
ALLEGHENY TWP.	CAMBRIA	PA	761	020,611	81-116
ALLEGHENY TWP.	SOMERSET	PA	828	444,796	289-311
ALLEGHENY TWP.	VENANGO	PA	832	444,800	395-422
ALLEGHENY TWP.	WESTMORELAND	PA	836	444,804	611-90
ALLEGHENY, WARD 1	ALLEGHENY	PA	744	020,594	1-106
ALLEGHENY, WARD 2	ALLEGHENY	PA	744	020,594	107-185
ALLEGHENY, WARD 3	ALLEGHENY	PA	744	020,594	187-340
ALLEGHENY, WARD 4	ALLEGHENY	PA	744	020,594	341-418
ALLEN	ALLEGANY	NY	476	017,052	445-67
ALLEN CO.		IN	135	007,748	158-581
ALLEN CO.		KY	190	007,843	201-378
ALLEN CO.		OH	657	020,205	467-759
ALLEN TWP.	NOBLE	IN	162	442,940	561-83
ALLEN TWP.	HILLSDALE	MI	351	443,567	809-833
ALLEN TWP.	GENTRY	MO	399	443,607	461-68, 485-88
ALLEN TWP.	DARKE	OH	674	020,222	539-46
ALLEN TWP.	HANCOCK	OH	692	444,685	1-24
ALLEN TWP.	UNION	OH	736	444,729	208-231
ALLEN TWP.	NORTHAMPTON	PA	803	444,771	595-622
ALLENDALE TWP.	OTTAWA	MI	361	443,577	125-28
ALLEN'S FRESH DIST.	CHARLES	MD	290	443,521	433-55, 536-52, 574-77
ALLENSTOWN	MERRIMACK	NH	435	443,639	391-403
ALLENTOWN BOR.	LEHIGH	PA	792	444,760	589-683
ALLIGATOR	COLUMBIA	FL	58	006,714	81-82
ALLISON TWP.	CLINTON	PA	768	444,736	125-34
ALMENA	VAN BUREN	MI	363	443,579	203-212

Almond

CITY, COUNTY, TOWN, OR TOWNSHIP	COUNTY	STATE	NA NO. M432	GD NO.	PAGES
ANDOVER	TOLLAND	CT	50	442,882	181, 739-46
ANDOVER	OXFORD	ME	262	443,499	383-99
ANDOVER	ESSEX	MA	314	014,708	641-806
ANDOVER	MERRIMACK	NH	436	443,640	369-98
ANDOVER	ALLEGANY	NY	475	017,051	229-60, 361-64
ANDOVER	ASHTABULA	OH	659	020,207	333-55
ANDOVER	WINDSOR	VT	931	444,930	471-88
ANDOVER NORTH SURPLUS	OXFORD	ME	262	443,499	401-2
ANDOVER TOWN	TOLLAND	CT	50	442,882	735-38
ANDREW	JACKSON	IA	184	007,793	672-75
ANDREW CO.		MO	391	014,871	57-264
ANDREWS DIST.	PITT	NC	641	444,654	141-55
ANGELICA	ALLEGANY	NY	476	017,052	401-440
ANGELINA CO.		TX	908	024,887	61-84
ANGOLA	STEUBEN	IN	173	442,951	302-7
ANN ARBOR	WASHTENAW	MI	364	443,580	355-470
ANNAPOLIS	ANNE ARUNDEL	MD	278	013,195	529-85
ANNE ARUNDEL CO.		MD	278	013,195	529-1043
ANNSBURG	WASHINGTON	ME	272	443,509	71-73
ANNSBURG PLANTATION	WASHINGTON	ME	272	443,509	74
ANNSVILLE	ONEIDA	NY	566	444,282	709-772
ANNUTTALIGA SET.	BENTON	FL	58	006,714	49-52
ANSON	SOMERSET	ME	269	443,506	333-53
ANSON CO.		NC	619	018,105	315-473
ANTHONY TWP.	LYCOMING	PA	795	444,763	363-86
ANTHONY TWP.	MONTOUR	PA	801	444,769	817-39
ANTIOCH	LAKE	IL	114	007,687	159-87
ANTIS TWP.	BLAIR	PA	755	020,605	411-69
ANTOINE TWP.	CLARK	AR	25	002,479	426-31
ANTOINE TWP.	PIKE	AR	29	002,483	374-75
ANTRIM	SHIAWASSEE	MI	363	443,579	160-66
ANTRIM	HILLSBORO	NH	434	443,638	137-64
ANTRIM	GUERNSEY	OH	684	444,677	781-86
ANTRIM TWP.	WYANDOT	OH	741	444,734	477-95
ANTRIM TWP.	FRANKLIN	PA	782	444,750	871-967
ANTWERP	VAN BUREN	MI	363	443,579	213-27
ANTWERP	JEFFERSON	NY	515	017,091	349-436
APOLACON TWP.	SUSQUEHANNA	PA	829	444,797	329-46
APOLLO BOR.	ARMSTRONG	PA	749	020,599	607-614
APPANOOSE	HANCOCK	IL	109	007,682	812-21
APPANOOSE CO.		IA	182	007,791	23-97
APPLETON	WALDO	ME	271	443,508	31-72
APPLING CO.		GA	61	007,057	1-63
APPOMATTOX CO.		VA	933	029,708	311-415
APPOQUINIMINK HUN.	NEW CASTLE	DE	54	006,438	423-96
AQUASCO DIST.	PRINCE GEORGES	MD	295	443,526	91-113
AQUAWKA	HENDERSON	IL	109	007,682	95-108
ARAMINGO BOR.	PHILADELPHIA	PA	823	444,791	1015-31
ARCADIA	WAYNE	NY	612	444,328	471-593
ARCADIA VILLAGE	WAYNE	NY	612	444,328	581-93
ARCHER TWP.	HARRISON	OH	693	444,686	925-46
ARENA	IOWA	WI	999	444,986	826-35
ARENZVILLE	CASS	IL	99	007,672	123, 125-26
ARGENTINE TWP.	GENESEE	MI	350	443,566	521-31
ARGYLE	PENOBSCOT	ME	266	443,503	503-511
ARGYLE	WASHINGTON	NY	610	444,326	267-344
ARGYLE	LAFAYETTE	WI	1001	444,988	899-909
ARIANA	GRUNDY	IL	108	007,681	345-48
ARIETTA	HAMILTON	NY	511	017,087	42-44

Arkadelphia

CITY, COUNTY, TOWN, OR TOWNSHIP	COUNTY	STATE	NA NO. M432	GD NO.	PAGES
ARKADELPHIA	CLARK	AR	25	002,479	454-57
ARKANSAS CO.		AR	25	002,479	1-48
ARKANSAS TWP.	ARKANSAS	AR	25	002,479	1-10
ARKWRIGHT	CHAUTAUQUA	NY	484	017,060	215-44
ARLINGTON	VAN BUREN	MI	363	443,579	229-34
ARLINGTON	BENNINGTON	VT	921	027,447	89-114
ARMADA	MACOMB	MI	357	443,573	25-52
ARMAGH BOR.	INDIANA	PA	785	444,753	253-56
ARMAGH TWP.	MIFFLIN	PA	797	444,765	337-80
ARMENIA TWP.	BRADFORD	PA	757	020,607	699-706
ARMICALOLA DIST.	LUMPKIN	GA	76	007,072	41-58
ARMSTRONG CO.		PA	749	020,599	1-725
ARMSTRONG TWP.	VANDERBURGH	IN	176	442,954	857-77
ARMSTRONG TWP.	INDIANA	PA	785	444,753	551-77
ARMSTRONG TWP.	LYCOMING	PA	795	444,763	399-409
AROOSTOOK CO.		ME	248	009,718	1-337
ARROWSIC	LINCOLN	ME	261	443,498	243-50
ASCENSION PARISH		LA	229	009,696	1-84
ASH TWP.	MONROE	MI	358	443,574	835-64
ASHBURNHAM	WORCESTER	MA	340	443,559	1-45
ASHBY	MIDDLESEX	MA	323	443,542	173-201
ASHBY	PIKE	MO	409	443,617	327-29
ASHBY DIST.	FAUQUIER	VA	943	444,933	397-531
ASHE CO.		NC	620	018,106	475-669
ASHEBORO	RANDOLPH	NC	641	444,654	165-67
ASHEVILLE	BUNCOMBE	NC	622	018,108	373-84
ASHFIELD	FRANKLIN	MA	316	443,535	361-94
ASHFORD	WINDHAM	CT	51	442,883	431-38, 443-50
ASHFORD	CATTARAUGUS	NY	480	017,056	705-712, 721-53
ASHFORD	FOND DU LAC	WI	997	444,984	821-36
ASHFORD TWP.	WINDHAM	CT	51	442,883	439-42, 451-62
ASHIPPUN	DODGE	WI	996	034,510	375-99
ASHLAND	MIDDLESEX	MA	326	443,545	963-94
ASHLAND	GREENE	NY	509	017,085	99-130
ASHLAND	ASHLAND	OH	658	020,206	845-875
ASHLAND		OH	658	020,206	761-1020, 1-332
ASHLAND CO.	SCHUYLER	IL	128	442,916	667-78
ASHLAND TWP.		AR	25	002,479	49-86
ASHLEY CO.	ASHTABULA	OH	659	020,207	377-409
ASHTABULA	ASHTABULA	OH	659	020,207	357-76
ASHTABULA BOR.		OH	659	020,207	333-1044
ASHTABULA CO.		LA	229	009,696	85-208
ASSUMPTION PARISH	BARRY	MI	346	014,808	249-56
ASSYRIA TWP.	DELAWARE	PA	776	444,744	75-112
ASTON TWP.	FULTON	IL	107	007,680	220-48
ASTORIA	BRADFORD	PA	757	020,607	605-624
ASYLUM	ST. MARTIN	LA	240	443,483	374-76
ATCHAFALAYA		MO	391	014,871	265-304
ATCHISON CO.	LIMESTONE	AL	8	002,350	188-201
ATHENS	SOMERSET	ME	269	443,506	1-35
ATHENS	CALHOUN	MI	348	014,810	229-41
ATHENS	GENTRY	MO	399	443,607	411-36, 469-76
ATHENS	GREENE	NY	509	017,085	197-270
ATHENS	ATHENS	OH	660	020,208	1-23
ATHENS	CRAWFORD	PA	771	444,739	793-815
ATHENS	WINDHAM	VT	929	444,928	43-51
ATHENS BEAT	DALLAS	AL	4	002,346	527-34, 561-62
ATHENS BOR.	BRADFORD	PA	756	020,606	577-94
ATHENS CO.		OH	660	020,208	1-446

CITY, COUNTY, TOWN, OR TOWNSHIP	COUNTY	STATE	NA NO. M432	GD NO.	PAGES
ATHENS DIST.	CLARKE	GA	65	007,061	1-48
ATHENS TWP.	ATHENS	OH	660	020,208	1-58
ATHENS TWP.	HARRISON	OH	693	444,686	431-57
ATHENS TWP.	BRADFORD	PA	756	020,606	595-646
ATHOL	WORCESTER	MA	340	443,559	465-513
ATHOL	WARREN	NY	609	444,325	380-416
ATKINSON	PISCATAQUIS	ME	267	443,504	597-619
ATKINSON	ROCKINGHAM	NH	438	443,642	189-203
ATLANTA DIST.	DE KALB	GA	67	007,063	398-452
ATLANTIC CO.		NJ	442	016,529	1-216
ATLANTIC TWP.	MONMOUTH	NJ	456	443,655	170-205
ATLAS TWP.	GENESEE	MI	350	443,566	589-617
ATTAKAYORT	ST. MARY PAR.	LA	240	443,483	417, 422
ATTALA CO.		MS	368	014,847	193-383
ATTEAN	SOMERSET	ME	269	443,506	548
ATTICA	LAPEER	MI	354	443,570	709-719
ATTICA	WYOMING	NY	616	444,332	249-305
ATTLEBORO	BRISTOL	MA	307	014,701	149-248
ATWATER TWP.	PORTAGE	OH	722	444,715	343-70
AUBBEENAUBBEE TWP.	FULTON	IN	146	442,924	929-38
AUBURN	SUTTER	CA	36	442,879	74-104
AUBURN	DE KALB	IN	142	007,755	411-17
AUBURN	CUMBERLAND	ME	250	009,720	1-68
AUBURN	WORCESTER	MA	341	443,560	717-37
AUBURN	ROCKINGHAM	NH	437	443,641	509-528
AUBURN	FOND DU LAC	WI	997	444,984	815-20
AUBURN PREC.	CLARK	IL	100	007,673	376-87
AUBURN, PRISON	CAYUGA	NY	482	017,058	630-46
AUBURN TWP.	CRAWFORD	OH	671	020,219	637-60
AUBURN TWP.	FAIRFIELD	OH	677	444,670	813-28
AUBURN TWP.	GEAUGA	OH	682	444,675	507-535
AUBURN TWP.	TUSCARAWAS	OH	734	444,727	35-66
AUBURN TWP.	SUSQUEHANNA	PA	829	444,797	89-124
AUBURN, WARD 1	CAYUGA	NY	482	017,058	419-71
AUBURN, WARD 2	CAYUGA	NY	482	017,058	472-519
AUBURN, WARD 3	CAYUGA	NY	482	017,058	520-74
AUBURN, WARD 4	CAYUGA	NY	482	017,058	575-629
AUDRAIN CO.		MO	391	014,871	305-377
AUGLAIZE CO.		OH	660	020,208	447-718
AUGLAIZE TWP.	ALLEN	OH	657	020,205	551-82
AUGLAIZE TWP.	PAULDING	OH	719	444,712	371-78
AUGUSTA	BRACKEN	KY	193	007,846	902-915
AUGUSTA	KENNEBEC	ME	256	443,493	1-208
AUGUSTA	WASHTENAW	MI	364	443,580	909-926
AUGUSTA	ONEIDA	NY	562	444,278	1-55
AUGUSTA CO.		VA	934	029,709	419-886
AUGUSTA TWP.	DES MOINES	IA	183	007,792	897-908
AUGUSTA TWP.	CARROLL	OH	664	020,212	263-89, 295-98
AURARIA DIST.	LUMPKIN	GA	76	007,072	61-80
AURELIUS	INGHAM	MI	351	443,567	131-42
AURELIUS	CAYUGA	NY	482	017,058	647-714
AURELIUS TWP.	WASHINGTON	OH	738	444,731	897-928
AURORA	KANE	IL	112	007,685	373-418
AURORA	HANCOCK	ME	255	443,492	862-67
AURORA	ERIE	NY	498	017,074	129-210
AURORA CENTRE TWP.	DEARBORN	IN	141	007,754	448-77
AURORA CITY	DEARBORN	IN	141	007,754	431-47
AURORA TWP.	PORTAGE	OH	722	444,715	85-104
AUSABLE	CLINTON	NY	489	017,065	383-489

CITY, COUNTY, TOWN, OR TOWNSHIP	COUNTY	STATE	NA NO. M432	GD NO.	PAGES
AUSTERLITZ	COLUMBIA	NY	492	017,068	205-251
AUSTIN	TRAVIS	TX	915	444,918	300-314
AUSTIN CO.		TX	908	024,887	87-141
AUSTINBURG TWP.	ASHTABULA	OH	659	020,207	781-811
AUSTINTOWN	MAHONING	OH	707	444,700	927-54
AUTAUGA CO.		AL	1	002,343	1-155
AUTAUGAVILLE	AUTAUGA	AL	1	002,343	8-10
AUX SABLE	GRUNDY	IL	108	007,681	316-24
AVA	ONEIDA	NY	565	444,281	235-60
AVERILL	ESSEX	VT	923	444,922	839
AVERYS GORE	CHITTENDEN	VT	923	444,922	427
AVERYS GORE	FRANKLIN	VT	924	444,923	467-68
AVOCA	STEUBEN	NY	600	444,316	241-79
AVON	HARTFORD	CT	39	003,067	523-46
AVON	LAKE	IL	114	007,687	303-327
AVON	FRANKLIN	ME	253	009,723	249-68
AVON	OAKLAND	MI	359	443,575	121-56
AVON	LIVINGSTON	NY	524	017,100	607-674
AVON	ROCK	WI	1005	444,992	749-62
AVON TWP.	LORAIN	OH	705	444,698	903-943
AVOYELLES PARISH		LA	229	009,696	209-308
AYR TWP.	FULTON	PA	783	444,751	71-96
AZTALAN	JEFFERSON	WI	1000	444,987	89-103
BABERSON CREEK	RUTHERFORD	NC	644	444,657	677
BACK CREEK DIST.	MECKLENBURG	NC	637	444,650	127-36
BACK RIVER DIST.	ELIZABETH	VA	942	444,932	113-20
BAD AX	CRAWFORD	WI	995	034,509	502-514, 516
BAD EGG	CRAWFORD	WI	995	034,509	515
BAD RIVER	LA POINTE	WI	1002	444,989	13
BAILEYVILLE	WASHINGTON	ME	273	443,510	377-87
BAINBRIDGE	CHENANGO	NY	488	017,064	839-918
BAINBRIDGE	ROSS	OH	725	444,718	742-56
BAINBRIDGE	LANCASTER	PA	787	444,755	617-28
BAINBRIDGE TWP.	SCHUYLER	IL	128	442,916	799-827
BAINBRIDGE TWP.	DUBOIS	IN	143	007,756	969-1004
BAINBRIDGE TWP.	GEAUGA	OH	682	444,675	597-621
BAIRD BEAT	JEFFERSON	AL	7	002,349	414-24
BAITS DIST.	COBB	GA	66	007,062	257-64, 357-72
BAKER CO.		GA	61	007,057	65-177
BAKER TWP.	MARTIN	IN	160	442,938	1-16
BAKER TWP.	MORGAN	IN	162	442,940	94-101
BAKERSFIELD	FRANKLIN	VT	924	444,923	97-133
BALD EAGLE TWP.	CLINTON	PA	768	444,736	18-34
BALDWIN	CUMBERLAND	ME	251	009,721	359-85
BALDWIN CO.		AL	1	002,343	159-211
BALDWIN CO.		GA	61	007,057	179-263
BALDWIN TWP.	ALLEGHENY	PA	747	020,597	251-89
BALL TWP.	BENTON	AR	25	002,479	103-113
BALLAHACK DIST.	PERQUIMANS	NC	640	444,653	790-807
BALLARD CO.		KY	190	007,843	501-612
BALLSTON	SARATOGA	NY	593	444,309	1051-1105
BALLVILLE TWP.	SANDUSKY	OH	726	444,719	844-47, 855-81, 968-76
BALTIMORE	FAIRFIELD	OH	677	444,670	372-83
BALTIMORE	WINDSOR	VT	931	444,930	963-65
BALTIMORE CO.		MD	279	013,196	1-400

CITY, COUNTY, TOWN, OR TOWNSHIP	COUNTY	STATE	NA NO. M432	GD NO.	PAGES
BALTIMORE CO.		MD	280	013,197	401-927
BALTIMORE CO.		MD	281-82	013,198-99	
BALTIMORE CO.		MD	283-87	443,514-18	
BALTIMORE HUN.	SUSSEX	DE	55	442,884	223-86
BALTIMORE TWP.	HENRY	IA	184	007,793	525-38
BALTIMORE TWP.	BARRY	MI	346	014,808	205-7
BALTIMORE, WARD 1	BALTIMORE	MD	281	013,198	1-348
BALTIMORE, WARD 2	BALTIMORE	MD	281	013,198	345-572
BALTIMORE, WARD 3	BALTIMORE	MD	282	013,199	573-850
BALTIMORE, WARD 4	BALTIMORE	MD	282	013,199	1-176
BALTIMORE, WARD 5	BALTIMORE	MD	283	443,514	177-311
BALTIMORE, WARD 6	BALTIMORE	MD	283	443,514	313-525
BALTIMORE, WARD 7	BALTIMORE	MD	283	443,514	527-708
BALTIMORE, WARD 8	BALTIMORE	MD	284	443,515	709-920
BALTIMORE, WARD 9	BALTIMORE	MD	284	443,515	1-110
BALTIMORE, WARD 10	BALTIMORE	MD	284	443,515	111-225
BALTIMORE, WARD 11	BALTIMORE	MD	284	443,515	227-433
BALTIMORE, WARD 12	BALTIMORE	MD	285	443,516	435-652
BALTIMORE, WARD 13	BALTIMORE	MD	285	443,516	653-779
BALTIMORE, WARD 14	BALTIMORE	MD	285	443,516	781-953
BALTIMORE, WARD 15	BALTIMORE	MD	286	443,517	1-238
BALTIMORE, WARD 16	BALTIMORE	MD	286	443,517	239-376
BALTIMORE, WARD 17	BALTIMORE	MD	286	443,517	377-610
BALTIMORE, WARD 18	BALTIMORE	MD	287	443,518	1-276
BALTIMORE, WARD 19	BALTIMORE	MD	287	443,518	277-463
BALTIMORE, WARD 20	BALTIMORE	MD	287	443,518	465-642
BANCROFT PLANTATION	AROOSTOOK	ME	248	009,718	35-38
BANDENBURG	MEDINA	TX	912	444,915	825-26
BANGOR	PENOBSCOT	ME	264	443,501	1-344
BANGOR	FRANKLIN	NY	505	017,081	111-62
BANKS TWP.	CARBON	PA	762	020,612	515-56
BARABOO TWP.	SAUK	WI	1006	444,993	104-114
BARABOO VILLAGE	SAUK	WI	1006	444,993	19-24
BARATARIA	JEFFERSON PAR.	LA	232	443,475	120-35
BARBOUR CO.		AL	1	002,343	213-521
BARBOUR CO.		VA	935	029,710	1-214
BARBOURVILLE	KNOX	KY	209	442,977	781-83
BAREFIELD DIST.	RUTHERFORD	TN	894	444,850	441-57
BARING	WASHINGTON	ME	273	443,510	365-374
BARKER	BROOME	NY	477	017,053	461-95
BARKHAMSTED	LITCHFIELD	CT	42	003,070	329-67
BARKLEY TWP.	JASPER	IN	152	442,930	471-84
BARLOW TWP.	WASHINGTON	OH	738	444,731	671-96
BARNARD	PISCATAQUIS	ME	267	443,504	705-9
BARNARD	WINDSOR	VT	931	444,930	793-832
BARNESVILLE	BELMONT	OH	661	020,209	719-37
BARNET	CALEDONIA	VT	922	027,448	155'-215
BARNETT TWP.	JEFFERSON	PA	786	444,754	12-25
BARNSTABLE	BARNSTABLE	MA	304	014,698	567-681
BARNSTABLE CO.		MA	303	014,697	1-425
BARNSTABLE CO.		MA	304	014,698	427-849
BARNSTEAD	BELKNAP	NH	425	014,938	393-436
BARNWELL CO.		SC	849	022,529	751-1052
BARNWELL DIST.	BARNWELL	SC	849	022,529	1013-20
BARR TWP.	DAVIESS	IN	140	007,753	302-345
BARRE	WORCESTER	MA	343	443,562	221-92
BARRE	ORLEANS	NY	575	444,291	130-85, 242-90
BARRE	WASHINGTON	VT	928	444,927	189-233
BARREE TWP.	HUNTINGDON	PA	784	444,752	245-76

11

CITY, COUNTY, TOWN, OR TOWNSHIP	COUNTY	STATE	NA NO. M432	GD NO.	PAGES
BARREN CO.		KY	191	007,844	613-988
BARREN CREEK	SOMERSET	MD	297	443,528	1011-49
BARREN TWP.	INDEPENDENCE	AR	26	002,480	635-42
BARRETTS DIST.	LUMPKIN	GA	76	007,072	151-62
BARRINGTON	COOK	IL	103	007,676	209-224
BARRINGTON	STRAFFORD	NH	440	443,644	489-530
BARRINGTON	YATES	NY	618	444,334	463-99
BARRINGTON	BRISTOL	RI	841	022,264	113-32
BARRON'S BEAT	PERRY	AL	12	002,354	585-92
BARRY	BARRY	MI	346	014,808	143-54
BARRY CO.		MI	346	014,808	129-260
BARRY CO.		MO	391	014,871	379-458
BARRY TWP.	SCHUYLKILL	PA	827	444,795	57-76
BART TWP.	LANCASTER	PA	787	444,755	85-140
BARTHOLOMEW CO.		IN	136	007,749	583-906
BARTHOLOMEW TWP.	DESHA	AR	26	002,480	126-29
BARTHOLOMEW TWP.	DREW	AR	26	002,480	177-82
BARTLETT	COOS	NH	429	443,633	21-39
BARTON	TIOGA	NY	604	444,320	1-85
BARTON	ORLEANS	VT	925	444,924	79-102
BARTON TWP.	GIBSON	IN	147	442,925	189-201
BASIL	FAIRFIELD	OH	677	444,670	384-88
BASTROP CO.		TX	908	024,887	145-96
BATAVIA	KANE	IL	112	007,685	285-306
BATAVIA	BRANCH	MI	347	014,809	569-86
BATAVIA	GENESEE	NY	508	017,084	409-520
BATAVIA TWP.	CLERMONT	OH	667	020,215	567-633
BATES CO.		MO	392	014,872	459-542
BATES TWP.	CRAWFORD	AR	25	002,479	561-66
BATESVILLE	INDEPENDENCE	AR	26	002,480	777-91
BATH	MASON	IL	120	442,908	302-9
BATH	LINCOLN	ME	261	443,498	251-442
BATH	GRAFTON	NH	431	443,635	171-208
BATH	STEUBEN	NY	600	444,316	353-500
BATH	MORGAN	VA	962	444,952	169-75
BATH CO.		KY	191	007,844	1-231
BATH CO.		VA	935	029,710	217-76
BATH DIST.	BEAUFORT	NC	620	018,106	717-22, 735-38, 765-67
BATH TWP.	FRANKLIN	IN	146	442,924	381-401
BATH TWP.	CLINTON	MI	349	014,811	127-32
BATH TWP.	ALLEN	OH	657	020,205	487-522
BATH TWP.	GREENE	OH	683	444,676	651-701
BATH TWP.	SUMMIT	OH	732	444,725	629-62
BATON ROUGE PAR., EAST		LA	229	009,696	309-443
BATON ROUGE PAR., WEST		LA	229	009,696	445-90
BATON ROUGE, WARD 3 BAT. ROU. EAST		LA	229	009,696	376-82
BATON ROUGE, WARD 4 BAT. ROU. EAST		LA	229	009,696	383-88
BATON ROUGE, WARD 5 BAT. ROU. EAST		LA	229	009,696	389-95
BATON ROUGE, WARD 6 BAT. ROU. EAST		LA	229	009,696	396-402
BATON ROUGE, WARD 7 BAT. ROU. EAST		LA	229	009,696	403-9
BATON ROUGE, WARD 8 BAT. ROU. EAST		LA	229	009,696	410-15
BATON ROUGE, WARD 9 BAT. ROU. EAST		LA	229	009,696	416-24
BATON ROUGE, WARD 10 BAT. ROU. EAST		LA	229	009,696	425-34
BATON ROUGE, WARD 11 BAT. ROU. EAST		LA	229	009,696	435-39
BATON ROUGE, WARD 12 BAT. ROU. EAST		LA	229	009,696	440-43
BATTLE CREEK	CALHOUN	MI	348	014,810	127-46
BATTLE CREEK VILLAGE	CALHOUN	MI	348	014,810	101-126
BAUGHMAN TWP.	WAYNE	OH	739	444,732	301-344

CITY, COUNTY, TOWN, OR TOWNSHIP	COUNTY	STATE	NA NO. M432	GD NO.	PAGES
BAUGO TWP.	ELKHART	IN	144	007,757	3-16
BAY TWP.	OTTAWA	OH	719	444,712	325-33
BAYOU BARTHOLOMEW TWP.	JEFFERSON	AR	27	002,481	168-73
BAYOU CHACBY	LAFOURCHE PAR.	LA	232	443,475	579-80, 584
BAYOU CHENE	ST. MARTIN	LA	240	443,483	377-81
BAYOU CHOUPIE	LAFOURCHE PAR.	LA	232	443,475	575-78
BAYOU LAFOURCHE	LAFOURCHE PAR.	LA	232	443,475	547-50, 553-67, 569, 571-74, 614-21, 623-25, 627-33, 635-43, 646-49, 658-70
BAYOU L'OURS	LAFOURCHE PAR.	LA	232	443,475	583
BAYOU MASON TWP.	CHICOT	AR	25	002,479	356-61
BAYOU METRE TWP.	PULASKI	AR	29	002,483	731-38
BAYOU SARA	WEST FELICIANA PAR.	LA	231	009,698	509-517
BAYOU SEC	LAFOURCHE PAR.	LA	232	443,475	595
BAYOU TWP.	JACKSON	AR	27	002,481	83-88
BAZETTA	TRUMBULL	OH	733	444,726	891-922
BEACH CREEK TWP.	ASHLEY	AR	25	002,479	74-78
BEACH ISLAND	HANCOCK	ME	254	443,491	425
BEAL BAR	SUTTER	CA	36	442,879	57
BEALE TWP.	JUNIATA	PA	786	444,754	421-37, 440
BEALLSVILLE	MONROE	OH	712	444,705	445-51
BEALS BAR (FORKSVILLE)	SUTTER	CA	36	442,879	37-45
BEAN BLOSSOM TWP.	MONROE	IN	161	442,939	509-532
BEAR CREEK PREC.	GALLATIN	IL	107	007,680	723-33
BEAR CREEK TWP.	SEARCY	AR	30	442,876	332-34
BEAR CREEK TWP.	JAY	IN	153	442,931	639-56
BEARDSTOWN	CASS	IL	99	007,672	136-71
BEARFIELD TWP.	PERRY	OH	719	444,712	529-69
BEARSVILLE	MONROE	OH	712	444,705	833-36
BEASE ISLAND	HANCOCK	ME	254	443,491	427
BEATIE TWP.	BENTON	AR	25	002,479	87-102
BEAUFORT	CARTERET	NC	623	018,109	272-99, 337-38
BEAUFORT	BEAUFORT	SC	849	022,529	1-22
BEAUFORT CO.		NC	620	018,106	671-874
BEAUFORT CO.		SC	849	022,529	1-163
BEAUVAIS TWP.	STE. GENEVIEVE	MO	413	443,621	459-74
BEAUX BRIDGE	ST. MARTIN	LA	240	443,483	335-36
BEAVER	CLARION	PA	767	444,735	501-567
BEAVER CO.		PA	750	020,600	1-661
BEAVER CREEK TWP.	GREENE	OH	683	444,676	891-941
BEAVER DAM	DODGE	WI	996	034,510	47-58, 143-67
BEAVER DAM DIST.	BEAUFORT	NC	620	018,106	739-56, 793-96
BEAVER DAM DIST.	GRANVILLE	NC	631	444,644	243-68
BEAVER DAM DIST.	JONES	NC	635	444,648	238-45, 270-82
BEAVER ISLAND	STOKES	NC	645	444,658	304-318
BEAVER TWP.	JASPER	IN	152	442,930	551-56
BEAVER TWP.	PULASKI	IN	166	442,944	674-77
BEAVER TWP.	GUERNSEY	OH	684	444,677	359-409, 650
BEAVER TWP.	MAHONING	OH	707	444,700	695-746
BEAVER TWP.	PIKE	OH	721	444,714	559-71
BEAVER TWP.	COLUMBIA	PA	769	444,737	520-35
BEAVER TWP.	CRAWFORD	PA	770	444,738	45-60
BEAVER TWP.	JEFFERSON	PA	786	444,754	100-115
BEAVER TWP.	UNION	PA	831	444,799	157-96
BECCARIA TWP.	CLEARFIELD	PA	768	444,736	747-62
BECKET	BERKSHIRE	MA	306	014,700	251-60
BECK'S CREEK DIST.	SHELBY	IL	128	442,916	296-310

13

CITY, COUNTY, TOWN, OR TOWNSHIP	COUNTY	STATE	NA NO. M432	GD NO.	PAGES
BEDDINGTON	WASHINGTON	ME	272	443,509	75-78
BEDFORD	TRIMBLE	KY	220	442,988	797-801
BEDFORD	MIDDLESEX	MA	324	443,543	977-1001
BEDFORD	CALHOUN	MI	348	014,810	187-205
BEDFORD	HILLSBORO	NH	433	443,637	489-537
BEDFORD	WESTCHESTER	NY	614	444,330	165-241
BEDFORD BOR.	BEDFORD	PA	751	020,601	1-30
BEDFORD CO.		PA	751	020,601	1-571
BEDFORD CO.		TN	869	024,560	157-554
BEDFORD CO.		VA	935	029,710	279-614
BEDFORD TWP.	MONROE	MI	358	443,574	569-91
BEDFORD TWP.	COSHOCTON	OH	670	020,218	31-60
BEDFORD TWP.	CUYAHOGA	OH	673	020,221	153-97
BEDFORD TWP.	MEIGS	OH	710	444,703	69-90
BEDFORD TWP.	BEDFORD	PA	751	020,601	31-74
BEDMINSTER	SOMERSET	NJ	463	443,662	909-952
BEDMINSTER TWP.	BUCKS	PA	758	020,608	477-522
BEE BRANCH TWP.	CHARITON	MO	395	443,603	364-72, 476
BEECH CREEK TWP.	GREENE	IN	148	442,926	655-83
BEECH CREEK TWP.	CLINTON	PA	768	444,736	1-17
BEEK DIST.	SURRY	NC	646	444,659	612
BEEKMAN	DUTCHESS	NY	496	017,072	527-60
BEEKMANTOWN	CLINTON	NY	489	017,065	1-43, 625-63
BEL AIR	HARFORD	MD	294	443,525	149-54
BELCHERTOWN	HAMPSHIRE	MA	321	443,540	819-90
BELEN	VALENCIA	NM	470	443,668	704-716
BELEN DE LOS CHAROIS	VALENCIA	NM	470	443,668	723-26
BELEN DE LOS CHAUSEL	VALENCIA	NM	470	443,668	717-22
BELEN DE LOS GABALDON	VALENCIA	NM	470	443,668	727
BELEN DE LOS IARALES	VALENCIA	NM	470	443,668	696-703
BELEN DE LOS PUBLITOS	VALENCIA	NM	470	443,668	689-95
BELFAST	WALDO	ME	270	443,507	217-337
BELFAST	ALLEGANY	NY	476	017,052	529-68
BELFAST ACAD. GRANT	AROOSTOOK	ME	248	009,718	153-59
BELFAST TWP.	FULTON	PA	783	444,751	51-69
BELGIUM	WASHINGTON	WI	1008	444,995	148-74
BELGRADE	KENNEBEC	ME	256	443,493	279-319
BELKNAP CO.		NH	425	014,938	1-436
BELL TWP.	CLEARFIELD	PA	768	444,736	712-23
BELLEFONTE	CENTRE	PA	763	020,613	313-41
BELLEVIEW PREC.	CALHOUN	IL	99	007,672	613-22
BELLEVILLE	ST. CLAIR	IL	126	442,914	842-905
BELLEVILLE PRAIRIE	ST. CLAIR	IL	126	442,914	763-78
BELLEVILLE TWP.	ESSEX	NJ	449	443,648	221-304
BELLEVUE	JACKSON	IA	184	007,793	607-9, 729-34
BELLEVUE	EATON	MI	349	014,811	165-83
BELLEVUE TWP.	JACKSON	IA	184	007,793	571-74, 584-87 592-98, 681-82
BELLEVUE TWP.	WASHINGTON	MO	421	443,629	209-246
BELLINGHAM	NORFOLK	MA	331	443,550	375-405
BELMONT	WALDO	ME	271	443,508	317-52
BELMONT	FRANKLIN	NY	505	017,081	523-38
BELMONT	BELMONT	OH	661	020,209	881
BELMONT	LAFAYETTE	WI	1001	444,988	923-30
BELMONT		OH	661	020,209	719-1018, 1-54
BELMONT CO.		AL	15	442,866	599-609
BELMONT DIV.	SUMTER				
BELOIT	ROCK	WI	1005	444,992	784-848
BELPRE TWP.	WASHINGTON	OH	738	444,731	539-77
BELVIDERE	BOONE	IL	98	007,671	1-47

CITY, COUNTY, TOWN, OR TOWNSHIP	COUNTY	STATE	NA NO. M432	GD NO.	PAGES
BELVIDERE	WARREN	NJ	465	443,664	771-94
BELVIDERE	LAMOILLE	VT	925	444,924	141-47
BELVILLE	HENDRICKS	IN	150	442,928	188-92
BEN HADEN DIST.	WAKULLA	FL	59	006,715	501, 504-6
BEN SMITHS DIST.	GWINNETT	GA	71	007,067	415-16, 418-26
BENDERSVILLE	ADAMS	PA	743	020,593	120-24
BENEDICTA PLANTATION	AROOSTOOK	ME	248	009,718	7-15
BENEZETTE TWP.	ELK	PA	776	444,744	721-26
BENGAL TWP.	CLINTON	MI	349	014,811	91-94
BENGAUL DIST.	GWINNETT	GA	71	007,067	355, 416-20, 424-26, 450-51
BENICIA	SOLANO	CA	36	442,879	1-12
BENNETT BAYOU TWP.	FULTON	AR	26	002,480	339-48
BENNINGTON	SHIAWASSEE	MI	363	443,579	127-41
BENNINGTON	HILLSBORO	NH	434	443,638	5-17
BENNINGTON	WYOMING	NY	616	444,332	191-248
BENNINGTON	BENNINGTON	VT	921	027,447	363-456
BENNINGTON CO.		VT	921	027,447	1-467
BENNINGTON TWP.	LICKING	OH	702	444,695	477-505
BENNINGTON TWP.	MORROW	OH	716	444,709	83-113
BENSALEM TWP.	BUCKS	PA	759	020,609	105-158
BENSON	RUTLAND	VT	927	444,926	283-314
BENTON	BOONE	IL	98	007,671	49-68
BENTON	LAKE	IL	114	007,687	213-30
BENTON	MC HENRY	IL	117	007,690	1001-8
BENTON	EATON	MI	349	014,811	291-99
BENTON	GRAFTON	NH	431	443,635	159-70
BENTON	YATES	NY	618	444,334	199-281
BENTON	LAFAYETTE	WI	1001	444,988	801-814, 816-54
BENTON CO.		AL	1	002,343	525-850
BENTON CO.		AR	25	002,479	87-174
BENTON CO.		FL	58	006,714	41-55
BENTON CO.		IN	136	007,749	1-28
BENTON CO.		IA	182	007,791	101-116
BENTON CO.		MN	367	014,834	1-10
BENTON CO.		MO	392	014,872	543-653
BENTON CO.		OR	742	020,298	1-20
BENTON CO.		TN	870	024,561	557-700
BENTON TWP.	CONWAY	AR	25	002,479	486-98
BENTON TWP.	FULTON	AR	26	002,480	299-304
BENTON TWP.	ELKHART	IN	144	007,757	265-91
BENTON TWP.	MONROE	IN	161	442,939	557-72
BENTON TWP.	DES MOINES	IA	183	007,792	805-820
BENTON TWP.	GREENE	MO	400	443,608	673-85
BENTON TWP.	KNOX	MO	403	443,611	184-97
BENTON TWP.	NEWTON	MO	408	443,616	686-703
BENTON TWP.	OSAGE	MO	408	443,616	897-921, 923-25
BENTON TWP.	TANEY	MO	420	443,628	770, 777-78
BENTON TWP.	HOCKING	OH	695	444,688	865-88
BENTON TWP.	OTTAWA	OH	719	444,712	276-77
BENTON TWP.	PAULDING	OH	719	444,712	395-96
BENTON TWP.	PIKE	OH	721	444,714	753-68
BENTON TWP.	LUZERNE	PA	793	444,761	415-35
BENTONVILLE	BENTON	AR	25	002,479	125-60
BENTONVILLE	ADAMS	OH	657	020,205	214-17
BENZINGER TWP.	ELK	PA	776	444,744	689-719
BERGEN	GENESEE	NY	507	017,083	85-130
BERGEN CO.		NJ	442	016,529	219-582
BERGEN TWP.	HUDSON	NJ	452	443,651	473-539

15

CITY, COUNTY, TOWN, OR TOWNSHIP	COUNTY	STATE	NA NO. M432	GD NO.	PAGES
BERKELEY CO.		VA	936	029,711	618-852
BERKLEY	BRISTOL	MA	307	014,701	537-58
BERKS CO.		PA	752	020,602	1-732
BERKS CO.		PA	753	020,603	733-942, 1-35
BERKS CO.		PA	754	020,604	359-944
BERKSHIRE	TIOGA	NY	604	444,320	583-608
BERKSHIRE	FRANKLIN	VT	924	444,923	391-438
BERKSHIRE CO.		MA	305	014,699	1-611
BERKSHIRE CO.		MA	306	014,700	1-612
BERKSHIRE DIST.	GWINNETT	GA	71	007,067	261-74, 276, 334-38, 350, 369, 379
BERKSHIRE TWP.	DELAWARE	OH	675	020,223	185-224
BERLIN	HARTFORD	CT	40	003,068	193-238
BERLIN	BUREAU	IL	99	007,672	367-69, 404-4
BERLIN	WORCESTER	MD	299	443,530	517-28
BERLIN	WORCESTER	MA	341	443,560	73-93
BERLIN	ST. CLAIR	MI	362	443,578	417-29
BERLIN	COOS	NH	429	443,633	207-211
BERLIN	RENSSELAER	NY	586	444,302	393-438
BERLIN	WASHINGTON	VT	928	444,927	235-70
BERLIN	MARQUETTE	WI	1002	444,989	242-67
BERLIN BOR.	SOMERSET	PA	828	444,796	313-28
BERLIN TWP.	IONIA	MI	352	443,568	323-32
BERLIN TWP.	DELAWARE	OH	675	020,223	465-92
BERLIN TWP.	ERIE	OH	676	338,044	906-943
BERLIN TWP.	HOLMES	OH	696	444,689	355-89
BERLIN TWP.	KNOX	OH	700	444,693	29-57
BERLIN TWP.	MAHONING	OH	707	444,700	1189-1221
BERLIN TWP.	WAYNE	PA	835	444,803	337-56
BERN TWP.	ATHENS	OH	660	020,208	221-40
BERN TWP.	FAIRFIELD	OH	677	444,670	859-922
BERN TWP.	BERKS	PA	753	020,603	849-90
BERNADOTTE	FULTON	IL	107	007,680	249-67
BERNALILLO CO.		NM	467	016,603	1-190
BERNARDS TWP.	SOMERSET	NJ	463	443,662	649-702
BERNARDSTON	FRANKLIN	MA	316	443,535	293-315
BERNE	ALBANY	NY	473	017,049	1-82
BERRIEN CO.		MI	346	014,808	261-532
BERRY TWP.	DANE	WI	995	034,509	868-72
BERRY'S DIST.	MONTGOMERY	MD	295	443,526	693-745
BERTIE CO.		NC	621	018,107	1-144
BERWICK	YORK	ME	276	443,513	325-75
BERWICK	ADAMS	PA	743	020,593	387-94
BERWICK BOR.	COLUMBIA	PA	769	444,737	317-28
BERWICK TWP.	ADAMS	PA	743	020,593	387-406
BETHANIA	FORSYTH	NC	630	444,643	533-34
BETHANY	NEW HAVEN	CT	45	003,073	495-516
BETHANY	GENESEE	NY	507	017,083	221-67
BETHANY BOR.	PAYNE	PA	835	444,803	483-90
BETHEL	OXFORD	ME	262	443,499	1-54
BETHEL	BRANCH	MI	347	014,809	769-85
BETHEL	SHELBY	MO	420	443,628	421-32
BETHEL	SULLIVAN	NY	603	444,319	143-92
BETHEL	WINDSOR	VT	930	444,929	355-96
BETHEL TWP.	POSEY	IN	166	442,944	503, 505-514
BETHEL TWP.	CLARK	OH	666	020,214	173-208, 226-4
BETHEL TWP.	MIAMI	OH	711	444,704	109-148
BETHEL TWP.	MONROE	OH	712	444,705	689-716

CITY, COUNTY, TOWN, OR TOWNSHIP	COUNTY	STATE	NA NO. M432	GD NO.	PAGES
BETHEL TWP.	BERKS	PA	752	020,602	287-332
BETHEL TWP.	DELAWARE	PA	776	444,744	235-45
BETHEL TWP.	FULTON	PA	783	444,751	97-124
BETHEL TWP.	LEBANON	PA	791	444,759	384-429
BETHLEHEM	LITCHFIELD	CT	43	003,071	801-820
BETHLEHEM	HAMILTON	IN	148	442,926	79-80
BETHLEHEM	GRAFTON	NH	431	443,635	278, 281-303
BETHLEHEM	ALBANY	NY	473	017,049	551-649
BETHLEHEM	STARK	OH	731	444,724	201-258
BETHLEHEM BEAT	JEFFERSON	AL	7	002,349	342-48
BETHLEHEM BOR.	NORTHAMPTON	PA	802	444,770	461-96
BETHLEHEM TWP.	CASS	IN	137	007,750	841-57
BETHLEHEM TWP.	CLARK	IN	138	007,751	63-90
BETHLEHEM TWP.	HUNTERDON	NJ	453	443,652	405-473
BETHLEHEM TWP.	COSHOCTON	OH	670	020,218	389-408
BETHLEHEM TWP.	NORTHAMPTON	PA	802	444,770	497-547
BEVERLY	ADAMS	IL	97	007,670	1-22
BEVERLY	ESSEX	MA	315	443,534	533-660
BEVERLY	RANDOLPH	VA	972	444,962	131-34
BEVERLY BOR.	BURLINGTON	NJ	443	016,530	131-45
BEVERLY DIST.	ANSON	NC	619	018,105	391-96
BEXAR CO.		TX	908	024,887	199-335
BIBB CO.		AL	2	002,344	1-170
BIBB CO.		GA	61	007,057	265-438
BIDDEFORD	YORK	ME	274	443,511	1-148
BIENVILLE PARISH		LA	230	009,697	491-577
BIG BEAVER TWP.	BEAVER	PA	750	020,600	193-214
BIG BEAVER TWP.	LAWRENCE	PA	790	444,758	171-86
BIG CREEK TWP.	CRAWFORD	AR	25	002,479	567-74
BIG CREEK TWP.	GREENE	AR	26	002,480	370-85
BIG CREEK TWP.	PHILLIPS	AR	29	002,483	285-98
BIG CREEK TWP.	HENRY	MO	401	443,609	73-87
BIG CREEK TWP.	TANEY	MO	420	443,628	761-69
BIG FLATS	CHEMUNG	NY	486	017,062	251-91
BIG GROVE	KENDALL	IL	113	007,686	563-94
BIG GROVE TWP.	JOHNSON	IA	185	442,960	359-68
BIG ISLAND TWP.	MARION	OH	708	444,701	65-79
BIG LAKE TWP.	MISSISSIPPI	AR	28	002,482	708-712
BIG NORTHFORK TWP.	FULTON	AR	26	002,480	321-31
BIG ROCK	KANE	IL	112	007,685	309-320
BIG ROCK TWP.	PULASKI	AR	29	002,483	671-87
BIG SHANTY DIST.	COBB	GA	66	007,062	273-76, 401-16
BIG SPRING DIST.	RUTHERFORD	TN	894	444,850	613-32
BIG SPRING TWP.	SENECA	OH	728	444,721	653-700
BIG STONE LAKE	DAKOTA	MN	367	014,834	15-16
BIGGER TWP.	JENNINGS	IN	155	442,933	709-717, 725-26, 737-43
BIGGS, THOMAS RANCH	VALENCIA	NM	470	443,668	654
BIGLICK TWP.	HANCOCK	OH	692	444,685	871-94
BILLERICA	MIDDLESEX	MA	324	443,543	385-424
BILLS CREEK	RUTHERFORD	NC	644	444,657	657-60
BINGHAM	SOMERSET	ME	269	443,506	473-90
BINGHAM	POTTER	PA	825	444,793	211-24
BINGHAM PURCHASE	FRANKLIN	ME	253	009,723	505-6
BINGHAM TWP.	CLINTON	MI	349	014,811	157-61
BIRD TWP.	JACKSON	AR	27	002,479	95-101
BIRDSALL	ALLEGANY	NY	476	017,052	1-15
BIRMINGHAM	VAN BUREN	IA	189	442,964	789-94
BIRMINGHAM	GUERNSEY	OH	684	444,677	819-23

17

CITY, COUNTY, TOWN, OR TOWNSHIP	COUNTY	STATE	NA NO. M432	GD NO.	PAGES
BIRMINGHAM BOR.	ALLEGHENY	PA	748	020,598	97-186
BIRMINGHAM BOR.	HUNTINGDON	PA	784	444,752	31-37
BIRMINGHAM TWP.	CHESTER	PA	766	020,616	831-38
BIRMINGHAM TWP.	DELAWARE	PA	776	444,744	199-212
BLACK BLUFF DIST.	SUMTER	AL	15	442,866	613-19
BLACK BROOK	CLINTON	NY	489	017,065	108-168
BLACK CREEK DIST.	DUVAL	FL	58	006,714	208-219
BLACK CREEK TWP.	MERCER	OH	710	444,703	574-85
BLACK CREEK TWP.	LUZERNE	PA	794	444,762	959-69
BLACK HAWK CO.		IA	182	007,791	119-24
BLACK HAWK TWP.	JEFFERSON	IA	185	442,960	241-46
BLACK ISLAND	HANCOCK	ME	254	443,491	333-34
BLACK JACK DIST.	RICHMOND	NC	642	444,655	588-99, 625-26
BLACK POINT	REFUGIO	TX	914	444,917	470
BLACK RIVER	CRAWFORD	WI	995	034,509	517-27
BLACK RIVER TWP.	INDEPENDENCE	AR	26	002,480	643-59
BLACK RIVER TWP.	LAWRENCE	AR	27	002,481	425-39
BLACK RIVER TWP.	LORAIN	OH	705	444,698	737-52
BLACK ROCK	ERIE	NY	500	017,076	357-535
BLACK THORN	PENDLETON	VA	968	444,958	115-19, 122-23
BLACK TWP.	POSEY	IN	166	442,944	363-422
BLACKBERRY	KANE	IL	112	007,685	321-38
BLACKFISH TWP.	CRITTENDEN	AR	25	002,479	745-51
BLACKFORD CO.		IN	136	007,749	29-98
BLACKHALL DIST.	DE KALB	GA	67	007,063	367-85
BLACKLICK TWP.	INDIANA	PA	785	444,753	287-336
BLACKSTONE	WORCESTER	MA	345	443,564	625-730
BLACKWATER	JOHNSON	MO	403	443,611	3
BLADEN CO.		NC	621	018,107	145-272
BLADENSBURG DIST.	PRINCE GEORGES	MD	295	443,526	1-34
BLAIR CO.		PA	755	020,605	1-526
BLAIR TWP.	BLAIR	PA	755	020,605	389-410
BLAIRSTOWN TWP.	WARREN	NJ	465	443,664	879-912
BLAIRSVILLE BOR.	INDIANA	PA	785	444,753	131-58
BLAKELY	LUZERNE	PA	794	444,762	127-67
BLANCHARD	PISCATAQUIS	ME	267	443,504	445-49
BLANCHARD TWP.	HANCOCK	OH	692	444,685	799-824
BLANCHARD TWP.	HARDIN	OH	692	444,685	317-22
BLANCHARD TWP.	PUTNAM	OH	723	444,716	61-94
BLANDFORD	HAMPDEN	MA	318	443,537	223-56
BLANDVILLE	BALLARD	KY	190	007,843	554-58
BLEDSOE CO.		TN	870	024,561	703-826
BLEECKER	FULTON	NY	506	017,082	271-83
BLENDON TWP.	FRANKLIN	OH	680	444,673	1-32
BLENHEIM	SCHOHARIE	NY	595	444,311	371-404
BLISSFIELD	LENAWEE	MI	355	443,571	354-75
BLOCKLEY TWP.	PHILADELPHIA	PA	824	444,792	1-141
BLOOM TWP.	COOK	IL	103	007,676	25, 30-31, 33-4 49-52
BLOOM TWP.	FAIRFIELD	OH	677	444,670	441-95
BLOOM TWP.	MORGAN	OH	715	444,708	181-214
BLOOM TWP.	SCIOTO	OH	727	444,720	313-52
BLOOM TWP.	SENECA	OH	728	444,721	257-300
BLOOM TWP.	WOOD	OH	741	444,734	273-88
BLOOM TWP.	COLUMBIA	PA	769	444,737	565-639
BLOOMFIELD	HARTFORD	CT	39	003,067	547-81
BLOOMFIELD	LA GRANGE	IN	157	442,935	103-126
BLOOMFIELD	DAVIS	IA	182	007,791	615-38
BLOOMFIELD	SOMERSET	ME	269	443,506	301-330

CITY, COUNTY, TOWN, OR TOWNSHIP	COUNTY	STATE	NA NO. M432	GD NO.	PAGES	
BLOOMFIELD	OAKLAND	MI	359	443,575	53-92	
BLOOMFIELD	TRUMBULL	OH	733	444,726	521-39	
BLOOMFIELD	ESSEX	VT	923	444,922	801-6	
BLOOMFIELD	WALWORTH	WI	1007	444,994	424-44	
BLOOMFIELD BOR.	PERRY	PA	805	444,773	989-1002	
BLOOMFIELD TWP.	GREENE	IN	148	442,926	627-32	
BLOOMFIELD TWP.	CLINTON	IA	182	007,791	421-32	
BLOOMFIELD TWP.	ESSEX	NJ	449	443,648	305-385	
BLOOMFIELD TWP.	JACKSON	OH	698	444,691	451-84	
BLOOMFIELD TWP.	LOGAN	OH	704	444,697	103-118	
BLOOMFIELD TWP.	CRAWFORD	PA	771	444,739	617-36	
BLOOMING GROVE	ORANGE	NY	573	444,289	637-88	
BLOOMING GROVE	DANE	WI	995	034,509	678-84	
BLOOMING GROVE TWP.	FRANKLIN	IN	146	442,924	321-56	
BLOOMING GROVE TWP.	RICHLAND	OH	724	444,717	311-45	
BLOOMINGDALE	DU PAGE	IL	105	007,678	181-201	
BLOOMINGDALE	VAN BUREN	MI	363	443,579	235-38	
BLOOMINGDALE	WINNEBAGO	WI	1009	444,996	1059-80	
BLOOMINGTON	MC LEON	IL	117	007,690	1-39	
BLOOMINGTON	MONROE	IN	161	442,939	437-58,	583-93
BLOOMINGTON	MUSCATINE	IA	187	442,962	737-41	
BLOOMINGTON PREC.	MC LEON	IL	117	007,690	40-62	
BLOOMINGTON TWP.	MONROE	IN	161	442,939	461-73, 594-604	477-80,
BLOOMINGTON TWP.	BUCHANAN	MO	393	014,873	187-219	
BLOSS TWP.	TIOGA	PA	830	444,798	1-21	
BLOSSOM HILL BEAT	CADDO PARISH	LA	230	009,697	639-45	
BLOSSOM HILL WARD	CADDO PARISH	LA	230	009,697	646-57	
BLOUNT CO.		AL	2	002,344	171-346	
BLOUNT CO.		TN	871	024,562	1-271	
BLOUNTS CREEK DIST.	BEAUFORT	NC	620	018,106	814-29	
BLUE BALL	LANCASTER	PA	789	444,757	339-86	
BLUE BAYOU TWP.	SEVIER	AR	30	442,876	424-27,	435-39
BLUE CREEK TWP.	ADAMS	IN	135	007,748	127-37	
BLUE MOUNDS TWP.	DANE	WI	995	034,509	886-93	
BLUE MOUNTAIN TWP.	IZARD	AR	27	002,481	15-22	
BLUE RIVER TWP.	HANCOCK	IN	149	442,927	417-37,	563-64
BLUE RIVER TWP.	HENRY	IN	151	442,929	385-405	
BLUE RIVER TWP.	JOHNSON	IN	155	442,933	207-230	
BLUE ROCK TWP.	MUSKINGUM	OH	718	444,711	163-98	
BLUE TWP.	JACKSON	MO	402	443,610	522-638	
BLUEHILL	HANCOCK	ME	254	443,491	123-69	
BLUFF BEAT	MARSHALL	AL	10	002,352	469-80	
BLUFF PORT DIV.	SUMTER	AL	15	442,866	536-40,	597-99
BLUFFTON	WELLS	IN	181	442,959	757-68	
BLYTHE TWP.	SCHUYLKILL	PA	827	444,795	157-247	
BOARDMAN TWP.	CLAYTON	IA	182	007,791	312-18,	325-27
BOARDMAN TWP.	MAHONING	OH	707	444,700	669-93	
BODCAW TWP.	HEMPSTEAD	AR	26	002,480	447-57	
BOGARD TWP.	DAVIESS	IN	140	007,753	269-83	
BOGGS TWP.	CENTRE	PA	763	020,613	441-86	
BOGGS TWP.	CLEARFIELD	PA	768	444,736	669-79	
BOGLE TWP.	GENTRY	MO	399	443,607	445-52	
BOGUE SOUND	CARTERET	NC	623	018,109	304-21	
BOIS BRULE TWP.	PERRY	MO	409	443,617	57-71	
BOIS D'ARC TWP.	HEMPSTEAD	AR	26	002,480	534-38	
BOISE TWP.	ATHENS	OH	660	020,208	445	
BOKES CREEK TWP.	LOGAN	OH	704	444,697	37-50	
BOLIVAR	ALLEGANY	NY	475	017,051	77-93	

19

Bolivar

CITY, COUNTY, TOWN, OR TOWNSHIP	COUNTY	STATE	NA NO. M432	GD NO.	PAGES
BOLIVAR	HARDEMAN	TN	881	444,837	159-69
BOLIVAR	JEFFERSON	VA	953	444,943	781-804
BOLIVAR CO.		MS	368	014,847	385-92
BOLIVAR DIST.	BOLIVAR	MS	368	014,847	385-92
BOLIVAR TWP.	JEFFERSON	AR	27	002,481	207-219
BOLIVAR TWP.	POINSETT	AR	29	002,483	418-31
BOLTON	TOLLAND	CT	50	442,882	719-33
BOLTON	WORCESTER	MA	341	443,560	1-31
BOLTON	WARREN	NY	609	444,325	19-46
BOLTON	CHITTENDEN	VT	923	444,922	451-65
BOMBAY	FRANKLIN	NY	505	017,081	407-453
BONAPARTE	VAN BUREN	IA	189	442,964	629-36
BOND CO.		IL	98	007,671	719-865
BONGCHITTO	DALLAS	AL	4	002,346	552-60, 568-73
BONHAM	FANNIN	TX	910	024,889	369-74
BONHOMME TWP.	ST. LOUIS	MO	414	443,622	708-744
BONO TWP.	LAWRENCE	IN	158	442,936	647-70
BONUS	BOONE	IL	98	007,671	89-109
BOON TWP.	WARRICK	IN	179	442,957	189-246
BOONE	BOONE	IL	98	007,671	69-88
BOONE CO.		IL	98	007,671	1-188
BOONE CO.		IN	136	007,749	101-377
BOONE CO.		IA	182	007,791	126-43
BOONE CO.		KY	192	007,845	233-499
BOONE CO.		MO	392	014,872	655-927
BOONE CO.		VA	936	029,711	1-73
BOONE TWP.	SCOTT	AR	30	442,876	281, 304-6, 311-23
BOONE TWP.	UNION	AR	30	442,876	481-87
BOONE TWP.	CASS	IN	137	007,750	769-83
BOONE TWP.	CRAWFORD	IN	139	007,752	157-69
BOONE TWP.	MADISON	IN	158	442,936	11-17
BOONE TWP.	PORTER	IN	165	442,943	273-86
BOONE TWP.	GREENE	MO	400	443,608	641-64
BOONSBORO	WASHINGTON	MD	298	443,529	357-77
BOONVILLE	WARRICK	IN	179	442,957	189-93
BOONVILLE	COPPER	MO	397	443,605	139-78
BOONVILLE	ONEIDA	NY	565	444,281	299-379
BOOTHBAY	LINCOLN	ME	260	443,497	77-136
BORDENTOWN	BURLINGTON	NJ	443	016,530	267-328
BOROUGH TWP.	BEAVER	PA	750	020,600	87-135
BOSCAWEN	MERRIMACK	NH	436	443,640	503-552
BOSSIER PARISH		LA	230	009,697	579-638
BOSTON	ERIE	NY	500	017,076	1-47
BOSTON CORNER	BERKSHIRE	MA	306	014,700	449-50
BOSTON TWP.	FRANKLIN	AR	26	002,480	209-216
BOSTON TWP.	WAYNE	IN	180	442,958	259-81
BOSTON TWP.	IONIA	MI	352	443,568	386-96
BOSTON TWP.	SUMMIT	OH	732	444,725	533-61
BOSTON, WARD 1	SUFFOLK	MA	334	443,553	1-239
BOSTON, WARD 2	SUFFOLK	MA	334	443,553	241-446
BOSTON, WARD 3	SUFFOLK	MA	334	443,553	447-675
BOSTON, WARD 4	SUFFOLK	MA	335	443,554	1-407
BOSTON, WARD 5	SUFFOLK	MA	335	443,554	409-645
BOSTON, WARD 6	SUFFOLK	MA	336	443,555	647-858
BOSTON, WARD 7	SUFFOLK	MA	336	443,555	1-127
BOSTON, WARD 8	SUFFOLK	MA	336	443,555	130-346
BOSTON, WARD 9	SUFFOLK	MA	337	443,556	347-606
BOSTON, WARD 10	SUFFOLK	MA	337	443,556	607-964

CITY, COUNTY, TOWN, OR TOWNSHIP	COUNTY	STATE	NA NO. M432	GD NO.	PAGES
BOSTON, WARD 11	SUFFOLK	MA	338	443,557	1-462
BOSTON, WARD 12	SUFFOLK	MA	339	443,558	463-779
BOTETOURT CO.		VA	936	029,711	77-344
BOURBOIS TWP.	GASCONADE	MO	399	443,607	373-84
BOURBON CO.		KY	192	007,845	451-627
BOURBONNAIS	WILL	IL	133	442,921	281-322
BOVINA	DELAWARE	NY	495	017,071	453-84
BOW	MERRIMACK	NH	435	443,639	321-46
BOW TWP.	SOMERSET	ME	269	443,506	560
BOWDOIN	LINCOLN	ME	261	443,498	639-83
BOWDOINHAM	LINCOLN	ME	261	443,498	581-638
BOWEN TWP.	MADISON	AR	27	002,481	573-88
BOWERBANK	PISCATAQUIS	ME	267	443,504	633-37
BOWIE CO.		TX	908	024,887	339-70
BOWLING GREEN	YUBA	CA	36	442,879	519-21
BOWLING GREEN	CLAY	IN	138	007,751	476-82
BOWLING GREEN	PIKE	MO	409	443,617	321-26
BOWLING GREEN	CAROLINE	VA	939	029,714	603-7
BOWLING GREEN TWP.	LICKING	OH	702	444,695	237-74
BOWLING GREEN TWP.	MARION	OH	708	444,701	54-64
BOWLWARE TWP.	GASCONADE	MO	399	443,607	319-42
BOWNE	KENT	MI	353	443,569	632-37
BOX ANKLE	STEWART	GA	82	442,891	126-47
BOXBORO	MIDDLESEX	MA	323	443,542	323-332
BOXFORD	ESSEX	MA	314	014,708	809-832
BOYLE CO.		KY	192	007,845	629-766
BOYLSTON	WORCESTER	MA	343	443,562	583-607
BOYLSTON	OSWEGO	NY	578	444,294	371-86
BOZRAH	NEW LONDON	CT	48	442,880	129-49
BRACEVILLE	GRUNDY	IL	108	007,681	375-77
BRACEVILLE TWP.	TRUMBULL	OH	733	444,726	923-45
BRACKEN CO.		KY	193	007,846	767-958
BRADFORD	PENOBSCOT	ME	265	443,502	399-427
BRADFORD	ESSEX	MA	315	443,534	417-48
BRADFORD	MERRIMACK	NH	436	443,640	147-78
BRADFORD	STEUBEN	NY	600	444,316	501-548
BRADFORD	ORANGE	VT	926	444,925	341-82
BRADFORD	ROCK	WI	1005	444,992	909-925
BRADFORD CO.		PA	756	020,606	529-768, 1-252
BRADFORD CO.		PA	757	020,607	253-826
BRADFORD TWP.	LEE	IL	116	007,689	221-24
BRADFORD TWP.	CLEARFIELD	PA	768	444,736	650-68
BRADFORD TWP.	MC KEAN	PA	795	444,763	44-67
BRADLEY	PENOBSCOT	ME	264	443,501	523-42
BRADLEY CO.		AR	25	002,479	175-239
BRADLEY CO.		TN	871	024,562	275-551
BRADLEY VALE	CALEDONIA	VT	922	027,448	251-53
BRADSHAW TWP.	GREENE	AR	26	002,480	360-66
BRADY	KALAMAZOO	MI	353	443,569	200-213
BRADY TWP.	WILLIAMS	OH	741	444,734	1-27
BRADY TWP.	CLEARFIELD	PA	768	444,736	839-64
BRADY TWP.	HUNTINGDON	PA	784	444,752	427-51
BRADYS BEND TWP.	ARMSTRONG	PA	749	020,599	63-116
BRADY'S ROCK	CANNON	TN	872	024,563	797-814
BRADYVILLE	CANNON	TN	872	024,563	815-32, 837
BRAINTREE	NORFOLK	MA	331	443,550	183-254
BRAINTREE	ORANGE	VT	926	444,925	613-42
BRAINTRIM TWP.	WYOMING	PA	838	444,806	1-20
BRANCH CO.		MI	347	014,809	533-847

CITY, COUNTY, TOWN, OR TOWNSHIP	COUNTY	STATE	NA NO. M432	GD NO.	PAGES	
BRANCH HILLS	PENDLETON	VA	968	444,958	48	
BRANCH TWP.	SCHUYLKILL	PA	826	444,794	565-629	
BRANCHBURG	SOMERSET	NJ	463	443,662	881-908	
BRANDON	FRANKLIN	NY	505	017,081	539-53	
BRANDON	RUTLAND	VT	927	444,926	157-224	
BRANDON TWP.	JACKSON	IA	184	007,793	621-25,	646-48
BRANDON TWP.	OAKLAND	MI	360	443,576	677-700	
BRANDYWINE TWP.	HANCOCK	IN	149	442,927	437-57	
BRANDYWINE TWP.	SHELBY	IN	172	442,950	722-40	
BRANFORD	NEW HAVEN	CT	45	003,073	311-45	
BRANT	ERIE	NY	499	017,075	661-85	
BRASHER	ST. LAWRENCE	NY	591	444,307	779-842	
BRATTLEBORO	WINDHAM	VT	929	444,928	265-355	
BRAWLEY	BUREAU	IL	99	007,672	561-63	
BRAXTON CO.		VA	937	029,712	345-443	
BRAZEAU TWP.	PERRY	MO	409	443,617	151-218	
BRAZIL DICK	CLAY	IN	138	007,751	605-621	
BRAZORIA CO.		TX	908	024,887	373-404	
BRAZOS CO.		TX	908	024,887	407-418	
BRAZOS DIST.	BRAZOS	TX	908	024,887	407-418	
BRAZOS DIST.	BURLESON	TX	908	024,887	421-49	
BREATHITT CO.		KY	193	007,846	1-88	
BRECKENRIDGE TWP.	JACKSON	AR	27	002,481	132-34	
BRECKINRIDGE CO.		KY	193	007,846	90-298	
BRECKNOCK TWP.	BERKS	PA	754	020,604	755-75	
BRECKNOCK TWP.	LANCASTER	PA	789	444,757	639-71	
BRECKSVILLE TWP.	CUYAHOGA	OH	673	020,221	267-93	
BREMEN	LINCOLN	ME	260	443,497	923-44	
BREMEN TWP.	COOK	IL	103	007,676	55-60	
BRENTWOOD	ROCKINGHAM	NH	437	443,641	307-328	
BRETON TWP.	WASHINGTON	MO	421	443,629	319-45	
BREWER	PENOBSCOT	ME	264	443,501	345-407	
BREWER TWP.	PIKE	AR	29	002,483	355-63,	381, 384-86
BREWERSVILLE DIV.	SUMTER	AL	15	442,866	529-32,	610-13, 666-67
BREWSTER	BARNSTABLE	MA	303	014,697	251-87	
BRIAR CREEK TWP.	COLUMBIA	PA	769	444,737	291-316	
BRICK BRAND DIST.	CLARKE	GA	65	007,061	87-90	
BRICK TWP.	OCEAN	NJ	460	443,659	1-38	
BRIDESBURG BOR.	PHILADELPHIA	PA	824	444,792	143-65	
BRIDGEPORT	FAIRFIELD	CT	37	003,065	554-56,	561-88
BRIDGEPORT	JACKSON	IA	184	007,793	726	
BRIDGEPORT BOR.	FAYETTE	PA	780	444,748	629-60	
BRIDGEPORT TWP.	SAGINAW	MI	361	443,577	192-200	
BRIDGEPORT, WARD 1	FAIRFIELD	CT	37	003,065	409-461	
BRIDGEPORT, WARD 2	FAIRFIELD	CT	37	003,065	462-92	
BRIDGEPORT, WARD 3	FAIRFIELD	CT	37	003,065	493-519	
BRIDGEPORT, WARD 4	FAIRFIELD	CT	37	003,065	520-53	
BRIDGETON TWP.	CUMBERLAND	NJ	446	016,533	379-437	
BRIDGEWATER	PLYMOUTH	MA	333	443,552	1-67	
BRIDGEWATER	WASHTENAW	MI	364	443,580	681-708	
BRIDGEWATER	GRAFTON	NH	430	443,634	269-84	
BRIDGEWATER	ONEIDA	NY	562	444,278	115-46	
BRIDGEWATER	WILLIAMS	OH	741	444,734	89-100	
BRIDGEWATER	WINDSOR	VT	930	444,929	323-54	
BRIDGEWATER ACAD. GT.	AROOSTOOK	ME	248	009,718	149-52	
BRIDGEWATER TWP.	SOMERSET	NJ	463	443,662	477-574	
BRIDGEWATER TWP.	SUSQUEHANNA	PA	829	444,797	577-614	

CITY, COUNTY, TOWN, OR TOWNSHIP	COUNTY	STATE	NA NO. M432	GD NO.	PAGES
BRIDGTON	CUMBERLAND	ME	251	009,721	549-613
BRIDPORT	ADDISON	VT	920	027,446	1-34
BRIGHTON	SOMERSET	ME	269	443,506	449-66
BRIGHTON	MIDDLESEX	MA	326	443,545	129-88
BRIGHTON	MONROE	NY	528	017,104	617-91
BRIGHTON	ESSEX	VT	923	444,922	813-17
BRIGHTON	KENOSHA	WI	1000	444,987	389-410
BRIGHTON TWP.	LIVINGSTON	MI	356	443,572	812-36
BRIGHTON TWP.	LORAIN	OH	705	444,698	585-600
BRIGHTON TWP.	BEAVER	PA	750	020,600	137-63
BRIMFIELD	HAMPDEN	MA	319	443,538	483-516
BRIMFIELD	PORTAGE	OH	722	444,715	801-826
BRINKLEYS DIST.	SOMERSET	MD	297	443,528	699-808
BRISTOL	HARTFORD	CT	40	003,068	695-763
BRISTOL	KENDALL	IL	113	007,686	543-61
BRISTOL	LINCOLN	ME	260	443,497	1-76
BRISTOL	GRAFTON	NH	430	443,634	333-59
BRISTOL	ONTARIO	NY	571	444,287	59-100
BRISTOL	TRUMBULL	OH	733	444,726	541-67
BRISTOL	BRISTOL	RI	841	022,264	1-111
BRISTOL	ADDISON	VT	920	027,446	637-68
BRISTOL	DANE	WI	995	034,509	809-819
BRISTOL	KENOSHA	WI	1000	444,987	413-39
BRISTOL BOR.	BUCKS	PA	759	020,609	1-60
BRISTOL CO.		MA	307	014,701	1-649
BRISTOL CO.		MA	308	014,702	651-860, 1-424
BRISTOL CO.		MA	309	014,703	425-973
BRISTOL CO.		RI	841	022,264	1-207
BRISTOL TWP.	MORGAN	OH	715	444,708	659-99
BRISTOL TWP.	BUCKS	PA	759	020,609	61-104
BRISTOL TWP.	PHILADELPHIA	PA	824	444,792	167-220
BROAD CREEK DIST.	BEAUFORT	NC	620	018,106	707-716
BROAD RIVER	RUTHERFORD	NC	644	444,657	505, 508, 510-11, 525-28, 531-36, 566-67, 591-92, 601-4, 611-13, 617-18
BROAD TOP TWP.	BEDFORD	PA	751	020,601	521-36
BROADALBIN	FULTON	NY	506	017,082	61-121
BROADKILN HUN.	SUSSEX	DE	55	442,884	1-84
BROCKVILLE	STEUBEN	IN	173	442,951	256-58
BROCKWAY	ST. CLAIR	MI	362	443,578	460-65
BROKENSTRAW TWP.	WARREN	PA	832	444,800	651-66
BRONSON	BRANCH	MI	347	014,809	533-49
BRONSON TWP.	HURON	OH	697	444,690	285-314
BROOKE CO.		VA	937	029,712	447-566
BROOKFIELD	FAIRFIELD	CT	37	003,065	131-63
BROOKFIELD	LA SALLE	IL	115	007,688	531-36
BROOKFIELD	WORCESTER	MA	343	443,562	105-144
BROOKFIELD	EATON	MI	349	014,811	196-202
BROOKFIELD	CARROLL	NH	426	014,939	1-14
BROOKFIELD	MADISON	NY	527	017,103	107-119, 275 7-23, 50-104,
BROOKFIELD	TRUMBULL	OH	733	444,726	347-81
BROOKFIELD	TIOGA	PA	830	444,798	487-505
BROOKFIELD	ORANGE	VT	926	444,925	489-528
BROOKFIELD	WAUKESHA	WI	1009	444,996	861-908
BROOKFIELD TWP.	MORGAN	OH	715	444,708	75-110
BROOKHAVEN	SUFFOLK	NY	601	444,317	291-497

CITY, COUNTY, TOWN, OR TOWNSHIP	COUNTY	STATE	NA NO. M432	GD NO.	PAGES
BROOKLIN	HANCOCK	ME	254	443,491	305-328
BROOKLIN	MARQUETTE	WI	1002	444,989	229-41
BROOKLINE	NORFOLK	MA	331	443,550	123-82
BROOKLINE	HILLSBORO	NH	434	443,638	457-74
BROOKLINE	WINDHAM	VT	929	444,928	35-41
BROOKLYN	WINDHAM	CT	51	442,883	183-219
BROOKLYN	MC HENRY	IL	117	007,690	675-98
BROOKLYN	GREEN	WI	999	444,986	533-45
BROOKLYN TWP.	LEE	IL	116	007,689	261-69
BROOKLYN TWP.	OGLE	IL	123	442,911	201-214
BROOKLYN TWP.	SCHUYLER	IL	128	442,916	697-712
BROOKLYN TWP.	CUYAHOGA	OH	673	020,221	1-152
BROOKLYN TWP.	SUSQUEHANNA	PA	829	444,797	617-43
BROOKLYN TWP.	SAUK	WI	1006	444,993	40-50
BROOKLYN, WARD 1	KINGS	NY	517	017,093	1-145
BROOKLYN, WARD 2	KINGS	NY	517	017,093	147-369
BROOKLYN, WARD 3	KINGS	NY	517	017,093	371-579
BROOKLYN, WARD 4	KINGS	NY	518	017,094	583-845
BROOKLYN, WARD 5	KINGS	NY	518	017,094	1-326
BROOKLYN, WARD 6	KINGS	NY	519	017,095	329-605
BROOKLYN, WARD 7	KINGS	NY	519	017,095	607-756
BROOKLYN, WARD 8	KINGS	NY	519	017,095	1-62
BROOKLYN, WARD 9	KINGS	NY	520	017,096	65-142
BROOKLYN, WARD 10	KINGS	NY	520	017,096	145-403
BROOKLYN, WARD 11	KINGS	NY	520	017,096	405-723
BROOKS	WALDO	ME	271	443,508	373-97
BROOKSVILLE	HANCOCK	ME	254	443,491	243-74
BROOKVILLE BOR.	JEFFERSON	PA	786	444,754	276-95
BROOKVILLE TWP.	OGLE	IL	123	442,911	90-102
BROOKVILLE TWP.	FRANKLIN	IN	146	442,924	553-640
BROOM TOWN VALLEY	CHATTOOGA	GA	64	007,060	681-708
BROOME	SCHOHARIE	NY	595	444,311	77-130
BROOME CO.		NY	477	017,053	207-536
BROOME CO.		NY	478	017,054	541-949
BROTHERSVALLEY TWP.	SOMERSET	PA	828	444,796	329-63
BROWARDS DIST.	DUVAL	FL	58	006,714	199-202
BROWN CO.		IL	98	007,671	191-366
BROWN CO.		IN	137	007,750	379-498
BROWN CO.		OH	662	020,210	543-981, 1-238
BROWN CO.		WI	994	034,508	9-166
BROWN MILL DIST.	RUTHERFORD	TN	894	444,850	545-57
BROWN TWP.	UNION	AR	30	442,876	479-80
BROWN TWP.	HANCOCK	IN	149	442,927	348-69
BROWN TWP.	HENDRICKS	IN	150	442,928	305-334, 338-4
BROWN TWP.	MARTIN	IN	160	442,938	32-47
BROWN TWP.	MONTGOMERY	IN	161	442,939	1064-1110
BROWN TWP.	MORGAN	IN	162	442,940	208-236
BROWN TWP.	RIPLEY	IN	169	442,947	567-614
BROWN TWP.	WASHINGTON	IN	179	442,957	497-536
BROWN TWP.	CARROLL	OH	664	020,212	355-404
BROWN TWP.	DARKE	OH	674	020,222	961-79
BROWN TWP.	DELAWARE	OH	675	020,223	599-627
BROWN TWP.	FRANKLIN	OH	680	444,673	383-99
BROWN TWP.	KNOX	OH	700	444,693	849-87
BROWN TWP.	MIAMI	OH	711	444,704	823-59
BROWN TWP.	PAULDING	OH	719	444,712	379-87
BROWN TWP.	LYCOMING	PA	795	444,763	413-26
BROWN TWP.	MIFFLIN	PA	797	444,765	381-406
BROWNFIELD	OXFORD	ME	262	443,499	135-66

CITY, COUNTY, TOWN, OR TOWNSHIP	COUNTY	STATE	NA NO. M432	GD NO.	PAGES
BROWNHELM TWP.	LORAIN	OH	705	444,698	677-702
BROWNING TWP.	SCHUYLER	IL	128	442,916	837-57
BROWNINGS DIST.	DE KALB	GA	67	007,063	201-214
BROWNINGTON	ORLEANS	VT	925	444,924	5-19
BROWNS DIST.	PITT	NC	641	444,654	157-62
BROWN'S GROVE	MC LEON	IL	117	007,690	247
BROWNSBURG	HENDRICKS	IN	150	442,928	335-37
BROWNSTOWN	WAYNE	MI	366	443,582	1041-65
BROWNSTOWN TWP.	JACKSON	IN	152	442,930	407-448
BROWNSVILLE	UNION	IN	176	442,954	583-89
BROWNSVILLE	LICKING	OH	702	444,695	242-53
BROWNSVILLE	FAYETTE	PA	780	444,748	571-627
BROWNSVILLE	HAYWOOD	TN	883	444,839	1-14
BROWNSVILLE TWP.	UNION	IN	176	442,954	583-617
BROWNVILLE	PISCATAQUIS	ME	267	443,504	717-35
BROWNVILLE	JEFFERSON	NY	514	017,090	349-455
BROWNVILLE	ROSS	OH	725	444,718	712-17
BRUCE	LA SALLE	IL	115	007,688	491, 515, 519-24, 527
BRUCE	MACOMB	MI	357	443,573	209-246
BRULE GRAND CHINE	LAFOURCHE PAR.	LA	232	443,475	650-56
BRUNSWICK	CUMBERLAND	ME	251	009,721	389-507
BRUNSWICK	CHARITON	MO	395	443,603	460-66, 469-73
BRUNSWICK	RENSSELAER	NY	585	444,301	131-206
BRUNSWICK	MEDINA	OH	709	444,702	729-62
BRUNSWICK	ESSEX	VT	923	444,922	809-811
BRUNSWICK CO.		NC	621	018,107	273-373
BRUNSWICK CO.		VA	937	029,712	569-699
BRUNSWICK TWP.	CHARITON	MO	395	443,603	433, 437-59
BRUSH CREEK BEAT	PERRY	AL	12	002,354	637-49
BRUSH CREEK TWP.	WASHINGTON	AR	31	442,877	685-700
BRUSH CREEK TWP.	HIGHLAND	OH	694	444,687	687-723
BRUSH CREEK TWP.	JEFFERSON	OH	699	444,692	891-920
BRUSH CREEK TWP.	MUSKINGUM	OH	718	444,711	113-46
BRUSH CREEK TWP.	SCIOTO	OH	727	444,720	167-83
BRUSH CREEK TWP.	FULTON	PA	783	444,751	141-50
BRUSH RUN TWP.	IOWA	IA	184	007,793	556-58
BRUSHTOWN	ADAMS	PA	743	020,593	553
BRUSHVALLEY TWP.	INDIANA	PA	785	444,753	159-94
BRUSHY FORK	PENDLETON	VA	968	444,958	112-13
BRUSHY RUN	PENDLETON	VA	968	444,958	34, 77
BRUTUS	CAYUGA	NY	482	017,058	771-843
BRYAN CO.		GA	62	007,058	439-67
BRYANTOWN	CHARLES	MD	290	443,521	456, 458-59, 503-4, 534-35, 553-73, 579-80, 583-88
BUCHANAN CO.		IA	182	007,791	149-58
BUCHANAN CO.		MO	393	014,873	1-297
BUCK CREEK TWP.	HANCOCK	IN	149	442,927	505-514
BUCK ISLAND	STOKES	NC	645	444,658	186-99
BUCK TWP.	HARDIN	OH	692	444,685	323-34
BUCK TWP.	LUZERNE	PA	794	444,762	1031-44
BUCKEYE	STEPHENSON	IL	129	442,917	529-59
BUCKEYSTOWN DIST.	FREDERICK	MD	293	443,524	383-474
BUCKFIELD	OXFORD	ME	263	443,500	201-240
BUCKHEAD DIST.	DE KALB	GA	67	007,063	275-85
BUCKHEART	FULTON	IL	107	007,680	629-55
BUCKINGHAM	WAYNE	PA	835	444,803	7-21

CITY, COUNTY, TOWN, OR TOWNSHIP	COUNTY	STATE	NA NO. M432	GD NO.	PAGES
BUCKINGHAM CO.		VA	937	029,712	703-838
BUCKINGHAM TWP.	BUCKS	PA	758	020,608	141-206
BUCKLAND	FRANKLIN	MA	317	443,536	397-422
BUCKLES' GROVE	MC LEON	IL	117	007,690	209-211, 213, 2
BUCKS CO.		PA	758	020,608	1-664
BUCKS CO.		PA	759	020,609	1-702
BUCKS DIST.	PITT	NC	641	444,654	105-111
BUCKS TWP.	TUSCARAWAS	OH	734	444,727	67-99
BUCKSKIN TWP.	ROSS	OH	725	444,718	369-420
BUCKSPORT	HANCOCK	ME	254	443,491	1-79
BUCYRUS TWP.	CRAWFORD	OH	671	020,219	841-900
BUDDY'S LAKE SET.	BENTON	FL	58	006,714	41-44
BUELS GORE	CHITTENDEN	VT	923	444,922	427
BUENA VISTA DIST.	MARION	GA	77	442,886	575-80
BUENA VISTA TOWN	MARION	GA	77	442,886	600-607
BUENA VISTA TWP.	SCHUYLER	IL	128	442,916	759-79
BUENA VISTA TWP.	SAGINAW	MI	361	443,577	201-6
BUENAVISTA	FAYETTE	OH	678	444,671	262-64
BUENAVISTA	ST. CROIX	WI	1006	444,993	1-6
BUFFALO	MARQUETTE	WI	1002	444,989	165-78
BUFFALO DIST.	WAKE	NC	647	444,660	297-309
BUFFALO GROVE	OGLE	IL	123	442,911	87
BUFFALO HILLS	PENDLETON	VA	968	444,958	44-46
BUFFALO LICK TWP.	CHARITON	MO	395	443,603	351-63, 468
BUFFALO TWP.	OGLE	IL	123	442,911	63, 67-86, 88-8
BUFFALO TWP.	MORGAN	MO	408	443,616	522-42
BUFFALO TWP.	PIKE	MO	409	443,617	370-431
BUFFALO TWP.	GUERNSEY	OH	684	444,677	593-620
BUFFALO TWP.	BUTLER	PA	760	020,610	1-69
BUFFALO TWP.	PERRY	PA	805	444,773	1199-1214
BUFFALO TWP.	UNION	PA	831	444,799	515-47
BUFFALO TWP.	WASHINGTON	PA	834	444,802	864-93
BUFFALO VILLAGE	OGLE	IL	123	442,911	64-66
BUFFALO, WARD 1	ERIE	NY	501	017,077	1-175
BUFFALO, WARD 2	ERIE	NY	501	017,077	177-380
BUFFALO, WARD 3	ERIE	NY	501	017,077	381-501
BUFFALO, WARD 4	ERIE	NY	502	017,078	505-879
BUFFALO, WARD 5	ERIE	NY	502	017,078	881-1014
BULLITT CO.		KY	193	007,846	299-428
BULLOCH CO.		GA	62	007,058	469-536
BULLSKIN TWP.	FAYETTE	PA	780	444,748	867-900
BUNCOMBE CO.		NC	622	018,108	373-662
BUNCOMBE DIST.	CLARKE	GA	65	007,061	97-107
BUNCOMBE TWP.	INDEPENDENCE	AR	26	002,480	700-704
BUNDY DIST.	SURRY	NC	646	444,659	685-90
BUNKER HILL	MACOUPIN	IL	118	442,906	595-98
BUNKER HILL	INGHAM	MI	351	443,567	39-47
BUREAU	BUREAU	IL	99	007,672	426-29
BUREAU CO.		IL	99	007,672	367-584
BURKE	FRANKLIN	NY	505	017,081	555-614
BURKE	CALEDONIA	VT	922	027,448	527-53
BURKE CO.		GA	62	007,058	537-660
BURKE CO.		NC	622	018,108	663-802
BURKES DIST.	STEWART	GA	82	442,891	93-104
BURKESVILLE	CUMBERLAND	KY	197	442,965	555-59
BURLESON CO.		TX	908	024,887	421-49
BURLESON DIST.	BRAZOS	TX	908	024,887	407-418
BURLESON DIST.	BURLESON	TX	908	024,887	421-49
BURLINGTON	HARTFORD	CT	40	003,068	765-92

CITY, COUNTY, TOWN, OR TOWNSHIP	COUNTY	STATE	NA NO. M432	GD NO.	PAGES	
BURLINGTON	KANE	IL	112	007,685	155-70	
BURLINGTON	BOONE	KY	192	007,845	349-54	
BURLINGTON	PENOBSCOT	ME	266	443,503	589-600	
BURLINGTON	MIDDLESEX	MA	325	443,544	413-26	
BURLINGTON	CALHOUN	MI	348	014,810	431-50	
BURLINGTON	BURLINGTON	NJ	443	016,530	1-108	
BURLINGTON	OTSEGO	NY	580	444,296	1-44	
BURLINGTON	CHITTENDEN	VT	923	444,922	529-710	
BURLINGTON	RACINE	WI	1004	444,991	299-337	
BURLINGTON CO.		NJ	443	016,530	1-571	
BURLINGTON CO.		NJ	444	016,531	573-1070	
BURLINGTON TWP.	DES MOINES	IA	183	007,792	909-938	
BURLINGTON TWP.	BURLINGTON	NJ	443	016,530	1-129	
BURLINGTON TWP.	LICKING	OH	703	444,696	841-74	
BURLINGTON TWP.	BRADFORD	PA	756	020,606	59-106	
BURLINGTON, WARD 1	DES MOINES	IA	183	007,792	939-68	
BURLINGTON, WARD 2	DES MOINES	IA	183	007,792	969-94	
BURLINGTON, WARD 3	DES MOINES	IA	183	007,792	995-1037	
BURNETTE	DODGE	WI	996	034,510	79-96	
BURNETTE DIST.	RUTHERFORD	TN	894	444,850	297-307	
BURNEYS DIST.	PITT	NC	641	444,654	93-104	
BURNHAM	WALDO	ME	270	443,507	471-90	
BURNS	SHIAWASSEE	MI	363	443,579	142-59	
BURNS	ALLEGANY	NY	476	017,052	151-74	
BURNSIDE TWP.	CLEARFIELD	PA	768	444,736	773-97	
BURNSVILLE	YANCEY	NC	649	444,662	763-65	
BURNSVILLE BEAT	DALLAS	AL	4	002,346	597-601	
BURNSVILLE DIST.	ANSON	NC	619	018,105	410-19	
BURR OAK TWP.	ST. JOSEPH	MI	362	443,578	681-96	
BURRILLVILLE	PROVIDENCE	RI	843	444,809	463-548	
BURRITT	WINNEBAGO	IL	134	442,922	669-83	
BURTCHVILLE	ST. CLAIR	MI	362	443,578	466-77	
BURTON	ADAMS	IL	97	007,670	23-52	
BURTON	CATTARAUGUS	NY	479	017,055	415-39	
BURTON TWP.	GEAUGA	OH	682	444,675	417-42	
BUSHKILL TWP.	NORTHAMPTON	PA	803	444,771	679-722	
BUSHNELL TWP.	MONTCALM	MI	358	443,574	889-90	
BUSHWICK TWP.	KINGS	NY	521	017,097	185-274	
BUSTI	CHAUTAUQUA	NY	485	017,061	29-76	
BUTLER	WINNEBAGO	IL	134	442,922	710-25	
BUTLER	WAYNE	NY	613	444,329	595-651	
BUTLER BOR.	BUTLER	PA	760	020,610	71-99	
BUTLER CO.		AL	2	002,344	351-523	
BUTLER CO.		KY	194	007,847	429-558	
BUTLER CO.		MO	393	014,873	299-336	
BUTLER CO.		OH	663	020,211	239-979	
BUTLER CO.		PA	760	020,610	1-758	
BUTLER TWP.	DE KALB	IN	142	007,755	375-90	
BUTLER TWP.	FRANKLIN	IN	146	442,924	501-527	
BUTLER TWP.	MIAMI	IN	160	442,938	373-78,	392-405
BUTLER TWP.	JACKSON	IA	184	007,793	615-19,	626-30
BUTLER TWP.	BRANCH	MI	347	014,809	809-823	
BUTLER TWP.	COLUMBIANA	OH	669	020,217	598-638	
BUTLER TWP.	DARKE	OH	674	020,222	843-77	
BUTLER TWP.	KNOX	OH	700	444,693	779-98	
BUTLER TWP.	MERCER	OH	710	444,703	515-19	
BUTLER TWP.	MONTGOMERY	OH	713	444,706	229-75	
BUTLER TWP.	RICHLAND	OH	724	444,717	497-524	
BUTLER TWP.	ADAMS	PA	743	020,593	1-31	

CITY, COUNTY, TOWN, OR TOWNSHIP	COUNTY	STATE	NA NO. M432	GD NO.	PAGES
BUTLER TWP.	LUZERNE	PA	794	444,762	971-89
BUTLER TWP.	SCHUYLKILL	PA	826	444,794	45-54
BUTTE CO.		CA	33	002,490	1-89
BUTTER ISLAND	HANCOCK	ME	254	443,491	428
BUTTERNUTS	OTSEGO	NY	580	444,296	399-444
BUTTS CO.		GA	62	007,058	661-748
BUXTON	YORK	ME	275	443,512	93-164
BYBERRY TWP.	PHILADELPHIA	PA	824	444,792	221-47
BYRAM TWP.	SUSSEX	NJ	464	443,663	461-94
BYRD TWP.	BROWN	OH	662	020,210	107-170
BYRON	MC HENRY	IL	117	007,690	953-72
BYRON	OXFORD	ME	262	443,499	403-410
BYRON	KENT	MI	353	443,569	499-506
BYRON	GENESEE	NY	507	017,083	133-70
BYRON	FOND DU LAC	WI	997	444,984	564-83
BYRON TWP.	OGLE	IL	123	442,911	220-30
BYRON VILLAGE	OGLE	IL	123	442,911	215-19
CABARRUS CO.		NC	622	018,108	803-971
CABELL CO.		VA	938	029,713	1-141
CABOT	CALEDONIA	VT	922	027,448	277-311
CACA COLORADO	VALENCIA	NM	470	443,668	545-58
CACHE CREEK TWP.	YOLO	CA	36	442,879	373-79
CACHE TWP.	JACKSON	AR	27	002,481	89-94
CACHE TWP.	MONROE	AR	28	002,482	752-63
CACHE TWP.	ST. FRANCIS	AR	30	442,876	79-82
CADDO PARISH		LA	230	009,697	639-802
CADDO PRAIRIE	CADDO PARISH	LA	230	009,697	709-714
CADDO TWP.	CLARK	AR	25	002,479	401-415
CADDO TWP.	MONTGOMERY	AR	28	002,482	805-811
CADIZ	HARRISON	OH	693	444,686	711-39
CADIZ	GREEN	WI	999	444,986	547-58
CADIZ TWP.	HARRISON	OH	693	444,686	711-72
CADRON TWP.	CONWAY	AR	25	002,479	508-513
CADRON TWP.	VAN BUREN	AR	31	442,877	649-56
CAERNARVON TWP.	BERKS	PA	754	020,604	777-800
CAERNARVON TWP.	LANCASTER	PA	789	444,757	773-810
CAESAR CREEK TWP.	DEARBORN	IN	141	007,754	839-50
CAESAR CREEK TWP.	GREENE	OH	683	444,676	845-89
CAHAWBA BEAT	DALLAS	AL	4	002,346	235-551
CAHAWBA VALLEY BEAT	JEFFERSON	AL	7	002,349	365-73
CAIN CREEK	RUTHERFORD	NC	644	444,657	585-90, 681-84
CAIN TWP.	FOUNTAIN	IN	145	442,923	243-66
CAINS DIST.	GWINNETT	GA	71	007,067	427, 429-42
CAIRO	ALEXANDER	IL	98	007,671	661-67
CAIRO	GREENE	NY	509	017,085	131-96
CALAIS	WASHINGTON	ME	273	443,510	249-362
CALAIS	MONROE	OH	712	444,705	499-501
CALAIS	WASHINGTON	VT	928	444,927	415-48
CALAMUS	DODGE	WI	996	034,510	189-200
CALAVERAS CO.		CA	33	002,490	93-492
CALAVERAS CREEK	BEXAR	TX	908	024,887	310-12
CALAVERAS DIST.	CALAVERAS	CA	33	002,490	93-492
CALCASIEU PARISH		LA	230	009,697	735-801
CALCUTTA TOWN	COLUMBIANA	OH	669	020,217	425-30
CALDWELL	WARREN	NY	609	444,325	1-18
CALDWELL CO.		KY	194	007,847	559-799

28

CITY, COUNTY, TOWN, OR TOWNSHIP	COUNTY	STATE	NA NO. M432	GD NO.	PAGES
CALDWELL CO.		MO	393	014,873	337-88
CALDWELL CO.		NC	623	018,109	1-122
CALDWELL CO.		TX	909	024,888	453-78
CALDWELL PARISH		LA	230	009,697	1-40
CALDWELL TWP.	APPANOOSE	IA	182	007,791	48-54
CALDWELL TWP.	ESSEX	NJ	449	443,648	135-91
CALEDONIA	BOONE	IL	98	007,671	111-28
CALEDONIA	PULASKI	IL	125	442,913	593-96
CALEDONIA	KENT	MI	353	443,569	525-27
CALEDONIA	SHIAWASSEE	MI	363	443,579	101-112
CALEDONIA	LIVINGSTON	NY	524	017,100	675-718
CALEDONIA	RACINE	WI	1004	444,991	205-230
CALEDONIA CO.		VT	922	027,448	1-600
CALF CREEK	SEARCY	AR	30	442,876	325-28
CALF ISLAND	HANCOCK	ME	254	443,491	333
CALHOUN CO.		FL	58	006,714	57-79
CALHOUN CO.		IL	99	007,672	585-668
CALHOUN CO.		MI	348	014,810	1-479
CALHOUN CO.		TX	909	024,888	481-503
CALIFORNIA	BRANCH	MI	347	014,809	787-98
CALIFORNIA DIST.	COBB	GA	66	007,062	265-68, 417-38
CALIFORNIA TWP.	STARKE	IN	172	442,950	237-40
CALLAWAY CO.		MO	393	014,873	389-625
CALLICOON	SULLIVAN	NY	603	443,648	297-344
CALLOWAY CO.		KY	194	007,847	800-971
CALUMET	FOND DU LAC	WI	997	444,984	723-64
CALUMET CO.		WI	994	034,508	169-211
CALUMET TWP.	PIKE	MO	409	443,617	432-82
CALVERT CO.		MD	288	443,519	1-127
CALVIN TWP.	CASS	MI	349	014,811	565-80
CAMANCHE TWP.	CLINTON	IA	182	007,791	372-83
CAMBRIA	NIAGARA	NY	561	444,277	557-613
CAMBRIA CO.		PA	761	020,611	1-437
CAMBRIA TWP.	HILLSDALE	MI	351	443,567	765-82
CAMBRIA TWP.	CAMBRIA	PA	761	020,611	331-64
CAMBRIDGE	WAYNE	IN	180	442,958	26-54
CAMBRIDGE	SOMERSET	ME	268	443,505	227-38
CAMBRIDGE	MIDDLESEX	MA	325	443,544	1-363
CAMBRIDGE	LENAWEE	MI	355	443,571	51-74
CAMBRIDGE	COOS	NH	429	443,633	285
CAMBRIDGE	WASHINGTON	NY	611	444,327	769-830
CAMBRIDGE	GUERNSEY	OH	684	444,677	527-53
CAMBRIDGE	LAMOILLE	VT	925	444,924	185-228
CAMBRIDGE TWP.	GUERNSEY	OH	684	444,677	527-92
CAMDEN	OUACHITA	AR	28	002,482	167-79
CAMDEN	WALDO	ME	270	443,507	339-434
CAMDEN	ONEIDA	NY	564	444,280	443-510
CAMDEN	KERSHAW	SC	854	444,817	141-57
CAMDEN	BENTON	TN	870	024,561	697-700
CAMDEN CO.		GA	62	007,058	749-98
CAMDEN CO.		MO	394	014,874	627-79
CAMDEN CO.		NJ	445	016,532	1-616
CAMDEN CO.		NC	623	018,109	123-215
CAMDEN, MIDDLE WARD	CAMDEN	NJ	445	016,532	61-128
CAMDEN, NORTH WARD	CAMDEN	NJ	445	016,532	1-60
CAMDEN, SOUTH WARD	CAMDEN	NJ	445	016,532	130-227
CAMDEN TWP.	SCHUYLER	IL	128	442,916	747-57
CAMDEN TWP.	HILLSDALE	MI	351	443,567	647-61
CAMDEN TWP.	LORAIN	OH	705	444,698	559-83

CITY, COUNTY, TOWN, OR TOWNSHIP	COUNTY	STATE	NA NO. M432	GD NO.	PAGES
CAMERON	STEUBEN	NY	599	444,315	657-98
CAMERON CO.		TX	909	024,888	507-709
CAMILLUS	ONONDAGA	NY	567	444,283	448-522
CAMP CREEK	RUTHERFORD	NC	644	444,657	702, 704-5
CAMP CREEK TWP.	PIKE	OH	721	444,714	711-20
CAMP POINT	ADAMS	IL	97	007,670	53-66
CAMPBELL	IONIA	MI	352	443,568	271-72
CAMPBELL	STEUBEN	NY	598	444,314	223-50
CAMPBELL CO.		GA	62	007,058	799-935
CAMPBELL CO.		KY	195	007,848	1-31C
CAMPBELL CO.		TN	872	024,563	553-689
CAMPBELL CO.		VA	938	029,713	145-441
CAMPBELL TWP.	SEARCY	AR	30	442,876	342-57
CAMPBELL TWP.	JENNINGS	IN	155	442,933	864-82
CAMPBELL TWP.	WARRICK	IN	179	442,957	283-311
CAMPBELL TWP.	GREENE	MO	400	443,608	489-532
CAMPBELL TWP.	TANEY	MO	420	443,628	771-76
CAMPBELLSVILLE	TAYLOR	KY	219	442,987	381-88
CAMPO SECO	TUOLUMNE	CA	36	442,879	167-74, 223-24, 229-30
CAMPTON	GRAFTON	NH	431	443,635	495-529
CANAAN	LITCHFIELD	CT	42	003,070	77-139
CANAAN	JEFFERSON	IN	154	442,932	459-61
CANAAN	SOMERSET	ME	268	443,505	125-65
CANAAN	GRAFTON	NH	430	443,634	149-89
CANAAN	COLUMBIA	NY	492	017,068	155-203
CANAAN	ESSEX	VT	923	444,922	823-34
CANAAN TWP.	GASCONADE	MO	399	443,607	357-72
CANAAN TWP.	ATHENS	OH	660	020,208	59-86
CANAAN TWP.	MADISON	OH	706	444,699	541-54
CANAAN TWP.	MORROW	OH	716	444,709	729-58
CANAAN TWP.	WAYNE	OH	740	444,733	767-814
CANAAN TWP.	WAYNE	PA	835	444,803	253-99
CANADA	JEFFERSON	NY	514	017,090	851 AFTER 943
CANADA LINE	SOMERSET	ME	269	443,506	537
CANADA ROAD	SOMERSET	ME	269	443,506	541
CANADIAN TWP.	MISSISSIPPI	AR	28	002,482	689-96
CANADICE	ONTARIO	NY	571	444,287	129-54
CANAJOHARIE	MONTGOMERY	NY	532	017,108	315-412
CANAL TWP.	VENANGO	PA	832	444,800	325-46
CANAL WINCHESTER	FAIRFIELD	OH	677	444,670	294-301
CANANDAIGUA	ONTARIO	NY	571	444,287	297-444
CANDIA	ROCKINGHAM	NH	437	443,641	473-508
CANDOR	TIOGA	NY	604	444,320	245-326
CANE CREEK PREC.	GALLATIN	IL	107	007,680	705-722
CANE HILL TWP.	WASHINGTON	AR	31	442,877	819-38
CANEADEA	ALLEGANY	NY	475	017,051	365-400
CANEBREAK	MACON	NC	636	444,649	741-42
CANFIELD TWP.	MAHONING	OH	707	444,700	1000-1103
CANISTEO	STEUBEN	NY	599	444,315	1-49
CANJAUNE	LAFOURCHE PAR.	LA	232	443,475	585
CANNON	KENT	MI	353	443,569	545-61
CANNON CO.		TN	872	024,563	693-895
CANOE TWP.	INDIANA	PA	785	444,753	449-71
CANONSBURG BOR.	WASHINGTON	PA	834	444,802	775-89
CANTERBURY	WINDHAM	CT	51	442,883	335-74
CANTERBURY	MERRIMACK	NH	436	443,640	399-437
CANTON	HARTFORD	CT	40	003,068	583-630
CANTON	FULTON	IL	107	007,680	301-338, 539-63

CITY, COUNTY, TOWN, OR TOWNSHIP	COUNTY	STATE	NA NO. M432	GD NO.	PAGES
CANTON	OXFORD	ME	263	443,500	241-64
CANTON	NORFOLK	MA	329	443,548	277-339
CANTON	WAYNE	MI	366	443,582	659-90
CANTON	ST. LAWRENCE	NY	590	444,306	583-700
CANTON TWP.	JACKSON	IA	184	007,793	665-66
CANTON TWP.	STARK	OH	730	444,723	695, 989-1092
CANTON TWP.	BRADFORD	PA	756	020,606	177-219
CANTON TWP.	WASHINGTON	PA	834	444,802	833-63
CANTWEEL'S BRIDGE	NEW CASTLE	DE	54	006,438	337-48
CANUSE TWP.	HEMPSTEAD	AR	26	002,480	458-80
CANYON CREEK	EL DORADO	CA	34	002,491	879-84
CAPE CINQUEHOMME TWP.	PERRY	MO	409	443,617	72-114, 120-50
CAPE ELIZABETH	CUMBERLAND	ME	251	009,721	651-700
CAPE FEAR	BLADEN	NC	621	018,107	145-204
CAPE FEAR RIVER	BLADEN	NC	621	018,107	205-272
CAPE GIRARDEAU CO.		MO	394	014,874	681-972
CAPE HATTERAS DIST.	HYDE	NC	634	444,647	785-98
CAPE MAY CO.		NJ	446	016,533	1-160
CAPE VINCENT	JEFFERSON	NY	514	017,090	769-841
CARBON CO.		PA	762	020,612	439-824
CARBONDALE	LUZERNE	PA	793	444,761	627-746
CARBONDALE TWP.	LUZERNE	PA	793	444,761	747-58
CARDINGTON	MORROW	OH	716	444,709	786-92
CARDINGTON TWP.	MORROW	OH	716	444,709	759-92
CAREY	WILL	IL	133	442,921	341-46
CARLINVILLE	MACOUPIN	IL	118	442,906	343-53
CARLISLE	MIDDLESEX	MA	324	443,543	961-76
CARLISLE	SCHOHARIE	NY	596	444,312	765-808
CARLISLE BOR.	CUMBERLAND	PA	773	444,741	655-764
CARLISLE TWP.	LORAIN	OH	705	444,698	867-902
CARLOWVILLE BEAT	DALLAS	AL	4	002,346	509-513, 515
CARLTON	ORLEANS	NY	575	444,291	1-71
CARLTON TWP.	BARRY	MI	346	014,808	223-29
CARMEL	PENOBSCOT	ME	265	443,502	699-730
CARMEL	EATON	MI	349	014,811	215-28
CARMEL	PUTNAM	NY	581	444,297	291-349
CARMI DIST.	WHITE	IL	132	442,920	529-33
CAROGA	FULTON	NY	506	017,082	461-75
CAROLINE	TOMPKINS	NY	605	444,321	1-61
CAROLINE CO.		MD	288	443,519	129-340
CAROLINE CO.		VA	939	029,714	445-630
CAROLINE TWP.	PRAIRIE	AR	29	002,483	597-609
CARONDELET	ST. LOUIS	MO	414	443,622	549-75
CARONDELET TWP.	ST. LOUIS	MO	414	443,622	549-75, 579-624
CAROTHERS TWP.	CLAY	IN	138	007,751	417-25
CARR TWP.	JACKSON	IN	152	442,930	335-58
CARROLL	PENOBSCOT	ME	266	443,503	655-64
CARROLL	COOS	NH	429	443,633	319-26
CARROLL	CHAUTAUQUA	NY	485	017,061	161-204
CARROLL CO.		AR	25	002,479	241-347
CARROLL CO.		GA	63	007,059	1-197
CARROLL CO.		IL	99	007,672	669-786
CARROLL CO.		IN	137	007,750	499-768
CARROLL CO.		KY	195	007,848	311-426
CARROLL CO.		MD	289	443,520	341-826
CARROLL CO.		MS	369	014,848	395-608
CARROLL CO.		MO	395	443,603	1-115
CARROLL CO.		NH	426	014,939	1-506
CARROLL CO.		OH	664	020,212	1-441

CITY, COUNTY, TOWN, OR TOWNSHIP	COUNTY	STATE	NA NO. M432	GD NO.	PAGES
CARROLL CO.		TN	873	024,564	1-314
CARROLL CO.		VA	939	029,714	633-770
CARROLL PARISH		LA	230	009,697	41-96
CARROLL TWP.	OUACHITA	AR	26	002,482	67-69
CARROLL TWP.	CARROLL	IL	99	007,672	775-86
CARROLL TWP.	PLATTE	MO	410	443,618	806-839
CARROLL TWP.	OTTAWA	OH	719	444,712	300-309
CARROLL TWP.	CAMBRIA	PA	761	020,611	33-59
CARROLL TWP.	PERRY	PA	805	444,773	957-85
CARROLL TWP.	WASHINGTON	PA	833	444,801	455-89
CARROLL TWP.	YORK	PA	840	444,808	641-60
CARROLLSVILLE BEAT	JEFFERSON	AL	7	002,349	336-41
CARROLLTON	PICKENS	AL	13	442,864	5-9
CARROLLTON	GREENE	IL	108	007,681	161-79
CARROLLTON	JEFFERSON PAR.	LA	232	443,475	87-119
CARROLLTON	CATTARAUGUS	NY	479	017,055	441-53
CARROLLTON	MONTGOMERY	OH	713	444,706	96-100
CARROLLTON TWP.	CARROLL	AR	25	002,479	241-60
CARROLLTON TWP.	CARROLL	IN	137	007,750	747-68
CARRYALL TWP.	PAULDING	OH	719	444,712	351-62
CARTER CO.		KY	195	007,848	427-571
CARTER CO.		TN	873	024,564	317-464
CARTER TWP.	ASHLEY	AR	25	002,479	84-86
CARTER TWP.	SPENCER	IN	172	442,950	1-21, 23-24
CARTERET CO.		NC	623	018,109	217-346
CARTHAGE	FRANKLIN	ME	253	009,723	29-38
CARTHAGE TWP.	ATHENS	OH	660	020,208	163-88
CARTOCGECHAYE TWP.	MACON	NC	636	444,649	765
CARVER	PLYMOUTH	MA	333	443,552	359-87
CASCADE	KENT	MI	353	443,569	517-24, 529
CASCADE TWP.	LYCOMING	PA	795	444,763	387-97
CASCO	CUMBERLAND	ME	249	009,719	241-67
CASCO	ST. CLAIR	MI	362	443,578	289-92
CASEY CO.		KY	196	007,849	573-718
CASEYS DIST.	DE KALB	GA	67	007,063	298-312
CASHIERS VALLEY	MACON	NC	636	444,649	738-39
CASS	FULTON	IL	107	007,680	588-603
CASS CO.		GA	63	007,059	199-444
CASS CO.		IL	99	007,672	1-172
CASS CO.		IN	137	007,750	769-1061
CASS CO.		MI	349	014,811	481-767
CASS CO.		MO	395	443,603	117-250
CASS CO.		TX	909	024,868	713-800
CASS TWP.	CLAY	IN	138	007,751	427-39
CASS TWP.	GREENE	IN	148	442,926	843-62
CASS TWP.	LA PORTE	IN	157	442,935	635-43
CASS TWP.	PULASKI	IN	166	442,944	678-79
CASS TWP.	GREENE	MO	400	443,608	699-721
CASS TWP.	TANEY	MO	420	443,628	729-35
CASS TWP.	HANCOCK	OH	692	444,685	107-122
CASS TWP.	RICHLAND	OH	724	444,717	387-421
CASS TWP.	HUNTINGDON	PA	784	444,752	409-425
CASS TWP.	SCHUYLKILL	PA	827	444,795	77-155
CASSOPOLIS VILLAGE	CASS	MI	349	014,811	621-29
CASSTOWN	MIAMI	OH	711	444,704	77-84
CASTILE	WYOMING	NY	616	444,332	307-365
CASTINE	HANCOCK	ME	254	443,491	173-201
CASTLETON	RICHMOND	NY	587	444,303	1-129, 133
CASTLETON	RUTLAND	VT	927	444,926	353-424

CITY, COUNTY, TOWN, OR TOWNSHIP	COUNTY	STATE	NA NO. M432	GD NO.	PAGES
CASTLETON TWP.	BARRY	MI	346	014,808	241-48
CASTOR TWP.	STODDARD	MO	420	443,628	522-66, 579-82
CASTROVILLE	MEDINA	TX	912	444,915	815-22
CASWELL CO.		NC	623	018,109	347-526
CATAHOULA PARISH		LA	230	009,697	97-184
CATAHOULAS DIST.	HANCOCK	MS	372	443,584	145
CATAWBA CO.		NC	624	444,637	527-700
CATAWISSA TWP.	COLUMBIA	PA	769	444,737	641-68
CATES DIST.	GWINNETT	GA	71	007,067	291-309, 317-22, 367, 397-98, 413
CATHARINE	CHEMUNG	NY	486	017,062	110-84
CATHERINE TWP.	BLAIR	PA	755	020,605	247-68
CATHIES CREEK	RUTHERFORD	NC	644	444,657	537-53, 615-16, 713
CATLIN	CHEMUNG	NY	486	017,062	1-36
CATO	CAYUGA	NY	481	017,057	1-56
CATOCTIN EL. DIST.	FREDERICK	MD	293	443,524	713-50
CATON	STEUBEN	NY	598	444,314	107-135
CATSKILL	GREENE	NY	510	017,086	675-806
CATTARAUGUS CO.		NY	479	017,055	1-590, 609-654
CATTARAUGUS CO.		NY	480	017,056	591-608, 655-980
CAVENDISH	WINDSOR	VT	931	444,930	605-642
CAVETOWN	WASHINGTON	MD	298	443,529	473-76
CAYUGA CO.		NY	481	017,057	1-418
CAYUGA CO.		NY	482	017,058	419-843
CAYUGA CO.		NY	483	017,059	1-519
CAYUTA	CHEMUNG	NY	486	017,062	293-317
CAZENOVIA	MADISON	NY	526	017,102	115-229
CEBOLLETA	VALENCIA	NM	470	443,668	411-25
CECIL CO.		MD	290	443,521	1-432
CECIL TWP.	WASHINGTON	PA	833	444,801	161-84
CEDAR CO.		IA	182	007,794	163-256
CEDAR CO.		MO	395	443,603	253-331
CEDAR CREEK DIST.	GRANVILLE	NC	631	444,644	271-85
CEDAR CREEK HUN.	SUSSEX	DE	55	442,884	128-84
CEDAR CREEK TWP.	MADISON	AR	27	002,481	565-70
CEDAR CREEK TWP.	ALLEN	IN	135	007,748	543-62
CEDAR CREEK TWP.	LAKE	IN	157	442,935	252-63
CEDAR HILL DIST.	ANSON	NC	619	018,105	397-409
CEDAR ISLAND	CARTERET	NC	623	018,109	226-29
CEDAR KEY	LEVY	FL	59	006,715	147-48
CEDAR TWP.	CLARK	AR	25	002,479	388-93
CEDAR TWP.	JEFFERSON	IA	185	442,960	1-15
CEDAR TWP.	JOHNSON	IA	185	442,960	337-40
CEDAR TWP.	MUSCATINE	IA	187	442,962	753-59
CEDAR TWP.	VAN BUREN	IA	189	442,964	555-69
CEDARBURG	WASHINGTON	WI	1008	444,995	226-54
CELINA	MERCER	OH	710	444,703	469-74
CENTER	BUREAU	IL	99	007,672	546-55
CENTER	FULTON	IL	107	007,680	604-628
CENTER	MC HENRY	IL	117	007,690	719-46
CENTER	MARION	IN	159	442,937	368-86
CENTER	STANLEY	NC	645	444,658	1-16
CENTER	LAFAYETTE	WI	1001	444,988	727-41
CENTER	ROCK	WI	1005	444,992	536-50
CENTER CREEK	JASPER	MO	402	443,610	755-56
CENTER DIST.	MECKLENBURG	NC	637	444,650	86-89
CENTER HARBOUR	BELKNAP	NH	425	014,938	1-14
CENTER TWP.	POLK	AR	29	002,483	455-58, 464-66

CITY, COUNTY, TOWN, OR TOWNSHIP	COUNTY	STATE	NA NO. M432	GD NO.	PAGES
CENTER TWP.	DEARBORN	IN	141	007,754	478-93
CENTER TWP.	DELAWARE	IN	143	007,756	738-43, 809-815
CENTER TWP.	GRANT	IN	147	442,925	505-552
CENTER TWP.	GREENE	IN	148	442,926	557-88
CENTER TWP.	HANCOCK	IN	149	442,927	329-48
CENTER TWP.	HENDRICKS	IN	150	442,928	64-74, 80-83, 260-61, 269, 274-80
CENTER TWP.	HOWARD	IN	151	442,929	903-926
CENTER TWP.	LAKE	IN	157	442,935	217-39
CENTER TWP.	LA PORTE	IN	157	442,935	481-503
CENTER TWP.	MARION	IN	159	442,937	345-584
CENTER TWP.	PORTER	IN	165	442,943	193-218
CENTER TWP.	RUSH	IN	170	442,948	971-1000
CENTER TWP.	ST. JOSEPH	IN	171	442,949	122-33
CENTER TWP.	STARKE	IN	172	442,950	225-56
CENTER TWP.	UNION	IN	176	442,954	618-57
CENTER TWP.	VANDERBURGH	IN	176	442,954	921-44
CENTER TWP.	WAYNE	IN	180	442,958	359-405
CENTER TWP.	CEDAR	IA	182	007,791	201-229
CENTER TWP.	HENRY	IA	184	007,793	371-91
CENTER TWP.	BUCHANAN	MO	393	014,873	138-63
CENTER TWP.	KNOX	MO	403	443,611	163-83
CENTER TWP.	CARROLL	OH	664	020,212	1-29
CENTER TWP.	COLUMBIANA	OH	669	020,217	639-705
CENTER TWP.	GUERNSEY	OH	684	444,677	331-57
CENTER TWP.	MERCER	OH	710	444,703	487-501
CENTER TWP.	MONROE	OH	712	444,705	869-939
CENTER TWP.	MORGAN	OH	715	444,708	587-622
CENTER TWP.	WILLIAMS	OH	741	444,734	129-50
CENTER TWP.	WOOD	OH	741	444,734	299-308
CENTER TWP.	BUTLER	PA	760	020,610	539-74
CENTER TWP.	COLUMBIA	PA	769	444,737	329-53
CENTER TWP.	GREENE	PA	783	444,751	529-70
CENTER TWP.	INDIANA	PA	785	444,753	257-85
CENTER TWP.	PERRY	PA	805	444,773	1003-1025
CENTERVILLE	EL DORADO	CA	34	002,491	861-62
CENTERVILLE	ST. CLAIR	IL	126	442,914	779-841
CENTERVILLE	WAYNE	IN	180	442,958	337-58
CENTERVILLE	WASHINGTON	ME	273	443,510	97-101
CENTERVILLE	ALLEGANY	NY	476	017,052	569-604
CENTERVILLE	MONTGOMERY	OH	713	444,706	42-44
CENTERVILLE	MANITOWOC	WI	1002	444,989	95-99
CENTERVILLE BOR.	BUTLER	PA	760	020,610	635-42
CENTRAL TWP.	ST. LOUIS	MO	414	443,622	689-707
CENTRE CO.		PA	763	020,613	1-577
CENTRE TWP.	BERKS	PA	752	020,602	143-74
CENTRE TWP.	UNION	PA	831	444,799	35-86
CERES TWP.	MC KEAN	PA	795	444,763	80-96
CERESCO	FOND DU LAC	WI	997	444,984	683-91
CESSNA TWP.	HARDIN	OH	692	444,685	417-22
CHAGRIN FALLS	CUYAHOGA	OH	673	020,221	843-74
CHALK BLUFF TWP.	GREENE	AR	26	002,480	367-68
CHAMBERS CO.		AL	2	002,344	527-832
CHAMBERSBURG	FRANKLIN	PA	781	444,749	427-506
CHAMPAGNOLLE TWP.	DALLAS	AR	26	002,480	8-11
CHAMPAGNOLLE TWP.	OUACHITA	AR	28	002,482	49-53
CHAMPAIGN CO.		IL	99	007,672	175-240
CHAMPAIGN CO.		OH	665	020,213	443-954

CITY, COUNTY, TOWN, OR TOWNSHIP	COUNTY	STATE	NA NO. M432	GD NO.	PAGES
CHAMPION	JEFFERSON	NY	516	017,092	749-98
CHAMPION	TRUMBULL	OH	733	444,726	415-40
CHAMPION TWP.	TRUMBULL	OH	733	444,726	427-37
CHAMPLAIN	CLINTON	NY	490	017,066	851-971
CHANCEFORD TWP.	YORK	PA	839	444,807	453-93
CHANNAHON	WILL	IL	133	442,921	203-217
CHAPLIN	WINDHAM	CT	51	442,883	819-39
CHAPMAN TWP.	CLINTON	PA	768	444,736	155-68
CHAPMAN TWP.	UNION	PA	831	444,799	291-326
CHARDON TWP.	GEAUGA	OH	682	444,675	443-506
CHARITON CO.		MO	395	443,603	333-476
CHARITON TWP.	APPANOOSE	IA	182	007,791	28-32
CHARITON TWP.	CHARITON	MO	395	443,603	399-408
CHARITON TWP.	RANDOLPH	MO	411	443,619	474-95
CHARLEMONT	FRANKLIN	MA	317	443,536	477-504
CHARLES CITY CO.		VA	939	029,714	773-830
CHARLES CO.		MD	290	443,521	433-589
CHARLESTON	COLES	IL	101	007,674	21-41
CHARLESTON	PENOBSCOT	ME	265	443,502	347-79
CHARLESTON	KALAMAZOO	MI	353	443,569	243-63
CHARLESTON	MONTGOMERY	NY	532	017,108	75-128
CHARLESTON	ORLEANS	VT	925	444,924	231-54
CHARLESTON	KANAWSA	VA	954	444,944	1-19
CHARLESTON CO.		SC	850	022,530	165-875
CHARLESTON NECK	CHARLESTON	SC	850	022,530	589-732
CHARLESTON PREC.	COLES	IL	101	007,674	42-76
CHARLESTON TWP.	TIOGA	PA	830	444,798	139-74
CHARLESTON, WARD 1	CHARLESTON	SC	850	022,530	165-238
CHARLESTON, WARD 2	CHARLESTON	SC	850	022,530	239-314
CHARLESTON, WARD 3	CHARLESTON	SC	850	022,530	315-431
CHARLESTON, WARD 4	CHARLESTON	SC	850	022,530	433-587
CHARLESTOWN	CLARK	IN	138	007,751	179-276
CHARLESTOWN	CECIL	MD	290	443,521	161-64
CHARLESTOWN	MIDDLESEX	MA	322	443,541	45-456
CHARLESTOWN	SULLIVAN	NH	441	443,645	377-416
CHARLESTOWN	WASHINGTON	RI	847	444,813	755-79
CHARLESTOWN	JEFFERSON	VA	953	444,943	585-611
CHARLESTOWN TWP.	PORTAGE	OH	722	444,715	299-318
CHARLESTOWN TWP.	CHESTER	PA	764	020,614	729-52
CHARLOTTE	WASHINGTON	ME	273	443,510	223-40
CHARLOTTE	CHAUTAUQUA	NY	484	017,060	409-449
CHARLOTTE	MECKLENBURG	NC	637	444,650	186-203
CHARLOTTE	CHITTENDEN	VT	923	444,922	155-93
CHARLOTTE CO.		VA	940	029,715	1-119
CHARLOTTE DIV.	CHARLOTTE	VA	940	029,715	1-119
CHARLOTTESVILLE	ALBEMARLE	VA	932	029,707	395-419
CHARLTON	WORCESTER	MA	345	443,564	365-412
CHARLTON	SARATOGA	NY	593	444,309	689-734
CHARTIERS TWP.	WASHINGTON	PA	834	444,802	633-72
CHASE'S RANCH	SUTTER	CA	36	442,879	48
CHATEAUGAY	FRANKLIN	NY	505	017,081	253-341
CHATFIELD TWP.	CRAWFORD	OH	671	020,219	1-34
CHATHAM	MIDDLESEX	CT	44	003,072	647-51, 654-83
CHATHAM	BARNSTABLE	MA	303	014,697	367-425
CHATHAM	CARROLL	NH	426	014,939	17-29
CHATHAM	COLUMBIA	NY	492	017,068	59-154
CHATHAM CO.		GA	64	007,060	445-680
CHATHAM CO.		NC	624	444,637	703-1001
CHATHAM TWP.	MORRIS	NJ	458	443,657	347-405

35

.

CITY, COUNTY, TOWN, OR TOWNSHIP	COUNTY	STATE	NA NO. M432	GD NO.	PAGES
CHATHAM TWP.	MEDINA	OH	709	444,702	451-79
CHATHAM TWP.	TIOGA	PA	830	444,798	273-301
CHATTANOOGA VALLEY	WALKER	GA	85	442,894	837-76
CHATTOOGA CO.		GA	64	007,060	681-804
CHAUTAUQUA	CHAUTAUQUA	NY	485	017,061	519-81
CHAUTAUQUA CO.		NY	484	017,060	1-618
CHAUTAUQUA CO.		NY	485	017,061	1-606
CHAWBA BEAT	DALLAS	AL	4	002,346	648-49
CHAZY	CLINTON	NY	490	017,066	665-767
CHEEKTOWAGA	ERIE	NY	499	017,075	489-561
CHELMSFORD	MIDDLESEX	MA	322	443,541	1-44
CHELSEA	SUFFOLK	MA	339	443,558	783-942
CHELSEA	ORANGE	VT	926	444,925	565-611
CHELTENHAM TWP.	MONTGOMERY	PA	800	444,768	691-721
CHEMUNG	MC HENRY	IL	117	007,690	863-86
CHEMUNG	CHEMUNG	NY	486	017,062	319-82
CHEMUNG CO.		NY	486	017,062	1-700
CHENANGO	BROOME	NY	478	017,054	597-804
CHENANGO CO.		NY	487	017,063	1-527
CHENANGO CO.		NY	488	017,064	529-989
CHENEY GROVE	MC LEON	IL	117	007,690	194-200
CHEQUEST TWP.	VAN BUREN	IA	189	442,964	713-29
CHEROKEE CO.		AL	3	002,345	1-290
CHEROKEE CO.		GA	65	007,061	805-1080
CHEROKEE CO.		NC	625	444,638	1-155
CHEROKEE CO.		TX	909	024,888	803-934
CHERRY CREEK	CHAUTAUQUA	NY	484	017,060	245-76
CHERRY GROVE	CARROLL	IL	99	007,672	675-81
CHERRY GROVE TWP.	WARREN	PA	832	444,800	725-26
CHERRY RIDGE TWP.	WAYNE	PA	835	444,803	357-72
CHERRY TWP.	BUTLER	PA	760	020,610	575-98
CHERRY TWP.	SULLIVAN	PA	828	444,796	665-703
CHERRY VALLEY	OTSEGO	NY	579	444,295	1-106
CHERRY VALLEY TWP.	ASHTABULA	OH	659	020,207	1025-44
CHERRYFIELD	WASHINGTON	ME	272	443,509	31-70
CHERRYTREE TWP.	VENANGO	PA	832	444,800	371-94
CHESAPEAKE CITY	CECIL	MD	290	443,521	53-63
CHESHIRE	NEW HAVEN	CT	46	003,074	153-91
CHESHIRE	BERKSHIRE	MA	305	014,699	199-230
CHESHIRE CO.		NH	427	014,940	1-349
CHESHIRE CO.		NH	428	014,941	351-751
CHESHIRE TWP.	GALLIA	OH	681	444,674	891-924
CHEST TWP.	CLEARFIELD	PA	768	444,736	763-72
CHESTER	MIDDLESEX	CT	44	003,072	595-618
CHESTER	RANDOLPH	IL	125	442,913	138-60
CHESTER	PENOBSCOT	ME	266	443,503	715-23
CHESTER	HAMPDEN	MA	318	443,537	85-121
CHESTER	EATON	MI	349	014,811	321-31
CHESTER	OTTAWA	MI	361	443,577	39-44
CHESTER	ROCKINGHAM	NH	437	443,641	529-59
CHESTER	ORANGE	NY	574	444,290	313-52
CHESTER	WARREN	NY	609	444,325	250-94
CHESTER	WINDSOR	VT	931	444,930	645-98
CHESTER	DODGE	WI	996	034,510	59-78
CHESTER BOR.	DELAWARE	PA	776	444,744	113-52
CHESTER CO.		PA	764	020,614	1-752
CHESTER CO.		PA	765	020,615	1-440
CHESTER CO.		PA	766	020,616	441-904
CHESTER CO.		SC	851	444,814	1-195

CITY, COUNTY, TOWN, OR TOWNSHIP	COUNTY	STATE	NA NO. M432	GD NO.	PAGES
CHESTER TWP.	DESHA	AR	26	002,480	140-43
CHESTER TWP.	WABASH	IN	178	442,956	741-78
CHESTER TWP.	WELLS	IN	181	442,959	669-82
CHESTER TWP.	BURLINGTON	NJ	443	016,530	169-254
CHESTER TWP.	MORRIS	NJ	458	443,657	65-96
CHESTER TWP.	CLINTON	OH	668	020,216	559-97
CHESTER TWP.	GEAUGA	OH	682	444,675	623-49
CHESTER TWP.	MEIGS	OH	710	444,703	91-129
CHESTER TWP.	MORROW	OH	716	444,709	875-914
CHESTER TWP.	WAYNE	OH	740	444,733	653-708
CHESTER TWP.	DELAWARE	PA	776	444,744	153-89
CHESTER VILLAGE	MEIGS	OH	710	444,703	125-26, 128-29
CHESTERFIELD	MACOUPIN	IL	118	442,906	363
CHESTERFIELD	HAMPSHIRE	MA	320	443,539	19-43
CHESTERFIELD	MACOMB	MI	357	443,573	185-208
CHESTERFIELD	CHESHIRE	NH	427	014,940	263-302
CHESTERFIELD	ESSEX	NY	504	017,080	441-540
CHESTERFIELD CO.		SC	851	444,814	197-361
CHESTERFIELD CO.		VA	940	029,715	121-333
CHESTERFIELD TWP.	BURLINGTON	NJ	443	016,530	255-362
CHESTERFIELD TWP.	FULTON	OH	681	444,674	537-50
CHESTERVILLE	FRANKLIN	ME	253	009,723	179-206
CHESTERVILLE	MORROW	OH	716	444,709	905-914
CHESTNUT BEAT	AUTAUGA	AL	1	002,343	96-116
CHESTNUT WOODS	PENDLETON	VA	968	444,958	98
CHESTNUTHILL TWP.	MONROE	PA	798	444,766	103-127
CHICAGO	COOK	IL	102	007,675	941-44
CHICAGO BOATS AND VESSELS COOK	COOK	IL	102	007,675	925-28, 397-40
CHICAGO CANAL BOATS	COOK	IL	102	007,675	929-36
CHICAGO, MISC.	COOK	IL	102	007,675	945-48
CHICAGO, WARD 1	COOK	IL	102	007,675	257-322, 337-40
CHICAGO, WARD 2	COOK	IL	102	007,675	323-36, 341-400
CHICAGO, WARD 3	COOK	IL	102	007,675	401-472
CHICAGO, WARD 4	COOK	IL	102	007,675	473-538
CHICAGO, WARD 5	COOK	IL	102	007,675	539-618
CHICAGO, WARD 6	COOK	IL	102	007,675	619-95
CHICAGO, WARD 7	COOK	IL	102	007,675	696-774
CHICAGO, WARD 8	COOK	IL	102	007,675	775-850
CHICAGO, WARD 9	COOK	IL	102	007,675	851-900
CHICAMACOMICO BANK	HYDE	NC	634	444,647	772-77
CHICHESTER	MERRIMACK	NH	436	443,640	39-62
CHICKALAH TWP.	YELL	AR	31	442,877	984-87
CHICKASAW CO.		MS	369	014,848	609-846
CHICKASAWBA TWP.	MISSISSIPPI	AR	28	002,482	684-88
CHICOPEE	HAMPDEN	MA	319	443,538	283-480
CHICOT CO.		AR	25	002,479	349-76
CHILI	MONROE	NY	528	017,104	561-615
CHILIAN CAMP	TUOLUMNE	CA	36	442,879	227-28
CHILLICOTHE	ROSS	OH	725	444,718	1-169
CHILLISQUAQUE TWP.	NORTHUMBERLAND	PA	804	444,772	235-66
CHILMARK	DUKES	MA	309	014,703	817-35
CHIMNEY ROCK	RUTHERFORD	NC	644	444,657	562-65
CHINA	KENNEBEC	ME	258	443,495	391-456
CHINA	ST. CLAIR	MI	362	443,578	263-87
CHINA	WYOMING	NY	617	444,333	685-731
CHINA TWP.	LEE	IL	116	007,689	195-211
CHINESE CAMP	TUOLUMNE	CA	36	442,879	195-98
CHIPPEWA	CHIPPEWA	WI	994	034,508	213-27
CHIPPEWA CO.		MI	349	014,811	1-22

CITY, COUNTY, TOWN, OR TOWNSHIP	COUNTY	STATE	NA NO. M432	GD NO.	PAGES
CHIPPEWA CO.		WI	994	034,508	213-27
CHIPPEWA TWP.	WAYNE	OH	739	444,732	201-264
CHIPPEWA TWP.	BEAVER	PA	750	020,600	171-92
CHITTENDEN	RUTLAND	VT	927	444,926	237-53
CHITTENDEN CO.		VT	923	444,922	1-710
CHOCOCHATTA SET.	BENTON	FL	58	006,714	45-48
CHOCONOLA SET.	HILLSBOROUGH	FL	58	006,714	516
CHOCONUT TWP.	SUSQUEHANNA	PA	829	444,797	311-28
CHOCOWINITY DIST.	BEAUFORT	NC	620	018,106	797-813
CHOCTAW CO.		AL	3	002,345	293-403
CHOCTAW CO.		MS	370	014,849	1-201
CHOWAN CO.		NC	625	444,638	157-232
CHRISTCHURCH PARISH	CHARLESTON	SC	850	022,530	753-68
CHRISTIAN CO.		IL	100	007,673	243-322
CHRISTIAN CO.		KY	196	007,849	719-997
CHRISTIAN TWP.	INDEPENDENCE	AR	26	002,480	729-40
CHRISTIANA	DANE	WI	995	034,509	703-728
CHRISTIANA HUN.	NEW CASTLE	DE	53	006,437	633-746
CHRISTIANSBURG	MONTGOMERY	VA	962	444,952	1-9
CHRYSTAL PLANTATION	AROOSTOOK	ME	248	009,718	20-24
CHUPEDEROS CREEK	BEXAR	TX	908	024,887	309-310
CHURCHVILLE	MONROE	NY	528	017,104	413-23
CIBOLO	BEXAR	TX	908	024,887	328-29
CIBOLO CREEK	BEXAR	TX	908	024,887	330-34
CICERO	ONONDAGA	NY	570	444,286	745-815
CICERO TWP.	TIPTON	IN	176	442,954	478-94
CINCINNATI	EL DORADO	CA	34	002,491	841-44
CINCINNATI, WARD 1	HAMILTON	OH	687	444,680	1-164
CINCINNATI, WARD 2	HAMILTON	OH	687	444,680	165-360
CINCINNATI, WARD 3	HAMILTON	OH	687	444,680	361-543
CINCINNATI, WARD 4	HAMILTON	OH	688	444,681	545-805
CINCINNATI, WARD 5	HAMILTON	OH	688	444,681	807-933
CINCINNATI, WARD 6	HAMILTON	OH	689	444,682	1-231
CINCINNATI, WARD 7	HAMILTON	OH	689	444,682	233-453
CINCINNATI, WARD 8	HAMILTON	OH	690	444,683	455-798
CINCINNATI, WARD 9	HAMILTON	OH	690	444,683	799-1054
CINCINNATI, WARD 10	HAMILTON	OH	691	444,684	1-311
CINCINNATI, WARD 11	HAMILTON	OH	691	444,684	313-776
CINCINNATUS	CORTLAND	NY	493	017,069	397-428
CIRCLEVILLE	PICKAWAY	OH	720	444,713	343-406
CIRCLEVILLE TWP.	PICKAWAY	OH	720	444,713	21-24, 343-414
CIRCLEVILLE, WARD 4	PICKAWAY	OH	720	444,713	1-20
CLACKAMAS CO.		OR	742	020,298	23-70
CLAIBORNE CO.		MS	370	014,849	203-291
CLAIBORNE CO.		TN	874	024,565	467-686
CLAIBORNE PARISH		LA	230	009,697	185-304
CLAIBOURNE TWP.	UNION	OH	736	444,729	13-34
CLARA	POTTER	PA	825	444,793	264-66
CLAREMONT	SULLIVAN	NH	441	443,645	289-374
CLARENCE	ERIE	NY	500	017,076	289-353
CLARENCE TWP.	CALHOUN	MI	348	014,810	369-80
CLARENDON	ORLEANS	NY	575	444,291	669-712
CLARENDON	RUTLAND	VT	927	444,926	795-830
CLARENDON TWP.	CALHOUN	MI	348	014,810	381-96
CLARIDON TWP.	MARION	OH	708	444,701	203-234
CLARINGTON	MONROE	OH	712	444,705	1019-27
CLARION	BUREAU	IL	99	007,672	373-86
CLARION BOR.	CLARION	PA	767	444,735	1-18
CLARION CO.		PA	767	444,735	1-567

CITY, COUNTY, TOWN, OR TOWNSHIP	COUNTY	STATE	NA NO. M432	GD NO.	PAGES
CLARION TWP.	CLARION	PA	767	444,735	19-60
CLARK CO.		AR	25	002,479	377-457
CLARK CO.		IL	100	007,673	325-556
CLARK CO.		IN	138	007,751	1-416
CLARK CO.		KY	196	007,849	1-190
CLARK CO.		MO	396	443,604	477-596
CLARK CO.		OH	666	020,214	1-566
CLARK TWP.		OR	742	020,298	73-88
CLARK TWP.	JOHNSON	AR	27	002,481	243-56
CLARK TWP.	LA FAYETTE	AR	27	002,481	359-72
CLARK TWP.	JOHNSON	IN	155	442,933	1-25
CLARK TWP.	MONTGOMERY	IN	161	442,939	1002-1034
CLARK TWP.	PERRY	IN	165	442,943	683-99
CLARK TWP.	CHARITON	MO	395	443,603	373-86
CLARK TWP.	BROWN	OH	662	020,210	687-721
CLARK TWP.	CLINTON	OH	668	020,216	483-525
CLARK TWP.	COSHOCTON	OH	670	020,218	369-88
CLARKE CO.		AL	3	002,345	407-524
CLARKE CO.		GA	65	007,061	1-162
CLARKE CO.		IA	182	007,791	259-62
CLARKE CO.		MS	370	014,849	293-384
CLARKE CO.		VA	940	029,715	337-425
CLARKSBURG	BERKSHIRE	MA	305	014,699	17-26
CLARKSBURG DIST.	MONTGOMERY	MD	295	443,526	677-92, 855-89
CLARKSFIELD TWP.	HURON	OH	697	444,690	703-737
CLARKSON	MONROE	NY	528	017,104	277-335
CLARKSON TWP.	COLUMBIANA	OH	669	020,217	347-49
CLARKSTOWN	ROCKLAND	NY	588	444,304	485-559
CLARKSVILLE	JOHNSON	AR	27	002,481	221-28
CLARKSVILLE	HABERSHAM	GA	72	007,068	661-68
CLARKSVILLE	PIKE	MO	409	443,617	432-38
CLARKSVILLE	COOS	NH	429	443,633	201-5
CLARKSVILLE DIST.	ALLEGANY	NY	475	017,051	261-76
CLARNO	MONTGOMERY	MD	295	443,526	855
CLATO	GREEN	WI	999	444,986	391-408
CLATSOP CO.	BEXAR	TX	908	024,887	329-30
CLAVERACK		OR	742	020,298	91-101
CLAY	COLUMBIA	NY	491	017,067	43-122
CLAY	LA GRANGE	IN	157	442,935	91-102
CLAY	ST. CLAIR	MI	362	443,578	303-322
CLAY	ONONDAGA	NY	570	444,286	584-664
CLAY CO.	MONTGOMERY	OH	714	444,707	843-88
CLAY CO.		IL	100	007,673	559-662
CLAY CO.		IN	138	007,751	417-622
CLAY CO.		KY	197	442,965	191-307
CLAY DIST.		MO	396	443,604	597-778
CLAY DIST.	CLAY	IL	100	007,673	559-662
CLAY HILL DIST.	RICHLAND	IL	125	442,913	267-362
CLAY TWP.	DUVAL	FL	58	006,714	221-24
CLAY TWP.	BRADLEY	AR	25	002,479	185-91
CLAY TWP.	BARTHOLOMEW	IN	136	007,749	809-824
CLAY TWP.	CASS	IN	137	007,750	825-40
CLAY TWP.	DEARBORN	IN	141	007,754	807-830, 836-37
CLAY TWP.	DECATUR	IN	142	007,755	51-101
CLAY TWP.	HAMILTON	IN	148	442,926	53-80
CLAY TWP.	HENDRICKS	IN	150	442,928	42-63
CLAY TWP.	HOWARD	IN	151	442,929	949-60
CLAY TWP.	KOSCIUSKO	IN	156	442,934	745-68
CLAY TWP.	MIAMI	IN	160	442,938	345-57

CITY, COUNTY, TOWN, OR TOWNSHIP	COUNTY	STATE	NA NO. M432	GD NO.	PAGES	
CLAY TWP.	MORGAN	IN	162	442,940	285-313	
CLAY TWP.	OWEN	IN	164	442,942	123-49	
CLAY TWP.	PIKE	IN	165	442,943	102-117	
CLAY TWP.	ST. JOSEPH	IN	171	442,949	167-83	
CLAY TWP.	WAYNE	IN	180	442,958	232-59	
CLAY TWP.	JONES	IA	185	442,960	432-42	
CLAY TWP.	DUNKLIN	MO	399	443,607	13-24	
CLAY TWP.	AUGLAIZE	OH	660	020,208	633-52	
CLAY TWP.	GALLIA	OH	681	444,674	163-85	
CLAY TWP.	HIGHLAND	OH	694	444,687	605-631	
CLAY TWP.	KNOX	OH	700	444,693	719-49	
CLAY TWP.	MUSKINGUM	OH	718	444,711	147-62	
CLAY TWP.	OTTAWA	OH	719	444,712	269-75	
CLAY TWP.	SCIOTO	OH	727	444,720	531-51	
CLAY TWP.	TUSCARAWAS	OH	734	444,727	273-303	
CLAY TWP.	HUNTINGDON	PA	784	444,752	453-69	
CLAYSVILLE	GUERNSEY	OH	684	444,677	926-30	
CLAYSVILLE BOR.	WASHINGTON	PA	834	444,802	1011-17	
CLAYTON	ADAMS	IL	97	007,670	67-85	
CLAYTON	JEFFERSON	NY	514	017,090	845-943	
CLAYTON	WINNEBAGO	WI	1009	444,996	977-86	
CLAYTON CO.		IA	182	007,791	265-362	
CLAYTON TWP.	GENESEE	MI	350	443,566	483-92	
CLAYTON TWP.	PERRY	OH	719	444,712	837-74	
CLEAR CREEK	HOT SPRINGS	AR	26	002,480	566-72, 582-84	576-79,
CLEAR CREEK	CLARK	IL	100	007,673	419-36	
CLEAR CREEK	GALVESTON	TX	910	024,889	566-69	
CLEAR CREEK	CUMBERLAND	IL	104	007,677	518-24	
CLEAR CREEK PREC.	SEVIER	AR	30	442,876	392-97	
CLEAR CREEK TWP.	WASHINGTON	AR	31	442,877	803-818	
CLEAR CREEK TWP.	MONROE	IN	161	442,939	632-55	
CLEAR CREEK TWP.	JOHNSON	IA	185	442,960	333-36	
CLEAR CREEK TWP.	ASHLAND	OH	658	020,206	1-30	
CLEAR CREEK TWP.	FAIRFIELD	OH	677	444,670	954-92	
CLEAR CREEK TWP.	WARREN	OH	737	444,730	837-903	
CLEAR LAKE TWP.	STEUBEN	IN	173	442,951	241-45	
CLEARFIELD	CLEARFIELD	PA	768	444,736	613-24	
CLEARFIELD CO.		PA	768	444,736	569-872	
CLEARFIELD TWP.	BUTLER	PA	760	020,610	331-79	
CLEARFIELD TWP.	CAMBRIA	PA	761	020,611	61-80	
CLEARSPRING	LA GRANGE	IN	157	442,935	18-34	
CLERMONT	COLUMBIA	NY	492	017,068	521-47	
CLERMONT		OH	667	020,215	567-973,	1-326
CLERMONT CO.		NC	625	444,638	233-439	
CLEVELAND CO.		OH	672	020,220	593-648	
CLEVELAND, EAST	CUYAHOGA	OH	672	020,220	181-372	
CLEVELAND TWP.	ELKHART	IN	144	007,757	19-28	
CLEVELAND, WARD 1	CUYAHOGA	OH	672	020,220	181-372	
CLEVELAND, WARD 2	CUYAHOGA	OH	672	020,220	373-503	
CLEVELAND, WARD 3	CUYAHOGA	OH	672	020,220	505-591	
CLEVES TWP.	HAMILTON	OH	686	444,679	529-34	
CLIFFORD TWP.	SUSQUEHANNA	PA	829	444,797	677-717	
CLIFTON	PENOBSCOT	ME	264	443,501	561-68	
CLIFTON	GREENE	OH	683	444,676	703-8	
CLIFTON PARK	SARATOGA	NY	593	444,309	981-1049	
CLIFTY TWP.	BARTHOLOMEW	IN	136	007,749	781-807	
CLIMAX	KALAMAZOO	MI	353	443,569	231-42	
CLINCH CO.		GA	65	007,061	163-75	
CLINTON	MIDDLESEX	CT	44	003,072	563-94	

40

CITY, COUNTY, TOWN, OR TOWNSHIP	COUNTY	STATE	NA NO. M432	GD NO.	PAGES
CLINTON	DE WITT	IL	104	007,677	845-53
CLINTON	VERMILLION	IN	177	442,955	1-8
CLINTON	KENNEBEC	ME	258	443,495	580-613
CLINTON	WORCESTER	MA	343	443,562	145-219
CLINTON	MACOMB	MI	357	443,573	73-123
CLINTON	CLINTON	NY	489	017,065	169-203
CLINTON	DUTCHESS	NY	497	017,073	575-619
CLINTON	ROCK	WI	1005	444,992	881-908
CLINTON CO.		IL	100	007,673	665-788
CLINTON CO.		IN	139	007,752	623-915
CLINTON CO.		IA	182	007,791	365-433
CLINTON CO.		KY	197	442,965	309-420
CLINTON CO.		MI	349	014,811	25-161
CLINTON CO.		MO	396	443,604	779-858
CLINTON CO.		NY	489	017,065	1-624
CLINTON CO.		NY	490	017,066	665-971
CLINTON CO.		OH	668	020,216	327-802
CLINTON CO.		PA	768	444,736	1-288
CLINTON GORE	KENNEBEC	ME	258	443,495	614-18
CLINTON TWP.	DE KALB	IL	104	007,677	709-717
CLINTON TWP.	CASS	IN	137	007,750	971-88
CLINTON TWP.	DECATUR	IN	142	007,755	1-20
CLINTON TWP.	ELKHART	IN	144	007,757	189-208
CLINTON TWP.	LA PORTE	IN	157	442,935	319-36
CLINTON TWP.	PUTNAM	IN	167	442,945	869-98
CLINTON TWP.	VERMILLION	IN	177	442,955	9-36
CLINTON TWP.	ESSEX	NJ	450	443,649	615-74
CLINTON TWP.	HUNTERDON	NJ	453	443,652	651-707
CLINTON TWP.	FRANKLIN	OH	680	444,673	123-51
CLINTON TWP.	FULTON	OH	681	444,674	651-68
CLINTON TWP.	KNOX	OH	700	444,693	507-526
CLINTON TWP.	SENECA	OH	728	444,721	845-949
CLINTON TWP.	SHELBY	OH	729	444,722	321-39
CLINTON TWP.	VINTON	OH	736	444,729	495-516
CLINTON TWP.	WAYNE	OH	739	444,732	1-28
CLINTON TWP.	LYCOMING	PA	795	444,763	743-63
CLINTON TWP.	WAYNE	PA	835	444,803	393-412
CLINTON TWP.	WYOMING	PA	838	444,806	239-51
CLOVER TWP.	JEFFERSON	PA	786	444,754	82-99
CLOVERDALE	PUTNAM	IN	167	442,945	1083-86
CLOVERDALE TWP.	PUTNAM	IN	167	442,945	1087-1114
CLYDE	ST. CLAIR	MI	362	443,578	443-59
CLYDE	IOWA	WI	999	444,986	841-44
CLYMAN	DODGE	WI	996	034,510	97-114
CLYMER	CHAUTAUQUA	NY	485	017,061	1-27
COAHOMA CO.		MS	370	014,849	385-418
COAL CREEK TWP.	MONTGOMERY	IN	161	442,939	905-920, 922-26, 928-41
COAL TWP.	NORTHUMBERLAND	PA	804	444,772	475-507
COBB CO.		GA	66	007,062	177-473
COBLESKILL	SCHOHARIE	NY	596	444,312	405-458
COCHECTON	SULLIVAN	NY	603	444,319	257-96
COCHRAN GROVE DIST.	SHELBY	IL	128	442,916	208-222
COCHRANVILLE	CHESTER	PA	766	020,616	728-30
COCKE CO.		TN	874	024,565	687-867
COEYMANS	ALBANY	NY	472	017,048	475-550
COFFEE CO.		AL	3	002,345	527-654
COFFEE CO.		TN	875	024,566	1-170
COGAN HOUSE	LYCOMING	PA	795	444,763	429-31

CITY, COUNTY, TOWN, OR TOWNSHIP	COUNTY	STATE	NA NO. M432	GD NO.	PAGES
COHANSEY TWP.	CUMBERLAND	NJ	446	016,533	463-87
COHASSETT	NORFOLK	MA	331	443,550	255-97
COHOCTON	STEUBEN	NY	599	444,315	51-100
COHOES	ALBANY	NY	474	017,050	339-438
COITSVILLE TWP.	MAHONING	OH	707	444,700	1289-1310
COKESBURY	ABBEVILLE	SC	848	022,528	373-80
COLBATH TWP.	CLARK	AR	25	002,479	394-400
COLCHESTER	NEW LONDON	CT	48	442,880	69-127
COLCHESTER	DELAWARE	NY	495	017,071	723-78
COLCHESTER	CHITTENDEN	VT	923	444,922	467-528
COLD SPRING	CATTARAUGUS	NY	479	017,055	1-16
COLD SPRING	PUTNAM	NY	581	444,297	173-226
COLDEN	ERIE	NY	500	017,076	129-60
COLDWATER TWP.	BRANCH	MI	347	014,809	669-720
COLE CO.		MO	397	443,605	1-137
COLE TWP.	BENTON	MO	392	014,872	543-53
COLEBROOK	LITCHFIELD	CT	42	003,070	141-75
COLEBROOK	COOS	NH	429	443,633	165-86
COLEBROOK TWP.	ASHTABULA	OH	659	020,207	1007-1023
COLEBROOK TWP.	CLINTON	PA	768	444,736	147-54
COLEBROOKDALE TWP.	BERKS	PA	754	020,604	635-61
COLERAIN TWP.	BELMONT	OH	661	020,209	985-1018
COLERAIN TWP.	HAMILTON	OH	686	444,679	671-747
COLERAIN TWP.	ROSS	OH	725	444,718	469-503
COLERAIN TWP.	BEDFORD	PA	751	020,601	163-93
COLERAIN TWP.	LANCASTER	PA	787	444,755	45-83
COLES CO.		IL	101	007,674	1-232
COLESVILLE	BROOME	NY	477	017,053	263-335
COLLEGE TWP.	KNOX	OH	700	444,693	551-63
COLLETON CO.		SC	851	444,814	365-539
COLLEY TWP.	SULLIVAN	PA	828	444,796	625-29
COLLIERVILLE	SHELBY	TN	895	444,851	369-73
COLLIN CO.		TX	910	024,889	1-49
COLLINS	ERIE	NY	499	017,075	565-660
COLLINS TWP.	ALLEGHENY	PA	747	020,597	654-82, 724-25, 732-33
COLLINSVILLE	MADISON	IL	119	442,907	1055-67
COLMA	EL DORADO	CA	34	002,491	789-803
COLON TWP.	ST. JOSEPH	MI	362	443,578	661-80
COLORADO CO.		TX	910	024,889	51-87
COLORADO SUBDIVISION	COLORADO	TX	910	024,889	51-86
COLRAIN	FRANKLIN	MA	316	443,535	1-43
COLTON	ST. LAWRENCE	NY	590	444,306	129-41
COLUMBIA	MONROE	IL	121	442,909	89-97
COLUMBIA	WASHINGTON	ME	272	443,509	211-38
COLUMBIA	JACKSON	MI	352	443,568	815-42
COLUMBIA	VAN BUREN	MI	363	443,579	239-45
COLUMBIA	COOS	NH	429	443,633	145-63
COLUMBIA	HERKIMER	NY	513	017,089	107-156
COLUMBIA	LANCASTER	PA	787	444,755	403-501
COLUMBIA	RICHLAND	SC	858	444,821	1-82
COLUMBIA	MAURY	TN	890	444,846	471-82
COLUMBIA BARRACKS	CLARK	OR	742	020,298	80-86
COLUMBIA CO.		FL	58	006,714	81-165
COLUMBIA CO.		GA	66	007,062	475-564
COLUMBIA CO.		NY	491	017,067	1-488
COLUMBIA CO.		NY	492	017,068	489-828, 1-251
COLUMBIA CO.		PA	769	444,737	291-721
COLUMBIA CO.		WI	994	034,508	231-468

CITY, COUNTY, TOWN, OR TOWNSHIP	COUNTY	STATE	NA NO. M432	GD NO.	PAGES
COLUMBIA TOWN	TOLLAND	CT	50	442,882	697-718
COLUMBIA TWP.	DUBOIS	IN	143	007,756	874-92
COLUMBIA TWP.	FAYETTE	IN	144	007,757	537-58
COLUMBIA TWP.	GIBSON	IN	147	442,925	251-81
COLUMBIA TWP.	JENNINGS	IN	155	442,933	639-62
COLUMBIA TWP.	MARTIN	IN	160	442,938	137-52
COLUMBIA TWP.	HAMILTON	OH	685	444,678	279-336
COLUMBIA TWP.	LORAIN	OH	705	444,698	807-836
COLUMBIA TWP.	MEIGS	OH	710	444,703	153-74
COLUMBIANA CO.	BRADFORD	PA	757	020,607	707-740
COLUMBUS		OH	669	020,217	1-824
COLUMBUS	MUSCOGEE	GA	79	442,888	591-678
COLUMBUS	ADAMS	IL	97	007,670	87-107
COLUMBUS	BARTHOLOMEW	IN	136	007,749	583-606
COLUMBUS	ST. CLAIR	MI	362	443,578	293-301
COLUMBUS	LOWNDES	MS	376	443,588	223-58
COLUMBUS	JOHNSON	MO	403	443,611	1-2
COLUMBUS	CHENANGO	NY	488	017,064	529-61
COLUMBUS CITY TWP.	LOUISA	IA	187	442,962	161-89
COLUMBUS CO.		NC	626	444,639	441-548
COLUMBUS TWP.	BARTHOLOMEW	IN	136	007,749	607-640
COLUMBUS TWP.	WARREN	PA	832	444,800	585-615
COLUMBUS TWP.	COLUMBIA	WI	994	034,508	231-46
COLUMBUS VILLAGE	COLUMBIA	WI	994	034,508	247-53
COLUMBUS, WARD 1	LOWNDES	MS	376	443,588	223-31
COLUMBUS, WARD 2	LOWNDES	MS	376	443,588	233-42
COLUMBUS, WARD 3	LOWNDES	MS	376	443,588	243-52
COLUMBUS, WARD 4	LOWNDES	MS	376	443,588	253-58
COLUMBUS, WARD 1	FRANKLIN	OH	679	444,672	715-806
COLUMBUS, WARD 2	FRANKLIN	OH	679	444,672	649-714
COLUMBUS, WARD 3	FRANKLIN	OH	679	444,672	569-648
COLUMBUS, WARD 4	FRANKLIN	OH	679	444,672	469-568
COLUMBUS, WARD 5	FRANKLIN	OH	679	444,672	373-468
COLUSA CO.		CA	36	442,879	495-97
COMAL	COMAL	TX	910	024,889	91-97
COMAL CO.		TX	910	024,889	91-132
COMANCHE SPRING CREEK	BEXAR	TX	908	024,887	334
COMMERCE TWP.	OAKLAND	MI	360	443,576	499-532
COMPTON	KANE	IL	112	007,685	187-207
COMSTOCK	KALAMAZOO	MI	353	443,569	265-93
CONCEPCION	BEXAR	TX	908	024,887	328
CONCORD	ADAMS	IL	97	007,670	109-127
CONCORD	BUREAU	IL	99	007,672	564-72
CONCORD	SOMERSET	ME	269	443,506	569-82
CONCORD	MIDDLESEX	MA	323	443,542	203-256
CONCORD	JACKSON	MI	352	443,568	515-38
CONCORD	MERRIMACK	NH	435	443,639	1-207
CONCORD	ERIE	NY	500	017,076	49-128
CONCORD	ESSEX	VT	923	444,922	715-42
CONCORD	JEFFERSON	WI	1000	444,987	177-94
CONCORD TWP.	GREENE	AR	26	002,480	369
CONCORD TWP.	DE KALB	IN	142	007,755	539-65
CONCORD TWP.	ELKHART	IN	144	007,757	31-64
CONCORD TWP.	WASHINGTON	MO	421	443,629	247-66
CONCORD TWP.	CHAMPAIGN	OH	665	020,213	617-42
CONCORD TWP.	DELAWARE	OH	675	020,223	493-525
CONCORD TWP.	FAYETTE	OH	678	444,671	265-87
CONCORD TWP.	HIGHLAND	OH	694	444,687	459-94
CONCORD TWP.	LAKE	OH	701	444,694	557-81

CITY, COUNTY, TOWN, OR TOWNSHIP	COUNTY	STATE	NA NO. M432	GD NO.	PAGES		
CONCORD TWP.	MIAMI	OH	711	444,704	149-232		
CONCORD TWP.	ROSS	OH	725	444,718	305-368		
CONCORD TWP.	DELAWARE	PA	776	444,744	247-71		
CONCORD TWP.	ERIE	PA	777	444,745	53-74		
CONCORDIA PARISH	CLAIBORNE PAR.	LA	230	009,697	305-324		
CONDEMNED BAR	SUTTER	CA	36	442,879	47		
CONECUH CO.		AL	3	002,345	657-772		
CONEMAUGH BOR.	CAMBRIA	PA	761	020,611	365-85		
CONEMAUGH TWP.	CAMBRIA	PA	761	020,611	209-281		
CONEMAUGH TWP.	INDIANA	PA	785	444,753	579-620		
CONEMAUGH TWP.	SOMERSET	PA	828	444,796	105-139		
CONESTOGA CENTER	LANCASTER	PA	787	444,755	514-22		
CONESTOGA TWP.	LANCASTER	PA	787	444,755	503-589		
CONESUS	LIVINGSTON	NY	525	017,101	425-58		
CONESVILLE	SCHOHARIE	NY	595	444,311	334-70		
CONEWAGO TWP.	ADAMS	PA	743	020,593	553-71		
CONEWAGO TWP.	DAUPHIN	PA	775	444,743	557-75		
CONEWAGO TWP.	YORK	PA	840	444,808	585-614		
CONEWANGO	CATTARAUGUS	NY	479	017,055	142-76		
CONEWANGO TWP.	WARREN	PA	832	444,800	771-92		
CONGRESS TWP.	MORROW	OH	716	444,709	915-54		
CONGRESS TWP.	WAYNE	OH	740	444,733	597-652		
CONKLIN	BROOME	NY	477	017,053	207-260		
CONNEAUT	ASHTABULA	OH	659	020,207	643-87		
CONNEAUT BOR.	ASHTABULA	OH	659	020,207	411-30		
CONNEAUT TWP.	CRAWFORD	PA	770	444,738	189-232		
CONNEAUT TWP.	ERIE	PA	778	444,746	898-944		
CONNEAUTVILLE BOR.	CRAWFORD	PA	770	444,738	169-87		
CONNELLSVILLE TWP.	FAYETTE	PA	780	444,748	795-832		
CONNERSVILLE TWP.	FAYETTE	IN	144	007,757	339-97		
CONOY TWP.	LANCASTER	PA	787	444,755	591-615		
CONQUEST	CAYUGA	NY	481	017,057	111-58		
CONSHOHOCKEN BOR.	MONTGOMERY	PA	800	444,768	1-19		
CONSTABLE	FRANKLIN	NY	505	017,081	487-521		
CONSTANTIA	OSWEGO	NY	578	444,294	613-76,	713, 7	
					722		
CONSTANTINE TWP.	ST. JOSEPH	MI	362	443,578	580-617		
CONTRA COSTA CO.		CA	LOST				
CONVIS	CALHOUN	MI	348	014,810	353-67		
CONWAY	FRANKLIN	MA	316	443,535	317-60		
CONWAY	CARROLL	NH	426	014,939	33-75		
CONWAY CO.		AR	25	002,479	459-538		
CONWAY TWP.	LIVINGSTON	MI	356	443,572	939-49		
CONWAY'S ISLAND	HANCOCK	ME	254	443,491	335		
COOK CO.		IL	102	007,675	233-948		
COOK CO.		IL	103	007,676	1-328		
COOKE CO.		TX	910	024,889	135-41		
COOK'S DIST.	FRANKLIN	NC	630	444,643	724-29,	766,	
					770-73		
COOKSTOWN BOR.	FAYETTE	PA	780	444,748	771-94		
COOKSVILLE	ANNE ARUNDEL	MD	278	013,195	997		
COOL SPRING DIST.	WASHINGTON	NC	648	444,661	163-88		
COOL SPRING TWP.	LA PORTE	IN	157	442,935	551-60		
COOLBAUGHS TWP.	MONROE	PA	798	444,766	309-314		
COOLSPRING TWP.	MERCER	PA	796	444,764	629-94		
COOPER	WASHINGTON	ME	272	443,509	445-58		
COOPER	KALAMAZOO	MI	353	443,569	81-98		
COOPER CO.		MO	397	443,605	139-376		
COOPER TWP.	MONTOUR	PA	801	444,769	753-60		

CITY, COUNTY, TOWN, OR TOWNSHIP	COUNTY	STATE	NA NO. M432	GD NO.	PAGES
COOPERSTOWN	MANITOWOC	WI	1002	444,989	39-40
COOS CO.		NH	429	443,633	1-328
COOSA CO.		AL	4	002,346	1-249
COOSA DIST.	COOSA	AL	4	002,346	10-172
COOSADA BEAT	AUTAUGA	AL	1	002,343	51-62
COPAKE	COLUMBIA	NY	491	017,067	243-84
COPIAH CO.		MS	371	443,583	419-570
COPLE PARISH	WESTMORELAND	VA	980	444,970	549-624
COPLEY TWP.	SUMMIT	OH	732	444,725	563-99
CORAL	MC HENRY	IL	117	007,690	795-818
CORINNA	PENOBSCOT	ME	265	443,502	97-135
CORINTH	PENOBSCOT	ME	265	443,502	307-345
CORINTH	SARATOGA	NY	593	444,309	559-94
CORINTH	ORANGE	VT	926	444,925	293-338
CORNIE TWP.	UNION	AR	30	442,876	473-78
CORNISH	YORK	ME	276	443,513	457-84
CORNISH	SULLIVAN	NH	441	443,645	149-87
CORNPLANTER TWP.	VENANGO	PA	832	444,800	185-201
CORNVILLE	SOMERSET	ME	269	443,506	36-65
CORNWALL	LITCHFIELD	CT	43	003,071	1-49
CORNWALL	ORANGE	NY	573	444,289	273-380
CORNWALL	ADDISON	VT	920	027,446	225-52
CORPUS CHRISTI	NUECES	TX	913	444,916	283-92
CORTLAND CO.		NY	493	017,069	253-862
CORTLANDT	WESTCHESTER	NY	614	444,330	319-503
CORTLANDVILLE	CORTLAND	NY	493	017,069	661-760, 763
CORYDON	HARRISON	IN	149	442,927	565-75
CORYDON TWP.	MC KEAN	PA	795	444,763	40-41
CORYDON TWP.	WARREN	PA	832	444,800	749-54
COSHOCTON	COSHOCTON	OH	670	020,218	235-56
COSHOCTON CO.		OH	670	020,218	1-636
COSUMNES RIVER	EL DORADO	CA	34	002,491	665-80, 707-716
COSUMNES RIVER	SACRAMENTO	CA	35	002,492	403-4, 483-90
COTAN CANJAUNE	LAFOURCHE PAR.	LA	232	443,475	586
COTEAU	ST. MARTIN	LA	240	443,483	340-52
COTTAGE GROVE	DANE	WI	995	034,509	729-47
COTTON TWP.	SWITZERLAND	IN	174	442,952	749-94
COTTONWOOD PREC.	CUMBERLAND	IL	104	007,677	503-517, 541
COTTRELLVILLE	ST. CLAIR	MI	362	443,578	339-60
COUDERSPORT BOR.	POTTER	PA	825	444,793	155-60
COUNCIL HILL PREC.	JO DAVIESS	IL	111	007,684	195-209
COUNCIL TWP.	CRITTENDEN	AR	25	002,479	757-58
COUNTY LINE DIST.	GRANVILLE	NC	631	444,644	355-68
COURT HOUSE DIST.	CURRITUCK	NC	627	444,640	347-54
COURTLAND	KENT	MI	353	443,569	569-78
COVE CREEK	WASHINGTON	AR	31	442,877	717-26
COVENTRY	TOLLAND	CT	50	442,882	623-26
COVENTRY	CHENANGO	NY	488	017,064	719-60
COVENTRY	KENT	RI	841	022,264	491-578
COVENTRY	ORLEANS	VT	925	444,924	309-329
COVENTRY TOWN	TOLLAND	CT	50	442,882	615-22, 627-62
COVENTRY TWP.	SUMMIT	OH	732	444,725	169-200
COVERT	SENECA	NY	597	444,313	57-111
COVINGTON	WYOMING	NY	617	444,333	367-97, 399-400
COVINGTON	MIAMI	OH	711	444,704	767-77
COVINGTON	LUZERNE	PA	794	444,762	169-84
COVINGTON	TIPTON	TN	897	444,853	619-23
COVINGTON CO.		AL	4	002,346	253-328
COVINGTON CO.		MS	371	443,583	571-624

45

CITY, COUNTY, TOWN, OR TOWNSHIP	COUNTY	STATE	NA NO. M432	GD NO.	PAGES
COVINGTON TWP.	FOUNTAIN	IN	145	442,923	113-40
COVINGTON TWP.	CLEARFIELD	PA	768	444,736	813-23
COVINGTON TWP.	TIOGA	PA	830	444,798	23-48
COVINGTON, WARD 1	KENTON	KY	208	442,976	411-51
COVINGTON, WARD 2	KENTON	KY	208	442,976	452-82
COVINGTON, WARD 3	KENTON	KY	208	442,976	483-504
COVINGTON, WARD 4	KENTON	KY	208	442,976	505-542
COVINGTON, WARD 5	KENTON	KY	208	442,976	543-87
COVINGTON, WARD 6	KENTON	KY	208	442,976	611-28
COVINGTON, WARD 7	KENTON	KY	208	442,976	588-610
COWANSHANNOCK TWP.	ARMSTRONG	PA	749	020,599	435-66
COWENJOCK DIST.	CURRITUCK	NC	627	444,640	381-89
COWETA CO.		GA	66	007,062	565-760
COWETA CO.		GA	66	007,062	377-83
COXES DIST.	COBB	GA	66	007,062	377-83
COXSACKIE	GREENE	NY	510	017,086	449-539
COYOTE CITY	YUBA	CA	36	442,879	579-82
CRACKLIN DIST.	MONTGOMERY	MD	295	443,526	629-76
CRAFTES	CANNON	TN	872	024,563	781-96
CRAFTSBURY	ORLEANS	VT	925	444,924	49-78
CRAIG TWP.	VAN BUREN	AR	31	442,877	631-36
CRAIG TWP.	SWITZERLAND	IN	174	442,952	701-746
CRANBERRY ISLAND	LINCOLN	ME	259	443,496	325
CRANBERRY ISLES	HANCOCK	ME	255	443,492	717-23
CRANBERRY TWP.	CRAWFORD	OH	671	020,219	901-927
CRANBERRY TWP.	BUTLER	PA	760	020,610	255-306
CRANBERRY TWP.	VENANGO	PA	832	444,800	45-76
CRANE TWP.	PAULDING	OH	719	444,712	363-70
CRANE TWP.	WYANDOT	OH	741	444,734	621-57
CRANSTON	PROVIDENCE	RI	843	444,809	359-461
CRAVEN CO.		NC	626	444,639	549-757
CRAWFORD	WASHINGTON	ME	272	443,509	461-68
CRAWFORD	ORANGE	NY	574	444,290	235-80
CRAWFORD CO.		AR	25	002,479	539-716
CRAWFORD CO.		GA	67	007,063	761-864
CRAWFORD CO.		IL	104	007,677	331-500
CRAWFORD CO.		IN	139	007,752	1-169
CRAWFORD CO.		MO	397	443,605	377-523
CRAWFORD CO.		OH	671	020,219	637-927 , 1-180
CRAWFORD CO.		PA	770	444,738	1-422
CRAWFORD CO.		PA	771	444,739	423-940
CRAWFORD CO.		WI	995	034,509	471-530
CRAWFORD DIST.	HARRIS	GA	73	007,069	230-37
CRAWFORD TWP.	BUCHANAN	MO	393	014,873	223-46
CRAWFORD TWP.	OSAGE	MO	408	443,616	872-96
CRAWFORD TWP.	COSHOCTON	OH	670	020,218	565-601
CRAWFORD TWP.	WYANDOT	OH	741	444,734	557-88
CRAWFORD TWP.	CLINTON	PA	768	444,736	223-30
CRAWFORDS PURCHASE	COOS	NH	429	443,633	311
CREAGERSTOWN EL. DIST.	FREDERICK	MD	292	443,523	209-283
CRETE	WILL	IL	133	442,921	323-40
CRITTENDEN	GRANT	KY	201	442,969	681-85
CRITTENDEN CO.		AR	25	002,479	717-60
CRITTENDEN CO.		KY	197	442,965	421-554
CROCKERY	OTTAWA	MI	361	443,577	54-59
CROCKETT	HOUSTON	TX	911	024,890	353-55
CROCKETT TWP.	ARKANSAS	AR	25	002,479	37-41
CROGHAN	LEWIS	NY	523	017,099	481-508
CROMMITS RUN	PENDLETON	VA	968	444,958	114
CROMWELL TWP.	HUNTINGDON	PA	784	444,752	535-65

CITY, COUNTY, TOWN, OR TOWNSHIP	COUNTY	STATE	NA NO. M432	GD NO.	PAGES
CROOKED CREEK PREC.	JASPER	IL	110	007,683	586-601
CROOKED TWP.	CARROLL	AR	25	002,479	316-28
CROSBY TWP.	HAMILTON	OH	686	444,679	607-670
CROSS CREEK TWP.	JEFFERSON	OH	699	444,692	175-220
CROSS CREEK TWP.	WASHINGTON	PA	834	444,802	925-70
CROSS CREEK VILLAGE	WASHINGTON	PA	834	444,802	951
CROSS KEYS	BURLINGTON	NJ	444	016,531	891, 894, 896-97
CROSS KEYS DIST.	DE KALB	GA	67	007,063	215-29
CROSS PLAINS TWP.	DANE	WI	995	034,509	878-85
CROSS ROAD DIST.	DE KALB	GA	67	007,063	240-49
CROSS ROADS DIST.	PITT	NC	641	444,654	41-54
CROSS ROADS DIST.	WAKE	NC	647	444,660	277-96
CROW VALLEYS	DAKOTA	MN	367	014,834	16
CROWN POINT	ESSEX	NY	504	017,080	699-754
CROYDON	SULLIVAN	NH	441	443,645	215-35
CRUMBY DIST.	LUMPKIN	GA	76	007,072	1-6
CUBA	LAKE	IL	114	007,687	131-38
CUBA	ALLEGANY	NY	476	017,052	473-526
CUIVRE TWP.	PIKE	MO	409	443,617	321-69
CULLOWHEE	MACON	NC	636	444,649	749-53
CULPEPER CO.		VA	941	444,931	429-562
CUMBERLAND	CUMBERLAND	ME	250	009,720	257-85
CUMBERLAND	GUERNSEY	OH	684	444,677	283-93
CUMBERLAND	PROVIDENCE	RI	843	444,809	199-357
CUMBERLAND CO.		IL	104	007,677	503-593
CUMBERLAND CO.		KY	197	442,965	555-690
CUMBERLAND CO.		ME	249	009,719	1-532
CUMBERLAND CO.		ME	250	009,720	535-724, 1-296
CUMBERLAND CO.		ME	251	009,721	299-744
CUMBERLAND CO.		ME	252	009,722	1-532
CUMBERLAND CO.		NJ	446	016,533	161-579
CUMBERLAND CO.		NC	627	444,640	1-323
CUMBERLAND CO.		PA	772	444,740	1-432
CUMBERLAND CO.		PA	773	444,741	433-858
CUMBERLAND CO.		VA	941	444,931	565-646
CUMBERLAND DIST.	CUMBERLAND	KY	197	442,965	560-689
CUMBERLAND ISLANDS	CUMBERLAND	ME	250	009,720	286-96
CUMBERLAND PREC.	CLARK	IL	100	007,673	533-40
CUMBERLAND TWP.	ADAMS	PA	743	020,593	219-52
CUMBERLAND TWP.	GREENE	PA	783	444,751	195-244
CUMBERLAND VALLEY TWP.	BEDFORD	PA	751	020,601	135-61
CUMMINGS TWP.	LYCOMING	PA	795	444,763	433-44
CUMMINGTON	MACOUPIN	IL	118	442,906	447-48
CUMMINGTON	HAMPSHIRE	MA	320	443,539	367-94
CUMRU TWP.	BERKS	PA	754	020,604	663-754
CURRAN PREC.	SALINE	IL	127	442,915	109-134
CURRITUCK CO.		NC	627	444,640	325-442
CURRITUCK DIST.	HYDE	NC	634	444,647	754-71
CURRY TWP.	SULLIVAN	IN	173	442,951	535-54
CURTISVILLE	TUOLUMNE	CA	36	442,879	199-204, 207
CUSHING	LINCOLN	ME	259	443,496	289-308
CUSSEWAGO TWP.	CRAWFORD	PA	770	444,738	61-97
CUTHBERT DIST.	RANDOLPH	GA	81	442,890	683-708
CUTLER	WASHINGTON	ME	272	443,509	411-30
CUYAHOGA CO.		OH	672	020,220	181-686
CUYAHOGA CO.		OH	673	020,221	687-874, 1-484
CYNTHIAN TWP.	SHELBY	OH	729	444,722	579-98
CYPRESS CREEK DIST.	JONES	NC	635	444,648	252-57

47

CITY, COUNTY, TOWN, OR TOWNSHIP	COUNTY	STATE	NA NO. M432	GD NO.	PAGES
DADE CO.		FL	58	006,714	167-70
DADE CO.		GA	67	007,063	1-62
DADE CO.		MO	398	443,606	523-617
DAGSBOROUGH HUN.	SUSSEX	DE	55	442,884	289-339, 346-4
DAHLONEGA DIST.	LUMPKIN	GA	76	007,072	193-216
DAHLONEGA VILLAGE	LUMPKIN	GA	76	007,072	203-216
DAKOTA CO.		MN	367	014,834	13-26
DALE CO.		AL	4	002,346	331-466
DALLAS	HENDERSON	IL	109	007,682	162
DALLAS CO.		AL	4	002,346	469-649
DALLAS CO.		AR	26	002,480	1-108
DALLAS CO.		IA	182	007,791	146, 438-58
DALLAS CO.		MO	398	443,606	619-704
DALLAS CO.		TX	910	024,889	145-205
DALLAS TWP.	CLINTON	MI	349	014,811	69-73
DALLAS TWP.	GREENE	MO	400	443,608	723-38
DALLAS TWP.	CRAWFORD	OH	671	020,219	107-118
DALLAS TWP.	LUZERNE	PA	793	444,761	61-82
DALTON	BERKSHIRE	MA	305	014,699	353-77
DALTON	COOS	NH	429	443,633	287-304
DALTON TWP.	WAYNE	IN	180	442,958	172-92
DAMARISCOTTA	LINCOLN	ME	260	443,497	859-88
DAMASCUS	HENRY	OH	693	444,686	63-68
DAMASCUS TWP.	WAYNE	PA	835	444,803	121-59
DAMES QUARTER DIST.	SOMERSET	MD	297	443,528	874-916
DANA	WORCESTER	MA	343	443,562	651-70
DANBURY	FAIRFIELD	CT	37	003,065	165-307
DANBURY	GRAFTON	NH	430	443,634	361-83
DANBURY TWP.	OTTAWA	OH	719	444,712	334-45
DANBY	IONIA	MI	352	443,568	252-58
DANBY	TOMPKINS	NY	605	444,321	63-120
DANBY	RUTLAND	VT	927	444,926	589-625
DANE CO.		WI	995	034,509	533-938
DANE TWP.	DANE	WI	995	034,509	847-53
DANFORTH TRACT	WASHINGTON	ME	273	443,510	405-8
DANSVILLE	STEUBEN	NY	599	444,315	179-240
DANUBE	HERKIMER	NY	513	017,089	573-616
DANVERS	ESSEX	MA	310	014,704	1-194
DANVILLE	VERMILION	IL	130	442,918	597-614
DANVILLE	HENDRICKS	IN	150	442,928	75-79, 270-7
DANVILLE	CUMBERLAND	ME	250	009,720	161-99
DANVILLE	ROCKINGHAM	NH	437	443,641	361-75
DANVILLE	CALEDONIA	VT	922	027,448	425-86
DANVILLE	PITTSYLVANIA	VA	968	444,958	320-40
DANVILLE BOR.	MONTOUR	PA	801	444,769	577-655
DANVILLE TWP.	DES MOINES	IA	183	007,792	843-68
DARBY TWP.	MADISON	OH	706	444,699	559-68
DARBY TWP.	PICKAWAY	OH	720	444,713	155-82
DARBY TWP.	UNION	OH	736	444,729	233-52
DARBY TWP.	DELAWARE	PA	776	444,744	581-612
DARDENELLE TWP.	YELL	AR	31	442,877	945-54
DARIEN	FAIRFIELD	CT	38	003,066	499-510, 533
DARIEN	GENESEE	NY	507	017,083	317-67
DARIEN	WALWORTH	WI	1007	444,994	635-59
DARIEN CITY	MC INTOSH	GA	77	442,886	441-48
DARIEN TOWN	FAIRFIELD	CT	38	003,066	511-32, 534-
DARKE CO.		OH	674	020,222	485-994

CITY, COUNTY, TOWN, OR TOWNSHIP	COUNTY	STATE	NA NO. M432	GD NO.	PAGES
DARLINGTON CO.		SC	851	444,814	541-702
DARLINGTON TWP.	BEAVER	PA	750	020,600	215-42
DARTMOUTH	BRISTOL	MA	309	014,703	813-905
DARWIN PREC.	CLARK	IL	100	007,673	437-68
DARYSAW TWP.	JEFFERSON	AR	27	002,481	197-206
DAUPHIN BOR.	DAUPHIN	PA	775	444,743	473-88
DAUPHIN CO.		PA	774	444,742	1-434
DAUPHIN CO.		PA	775	444,743	435-893
DAVENPORT	DELAWARE	NY	494	017,070	257-312
DAVIDSON COLLEGE	MECKLENBURG	NC	637	444,650	70-75
DAVIDSON CO.		NC	628	444,641	443-746
DAVIDSON CO.		TN	875	024,566	173-771
DAVIDSON TWP.	SULLIVAN	PA	828	444,796	641-53
DAVIE CO.		NC	628	444,641	747-884
DAVIESS CO.		IN	140	007,753	169-428
DAVIESS CO.		KY	198	442,966	691-918
DAVIESS CO.		MO	398	443,606	705-825
DAVIS CO.		IA	182	007,791	461-641
DAVIS CO.		UT	919	025,540	1-34
DAVIS DIST.	LUMPKIN	GA	76	007,072	99-115
DAVIS DIST.	FRANKLIN	NC	630	444,643	730-50, 769
DAVIS SHORE	CARTERET	NC	623	018,109	244-47
DAVIS TWP.	FOUNTAIN	IN	145	442,923	267-80
DAVISON TWP.	GENESEE	MI	350	443,566	618-26
DAY	SARATOGA	NY	593	444,309	735-60
DAYSVILLE	OGLE	IL	123	442,911	113-17
DAYTON	LA SALLE	IL	115	007,688	541, 585-98
DAYTON	CATTARAUGUS	NY	479	017,055	501-534, 703-4
DAYTON, WARD 1	MONTGOMERY	OH	713	444,706	277-307
DAYTON, WARD 2	MONTGOMERY	OH	713	444,706	309-356
DAYTON, WARD 3	MONTGOMERY	OH	713	444,706	358-406
DAYTON, WARD 4	MONTGOMERY	OH	713	444,706	409-460
DAYTON, WARD 5	MONTGOMERY	OH	713	444,706	461-520
DAYTON, WARD 6	MONTGOMERY	OH	713	444,706	521-47
DAYTON PLANTATION	AROOSTOOK	ME	248	009,718	24-25
DE BASTROP TWP.	ASHLEY	AR	25	002,479	79-80
DE KALB	ST. LAWRENCE	NY	590	444,306	701-760
DE KALB CO.		AL	5	002,347	653-838
DE KALB CO.		GA	67	007,063	175-452
DE KALB CO.		IL	104	007,677	597-790
DE KALB CO.		IN	142	007,755	375-584
DE KALB CO.		MO	398	443,606	827-74
DE KALB TWP.	DE KALB	TN	876	444,832	1-175
DE PEYSTER	ST. LAWRENCE	IL	104	007,677	755-66
DE RUYTER	MADISON	NY	589	444,305	133-54
DE SOTO CO.		NY	527	017,103	545-95
DE SOTO PARISH		MS	371	443,583	625-856
DE WITT	ONONDAGA	LA	231	009,698	325-410
DE WITT CO.		NY	570	444,286	665-743
DE WITT CO.		IL	104	007,677	793-913
DE WITT TWP.	CLINTON	TX	910	024,889	229-56
DE WITT TWP.	CLINTON	IA	182	007,791	365-72, 408, 419-21, 432
DEAD MAN'S BAR	SUTTER	MI	349	014,811	95-111
DEARBORN	WAYNE	CA	36	442,879	57
DEARBORN CO.		MI	366	443,582	581-614
DECATUR	ADAMS	IN	141	007,754	431-931
DECATUR	VAN BUREN	IN	135	007,748	1-6
		MI	363	443,579	247-56

CITY, COUNTY, TOWN, OR TOWNSHIP	COUNTY	STATE	NA NO. M432	GD NO.	PAGES
DECATUR	OTSEGO	NY	579	444,295	167-90
DECATUR	GREEN	WI	999	444,986	491-504
DECATUR CO.		GA	67	007,063	63-173
DECATUR CO.		IN	142	007,755	1-374
DECATUR CO.		IA	183	007,792	646-68
DECATUR CO.		TN	876	444,832	775-900
DECATUR DIST.		GA	67	007,063	386-97
DECATUR TWP.	DE KALB	IN	159	442,937	585-609
DECATUR TWP.	MARION	IN	701	444,694	645-70
DECATUR TWP.	LAWRENCE	OH	738	444,731	769-88
DECATUR TWP.	WASHINGTON	PA	768	444,736	680-89
DECATUR TWP.	CLEARFIELD	PA	797	444,765	609-633
DEDHAM	MIFFLIN	ME	255	443,492	827-39
DEDHAM	HANCOCK	MA	330	443,549	441-546
DEEP CREEK	NORFOLK	NC	636	444,649	684-91, 766-67
DEEP CREEK TWP.	MACON	IA	182	007,791	404-8
DEEPWATER TWP.	CLINTON	MO	401	443,609	61-70
DEER CREEK	HENRY	CA	36	442,879	522-30
DEER CREEK MINES	YUBA	CA	36	442,879	523-30
DEER CREEK TWP.	YUBA	IN	137	007,750	935-53
DEER CREEK TWP.	CASS	IN	160	442,938	419-36
DEER CREEK TWP.	MIAMI	IN	165	442,943	760-77
DEER CREEK TWP.	PERRY	OH	706	444,699	497-507
DEER CREEK TWP.	MADISON	OH	720	444,713	265-98
DEER ISLAND	PICKAWAY	ME	267	443,504	519
DEER ISLE	PISCATAQUIS	ME	254	443,491	351-423
DEER PARK	HANCOCK	IL	115	007,688	501-3, 506-511
DEERFIELD	LA SALLE	IL	107	007,680	498-509
DEERFIELD	FULTON	IL	114	007,687	63-82
DEERFIELD	LAKE	IN	168	442,946	273-76
DEERFIELD	RANDOLPH	MA	316	443,535	66-123
DEERFIELD	FRANKLIN	NH	438	443,642	601-649
DEERFIELD	ROCKINGHAM	NY	566	444,282	595-649
DEERFIELD	ONEIDA	WI	995	034,509	748-64
DEERFIELD SCHOOL GT.	DANE	ME	248	009,718	324
DEERFIELD TWP.	AROOSTOOK	MI	356	443,572	905-925
DEERFIELD TWP.	LIVINGSTON	NJ	446	016,533	439-61
DEERFIELD TWP.	CUMBERLAND	OH	715	444,708	421-52
DEERFIELD TWP.	MORGAN	OH	722	444,715	371-404
DEERFIELD TWP.	PORTAGE	OH	725	444,718	273-304
DEERFIELD TWP.	ROSS	OH	737	444,730	92-135
DEERFIELD TWP.	WARREN	PA	830	444,798	469-86
DEERFIELD TWP.	TIOGA	PA	832	444,800	693-717
DEERFIELD TWP.	WARREN	NH	434	443,638	113-34
DEERING	HILLSBORO	NY	574	444,290	549-644
DEERPARK	ORANGE	OH	693	444,686	805-812
DEERSVILLE	HARRISON	OH	674	020,222	1-184
DEFIANCE CO.		OH	674	020,222	1-33
DEFIANCE TWP.	DEFIANCE	WI	994	034,508	336-51
DEKORRA TWP.	COLUMBIA	WI	1009	444,996	759-85
DELAFIELD	WAUKESHA	OH	675	020,223	323-74
DELAWARE	DELAWARE	IN	143	007,756	585-849
DELAWARE CO.		IA	183	007,792	671-712
DELAWARE CO.		NY	494	017,070	1-452
DELAWARE CO.		NY	495	017,071	453-994
DELAWARE CO.		OH	675	020,223	185-742
DELAWARE CO.		PA	776	444,744	1-612
DELAWARE CO.		IN	143	007,756	639-61
DELAWARE TWP.	DELAWARE	IN	148	442,926	81-102
DELAWARE TWP.	HAMILTON				

CITY, COUNTY, TOWN, OR TOWNSHIP	COUNTY	STATE	NA NO. M432	GD NO.	PAGES
DELAWARE TWP.	RIPLEY	IN	169	442,947	399-429
DELAWARE TWP.	CAMDEN	NJ	445	016,532	229-90
DELAWARE TWP.	HUNTERDON	NJ	453	443,652	205-266
DELAWARE TWP.	DEFIANCE	OH	674	020,222	108-119
DELAWARE TWP.	DELAWARE	OH	675	020,223	376-405
DELAWARE TWP.	HANCOCK	OH	692	444,685	139-63
DELAWARE TWP.	JUNIATA	PA	786	444,754	507-34
DELAWARE TWP.	MERCER	PA	796	444,764	269-337
DELAWARE TWP.	NORTHUMBERLAND	PA	804	444,772	1-46
DELAWARE TWP.	PIKE	PA	825	444,793	135-53
DELEVAN	WALWORTH	WI	1007	444,994	603-633
DELHI	INGHAM	MI	351	443,567	29-38
DELHI	DELAWARE	NY	495	017,071	485-554
DELHI TWP.	HAMILTON	OH	686	444,679	963-1009
DELMAR TWP.	TIOGA	PA	830	444,798	423-60
DELTA	EATON	MI	349	014,811	285-90
DENMARK	OXFORD	ME	262	443,499	297-381
DENMARK	LEWIS	NY	523	017,099	413-80
DENMARK	ASHTABULA	OH	659	020,207	543-48
DENNING	ULSTER	NY	608	444,324	763-74
DENNIS	BARNSTABLE	MA	304	014,698	427-504
DENNIS TWP.	CAPE MAY	NJ	446	016,533	35-74
DENNISON	LUZERNE	PA	794	444,762	931-54, 1-13
DENNYSVILLE	WASHINGTON	ME	272	443,509	195-206
DENTON CO.		TX	910	024,889	209-225
DEPERE	BROWN	WI	994	034,508	45-63
DEPTFORD TWP.	GLOUCESTER	NJ	451	443,650	121-200
DERBY	NEW HAVEN	CT	46	003,074	539-632
DERBY	ORLEANS	VT	925	444,924	331-72
DERRY	ROCKINGHAM	NH	438	443,642	141-85
DERRY TWP.	DAUPHIN	PA	774	444,742	241-88
DERRY TWP.	MIFFLIN	PA	797	444,765	545-78
DERRY TWP.	MONTOUR	PA	801	444,769	793-813
DERRY TWP.	WESTMORELAND	PA	837	444,805	747-880
DES ARC TWP.	WHITE	AR	31	442,877	905-910
DES MOINES CO.		IA	183	007,792	715-1037
DES MOINES TWP.	JEFFERSON	IA	185	442,960	180-203
DES MOINES TWP.	VAN BUREN	IA	189	442,964	731-47
DESHA CO.		AR	26	002,480	109-150
DETROIT	SOMERSET	ME	268	443,505	41-53
DETROIT	WAYNE	MI	365	443,581	1-500
DEXTER	PENOBSCOT	ME	265	443,502	137-85
DEXTER TWP.	WASHTENAW	MI	364	443,580	1021-39
DEXTER VILLAGE	WASHTENAW	MI	364	443,580	1041-57
D'HANIS	MEDINA	TX	912	444,915	827-28
DIAMOND DIST.	DE KALB	GA	67	007,063	175-87
DIAMOND GROVE	MC LEON	IL	117	007,690	150
DIAMOND HILL DIST.	ANSON	NC	619	018,105	420-31
DIAMOND SPRINGS	EL DORADO	CA	34	002,491	685-88, 693-98
DIANA	LEWIS	NY	523	017,099	509-532
DICKINSON	FRANKLIN	NY	505	017,081	219-46
DICKINSONS BAYOU	GALVESTON	TX	910	024,889	566-69
DICKSON CO.		TN	876	444,832	179-328
DIGHTON	BRISTOL	MA	307	014,701	559-98
DILLSBORO	DEARBORN	IN	141	007,754	831-35
DILLSBURG BOR.	YORK	PA	840	444,808	661-67
DILLSONS ENLARGEMENT	VANDERBURGH	IN	176	442,954	809-816
DIMMICK	LA SALLE	IL	115	007,688	549-50, 555, 575-78, 582-83

51

CITY, COUNTY, TOWN, OR TOWNSHIP	COUNTY	STATE	NA NO. M432	GD NO.	PAGES	
DIMOCK TWP.	SUSQUEHANNA	PA	829	444,797	29-54	
DINGMAN TWP.	PIKE	PA	825	444,793	119-34	
DINSMORE TWP.	SHELBY	OH	729	444,722	411-28	
DINWIDDIE CO.		VA	941	444,931	649-992	
DIRT TOWN DIST.	CHATTOOGA	GA	64	007,060	770-804	
DISTRICT TWP.	BERKS	PA	753	020,603	337-57	
DIX	CHEMUNG	NY	486	017,062	37-109	
DIXFIELD	OXFORD	ME	263	443,500	431-59	
DIXMONT	PENOBSCOT	ME	265	443,502	765-803	
DIXON TWP.	LEE	IL	116	007,689	167-92	
DIXON TWP.	PREBLE	OH	723	444,716	696-723	
DIXVILLE	COOS	NH	429	443,633	313	
DODDRIDGE CO.		VA	942	444,932	1-66	
DODGE CO.		MO	399	443,607	1-12	
DODGE CO.		WI	996	034,510	1-480	
DODGEVILLE	IOWA	WI	999	444,986	757-808	
DODSON TWP.	HIGHLAND	OH	694	444,687	531-60	
DONA ANA	VALENCIA	NM	470	443,668	585-96	
DONEGAL TWP.	BUTLER	PA	760	020,610	381-410	
DONEGAL TWP.	WASHINGTON	PA	834	444,802	971-1010	
DONEGAL TWP.	WESTMORELAND	PA	836	444,804	139-201	
DONNELSVILLE	CLARK	OH	666	020,214	198-202	
DOOLY CO.		GA	68	007,064	453-588	
DORCHESTER	NORFOLK	MA	329	443,548	1-190	
DORCHESTER	GRAFTON	NH	430	443,634	225-41	
DORCHESTER CO.		MD	291	443,522	591-940	
DORR	ALLEGAN	MI	346	014,808	103-5	
DORRANCE TWP.	LUZERNE	PA	794	444,762	991-1002	
DORSET	BENNINGTON	VT	921	027,447	145-85	
DORSET TWP.	ASHTABULA	OH	659	020,207	985-90	
DOTON'S BAR	SUTTER	CA	36	442,879	49-50	
DOUGLAS	WORCESTER	MA	341	443,560	669-714	
DOUGLASS TWP.	ARKANSAS	AR	25	002,479	15-21	
DOUGLASS TWP.	BERKS	PA	754	020,604	609-633	
DOUGLASS TWP.	MONTGOMERY	PA	799	444,767	377-407	412-25
DOVER	BUREAU	IL	99	007,672	369-73	
DOVER	PISCATAQUIS	ME	267	443,504	549-94	
DOVER	NORFOLK	MA	330	443,549	549-64	
DOVER	LENAWEE	MI	355	443,571	171-200	
DOVER	STRAFFORD	NH	439	443,643	1-196	
DOVER	DUTCHESS	NY	497	017,073	621-72	
DOVER	WINDHAM	VT	929	444,928	427-43	
DOVER	RACINE	WI	1004	444,991	379-98	
DOVER HUN.	KENT	DE	52	006,436	305-404	
DOVER TWP.	OCEAN	NJ	460	443,659	147-204	
DOVER TWP.	ATHENS	OH	660	020,208	277-306	
DOVER TWP.	CUYAHOGA	OH	673	020,221	421-47	
DOVER TWP.	FULTON	OH	681	444,674	551-60	
DOVER TWP.	TUSCARAWAS	OH	734	444,727	129-208	
DOVER TWP.	UNION	OH	736	444,729	112-28	
DOVER TWP.	YORK	PA	839	444,807	567-622	
DOWAGIAC STATION	CASS	MI	349	014,811	644-47	
DOWDELL'S DIST.	HARRIS	GA	73	007,069	122-35	
DOWNE TWP.	CUMBERLAND	NJ	446	016,533	215-70	
DOWNERS GROVE	DU PAGE	IL	105	007,678	67-89	
DOYLESTOWN BOR.	BUCKS	PA	759	020,609	647-70	
DOYLESTOWN TWP.	BUCKS	PA	759	020,609	671-702	
DRACUT	MIDDLESEX	MA	322	443,541	540-623	
DRAKESVILLE	DAVIS	IA	182	007,791	639-41	

CITY, COUNTY, TOWN, OR TOWNSHIP	COUNTY	STATE	NA NO. M432	GD NO.	PAGES
DRESDEN	LINCOLN	ME	261	443,498	495-528
DRESDEN	WASHINGTON	NY	610	444,326	247-63
DRESDEN	WEAKLEY	TN	899	444,855	957-66
DREW CO.		AR	26	002,480	151-208
DRIFTWOOD TWP.	JACKSON	IN	152	442,930	359-74
DRUMORE TWP.	LANCASTER	PA	787	444,755	141-208
DRY CREEK	EL DORADO	CA	34	002,491	850-54
DRY GROVE	MC LEON	IL	117	007,690	69-75
DRY RUN, NORTH FORK	PENDLETON	VA	968	444,958	89-92
DRY RUN, SOUTH FORK	PENDLETON	VA	968	444,958	96-97
DRYDEN	LAPEER	MI	354	443,570	681-707
DRYDEN	TOMPKINS	NY	605	444,321	121-242
DRYSDALE PARISH	KING AND QUEEN	VA	954	444,944	384-400, 405
DU PAGE	DU PAGE	IL	105	007,678	1-27
DU PAGE	WILL	IL	133	442,921	109-123
DU PAGE CO.		IL	105	007,678	1-222
DUANE	FRANKLIN	NY	505	017,081	213-18
DUANESBURG	SCHENECTADY	NY	594	444,310	1-84
DUBLIN	WAYNE	IN	180	442,958	9-25
DUBLIN	CHESHIRE	NH	428	014,941	535-61
DUBLIN	FRANKLIN	OH	680	444,673	375-82
DUBLIN BEAT	PERRY	AL	12	002,354	710-718
DUBLIN DIST.	SOMERSET	MD	297	443,528	809-832
DUBLIN TWP.	MERCER	OH	710	444,703	547-68
DUBLIN TWP.	FULTON	PA	783	444,751	151-67
DUBLIN TWP.	HUNTINGDON	PA	784	444,752	487-508
DUBOIS CO.		IN	143	007,756	851-1004
DUBUQUE CO.		IA	183	007,792	1-259
DUCHOUQUET TWP.	AUGLAIZE	OH	660	020,208	677-710
DUCK CREEK HUN.	KENT	DE	52	006,436	1-108
DUCK ISLAND	HANCOCK	ME	254	443,491	334
DUDLEY	WORCESTER	MA	340	443,559	137-72
DUDLEY TWP.	HENRY	IN	151	442,929	435-65
DUDLEY TWP.	HARDIN	OH	692	444,685	261-74
DUKE CREEK TWP.	STODDARD	MO	420	443,628	505-521
DUKES CO.		MA	309	014,703	739-880
DUMAS SHOP DIST.	ANSON	NC	619	018,105	450-59
DUMMER	COOS	NH	429	443,633	99-103
DUMMERSTON	WINDHAM	VT	929	444,928	387-426
DUNBAR TWP.	FAYETTE	PA	780	444,748	451-502
DUNBARTON	MERRIMACK	NH	435	443,639	245-66
DUNCANS CREEK	RUTHERFORD	NC	644	444,657	677-80, 695-700, 703
DUNDAFF BOR.	SUSQUEHANNA	PA	829	444,797	710-17
DUNDEE	KANE	IL	112	007,685	81-113
DUNDEE TWP.	MONROE	MI	358	443,574	777-806
DUNKARD TWP.	GREENE	PA	783	444,751	307-340
DUNKIRK	DANE	WI	995	034,509	568, 571-88
DUNKLIN CO.		MO	399	443,607	13-42
DUNN	DANE	WI	995	034,509	624-31
DUNNSTABLE TWP.	CLINTON	PA	768	444,736	237-45
DUN'S DIST.	FRANKLIN	NC	630	444,643	633-52
DUNSTABLE	MIDDLESEX	MA	322	443,541	457-71
DUPLAIN TWP.	CLINTON	MI	349	014,811	139-48
DUPLIN CO.		NC	629	444,642	1-182
DUPRES DIST.	CLARKE	GA	65	007,061	59-66
DUQUESNE BOR.	ALLEGHENY	PA	744	020,594	483-503
DURANTS NECK DIST.	PERQUIMANS	NC	640	444,653	771-89
DURELL	BRADFORD	PA	757	020,607	493-523

CITY, COUNTY, TOWN, OR TOWNSHIP	COUNTY	STATE	NA NO. M432	GD NO.	PAGES
DURHAM	MIDDLESEX	CT	44	003,072	619-43
DURHAM	CUMBERLAND	ME	249	009,719	333-77
DURHAM	STRAFFORD	NH	440	443,644	441-76
DURHAM	GREENE	NY	509	017,085	271-333
DURHAM CREEK DIST.	BEAUFORT	NC	620	018,106	830, 837-38, 85: 58
DURHAM TWP.	BUCKS	PA	759	020,609	465-88
DUTCH	CLAIBORNE PAR.	LA	230	009,697	260
DUTCH CREEK	EL DORADO	CA	34	002,491	834-40, 845-49
DUTCH DIST.	GRANVILLE	NC	631	444,644	239-42, 287-96
DUTCHESS CO.		NY	496	017,072	1-640, 1-54
DUTCHESS CO.		NY	497	017,073	57-798
DUTCHESS CREEK TWP.	YELL	AR	31	442,877	1009-1013
DUVAL CO.		FL	58	006,714	171-232
DUXBURY	PLYMOUTH	MA	333	443,552	113-76
DUXBURY	WASHINGTON	VT	928	444,927	271-91
DYBERRY TWP.	WAYNE	PA	835	444,803	373-91
DYER CO.		TN	877	444,833	333-458
EAGLE	LA SALLE	IL	115	007,688	485-90, 525-26
EAGLE	WYOMING	NY	617	444,333	651-83
EAGLE	WAUKESHA	WI	1009	444,996	493-514
EAGLE CREEK TWP.	LAKE	IN	157	442,935	264-71
EAGLE HARBOR	HOUGHTON	MI	351	443,567	4-6
EAGLE ISLAND	HANCOCK	ME	254	443,491	429
EAGLE PASS	BEXAR	TX	908	024,887	282-85, 287-90
EAGLE PREC.	GALLATIN	IL	107	007,680	788-801
EAGLE PREC.	MONROE	IL	121	442,909	58A, 80-91, 98-110
EAGLE TWP.	PULASKI	AR	29	002,483	647-64
EAGLE TWP.	OGLE	IL	123	442,911	135-50
EAGLE TWP.	CLINTON	MI	349	014,811	33-45
EAGLE TWP.	BROWN	OH	662	020,210	853-84
EAGLE TWP.	HANCOCK	OH	692	444,685	185-208
EAGLE TWP.	VINTON	OH	736	444,729	599-611
EAGLE TWP.	SAUK	WI	1006	444,993	115-23
EARL	LA SALLE	IL	115	007,688	757-76
EARL TWP.	BERKS	PA	754	020,604	919-44
EARL TWP.	LANCASTER	PA	789	444,757	387-451
EARLY CO.		GA	68	007,064	589-677
EAST ALLEN TWP.	NORTHAMPTON	PA	803	444,771	561-64
EAST ALLENTOWN	LEHIGH	PA	792	444,760	685-98
EAST AMWELL TWP.	HUNTERDON	NJ	453	443,652	1-60
EAST ARMUCHY	WALKER	GA	85	442,894	725-44
EAST BATON ROUGE PAR.		LA	229	009,696	309-443
EAST BERLIN	ADAMS	PA	743	020,593	427-39
EAST BETHLEHEM	WASHINGTON	PA	833	444,801	215-69
EAST BIRMINGHAM	ALLEGHENY	PA	748	020,598	51-95
EAST BLOOMFIELD	ONTARIO	NY	571	444,287	243-96
EAST BOSTON	SUFFOLK	MA	335	443,554	1-244
EAST BRADFORD	CHESTER	PA	764	020,614	441-72
EAST BRANDYWINE TWP.	CHESTER	PA	766	020,616	555-82
EAST BRIDGEPORT	FAIRFIELD	CT	37	003,065	557-60
EAST BRIDGEWATER	PLYMOUTH	MA	332	443,551	473-533
EAST BRUNSWICK	SCHUYLKILL	PA	826	444,794	355-95
EAST BUFFALO TWP.	UNION	PA	831	444,799	569-92
EAST CALN TWP.	CHESTER	PA	766	020,616	463-518

CITY, COUNTY, TOWN, OR TOWNSHIP	COUNTY	STATE	NA NO. M432	GD NO.	PAGES
EAST CANYON	EL DORADO	CA	34	002,491	887
EAST CHICAGO	COOK	IL	102	007,675	901-912
EAST CHICKAMAUGA	WALKER	GA	85	442,894	683-724, 761-74
EAST CLEVELAND	CUYAHOGA	OH	672	020,220	593-648
EAST COCALICO TWP.	LANCASTER	PA	789	444,757	673-723
EAST CONNOQUENESSING	BUTLER	PA	760	020,610	227-54
EAST COVENTRY TWP.	CHESTER	PA	765	020,615	307-337
EAST DEER TWP.	ALLEGHENY	PA	747	020,597	1-49
EAST DONEGAL TWP.	LANCASTER	PA	788	444,756	99-164
EAST FALLOWFIELD TWP.	CHESTER	PA	766	020,616	731-62
EAST FALLOWFIELD TWP.	CRAWFORD	PA	771	444,739	837-54
EAST FELICIANA PARISH		LA	231	009,698	411-508
EAST FINLEY TWP.	WASHINGTON	PA	834	444,802	1069-99
EAST FISHKILL	DUTCHESS	NY	496	017,072	219-83
EAST FORK PREC.	JO DAVIESS	IL	111	007,684	210-31
EAST GENESEE	GENESEE	MI	350	443,566	432-52
EAST GOSHEN TWP.	CHESTER	PA	764	020,614	513-32
EAST GREENFIELD	LA GRANGE	IN	157	442,935	207-216
EAST GREENWICH	KENT	RI	841	022,264	431-87
EAST HADDAM	MIDDLESEX	CT	44	003,072	381-443
EAST HAMPTON	HAMPSHIRE	MA	320	443,539	333-66
EAST HAMPTON	SUFFOLK	NY	602	444,318	831-81
EAST HANOVER TWP.	DAUPHIN	PA	775	444,743	697-736
EAST HANOVER TWP.	LEBANON	PA	791	444,759	469-512
EAST HARTFORD	HARTFORD	CT	41	003,069	669-728
EAST HAVEN	NEW HAVEN	CT	45	003,073	347-86
EAST HAVEN	ESSEX	VT	923	444,922	789-91
EAST HEMPFIELD TWP.	LANCASTER	PA	788	444,756	267-322
EAST HUNTINGDON TWP.	WESTMORELAND	PA	836	444,804	281-325
EAST INDIAN	PENOBSCOT	ME	266	443,503	673-77
EAST KINGSTON	ROCKINGHAM	NH	438	443,642	85-97
EAST LACKAWANNOCK TWP.	MERCER	PA	796	444,764	397-418
EAST LAMPETER TWP.	LANCASTER	PA	788	444,756	389-436
EAST LIMA	LA GRANGE	IN	157	442,935	173-94
EAST LIVERMORE	KENNEBEC	ME	257	443,494	153-74
EAST LYME	NEW LONDON	CT	49	442,881	803-836
EAST MACHIAS	WASHINGTON	ME	272	443,509	83-128
EAST MAHONING TWP.	INDIANA	PA	785	444,753	493-513
EAST MAIMA	BURLINGTON	NJ	444	016,531	962-63
EAST MARLBOROUGH TWP.	CHESTER	PA	764	020,614	331-64
EAST MONTPELIER	WASHINGTON	VT	928	444,927	379-413
EAST NANTMEAL TWP.	CHESTER	PA	766	020,616	441-62
EAST NORWEGIAN TWP.	SCHUYLKILL	PA	827	444,795	349-424
EAST NOTTINGHAM TWP.	CHESTER	PA	764	020,614	19-78
EAST PENN	CARBON	PA	762	020,612	497-514
EAST PIKELAND TWP.	CHESTER	PA	765	020,615	1-18
EAST PIKERUN	WASHINGTON	PA	833	444,801	304-9, 311-37
EAST PROVIDENCE TWP.	BEDFORD	PA	751	020,601	231-54
EAST TOWN TWP.	CHESTER	PA	764	020,614	669-85
EAST TWP.	CARROLL	OH	664	020,212	291-94, 299-318
EAST TROY	WALWORTH	WI	1007	444,994	329-60
EAST UNION TWP.	WAYNE	OH	739	444,732	397-444
EAST VAN BUREN	LA GRANGE	IN	157	442,935	157-64
EAST VINCENT TWP.	CHESTER	PA	765	020,615	119-54
EAST WHITELAND	CHESTER	PA	766	020,616	875-904
EAST WINDSOR	HARTFORD	CT	39	003,067	109-172
EAST WINDSOR TWP.	MERCER	NJ	454	443,653	111-72
EASTBROOK	HANCOCK	ME	255	443,492	496-500
EASTCHESTER	WESTCHESTER	NY	615	444,331	493-532

55

CITY, COUNTY, TOWN, OR TOWNSHIP	COUNTY	STATE	NA NO. M432	GD NO.	PAGES
EASTERN DIST.	STAFFORD	VA	978	444,968	1-113
EASTFORD TWP.	WINDHAM	CT	51	442,883	463-90
EASTHAM	BARNSTABLE	MA	303	014,697	185-205
EASTON	FAIRFIELD	CT	38	003,066	89-123
EASTON	TALBOT	MD	297	443,528	129-55
EASTON	BRISTOL	MA	307	014,701	1-56
EASTON	IONIA	MI	352	443,568	352-61
EASTON	WASHINGTON	NY	611	444,327	691-767
EASTON BOR.	NORTHAMPTON	PA	802	444,770	189-364
EASTON DIST.	TALBOT	MD	297	443,528	1-17
EASTPORT	WASHINGTON	ME	273	443,510	437-535
EATON	EATON	MI	349	014,811	229-41
EATON	CARROLL	NH	426	014,939	77-118
EATON	MADISON	NY	527	017,103	625, 649, 651-749
EATON	PREBLE	OH	723	444,716	461-92
EATON CO.		MI	349	014,811	165-342
EATON GRANT	AROOSTOOK	ME	248	009,718	207-211
EATON RAPIDS	EATON	MI	349	014,811	242-78
EATON TWP.	LORAIN	OH	705	444,698	839-65
EATON TWP.	WYOMING	PA	838	444,806	155-76
EBENSBURG BOR.	CAMBRIA	PA	761	020,611	315-29
ECKFORD	CALHOUN	MI	348	014,610	397-414
ECONOMY	WAYNE	IN	180	442,958	151-54
ECONOMY TWP.	BEAVER	PA	750	020,600	577-610
ECORE FABRA TWP.	OUACHITA	AR	28	002,482	159-65
ECORSE TWP.	WAYNE	MI	366	443,582	549-64
EDDINGTON	PENOBSCOT	ME	264	443,501	543-59
EDEN	LA SALLE	IL	115	007,688	447, 459-60, 463-71
EDEN	LA GRANGE	IN	157	442,935	1-17
EDEN	HANCOCK	ME	255	443,492	681-707
EDEN	ERIE	NY	499	017,075	687-746
EDEN	LAMOILLE	VT	925	444,924	169-84
EDEN	FOND DU LAC	WI	997	444,984	795-814
EDEN TWP.	SCHUYLER	IL	128	442,916	713-32
EDEN TWP.	LICKING	OH	703	444,696	781-805
EDEN TWP.	SENECA	OH	728	444,721	745-83
EDEN TWP.	WYANDOT	OH	741	444,734	497-512
EDENTON	CHOWAN	NC	625	444,638	209-218, 220-23
EDGAR CO.		IL	105	007,678	226-487
EDGARTOWN	DUKES	MA	309	014,703	769-816
EDGECOMB	LINCOLN	ME	260	443,497	827-58
EDGECOMB CO.		NC	629	444,642	183-395
EDGEFIELD	DAVIDSON	TN	875	024,566	504-522
EDGEFIELD CO.		SC	852	444,815	1-397
EDGEMONT TWP.	DELAWARE	PA	776	444,744	421-36
EDINA	KNOX	MO	403	443,611	163-66
EDINBORO	ERIE	PA	778	444,746	673-79
EDINBURG	PENOBSCOT	ME	266	443,503	538-40
EDINBURG	SARATOGA	NY	593	444,309	795-826
EDINBURG	PORTAGE	OH	722	444,715	433-60
EDMESTON	OTSEGO	NY	580	444,296	154-98
EDMONSON CO.		KY	198	442,966	1-91
EDMUNDS	WASHINGTON	ME	272	443,509	185-93
EDWARDS	ST. LAWRENCE	NY	589	444,305	515-39
EDWARDS CO.		IL	105	007,678	491-576
EDWARDSBURG VILLAGE	CASS	MI	349	014,811	503-8
EDWARDSVILLE	MADISON	IL	119	442,907	993-1008
EEL RIVER TWP.	ALLEN	IN	135	007,748	505-520

CITY, COUNTY, TOWN, OR TOWNSHIP	COUNTY	STATE	NA NO. M432	GD NO.	PAGES
EEL RIVER TWP.	GREENE	IN	148	442,926	795-810
EEL RIVER TWP.	HENDRICKS	IN	150	442,928	101-132
EEL TWP.	CASS	IN	137	007,750	889-910, 1007-1038
EFFINGHAM	CARROLL	NH	426	014,939	121-50
EFFINGHAM CO.		GA	68	007,064	679-726
EFFINGHAM CO.		IL	105	007,678	579-670
EGG HARBOR TWP.	ATLANTIC	NJ	442	016,529	1-64
EGG HARBOR TWP.	BURLINGTON	NJ	444	016,531	735-86
EGREMONT	BERKSHIRE	MA	306	014,700	423-47
EGYPT TWP.	ASHLEY	AR	25	002,479	69-70
EL DORADO CO.		CA	34	002,491	501-978
EL DORADO TWP.	UNION	AR	30	442,876	449-72
EL IOLLAL	VALENCIA	NM	470	443,668	559-69
EL IOLLITAL	VALENCIA	NM	470	443,668	570-74
EL PUEBLO DE NOMBE	SANTA FE	NM	468	443,666	754-56
EL PUEBLO DE TESUGNE	SANTA FE	NM	468	443,666	751-53
EL PUEBLO SAN ILDEFONSO	SANTA FE	NM	468	443,666	601-3
ELA	LAKE	IL	114	007,687	329-52
ELBA	LAPEER	MI	354	443,570	761-67
ELBA	GENESEE	NY	508	017,084	669-713
ELBA	DODGE	WI	996	034,510	201-218
ELBERT CO.		GA	68	007,064	727-884
ELBRIDGE	ONONDAGA	NY	568	444,284	725-818
ELDORADO	FOND DU LAC	WI	997	444,984	617-28
ELDRED TWP.	JEFFERSON	PA	786	444,754	26-37
ELDRED TWP.	MC KEAN	PA	795	444,763	67-80
ELDRID TWP.	WARREN	PA	832	444,800	677-81
ELGIN	KANE	IL	112	007,685	17-57
ELGIN VILLAGE	KANE	IL	112	007,685	1-16
ELIDA	WINNEBAGO	IL	134	442,922	684-95
ELIZABETH	LANCASTER	PA	789	444,757	535-48
ELIZABETH BOR.	ALLEGHENY	PA	747	020,597	291-318
ELIZABETH CITY CO.		VA	942	444,932	69-127
ELIZABETH RIVER PAR.	NORFOLK	VA	964	444,954	481-504
ELIZABETH PREC.	JO DAVIESS	IL	111	007,684	345-57, 365-66, 379-87
ELIZABETH TWP.	ESSEX	NJ	449	443,648	1-134
ELIZABETH TWP.	LAWRENCE	OH	701	444,694	583-643
ELIZABETH TWP.	MIAMI	OH	711	444,704	1-36
ELIZABETH TWP.	ALLEGHENY	PA	747	020,597	319-412
ELIZABETH TWP.	LANCASTER	PA	789	444,757	493-534
ELIZABETH VILLAGE	JO DAVIESS	IL	111	007,684	367-78
ELIZABETHTON	CARTER	TN	873	024,564	379-86
ELIZABETHTOWN	HARDIN	IL	109	007,682	1-6
ELIZABETHTOWN	ESSEX	NY	503	017,079	277-315
ELIZABETHTOWN	GUERNSEY	OH	684	444,677	465-67
ELIZABETHTOWN	MARSHALL	VA	959	444,949	707-712, 714
ELIZABETHTOWN ADDITION	MARSHALL	VA	959	444,949	715-19
ELK	CLARION	PA	767	444,735	466-500
ELK CO.		PA	776	444,744	615-726
ELK CREEK TWP.	ERIE	PA	778	444,746	699-736
ELK GROVE	COOK	IL	103	007,676	265-80
ELK GROVE	LAFAYETTE	WI	1001	444,988	677-91
ELK LICK TWP.	SOMERSET	PA	828	444,796	559-85
ELK RIDGE LANDING	ANNE ARUNDEL	MD	278	013,195	827-35
ELK RIVER TWP.	CLINTON	IA	182	007,791	394-404
ELK TWP.	MONROE	OH	712	444,705	629-52
ELK TWP.	VINTON	OH	736	444,729	435-64

CITY, COUNTY, TOWN, OR TOWNSHIP	COUNTY	STATE	NA NO. M432	GD NO.	PAGES	
ELK TWP.	WARREN	PA	832	444,800	739-48	
ELKHART CO.		IN	144	007,757	3-337	
ELKHART TWP.	ELKHART	IN	144	007,757	162-87	
ELKHART TWP.	NOBLE	IN	162	442,940	415-29	
ELKHORN	WALWORTH	WI	1007	444,994	496	
ELKHORN GROVE TWP.	CARROLL	IL	99	007,672	747-57	
ELKINS TWP.	CLARK	AR	25	002,479	422-25	
ELKLAND	TIOGA	PA	830	444,798	115-37	
ELKLAND TWP.	SULLIVAN	PA	828	444,796	631-40	
ELKRUN TWP.	COLUMBIANA	OH	669	020,217	387-424	
ELKTON	CECIL	MD	290	443,521	1-26	
ELLENBURG	CLINTON	NY	489	017,065	347-82	
ELLERSLIE DIST.	HARRIS	GA	73	007,069	103-117	
ELLERY	CHAUTAUQUA	NY	484	017,060	325-75	
ELLETTSVILLE	MONROE	IN	161	442,939	505-7	
ELLICOTT	CHAUTAUQUA	NY	485	017,061	77-160	
ELLICOTTS MILLS	ANNE ARUNDEL	MD	278	013,195	840-44,	901-920
ELLICOTTVILLE	CATTARAUGUS	NY	479	017,055	457-99	
ELLINGTON	TOLLAND	CT	50	442,882	39-72	
ELLINGTON	ADAMS	IL	97	007,670	129-63	
ELLINGTON	CHAUTAUQUA	NY	484	017,060	277-324	
ELLINGTON	BROWN	WI	994	034,508	33-34	
ELLIOT	YORK	ME	274	443,511	473-516	
ELLIOTTSVILLE	PISCATAQUIS	ME	267	443,504	481-83	
		TX	910	024,889	259-78,	184, 279
ELLIS CO.	JEFFERSON	NY	516	017,092	573-704	
ELLISBURG	HANCOCK	ME	255	443,492	583-678	
ELLSWORTH	GRAFTON	NH	431	443,635	305-312	
ELLSWORTH	CHEMUNG	NY	486	017,062	383-580	
ELMIRA	LAMOILLE	VT	925	444,924	377-88	
ELMORE	DAVIESS	IN	140	007,753	284-301	
ELMORE TWP.	SALEM	NJ	462	443,661	1-16	
ELSINBORO TWP.	MAHONING	OH	707	444,700	1223-46	
ELSWORTH TWP.	LORAIN	OH	705	444,698	1057-84	
ELYRIA TWP.	LORAIN	OH	705	444,698	1021-56	
ELYRIA VILLAGE	JEFFERSON	AL	7	002,349	445-55	
ELYTON BEAT		GA	68	007,064	885-971	
EMANUEL CO.	EDGAR	IL	105	007,678	455-87	
EMBARRASS PREC.	SOMERSET	ME	269	443,506	425-48	
EMBDEN	CALHOUN	MI	346	014,810	148-85	
EMMETT	DODGE	WI	996	034,510	303-332	
EMMETT	RANDOLPH	IN	168	442,946	277	
EMMETTSVILLE	FREDERICK	MD	292	443,523	317-36	
EMMITSBURG	EL DORADO	CA	34	002,491	865-66	
EMPIRE CANYON	HARTFORD	CT	39	003,067	1-107	
ENFIELD	PENOBSCOT	ME	266	443,503	541-50	
ENFIELD	HAMPSHIRE	MA	321	443,540	673-98	
ENFIELD	GRAFTON	NH	430	443,634	385-426	
ENFIELD	TOMPKINS	NY	606	444,322	663-716	
ENFIELD	IOWA	IA	184	007,793	552-55	
ENGLISH RIVER	MONROE	OH	712	444,705	653-88	
ENOCH TWP.	CLARK	OH	666	020,214	148-55	
ENON	FRANKLIN	VT	924	444,923	339-87	
ENOSBURG	LANCASTER	PA	789	444,757	289-338	
EPHRATA TWP.	FULTON	NY	506	017,082	355-404	
EPHRATAH	ROCKINGHAM	NH	437	443,641	261-304	
EPPING	GRANVILLE	NC	631	444,644	139-51	
EPPING FOREST DIST.	MERRIMACK	NH	435	443,639	409-441	
EPSOM	GALLATIN	IL	107	007,680	802-821	
EQUALITY PREC.						

CITY, COUNTY, TOWN, OR TOWNSHIP	COUNTY	STATE	NA NO. M432	GD NO.	PAGES
ERIE CO.		NY	498	017,074	1-324
ERIE CO.		NY	499	017,075	325-798
ERIE CO.		NY	500	017,076	1-638
ERIE CO.		NY	501	017,077	1-501
ERIE CO.		NY	502	017,078	505-1014
ERIE CO.		OH	676	338,044	743-943, 1-256
ERIE CO.		PA	777	444,745	1-506
ERIE CO.		PA	778	444,746	507-944
ERIE, EAST WARD	ERIE	PA	777	444,745	367-436
ERIE TWP.	MIAMI	IN	160	442,938	203-212
ERIE TWP.	MONROE	MI	358	443,574	611-24, 626-38
ERIE TWP.	OTTAWA	OH	719	444,712	293-99
ERIE, WEST WARD	ERIE	PA	777	444,745	437-506
ERIN	STEPHENSON	IL	129	442,917	645-66
ERIN	MACOMB	MI	357	443,573	361-84
ERIN	CHEMUNG	NY	486	017,062	581-624
ERIN	WASHINGTON	WI	1008	444,995	281-300
ERROL	COOS	NH	429	443,633	315-18
ERVIN TWP.	HOWARD	IN	151	442,929	881-902
ERVING	FRANKLIN	MA	317	443,536	615-26
ERWIN	STEUBEN	NY	598	444,314	155-89
ESCAMBIA CO.		FL	58	006,714	233-307
ESOPUS	ULSTER	NY	608	444,324	495-565
ESPADA MISSION	BEXAR	TX	908	024,887	319-21
ESPERANCE	SCHOHARIE	NY	595	444,311	42-76
ESSEX	MIDDLESEX	CT	44	003,072	473-75, 477-93
ESSEX	ESSEX	MA	314	014,708	553-90
ESSEX	ESSEX	NY	503	017,079	130-85
ESSEX	CHITTENDEN	VT	923	444,922	279-327
ESSEX CO.		MA	310	014,704	1-423
ESSEX CO.		MA	311	014,705	427-768
ESSEX CO.		MA	312	014,706	1-489
ESSEX CO.		MA	313	014,707	491-830, 1-292
ESSEX CO.		MA	314	014,708	293-832, 1-106
ESSEX CO.		MA	315	443,534	109-748
ESSEX CO.		NJ	447	443,646	1-610
ESSEX CO.		NJ	448	443,647	611-940
ESSEX CO.		NJ	449	443,648	1-522
ESSEX CO.		NJ	450	443,649	523-852
ESSEX CO.		NY	503	017,079	1-376
ESSEX CO.		NY	504	017,080	377-754
ESSEX CO.		VT	923	444,922	715-841
ESSEX TWP.		VA	942	444,932	131-214
ESSEX TWP.	PORTER	IN	165	442,943	241-42
ESTILL CO.	CLINTON	MI	349	014,811	81-90
ETNA		KY	198	442,966	93-225
ETNA TWP.	PENOBSCOT	ME	265	443,502	55-74
EUCLID	LICKING	OH	703	444,696	603-634
EUGENE TWP.	CUYAHOGA	OH	673	020,221	779-814
EULALIA	VERMILLION	IN	177	442,955	149-76
EUPHEMIA	POTTER	PA	825	444,793	161-67
EUREKA CITY	PREBLE	OH	723	444,716	830-34
EUREKA TWP.	TRINITY	CA	36	442,879	128-29
EVANS	MONTCALM	MI	358	443,574	868-78
EVANSPORT	ERIE	NY	499	017,075	747-98
EVANSVILLE	DEFIANCE	OH	674	020,222	97-101
EVANSVILLE, WARD 1	VANDERBURGH	IN	176	442,954	727-816
EVANSVILLE, WARD 2	VANDERBURGH	IN	176	442,954	790-804
	VANDERBURGH	IN	176	442,954	782-89

CITY, COUNTY, TOWN, OR TOWNSHIP	COUNTY	STATE	NA NO. M432	GD NO.	PAGES
EVANSVILLE, WARD 3	VANDERBURGH	IN	176	442,954	773-81
EVANSVILLE, WARD 4	VANDERBURGH	IN	176	442,954	753-72
EVANSVILLE, WARD 5	VANDERBURGH	IN	176	442,954	746-52
EVANSVILLE, WARD 6	VANDERBURGH	IN	176	442,954	740-45
EVANSVILLE, WARD 7	VANDERBURGH	IN	176	442,954	732-39
EVANSVILLE, WARD 8	VANDERBURGH	IN	176	442,954	727-31
EVESHAM TWP.	BURLINGTON	NJ	444	016,531	941-1018
EWING TWP.	MERCER	NJ	454	443,653	463-98
EXETER	SCOTT	IL	128	442,916	26, 46-50
EXETER	PENOBSCOT	ME	265	443,502	231-75
EXETER	ROCKINGHAM	NH	438	443,642	393-470
EXETER	OTSEGO	NY	580	444,296	45-81
EXETER	WASHINGTON	RI	847	444,813	441-80
EXETER	GREEN	WI	999	444,986	559-69
EXETER TWP.	MONROE	MI	358	443,574	823-33
EXETER TWP.	BERKS	PA	753	020,603	733-82
EXETER TWP.	LUZERNE	PA	793	444,761	116-35
EXETER TWP.	WYOMING	PA	838	444,806	197-202
EXTRA TWP.	ASHLEY	AR	25	002,479	71-73
FABIUS	ONONDAGA	NY	567	444,283	247-304
FABIUS TWP.	DAVIS	IA	182	007,791	569-79, 589
FABIUS TWP.	ST. JOSEPH	MI	362	443,578	483-94
FABIUS TWP.	KNOX	MO	403	443,611	212-27
FABIUS TWP.	MARION	MO	406	443,614	517-39
FAIR GROUND DIST.	RICHMOND	NC	642	444,655	600-624
FAIR HAVEN	RUTLAND	VT	927	444,926	481-502
FAIRBANKS TWP.	SULLIVAN	IN	173	442,951	555-78
FAIRFAX	FRANKLIN	VT	924	444,923	223-73
FAIRFAX	CULPEPER	VA	941	444,931	554-62
FAIRFAX CO.		VA	942	444,932	217-393
FAIRFIELD	FAIRFIELD	CT	38	003,066	1-87
FAIRFIELD	BUREAU	IL	99	007,672	443-47
FAIRFIELD	WAYNE	IL	131	442,919	523-27
FAIRFIELD	JEFFERSON	IA	185	442,960	133-33
FAIRFIELD	SOMERSET	ME	269	443,506	241-99
FAIRFIELD	LENAWEE	MI	355	443,571	303-334
FAIRFIELD	HERKIMER	NY	512	017,088	357-96
FAIRFIELD	MACON	NC	636	444,649	744
FAIRFIELD	FRANKLIN	VT	924	444,923	275-336
FAIRFIELD	DODGE	WI	996	034,510	115-42
FAIRFIELD CO.		CT	37	003,065	1-737
FAIRFIELD CO.		CT	38	003,066	1-723
FAIRFIELD CO.		OH	677	444,670	259-992
FAIRFIELD CO.		SC	852	444,815	399-573
FAIRFIELD TWP.	DE KALB	IN	142	007,755	457-71
FAIRFIELD TWP.	FRANKLIN	IN	146	442,924	357-80
FAIRFIELD TWP.	TIPPECANOE	IN	175	442,953	79-81, 231-60
FAIRFIELD TWP.	JACKSON	IA	184	007,793	679, 704-7
FAIRFIELD TWP.	JEFFERSON	IA	185	442,960	36-44, 134-50
FAIRFIELD TWP.	CUMBERLAND	NJ	446	016,533	327-78
FAIRFIELD TWP.	BUTLER	OH	663	020,211	427-569
FAIRFIELD TWP.	COLUMBIANA	OH	669	020,217	159-216
FAIRFIELD TWP.	HIGHLAND	OH	694	444,687	187-264
FAIRFIELD TWP.	HURON	OH	697	444,690	315-53
FAIRFIELD TWP.	MADISON	OH	706	444,699	405-424
FAIRFIELD TWP.	TUSCARAWAS	OH	735	444,728	645-66

CITY, COUNTY, TOWN, OR TOWNSHIP	COUNTY	STATE	NA NO. M432	GD NO.	PAGES
FAIRFIELD TWP.	CRAWFORD	PA	771	444,739	857-86
FAIRFIELD TWP.	LYCOMING	PA	795	444,763	985-1016
FAIRFIELD TWP.	WESTMORELAND	PA	836	444,804	203-280
FAIRHAVEN	BRISTOL	MA	308	014,702	317-424
FAIRLEE	ORANGE	VT	926	444,925	181-94
FAIRMONT	MARION	VA	958	444,948	362-76
FAIRMOUNT TWP.	LUZERNE	PA	793	444,761	316-38
FAIRPLAIN	MONTCALM	MI	358	443,574	883-88
FAIRPLAY TWP.	GREENE	IN	148	442,926	863-74
FAIRVIEW	FULTON	IL	107	007,680	439-63, 467
FAIRVIEW	RANDOLPH	IN	168	442,946	293-95
FAIRVIEW	GUERNSEY	OH	684	444,677	469-80
FAIRVIEW TWP.	JONES	IA	185	442,960	389-405
FAIRVIEW TWP.	BUTLER	PA	760	020,610	443-68
FAIRVIEW TWP.	ERIE	PA	777	444,745	323-65
FAIRVIEW TWP.	YORK	PA	840	444,808	731-42, 747-81
FALKLAND DIST.	PITT	NC	641	444,654	30-39
FALL CREEK	ADAMS	IL	97	007,670	165-87
FALL CREEK DIST.	RUTHERFORD	TN	894	444,850	319-31
FALL CREEK TWP.	HAMILTON	IN	148	442,926	103-134
FALL CREEK TWP.	HENRY	IN	151	442,929	617-49
FALL CREEK TWP.	MADISON	IN	158	442,936	203-224, 230-53
FALL RIVER	BRISTOL	MA	308	014,702	1-275
FALL RIVER VILLAGE	COLUMBIA	WI	994	034,508	276-78
FALLOWFIELD TWP.	WASHINGTON	PA	834	444,802	543-70
FALLS CREEK DIST.	CURRITUCK	NC	627	444,640	337-46
FALLS OF ST. CROIX PREC.	WASHINGTON	MN	367	014,834	152-53
FALLS ST. CROIX	ST. CROIX	WI	1006	444,993	8-11
FALLS TWP.	HOCKING	OH	695	444,688	65-106
FALLS TWP.	MUSKINGUM	OH	717	444,710	195-245
FALLS TWP.	BUCKS	PA	758	020,608	257-311
FALLS TWP.	WYOMING	PA	838	444,806	219-37
FALLSBURG	SULLIVAN	NY	603	444,319	363-423
FALLSBURY TWP.	LICKING	OH	703	444,696	727-55
FALLSTON	BEAVER	PA	750	020,600	73-86
FALMOUTH	CUMBERLAND	ME	250	009,720	230-54
FALMOUTH	BARNSTABLE	MA	304	014,698	787-846
FALSINGTON TWP.	BUCKS	PA	758	020,608	306-311
FANNETT TWP.	FRANKLIN	PA	782	444,750	755-802
FANNIN CO.		TX	910	024,889	283-374
FANNING BEAT	AUTAUGA	AL	1	002,343	123-28
FARM RIDGE	LA SALLE	IL	115	007,688	500, 512-14, 516-18
FARMER TWP.	DEFIANCE	OH	674	020,222	131-53
FARMERS	FULTON	IL	107	007,680	139-58
FARMERS CREEK TWP.	JACKSON	IA	184	007,793	634, 639-40, 644-45, 649-52, 654-55
FARMERSBURG TWP.	CLAYTON	IA	182	007,791	319-24
FARMERSVILLE	CATTARAUGUS	NY	480	017,056	822-58
FARMERSVILLE TWP.	DANE	WI	995	034,509	873-77
FARMINGHAM ACAD. GT.	AROOSTOOK	ME	248	009,718	163
FARMINGTON	HARTFORD	CT	40	003,068	631-93
FARMINGTON	FULTON	IL	107	007,680	464-66, 468-97
FARMINGTON	VAN BUREN	IA	189	442,964	637-50
FARMINGTON	FRANKLIN	ME	253	009,723	343-405
FARMINGTON	STRAFFORD	NH	440	443,644	609-649
FARMINGTON	ONTARIO	NY	572	444,288	555-601
FARMINGTON	BELMONT	OH	661	020,209	1009

CITY, COUNTY, TOWN, OR TOWNSHIP	COUNTY	STATE	NA NO. M432	GD NO.	PAGES	
FARMINGTON	CLARION	PA	767	444,735	380-406	
FARMINGTON	JEFFERSON	WI	1000	444,987	197-214	
FARMINGTON	WASHINGTON	WI	1008	444,995	88-99	
FARMINGTON DIST.	CLARKE	GA	65	007,061	133-38	
FARMINGTON TWP.	VAN BUREN	IA	189	442,964	593-627	
FARMINGTON TWP.	OAKLAND	MI	359	443,575	353-96	
FARMINGTON TWP.	TRUMBULL	OH	733	444,726	465-95	
FARMINGTON TWP.	TIOGA	PA	830	444,798	251-72	
FARNHAM PARISH	RICHMOND	VA	972	444,962	315-60,	412
FAUQUIER CO.		VA	943	444,933	397-655	
FAUSSE POINTE	ST. MARTIN	LA	240	443,483	276-88,	371-73
FAWN RIVER TWP.	ST. JOSEPH	MI	362	443,578	509-520	
FAWN TWP.	YORK	PA	839	444,807	273-99	
FAYETTE	KENNEBEC	ME	257	443,494	825-50	
FAYETTE	JEFFERSON	MS	374	443,586	194-98	
FAYETTE	SENECA	NY	597	444,313	265-355	
FAYETTE	LAFAYETTE	WI	1001	444,988	743-60	
FAYETTE CO.		AL	5	002,347	1-203	
FAYETTE CO.		GA	69	007,065	1-164	
FAYETTE CO.		IL	106	007,679	673-886	
FAYETTE CO.		IN	144	007,757	339-592	
FAYETTE CO.		IA	184	007,793	263-82	
FAYETTE CO.		KY	199	442,967	227-510	
FAYETTE CO.		OH	678	444,671	1-317	
FAYETTE CO.		PA	779	444,747	1-357	
FAYETTE CO.		PA	780	444,748	415-957	
FAYETTE CO.		TN	877	444,833	461-750	
FAYETTE CO.		TX	910	024,889	377-445	
FAYETTE CO.		VA	943	444,933	659-749	
FAYETTE TWP.	VIGO	IN	177	442,955	351-82	
FAYETTE TWP.	HILLSDALE	MI	351	443,567	747, 1039-60	
FAYETTE TWP.	LAWRENCE	OH	701	444,694	869-95	
FAYETTE TWP.	JUNIATA	PA	786	444,754	567-603	
FAYETTEVILLE	WASHINGTON	AR	31	442,877	871-80	
FAYETTEVILLE DIST.	CUMBERLAND	NC	627	444,640	1-50, 217-40	
FAYSTON	WASHINGTON	VT	928	444,927	53-69	
FEARING TWP.	WASHINGTON	OH	738	444,731	609-638	
FELICIANA PARISH, EAST		LA	231	009,698	411-508	
FELICIANA PARISH, WEST		LA	231	009,698	509-570	
FELL TWP.	LUZERNE	PA	793	444,761	467-75	
FENNER	MADISON	NY	526	017,102	231-71	
FENTER	HOT SPRINGS	AR	26	002,480	573-75,	585-86
FENTER TWP.	HOT SPRINGS	AR	26	002,480	554-56,	559-65
FENTON TWP.	GENESEE	MI	350	443,566	533-53	
FENTRESS CO.		TN	877	444,833	753-855	
FERDINAND TWP.	DUBOIS	IN	143	007,756	918-30	
FERGUSON TWP.	CENTRE	PA	763	020,613	245-83	
FERGUSON TWP.	CLEARFIELD	PA	768	444,736	724-31	
FERMANAGH TWP.	JUNIATA	PA	786	444,754	546-66	
FERRISBURG	ADDISON	VT	920	027,446	587-636	
FILLMORE	ALLEGAN	MI	346	014,808	30-42	
FINDLAY	HANCOCK	OH	692	444,685	45-76	
FINDLAY TWP.	HANCOCK	OH	692	444,685	25-44	
FINDLEY TWP.	ALLEGHENY	PA	748	020,598	623-54	
FINDLEY TWP.	MERCER	PA	796	444,764	339-64	
FINE	ST. LAWRENCE	NY	589	444,305	493-500	
FINLEY'S	GREENE	MO	400	443,608	601-640	
FISH RIVER DIST.	SURRY	NC	646	444,659	613-23,	625-29
					703	

CITY, COUNTY, TOWN, OR TOWNSHIP	COUNTY	STATE	NA NO. M432	GD NO.	PAGES
FISHING CREEK DIST.	GRANVILLE	NC	631	444,644	171-80
FISHING RIVER TWP.	CLAY	MO	396	443,604	742-78
FISHINGCREEK TWP.	COLUMBIA	PA	769	444,737	380-406
FISHKILL	DUTCHESS	NY	496	017,072	1-218
FITCHBURG	WORCESTER	MA	340	443,559	265-387
FITCHVILLE TWP.	HURON	OH	697	444,690	841-69
FITZWILLIAM	CHESHIRE	NH	428	014,941	351-86
FIVE MILE BEAT	JEFFERSON	AL	7	002,349	349-63
FIVE MILE BEAT	PERRY	AL	12	002,354	651-61
FLAGG TWP.	OGLE	IL	123	442,911	103-110
FLAGSTAFF	SOMERSET	ME	269	443,506	533-35
FLAT BRANCH DIST.	SHELBY	IL	128	442,916	273-81
FLAT ROCK TWP.	BARTHOLOMEW	IN	136	007,749	825-44
FLAT SHOALS DIST.	DE KALB	GA	67	007,063	336-38
FLAT TWP.	TANEY	MO	420	443,628	710-20
FLATBUSH TWP.	KINGS	NY	521	017,097	109-184
FLATLANDS	KINGS	NY	521	017,097	1-28
FLATROCK TWP.	HENRY	OH	693	444,686	15-24
FLEMING	CAYUGA	NY	483	017,059	387-416
FLEMING CO.		KY	199	442,967	511-812
FLEMINGS DIST.	RUTHERFORD	TN	894	444,850	559-73
FLEMINGSBURG	FLEMING	KY	199	442,967	511-24
FLETCHER	MIAMI	OH	711	444,704	823-28
FLETCHER	FRANKLIN	VT	924	444,923	1-26
FLINN TWP.	LAWRENCE	IN	158	442,936	836-37, 854-79
FLINT	GENESEE	MI	350	443,566	345-423
FLINT RIVER TWP.	DES MOINES	IA	183	007,792	821-42
FLORA TWP.	SAUK	WI	1006	444,993	93-98
FLORENCE	LAUDERDALE	AL	7	002,349	578-89
FLORENCE	STEPHENSON	IL	129	442,917	679-82
FLORENCE	ONEIDA	NY	564	444,280	381-442
FLORENCE	WASHINGTON	PA	833	444,801	152-59
FLORENCE DIST.	STEWART	GA	82	442,891	254-64
FLORENCE TWP.	LOUISA	IA	187	442,962	217-35
FLORENCE TWP.	ST. JOSEPH	MI	362	443,578	620-37
FLORENCE TWP.	ERIE	OH	676	338,044	831-66
FLORENCE TWP.	WILLIAMS	OH	741	444,734	111-27
FLORIDA	BERKSHIRE	MA	305	014,699	1-16
FLORIDA	MONTGOMERY	NY	532	017,108	129-214
FLOWERFIELD TWP.	ST. JOSEPH	MI	362	443,578	495-508
FLOYD	ONEIDA	NY	565	444,281	261-97
FLOYD CO.		GA	69	007,065	165-288
FLOYD CO.		IN	145	442,923	593-951
FLOYD CO.		KY	200	442,968	813-947
FLOYD CO.		VA	943	444,933	753-896
FLOYD TWP.	PUTNAM	IN	167	442,945	774-806
FLOYDS CREEK	RUTHERFORD	NC	644	444,657	509, 512-20, 605-6
FLUSHING	QUEENS	NY	583	444,299	491-619
FLUSHING TWP.	GENESEE	MI	350	443,566	465-81
FLUSHING TWP.	BELMONT	OH	661	020,209	317-60
FLUVANNA CO.		VA	944	444,934	1-114
FOND DU LAC	FOND DU LAC	WI	997	444,984	487-534
FOND DU LAC CO.		WI	997	444,984	487-836
FOND DU LAC VILLAGE	LA POINTE	WI	1002	444,989	1
FOREST	FOND DU LAC	WI	997	444,984	765-94
FOREST LAKE TWP.	SUSQUEHANNA	PA	829	444,797	189-207
FOREST TWP.	GENESEE	MI	350	443,566	639-43
FORESTBURGH	SULLIVAN	NY	603	444,319	345-62

CITY, COUNTY, TOWN, OR TOWNSHIP	COUNTY	STATE	NA NO. M432	GD NO.	PAGES
FORESTVILLE VILLAGE	CHAUTAUQUA	NY	484	017,060	145-58
FORK BROOK (TAMPA)	HILLSBOROUGH	FL	58	006,714	481-94
FORKS, THE	SOMERSET	ME	269	443,506	549-53
FORKS TWP.	NORTHAMPTON	PA	802	444,770	133-88
FORKS TWP.	SULLIVAN	PA	828	444,796	655-63
FORKSTON TWP.	WYOMING	PA	838	444,806	117-33
FORKSVILLE	SUTTER	CA	36	442,879	37-45
FORSYTH	FORSYTH	NC	630	444,643	398
FORSYTH CO.		GA	69	007,065	289-475
FORSYTH CO.		NC	630	444,643	397-631
FORT ANN	WASHINGTON	NY	610	444,326	137-217
FORT ATKINSON	JEFFERSON	WI	1000	444,987	243-50
FORT BEND CO.		TX	910	024,889	449-72
FORT CAMP DIST.	RUTHERFORD	TN	894	444,850	677-86
FORT COVINGTON	FRANKLIN	NY	505	017,081	343-405
FORT CREEK DIST.	GRANVILLE	NC	631	444,644	219-38
FORT DES MOINES	POLK	IA	188	442,963	43-54
FORT DUNCAN	BEXAR	TX	908	024,887	287-90
FORT EDWARD	WASHINGTON	NY	611	444,327	347-402
FORT GAINES	MANKAHTA	MN	367	014,834	35-38
FORT INGE	BEXAR	TX	908	024,887	277-78
FORT LAWRENCE	LUCAS	OH	706	444,699	59-144
FORT LINCOLN	MEDINA	TX	912	444,915	829-32
FORT MADISON	LEE	IA	186	442,961	561-96
FORT MARKE RIVER	GONZALES	TX	910	024,889	660-62
FORT MARTIN SCOTT	GILLESPIE	TX	910	024,889	626-28
FORT OSAGE TWP.	JACKSON	MO	402	443,610	639-57
FORT SMITH	CRAWFORD	AR	25	002,479	575-94
FORT SNELLING	DAKOTA	MN	367	014,834	20-26
FORT WINNEBAGO TWP.	COLUMBIA	WI	994	034,508	387-95, 399
FORT WINNEBAGO VILLAGE	COLUMBIA	WI	994	034,508	352-82
FOSTER	PROVIDENCE	RI	846	444,812	1-47
FOSTERVILLE DIST.	RUTHERFORD	TN	894	444,850	655-76
FOUNTAIN CO.		IN	145	442,923	1-322
FOUNTAIN PRARIE	COLUMBIA	WI	994	034,508	266-75
FOUNTAIN PREC.	MONROE	IL	121	442,909	41, 58, 59, 6 62, 111-30
FOURCHE, LOWER, TWP.	YELL	AR	31	442,877	1000-1008
FOURCHE TWP.	PULASKI	AR	29	002,483	640-46
FOURCHE, UPPER, TWP.	YELL	AR	31	442,877	988-99
FOWLER	ST. LAWRENCE	NY	589	444,305	449-92
FOWLER	TRUMBULL	OH	733	444,726	843-68
FOX	KENDALL	IL	113	007,686	595-614
FOX HILL DIST.	ELIZABETH	VA	942	444,932	69-83
FOX SQUIRREL DIST.	RUTHERFORD	NC	644	444,657	593-600
FOX TWP.	DAVIS	IA	182	007,791	550-68
FOX TWP.	CARROLL	OH	664	020,212	319-53
FOX TWP.	CLEARFIELD	PA	768	444,736	831-32
FOX TWP.	ELK	PA	776	444,744	621-59
FOX TWP.	SULLIVAN	PA	828	444,796	607-612
FOXBORO	NORFOLK	MA	330	443,549	1-45
FOXCROFT	PISCATAQUIS	ME	267	443,504	521-45
FRAILEY TWP.	SCHUYLKILL	PA	826	444,794	747-62
FRAMINGHAM	MIDDLESEX	MA	323	443,542	507-1008
FRANCESTOWN	HILLSBORO	NH	434	443,638	65-91
FRANCONIA	GRAFTON	NH	431	443,635	107-120
FRANCONIA	MONTGOMERY	PA	799	444,767	1-31
FRANKFORD BOR.	PHILADELPHIA	PA	824	444,792	249-378
FRANKFORD TWP.	SUSSEX	NJ	464	443,663	495-541

CITY, COUNTY, TOWN, OR TOWNSHIP	COUNTY	STATE	NA NO. M432	GD NO.	PAGES
FRANKFORD TWP.	CUMBERLAND	PA	772	444,740	162-91
FRANKFORT	WILL	IL	133	442,921	251-71
FRANKFORT	CLINTON	IN	139	007,752	623-36
FRANKFORT	WALDO	ME	270	443,507	75-175
FRANKFORT	HERKIMER	NY	512	017,088	157-228
FRANKLIN	NEW LONDON	CT	48	442,880	1-22
FRANKLIN	KENDALL	IL	113	007,686	519-27
FRANKLIN	ST. MARY PAR.	LA	240	443,483	479-95
FRANKLIN	HANCOCK	ME	255	443,492	458-75
FRANKLIN	NORFOLK	MA	331	443,550	583-626
FRANKLIN	LENAWEE	MI	355	443,571	75-104
FRANKLIN	MERRIMACK	NH	436	443,640	471-500
FRANKLIN	DELAWARE	NY	494	017,070	57-131
FRANKLIN	FRANKLIN	NY	505	017,081	163-80
FRANKLIN	HARRISON	OH	693	444,686	814-18
FRANKLIN	WARREN	OH	737	444,730	784-806
FRANKLIN	YORK	PA	840	444,808	855-56
FRANKLIN	ROBERTSON	TX	914	444,917	494
FRANKLIN	FRANKLIN	VT	924	444,923	679-718
FRANKLIN	PENDLETON	VA	968	444,958	127-31
FRANKLIN	MILWAUKEE	WI	1003	444,990	883-910
FRANKLIN BOR.	VENANGO	PA	832	444,800	279-302
FRANKLIN CO.		AL	5	002,347	207-483
FRANKLIN CO.		AR	26	002,480	209-298
FRANKLIN CO.		FL	58	066,714	309-337
FRANKLIN CO.		GA	70	007,066	477-694
FRANKLIN CO.		IL	106	007,679	1-136
FRANKLIN CO.		IN	146	442,924	321-800
FRANKLIN CO.		KY	200	442,968	1-219
FRANKLIN CO.		ME	253	009,723	1-516
FRANKLIN CO.		MA	316	443,535	1-394
FRANKLIN CO.		MA	317	443,536	397-779
FRANKLIN CO.		MS	372	443,584	1-61
FRANKLIN CO.		MO	399	443,607	43-270
FRANKLIN CO.		NY	505	017,081	1-614
FRANKLIN CO.		NC	630	444,643	633-780
FRANKLIN CO.		OH	679	444,672	319-841
FRANKLIN CO.		OH	680	444,673	1-536
FRANKLIN CO.		PA	781	444,749	1-506
FRANKLIN CO.		PA	782	444,750	507-967
FRANKLIN CO.		TN	878	444,834	1-242
FRANKLIN CO.		VT	924	444,923	1-718
FRANKLIN PARISH		VA	944	444,934	117-392
FRANKLIN PLANTATION	.OXFORD	LA	231	009,698	571-611
FRANKLIN PREC.	CRAWFORD	ME	263	443,500	325-30
FRANKLIN TWP.	CHICOT	IL	104	007,677	454-65
FRANKLIN TWP.	DESHA	AR	25	002,479	368-70
FRANKLIN TWP.	FULTON	AR	26	002,480	123-25
FRANKLIN TWP.	IZARD	AR	26	002,480	333-37
FRANKLIN TWP.	OUACHITA	AR	27	002,481	54-68
FRANKLIN TWP.	SEVIER	AR	28	002,482	43-47
FRANKLIN TWP.	UNION	AR	30	442,876	388-91
FRANKLIN TWP.	DE KALB	AR	30	442,876	567-89
FRANKLIN TWP.	DE KALB	IL	104	007,677	615-32
FRANKLIN TWP.	FLOYD	IN	142	007,755	419-40
FRANKLIN TWP.	HENDRICKS	IN	145	442,923	878-95
FRANKLIN TWP.	HENRY	IN	150	442,928	21-41
FRANKLIN TWP.	JOHNSON	IN	151	442,929	467-99
		IN	155	442,933	131-206

65

Franklin Twp.

CITY, COUNTY, TOWN, OR TOWNSHIP	COUNTY	STATE	NA NO. M432	GD NO.	PAGES
FRANKLIN TWP.	KOSCIUSKO	IN	156	442,934	769-96
FRANKLIN TWP.	MARION	IN	159	442,937	669-705
FRANKLIN TWP.	MONTGOMERY	IN	161	442,939	543-76
FRANKLIN TWP.	OWEN	IN	164	442,942	209-236
FRANKLIN TWP.	PUTNAM	IN	167	442,945	745-73
FRANKLIN TWP.	RIPLEY	IN	169	442,947	485-528
FRANKLIN TWP.	WASHINGTON	IN	179	442,957	689-764
FRANKLIN TWP.	WAYNE	IN	180	442,958	501-533
FRANKLIN TWP.	DES MOINES	IA	183	007,792	737-63
FRANKLIN TWP.	BERGEN	NJ	442	016,529	405-448
FRANKLIN TWP.	GLOUCESTER	NJ	451	443,650	1-72
FRANKLIN TWP.	HUNTERDON	NJ	453	443,652	169-204
FRANKLIN TWP.	SOMERSET	NJ	463	443,662	575-648
FRANKLIN TWP.	WARREN	NJ	465	443,664	913-50
FRANKLIN TWP.	ADAMS	OH	657	020,205	1-47
FRANKLIN TWP.	BROWN	OH	662	020,210	781-808
FRANKLIN TWP.	CLERMONT	OH	667	020,215	749-825
FRANKLIN TWP.	COLUMBIANA	OH	669	020,217	459-86
FRANKLIN TWP.	COSHOCTON	OH	670	020,218	513-35
FRANKLIN TWP.	DARKE	OH	674	020,222	657-70
FRANKLIN TWP.	FRANKLIN	OH	680	444,673	489-536
FRANKLIN TWP.	FULTON	OH	681	444,674	669-86
FRANKLIN TWP.	HARRISON	OH	693	444,686	813-40
FRANKLIN TWP.	JACKSON	OH	698	444,691	587-619
FRANKLIN TWP.	LICKING	OH	703	444,696	909-934
FRANKLIN TWP.	MERCER	OH	710	444,703	520-28
FRANKLIN TWP.	MONROE	OH	712	444,705	941-78
FRANKLIN TWP.	MORROW	OH	716	444,709	955-89
FRANKLIN TWP.	PORTAGE	OH	722	444,715	133-74
FRANKLIN TWP.	RICHLAND	OH	724	444,717	605-635
FRANKLIN TWP.	ROSS	OH	725	444,718	607-622
FRANKLIN TWP.	SHELBY	OH	729	444,722	341-60
FRANKLIN TWP.	SUMMIT	OH	732	444,725	83-122
FRANKLIN TWP.	WARREN	OH	737	444,730	775-835
FRANKLIN TWP.	WAYNE	OH	739	444,732	29-64
FRANKLIN TWP.	ADAMS	PA	743	020,593	320-62
FRANKLIN TWP.	ALLEGHENY	PA	744	020,594	633-64
FRANKLIN TWP.	ARMSTRONG	PA	749	020,599	117-74
FRANKLIN TWP.	BEAVER	PA	750	020,600	337-51
FRANKLIN TWP.	BRADFORD	PA	756	020,606	107-125
FRANKLIN TWP.	BUTLER	PA	760	020,610	469-84, 493-50
FRANKLIN TWP.	ERIE	PA	778	444,746	681-98
FRANKLIN TWP.	FAYETTE	PA	780	444,748	415-49
FRANKLIN TWP.	GREENE	PA	783	444,751	490-528
FRANKLIN TWP.	HUNTINGDON	PA	784	444,752	209-244
FRANKLIN TWP.	LUZERNE	PA	793	444,761	100-115
FRANKLIN TWP.	LYCOMING	PA	795	444,763	931-56, 961
FRANKLIN TWP.	MONTOUR	PA	801	444,769	899-916
FRANKLIN TWP.	SUSQUEHANNA	PA	829	444,797	239-55
FRANKLIN TWP.	WESTMORELAND	PA	836	444,804	549-609
FRANKLIN TWP.	YORK	PA	840	444,808	857-76
FRANKLINTON	FRANKLIN	OH	680	444,673	489-503
FRANKLINTON DIST.	FRANKLIN	NC	630	444,643	684-95
FRANKLINVILLE	CATTARAUGUS	NY	480	017,056	755-95
FRANKS TWP.	ST. FRANCIS	AR	30	442,876	115-17, 122-2 125-27, 139-4 150, 152-53, 162-65
FRANKSTOWN TWP.	BLAIR	PA	755	020,605	311-46

CITY, COUNTY, TOWN, OR TOWNSHIP	COUNTY	STATE	NA NO. M432	GD NO.	PAGES
FREDERICK CO.		MD	292	443,523	1-381
FREDERICK CO.		MD	293	443,524	383-906
FREDERICK CO.		VA	945	444,935	395-722
FREDERICK TWP.	SCHUYLER	IL	128	442,916	829-36
FREDERICK TWP.	MONTGOMERY	PA	799	444,767	301-335
FREDERICKSBURG	LEBANON	PA	791	444,759	384-93
FREDERICKSBURG	GILLESPIE	TX	910	024,889	607-624
FREDERICKSBURG	SPOTSYLVANIA	VA	977	444,967	673-742
FREDERICKTOWN	FREDERICK	MD	292	443,523	1-134
FREDERICKTOWN	KNOX	OH	700	444,693	84-100
FREDERICKTOWN EL. DIST. FREDERICK		MD	292	443,523	137-207
FREDONIA	CALHOUN	MI	348	014,810	465-79
FREDONIA	WASHINGTON	WI	1008	444,995	112-27
FREDONIA TWP.	LOUISA	IA	187	442,962	191-99
FREEBORN TWP.	DUNKLIN	MO	399	443,607	36-42
FREEDOM	LA SALLE	IL	115	007,688	733-55
FREEDOM	WALDO	ME	270	443,507	531-54
FREEDOM	WASHTENAW	MI	364	443,580	749-77
FREEDOM	CARROLL	NH	426	014,939	153-74
FREEDOM	CATTARAUGUS	NY	480	017,056	859-99
FREEDOM BOR.	BEAVER	PA	750	020,600	419-31
FREEDOM TWP.	POLK	AR	29	002,483	471-74
FREEDOM TWP.	CARROLL	IL	99	007,672	693-700
FREEDOM TWP.	HENRY	OH	693	444,686	43-44
FREEDOM TWP.	PORTAGE	OH	722	444,715	319-42
FREEDOM TWP.	WOOD	OH	741	444,734	363-74
FREEDOM TWP.	ADAMS	PA	743	020,593	253-64
FREEHOLD TWP.	MONMOUTH	NJ	456	443,655	315-67
FREEHOLD TWP.	WARREN	PA	832	444,800	557-84
FREEMAN	FRANKLIN	ME	253	009,723	449-67
FREEMAN	STANLEY	NC	645	444,658	17-29
FREEPORT	STEPHENSON	IL	129	442,917	473-507
FREEPORT	CUMBERLAND	ME	249	009,719	1-63
FREEPORT	ARMSTRONG	PA	749	020,599	229-54
FREEPORT TWP.	HARRISON	OH	693	444,686	679-710
FREETOWN	JEFFERSON PAR.	LA	232	443,475	181-91
FREETOWN	BRISTOL	MA	308	014,702	277-315
FREETOWN	CORTLAND	NY	493	017,069	479-503
FRELINGHUYSEN TWP.	WARREN	NJ	465	443,664	951-82
FREMONT	YOLO	CA	36	442,879	369-72
FREMONT	LAKE	IL	114	007,687	139-57
FREMONT	SANDUSKY	OH	726	444,719	785-819
FREMONT	SCHUYLKILL	PA	826	444,794	915-44
FREMONT CO.		IA	184	007,793	285-314
FREMONT TWP.	STEUBEN	IN	173	442,951	245-58
FRENCH CANYON	EL DORADO	CA	34	002,491	809, 812-14
FRENCH CREEK	CHAUTAUQUA	NY	484	017,060	573-90
FRENCH CREEK TWP.	MERCER	PA	796	444,764	545-61
FRENCH LICK TWP.	ORANGE	IN	163	442,941	932-61
FRENCH TWP.	ADAMS	IN	135	007,748	85-93
FRENCHCREEK TWP.	VENANGO	PA	832	444,800	1-24
FRENCHTOWN TWP.	MONROE	MI	358	443,574	497-523
FRENCHVILLE BOR.	SUSQUEHANNA	PA	829	444,797	305-9
FRIARS POINT	COAHOMA	MS	370	014,849	417-18
FRIENDSHIP	LINCOLN	ME	259	443,496	308-325
FRIENDSHIP	ALLEGANY	NY	475	017,051	97-136
FRIENDSHIP	FOND DU LAC	WI	997	444,984	554-63
FRISCO TWP.	OUACHITA	AR	28	002,482	71-79
FRISTOE TWP.	BENTON	MO	392	014,872	554-68

67

CITY, COUNTY, TOWN, OR TOWNSHIP	COUNTY	STATE	NA NO. M432	GD NO.	PAGES
FROGTOWN DIST.	LUMPKIN	GA	76	007,072	179-92
FRONT ROYAL	WARREN	VA	980	444,970	109-116
FRYEBURG	OXFORD	ME	262	443,499	201-237
FRYEBURG ACADEMY GRANTS	OXFORD	ME	262	443,499	473-74
FUGIT TWP.	DECATUR	IN	142	007,755	123-66
FULDA	SPENCER	IN	172	442,950	199
FULTON	ISSAQUENA	MS	373	443,585	873-78
FULTON	OSWEGO	NY	577	444,293	585-640
FULTON	SCHOHARIE	NY	596	444,312	459-520
FULTON	OHIO	VA	966	444,956	109-121
FULTON	ROCK	WI	1005	444,992	631-38, 737-48
FULTON CO.		AR	26	002,480	299-348
FULTON CO.		IL	107	007,680	139-690
FULTON CO.		IN	146	442,924	801-956
FULTON CO.		KY	200	442,968	219-302
FULTON CO.		NY	506	017,082	1-496
FULTON CO.		OH	681	444,674	537-734
FULTON CO.		PA	783	444,751	1-192
FULTON TWP.	POLK	AR	29	002,483	459-63
FULTON TWP.	FOUNTAIN	IN	145	442,923	29-52
FULTON TWP.	FULTON	OH	681	444,674	599-614
FULTON TWP.	HAMILTON	OH	685	444,678	411-88
FULTON TWP.	LANCASTER	PA	788	444,756	221-66
FUNK'S GROVE	MC LEON	IL	117	007,690	233-36
FUNKSTOWN DIST.	WASHINGTON	MD	298	443,529	337-351
FURR	STANLEY	NC	645	444,658	74-86
GADSDEN CO.		FL	58	006,714	339-432
GAINES	KENT	MI	353	443,569	509-516
GAINES	ORLEANS	NY	575	444,291	291-358
GAINES TWP.	GENESEE	MI	350	443,566	493-99
GAINES TWP.	TIOGA	PA	830	444,798	515-27
GAINESVILLE	SUMTER	AL	15	442,866	565-80, 634-43 660, 667-68
GAINESVILLE	HANCOCK	MS	372	443,584	128-36, 154-55
GAINESVILLE	WYOMING	NY	617	444,333	401-442
GALEN	WAYNE	NY	613	444,329	653-762
GALENA	JO DAVIESS	IL	111	007,684	495-638
GALENA PREC.	JO DAVIESS	IL	111	007,684	460-94
GALENA TWP.	LA PORTE	IN	157	442,935	449-64
GALESBURG	KNOX	IL	113	007,686	685-705
GALLA ROCK TWP.	YELL	AR	31	442,877	969-71
GALLAHER TWP.	CLINTON	PA	768	444,736	231-36
GALLATIN	COPIAH	MS	371	443,583	565-67
GALLATIN	COLUMBIA	NY	491	017,067	163-202
GALLATIN CO.		IL	107	007,680	691-821
GALLATIN CO.		KY	200	442,968	303-408
GALLATIN TWP.	CLAY	MO	396	443,604	642-78
GALLEDGER DIST.	ANSON	NC	619	018,105	347-60
GALLIA CO.		OH	681	444,674	735-949, 1-21.
GALLIPOLIS TWP.	GALLIA	OH	681	444,674	1-54
GALLOWAY TWP.	ATLANTIC	NJ	442	016,529	65-120
GALMAN WORKS PLANT.	AROOSTOOK	ME	248	009,718	325-29
GALVESTON	GALVESTON	TX	910	024,889	475-561
GALVESTON CO.		TX	910	024,889	475-569
GALVESTON ISLAND	GALVESTON	TX	910	024,889	564-65
GALWAY	SARATOGA	NY	593	444,309	827-78

CITY, COUNTY, TOWN, OR TOWNSHIP	COUNTY	STATE	NA NO. M432	GD NO.	PAGES	
GAMBIER	KNOX	OH	700	444,693	556-63	
GAMBRILL DIST.	RUTHERFORD	TN	894	444,850	363-76	
GAP TWP.	MONTGOMERY	AR	28	002,482	777-88	
GARDINER	KENNEBEC	ME	257	443,494	521-665	
GARDNER	WORCESTER	MA	340	443,559	49-85	
GARLAND	PENOBSCOT	ME	265	443,502	277-306	
GARLANDVILLE	JASPER	MS	374	443,586	93	
GARNAVILLO TWP.	CLAYTON	IA	182	007,791	328-44	
GARRARD CO.		KY	201	442,969	409-578	
GASCONADE CO.		MO	399	443,607	271-388	
GASKILL TWP.	JEFFERSON	PA	786	444,754	194-208	
GASTON	NORTHAMPTON	NC	639	444,652	161	
GASTON CO.		NC	630	444,643	781-928	
GASTON DIV.	SUMTER	AL	15	442,866	619-23,	629-33,
					689-90	
GATES	MONROE	NY	528	017,104	513-60	
GATES CO.		NC	631	444,644	1-109	
GAUGES	ALLEGAN	MI	346	014,808	7-12	
GAYSPORT TWP.	BLAIR	PA	755	020,605	295-309	
GEAUGA CO.		OH	682	444,675	213-649	
GEDDES	ONONDAGA	NY	568	444,284	963-1010	
GENESEE	ALLEGANY	NY	475	017,051	61-76	
GENESEE	POTTER	PA	825	444,793	225-32	
GENESEE	WAUKESHA	WI	1009	444,996	514-45	
GENESEE CO.		MI	350	443,566	345-643	
GENESEE CO.		NY	507	017,083	3-367	
GENESEE CO.		NY	508	017,084	369-713	
GENESEE FALLS	WYOMING	NY	617	444,333	487-518	
GENESEO	LIVINGSTON	NY	524	017,100	719-89	
GENEVA	KANE	IL	112	007,685	261-82	
GENEVA	ASHTABULA	OH	659	020,207	431-63	
GENEVA	WALWORTH	WI	1007	444,994	497-533	
GENEVA TWP.	JENNINGS	IN	155	442,933	579-621	
GENOA	CAYUGA	NY	483	017,059	113-72	
GENOA TWP.	DE KALB	IL	104	007,677	649-64	
GENOA TWP.	LIVINGSTON	MI	356	443,572	771-88	
GENOA TWP.	DELAWARE	OH	675	020,223	227-59	
GENTRY CO.		MO	399	443,607	389-488	
GENTRYVILLE	GENTRY	MO	399	443,607	401-3	
GEORGES TWP.	FAYETTE	PA	779	444,747	91-151	
GEORGETOWN	EL DORADO	CA	34	002,491	867,	869-76,
					910-11	
GEORGETOWN	TUOLUMNE	CA	36	442,879	231-32,	234-44
GEORGETOWN	SUSSEX	DE	55	442,884	1-15	
GEORGETOWN		DC	57	006,703	295-479	
GEORGETOWN	LINCOLN	ME	261	443,498	215-41	
GEORGETOWN	ESSEX	MA	315	443,534	449-500	
GEORGETOWN	MADISON	NY	527	017,103	751-86	
GEORGETOWN	HARRISON	OH	693	444,686	897-900	
GEORGETOWN	GEORGETOWN	SC	853	444,816	575-91	
GEORGETOWN COLLEGE		DC	57	006,703	359-68	
GEORGETOWN CO.		SC	853	444,816	575-634	
GEORGETOWN, NORTHWEST WARD		DC	57	006,703	295-357	
GEORGETOWN TWP.	FLOYD	IN	145	442,923	896-924	
GEORGETOWN TWP.	OTTAWA	MI	361	443,577	119-23	
GEORGIA	FRANKLIN	VT	924	444,923	29-92	
GEORGIA FACTORY DIST.	CLARKE	GA	65	007,061	67-78	
GERMAN	CHENANGO	NY	487	017,063	193-214	
GERMAN FLATTS	HERKIMER	NY	513	017,089	159-244	

CITY, COUNTY, TOWN, OR TOWNSHIP	COUNTY	STATE	NA NO. M432	GD NO.	PAGES
GERMAN TWP.	BARTHOLOMEW	IN	136	007,749	845-67
GERMAN TWP.	ST. JOSEPH	IN	171	442,949	90-104
GERMAN TWP.	VANDERBURGH	IN	176	442,954	878-903
GERMAN TWP.	ALLEN	OH	657	020,205	605-628
GERMAN TWP.	AUGLAIZE	OH	660	020,208	447-500
GERMAN TWP.	CLARK	OH	666	020,214	47-94
GERMAN TWP.	DARKE	OH	674	020,222	747-83
GERMAN TWP.	FULTON	OH	681	444,674	709-734
GERMAN TWP.	HARRISON	OH	693	444,686	499-531
GERMAN TWP.	HOLMES	OH	696	444,689	417-53
GERMAN TWP.	MONTGOMERY	OH	714	444,707	597-663
GERMAN TWP.	FAYETTE	PA	779	444,747	45-90
GERMANTOWN	WAYNE	IN	180	442,958	55-65
GERMANTOWN	COLUMBIA	NY	492	017,068	549-73
GERMANTOWN	STOKES	NC	645	444,658	200-211
GERMANTOWN	PHILADELPHIA	PA	824	444,792	379-582
GERMANTOWN	SHELBY	TN	895	444,851	395-98
GERMANTOWN	WASHINGTON	WI	1008	444,995	185-225
GERMANY TWP.	ADAMS	PA	743	020,593	501-527
GEROTE	TUOLUMNE	CA	36	442,879	221-22, 225-26
GERRY	CHAUTAUQUA	NY	484	017,060	377-408
GETTYSBURG BOR.	ADAMS	PA	743	020,593	33-84
GHENT	COLUMBIA	NY	492	017,068	577-632
GIBOLETITA	VALENCIA	NM	470	443,668	469
GIBSON CO.		IN	147	442,925	1-281
GIBSON CO.		TN	878	444,834	245-612
GIBSON TWP.	WASHINGTON	IN	179	442,957	801-828
GIBSON TWP.	MERCER	OH	710	444,703	596-607
GIBSON TWP.	ELK	PA	776	444,744	675-82
GIBSON TWP.	SUSQUEHANNA	PA	829	444,797	539-76
GIBSONS COMPANY	SUTTER	CA	36	442,879	48
GILBOA	SCHOHARIE	NY	595	444,311	265-333
GILEAD	OXFORD	ME	262	443,499	463-71
GILEAD	BRANCH	MI	347	014,809	639-50
GILEAD DIST.	MECKLENBURG	NC	637	444,650	76-77
GILEAD PREC.	CALHOUN	IL	99	007,672	633-46
GILEAD TWP.	MORROW	OH	716	444,709	991-1032
GILES CO.		TN	879	444,835	615-1013
GILES CO.		VA	945	444,935	725-865
GILES TWP.	VAN BUREN	AR	31	442,877	609-617
GILFORD	BELKNAP	NH	425	014,938	289-346
GILL	FRANKLIN	MA	316	443,535	209-227
GILL TWP.	SULLIVAN	IN	173	442,951	579-610
GILLAM	JASPER	IN	152	442,930	524-33
GILLESPIE CO.		TX	910	024,889	603-632
GILMAN	HAMILTON	NY	511	017,087	31-34
GILMANTON	BELKNAP	NH	425	014,938	209-287
GILMER	ADAMS	IL	97	007,670	189-213
GILMER CO.		GA	70	007,066	695-891
GILMER CO.		VA	946	444,936	1-82
GILSUM	CHESHIRE	NH	428	014,941	719-34
GIRARD BOR.	ERIE	PA	778	444,746	737-46
GIRARD TWP.	BRANCH	MI	347	014,809	587-609
GIRARD TWP.	CLEARFIELD	PA	768	444,736	643-49
GIRARD TWP.	ERIE	PA	778	444,746	793-851
GLADE TWP.	WARREN	PA	832	444,800	761-70
GLASGOW	BARREN	KY	191	007,844	792-808
GLASTENBURY	BENNINGTON	VT	921	027,447	337-41
GLASTONBURY	HARTFORD	CT	41	003,069	729-807

CITY, COUNTY, TOWN, OR TOWNSHIP	COUNTY	STATE	NA NO. M432	GD NO.	PAGES
GLEN	MONTGOMERY	NY	532	017,108	1-74
GLENBURN	PENOBSCOT	ME	264	443,501	603-624
GLENS FALLS VILLAGE	WARREN	NY	609	444,325	47-111
GLENVILLE	SCHENECTADY	NY	594	444,310	407-488
GLOCESTER	PROVIDENCE	RI	846	444,812	299-367
GLOUCESTER	ESSEX	MA	315	443,534	109-294
GLOUCESTER	CAMDEN	NJ	445	016,532	361-411
GLOUCESTER CO.		NJ	451	443,650	1-352
GLOUCESTER CO.		VA	946	444,936	85-203
GLOUCESTER TWP.	CAMDEN	NJ	445	016,532	519-76
GLOVER	ORLEANS	VT	925	444,924	21-48
GLYNN CO.		GA	71	007,067	1-17
GOFFSTOWN	HILLSBORO	NH	432	443,636	373-427
GOLD	BUREAU	IL	99	007,672	450
GOLD HILL DIST.	ROWAN	NC	643	444,656	230-44
GOLD SPRING	JEFFERSON	WI	1000	444,987	327-40
GOLDEN RIDGE PLANT.	AROOSTOOK	ME	248	009,718	15-20
GOLDSTONE DIST.	GWINNETT	GA	71	007,067	339-46, 348, 352-54, 456
GOLIAD	GOLIAD	TX	910	024,889	635-39
GOLIAD CO.		TX	910	024,889	635-46
GONZALES	GONZALES	TX	910	024,889	656-59
GONZALES CO.		TX	910	024,889	649-70
GOOCHLAND CO.		VA	946	444,936	207-314
GOOD HOPE TWP.	HOCKING	OH	695	444,688	21-36
GOODALE	LAKE	IL	114	007,687	121-30
GOODFARM	GRUNDY	IL	108	007,681	367-69
GOODMANS DIST.	HARRIS	GA	73	007,069	165-80
GOODSELS ENLARGEMENT	VANDERBURGH	IN	176	442,954	805-8
GOODWINS DIST.	GWINNETT	GA	71	007,067	351, 368, 380-81, 399-400, 412, 457-62
GOOSE CREEK DIST.	BEAUFORT	NC	620	018,106	839-49
GORDON CO.		GA	71	007,067	19-142
GORHAM	CUMBERLAND	ME	250	009,720	535-608
GORHAM	COOS	NH	429	443,633	41-46
GORHAM	ONTARIO	NY	571	444,287	491-554
GORHAM TWP.	FULTON	OH	681	444,674	684-708
GOSHEN	LITCHFIELD	CT	42	003,070	177-214
GOSHEN	HAMPSHIRE	MA	320	443,539	415-27
GOSHEN	SULLIVAN	NH	441	443,645	133-48
GOSHEN	ORANGE	NY	574	444,290	353-427
GOSHEN	CHAMPAIGN	OH	665	020,213	443-92
GOSHEN	ADDISON	VT	920	027,446	53-64
GOSHEN DIST.	GRANVILLE	NC	631	444,644	379-96
GOSHEN GORE	CALEDONIA	VT	922	027,448	509-513
GOSHEN GORE SOUTH	CALEDONIA	VT	922	027,448	313
GOSHEN TWP.	AUGLAIZE	OH	660	020,208	585-92
GOSHEN TWP.	BELMONT	OH	661	020,209	841-90
GOSHEN TWP.	CLERMONT	OH	667	020,215	279-326
GOSHEN TWP.	HARDIN	OH	692	444,685	301-316
GOSHEN TWP.	MAHONING	OH	707	444,700	1247-88
GOSHEN TWP.	TUSCARAWAS	OH	735	444,728	479-520
GOSHEN TWP.	CLEARFIELD	PA	768	444,736	639-42
GOSHEN VILLAGE	ELKHART	IN	144	007,757	319-37
GOSPORT	OWEN	IN	164	442,942	1-14
GOSPORT	ROCKINGHAM	NH	437	443,641	257-59
GOULDSBORO	HANCOCK	ME	255	443,492	501-534
GOUVERNEUR	ST. LAWRENCE	NY	589	444,305	345-412

CITY, COUNTY, TOWN, OR TOWNSHIP	COUNTY	STATE	NA NO. M432	GD NO.	PAGES
GRACEVILLE DIST.	HOUSTON	GA	74	007,070	739-47
GRAFTON	JERSEY	IL	111	007,684	21-26
GRAFTON	MC HENRY	IL	117	007,690	747-58
GRAFTON	WORCESTER	MA	344	443,563	747-50, 811-901
GRAFTON	GRAFTON	NH	430	443,634	429-58
GRAFTON	RENSSELAER	NY	586	444,302	503-551
GRAFTON	WINDHAM	VT	929	444,928	611-40
GRAFTON	WASHINGTON	WI	1008	444,995	451-67
GRAFTON		NH	430	443,634	1-504
GRAFTON CO.		NH	431	443,635	1-555
GRAFTON CO.	LORAIN	OH	705	444,698	981-1003
GRAFTON TWP.	JEFFERSON	IN	154	442,932	480-516
GRAHAM TWP.		TN	880	444,836	1-272
GRAINGER CO.	HARTFORD	CT	39	003,067	285-344
GRANBY	HAMPSHIRE	MA	321	443,540	583-609
GRANBY	OSWEGO	NY	576	444,292	1-81
GRANBY	ESSEX	VT	923	444,922	835-38
GRANBY	LAFOURCHE PAR.	LA	232	443,475	581-82
GRAND BAYOU	GENESEE	MI	350	443,566	561-88
GRAND BLANC TWP.	ST. MARTIN	LA	240	443,483	325-31
GRAND CHARPENTIER	BROWN	WI	994	034,508	130-43
GRAND CHUTE	LAFOURCHE PAR.	LA	232	443,475	551-52
GRAND COTEAU	OGLE	IL	123	442,911	241-50
GRAND DETOUR	CLAIBORNE	MS	370	014,849	218-27
GRAND GULF	SCHOOLCRAFT	MI	363	443,579	55
GRAND ISLAND	GRANDE ISLE	VT	924	444,923	20-35
GRAND ISLE	ST. MARTIN	LA	240	443,483	309-324
GRAND POINT	MARION	OH	708	444,701	292-303
GRAND PRARIE TWP.	LA SALLE	IL	115	007,688	495-96, 528-30, 537, 688-689
GRAND RAPIDS	PORTAGE	WI	1004	444,991	9-17
GRAND RAPIDS	KENT	MI	353	443,569	335-97
GRAND RAPIDS CITY	KENT	MI	353	443,569	398-409
GRAND RAPIDS TOWN	HENRY	MO	401	443,609	45-60
GRAND RIVER TWP.	MARION	OH	708	444,701	95-102
GRAND TWP.		VT	924	444,923	1-106
GRANDE ISLE CO.	EDGAR	IL	105	007,678	455-87
GRANDVIEW PREC.	LOUISA	IA	187	442,962	135-59
GRANDVIEW TWP.	WASHINGTON	OH	738	444,731	1035-62
GRANDVIEW TWP.	ALLEGANY	NY	475	017,051	1-32
GRANGER	MEDINA	OH	709	444,702	663-94
GRANGER	EL DORADO	CA	34	002,491	858-60
GRANITE CREEK		IN	147	442,925	286-554
GRANT CO.		KY	201	442,969	579-723
GRANT CO.		WI	998	444,985	1-388
GRANT CO.	SULLIVAN	NH	441	443,645	237-55
GRANTHAM	HAMPDEN	MA	318	443,537	491-522
GRANVILLE	WASHINGTON	NY	610	444,326	603-84
GRANVILLE	LICKING	OH	702	444,695	124-42
GRANVILLE	ADDISON	VT	920	027,446	37-52
GRANVILLE	MILWAUKEE	WI	1003	444,990	1011-52
GRANVILLE		NC	631	444,644	111-423
GRANVILLE CO.	LICKING	OH	702	444,695	124-75
GRANVILLE TWP.	MERCER	OH	710	444,703	502-514
GRANVILLE TWP.	BRADFORD	PA	756	020,606	151-76
GRANVILLE TWP.	MIFFLIN	PA	797	444,765	581-607
GRANVILLE TWP.	JACKSON	MI	352	443,568	843-73
GRASS LAKE	SPENCER	IN	172	442,950	22, 43-64
GRASS TWP.	YUBA	CA	36	442,879	547-54, 619-22
GRASS VALLEY					

CITY, COUNTY, TOWN, OR TOWNSHIP	COUNTY	STATE	NA NO. M432	GD NO.	PAGES	
GRASSY FORK TWP.	JACKSON	IN	152	442,930	451-70	
GRATIOT	LAFAYETTE	WI	1001	444,988	911-22	
GRATIS TWP.	PREBLE	OH	723	444,716	646-95	
GRATTAN	KENT	MI	353	443,569	601-616	
GRAVES CO.		KY	201	442,969	725-974	
GRAVESEND TWP.	KINGS	NY	521	017,097	29-54	
GRAY	CUMBERLAND	ME	249	009,719	407-449	
GRAY TWP.	PULASKI	AR	29	002,483	665-70	
GRAY TWP.	WHITE	AR	31	442,877	894-904	
GRAYSON CO.		KY	202	442,970	1-156	
GRAYSON CO.		TX	910	024,889	673-721	
GRAYSON CO.		VA	947	444,937	317-464	
GRAYSVILLE	MONROE	OH	712	444,705	749-50	
GRAYVILLE	WHITE	IL	132	442,920	601-9	
GREASY CREEK PREC.	COLES	IL	101	007,674	199-209	
GREAT BARRINGTON	BERKSHIRE	MA	306	014,700	331-409	
GREAT BEND TWP.	SUSQUEHANNA	PA	829	444,797	371-98	
GREAT SALT LAKE CO.		UT	919	025,540	47-136	
GREAT SPRUCE HEADS ISLE	HANCOCK	ME	254	443,491	426	
GREAT VALLEY	CATTARAUGUS	NY	479	017,055	289-327	
GREECE	MONROE	NY	529	017,105	227-331	
GREEN	MADISON	IN	158	442,936	161-72	
GREEN BAY	BROWN	WI	994	034,508	64-109	
GREEN CAMP TWP.	MARION	OH	708	444,701	45-54	
GREEN CO.		KY	202	442,970	157-311	
GREEN CO.		WI	999	444,986	391-613	
GREEN CREEK TWP.	SANDUSKY	OH	726	444,719	843-44, 847-55, 881-901	
GREEN LAKE	MARQUETTE	WI	1002	444,989	138-55	
GREEN OAK TWP.	LIVINGSTON	MI	356	443,572	789-811	
GREEN RIVER	BUREAU	IL	99	007,672	448-49	
GREEN TWP.	GRANT	IN	147	442,925	327-35	
GREEN TWP.	HANCOCK	IN	149	442,927	536-61	
GREEN TWP.	HOWARD	IN	151	442,929	929-48	
GREEN TWP.	MADISON	IN	158	442,936	158-72	
GREEN TWP.	NOBLE	IN	162	442,940	477-78, 482-87	
GREEN TWP.	RANDOLPH	IN	166	442,946	278-92	
GREEN TWP.	WAYNE	IN	180	442,958	193-231	
GREEN TWP.	GENTRY	MO	399	443,607	453-56	
GREEN TWP.	PLATTE	MO	410	443,618	726-52, 754-75	
GREEN TWP.	SUSSEX	NJ	464	443,663	543-62	
GREEN TWP.	ADAMS	OH	657	020,205	85-121	
GREEN TWP.	ASHLAND	OH	658	020,206	195-242	
GREEN TWP.	BROWN	OH	662	020,210	833-49	
GREEN TWP.	CLINTON	OH	668	020,216	327-76	
GREEN TWP.	FAYETTE	OH	678	444,671	239-64	
GREEN TWP.	GALLIA	OH	681	444,674	55-86	
GREEN TWP.	HAMILTON	OH	686	444,679	867-961	
GREEN TWP.	HARRISON	OH	693	444,686	459-97	
GREEN TWP.	HOCKING	OH	695	444,688	791-822	
GREEN TWP.	MAHONING	OH	707	444,700	957-99	
GREEN TWP.	MONROE	OH	712	444,705	717-46	
GREEN TWP.	ROSS	OH	725	444,718	421-68	
GREEN TWP.	SCIOTO	OH	727	444,720	257-312	
GREEN TWP.	SHELBY	OH	729	444,722	361-88	
GREEN TWP.	SUMMIT	OH	732	444,725	1-47	
GREEN TWP.	WAYNE	OH	739	444,732	345-95	
GREEN TWP.	INDIANA	PA	785	444,753	57-111	
GREENBRIER CO.		VA	947	444,937	467-674	

CITY, COUNTY, TOWN, OR TOWNSHIP	COUNTY	STATE	NA NO. M432	GD NO.	PAGES
GREENBRIER TWP.	INDEPENDENCE	AR	26	002,480	705-718
GREENBURGH	WESTCHESTER	NY	615	444,331	1-104
GREENBUSH	PENOBSCOT	ME	266	443,503	551-61
GREENBUSH	RENSSELAER	NY	586	444,302	553-670
GREENBUSH	SHEBOYGAN	WI	1006	444,993	291-96
GREENBUSH TWP.	CLINTON	MI	349	014,811	149-56
GREENCASTLE	PUTNAM	IN	167	442,945	987-1019
GREENCASTLE	FRANKLIN	PA	782	444,750	871-97
GREENCASTLE TWP.	PUTNAM	IN	167	442,945	1020-49
GREENE	KENNEBEC	ME	258	443,495	661-94
GREENE	CHENANGO	NY	488	017,064	627-717
GREENE	TRUMBULL	OH	733	444,726	693-715
GREENE	GREENE	PA	783	444,751	421-37
GREENE CO.		AL	6	002,348	487-708
GREENE CO.		AR	26	002,480	349-409
GREENE CO.		GA	71	007,067	143-259
GREENE CO.		IL	108	007,681	1-300
GREENE CO.		IN	148	442,926	557-875
GREENE CO.		MS	372	443,584	63-96
GREENE CO.		MO	400	443,608	489-770
GREENE CO.		NY	509	017,085	1-391
GREENE CO.		NY	510	017,086	394-806
GREENE CO.		NC	632	444,645	427-507
GREENE CO.		OH	683	444,676	651-941, 1-244
GREENE CO.		PA	783	444,751	195-732
GREENE CO.		TN	880	444,836	273-673
GREENE CO.		VA	947	444,937	677-740
GREENE CO.		IN	153	442,931	727-36
GREENE TWP.	JAY	IN	162	442,940	1-32
GREENE TWP.	MORGAN	IN	164	442,942	402-437
GREENE TWP.	PARKE	IN	171	442,949	108-121
GREENE TWP.	ST. JOSEPH	IA	184	007,793	547-51
GREENE TWP.	IOWA	OH	666	020,214	95-126
GREENE TWP.	CLARK	PA	750	020,600	531-76
GREENE TWP.	BEAVER	PA	768	444,736	265-88
GREENE TWP.	CLINTON	PA	777	444,745	285-322
GREENE TWP.	ERIE	PA	781	444,749	351-426
GREENE TWP.	FRANKLIN	PA	796	444,764	771-94
GREENE TWP.	MERCER	PA	825	444,793	1-9
GREENE TWP.	PIKE	VA	947	444,937	743-87
GREENESVILLE CO.		IL	108	007,681	372-74
GREENFIELD	GRUNDY	ME	255	443,492	868-75
GREENFIELD	HANCOCK	MA	316	443,535	229-90
GREENFIELD	FRANKLIN	MI	366	443,582	617-57
GREENFIELD	WAYNE	NH	434	443,638	93-110
GREENFIELD	HILLSBORO	NY	593	444,309	595-664
GREENFIELD	SARATOGA	OH	694	444,687	265-88
GREENFIELD	HIGHLAND	PA	833	444,801	294-303
GREENFIELD	WASHINGTON	WI	995	034,509	609-623
GREENFIELD	DANE	WI	1003	444,990	911-58
GREENFIELD	MILWAUKEE	AR	29	002,483	432-47
GREENFIELD TWP.	POINSETT	IN	163	442,941	777-94
GREENFIELD TWP.	ORANGE	IA	185	442,960	371-74
GREENFIELD TWP.	JONES	OH	677	444,670	717-67
GREENFIELD TWP.	FAIRFIELD	OH	681	444,674	117-39
GREENFIELD TWP.	GALLIA	OH	697	444,690	389-420
GREENFIELD TWP.	HURON	PA	755	020,605	269-93
GREENFIELD TWP.	BLAIR	PA	777	444,745	151-68
GREENFIELD TWP.	ERIE	PA	793	444,761	479-504
GREENFIELD TWP.	LUZERNE				

CITY, COUNTY, TOWN, OR TOWNSHIP	COUNTY	STATE	NA NO. M432	GD NO.	PAGES
GREENLAND	ROCKINGHAM	NH	438	443,642	283-300
GREENPORT	COLUMBIA	NY	492	017,068	489-520
GREENS BEAT	JEFFERSON	AL	7	002,349	425-34
GREENS GRANT	COOS	NH	429	443,633	283
GREENSBORO	ORLEANS	VT	925	444,924	171-94
GREENSBORO TWP.	HENRY	IN	151	442,929	587-616
GREENSBURG	DECATUR	IN	142	007,755	21-49
GREENSBURG BOR.	WESTMORELAND	PA	837	444,805	335-62
GREENSBURG TWP.	PUTNAM	OH	723	444,716	1-16
GREENSFORK TWP.	RANDOLPH	IN	168	442,946	297-338
GREENTOWN	STARK	OH	731	444,724	5-9
GREENUP CO.		KY	202	442,970	313-529
GREENUP PREC.	CUMBERLAND	IL	104	007,677	571-93
GREENVILLE	BOND	IL	98	007,671	771
GREENVILLE	BUREAU	IL	99	007,672	437-42
GREENVILLE	PISCATAQUIS	ME	267	443,504	505-512
GREENVILLE	GREENE	NY	510	017,086	394-448
GREENVILLE	DARKE	OH	674	020,222	485-510
GREENVILLE	GREENVILLE	SC	853	444,816	547-63
GREENVILLE	GREENE	TN	880	444,836	273-385
GREENVILLE	BROWN	WI	994	034,508	42-44
GREENVILLE CO.		SC	853	444,816	635-963
GREENVILLE DIST.	PITT	NC	641	444,654	1-20
GREENVILLE TWP.	CLARK	AR	25	002,479	438-43
GREENVILLE TWP.	FLOYD	IN	145	442,923	743-66, 925-45
GREENVILLE TWP.	DARKE	OH	674	020,222	547-603
GREENVILLE TWP.	SOMERSET	PA	828	444,796	587-604
GREENWICH	FAIRFIELD	CT	38	003,066	396, 388, 390-91, 409, 411-12, 414-15, 418-25, 427, 430-31, 454, 475, 480-97
GREENWICH	HAMPSHIRE	MA	321	443,540	701-721
GREENWICH	WASHINGTON	NY	611	444,327	403-493
GREENWICH TOWN	FAIRFIELD	CT	38	003,066	377-85, 387, 389, 392-408, 410, 413, 416-17, 426, 428-29, 432-53, 455-74, 476-79
GREENWICH TWP.	CUMBERLAND	NJ	446	016,533	525-52
GREENWICH TWP.	GLOUCESTER	NJ	451	443,650	201-274
GREENWICH TWP.	WARREN	NJ	465	443,664	605-694
GREENWICH TWP.	HURON	OH	697	444,690	815-40
GREENWICH TWP.	BERKS	PA	753	020,603	259-302
GREENWOOD	MC HENRY	IL	117	007,690	931-52
GREENWOOD	OXFORD	ME	262	443,499	75-101
GREENWOOD	STEUBEN	NY	599	444,315	603-631
GREENWOOD	ABBEVILLE	SC	848	022,528	331-39
GREENWOOD TWP.	COLUMBIA	PA	769	444,737	448-77
GREENWOOD TWP.	CRAWFORD	PA	771	444,739	889-918
GREENWOOD TWP.	JUNIATA	PA	786	444,754	604-643
GREENWOOD TWP.	PERRY	PA	805	444,773	1159-82
GREENWOOD VALLEY	EL DORADO	CA	34	002,491	894-98, 907-9
GREENWOOD WARD	CADDO PARISH	LA	230	009,697	695-704, 707-8
GREERVILLE	BUTLER	AL	2	002,344	513-16
GREGG TWP.	MORGAN	IN	162	442,940	351-67
GREGG TWP.	CENTRE	PA	763	020,613	104-141
GREIG	LEWIS	NY	523	017,099	387-412
GRETNA	JEFFERSON PAR.	LA	232	443,475	168-80

CITY, COUNTY, TOWN, OR TOWNSHIP	COUNTY	STATE	NA NO. M432	GD NO.	PAGES	
GRIFFIN TWP.	CONWAY	AR	25	002,479	514-23	
GRIFFINS DIST.	PITT	NC	641	444,654	65-80	
GRIGGS TWP.	VAN BUREN	AR	31	442,877	643-48	
GRIGGSVILLE	PIKE	IL	124	442,912	130-43	
GRIMES CO.		TX	910	024,889	725-80	
GRISWOLD	NEW LONDON	CT	49	442,881	45-95	
GROSSE POINT	WAYNE	MI	366	443,582	965-98	
GROTON	NEW LONDON	CT	49	442,881	735-37	
GROTON	MIDDLESEX	MA	323	443,542	29-88	
GROTON	GRAFTON	NH	430	443,634	205-223	
GROTON	TOMPKINS	NY	605	444,321	243-322	
GROTON	CALEDONIA	VT	922	027,448	255-76	
GROTON TWP.	ERIE	OH	676	338,044	743-64	
GROVE	ALLEGANY	NY	475	017,051	33-60	
GROVE TWP.	DAVIS	IA	182	007,791	595-605	
GROVE TWP.	CLINTON	PA	768	444,736	175-81	
GROVELAND	ESSEX	MA	315	443,534	501-531	
GROVELAND	LIVINGSTON	NY	524	017,100	791-832	
GROVELAND TWP.	OAKLAND	MI	360	443,576	653-76	
GROVEPORT	FRANKLIN	OH	680	444,673	449-60	
GRUNDY CO.		IL	108	007,681	301-379	
GRUNDY CO.		MO	400	443,608	771-839	
GRUNDY CO.		TN	881	444,837	675-736	
GUADALUPE CO.		TX	910	024,889	475-601	
GUADALUPE RIVER	GONZALES	TX	910	024,889	663-66	
GUBIERO	VALENCIA	NM	470	443,668	459-68	
GUERNSEY CO.		OH	684	444,677	245-1032	
GUILDERLAND	ALBANY	NY	474	017,050	694-771	
GUILDHALL	ESSEX	VT	923	444,922	749-60	
GUILFORD	MIDDLESEX	CT	44	003,072	476	
GUILFORD	NEW HAVEN	CT	45	003,073	203-266	
GUILFORD	WINNEBAGO	IL	134	442,922	726-47	
GUILFORD	PISCATAQUIS	ME	267	443,504	485-504	
GUILFORD	CHENANGO	NY	488	017,064	563-626	
GUILFORD	WINDHAM	VT	929	444,928	121-54	
GUILFORD CO.		NC	632	444,645	509-901	
GUILFORD TWP.	HENDRICKS	IN	150	442,928	193-202, 208-22
GUILFORD TWP.	MEDINA	OH	709	444,702	555-98	
GUILFORD TWP.	FRANKLIN	PA	781	444,749	179-262	
GULL LAKE	MANKAHTA	MN	367	014,834	39	
GUNIE	VALENCIA	NM	470	443,668	426-58	
GUNPLAIN	ALLEGAN	MI	346	014,808	16-29	
GUSTAVUS	TRUMBULL	OH	733	444,726	593-622	
GUYAN TWP.	GALLIA	OH	681	444,674	749-62	
GWINNETT CO.		GA	71	007,067	261-476	
GWYNEDD TWP.	MONTGOMERY	PA	800	444,768	141-78	
HABERSHAM CO.		GA	72	007,068	477-668	
HABOLOCHITTO DIST.	HANCOCK	MS	372	443,584	146-52	
HACKATASK	HANCOCK	ME	254	443,491	430	
HACKENSACK TWP.	BERGEN	NJ	442	016,529	219-302	
HADDAM	MIDDLESEX	CT	44	003,072	789-843	
HADDOCKS DIST.	PITT	NC	641	444,654	81-90	
HADDON TWP.	SULLIVAN	IN	173	442,951	395-468	
HADDONFIELD	CAMDEN	NJ	445	016,532	291-310	
HADLEY	HAMPSHIRE	MA	320	443,539	431-78	
HADLEY	LAPEER	MI	354	443,570	740-60	

CITY, COUNTY, TOWN, OR TOWNSHIP	COUNTY	STATE	NA NO. M432	GD NO.	PAGES
HADLEY	SARATOGA	NY	593	444,309	665-88
HAGERSTOWN	WAYNE	IN	180	442,958	136-50
HAGERSTOWN DIV.	WASHINGTON	MD	298	443,529	241-333
HAGUE	WARREN	NY	609	444,325	323-40
HAINES J. PENN TWP.	CENTRE	PA	763	020,613	1-59
HALBERT TWP.	MARTIN	IN	160	442,938	73-82
HALE TWP.	HARDIN	OH	692	444,685	275-86
HALF MOON	ONSLOW	NC	639	444,652	177-89
HALFMOON	SARATOGA	NY	592	444,308	65-131
HALFMOON TWP.	CENTRE	PA	763	020,613	519-35
HALIFAX	PLYMOUTH	MA	333	443,552	69-87
HALIFAX	DAUPHIN	PA	775	444,743	607-617
HALIFAX	WINDHAM	VT	929	444,928	237-64
HALIFAX CO.		NC	633	444,646	1-180, 263-64
HALIFAX CO.		VA	948	444,938	1-276
HALIFAX TWP.	DAUPHIN	PA	775	444,743	577-606
HALL CO.		GA	72	007,068	669-844
HALL DIST.	DE KALB	GA	67	007,063	366
HALL TWP.	DUBOIS	IN	143	007,756	893-917
HALLOCA	MUSCOGEE	GA	79	442,888	679-702
HALLOWELL	KENNEBEC	ME	256	443,493	323-436
HALSEYS DIST.	DE KALB	GA	67	007,063	286-97
HAMBDEN TWP.	GEAUGA	OH	682	444,675	377-98
HAMBLEN TWP.	BROWN	IN	137	007,750	436-68
HAMBURG	PERRY	AL	12	002,354	615-16
HAMBURG	ERIE	NY	498	017,074	1-127
HAMBURG	MACON	NC	636	444,649	745-46
HAMBURG	EDGEFIELD	SC	852	444,815	257-72
HAMBURG BEAT	PERRY	AL	12	002,354	593-603
HAMBURG BOR.	BERKS	PA	754	020,604	481-506
HAMBURG PREC.	CALHOUN	IL	99	007,672	623-32
HAMBURG TWP.	LIVINGSTON	MI	356	443,572	749-70
HAMDEN	NEW HAVEN	CT	45	003,073	411-62
HAMDEN	DELAWARE	NY	495	017,071	555-602
HAMER TWP.	HIGHLAND	OH	694	444,687	561-83
HAMILTON	ESSEX	MA	314	014,708	617-38
HAMILTON	VAN BUREN	MI	363	443,579	265-73
HAMILTON	MADISON	NY	527	017,103	121-32, 157-230
HAMILTON	BUTLER	OH	663	020,211	427-28
HAMILTON CO.		FL	58	006,714	433-80
HAMILTON CO.		IL	108	007,681	383-536
HAMILTON CO.		IN	148	442,926	1-328
HAMILTON CO.		NY	511	017,087	1-55
HAMILTON CO.		OH	685	444,678	1-488
HAMILTON CO.		OH	686	444,679	489-1009
HAMILTON CO.		OH	687	444,680	1-543
HAMILTON CO.		OH	688	444,681	545-933
HAMILTON CO.		OH	689	444,682	1-453
HAMILTON CO.		OH	690	444,683	455-1054
HAMILTON CO.		OH	691	444,684	1-776
HAMILTON CO.		TN	881	444,837	737-960
HAMILTON DIST.	HARRIS	GA	73	007,069	149-64
HAMILTON DIST.	LARUE	KY	209	442,977	785-910
HAMILTON TWP.	PRAIRIE	AR	29	002,483	617-22
HAMILTON TWP.	LEE	IL	116	007,689	241-48
HAMILTON TWP.	DELAWARE	IN	143	007,756	816-26
HAMILTON TWP.	JACKSON	IN	152	442,930	193-220
HAMILTON TWP.	SULLIVAN	IN	173	442,951	469-507
HAMILTON TWP.	ATLANTIC	NJ	442	016,529	121-68

CITY, COUNTY, TOWN, OR TOWNSHIP	COUNTY	STATE	NA NO. M432	GD NO.	PAGES
HAMILTON TWP.	MERCER	NJ	454	443,653	499-565
HAMILTON TWP.	FRANKLIN	OH	680	444,673	313-50
HAMILTON TWP.	JACKSON	OH	698	444,691	675-90
HAMILTON TWP.	WARREN	OH	737	444,730	136-85
HAMILTON TWP.	ADAMS	PA	743	020,593	411-39
HAMILTON TWP.	FRANKLIN	PA	782	444,750	507-552
HAMILTON TWP.	MC KEAN	PA	795	444,763	41-44
HAMILTON TWP.	MONROE	PA	798	444,766	1-48
HAMILTONBAN TWP.	ADAMS	PA	743	020,593	283-319
HAMLIN TWP.	MC KEAN	PA	795	444,763	29-31
HAMLIN'S GRANT	OXFORD	ME	262	443,499	491-93
HAMMOND	ST. LAWRENCE	NY	589	444,305	1-46
HAMMOND TWP.	SPENCER	IN	172	442,950	141-63
HAMPDEN	PENOBSCOT	ME	265	443,502	625-98
HAMPDEN	COLUMBIA	WI	994	034,508	254-65
HAMPDEN CO.		MA	318	443,537	1-616
HAMPDEN CO.		MA	319	443,538	1-641
HAMPDEN TWP.	CUMBERLAND	PA	773	444,741	815-58
HAMPSHIRE	KANE	IL	112	007,685	135-53
HAMPSHIRE	LEWIS	TN	887	444,843	837
HAMPSHIRE CO.		MA	320	443,539	1-478
HAMPSHIRE CO.		MA	321	443,540	483-918
HAMPSHIRE CO.		VA	948	444,938	279-579
HAMPSTEAD	ROCKINGHAM	NH	438	443,642	21-39
HAMPTON	WINDHAM	CT	51	442,883	795-817
HAMPTON	ROCKINGHAM	NH	438	443,642	479-507
HAMPTON	WASHINGTON	NY	610	444,326	221-45
HAMPTON	ADAMS	PA	743	020,593	468-71
HAMPTON	ELIZABETH	VA	942	444,932	84-102
HAMPTON FALLS	ROCKINGHAM	NH	438	443,642	509-524
HAMPTON TWP.	MONROE	AR	28	002,482	730-38
HAMPTON TWP.	SAGINAW	MI	361	443,577	207-219
HAMPTONBURGH	ORANGE	NY	574	444,290	281-312
HAMTRAMCK TWP.	WAYNE	MI	366	443,582	999-1039
HANCOCK	HANCOCK	ME	255	443,492	435-57
HANCOCK	BERKSHIRE	MA	305	014,699	261-80
HANCOCK	HILLSBORO	NH	433	443,637	757-81
HANCOCK	DELAWARE	NY	495	017,071	679-722
HANCOCK	ADDISON	VT	920	027,446	121-31
HANCOCK CO.		AL	6	002,348	711-46
HANCOCK CO.		GA	72	007,068	1-102
HANCOCK CO.		IL	109	007,682	537-890
HANCOCK CO.		IN	149	442,927	329-564
HANCOCK CO.		KY	202	442,970	531-607
HANCOCK CO.		ME	254	443,491	1-430
HANCOCK CO.		ME	255	443,492	435-878
HANCOCK CO.		MS	372	443,584	97-155
HANCOCK CO.		OH	692	444,685	777-992, 1-208
HANCOCK CO.		TN	881	444,837	1-131
HANCOCK CO.		VA	949	444,939	583-680
HANCOCK PLANTATION	AROOSTOOK	ME	248	009,718	249-63
HANDY TWP.	LIVINGSTON	MI	356	443,572	950-61
HANNIBAL	MARION	MO	406	443,614	609-957
HANNIBAL	OSWEGO	NY	576	444,292	83-151
HANOVER	COOK	IL	103	007,676	237-52
HANOVER	OXFORD	ME	262	443,499	455-61
HANOVER	PLYMOUTH	MA	332	443,551	199-235
HANOVER	JACKSON	MI	352	443,568	471-93
HANOVER	GRAFTON	NH	430	443,634	53-108

CITY, COUNTY, TOWN, OR TOWNSHIP	COUNTY	STATE	NA NO. M432	GD NO.	PAGES
HANOVER	CHAUTAUQUA	NY	484	017,060	53-175
HANOVER	LUZERNE	PA	794	444,762	895-930
HANOVER BOR.	YORK	PA	839	444,807	537-66
HANOVER CO.		VA	949	444,939	683-844
HANOVER TWP.	JEFFERSON	IN	154	442,932	325, 329-30, 337-38
HANOVER TWP.	SHELBY	IN	172	442,950	741-66
HANOVER TWP.	MORRIS	NJ	458	443,657	261-346
HANOVER TWP.	ASHLAND	OH	656	020,206	243-88
HANOVER TWP.	BUTLER	OH	663	020,211	301-336
HANOVER TWP.	COLUMBIANA	OH	669	020,217	707-773
HANOVER TWP.	LICKING	OH	703	444,696	665-94
HANOVER TWP.	BEAVER	PA	750	020,600	477-518
HANOVER TWP.	LEHIGH	PA	792	444,760	325-82
HANOVER TWP.	NORTHAMPTON	PA	803	444,771	549-59
HANOVER VILLAGE	WASHINGTON	PA	833	444,801	109-159
HANSON	JO DAVIESS	IL	111	007,684	396-99
HANSTOWN	PLYMOUTH	MA	332	443,551	237-65
HARBINS DIST.	LANCASTER	PA	789	444,757	304
	GWINNETT	GA	71	007,067	310-16, 323-33, 414, 447-49, 452
HARBISON TWP.	DUBOIS	IN	143	007,756	851-73
HARBOR ISLAND	LINCOLN	ME	259	443,496	325
HARBORCREEK TWP.	ERIE	PA	777	444,745	169-216
HARDEMAN CO.		TN	881	444,837	135-381
HARDIN CO.		IL	109	007,682	1-70
HARDIN CO.		KY	203	442,971	609-899
HARDIN CO.		OH	692	444,685	209-422
HARDIN CO.		TN	882	444,838	385-613
HARDIN PREC.	CALHOUN	IL	99	007,672	585-99
HARDIN TWP.	CONWAY	AR	25	002,479	504-7
HARDWICK	WORCESTER	MA	344	443,563	671-709
HARDWICK	WARREN	NJ	465	443,664	983-1000
HARDWICK	CALEDONIA	VT	922	027,448	389-422
HARDY CO.		VA	950	444,940	1-199
HARDY TWP.	HOLMES	OH	696	444,689	167-224
HARDYSTON TWP.	SUSSEX	NJ	464	443,663	289-320
HARFORD	CORTLAND	NY	493	017,069	840-62
HARFORD CO.		MD	294	443,525	1-414
HARFORD TWP.	SUSQUEHANNA	PA	829	444,797	645-75
HARKERS ISLAND	CARTERET	NC	623	018,109	339-46
HARLAN CO.		KY	203	442,971	1-100
HARLEM	WINNEBAGO	IL	134	442,922	748-66
HARLEM TWP.	CARROLL	IL	99	007,672	729-38
HARLEM TWP.	DELAWARE	OH	675	020,223	261-91
HARLOWS CREEK	CARTERET	NC	623	018,109	300-303, 335-36
HARMON TWP.	LEE	IL	116	007,689	249-60
HARMONY	SOMERSET	ME	268	443,505	195-225
HARMONY	CHAUTAUQUA	NY	484	017,060	451-540
HARMONY	ROCK	WI	1005	444,992	639-58
HARMONY BOR.	BUTLER	PA	760	020,610	309-320
HARMONY TWP.	POSEY	IN	166	442,944	503, 515-58
HARMONY TWP.	UNION	IN	176	442,954	706-726
HARMONY TWP.	WASHINGTON	MO	421	443,629	347-63
HARMONY TWP.	WARREN	NJ	465	443,664	733-70
HARMONY TWP.	CLARK	OH	666	020,214	1-46
HARMONY TWP.	MORROW	OH	716	444,709	57-81
HARMONY TWP.	SUSQUEHANNA	PA	829	444,797	435-73
HARPERS FERRY	JEFFERSON	VA	953	444,943	805-843

79

CITY, COUNTY, TOWN, OR TOWNSHIP	COUNTY	STATE	NA NO. M432	GD NO.	PAGES
HARPERSFIELD	DELAWARE	NY	494	017,070	313-54
HARPERSFIELD TWP.	ASHTABULA	OH	659	020,207	814-44
HARPSWELL	CUMBERLAND	ME	251	009,721	509-545
HARRIETSTOWN	FRANKLIN	NY	505	017,081	247-51
HARRINGTON	WASHINGTON	ME	272	443,509	239-61
HARRINGTON TWP.	BERGEN	NJ	442	016,529	553-82
HARRIS	STANLEY	NC	645	444,658	39-47
HARRIS CO.		GA	73	007,069	103-267
HARRIS CO.		TX	911	024,890	1-96
HARRIS DIST.	MUSCOGEE	GA	79	442,888	737-62
HARRIS DIST.	FRANKLIN	NC	630	444,643	653-65
HARRIS GORE	CALEDONIA	VT	922	027,448	315
HARRIS TWP.	ST. JOSEPH	IN	171	442,949	184-95
HARRIS TWP.	OTTAWA	OH	719	444,712	278-87
HARRIS TWP.	CENTRE	PA	763	020,613	197-243
HARRISBURG	LEWIS	NY	523	017,099	265-97
HARRISBURG	FRANKLIN	OH	680	444,673	119-21
HARRISBURG BOR.	DAUPHIN	PA	774	444,742	1-194
HARRISBURG, EAST WARD	DAUPHIN	PA	774	444,742	145-93
HARRISBURG, NORTH WARD	DAUPHIN	PA	774	444,742	91-143
HARRISBURG, SOUTH WARD	DAUPHIN	PA	774	444,742	1-33
HARRISBURG TWP.	VAN BUREN	IA	189	442,964	571-92
HARRISBURG, WEST WARD	DAUPHIN	PA	774	444,742	35-89
HARRISON	WINNEBAGO	IL	134	442,922	658-68
HARRISON	CUMBERLAND	ME	251	009,721	614-47
HARRISON	MACOMB	MI	357	443,573	157-68
HARRISON	HUDSON	NJ	452	443,651	355
HARRISON	WESTCHESTER	NY	615	444,331	221-50
HARRISON	HAMILTON	OH	686	444,679	647-70
HARRISON	POTTER	PA	825	444,793	293-311
HARRISON CO.		IN	149	442,927	565-928
HARRISON CO.		KY	203	442,971	101-340
HARRISON CO.		MS	372	443,584	157-240
HARRISON CO.		MO	400	443,608	841-900
HARRISON CO.		OH	693	444,686	423-947
HARRISON CO.		TX	911	024,890	99-236
HARRISON CO.		VA	950	444,940	203-473
HARRISON TWP.	OUACHITA	AR	28	002,482	201, 203-210
HARRISON TWP.	UNION	AR	30	442,876	533-40
HARRISON TWP.	WHITE	AR	31	442,877	929-39
HARRISON TWP.	OGLE	IL	123	442,911	189-200
HARRISON TWP.	BARTHOLOMEW	IN	136	007,749	643-57
HARRISON TWP.	BLACKFORD	IN	136	007,749	81-98
HARRISON TWP.	CASS	IN	137	007,750	785-803
HARRISON TWP.	CLAY	IN	138	007,751	565-81
HARRISON TWP.	DAVIESS	IN	140	007,753	412-28
HARRISON TWP.	DEARBORN	IN	141	007,754	611-34
HARRISON TWP.	DELAWARE	IN	143	007,756	762-80
HARRISON TWP.	ELKHART	IN	144	007,757	244-63
HARRISON TWP.	FAYETTE	IN	144	007,757	399-435
HARRISON TWP.	HANCOCK	IN	149	442,927	403-415
HARRISON TWP.	HENRY	IN	151	442,929	683-716
HARRISON TWP.	HOWARD	IN	151	442,929	841-63
HARRISON TWP.	KOSCIUSKO	IN	156	442,934	797-815
HARRISON TWP.	MIAMI	IN	160	442,938	359-71
HARRISON TWP.	MORGAN	IN	162	442,940	272-82
HARRISON TWP.	OWEN	IN	164	442,942	81-90
HARRISON TWP.	PULASKI	IN	166	442,944	696-702
HARRISON TWP.	SPENCER	IN	172	442,950	189-219

CITY, COUNTY, TOWN, OR TOWNSHIP	COUNTY	STATE	NA NO. M432	GD NO.	PAGES
HARRISON TWP.	UNION	IN	176	442,954	686-705
HARRISON TWP.	VIGO	IN	177	442,955	427-543
HARRISON TWP.	WAYNE	IN	180	442,958	85-103
HARRISON TWP.	WELLS	IN	181	442,959	757-92
HARRISON TWP.	SCOTLAND	MO	419	443,627	273-82
HARRISON TWP.	GLOUCESTER	NJ	451	443,650	73-120
HARRISON TWP.	HUDSON	NJ	452	443,651	355-86
HARRISON TWP.	CARROLL	OH	664	020,212	231-61
HARRISON TWP.	CHAMPAIGN	OH	665	020,213	643-67
HARRISON TWP.	DARKE	OH	674	020,222	705-745
HARRISON TWP.	GALLIA	OH	681	444,674	187-212
HARRISON TWP.	HENRY	OH	693	444,686	45-57
HARRISON TWP.	KNOX	OH	700	444,693	799-817
HARRISON TWP.	LICKING	OH	703	444,696	541-75
HARRISON TWP.	LOGAN	OH	704	444,697	371-94
HARRISON TWP.	MONTGOMERY	OH	714	444,707	547-96
HARRISON TWP.	MUSKINGUM	OH	718	444,711	75-111
HARRISON TWP.	PAULDING	OH	719	444,712	393-94
HARRISON TWP.	PERRY	OH	719	444,712	875-900
HARRISON TWP.	PICKAWAY	OH	720	444,713	93-120
HARRISON TWP.	PREBLE	OH	723	444,716	797-846
HARRISON TWP.	ROSS	OH	725	444,718	505-526
HARRISON TWP.	SCIOTO	OH	727	444,720	209-235
HARRISON TWP.	VAN WERT	OH	736	444,729	420-32
HARRISON TWP.	VINTON	OH	736	444,729	559-72
HARRISON TWP.	BEDFORD	PA	751	020,601	367-99
HARRISONBURG	CATAHOULA PAR.	LA	230	009,697	180-83
HARRISONBURG	ROCKINGHAM	VA	974	444,964	2-18
HARRISONVILLE	KNOX	IL	113	007,686	871-72
HARRISONVILLE	TIPPECANOE	IN	175	442,953	70-71
HARRISVILLE	HARRISON	OH	693	444,686	873-80
HARRISVILLE BOR.	BUTLER	PA	760	020,610	674-79
HARRISVILLE PREC.	MONROE	IL	121	442,909	44, 52-57, 59A, 63-66
HARRISVILLE TWP.	MEDINA	OH	709	444,702	335-70
HARRODSBURG	JOHNSON	MO	403	443,611	76
HARRODSBURG DIST.	MEADE	KY	213	442,981	719-33
HART CO.		KY	204	442,972	341-538
HART TWP.	WARRICK	IN	179	442,957	371-405
HART'S LOCATION	COOS	NH	429	443,633	1-2
HARTFORD	BLACKFORD	IN	136	007,749	29-34
HARTFORD	OXFORD	ME	263	443,500	169-200
HARTFORD	VAN BUREN	MI	363	443,579	257-64
HARTFORD	WASHINGTON	NY	610	444,326	491-540
HARTFORD	GUERNSEY	OH	684	444,677	618-20
HARTFORD	TRUMBULL	OH	733	444,726	813-42
HARTFORD	WINDSOR	VT	930	444,929	271-322
HARTFORD	WASHINGTON	WI	1008	444,995	328-52
HARTFORD CITY	HARTFORD	CT	41	003,069	345-667
HARTFORD CO.		CT	39	003,067	1-581
HARTFORD CO.		CT	40	003,068	583-792, 1-238
HARTFORD CO.		CT	41	003,069	239-903
HARTFORD TOWN	HARTFORD	CT	41	003,069	239-344
HARTFORD TWP.	ADAMS	IN	135	007,748	78-84
HARTFORD TWP.	PIKE	MO	409	443,617	486-501
HARTFORD TWP.	LICKING	OH	702	444,695	443-76
HARTLAND	HARTFORD	CT	39	003,067	345-65
HARTLAND	MC HENRY	IL	117	007,690	819-42
HARTLAND	SOMERSET	ME	268	443,505	54-76

CITY, COUNTY, TOWN, OR TOWNSHIP	COUNTY	STATE	NA NO. M432	GD NO.	PAGES
HARTLAND	NIAGARA	NY	561	444,277	615-87
HARTLAND	WINDSOR	VT	931	444,930	553-602
HARTLAND TWP.	LIVINGSTON	MI	356	443,572	860-83
HARTLAND TWP.	HURON	OH	697	444,690	789-813
HARTLEY TWP.	UNION	PA	831	444,799	327-78
HARTON	COMAL	TX	910	024,889	129-32
HARTSGROVE TWP.	ASHTABULA	OH	659	020,207	905-920
HARTSUGG	VAN BUREN	AR	31	442,877	591-96
HARTSVILLE	STEUBEN	NY	600	444,316	331-51
HARTWICK	OTSEGO	NY	579	444,295	407-462
HARVARD	WORCESTER	MA	341	443,560	33-71
HARVEYSBURG	WARREN	OH	737	444,730	718-24
HARWICH	BARNSTABLE	MA	303	014,697	289-365
HARWINTON	LITCHFIELD	CT	42	003,070	477-504
HASTINGS	OSWEGO	NY	578	444,294	541-611
HASTINGS TWP.	BARRY	MI	346	014,808	209-222
HATCHET CREEK DIST.	COOSA	AL	4	002,346	173-249
HATFIELD	HAMPSHIRE	MA	320	443,539	73-98
HATFIELD TWP.	MONTGOMERY	PA	800	444,768	409-434
HAVANA	MASON	IL	120	442,908	369-79
HAVERFORD TWP.	DELAWARE	PA	776	444,744	491-524
HAVERHILL	ESSEX	MA	313	014,707	153-292
HAVERHILL	GRAFTON	NH	431	443,635	49-106
HAVERSTRAW	ROCKLAND	NY	588	444,304	561-700
HAVRE DE GRACE	HARFORD	MD	294	443,525	289-318
HAW CREEK TWP.	BARTHOLOMEW	IN	136	007,749	869-906
HAW CREEK TWP.	MORGAN	MO	408	443,616	470-76
HAWKINS CO.		TN	882	444,838	614-904
HAWLEY	FRANKLIN	MA	317	443,536	521-41
HAYCOCK TWP.	BUCKS	PA	759	020,609	383-410
HAYESVILLE DIST.	FRANKLIN	NC	630	444,643	696-707
HAYFIELD TWP.	CRAWFORD	PA	770	444,739	99-140
HAYNESVILLE PLANT.	AROOSTOOK	ME	248	009,718	25-27
HAYS CO.		TX	911	024,890	239-45
HAYSVILLE	ASHLAND	OH	658	020,206	795-805
HAYWOOD CO.		NC	633	444,646	267-426
HAYWOOD CO.		TN	883	444,839	1-215
HAZELTON	SHIAWASSEE	MI	363	443,579	100
HAZLE	LUZERNE	PA	794	444,762	15-64
HEARD CO.		GA	73	007,069	269-376
HEARD'S BEAT	PERRY	AL	12	002,354	704-9
HEATH	FRANKLIN	MA	317	443,536	457-76
HEATH TWP.	JEFFERSON	PA	786	444,754	7-11
HEATHSVILLE	NORTHUMBERLAND	VA	965	444,955	713-15, 171
HEBRON	TOLLAND	CT	50	442,882	663-82
HEBRON	MC HENRY	IL	117	007,690	913-30
HEBRON	OXFORD	ME	263	443,500	65-85
HEBRON	GRAFTON	NH	430	443,634	285-99
HEBRON	WASHINGTON	NY	610	444,326	541-602
HEBRON	LICKING	OH	702	444,695	278-93
HEBRON	POTTER	PA	825	444,793	285-92
HEBRON	JEFFERSON	WI	1000	444,987	311-26
HEBRON TOWN	TOLLAND	CT	50	442,882	683-95
HECTOR	TOMPKINS	NY	606	444,322	717-865
HECTOR	POTTER	PA	825	444,793	244-51
HEIDELBERG TWP.	ADAMS	PA	743	020,593	144-46
HEIDELBERG TWP.	LEBANON	PA	791	444,759	1-50
HEIDELBERG TWP.	LEHIGH	PA	792	444,760	707-739
HEIDELBERG TWP.	YORK	PA	839	444,807	669-708

CITY, COUNTY, TOWN, OR TOWNSHIP	COUNTY	STATE	NA NO. M432	GD NO.	PAGES
HELEN	CLARION	PA	767	444,735	407-421
HELENA	PHILLIPS	AR	29	002,483	273-84
HELLAM	YORK	PA	840	444,808	265-304
HELT TWP.	VERMILLION	IN	177	442,955	39-89
HEMLOCK TWP.	COLUMBIA	PA	769	444,737	669-94
HEMPFIELD TWP.	WESTMORELAND	PA	837	444,805	363-476
HEMPSTEAD	QUEENS	NY	583	444,299	281-490
HEMPSTEAD CO.		AR	26	002,480	411-544
HENDERSON	HENDERSON	KY	204	442,972	539-60
HENDERSON	JEFFERSON	NY	515	017,091	437-91
HENDERSON CO.		IL	109	007,682	73-785
HENDERSON CO.		KY	204	442,972	539-725
HENDERSON CO.		NC	634	444,647	427-570
HENDERSON CO.		TN	883	444,839	219-477
HENDERSON CO.		TX	911	024,890	249-76
HENDERSON DIST.	HOUSTON	GA	74	007,070	673-84
HENDERSON DIST.	GRANVILLE	NC	631	444,644	119-38
HENDERSON TWP.	HUNTINGDON	PA	784	444,752	121-41
HENDERSONVILLE	KNOX	IL	113	007,666	789-97
HENDRICKS CO.		IN	150	442,928	1-340
HENDRICKS TWP.	SHELBY	IN	172	442,950	433-63
HENNEPIN	PUTNAM	IL	125	442,913	723-33
HENNIKER	MERRIMACK	NH	436	443,640	105-145
HENRICO CO.		VA	951	444,941	477-1135
HENRIETTA	JACKSON	MI	352	443,568	757-76
HENRIETTA	MONROE	NY	529	017,105	539-98
HENRIETTA TWP.	LORAIN	OH	705	444,698	651-75
HENRY	MARSHALL	IL	120	442,908	205-214
HENRY CLAY TWP.	FAYETTE	PA	779	444,747	227-53
HENRY CO.		AL	6	002,348	749-912
HENRY CO.		GA	73	007,069	377-609
HENRY CO.		IL	109	007,682	187-278
HENRY CO.		IN	151	442,929	341-784
HENRY CO.		IA	184	007,793	317-538
HENRY CO.		KY	204	442,972	727-929
HENRY CO.		MO	401	443,609	1-87
HENRY CO.		OH	693	444,686	1-88
HENRY CO.		TN	884	444,840	481-829
HENRY LOCKETS BAR		VA	952	444,942	1-130
HENRY TWP.	SUTTER	CA	36	442,879	48
HENRY TWP.	FULTON	IN	146	442,924	801-824
HENRY TWP.	HENRY	IN	151	442,929	717-63
HENSLEY TWP.	WOOD	OH	741	444,734	265-72
HEPBURN TWP.	JOHNSON	IN	155	442,933	231-62
HEREFORD TWP.	LYCOMING	PA	795	444,763	455-88
HERKIMER	BERKS	PA	753	020,603	73-102
HERKIMER CO.	HERKIMER	NY	513	017,089	1-63
HERKIMER CO.		NY	512	017,088	1-512
HERMAN		NY	513	017,089	513-756, 1-244
HERMANN	DODGE	WI	996	034,510	401-422
HERMER	GASCONADE	MO	399	443,607	271-93
HERMON	WASHINGTON	OH	738	444,731	455-78
HERMON	PENOBSCOT	ME	264	443,501	569-601
HERRICK	ST. LAWRENCE	NY	589	444,305	541-81
HERRICK TWP.	BRADFORD	PA	757	020,607	383-402
HERTFORD	SUSQUEHANNA	PA	829	444,797	515-35
HERTFORD	CHOWAN	NC	625	444,638	219
HERTFORD CO.	PERQUIMANS	NC	640	444,653	804-7
		NC	634	444,647	571-681

CITY, COUNTY, TOWN, OR TOWNSHIP	COUNTY	STATE	NA NO. M432	GD NO.	PAGES
HESTER BEAT	AUTAUGA	AL	1	002,343	17-23
HESTER TWP.	JACKSON	AR	27	002,481	112-15
HICKMAN CO.		KY	205	442,973	1-95
HICKMAN CO.		TN	884	444,840	1-180
HICKMAN TOWN	FULTON	KY	200	442,968	219-25
HICKMAN TWP.	SCOTT	AR	30	442,876	253-54, 257-61, 264-68, 279-80, 289-90
HICKORY	FULTON	IL	107	007,680	419-37
HICKORY CO.		MO	401	443,609	89-140
HICKORY TWP.	SCHUYLER	IL	128	442,916	858-68
HICKORY TWP.	MERCER	PA	796	444,764	129-78
HICKSVILLE TWP.	DEFIANCE	OH	674	020,222	171-83
HIGGINSPORT	BROWN	OH	662	020,210	937-49
HIGH PRAIRIE	ST. CLAIR	IL	126	442,914	734-62
HIGH SHOALS DIST.	CLARKE	GA	65	007,061	109-116
HIGH SHOALS DIST.	RUTHERFORD	NC	644	444,657	521-24, 529-30, 607-610, 614, 619-24, 661-62, 664-65, 668, 672
HIGHGATE	FRANKLIN	VT	924	444,923	609-675
HIGHLAND	GRUNDY	IL	108	007,681	370-71
HIGHLAND	MADISON	IL	119	442,907	1160-72
HIGHLAND	OAKLAND	MI	359	443,575	331-51
HIGHLAND	IOWA	WI	999	444,986	712-40
HIGHLAND CO.		OH	694	444,687	89-723
HIGHLAND CO.		VA	952	444,942	133-226
HIGHLAND TWP.	FRANKLIN	IN	146	442,924	673-714
HIGHLAND TWP.	GREENE	IN	148	442,926	684-706
HIGHLAND TWP.	VERMILLION	IN	177	442,955	111-47
HIGHLAND TWP.	DEFIANCE	OH	674	020,222	34-43
HIGHLAND TWP.	MUSKINGUM	OH	718	444,711	839-61
HIGHLAND TWP.	ELK	PA	776	444,744	683-84
HIGHSPIRE	DAUPHIN	PA	774	444,742	369-75
HILBURN TWP.	MADISON	AR	27	002,481	517-30
HILL	GRAFTON	NH	430	443,634	245-68
HILL TOP DIST.	CHARLES	MD	290	443,521	461-97, 526-27, 529, 589
HILLSBORO	SCOTT	MS	381	443,593	517-20
HILLSBORO CO.		NH	432	443,636	1-486
HILLSBORO CO.		NH	433	443,637	489-781
HILLSBORO CO.		NH	434	443,638	1-647
HILLSBOROUGH	HILLSBORO	NH	434	443,638	21-61
HILLSBOROUGH	SOMERSET	NJ	463	443,662	799-880
HILLSBOROUGH	ORANGE	NC	639	444,652	344-57
HILLSBOROUGH	HIGHLAND	OH	694	444,687	89-122
HILLSBOROUGH CO.		FL	58	006,714	481-522
HILLSDALE	COLUMBIA	NY	492	017,068	633-84
HILLSDALE CO.		MI	351	443,567	647-1060
HILLSDALE VILLAGE	HILLSDALE	MI	351	443,567	999-1024
HILLSVILLE	CARROLL	VA	939	029,714	766-70
HILLTOWN TWP.	BUCKS	PA	758	020,608	523-77
HINCKLEY	MEDINA	OH	709	444,702	695-728
HINDS CO.		MS	372	443,584	241-450
HINESBURG	CHITTENDEN	VT	923	444,922	195-238
HINGHAM	PLYMOUTH	MA	332	443,551	1-93
HINLITETOWN	LANCASTER	PA	789	444,757	303
HINSDALE	BERKSHIRE	MA	305	014,699	401-431
HINSDALE	CHESHIRE	NH	427	014,940	135-80

CITY, COUNTY, TOWN, OR TOWNSHIP	COUNTY	STATE	NA NO. M432	GD NO.	PAGES
HINSDALE	CATTARAUGUS	NY	479	017,055	257-87
HIRAM	OXFORD	ME	262	443,499	169-97
HIRAM TWP.	PORTAGE	OH	722	444,715	1-28
HITESVILLE PREC.	COLES	IL	101	007,674	211-32
HOAGLIN TWP.	VAN WERT	OH	736	444,729	369-71
HOBART TWP.	LAKE	IN	157	442,935	308-313
HOBOKEN TWP.	HUDSON	NJ	452	443,651	541-604
HOCK FARM	SUTTER	CA	36	442,879	113
HOCKING CO.		OH	695	444,688	725-908 , 1-166
HOCKING TWP.	FAIRFIELD	OH	677	444,670	625-68
HODGDON	AROOSTOOK	ME	248	009,718	53-73
HOG ISLAND	NORTHAMPTON	VA	965	444,955	606
HOG MOUNTAIN DIST.	GWINNETT	GA	71	007,067	347, 361, 403, 405-411, 428, 443-46
HOGSEACK	MACON	NC	636	444,649	740
HOHOKUS TWP.	BERGEN	NJ	442	016,529	449-505
HOLDEN	WORCESTER	MA	343	443,562	535-82
HOLDEN PLANTATION	SOMERSET	ME	269	443,506	542-43
HOLDERNESS	GRAFTON	NH	430	443,634	461-504
HOLLAND	HAMPDEN	MA	318	443,537	211-21
HOLLAND	ERIE	NY	500	017,076	167-92
HOLLAND	ORLEANS	VT	925	444,924	283-96
HOLLAND	SHEBOYGAN	WI	1006	444,993	153-77, 188, 190-94
HOLLAND TWP.	OTTAWA	MI	361	443,577	73-116
HOLLENBACH	LUZERNE	PA	794	444,762	87-105
HOLLIDAYSBURG BOR.	BLAIR	A	755	020,605	161-218
HOLLIS	YORK	ME	275	443,512	165-228
HOLLIS	HILLSBORO	NH	434	443,638	617-47
HOLLISTON	MIDDLESEX	MA	326	443,545	735-93
HOLLOW SPRING DIST.	SURRY	NC	646	444,659	573-87
HOLLY TWP.	OAKLAND	MI	360	443,576	771-93
HOLMES CO.		FL	58	006,714	523-47
HOLMES CO.		MS	373	443,585	455-587
HOLMES CO.		OH	696	444,689	167-669
HOLMES TWP.	CRAWFORD	OH	671	020,219	149-80
HOLT CO.		MO	401	443,609	141-234
HOLYOKE	HAMPDEN	MA	318	443,537	539-616
HOMER	CHAMPAIGN	IL	99	007,672	175-76
HOMER	WILL	IL	133	442,921	125-44
HOMER	CLAIBORNE PAR.	LA	230	009,697	292-96
HOMER	CALHOUN	MI	348	014,810	77-99
HOMER	CORTLAND	NY	493	017,069	537-628
HOMER	LICKING	OH	703	444,696	868-73
HOMER	POTTER	PA	825	444,793	168-71
HOMER TWP.	MEDINA	OH	709	444,702	307-333
HOMER TWP.	MORGAN	OH	715	444,708	111-48
HONESDALE BOR.	PAYNE	PA	835	444,803	491-546
HONEY CREEK	ADAMS	IL	97	007,670	215-36
HONEY CREEK TWP.	CLINTON	IN	139	007,752	767-88
HONEY CREEK TWP.	VIGO	IN	177	442,955	259-95
HONEY CREEK TWP.	SAUK	WI	1006	444,993	85-92
HONEYBROOK TWP.	CHESTER	PA	766	020,616	763-810
HOOKSETT	MERRIMACK	NH	435	443,639	209-244
HOOSICK	RENSSELAER	NY	585	444,301	691-779
HOPE	LA SALLE	IL	115	007,688	448-55, 457
HOPE	WALDO	ME	271	443,508	1-27
HOPE	BARRY	MI	346	014,808	155-57

CITY, COUNTY, TOWN, OR TOWNSHIP	COUNTY	STATE	NA NO. M432	GD NO.	PAGES
HOPE	HAMILTON	NY	511	017,087	13-31
HOPE TWP.	WARREN	NJ	465	443,664	837-78
HOPEWELL	ONTARIO	NY	571	444,287	445-90
HOPEWELL DIST.	MECKLENBURG	NC	637	444,650	55-69
HOPEWELL TWP.	CUMBERLAND	NJ	446	016,533	489-524
HOPEWELL TWP.	MERCER	NJ	454	443,653	173-260
HOPEWELL TWP.	LICKING	OH	703	444,696	935-64
HOPEWELL TWP.	MERCER	OH	710	444,703	481-87
HOPEWELL TWP.	MUSKINGUM	OH	717	444,710	137-93
HOPEWELL TWP.	PERRY	OH	719	444,712	760-92
HOPEWELL TWP.	SENECA	OH	728	444,721	581-612
HOPEWELL TWP.	BEAVER	PA	750	020,600	365-89
HOPEWELL TWP.	BEDFORD	PA	751	020,601	551-71
HOPEWELL TWP.	CUMBERLAND	PA	772	444,740	319-44
HOPEWELL TWP.	HUNTINGDON	PA	784	444,752	597-603
HOPEWELL TWP.	WASHINGTON	PA	834	444,802	1019-60
HOPEWELL TWP.	YORK	PA	839	444,807	301-361
HOPKINS CO.		KY	205	442,973	97-346
HOPKINS CO.		TX	911	024,890	279-338
HOPKINTON	MIDDLESEX	MA	326	443,545	795-861
HOPKINTON	MERRIMACK	NH	435	443,639	269-320
HOPKINTON	ST. LAWRENCE	NY	591	444,307	619-54
HOPKINTON	WASHINGTON	RI	847	444,813	525-86
HORICON	WARREN	NY	609	444,325	295-322
HORNBY	STEUBEN	NY	598	444,314	191-222
HORNELLSVILLE	STEUBEN	NY	599	444,315	717-80
HORRY CO.		SC	854	444,817	1-140
HORSE COVE	MACON	NC	636	444,649	737
HORSEHEAD TWP.	JOHNSON	AR	27	002,481	265-87
HORSESHOE BAR	SUTTER	CA	36	442,879	53-56
HORSHAM TWP.	MONTGOMERY	PA	800	444,768	77-108
HORTONIA	BROWN	WI	994	034,508	36-41
HOT SPRINGS	HOT SPRINGS	AR	26	002,480	598-618
HOT SPIRNGS CO.		AR	26	002,480	545-622
HOT SPRINGS TWP.	HOT SPRINGS	AR	26	002,480	545-46
HOTEL DIST.	SURRY	NC	646	444,659	652-63
HOUGHTON	HOUGHTON	MI	351	443,567	7-17
HOUGHTON CO.		MI	351	443,567	1-17
HOULTON	AROOSTOOK	ME	248	009,718	99-133
HOUNSFIELD	JEFFERSON	NY	514	017,090	245-346
HOUSTON	ADAMS	IL	97	007,670	237-48
HOUSTON	HARRIS	TX	911	024,890	1-47
HOUSTON CO.		GA	74	007,070	611-775
HOUSTON CO.		TX	911	024,890	341-92
HOWARD	WINNEBAGO	IL	134	442,922	615-36
HOWARD	STEUBEN	NY	599	444,315	101-178
HOWARD	BROWN	WI	994	034,508	110-23
HOWARD	SHEBOYGAN	WI	1006	444,993	268-69, 322-26
HOWARD CO.		IN	151	442,929	785-960
HOWARD CO.		MO	401	443,609	235-451
HOWARD DIST.	ANNE ARUNDEL	MD	278	013,195	823-1043
HOWARD TWP.	HOWARD	IN	151	442,929	809-824
HOWARD TWP.	CASS	MI	349	014,811	663-82
HOWARD TWP.	GENTRY	MO	399	443,607	477-84
HOWARD TWP.	KNOX	OH	700	444,693	599-624
HOWARD TWP.	CENTRE	PA	763	020,613	352-83
HOWELL TWP.	LIVINGSTON	MI	356	443,572	672-99
HOWELL TWP.	MONMOUTH	NJ	456	443,655	206-313
HOWLAND	PENOBSCOT	ME	266	443,503	567-72

CITY, COUNTY, TOWN, OR TOWNSHIP	COUNTY	STATE	NA NO. M432	GD NO.	PAGES
HOWLAND	TRUMBULL	OH	733	444,726	869-90
HUBBARD	TRUMBULL	OH	733	444,726	315-45
HUBBARD	DODGE	WI	996	034,510	333-53
HUBBARDSTON	WORCESTER	MA	342	443,561	699-742
HUBBARDTON	RUTLAND	VT	927	444,926	333-49
HUDDLESTON BEAT	AUTAUGA	AL	1	002,343	40-50
HUDSON	LENAWEE	MI	355	443,571	201-237
HUDSON	HILLSBORO	NH	434	443,638	205-236
HUDSON	WALWORTH	WI	1007	444,994	395-423
HUDSON CO.		NJ	452	443,651	355-878
HUDSON, NORTH	ESSEX	NY	504	017,080	681-96
HUDSON PREC.	MC LEON	IL	117	007,690	96-108, 117
HUDSON TWP.	LA PORTE	IN	157	442,935	421-31
HUDSON TWP.	SUMMIT	OH	732	444,725	869-903
HUDSON, WARD 1	COLUMBIA	NY	491	017,067	335-406
HUDSON, WARD 2	COLUMBIA	NY	491	017,067	407-488
HUFF TWP.	SPENCER	IN	172	442,950	165-78, 181-68
HULL	PLYMOUTH	MA	332	443,551	95-101
HUME	ALLEGANY	NY	476	017,052	605-656
HUMMELSTOWN	DAUPHIN	PA	774	444,742	225-39
HUMPHREY	CATTARAUGUS	NY	479	017,055	217-36
HUMPHREYS CO.		TN	884	444,840	185-313
HUNGARY NECK DIST.	SOMERSET	MD	297	443,528	917-33
HUNT CO.		TX	911	024,890	395-430
HUNTER	GREENE	NY	510	017,086	595-637
HUNTERDON CO.		NJ	453	443,652	1-707
HUNTERSTOWN	ADAMS	PA	743	020,593	649-52
HUNTERSVILLE	HARDIN	OH	692	444,685	385-86
HUNTERSVILLE	MIAMI	OH	711	444,704	625-31
HUNTING QUARTERS	CARTERET	NC	623	018,109	230-43
HUNTINGDON BOR.	HUNTINGDON	PA	784	444,752	83-119
HUNTINGDON CO.		PA	784	444,752	1-634
HUNTINGTON	FAIRFIELD	CT	37	003,065	707-737
HUNTINGTON	HUNTINGTON	IN	152	442,930	69-83
HUNTINGTON	SUFFOLK	NY	601	444,317	1-189
HUNTINGTON	CARROLL	TN	873	024,564	27-32
HUNTINGTON	CHITTENDEN	VT	923	444,922	429-50
HUNTINGTON CO.		IN	152	442,930	1-192
HUNTINGTON TWP.	BROWN	OH	662	020,210	175-238
HUNTINGTON TWP.	GALLIA	OH	681	444,674	763-94
HUNTINGTON TWP.	LORAIN	OH	705	444,698	623-50
HUNTINGTON TWP.	ROSS	OH	725	444,718	623-62
HUNTINGTON TWP.	ADAMS	PA	743	020,593	147-89
HUNTSBURG TWP.	LUZERNE	PA	793	444,761	274-315
HUNTSVILLE	GEAUGA	OH	682	444,675	323-46
HUNTSVILLE	MADISON	AL	9	002,351	917-54
HUNTSVILLE	MADISON	AR	27	002,481	615-20
HUNTSVILLE	MADISON	IN	158	442,936	225-29
HUNTSVILLE TWP.	RANDOLPH	IN	168	442,946	341-44
HURLEY	SCHUYLER	IL	128	442,916	733-46
HURON	ULSTER	NY	608	444,324	447-94
HURON	WAYNE	MI	366	443,582	1065-77
HURON CO.	WAYNE	NY	613	444,329	763-809
HURON CO.		MI	351	443,567	21-26
HURON TWP.	DES MOINES	OH	697	444,690	671-869, 1-450
HURON TWP.	ERIE	IA	183	007,792	789-803
HURRICANE PREC.	CUMBERLAND	OH	676	338,044	797-830
HURRICANE TWP.	BRADLEY	IL	104	007,677	545-57
		AR	25	002,479	222-26

CITY, COUNTY, TOWN, OR TOWNSHIP	COUNTY	STATE	NA NO. M432	GD NO.	PAGES
HURSTVILLE	JEFFERSON PAR.	LA	232	443,475	80
HUSTISFORD	DODGE	WI	996	034,510	423-38
HUSTON TWP.	BLAIR	PA	755	020,605	219-46
HUSTON TWP.	CENTRE	PA	763	020,613	487-95
HUSTON TWP.	CLEARFIELD	PA	768	444,736	833-38
HYDE CO.		NC	634	444,647	683-809
HYDE PARK	DUTCHESS	NY	497	017,073	443-503
HYDE PARK	LAMOILLE	VT	925	444,924	349-75
IBERIA	ST. MARTIN	LA	240	443,483	362-68
IBERIA	MORROW	OH	716	444,709	723-28
IBERVILLE PARISH		LA	231	009,698	613-700
IDA	MONROE	MI	358	443,574	547-55
ILCHESTER	ANNE ARUNDEL	MD	278	013,195	924-25
ILES BEAT	CADDO PARISH	LA	230	009,697	717-30
ILLINOIS CANYON	EL DORADO	CA	34	002,491	877-78
ILLINOIS PREC.	CALHOUN	IL	99	007,672	600-612
ILLINOIS TWP.	WASHINGTON	AR	31	442,877	855-68
IMLAY	LAPEER	MI	354	443,570	676-80
INDEPENDENCE	WARREN	IN	178	442,956	163-68
INDEPENDENCE	KENTON	KY	208	442,976	251-55
INDEPENDENCE	ALLEGANY	NY	475	017,051	317-57
INDEPENDENCE BEAT	AUTAUGA	AL	1	002,343	129-39
INDEPENDENCE CO.		AR	26	002,480	623-791
INDEPENDENCE PREC.	COLES	IL	101	007,674	177-98
INDEPENDENCE TWP.	PHILLIPS	AR	29	002,483	335-43
INDEPENDENCE TWP.	VAN BUREN	AR	31	442,877	637-42
INDEPENDENCE TWP.	APPANOOSE	IA	182	007,791	23-27
INDEPENDENCE TWP.	OAKLAND	MI	360	443,576	621-51
INDEPENDENCE TWP.	DUNKLIN	MO	399	443,607	25-35
INDEPENDENCE TWP.	WARREN	NJ	465	443,664	1001-1066
INDEPENDENCE TWP.	CUYAHOGA	OH	673	020,221	231-66
INDEPENDENCE TWP.	WASHINGTON	OH	738	444,731	1063-81
INDEPENDENCE TWP.	BEAVER	PA	750	020,600	457-76
INDIAN CREEK TWP.	LAWRENCE	IN	158	442,936	744-75
INDIAN CREEK TWP.	MONROE	IN	161	442,939	683-712
INDIAN CREEK TWP.	PULASKI	IN	166	442,944	664-73
INDIAN CREEK TWP.	PIKE	MO	409	443,617	502-513
INDIAN GROVE	LIVINGSTON	IL	116	007,689	299-304
INDIAN LAKE SETTLEMENT	HAMILTON	NY	511	017,087	50-51
INDIAN LANDS	MARQUETTE	WI	1002	444,989	268-336
INDIAN RIDGE DIST.	CURRITUCK	NC	627	444,640	368-80
INDIAN RIVER HUN.	SUSSEX	DE	55	442,884	351-88
INDIAN TWP.	PENOBSCOT	ME	266	443,503	759
INDIANA BOR.	INDIANA	PA	785	444,753	1-24
INDIANA CO.		PA	785	444,753	1-667
INDIANA TWP.	ALLEGHENY	PA	747	020,597	107-65
INDIANAPOLIS	MARION	IN	159	442,937	389-584
INDIANOLA	CALHOUN	TX	909	024,888	487-96
INDIANTOWN	BUREAU	IL	99	007,672	451-61
INDUSTRY	FRANKLIN	ME	253	009,723	135-59
INGHAM	INGHAM	MI	351	443,567	64-81
INGHAM CO.		MI	351	443,567	29-243
INTERCOURSE DIST.	SUMTER	AL	15	442,866	624-28, 670-76 691
IONIA CO.		MI	352	443,568	245-439
IONIA TWP.	IONIA	MI	352	443,568	333-51

CITY, COUNTY, TOWN, OR TOWNSHIP	COUNTY	STATE	NA NO. M432	GD NO.	PAGES
IOSCO TWP.	LIVINGSTON	MI	356	443,572	962-76
IOWA CITY	JOHNSON	IA	185	442,960	295-324
IOWA CITY TWP.	JOHNSON	IA	185	442,960	325-32
IOWA CO.		IA	184	007,793	539-60
IOWA CO.		WI	999	444,986	619-849
IOWA TWP.	CEDAR CO.	IA	182	007,791	163-75
IPSWICH	ESSEX	MA	314	014,708	1-80
IRA	ST. CLAIR	MI	362	443,578	323-37
IRA	CAYUGA	NY	481	017,057	57-109
IRA	RUTLAND	VT	927	444,926	1-10
IRASBURG	ORLEANS	VT	925	444,924	129-54
IREDELL CO.		NC	633	444,646	181-254
IREDELL CO.		NC	634	444,647	811-984
IRISH CREEK	EL DORADO	CA	34	002,491	855-57, 864, 868, 893
IRISH HOLLOW PREC.	JO DAVIESS	IL	111	007,684	407-424
IRON CO.		UT	919	025,540	35-45
IRONDEQUOIT	MONROE	NY	528	017,104	693-751
IROQUOIS CO.		IL	110	007,683	281-381
IROQUOIS TWP.	JASPER	IN	152	442,930	534-43
IRVING	BARRY	MI	346	014,808	193-98
IRWIN CO.		GA	74	007,070	777-845
IRWIN TWP.	VENANGO	PA	832	444,800	77-112
ISABEL	FULTON	IL	107	007,680	385-96
ISLAND CREEK DIST.	GRANVILLE	NC	631	444,644	371-77
ISLAND CREEK TWP.	JEFFERSON	OH	699	444,692	1023-70
ISLAND GROVE PREC.	JASPER	IL	110	007,683	562-67
ISLAND TWP.	DESHA	AR	26	002,480	137-39
ISLE LA MOTTE	GRANDE ISLE	VT	924	444,923	95-106
ISLE OF SHOALS	YORK	ME	274	443,511	471-72
ISLE OF SHOALS	ROCKINGHAM	NH	437	443,641	257-59
ISLE OF WIGHT CO.		VA	952	444,942	227-370
ISLESBOROUGH	WALDO	ME	271	443,508	483-506
ISLIP	SUFFOLK	NY	601	444,317	191-242
ISRAEL TWP.	PREBLE	OH	723	444,716	724-63
ISSAQUENA CO.		MS	373	443,585	591-600
ITALY	YATES	NY	618	444,334	159-97
ITASCA CO.		MN	367	014,834	31-33
ITAWAMBA CO.		MS	373	443,585	603-878
ITEHPOESASSA SET.	HILLSBOROUGH	FL	58	006,714	499-502
ITHACA	TOMPKINS	NY	606	444,322	403-568
IXONIA	JEFFERSON	WI	1000	444,987	149-75
IZARD CO.		AR	27	002,481	1-68
IZARD CO.		AR	28	002,482	713-18
JACKSON	WILL	IL	133	442,921	407-417
JACKSON	FAYETTE	IN	144	007,757	561-92
JACKSON	SOMERSET	ME	269	443,506	546
JACKSON	WALDO	ME	270	443,507	29-48
JACKSON	JACKSON	MI	352	443,568	625-723
JACKSON	HINDS	MS	372	443,584	241
JACKSON	COOS	NH	429	443,633	5-20
JACKSON	WASHINGTON	NY	611	444,327	639-89
JACKSON	JACKSON	OH	698	444,691	549-60
JACKSON	MAHONING	OH	707	444,700	1104-1161
JACKSON	POTTER	PA	825	444,793	234-35
JACKSON	MADISON	TN	889	444,845	429-62

Jackson

CITY, COUNTY, TOWN, OR TOWNSHIP	COUNTY	STATE	NA NO. M432	GD NO.	PAGES
JACKSON TWP.	WASHINGTON	IN	179	442,957	537-606
JACKSON TWP.	WAYNE	IN	180	442,958	1-25, 55-84
JACKSON TWP.	WELLS	IN	181	442,959	683-98
JACKSON TWP.	HENRY	IA	184	007,793	511-24
JACKSON TWP.	JACKSON	IA	184	007,793	588-91, 599
JACKSON TWP.	VAN BUREN	IA	189	442,964	749-63
JACKSON TWP.	ANDREW	MO	391	014,871	234-64
JACKSON TWP.	BUCHANAN	MO	393	014,873	261-74
JACKSON TWP.	GENTRY	MO	399	443,607	399-96
JACKSON TWP.	GREENE	MO	400	443,608	753-70
JACKSON TWP.	JASPER	MO	402	443,610	741-42, 744-52
JACKSON TWP.	JOHNSON	MO	403	443,611	115-61
JACKSON TWP.	NEWTON	MO	408	443,616	664-69, 674-75
JACKSON TWP.	OSAGE	MO	408	443,616	849-71
JACKSON TWP.	STE. GENEVIEVE	MO	413	443,621	513-25
JACKSON TWP.	OCEAN	NJ	460	443,659	39-70
JACKSON TWP.	ALLEN	OH	657	020,205	523-50
JACKSON TWP.	ASHLAND	OH	658	020,206	157-93
JACKSON TWP.	BROWN	OH	662	020,210	951-81
JACKSON TWP.	CHAMPAIGN	OH	665	020,213	911-54
JACKSON TWP.	CLERMONT	OH	667	020,215	107-134
JACKSON TWP.	COSHOCTON	OH	670	020,218	275-323
JACKSON TWP.	CRAWFORD	OH	671	020,219	693-737
JACKSON TWP.	DARKE	OH	674	020,222	981-94
JACKSON TWP.	FRANKLIN	OH	680	444,673	275-311
JACKSON TWP.	GUERNSEY	OH	684	444,677	649, 651-79
JACKSON TWP.	HANCOCK	OH	692	444,685	165-84
JACKSON TWP.	HARDIN	OH	692	444,685	335-48
JACKSON TWP.	HIGHLAND	OH	694	444,687	495-529
JACKSON TWP.	JACKSON	OH	698	444,691	725-42
JACKSON TWP.	KNOX	OH	700	444,693	751-77
JACKSON TWP.	LICKING	OH	702	444,695	231-36
JACKSON TWP.	MONROE	OH	712	444,705	841-68
JACKSON TWP.	MONTGOMERY	OH	714	444,707	665-712
JACKSON TWP.	MORGAN	OH	715	444,708	557-86
JACKSON TWP.	MUSKINGUM	OH	718	444,711	645-74
JACKSON TWP.	PAULDING	OH	719	444,712	397-98
JACKSON TWP.	PERRY	OH	719	444,712	399-439
JACKSON TWP.	PICKAWAY	OH	720	444,713	223-48
JACKSON TWP.	PIKE	OH	721	444,714	629-64
JACKSON TWP.	PREBLE	OH	723	444,716	893-926
JACKSON TWP.	PUTNAM	OH	723	444,716	147-52
JACKSON TWP.	RICHLAND	OH	724	444,717	793-820
JACKSON TWP.	SANDUSKY	OH	726	444,719	77-102
JACKSON TWP.	SENECA	OH	728	444,721	821-44
JACKSON TWP.	SHELBY	OH	729	444,722	638-56
JACKSON TWP.	STARK	OH	731	444,724	107-144
JACKSON TWP.	UNION	OH	736	444,729	1-11
JACKSON TWP.	VINTON	OH	736	444,729	613-32
JACKSON TWP.	WOOD	OH	741	444,734	257-58
JACKSON TWP.	WYANDOT	OH	741	444,734	611-20
JACKSON TWP.	CAMBRIA	PA	761	020,611	387-406
JACKSON TWP.	COLUMBIA	PA	769	444,737	439-47
JACKSON TWP.	DAUPHIN	PA	775	444,743	619-41
JACKSON TWP.	GREENE	PA	783	444,751	623-52
JACKSON TWP.	HUNTINGDON	PA	784	444,752	277-312
JACKSON TWP.	LEBANON	PA	791	444,759	82-150
JACKSON TWP.	LUZERNE	PA	793	444,761	85-99
JACKSON TWP.	LYCOMING	PA	795	444,763	445-54

CITY, COUNTY, TOWN, OR TOWNSHIP	COUNTY	STATE	NA NO. M432	GD NO.	PAGES	
JACKSON TWP.	MONROE	PA	798	444,766	49-66	
JACKSON TWP.	NORTHUMBERLAND	PA	804	444,772	541-607	
JACKSON TWP.	PERRY	PA	805	444,773	817-38	
JACKSON TWP.	SUSQUEHANNA	PA	829	444,797	491-514	
JACKSON TWP.	TIOGA	PA	830	444,798	203-238	
JACKSON TWP.	VENANGO	PA	832	444,800	347-70	
JACKSONVILLE	BENTON	AL	1	002,343	655-64	
JACKSONVILLE	TUOLUMNE	CA	36	442,879	208-213	
JACKSONVILLE	MORGAN	IL	122	442,910	335-400	
JACKSONVILLE DIST.	DUVAL	FL	58	006,714	171-98	
JACKSONVILLE DIST.	TELFAIR	GA	83	442,892	793-94	
JACOBSPORT	COSHOCTON	OH	670	020,218	165-70	
JAFFREY	CHESHIRE	NH	428	014,941	467-502	
JAMAICA	QUEENS	NY	582	444,298	521-622	
JAMAICA	WINDHAM	VT	929	444,928	489-527	
JAMES CITY CO.		VA	953	444,943	531-82	
JAMES POINT	SUTTER	CA	36	442,879	61-62	
JAMES RIVER DIST.	ELIZABETH	VA	942	444,932	121-27	
JAMES TWP.	TANEY	MO	420	443,628	704-9	
JAMESTOWN	TUOLUMNE	CA	36	442,879	175-86, 245-46,	205-6, 363-66
JAMESTOWN	MONROE	OH	712	444,705	777-79	
JAMESTOWN	NEWPORT	RI	842	022,265	33-41	
JAMESTOWN TWP.	STEUBEN	IN	173	442,951	258-68	
JAMESTOWN TWP.	OTTAWA	MI	361	443,577	117-18	
JANESVILLE	ROCK	WI	1005	444,992	425-507	
JASPER	HAMILTON	FL	58	006,714	460-61	
JASPER	STEUBEN	NY	599	444,315	561-602	
JASPER CO.		GA	74	007,070	165-276	
JASPER CO.		IL	110	007,683	525-601	
JASPER CO.		IN	152	442,930	471-556	
JASPER CO.		IA	184	007,793	737-67	
JASPER CO.		MS	374	443,586	59-161	
JASPER CO.		MO	402	443,610	717-812	
JASPER CO.		TX	912	444,915	448-79	
JASPER TWP.	CRAWFORD	AR	25	002,479	663-78	
JASPER TWP.	CRITTENDEN	AR	25	002,479	717-24	
JASPER TWP.	TANEY	MO	420	443,628	739-40	
JASPER TWP.	FAYETTE	OH	678	444,671	289-317	
JASPER TWP.	PREBLE	OH	723	444,716	534-55	
JAVA	WYOMING	NY	616	444,332	99-153	
JAY	FRANKLIN	ME	253	009,723	41-81	
JAY	ESSEX	NY	504	017,080	377-440	
JAY	ORLEANS	VT	925	444,924	273-81	
JAY CO.		IN	153	442,931	557-736	
JAY TWP.	ELK	PA	776	444,744	661-68	
JEFFERSON	COOK	IL	103	007,676	313-28	
JEFFERSON	CLINTON	IN	139	007,752	678-84	
JEFFERSON	JEFFERSON PAR.	LA	232	443,475	42-78	
JEFFERSON	LINCOLN	ME	260	443,497	647-700	
JEFFERSON	FREDERICK	MD	293	443,524	795-800	
JEFFERSON	COOS	NH	429	443,633	77-91	
JEFFERSON	SCHOHARIE	NY	596	444,312	521-62	
JEFFERSON	GREEN	WI	999	444,986	409-425	
JEFFERSON	JEFFERSON	WI	1000	444,987	271-310	
JEFFERSON BARRACKS	ST. LOUIS	MO	414	443,622	531-48	
JEFFERSON BOR.	ASHTABULA	OH	659	020,207	755-65	
JEFFERSON CO.		AL	7	002,349	287-455	
JEFFERSON CO.		AR	27	002,481	135-219	

CITY, COUNTY, TOWN, OR TOWNSHIP	COUNTY	STATE	NA NO. M432	GD NO.	PAGES
JEFFERSON CO.		FL	59	006,715	1-62
JEFFERSON CO.		GA	75	007,071	269-360
JEFFERSON CO.		IL	110	007,683	605-831
JEFFERSON CO.		IN	154	442,932	1-578
JEFFERSON CO.		IA	185	442,960	1-248
JEFFERSON CO.		KY	205	442,973	347-611
JEFFERSON CO.		KY	206	442,974	1-459
JEFFERSON CO.		KY	207	442,975	461-907
JEFFERSON CO.		MS	374	443,586	163-227
JEFFERSON CO.		MO	402	443,610	813-965
JEFFERSON CO.		NY	514	017,090	245-943
JEFFERSON CO.		NY	515	017,091	1-491
JEFFERSON CO.		NY	516	017,092	493-971
JEFFERSON CO.		OH	699	444,692	769-1070, 1-410
JEFFERSON CO.		PA	786	444,754	1-329
JEFFERSON CO.		TN	885	444,841	657-934
JEFFERSON CO.		TX	912	444,915	483-520
JEFFERSON CO.		VA	953	444,943	585-849
JEFFERSON CO.		WI	1000	444,987	1-386
JEFFERSON DIST.	FREDERICK	MD	293	443,524	801-818
JEFFERSON DIST.	RUTHERFORD	TN	894	444,850	349-62
JEFFERSON PARISH		LA	232	443,475	1-454
JEFFERSON TWP.	CARROLL	AR	25	002,479	329-47
JEFFERSON TWP.	INDEPENDENCE	AR	26	002,480	623-34
JEFFERSON TWP.	JACKSON	AR	27	002,481	102-111
JEFFERSON TWP.	OUACHITA	AR	28	002,482	181-91, 202
JEFFERSON TWP.	SEVIER	AR	30	442,876	406-415
JEFFERSON TWP.	ADAMS	IN	135	007,748	119-26
JEFFERSON TWP.	ALLEN	IN	135	007,748	355-68
JEFFERSON TWP.	CARROLL	IN	137	007,750	661-75
JEFFERSON TWP.	CASS	IN	137	007,750	805-822
JEFFERSON TWP.	ELKHART	IN	144	007,757	114-30
JEFFERSON TWP.	GRANT	IN	147	442,925	368-92
JEFFERSON TWP.	GREENE	IN	148	442,926	775-86
JEFFERSON TWP.	HENRY	IN	151	442,929	765-84
JEFFERSON TWP.	JAY	IN	153	442,931	691-708
JEFFERSON TWP.	KOSCIUSKO	IN	156	442,934	624-28
JEFFERSON TWP.	MIAMI	IN	160	442,938	241-69
JEFFERSON TWP.	MORGAN	IN	162	442,940	163-84
JEFFERSON TWP.	NOBLE	IN	162	442,940	491-508
JEFFERSON TWP.	OWEN	IN	164	442,942	237-65
JEFFERSON TWP.	PIKE	IN	165	442,943	118-57
JEFFERSON TWP.	PUTNAM	IN	167	442,945	931-56
JEFFERSON TWP.	SWITZERLAND	IN	174	442,952	797-874
JEFFERSON TWP.	TIPTON	IN	176	442,954	540-58
JEFFERSON TWP.	WAYNE	IN	180	442,958	105-150
JEFFERSON TWP.	WELLS	IN	181	442,959	635-54
JEFFERSON TWP.	CLAYTON	IA	182	007,791	281-93
JEFFERSON TWP.	HENRY	IA	184	007,793	423-41
JEFFERSON TWP.	LOUISA	IA	187	442,962	201-216
JEFFERSON TWP.	CASS	MI	349	014,811	581-602
JEFFERSON TWP.	HILLSDALE	MI	351	443,567	745-46, 748-64
JEFFERSON TWP.	ANDREW	MO	391	014,871	164-96
JEFFERSON TWP.	JOHNSON	MO	403	443,611	57-75
JEFFERSON TWP.	OSAGE	MO	408	443,616	837-48
JEFFERSON TWP.	SCOTLAND	MO	419	443,627	232-35, 238-56
JEFFERSON TWP.	MORRIS	NJ	459	443,658	705-737
JEFFERSON TWP.	ADAMS	OH	657	020,205	397-434
JEFFERSON TWP.	ASHTABULA	OH	659	020,207	766-80

CITY, COUNTY, TOWN, OR TOWNSHIP	COUNTY	STATE	NA NO. M432	GD NO.	PAGES
JEFFERSON TWP.	CLINTON	OH	668	020,216	463-82
JEFFERSON TWP.	COSHOCTON	OH	670	020,218	325-47
JEFFERSON TWP.	FAYETTE	OH	678	444,671	1-45
JEFFERSON TWP.	FRANKLIN	OH	680	444,673	245-74
JEFFERSON TWP.	GUERNSEY	OH	684	444,677	847-67
JEFFERSON TWP.	JACKSON	OH	698	444,691	523-47
JEFFERSON TWP.	KNOX	OH	700	444,693	889-926
JEFFERSON TWP.	LOGAN	OH	704	444,697	395-445
JEFFERSON TWP.	MADISON	OH	706	444,699	513-28
JEFFERSON TWP.	MERCER	OH	710	444,703	469-80
JEFFERSON TWP.	MONTGOMERY	OH	714	444,707	713-56
JEFFERSON TWP.	MUSKINGUM	OH	717	444,710	283-350
JEFFERSON TWP.	PREBLE	OH	723	444,716	927-80
JEFFERSON TWP.	RICHLAND	OH	724	444,717	845-907
JEFFERSON TWP.	ROSS	OH	725	444,718	585-606
JEFFERSON TWP.	SCIOTO	OH	727	444,720	237-56
JEFFERSON TWP.	TUSCARAWAS	OH	734	444,727	101-127
JEFFERSON TWP.	WILLIAMS	OH	741	444,734	29-53
JEFFERSON TWP.	ALLEGHENY	PA	747	020,597	215-42
JEFFERSON TWP.	DAUPHIN	PA	775	444,743	647-64
JEFFERSON TWP.	FAYETTE	PA	780	444,748	535-70
JEFFERSON TWP.	GREENE	PA	783	444,751	245-78
JEFFERSON TWP.	LUZERNE	PA	793	444,761	455-65
JEFFERSON TWP.	SOMERSET	PA	828	444,796	23-41
JEFFERSONVILLE	CLARK	IN	138	007,751	321-74
JEFFERSONVILLE TWP.	CLARK	IN	138	007,751	277-320, 415
JENKS TWP.	JEFFERSON	PA	786	444,754	1-3
JENNER TWP.	SOMERSET	PA	828	444,796	163-99
JENNINGS CO.		IN	155	442,933	579-882
JENNINGS TWP.	CRAWFORD	IN	139	007,752	103-136
JENNINGS TWP.	FAYETTE	IN	144	007,757	437-57
JENNINGS TWP.	OWEN	IN	164	442,942	111-22
JENNINGS TWP.	SCOTT	IN	171	442,949	381-419
JENNINGS TWP.	PUTNAM	OH	723	444,716	39-46
JENNINGS TWP.	VAN WERT	OH	736	444,729	413-17
JERICHO	CHITTENDEN	VT	923	444,922	41-84
JEROME TWP.	UNION	OH	736	444,729	253-82
JERSEY CITY	HUDSON	NJ	452	443,651	617-768
JERSEY CITY TWP.	HUDSON	NJ	452	443,651	605-616
JERSEY CO.		IL	111	007,684	1-192
JERSEY SHORE BOR.	LYCOMING	PA	795	444,763	489-504
JERSEY TWP.	LICKING	OH	702	444,695	413-42
JERSEYVILLE	JERSEY	IL	111	007,684	1-19
JERUSALEM	YATES	NY	618	444,334	89-158
JESSAMINE CO.		KY	208	442,976	1-157
JESSUP TWP.	SUSQUEHANNA	PA	829	444,797	69-88
JEWETT	GREENE	NY	510	017,086	639-73
JO DAVIESS CO.		IL	111	007,684	195-638
JOHN Q. ADAMS TWP.	WARREN	IN	178	442,956	111-24
JOHN'S RIVER DIST.	CALDWELL	NC	623	018,109	1-18, 84, 101
JOHNSBURG	WARREN	NY	609	444,325	343-79
JOHNSON	LA GRANGE	IN	157	442,935	35-56
JOHNSON	CHAMPAIGN	OH	665	020,213	705-744
JOHNSON	LAMOILLE	VT	925	444,924	107-139
JOHNSON CO.		AR	27	002,481	221-332
JOHNSON CO.		IL	112	007,685	641-748
JOHNSON CO.		IN	155	442,933	1-302
JOHNSON CO.		IA	185	442,960	253-368
JOHNSON CO.		KY	208	442,976	159-250

CITY, COUNTY, TOWN, OR TOWNSHIP	COUNTY	STATE	NA NO. M432	GD NO.	PAGES
JOHNSON CO.		MO	403	443,611	1-161
JOHNSON CO.		TN	886	444,842	1-89
JOHNSON PREC.	CLARK	IL	100	007,673	541-56
JOHNSON TWP.	ST. FRANCIS	AR	30	442,876	75, 95-96, 104-111, 114, 124, 161
JOHNSON TWP.	UNION	AR	30	442,876	505-525
JOHNSON TWP.	BROWN	IN	137	007,750	487-98
JOHNSON TWP.	CLAY	IN	138	007,751	605-621
JOHNSON TWP.	CLINTON	IN	139	007,752	791-809
JOHNSON TWP.	GIBSON	IN	147	442,925	211-50
JOHNSON TWP.	RIPLEY	IN	169	442,947	431-84
JOHNSON TWP.	SCOTLAND	MO	419	443,627	283-95
JOHNSON TWP.	WASHINGTON	MO	421	443,629	307-317
JOHNSONVILLE	MORROW	OH	716	444,709	868-70
JOHNSTON	TRUMBULL	OH	733	444,726	643-69
JOHNSTON	PROVIDENCE	RI	846	444,812	369-440
JOHNSTON CO.		NC	635	444,648	1-222
JOHNSTOWN	BARRY	MI	346	014,808	167-77
JOHNSTOWN	FULTON	NY	506	017,082	123-270
JOHNSTOWN	LICKING	OH	702	444,695	377-85
JOHNSTOWN	CAMBRIA	PA	761	020,611	407-437
JOHNSTOWN	ROCK	WI	1005	444,992	685-715
JOLIET	WILL	IL	133	442,921	41-56, 359-406
JOLLEY TWP.	WASHINGTON	OH	738	444,731	1009-1033
JONES	CANNON	TN	872	024,563	833-46, 859
JONES BLUFF DIV.	SUMTER	AL	15	442,866	541-42, 580, 595-97, 599, 693
JONES CO.		GA	75	007,071	361-457
JONES CO.		IA	185	442,960	371-442
JONES CO.		MS	374	443,586	229-75
JONES CO.		NC	635	444,648	223-82
JONES TWP.	HANCOCK	IN	149	442,927	476-92
JONES TWP.	ELK	PA	776	444,744	615-20
JONESBORO	UNION	IL	130	442,918	457-71
JONESBORO	WASHINGTON	ME	273	443,510	21-32
JONESBORO bEAT	JEFFERSON	AL	7	002,349	287-304
JONESBORO MILL TWP.	GRANT	IN	147	442,925	315-21
JONESPORT	WASHINGTON	ME	273	443,510	1-20
JONESTOWN	LEBANON	PA	791	444,759	339-53
JONESVILLE VILLAGE	HILLSDALE	MI	351	443,567	1025-38
JORDON	GREEN	WI	999	444,986	571-80
JORDAN RIVER	HANCOCK	MS	372	443,584	137-40
JORDAN TWP.	JASPER	IN	152	442,930	517-23
JORDAN TWP.	WARREN	IN	178	442,956	79-86
JORDAN TWP.	CLEARFIELD	PA	768	444,736	732-46
JOSHUA	FULTON	IL	107	007,680	518-38
JUNIATA CO.		PA	786	444,754	333-643
JUNIATA TWP.	BLAIR	PA	755	020,605	347-88
JUNIATA TWP.	PERRY	PA	805	444,773	781-815
JUNIUS	SENECA	NY	597	444,313	447-83
KALAMAZOO CO.		MI	353	443,569	1-331
KALAMAZOO VILLAGE	KALAMAZOO	MI	353	443,569	1-79
KALAMO	EATON	MI	349	014,811	203-213
KANASHA CO.		VA	954	444,944	1-293
KANE CO.		IL	112	007,685	1-416

CITY, COUNTY, TOWN, OR TOWNSHIP	COUNTY	STATE	NA NO. M432	GD NO.	PAGES
KANEVILLE	KANE	IL	112	007,685	339-53
KANKAKEE TWP.	LA PORTE	IN	157	442,935	385-407
KARTHAUS TWP.	CLEARFIELD	PA	768	444,736	824-30
KASKASKIA	RANDOLPH	IL	125	442,913	244-55
KATAHDIN IRON WORKS	PISCATAQUIS	ME	267	443,504	737-40
KAUFMAN CO.		TX	912	444,915	523-46
KAUKAULIN	BROWN	WI	994	034,503	145-61
KAW TWP.	JACKSON	MO	402	443,610	453-501
KEATING TWP.	CLINTON	PA	768	444,736	169-74
KEATING TWP.	MC KEAN	PA	795	444,763	1-29
KEELER	VAN BUREN	MI	363	443,579	275-86
KEENE	ADAMS	IL	97	007,670	249-64
KEENE	CHESHIRE	NH	427	014,940	181-261
KEENE	ESSEX	NY	503	017,079	359-76
KEENE TWP.	IONIA	MI	352	443,568	397-414
KEENE TWP.	COSHOCTON	OH	670	020,218	409-434
KEITHS DIST.	LUMPKIN	GA	76	007,072	21-28
KEITHSBURG	MERCER	IL	120	442,908	677-82
KELLEYS ISLAND	ERIE	OH	676	338,044	791-95
KELLY TWP.	UNION	PA	831	444,799	497-514
KELSEY'S	EL DORADO	CA	34	002,491	815-31
KELSO TWP.	DEARBORN	IN	141	007,754	653-90
KEMPER CO.		MS	374	443,586	277-447
KENDALL	KENDALL	IL	113	007,686	419-38
KENDALL	ORLEANS	NY	575	444,291	72-129
KENDALL	LAFAYETTE	WI	1001	444,988	669-676
KENDALL CO.		IL	113	007,686	419-616
KENNEBEC CO.		ME	256	443,493	1-520
KENNEBEC CO.		ME	257	443,494	521-850, 1-17
KENNEBEC CO.		ME	258	443,495	179-694
KENNEBUNK	YORK	ME	274	443,511	151-216
KENNEBUNKPORT	YORK	ME	274	443,511	219-84
KENNEKEET BANKS DIST.	HYDE	NC	634	444,647	778-84
KENNETT	CHESTER	PA	764	020,614	365-405
KENOSHA CO.		WI	1000	444,987	389-657
KENOSHA, WARD 1	KENOSHA	WI	1000	444,987	461-96
KENOSHA, WARD 2	KENOSHA	WI	1000	444,987	441-60
KENOSHA, WARD 3	KENOSHA	WI	1000	444,987	497-523
KENSINGTON	ROCKINGHAM	NH	438	443,642	529-45
KENSINGTON, WARD 1	PHILADELPHIA	PA	806	444,774	1-109
KENSINGTON, WARD 2	PHILADELPHIA	PA	806	444,774	111-236
KENSINGTON, WARD 3	PHILADELPHIA	PA	806	444,774	237-475
KENSINGTON, WARD 4	PHILADELPHIA	PA	806	444,774	477-600
KENSINGTON, WARD 5	PHILADELPHIA	PA	807	444,775	601-800
KENSINGTON, WARD 6	PHILADELPHIA	PA	807	444,775	803-968
KENSINGTON, WARD 7	PHILADELPHIA	PA	807	444,775	969-1085
KENSINGTON, WARD 8	PHILADELPHIA	PA	807	444,775	1087-1124
KENT	LITCHFIELD	CT	43	003,071	135-79
KENT	JEFFERSON	IN	154	442,932	310-12
KENT	PUTNAM	NY	581	444,297	253-90
KENT CO.		DE	52	006,436	1-540
KENT CO.		MD	294	443,525	415-628
KENT CO.		MI	353	443,569	335-637
KENT CO.		RI	841	022,264	211-578
KENTON	HARDIN	OH	692	444,685	209-234
KENTON CO.		KY	208	442,976	251-628
KENTUCKY DIST.	CLAY	KY	197	442,965	191-307
KENTUCKY DIST.	MEADE	KY	213	442,981	339-478
KENTUCKY DIST.	OWSLEY	KY	216	442,984	555-643

CITY, COUNTY, TOWN, OR TOWNSHIP	COUNTY	STATE	NA NO. M432	6D NO.	PAGES
KEOKUK	LEE	IA	186	442,961	821-79
KEOKUK CO.		IA	185	442,960	445-560
KEOSAUQUA	VAN BUREN	IA	189	442,964	651-67
KERSHAW CO.		SC	854	444,817	141-259
KERTON	FULTON	IL	107	007,680	293-300
KEYTESVILLE TWP.	CHARITON	MO	395	443,603	409-432, 434-36
KIDDER TWP.	CARBON	PA	762	020,612	483-95
KILAUGH'S DIST.	LUMPKIN	GA	76	007,072	163-70
KILLBUCK TWP.	HOLMES	OH	696	444,689	225-54
KILLINGLY	WINDHAM	CT	51	442,883	641-749
KILLINGWORTH	MIDDLESEX	CT	44	003,072	445-71
KILMARNOCK	PISCATAQUIS	ME	267	443,504	641-48
KINCHAFOONEE DIST.	MARION	GA	77	442,886	569-74
KINDERHOOK	COLUMBIA	NY	492	017,068	685-782
KINDERHOOK TWP.	BRANCH	MI	347	014,809	799-807
KINEO BAY'S ACAD. GT.	PISCATAQUIS	ME	267	443,504	517
KING AND QUEEN CO.		VA	954	444,944	297-405
KING GEORGE	KING GEORGE	VA	954	444,944	409-448
KING GEORGE CO.		VA	954	444,944	409-470
KING WILLIAM CO.		VA	955	444,945	473-545
KINGFIELD	FRANKLIN	ME	253	009,723	433-48
KINGS CO.		NY	517	017,093	1-579
KINGS CO.		NY	518	017,094	583-845, 1-326
KINGS CO.		NY	519	017,095	329-756, 1-62
KINGS CO.		NY	520	017,096	65-723
KINGS CO.		NY	521	017,097	1-274
KINGS CO.		NY	522	017,098	277-1010
KINGS CREEK DIST.	CALDWELL	NC	623	018,109	58-60, 73-79
KINGS RIVER TWP.	MADISON	AR	27	002,481	549-63
KINGSBURY	PISCATAQUIS	ME	267	443,504	423-27
KINGSBURY	WASHINGTON	NY	610	444,326	417-89
KINGSESSING TWP.	PHILADELPHIA	PA	808	444,776	1-43
KINGSTON	PLYMOUTH	MA	333	443,552	177-214
KINGSTON	ROCKINGHAM	NH	437	443,641	329-57
KINGSTON	ULSTER	NY	607	444,323	79-250
KINGSTON	ROSS	OH	725	444,718	421-28
KINGSTON	ROANE	TN	893	444,849	891-97
KINGSTON	MARQUETTE	WI	1002	444,989	179-91
KINGSTON BEAT	AUTAUGA	AL	1	002,343	117-22
KINGSTON TWP.	DE KALB	IL	104	007,677	633-47
KINGSTON TWP.	DELAWARE	OH	675	020,223	655-73
KINGSTON TWP.	LUZERNE	PA	793	444,761	1-59
KINGSTON TWP.	SAUK	WI	1006	444,993	51-60
KINGSTON VILLAGE	ULSTER	NY	607	444,323	1-77
KINGSVILLE	ASHTABULA	OH	659	020,207	465-500
KINGWOOD TWP.	HUNTERDON	NJ	453	443,652	267-309
KINSMAN	TRUMBULL	OH	733	444,726	569-92
KINSTON	LENOIR	NC	635	444,648	366-72
KINZUA TWP.	WARREN	PA	832	444,800	755-60
KIRBY	CALEDONIA	VT	922	027,448	75-87
KIRKERSVILLE	LICKING	OH	703	444,696	561-67
KIRKLAND	PENOBSCOT	ME	265	443,502	391-96
KIRKLAND	ONEIDA	NY	562	444,278	221-302
KIRKLAND TWP.	ADAMS	IN	135	007,748	103-107
KIRKLIN	CLINTON	IN	139	007,752	822-40
KIRKWOOD TWP.	BELMONT	OH	661	020,209	157-210
KIRTLAND	LAKE	OH	701	444,694	423-62
KISKIMINETAS TWP.	ARMSTRONG	PA	749	020,599	615-72
KITTANNING BOR.	ARMSTRONG	PA	749	020,599	399-434

CITY, COUNTY, TOWN, OR TOWNSHIP	COUNTY	STATE	NA NO. M432	GD NO.	PAGES
KITTANNING TWP.	ARMSTRONG	PA	749	020,599	371-98
KITTERY	YORK	ME	275	443,512	517-81
KNIGHT TWP.	VANDERBURGH	IN	176	442,954	545-60
KNOB DIST.	SHELBY	IL	128	442,916	282-95
KNOTTS ISLAND DIST.	CURRITUCK	NC	627	444,640	355-67
KNOWLTON TWP.	WARREN	NJ	465	443,664	1068-1100
KNOX	WALDO	ME	271	443,508	595-621
KNOX	ALBANY	NY	474	017,050	643-93
KNOX CO.		IL	113	007,686	617-934
KNOX CO.		IN	156	442,934	303-586
KNOX CO.		KY	209	442,977	629-783
KNOX CO.		MO	403	443,611	163-227
KNOX CO.		OH	700	444,693	411-926, 1-22
KNOX CO.		TN	886	444,842	93-490
KNOX TWP.	JAY	IN	153	442,931	719-26
KNOX TWP.	COLUMBIANA	OH	669	020,217	547-97
KNOX TWP.	GUERNSEY	OH	684	444,677	951-70
KNOX TWP.	HOLMES	OH	696	444,689	531-59
KNOX TWP.	JEFFERSON	OH	699	444,692	975-1022
KNOXVILLE	KNOX	IL	113	007,686	633-51
KNOXVILLE	JEFFERSON	OH	699	444,692	1007-1010
KNOXVILLE	KNOX	TN	886	444,842	185-223
KORTRIGHT	DELAWARE	NY	494	017,070	399-452
KOSCIUSKO	ATTALA	MS	368	014,847	369-75
KOSCIUSKO CO.		IN	156	442,934	587-833
KOSHKONONG	JEFFERSON	WI	1000	444,987	215-42
KOSSUTH	AUGLAIZE	OH	660	020,208	562-63
KOSSUTH TWP.	COLUMBIA	WI	994	034,508	301-8, 319-20
KULENHOURS	STANLEY	NC	645	444,658	48-55
KUTZTOWN BOR.	BERKS	PA	753	020,603	193-208
LA CUESTA	SAN MIGUEL	NM	469	443,667	39-96
LA FAVE TWP.	SCOTT	AR	30	442,876	275-78
LA FAYETTE CO.		AR	27	002,481	333-78
LA FAYETTE TWP.	OUACHITA	AR	28	002,482	89-107
LA GRANGE	TROUP	GA	84	442,893	223-43
LA GRANGE	BROWN	IL	98	007,671	249-50
LA GRANGE	PENOBSCOT	ME	266	443,503	519-30
LA GRANGE	DUTCHESS	NY	496	017,072	479-525
LA GRANGE	JEFFERSON	OH	699	444,692	845, 851-58
LA GRANGE	WALWORTH	WI	1007	444,994	731-55
LA GRANGE CO.		IN	157	442,935	1-216
LA GRANGE TWP.	LA FAYETTE	AR	27	002,481	340, 342-44, 373-76
LA GRANGE TWP.	CASS	MI	349	014,811	603-635
LA GRANGE TWP.	LORAIN	OH	705	444,698	947-80
LA POINTE CO.		WI	1002	444,989	1-13
LA POINTE VILLAGE	LA POINTE	WI	1002	444,989	2-12
LA PORTE	LA PORTE	IN	157	442,935	505-550
LA PORTE CO.		IN	157	442,935	319-645
LA PRARIE	ROCK	WI	1005	444,992	872-80
LA SALLE	MONROE	MI	358	443,574	639-65
LA SALLE CO.		IL	115	007,688	355-786
LA VACA	CALHOUN	TX	909	024,888	497-502
LAC QUI PARLE	DAKOTA	MN	367	014,834	15
LACK TWP.	JUNIATA	PA	786	444,754	333-58, 360,
LACKAWANNA	LUZERNE	PA	794	444,762	255-64

CITY, COUNTY, TOWN, OR TOWNSHIP	COUNTY	STATE	NA NO. M432	GD NO.	PAGES
LACKAWAXEN TWP.	PIKE	PA	825	444,793	71-104
LACLEDE CO.		MO	403	443,611	229-85
LACON	MARSHALL	IL	120	442,908	182-204
LACY'S BAR	SUTTER	CA	36	442,879	64-73
LAFAYETTE	WALKER	GA	85	442,894	827-36
LAFAYETTE	FULTON	IL	107	007,680	269-91
LAFAYETTE	TIPPECANOE	IN	175	442,953	83-230
LAFAYETTE	ONONDAGA	NY	567	444,283	387-447
LAFAYETTE	WALWORTH	WI	1007	444,994	471-95
LAFAYETTE CO.		MS	375	443,587	449-647
LAFAYETTE CO.		MO	403	443,611	287-531
LAFAYETTE CO.		WI	1001	444,988	661-946
LAFAYETTE PARISH		LA	232	443,475	455-546
LAFAYETTE TWP.	CRAWFORD	AR	25	002,479	621-33
LAFAYETTE TWP.	SCOTT	AR	30	442,876	262-63
LAFAYETTE TWP.	OGLE	IL	123	442,911	128-34
LAFAYETTE TWP.	ALLEN	IN	135	007,748	451-63
LAFAYETTE TWP.	FLOYD	IN	145	442,923	721-42, 946-51
LAFAYETTE TWP.	MADISON	IN	158	442,936	85-101
LAFAYETTE TWP.	OWEN	IN	164	442,942	291-311
LAFAYETTE TWP.	VAN BUREN	MI	363	443,579	301-328
LAFAYETTE TWP.	SUSSEX	NJ	464	443,663	185-207
LAFAYETTE TWP.	COSHOCTON	OH	670	020,218	487-511
LAFAYETTE TWP.	MADISON	OH	706	444,699	509-512
LAFAYETTE TWP.	MEDINA	OH	709	444,702	481-513
LAFAYETTE TWP.	MC KEAN	PA	795	444,763	36-39
LAFAYETTE, WARD 1	TIPPECANOE	IN	175	442,953	83-125
LAFAYETTE, WARD 2	TIPPECANOE	IN	175	442,953	126-42
LAFAYETTE, WARD 3	TIPPECANOE	IN	175	442,953	143-63
LAFAYETTE, WARD 4	TIPPECANOE	IN	175	442,953	164-97
LAFAYETTE, WARD 5	TIPPECANOE	IN	175	442,953	198-230
LAFAYETTE, WARD 1	JEFFERSON PAR.	LA	232	443,475	193-256
LAFAYETTE, WARD 2	JEFFERSON PAR.	LA	232	443,475	257-324
LAFAYETTE, WARD 3	JEFFERSON PAR.	LA	232	443,475	325-40, 403-454
LAFAYETTE, WARD 4	JEFFERSON PAR.	LA	232	443,475	341-402
LAFAYETTE, WARD 5	JEFFERSON PAR.	LA	232	443,475	1-41
LAFOURCHE	LAFOURCHE PAR.	LA	232	443,475	609-613, 622, 626, 634, 644-45, 657
LAFOURCHE PARISH		LA	232	443,475	547-670
LAGRO TWP.	WABASH	IN	178	442,956	593-655
LAGUNA	VALENCIA	NM	470	443,668	476-93
LAKE	MILWAUKEE	WI	1003	444,990	817-52
LAKE CO.		IL	114	007,687	1-352
LAKE CO.		IN	157	442,935	217-317
LAKE CO.		OH	701	444,694	223-582
LAKE MILLS	JEFFERSON	WI	1000	444,987	105-28
LAKE PLEASANT	HAMILTON	NY	511	017,087	34-41
LAKE PRAIRIE TWP.	MARION	IA	187	442,962	561-87
LAKE TWP.	COOK	IL	103	007,676	1-6, 8, 121-22
LAKE TWP.	ALLEN	IN	135	007,748	317-30
LAKE TWP.	BUCHANAN	MO	393	014,873	172-80
LAKE TWP.	ASHLAND	OH	658	020,206	311-32
LAKE TWP.	LOGAN	OH	704	444,697	263-307
LAKE TWP.	STARK	OH	731	444,724	1-54
LAKE TWP.	WOOD	OH	741	444,734	419-22
LAKE TWP.	LUZERNE	PA	793	444,761	186-95
LAMAR CO.		TX	912	444,915	549-629
LAMAR TWP.	CLINTON	PA	768	444,736	72-101

CITY, COUNTY, TOWN, OR TOWNSHIP	COUNTY	STATE	NA NO. M432	GD NO.	PAGES
LAMARTINE	FOND DU LAC	WI	997	444,984	603-616
LAMASCO	VANDERBURGH	IN	176	442,954	817-51
LAMBERTVILLE	HUNTERDON	NJ	453	443,652	61-94
LAMOILLE	BUREAU	IL	99	007,672	387-97
LAMOILLE CO.		VT	925	444,924	107-388
LANCASTER	STEPHENSON	IL	129	442,917	509-528
LANCASTER	WORCESTER	MA	343	443,562	317-58
LANCASTER	COOS	NH	429	443,633	105-143
LANCASTER	ERIE	NY	499	017,075	325-415
LANCASTER CO.		PA	787	444,755	1-826
LANCASTER CO.		PA	786	444,756	1-795
LANCASTER CO.		PA	789	444,757	1-810
LANCASTER CO.		SC	854	444,817	261-424
LANCASTER CO.		VA	955	444,945	549-99
LANCASTER CORPORATION	FAIRFIELD	OH	677	444,670	541-623
LANCASTER, N.E. WARD	LANCASTER	PA	788	444,756	601-671
LANCASTER, N.W. WARD	LANCASTER	PA	788	444,756	499-600
LANCASTER, S.E. WARD	LANCASTER	PA	788	444,756	673-740
LANCASTER, S.W. WARD	LANCASTER	PA	788	444,756	741-95
LANCASTER TWP.	JEFFERSON	IN	154	442,932	517-52
LANCASTER TWP.	WELLS	IN	181	442,959	737-56
LANCASTER TWP.	LANCASTER	PA	788	444,756	479-98
LANCASTER VILLAGE	LANCASTER	SC	854	444,817	261-66
LANCE	HOUGHTON	MI	351	443,567	1-3
LANDAFF	GRAFTON	NH	431	443,635	210-32
LANDGROVE	BENNINGTON	VT	921	027,447	81-88
LANDIES CREEK	GONZALES	TX	910	024,889	667-70
LANDISBURG BOR.	PERRY	PA	805	444,773	717-26
LANESBORO	BERKSHIRE	MA	305	014,699	231-60
LANESBORO	SUSQUEHANNA	PA	829	444,797	465-73
LANESBORO DIST.	ANSON	NC	619	018,105	460-73
LANGDON	SULLIVAN	NH	441	443,645	417-30
L'ANGUILLE TWP.	PHILLIPS	AR	29	002,483	323-33
L'ANGUILLE TWP.	ST. FRANCIS	AR	30	442,876	94, 112-13, 118-21
LANIER TWP.	PREBLE	OH	723	444,716	606-645
LANNAHAPIE DIST.	STEWART	GA	82	442,891	157-72
LANSING	INGHAM	MI	351	443,567	101-130
LANSING	TOMPKINS	NY	605	444,321	322-402
LANSING	BROWN	WI	994	034,508	26-32
LANSINGBURG	RENSSELAER	NY	586	444,302	207-344
LAONA	WINNEBAGO	IL	134	442,922	637-48
LAPEER	LAPEER	MI	354	443,570	778-814
LAPEER	CORTLAND	NY	493	017,069	820-39
LAPEER CO.		MI	354	443,570	641-814
LAPILE TWP.	UNION	AR	30	442,876	527-32
LARUE CO.		KY	209	442,977	785-910
LAS CRUCES	VALENCIA	NM	470	443,668	597-606
LAS VEGAS	SAN MIGUEL	NM	469	443,667	1-38
LATHROPE TWP.	SUSQUEHANNA	PA	829	444,797	55-67
LATIMORE TWP.	ADAMS	PA	743	020,593	190-217
LAUDERDALE CO.		AL	7	002,349	459-726
LAUDERDALE CO.		MS	375	443,587	649-823
LAUDERDALE CO.		TN	886	444,842	493-575
LAUGHERY TWP.	DEARBORN	IN	141	007,754	851-76
LAUGHERY TWP.	RIPLEY	IN	169	442,947	377-97
LAURAMIE TWP.	TIPPECANOE	IN	175	442,953	344-84
LAUREL CO.		KY	209	442,977	1-98
LAUREL HILL DIST.	RICHMOND	NC	642	444,655	519-40

CITY, COUNTY, TOWN, OR TOWNSHIP	COUNTY	STATE	NA NO. M432	GD NO.	PAGES
LAUREL TWP.	FRANKLIN	IN	146	442,924	427-71, 473-74
LAUREL TWP.	HOCKING	OH	695	444,688	37-64
LAURENS	OTSEGO	NY	580	444,296	445-96
LAURENS CO.		GA	75	007,071	459-541
LAURENS CO.		SC	855	444,818	425-697
LAUSANNE TWP.	CARBON	PA	762	020,612	449-81
LAVACA CO.		TX	912	444,915	633-60
LAWRENCE	ESSEX	MA	314	014,708	293-490
LAWRENCE	VAN BUREN	MI	363	443,579	287-99
LAWRENCE	ST. LAWRENCE	NY	591	444,307	655-708
LAWRENCE	TIOGA	PA	830	444,798	303-328
LAWRENCE	BROWN	WI	994	034,508	124-29
LAWRENCE CO.		AL	8	002,350	729-932
LAWRENCE CO.		AR	27	002,481	379-495
LAWRENCE CO.		IL	115	007,688	1-147
LAWRENCE CO.		IN	158	442,936	647-940
LAWRENCE CO.		KY	209	442,977	99-248
LAWRENCE CO.		MS	375	443,587	825-909
LAWRENCE CO.		MO	404	443,612	533-643
LAWRENCE CO.		OH	701	444,694	583-956
LAWRENCE CO.		PA	790	444,758	1-518
LAWRENCE CO.		TN	886	444,842	579-774
LAWRENCE TWP.	MARION	IN	159	442,937	749-96
LAWRENCE TWP.	MERCER	NJ	454	443,653	261-304
LAWRENCE TWP.	LAWRENCE	OH	701	444,694	855-68
LAWRENCE TWP.	STARK	OH	731	444,724	145-99
LAWRENCE TWP.	TUSCARAWAS	OH	734	444,727	369-99
LAWRENCE TWP.	WASHINGTON	OH	738	444,731	963-82
LAWRENCE TWP.	CLEARFIELD	PA	768	444,736	599-612, 625-38
LAWRENCEBURG	DEARBORN	IN	141	007,754	515-76
LAWRENCEBURG TWP.	DEARBORN	IN	141	007,754	495-514, 579-82
LAWRENCEVILLE	ALLEGHENY	PA	747	020,597	683, 691-96, 711-13, 717-19, 721-24
LAWRENCEVILLE BOR.	ALLEGHENY	PA	747	020,597	684-90, 697-710, 714-16, 720-21
LAWRENCEVILLE BOR.	TIOGA	PA	830	444,798	239-50
LE BOUF TWP.	ERIE	PA	777	444,745	101-124
LE RAY	JEFFERSON	NY	515	017,091	213-300
LE ROY	CALHOUN	MI	348	014,810	208-228
LE ROY	GENESEE	NY	507	017,083	3-84
LE ROY	DODGE	WI	996	034,510	267-76
LE ROY TWP.	INGHAM	MI	351	443,567	186-92
LE ROY TWP.	BRADFORD	PA	756	020,606	127-49
LEACHVILLE DIST	BEAUFORT	NC	620	018,106	699-702
LEACOCK TWP.	LANCASTER	PA	789	444,757	195-241
LEAF RIVER TWP.	OGLE	IL	123	442,911	231-40
LEAKE CO.		MS	376	443,588	1-96
LEBANON	NEW LONDON	CT	48	442,880	23-68
LEBANON	ST. CLAIR	IL	126	442,914	994-1005
LEBANON	YORK	ME	275	443,512	37-90
LEBANON	GRAFTON	NH	430	443,634	1-52
LEBANON	MADISON	NY	527	017,103	231-74
LEBANON	WARREN	OH	737	444,730	42-91
LEBANON	WILSON	TN	901	444,857	732-57
LEBANON	RUSSELL	VA	975	444,965	693-69
LEBANON	DODGE	WI	996	034,510	276-301
LEBANON BOR.	LEBANON	PA	791	444,759	229-80
LEBANON CO.		PA	791	444,759	1-631

CITY, COUNTY, TOWN, OR TOWNSHIP	COUNTY	STATE	NA NO. M432	GD NO.	PAGES
LEBANON TWP.	LAWRENCE	AR	27	002,481	397-400
LEBANON TWP.	CLINTON	MI	349	014,811	75-79
LEBANON TWP.	HUNTERDON	NJ	453	443,652	475-525
LEBANON TWP.	MEIGS	OH	710	444,703	278-301
LEBANON TWP.	WAYNE	PA	835	444,803	109-119
LEDGE OF ROCKS DIST.	GRANVILLE	NC	631	444,644	299-317
LEDYARD	NEW LONDON	CT	49	442,881	121-58
LEDYARD	CAYUGA	NY	483	017,059	471-519
LEE	FULTON	IL	107	007,680	510-17
LEE	PENOBSCOT	ME	266	443,503	619-40
LEE	BERKSHIRE	MA	306	014,700	63-139
LEE	STRAFFORD	NH	440	443,644	417-37
LEE	ONEIDA	NY	564	444,280	511-83
LEE CENTRE TWP.	LEE	IL	116	007,689	213-20
LEE CO.		GA	75	007,071	543-615
LEE CO.		IL	116	007,689	151-290
LEE CO.		IA	186	442,961	561-1016
LEE CO.		VA	955	444,945	603-828
LEE TWP.	CALHOUN	MI	348	014,810	65-74
LEE TWP.	PLATTE	MO	410	443,618	691-725, 753
LEE TWP.	ATHENS	OH	660	020,208	341-63
LEE TWP.	CARROLL	OH	664	020,212	174-203
LEEDS	KENNEBEC	ME	258	443,495	621-60
LEES CREEK TWP.	CRAWFORD	AR	25	002,479	679-90
LEES MILL DIST.	WASHINGTON	NC	648	444,661	129-40, 158-60
LEESBURG	KOSCIUSKO	IN	156	442,934	699-703
LEESBURG	LOUDOUN	VA	957	444,947	687-716
LEESBURG TWP.	UNION	OH	736	444,729	35-51
LEESVILLE	CAMPBELL	VA	938	029,713	311
LEHIGH CO.		PA	792	444,760	1-801
LEHIGH TWP.	NORTHAMPTON	PA	803	444,771	623-78
LEHIGHTON	CARBON	PA	762	020,612	747-53
LEHMAN TWP.	LUZERNE	PA	793	444,761	172-85
LEHMAN TWP.	PIKE	PA	825	444,793	31-51
LEICESTER	WORCESTER	MA	342	443,561	621-77
LEICESTER	LIVINGSTON	NY	524	017,100	1-51
LEICESTER	ADDISON	VT	920	027,446	105-120
LEIDY TWP.	CLINTON	PA	768	444,736	186-92
LEIGHTON	ALLEGAN	MI	346	014,808	106-8
LEITERSBURG DIST.	WASHINGTON	MD	298	443,529	557-63
LEMINGTON	ESSEX	VT	923	444,922	743-47
LEMINTON DIST.	CALCASIEN PAR.	LA	230	009,697	731
LEMINTON RIVER	CADDO PARISH	LA	230	009,697	732-34
LEMITAR	VALENCIA	NM	470	443,668	655-64
LEMON TWP.	BUTLER	OH	663	020,211	895-940
LEMON TWP.	WYOMING	PA	838	444,806	93-99
LEMONT TWP.	COOK	IL	103	007,676	72-76
LEMPSTER	SULLIVAN	NH	441	443,645	109-130
LENAWEE CO.		MI	355	443,571	1-647
LENOIR CO.		NC	635	444,648	283-372
LENOX	BERKSHIRE	MA	306	014,700	1-39
LENOX	MACOMB	MI	357	443,573	169-84
LENOX	MADISON	NY	526	017,102	325-503
LENOX TWP.	ASHTABULA	OH	659	020,207	887-904
LENOX TWP.	SUSQUEHANNA	PA	829	444,797	153-87
LEOMINSTER	WORCESTER	MA	340	443,559	389-463
LEON	CATTARAUGUS	NY	479	017,055	73-105
LEON CO.		FL	59	006,715	65-143
LEON CO.		TX	912	444,915	663-94

CITY, COUNTY, TOWN, OR TOWNSHIP	COUNTY	STATE	NA NO. M432	GD NO.	PAGES	
LEON CREEK	BEXAR	TX	908	024,887	334-35	
LEON DIV.	LEON	TX	912	444,915	663-94	
LEONI	JACKSON	MI	352	443,568	725-55	
LEONIDAS TWP.	ST. JOSEPH	MI	362	443,578	639-59	
LEOPOLD TWP.	PERRY	IN	165	442,943	820-31	
LEROY	BOONE	IL	98	007,671	129-50	
LEROY TWP.	LAKE	OH	701	444,694	491-518	
LESLIE TWP.	INGHAM	MI	351	443,567	206-222	
LETART TWP.	MEIGS	OH	710	444,703	302-24	
LETCHER CO.		KY	209	442,977	249-310	
LETTERKENNY TWP.	FRANKLIN	PA	782	444,750	601-649	
LEVANT	PENOBSCOT	ME	265	443,502	187-230	
LEVERETT	FRANKLIN	MA	317	443,536	737-59	
LEVY CO.		FL	59	006,715	147-55	
LEWIS	ESSEX	NY	503	017,079	232-76,	316-19
LEWIS CO.		KY	210	442,978	311-481	
LEWIS CO.		MO	404	443,612	645-776	
LEWIS CO.		NY	523	017,099	1-606	
LEWIS CO.		OR	742	020,298	105-118	
LEWIS CO.		TN	887	444,843	777-865	
LEWIS CO.		VA	956	444,946	1-231	
LEWIS HUN.	SUSSEX	DE	55	442,884	85-127	
LEWIS TWP.	CLAY	IN	138	007,751	515-528	
LEWIS TWP.	BROWN	OH	662	020,210	885-949	
LEWIS TWP.	LYCOMING	PA	795	444,763	505-519	
LEWIS TWP.	NORTHUMBERLAND	PA	804	444,772	47-82	
LEWISBERRY BOR.	YORK	PA	840	444,808	669-74	
LEWISBORO	WESTCHESTER	NY	614	444,330	243-81	
LEWISBURG	CHAMPAIGN	OH	665	020,213	509-516	
LEWISBURG	PREBLE	OH	723	444,716	835-43	
LEWISBURG	UNION	PA	831	444,799	593-640	
LEWISTON	LINCOLN	ME	261	443,498	733-818	
LEWISTON	NIAGARA	NY	561	444,277	819-92	
LEWISTON BOR.	MIFFLIN	PA	797	444,765	473-543	
LEWISTOWN	SUSSEX	DE	55	442,884	87-111	
LEWISTOWN	FULTON	IL	107	007,680	347-84	
LEWISVILLE	HENRY	IN	151	442,929	495-99	
LEXINGTON	SCOTT	IN	171	442,949	374-80	
LEXINGTON	SOMERSET	ME	269	443,506	509-521	
LEXINGTON	MIDDLESEX	MA	325	443,544	365-410	
LEXINGTON	SANILAC	MI	363	443,579	9-36	
LEXINGTON	HOLMES	MS	373	443,585	489-93,	495-96
LEXINGTON	GREENE	NY	510	017,086	541-94	
LEXINGTON	ROCKBRIDGE	VA	973	444,963	917-46	
LEXINGTON BEAT	DALLAS	AL	4	002,346	523-26	
LEXINGTON CO.		SC	855	444,818	699-876	
LEXINGTON POLICE BEAT	HOLMES	MS	373	443,585	455-88,	494
LEXINGTON TWP.	SCOTT	IN	171	442,949	328-80	
LEXINGTON TWP.	STARK	OH	730	444,723	879-926	
LEYDEN	COOK	IL	103	007,676	295-312	
LEYDEN	FRANKLIN	MA	316	443,535	45-62	
LEYDEN	LEWIS	NY	523	017,099	145-98	
LIBERTY	ADAMS	IL	97	007,670	265-90	
LIBERTY	RANDOLPH	IL	125	442,913	112	
LIBERTY	UNION	IN	176	442,954	618, 622-31	
LIBERTY	WALDO	ME	271	443,508	75-101	
LIBERTY	JACKSON	MI	352	443,568	791-812	
LIBERTY	CLAY	MO	396	443,604	679-93	
LIBERTY	SULLIVAN	NY	603	444,319	193-256	

Liberty

CITY, COUNTY, TOWN, OR TOWNSHIP	COUNTY	STATE	NA NO. M432	GD NO.	PAGES
LIBERTY	FORSYTH	NC	630	444,643	511-13
LIBERTY	GUERNSEY	OH	684	444,677	877-81
LIBERTY	TRUMBULL	OH	733	444,726	243-74
LIBERTY	TIOGA	PA	830	444,798	529-64
LIBERTY CO.		GA	75	007,071	617-65
LIBERTY CO.		TX	912	444,915	697-735
LIBERTY TWP.	OUACHITA	AR	28	002,482	145-57
LIBERTY TWP.	ST. FRANCIS	AR	30	442,876	129-31
LIBERTY TWP.	WHITE	AR	31	442,877	921-28
LIBERTY TWP.	CRAWFORD	IN	139	007,752	65-77
LIBERTY TWP.	DELAWARE	IN	143	007,756	611-38
LIBERTY TWP.	FULTON	IN	146	442,924	879-94
LIBERTY TWP.	GRANT	IN	147	442,925	336-54
LIBERTY TWP.	HENDRICKS	IN	150	442,928	1-20, 165-87
LIBERTY TWP.	HENRY	IN	151	442,929	341-83
LIBERTY TWP.	PARKE	IN	164	442,942	358-72, 439-53
LIBERTY TWP.	PORTER	IN	165	442,943	307-312
LIBERTY TWP.	ST. JOSEPH	IN	171	442,949	150-66
LIBERTY TWP.	SHELBY	IN	172	442,950	621-47
LIBERTY TWP.	TIPTON	IN	176	442,954	495-98
LIBERTY TWP.	UNION	IN	176	442,954	559-82
LIBERTY TWP.	WABASH	IN	178	442,956	657-92
LIBERTY TWP.	WARREN	IN	178	442,956	57-78
LIBERTY TWP.	WELLS	IN	181	442,959	729-36
LIBERTY TWP.	CLINTON	IA	182	007,791	414-19
LIBERTY TWP.	JEFFERSON	IA	185	442,960	151-79
LIBERTY TWP.	JOHNSON	IA	185	442,960	263-72
LIBERTY TWP.	CLAY	MO	396	443,604	597-641
LIBERTY TWP.	MARION	MO	406	443,614	563-80
LIBERTY TWP.	STODDARD	MO	420	443,628	567-76
LIBERTY TWP.	WASHINGTON	MO	421	443,629	276-87
LIBERTY TWP.	ADAMS	OH	657	020,205	229-64
LIBERTY TWP.	BUTLER	OH	663	020,211	623-58
LIBERTY TWP.	CLINTON	OH	668	020,216	599-628
LIBERTY TWP.	CRAWFORD	OH	671	020,219	795-840
LIBERTY TWP.	DELAWARE	OH	675	020,223	409-433
LIBERTY TWP.	FAIRFIELD	OH	677	444,670	319-88
LIBERTY TWP.	GUERNSEY	OH	684	444,677	869-93
LIBERTY TWP.	HANCOCK	OH	692	444,685	777-98
LIBERTY TWP.	HARDIN	OH	692	444,685	359-70
LIBERTY TWP.	HENRY	OH	693	444,686	69-78
LIBERTY TWP.	HIGHLAND	OH	694	444,687	89-186
LIBERTY TWP.	JACKSON	OH	698	444,691	743-67
LIBERTY TWP.	KNOX	OH	700	444,693	130-62
LIBERTY TWP.	LICKING	OH	703	444,696	635-63
LIBERTY TWP.	LOGAN	OH	704	444,697	51-81
LIBERTY TWP.	MERCER	OH	710	444,703	569-73
LIBERTY TWP.	PUTNAM	OH	723	444,716	17-24
LIBERTY TWP.	ROSS	OH	725	444,718	557-84
LIBERTY TWP.	SENECA	OH	728	444,721	709, 785-819
LIBERTY TWP.	UNION	OH	736	444,729	129-58
LIBERTY TWP.	VAN WERT	OH	736	444,729	381-91
LIBERTY TWP.	WASHINGTON	OH	738	444,731	579-608
LIBERTY TWP.	WOOD	OH	741	444,734	251-56
LIBERTY TWP.	ADAMS	PA	743	020,593	265-82
LIBERTY TWP.	BEDFORD	PA	751	020,601	537-49
LIBERTY TWP.	CENTRE	PA	763	020,613	343-51
LIBERTY TWP.	MC KEAN	PA	795	444,763	96-110
LIBERTY TWP.	MONTOUR	PA	801	444,769	701-730

CITY, COUNTY, TOWN, OR TOWNSHIP	COUNTY	STATE	NA NO. M432	GD NO.	PAGES
LIBERTY TWP.	SUSQUEHANNA	PA	829	444,797	257-76
LIBERTYVILLE	LAKE	IL	114	007,687	83-100
LICK CREEK TWP.	DAVIS	IA	182	007,791	514-27
LICK CREEK TWP.	VAN BUREN	IA	189	442,964	669-88
LICK MOUNTAIN TWP.	CONWAY	AR	25	002,479	524-30
LICK TWP.	JACKSON	OH	698	444,691	561-85
LICKING CO.		OH	702	444,695	1-505
LICKING CO.		OH	703	444,696	507-964
LICKING CREEK TWP.	FULTON	PA	783	444,751	27-49
LICKING TWP.	BLACKFORD	IN	136	007,749	29-58
LICKING TWP.	LICKING	OH	702	444,695	203-236
LICKING TWP.	MUSKINGUM	OH	718	444,711	676-710
LIGONIER BOR.	WESTMORELAND	PA	836	444,804	1-10
LIGONIER TWP.	WESTMORELAND	PA	836	444,804	11-62
LIMA	ADAMS	IL	97	007,670	291-312
LIMA	WASHTENAW	MI	364	443,580	623-46
LIMA	LIVINGSTON	NY	525	017,101	365-422
LIMA	ROCK	WI	1005	444,992	717-36
LIMA	SHEBOYGAN	WI	1006	444,993	181-87, 268, 273-74
LIMA TWP.	CARROLL	IL	99	007,672	669-73
LIMA TWP.	ALLEN	OH	657	020,205	467-86
LIMA TWP.	LICKING	OH	703	444,696	577-601
LIMERICK	YORK	ME	276	443,513	485-520
LIMERICK TWP.	MONTGOMERY	PA	799	444,767	149-200
LIMESTONE CO.		AL	8	002,350	1-201
LIMESTONE CO.		TX	912	444,915	739-86
LIMESTONE TWP.	CLARION	PA	767	444,735	61-87, 89-95
LIMESTONE TWP.	LYCOMING	PA	795	444,763	553-76
LIMESTONE TWP.	MONTOUR	PA	801	444,769	733-51
LIMESTONE TWP.	UNION	PA	831	444,799	403-422
LIMESTONE TWP.	WARREN	PA	832	444,800	793-800
LIMINGTON	YORK	ME	276	443,513	555-605
LINCKLAEN	CHENANGO	NY	487	017,063	129-57
LINCOLN	PENOBSCOT	ME	266	443,503	681-713
LINCOLN	MIDDLESEX	MA	324	443,543	541-58
LINCOLN	GRAFTON	NH	431	443,635	209-210
LINCOLN	ADDISON	VT	920	027,446	561-86
LINCOLN CO.		GA	75	007,071	667-719
LINCOLN CO.		KY	210	442,978	482-648
LINCOLN CO.		ME	259	443,496	1-646
LINCOLN CO.		ME	260	443,497	647-944, 1-213
LINCOLN CO.		ME	261	443,498	215-885
LINCOLN CO.		MO	404	443,612	779-955
LINCOLN CO.		NC	636	444,649	373-508
LINCOLN CO.		TN	887	444,843	1-439
LINCOLN TWP.	MORROW	OH	716	444,709	35-56
LINCOLNVILLE	WALDO	ME	271	443,508	401-452
LINDEN	WASHTENAW	MI	364	443,580	621-22
LINDEN	IOWA	WI	999	444,986	688-711
LINDLEY	STEUBEN	NY	598	444,314	137-53
LINDSEY TWP.	BENTON	MO	392	014,872	619-38
LINN	WALWORTH	WI	1007	444,994	534-49
LINN CO.		IA	186	442,961	1-132
LINN CO.		MO	405	443,613	1-88
LINN CO.		OR	742	020,298	121-44
LINN TWP.	CEDAR	IA	182	007,791	230-39
LINN TWP.	OSAGE	MO	408	443,616	927-54
LINN TWP.	TANEY	MO	420	443,628	736-38, 752-60

CITY, COUNTY, TOWN, OR TOWNSHIP	COUNTY	STATE	NA NO. M432	GD NO.	PAGES
LINNEUS	AROOSTOOK	ME	248	009,718	74-89
LINNVILLE	LICKING	OH	702	444,695	237-41
LINTON TWP.	VIGO	IN	177	442,955	547-70
LINTON TWP.	COSHOCTON	OH	670	020,218	165-204
LISBON	NEW LONDON	CT	49	442,881	97-119
LISBON	KENDALL	IL	113	007,686	529-41
LISBON	LINCOLN	ME	261	443,498	820-57
LISBON	ANNE ARUNDEL	MD	278	013,195	1014-17
LISBON	GRAFTON	NH	431	443,635	1-45
LISBON	ST. LAWRENCE	NY	591	444,307	325-451
LISBON	WAUKESHA	WI	1009	444,996	810-34
LISLE	BROOME	NY	478	017,054	541-80
LITCHFIELD	LITCHFIELD	CT	42	003,070	505-600
LITCHFIELD	KENNEBEC	ME	257	443,494	667-716
LITCHFIELD	HILLSBORO	NH	434	443,638	165-75
LITCHFIELD	HERKIMER	NY	512	017,088	229-68
LITCHFIELD	MEDINA	OH	709	444,702	879-910
LITCHFIELD	BRADFORD	PA	757	020,607	403-429
LITCHFIELD CO.		CT	42	003,070	1-600
LITCHFIELD CO.		CT	43	003,071	601-820, 1-348
LITCHFIELD TWP.	HILLSDALE	MI	351	443,567	835-67
LITTLE BEAVER TWP.	LAWRENCE	PA	790	444,758	147-69
LITTLE BRITAIN TWP.	LANCASTER	PA	787	444,755	1-44
LITTLE CANADA PREC.	RAMSEY	MN	367	014,834	75-79
LITTLE COMPTON	NEWPORT	RI	842	022,265	579-614
LITTLE CREEK HUN.	KENT	DE	52	006,436	109-164
LITTLE FALLS	HERKIMER	NY	512	017,088	397-512
LITTLE MAHONOY TWP.	NORTHUMBERLAND	PA	804	444,772	608-615
LITTLE RIVER	PERQUIMANS	NC	640	444,653	771-89
LITTLE RIVER DIST.	CALDWELL	NC	623	018,109	85-100
LITTLE RIVER DIST.	WAKE	NC	647	444,660	323-40
LITTLE ROCK	PULASKI	AR	29	002,483	691-729
LITTLE ROCK	KENDALL	IL	113	007,686	439-60
LITTLE VALLEY	CATTARAUGUS	NY	479	017,055	377-409
LITTLESTOWN	ADAMS	PA	743	020,593	501-510
LITTLETON	MIDDLESEX	MA	323	443,542	299-322
LITTLETON	GRAFTON	NH	431	443,635	233-77, 279-80
LIVE OAK CREEK	GILLESPIE	TX	910	024,889	604-5
LIVE OAK DIST.	GILLESPIE	TX	910	024,889	603
LIVERMORE	OXFORD	ME	262	443,499	503-546
LIVERPOOL	FULTON	IL	107	007,680	674-90
LIVERPOOL	MEDINA	OH	709	444,702	763-815
LIVERPOOL BOR.	PERRY	PA	805	444,773	1119-34
LIVERPOOL TWP.	COLUMBIANA	OH	669	020,217	217-55
LIVERPOOL TWP.	PERRY	PA	805	444,773	1095-1118
LIVERTON	NEWPORT	RI	842	022,265	89-198
LIVINGSTON	SUMTER	AL	15	442,866	517-28, 545, 582-84, 592, 6 663-66, 693
LIVINGSTON	CLARK	IL	100	007,673	357-75
LIVINGSTON	COLUMBIA	NY	491	017,067	285-334
LIVINGSTON CO.		IL	116	007,689	291-328
LIVINGSTON CO.		KY	210	442,978	649-775
LIVINGSTON CO.		MI	356	443,572	651-976
LIVINGSTON CO.		MO	405	443,613	89-183
LIVINGSTON CO.		NY	524	017,100	607-832, 1-299
LIVINGSTON CO.		NY	525	017,101	301-783
LIVINGSTON PARISH		LA	233	443,476	671-732
LIVINGSTON TWP.	ESSEX	NJ	449	443,648	193-220

CITY, COUNTY, TOWN, OR TOWNSHIP	COUNTY	STATE	NA NO. M432	GD NO.	PAGES
LIVONIA	LIVINGSTON	NY	525	017,101	301-363
LIVONIA TWP.	WAYNE	MI	366	443,582	731-63
LLOYD	ULSTER	NY	608	444,324	567-616
LOCK HAVEN TWP.	CLINTON	PA	768	444,736	103-123
LOCKBOURNE	FRANKLIN	OH	680	444,673	345-50
LOCKE	CAYUGA	NY	483	017,059	173-208
LOCKE TWP.	ELKHART	IN	144	007,757	221-24
LOCKE TWP.	INGHAM	MI	351	443,567	178-85
LOCKPORT	WILL	IL	133	442,921	1-40
LOCKPORT	CARROLL	IN	137	007,750	693-95
LOCKPORT	LAFOURCHE PAR.	LA	232	443,475	626
LOCKPORT	NIAGARA	NY	560	444,276	1-294
LOCKPORT	LICKING	OH	702	444,695	88-91
LOCKPORT TWP.	TUSCARAWAS	OH	735	444,728	516-20
LOCKRIDGE TWP.	ST. JOSEPH	MI	362	443,578	777-804
LOCKWOODS FOLLY DIST.	JEFFERSON	IA	185	442,960	45-70
LOCUST BAYOU TWP.	BRUNSWICK	NC	621	018,107	337-48
LOCUST GROVE DIST.	OUACHITA	AR	28	002,482	55-66
LOCUST GROVE TWP.	SHELBY	IL	128	442,916	329-36
LODI	JEFFERSON	IA	185	442,960	204-225
LODI	WASHTENAW	MI	364	443,580	991-1020
LODI TWP.	SENECA	NY	597	444,313	1-55
LODI TWP.	BERGEN	NJ	442	016,529	357-83
LODI TWP.	ATHENS	OH	660	020,208	307-339
LODI VILLAGE	COLUMBIA	WI	994	034,508	297-300, 313-16
LODOMILLO TWP.	COLUMBIA	WI	994	034,508	313-14
LOGAN	CLAYTON	IA	182	007,791	300-306
LOGAN CO.		KY	211	442,979	1-269
LOGAN CO.		IL	116	007,689	331-454
LOGAN CO.		OH	704	444,697	1-482
LOGAN TWP.		VA	956	444,946	235-379
LOGAN TWP.	DEARBORN	IN	141	007,754	635-52
LOGAN TWP.	FOUNTAIN	IN	145	442,923	281-322
LOGAN TWP.	PIKE	IN	165	442,943	83-101
LOGAN TWP.	AUGLAIZE	OH	660	020,208	711-18
LOGAN TWP.	HOCKING	OH	695	444,688	1-20
LOGAN VILLE	CLINTON	PA	768	444,736	247-64
LOGTOWN	CLINTON	PA	768	444,736	277-88
LOMIRA	EL DORADO	CA	34	002,491	717-25
LONDON BRITAIN TWP.	DODGE	WI	996	034,510	251-66
LONDON GROVE TWP.	CHESTER	PA	764	020,614	251-68
LONDON TWP.	CHESTER	PA	764	020,614	165-98
LONDON TWP.	MONROE	MI	358	443,574	807-821
LONDON TWP.	CARROLL	OH	664	020,212	152-71
LONDON TWP.	MADISON	OH	706	444,699	391-403
LONDONDERRY	ROCKINGHAM	NH	437	443,641	561-602
LONDONDERRY	WINDHAM	VT	929	444,928	579-611
LONDONDERRY TWP.	GUERNSEY	OH	684	444,677	971-1008
LONDONDERRY TWP.	BEDFORD	PA	751	020,601	401-420
LONDONDERRY TWP.	CHESTER	PA	764	020,614	269-84
LONDONDERRY TWP.	DAUPHIN	PA	774	444,742	345-75, 397-434
LONDONDERRY TWP.	LEBANON	PA	791	444,759	594-631
LONG ACRE DIST.	BEAUFORT	NC	620	018,106	757-64
LONG BAR	SUTTER	CA	36	442,879	52
LONG CREEK TWP.	CARROLL	AR	25	002,479	261-67
LONG ISLAND PLANT.	HANCOCK	ME	254	443,491	329-32
LONG LAKE	HAMILTON	NY	511	017,087	51-55
LONG MEADOW	HAMPDEN	MA	318	443,537	1-32
LONG POINT PREC.	CUMBERLAND	IL	104	007,677	558-70

CITY, COUNTY, TOWN, OR TOWNSHIP	COUNTY	STATE	NA NO. M432	GD NO.	PAGES
LONG POND PLANTATION	SOMERSET	ME	269	443,506	545
LONG PRAIRIE	WAHNAHTA	MN	367	014,834	143-46
LONG'S BAR	BUTTE	CA	33	002,490	38-39
LONG'S BAR	SUTTER	CA	36	442,879	50
LONGSWAMP TWP.	BERKS	PA	753	020,603	103-149
LOOKOUT VALLEY	WALKER	GA	85	442,894	934-55
LORAIN CO.		OH	705	444,698	483-1122
LORAMIE TWP.	SHELBY	OH	729	444,722	472-98
LORAN	STEPHENSON	IL	129	442,917	691-706
LORDSTOWN	TRUMBULL	OH	733	444,726	383-414
LORRAINE	JEFFERSON	NY	516	017,092	713-48
LOS ANGELES	LOS ANGELES	CA	35	002,492	1-39
LOS ANGELES CO.		CA	35	002,492	1-85
LOS EN LAMES	VALENCIA	NM	470	443,668	539-44
LOS LENTES	VALENCIA	NM	470	443,668	735-40
LOS LOPES	VALENCIA	NM	470	443,668	641-45
LOS LUNAS	VALENCIA	NM	470	443,668	728-33
LOST CREEK TWP.	VIGO	IN	177	442,955	321-50
LOST CREEK TWP.	NEWTON	MO	408	443,616	723-33
LOST CREEK TWP.	MIAMI	OH	711	444,704	73-108
LOST MOUNTAIN DIST.	COBB	GA	66	007,062	285-304
LOUDON	MERRIMACK	NH	436	443,640	1-37
LOUDON TWP.	SENECA	OH	728	444,721	701-8, 710-44
LOUDOUN CO.		VA	957	444,947	323-716
LOUISA CO.		IA	187	442,962	135-259
LOUISA CO.		VA	957	444,947	721-883
LOUISBURG DIST.	FRANKLIN	NC	630	444,643	751-65, 768
LOUISIANA CITY	PIKE	MO	409	443,617	370-90
LOUISIANA TWP.	CHICOT	AR	25	002,479	362-64
LOUISVILLE	EL DORADO	CA	34	002,491	832-33, 899-906
LOUISVILLE	TUOLUMNE	CA	36	442,879	214, 217
LOUISVILLE	JEFFERSON	KY	206	442,974	1-459
LOUISVILLE	JEFFERSON	KY	207	442,975	461-552
LOUISVILLE	ST. LAWRENCE	NY	591	444,307	453-502
LOUISVILLE	MONROE	OH	712	444,705	889-91
LOUISVILLE, WARD 6	JEFFERSON	KY	207	442,975	553-59
LOUISVILLE, WARD 7	JEFFERSON	KY	207	442,975	663-764
LOUISVILLE, WARD 8	JEFFERSON	KY	207	442,975	767-907
LOWELL	JACKSON	IA	184	007,793	723-24
LOWELL	OXFORD	ME	262	443,499	241-69
LOWELL	PENOBSCOT	ME	266	443,503	580-88
LOWELL	MIDDLESEX	MA	327	443,546	395-1048
LOWELL	KENT	MI	353	443,569	626-32
LOWELL	ORLEANS	VT	925	444,924	155-70
LOWELL	DODGE	WI	996	034,510	169-88
LOWELL, WARD 5	MIDDLESEX	MA	326	443,545	189-329
LOWER ALBANY	FLOYD	IN	145	442,923	861-62
LOWER ALLEN TWP.	CUMBERLAND	PA	772	444,740	31-58
LOWER ALLOWAYS CREEK TWP.	SALEM	NJ	462	443,661	17-50
LOWER ALLSAINTS	GEORGETOWN	SC	853	444,816	629-34
LOWER AUGUSTA TWP.	NORTHUMBERLAND	PA	804	444,772	310-59
LOWER CHANCEFORD TWP.	YORK	PA	839	444,807	411-51
LOWER CHICHESTER TWP.	DELAWARE	PA	776	444,744	63-73
LOWER CREEK DIST	CALDWELL	NC	623	018,109	19-29, 46-57, 66, 80-83, 112-
LOWER DICKINSON TWP.	CUMBERLAND	PA	772	444,740	245-63
LOWER DUBLIN TWP.	PHILADELPHIA	PA	808	444,776	57-162
LOWER HEIDELBERG	BERKS	PA	753	020,603	891-942
LOWER MACUNGIE	LEHIGH	PA	792	444,760	269-324

CITY, COUNTY, TOWN, OR TOWNSHIP	COUNTY	STATE	NA NO. M432	GD NO.	PAGES
LOWER MAHANTONGO TWP.	SCHUYLKILL	PA	826	444,794	703-738
LOWER MAHONOY TWP.	NORTHUMBERLAND	PA	804	444,772	437-74
LOWER MAKEFIELD	BUCKS	PA	758	020,608	1-42
LOWER MERION TWP.	MONTGOMERY	PA	800	444,768	297-380
LOWER MT. BETHEL TWP.	NORTHAMPTON	PA	803	444,771	829-903
LOWER NAZARETH TWP.	NORTHAMPTON	PA	802	444,770	429-59
LOWER OKAW PREC.	COLES	IL	101	007,674	111-21
LOWER OXFORD TWP.	CHESTER	PA	764	020,614	105-137
LOWER PAXTON TWP.	DAUPHIN	PA	775	444,743	519-56
LOWER PENNS NECK	SALEM	NJ	462	443,661	51-85
LOWER PROVIDENCE TWP.	MONTGOMERY	PA	800	444,768	205-251
LOWER REGIMENT	CHATHAM	NC	624	444,637	879-1001
LOWER RICHLAND	ONSLOW	NC	639	444,652	293-308
LOWER ST. CLAIR TWP.	ALLEGHENY	PA	748	020,598	233-374
LOWER SALFORD TWP.	MONTGOMERY	PA	799	444,767	33-62
LOWER SOUTHWEST	ONSLOW	NC	639	444,652	263-75
LOWER SWATARA	DAUPHIN	PA	774	444,742	377-95, 321
LOWER TOWAMENSING	CARBON	PA	762	020,612	557-85
LOWER TWP.	FRANKLIN	AR	26	002,480	289-94
LOWER TWP.	CAPE MAY	NJ	446	016,533	121-60
LOWER TURKEYFOOT TWP.	SOMERSET	PA	828	444,796	435-50
LOWER WINDSOR TWP.	YORK	PA	840	444,808	401-449
LOWHILL TWP.	LEHIGH	PA	792	444,760	777-801
LOWNDES CO.		AL	8	002,350	205-379
LOWNDES CO.		GA	75	007,071	721-848
LOWNDES CO.		MS	376	443,588	97-258
LOWNDES DIST.	LOWNDES	AL	8	002,350	205-349
LOWVILLE	LEWIS	NY	523	017,099	329-85
LOWVILLE TWP.	COLUMBIA	WI	994	034,508	289-96
LOYALHANNA TWP.	WESTMORELAND	PA	836	444,804	855-84
LOYALSOCK TWP.	LYCOMING	PA	795	444,763	611-48
LOZETTO BOR.	CAMBRIA	PA	761	020,611	117-21
LUBEC	WASHINGTON	ME	272	443,509	319-86
LUCAS CO.		IA	187	442,962	263-74
LUCAS CO.		OH	706	444,699	1-306
LUCAS TWP.	CRITTENDEN	AR	25	002,479	759-60
LUCE TWP.	SPENCER	IN	172	442,950	65-90
LUDLOW	HAMPDEN	MA	319	443,538	613-41
LUDLOW	WINDSOR	VT	931	444,930	513-51
LUDLOW TWP.	WASHINGTON	OH	738	444,731	983-1008
LUMBER TWP.	CLINTON	PA	768	444,736	182-85
LUMBERLAND	SULLIVAN	NY	603	444,319	1-64
LUMBERTON	BURLINGTON	NJ	444	016,531	864-66, 868
LUMPKIN CO.		GA	76	007,072	1-216
LUMPKIN DIST.	STEWART	GA	82	442,891	173-209
LUNENBURG	WORCESTER	MA	340	443,559	233-63
LUNENBURG	ESSEX	VT	923	444,922	761-87
LUNENBURG CO.		VA	958	444,948	1-108
LUNENBURG PARISH	RICHMOND	VA	972	444,962	361-411
LURAY	LICKING	OH	702	444,695	275-77
LURGAN TWP.	FRANKLIN	PA	782	444,750	725-54
LUZERNE	WARREN	NY	609	444,325	174-204
LUZERNE CO.		PA	793	444,761	1-758
LUZERNE CO.		PA	794	444,762	759-1044, 1-360
LUZERNE TWP.	FAYETTE	PA	780	444,748	693-738
LYCOMING CO.		PA	795	444,763	363-1021
LYCOMING TWP.	LYCOMING	PA	795	444,763	521-51
LYKENS TWP.	CRAWFORD	OH	671	020,219	119-48
LYKENS TWP.	DAUPHIN	PA	775	444,743	768-800

CITY, COUNTY, TOWN, OR TOWNSHIP	COUNTY	STATE	NA NO. M432	GD NO.	PAGES
LYMAN	YORK	ME	274	443,511	287-320
LYMAN	GRAFTON	NH	431	443,635	123-57
LYME	NEW LONDON	CT	49	442,881	739-802
LYME	GRAFTON	NH	430	443,634	109-147
LYME	JEFFERSON	NY	514	017,090	697-766
LYME TWP.	HURON	OH	697	444,690	143-88
LYNCHBURG	CAMPBELL	VA	938	029,713	145-256
LYNDEBOROUGH	HILLSBORO	NH	433	443,637	733-56
LYNDON	WASHTENAW	MI	364	443,580	601-620
LYNDON	CATTARAUGUS	NY	480	017,056	796-821
LYNDON	CALEDONIA	VT	922	027,448	317-58
LYNDON	SHEBOYGAN	WI	1006	444,993	183-84, 189, 201-5, 249-54, 268-71, 275-77, 288-90, 306-7
LYNN	ESSEX	MA	311	014,705	427-768
LYNN	ST. CLAIR	MI	362	443,578	478-79
LYNN TWP.	POSEY	IN	166	442,944	423-54
LYNN TWP.	LEHIGH	PA	792	444,760	220-67
LYNNFIELD	ESSEX	MA	310	014,704	345-86
LYNNVILLE TWP.	OGLE	IL	123	442,911	151-54
LYON TWP.	OAKLAND	MI	360	443,576	569-95
LYONS	IONIA	MI	352	443,568	293-314
LYONS	WAYNE	NY	613	444,329	811-928
LYONS TWP.	COOK	IL	103	007,676	61-71, 109-119
LYONS TWP.	CLINTON	IA	182	007,791	383-94
LYONS VILLAGE	SAUK	WI	1006	444,993	37-38
LYSANDER	WINNEBAGO	IL	134	442,922	601-614
LYSANDER	ONONDAGA	NY	570	444,286	511-1050
LYTHOPOLIS	FAIRFIELD	OH	677	444,670	442-50
MC ARTHUR TWP.	LOGAN	OH	704	444,697	337-70
MC ARTHURSTOWN	VINTON	OH	736	444,729	465-76
MC CAMERON TWP.	MARTIN	IN	160	442,938	17-29
MC CONNELLSBURG	FULTON	PA	783	444,751	1-12
MC CRACKEN CO.		KY	211	442,979	271-397
MC CRACKINS DIST.	RUTHERFORD	TN	894	444,850	497-512
MC DONALD CO.		MO	405	443,613	185-236
MC DONALD TWP.	HARDIN	OH	692	444,685	371-84
MC DONOUGH	CHENANGO	NY	487	017,063	217-53
MC DONOUGH CO.		IL	116	007,689	455-636
MC DOWELL CO.		NC	636	444,649	509-627
MACEDON	WAYNE	NY	612	444,328	97-154
MC HENRY	MC HENRY	IL	117	007,690	973-1000
MC HENRY CO.		IL	117	007,690	637-1008
MACHIAS	WASHINGTON	ME	273	443,510	33-70
MACHIAS	CATTARAUGUS	NY	480	017,056	948-80
MACHIASPORT	WASHINGTON	ME	272	443,509	131-61
MACIAL	VALENCIA	NM	470	443,668	607-623
MC INTOSH CO.		GA	77	442,886	413-48
MACK COM	WALKER	GA	85	442,894	910-33
MC KEAN CO.		PA	795	444,763	1-126
MC KEAN TWP.	LICKING	OH	703	444,696	507-539
MC KEAN TWP.	ERIE	PA	778	444,746	747-92
MC KEESPORT BOR.	ALLEGHENY	PA	747	020,597	453-86
MACKENTIRE TWP.	LYCOMING	PA	795	444,763	605-610
MACKFORD	MARQUETTE	WI	1002	444,989	125-37

CITY, COUNTY, TOWN, OR TOWNSHIP	COUNTY	STATE	NA NO. M432	GD NO.	PAGES
MACKINAC CO.		MI	357	443,573	399-489
MACKINAW	MC LEON	IL	117	007,690	119-31, 133-39, 141-42, 144, 146-49
MC KINNEY	COLLIN	TX	910	024,889	13-14, 17
MC LEAN TWP.	SHELBY	OH	729	444,722	429-47
MC LEANSBORO	HAMILTON	IL	108	007,681	383-88
MC LEON CO.		IL	117	007,690	1-248
MC MINN CO.		TN	887	444,843	443-736
MC NAIRY CO.		TN	888	444,844	1-275
MC NORTONS DIST.	MUSCOGEE	GA	79	442,888	783-817
MACOMB	MACOMB	MI	357	443,573	53-71
MACOMB	ST. LAWRENCE	NY	589	444,305	103-132
MACOMB CO.		MI	357	443,573	1-384
MACON	BIBB	GA	61	007,057	265-345
MACON	BUREAU	IL	99	007,672	573-74
MACON	LENAWEE	MI	355	443,571	1-25
MACON CO.		AL	9	002,351	383-656
MACON CO.		GA	76	007,072	217-321
MACON CO.		IL	118	442,906	247-342
MACON CO.		MO	405	443,613	237-387
MACON CO.		NC	636	444,649	629-768
MACON CO.		TN	888	444,844	279-426
MACON DIST.	MACON	IL	118	442,906	247-334
MACOUPIN CO.		IL	118	442,906	343-656
MC SHERRYSTOWN	ADAMS	PA	743	020,593	561-65
MC VEYTOWN BOR.	MIFFLIN	PA	797	444,765	723-37
MAD RIVER TWP.	CHAMPAIGN	OH	665	020,213	863-910
MAD RIVER TWP.	CLARK	OH	666	020,214	127-71
MAD RIVER TWP.	MONTGOMERY	OH	713	444,706	165-200
MADAWASKA PLANTATION	AROOSTOOK	ME	248	009,718	290-320
MADBURY	STRAFFORD	NH	440	443,644	477-88
MADISON	NEW HAVEN	CT	45	003,073	267-310
MADISON	JEFFERSON	IN	154	442,932	58-62
MADISON	SOMERSET	ME	269	443,506	103-145
MADISON	LENAWEE	MI	355	443,571	403-460
MADISON	MADISON	NY	527	017,103	1-6, 24-49, 105-6, 133-56
MADISON	PERRY	OH	719	444,712	747-59
MADISON	SANDUSKY	OH	726	444,719	35-45
MADISON	DANE	WI	995	034,509	632-40
MADISON CITY	JEFFERSON	IN	154	442,932	63-150
MADISON CO.		AL	9	002,351	659-954
MADISON CO.		AR	27	002,481	497-620
MADISON CO.		FL	59	006,715	159-223
MADISON CO.		GA	76	007,072	323-412
MADISON CO.		IL	119	442,907	657-1173
MADISON CO.		IN	158	442,936	1-300
MADISON CO.		IA	187	442,962	277-305
MADISON CO.		KY	211	442,979	399-650
MADISON CO.		MS	376	443,588	259-362
MADISON CO.		MO	405	443,613	389-516
MADISON CO.		NY	526	017,102	1-544
MADISON CO.		NY	527	017,103	545-786, 1-274
MADISON CO.		OH	706	444,699	319-586
MADISON CO.		TN	889	444,845	429-747
MADISON CO.		VA	958	444,948	111-222
MADISON PARISH		LA	233	443,476	733-68
MADISON TWP.	SEVIER	AR	30	442,876	416-23

CITY, COUNTY, TOWN, OR TOWNSHIP	COUNTY	STATE	NA NO. M432	GD NO.	PAGES
MADISON TWP.	ALLEN	IN	135	007,748	331-44
MADISON TWP.	CLINTON	IN	139	007,752	685-701
MADISON TWP.	DAVIESS	IN	140	007,753	346-68
MADISON TWP.	JAY	IN	153	442,931	595-610
MADISON TWP.	JEFFERSON	IN	154	442,932	1-50, 267-70, 283, 285-94, 314
MADISON TWP.	MONTGOMERY	IN	161	442,939	890-904
MADISON TWP.	MORGAN	IN	162	442,940	187-207
MADISON TWP.	PIKE	IN	165	442,943	1-70, 81-82
MADISON TWP.	PUTNAM	IN	167	442,945	957-85
MADISON TWP.	ST. JOSEPH	IN	171	442,949	271-80
MADISON TWP.	TIPTON	IN	176	442,954	521-39
MADISON TWP.	JOHNSON	MO	403	443,611	98-113
MADISON TWP.	BUTLER	OH	663	020,211	659-712
MADISON TWP.	CLARK	OH	666	020,214	281-92, 304-316
MADISON TWP.	COLUMBIANA	OH	669	020,217	511-44
MADISON TWP.	FAIRFIELD	OH	677	444,670	923-50
MADISON TWP.	FAYETTE	OH	678	444,671	79-99
MADISON TWP.	FRANKLIN	OH	680	444,673	401-460
MADISON TWP.	GUERNSEY	OH	684	444,677	781-618
MADISON TWP.	HANCOCK	OH	692	444,685	123-38
MADISON TWP.	HIGHLAND	OH	694	444,687	265-316
MADISON TWP.	JACKSON	OH	698	444,691	485-521
MADISON TWP.	LAKE	OH	701	444,694	223-94
MADISON TWP.	LICKING	OH	702	444,695	177-201
MADISON TWP.	MONTGOMERY	OH	714	444,707	803-842
MADISON TWP.	MUSKINGUM	OH	718	444,711	571-95
MADISON TWP.	PICKAWAY	OH	720	444,713	69-90
MADISON TWP.	RICHLAND	OH	724	444,717	187-309
MADISON TWP.	SCIOTO	OH	727	444,720	497-529
MADISON TWP.	WILLIAMS	OH	741	444,734	65-70
MADISON TWP.	ARMSTRONG	PA	749	020,599	501-528
MADISON TWP.	CLARION	PA	767	444,735	181-213
MADISON TWP.	COLUMBIA	PA	769	444,737	705-721
MADISON TWP.	LUZERNE	PA	793	444,761	441-54
MADISON TWP.	MONTOUR	PA	801	444,769	761-90
MADISON TWP.	PERRY	PA	805	444,773	865-95
MADISON VILLAGE	DANE	WI	995	034,509	641-77
MADISON, WARD 4	JEFFERSON	IN	154	442,932	167-80
MADISON, WARD 5	JEFFERSON	IN	154	442,932	181-97
MADISON, WARD 6	JEFFERSON	IN	154	442,932	198-218
MADISON, WARD 7	JEFFERSON	IN	154	442,932	219-32
MADISON, WARD 8	JEFFERSON	IN	154	442,932	233-66
MADRID	FRANKLIN	ME	253	009,723	309-318
MADRID	ST. LAWRENCE	NY	591	444,307	503-618
MAGAZINE TWP.	YELL	AR	31	442,877	955-65
MAGNOLIA	ROCK	WI	1005	444,992	569-83
MAGOTHA BAY	NORTHAMPTON	VA	965	444,955	546-54
MAHASKA CO.		IA	187	442,962	309-452
MAHONING CO.		OH	707	444,700	631-1310
MAHONING TWP.	CARBON	PA	762	020,612	747-83
MAHONING TWP.	LAWRENCE	PA	790	444,758	1-44
MAHONING TWP.	MONTOUR	PA	801	444,769	657-77
MAIDENCREEK TWP.	BERKS	PA	754	020,604	385-416
MAIDSTONE	ESSEX	VT	923	444,922	793-98
MAINE	COOK	IL	103	007,676	281-94
MAINE	BROOME	NY	478	017,054	805-848
MAINE TWP.	COLUMBIA	PA	769	444,737	536-49
MAJORS DIST.	MARION	GA	77	442,886	581-83

CITY, COUNTY, TOWN, OR TOWNSHIP	COUNTY	STATE	NA NO. M432	GD NO.	PAGES	
MALAGA	MONROE	OH	712	444,705	457-60	
MALAGA TWP.	MONROE	OH	712	444,705	452-98	
MALDEN	MIDDLESEX	MA	323	443,542	723-806	
MALLARD CREEK DIST.	MECKLENBURG	NC	637	444,650	106-121	
MALLORY TWP.	CLAYTON	IA	182	007,791	273-80	
MALONE	FRANKLIN	NY	505	017,081	1-109	
MALTA	SARATOGA	NY	592	444,308	133-65	
MALTA	MORGAN	OH	715	444,708	215-27	
MALTA TWP.	MORGAN	OH	715	444,708	215-58	
MAMAKATING	SULLIVAN	NY	603	444,319	509-606	
MAMARONECK	WESTCHESTER	NY	615	444,331	295-317	
MANALAPAN TWP.	MONMOUTH	NJ	457	443,656	509-554	
MANATEE SET.	HILLSBOROUGH	FL	58	006,714	512-15	
MANAYUNK, LOWER WARD	PHILADELPHIA	PA	808	444,776	239-309	
MANAYUNK, UPPER WARD	PHILADELPHIA	PA	808	444,776	163-238	
MANCHESTER	HARTFORD	CT	41	003,069	809-872	
MANCHESTER	BOONE	IL	98	007,671	151-71	
MANCHESTER	SCOTT	IL	128	442,916	104-9	
MANCHESTER	CARROLL	MD	289	443,520	655-67	
MANCHESTER	ESSEX	MA	315	443,534	661-700	
MANCHESTER	WASHTENAW	MI	364	443,580	801-831	
MANCHESTER	HILLSBORO	NH	432	443,636	1-332	
MANCHESTER	ONTARIO	NY	572	444,288	603-676	
MANCHESTER	ADAMS	OH	657	020,205	178-85	
MANCHESTER	WAYNE	PA	835	444,803	161-78	
MANCHESTER	COFFEE	TN	875	024,566	83-85	
MANCHESTER	BENNINGTON	VT	921	027,447	225-67	
MANCHESTER BOR.	ALLEGHENY	PA	744	020,594	535-78	
MANCHESTER TWP.	DALLAS	AR	26	002,480	64-75	
MANCHESTER TWP.	DEARBORN	IN	141	007,754	693-759	
MANCHESTER TWP.	PASSAIC	NJ	461	443,660	739-808	
MANCHESTER TWP.	MORGAN	OH	715	444,708	43-74	
MANCHESTER TWP.	YORK	PA	840	444,808	451-516	
MANCHESTER VILLAGE	SAUK	WI	1006	444,993	38-40	
MANDARIN DIST.	DUVAL	FL	58	006,714	203-7	
MANHATTAN BAR	SUTTER	CA	36	442,879	64-73	
MANHATTAN TWP.	LUCAS	OH	706	444,699	153-64	
MANHEIM	HERKIMER	NY	513	017,089	709-756	
MANHEIM BOR.	LANCASTER	PA	787	444,755	679-97	
MANHEIM TWP.	LANCASTER	PA	787	444,755	629-78	
MANHEIN TWP.	YORK	PA	839	444,807	623-67	
MANITOWOC	MANITOWOC	WI	1002	444,989	45-62	
MANITOWOC CO.		WI	1002	444,989	17-105	
MANITOWOC RAPIDS	MANITOWOC	WI	1002	444,989	41-44,	63-81
MANKAHTA CO.		MN	367	014,834	35-39	
MANLIUS	LA SALLE	IL	115	007,688	623-37	
MANLIUS	ALLEGAN	MI	346	014,808	13-14	
MANLIUS	ONONDAGA	NY	567	444,283	1-150	
MANNINGTON TWP.	SALEM	NJ	462	443,661	87-139	
MANON BEAT	PERRY	AL	12	002,354	729-42	
MANOR TWP.	ARMSTRONG	PA	749	020,599	587-605	
MANOR TWP.	LANCASTER	PA	787	444,755	287-401	
MANSFIELD	TOLLAND	CT	50	442,882	431-90	
MANSFIELD	BRISTOL	MA	307	014,701	105-147	
MANSFIELD	CATTARAUGUS	NY	480	017,056	591-608,	713-20
MANSFIELD TWP.	BURLINGTON	NJ	443	016,530	363-433	
MANSFIELD TWP.	WARREN	NJ	465	443,664	565-603	
MANTUA TWP.	PORTAGE	OH	722	444,715	105-132	
MANZANO	VALENCIA	NM	470	443,668	746-55	

CITY, COUNTY, TOWN, OR TOWNSHIP	COUNTY	STATE	NA NO. M432	GD NO.	PAGES
MAPLE GROVE	BARRY	MI	346	014,808	257-60
MAQUOKETA	JACKSON	IA	184	007,793	718-21
MAQUOKETA TWP.	JACKSON	IA	184	007,793	637, 656-58, 677-78, 708, 725
MAQUON	KNOX	IL	113	007,686	885-87
MARATHON	LAPEER	MI	354	443,570	773-77
MARATHON	CORTLAND	NY	493	017,069	451-78
MARATHON CO.		WI	1002	444,989	109-121
MARBLEHEAD	ESSEX	MA	310	014,704	197-344
MARBLETOWN	ULSTER	NY	607	444,323	309-402
MARCELLON TWP.	COLUMBIA	WI	994	034,508	403-413
MARCELLUS	ONONDAGA	NY	568	444,284	659-724
MARCELLUS TWP.	CASS	MI	349	014,811	713-19
MARCUS HOOK BOR.	DELAWARE	PA	776	444,744	37-48
MARCY	ONEIDA	NY	566	444,282	549-93
MARENGO	MC HENRY	IL	117	007,690	637-62
MARENGO	IOWA	IA	184	007,793	559-60
MARENGO	CALHOUN	MI	348	014,810	311-35
MARENGO CO.		AL	10	002,352	1-182
MARENGO TWP.	IOWA	IA	164	007,793	539-46
MARGARETTA TWP.	ERIE	OH	676	338,044	219-56
MARIAVILLE	HANCOCK	ME	255	443,492	843-51
MARIETTA	COBB	GA	66	007,062	305-332
MARIETTA	FULTON	IL	107	007,680	577-87
MARIETTA	LANCASTER	PA	787	444,755	775-826
MARIETTA DIST.	COBB	GA	66	007,062	177-205, 246-52, 459-71
MARIETTA TWP.	WASHINGTON	OH	738	444,731	427-53
MARIETTA, WARD 1	WASHINGTON	OH	738	444,731	390-426
MARIETTA, WARD 2	WASHINGTON	OH	738	444,731	351-89
MARIN CO.		CA	35	002,492	89-96
MARINE PREC.	WASHINGTON	MN	367	014,834	149-51
MARINE SETTLEMENT	MADISON	IL	119	442,907	1103-18, 1122-2,
MARINE TOWN	MADISON	IL	119	442,907	1119-21
MARINETTE DIST.	BROWN	WI	994	034,508	9-15
MARION	PERRY	AL	12	002,354	555-74
MARION	DE WITT	IL	104	007,677	886-87
MARION	WASHINGTON	ME	272	443,509	175-79
MARION	WAYNE	NY	612	444,328	427-70
MARION	MC DOWELL	NC	636	444,649	621-24
MARION	MARION	OH	708	444,701	131-61
MARION CO.		AL	10	002,352	183-350
MARION CO.		AR	26	002,482	621-73
MARION CO.		FL	59	006,715	227-77
MARION CO.		GA	77	442,886	449-607
MARION CO.		IL	119	442,907	1-160
MARION CO.		IN	159	442,937	301-896
MARION CO.		IA	187	442,962	455-587
MARION CO.		KY	212	442,980	651-858
MARION CO.		MS	376	443,588	363-416
MARION CO.		MO	406	443,614	517-744
MARION CO.		OH	708	444,701	1-306
MARION CO.		OR	742	020,298	147-212
MARION CO.		SC	856	444,819	1-242
MARION CO.		TN	889	444,845	751-892
MARION CO.		VA	958	444,948	225-474
MARION TWP.	CRAWFORD	AR	25	002,479	595-609
MARION TWP.	DREW	AR	26	002,480	151-64
MARION TWP.	OUACHITA	AR	28	002,482	109-121

CITY, COUNTY, TOWN, OR TOWNSHIP	COUNTY	STATE	NA NO. M432	GD NO.	PAGES	
MARION TWP.	WHITE	AR	31	442,877	911-20	
MARION TWP.	OGLE	IL	123	442,911	173-82,	184-88
MARION TWP.	ALLEN	IN	135	007,748	369-95	
MARION TWP.	DECATUR	IN	142	007,755	167-206	
MARION TWP.	GRANT	IN	147	442,925	536-52	
MARION TWP.	HENDRICKS	IN	150	442,928	133-64	
MARION TWP.	JASPER	IN	152	442,930	485-506	
MARION TWP.	JENNINGS	IN	155	442,933	783-95,	803-821
MARION TWP.	LAWRENCE	IN	158	442,936	671-720	
MARION TWP.	MONROE	IN	161	442,939	573-80	
MARION TWP.	OWEN	IN	164	442,942	267-90	
MARION TWP.	PUTNAM	IN	167	442,945	899-930	
MARION TWP.	SHELBY	IN	172	442,950	767-86	
MARION TWP.	DAVIS	IA	182	007,791	541-51	
MARION TWP.	HENRY	IA	184	007,793	443-54	
MARION TWP.	LIVINGSTON	MI	356	443,572	651-71	
MARION TWP.	BUCHANAN	MO	393	014,873	98-116	
MARION TWP.	NEWTON	MO	408	443,616	703-711	
MARION TWP.	TANEY	MO	420	443,628	741-47	
MARION TWP.	ALLEN	OH	657	020,205	647-71	
MARION TWP.	CLINTON	OH	668	020,216	437-62	
MARION TWP.	FAYETTE	OH	678	444,671	101-121	
MARION TWP.	HANCOCK	OH	692	444,685	895-918	
MARION TWP.	HARDIN	OH	692	444,685	387-96	
MARION TWP.	HENRY	OH	693	444,686	87-88	
MARION TWP.	HOCKING	OH	695	444,688	823-64	
MARION TWP.	MARION	OH	708	444,701	131-84	
MARION TWP.	MERCER	OH	710	444,703	435-68	
MARION TWP.	MORGAN	OH	715	444,708	293-337	
MARION TWP.	PIKE	OH	721	444,714	523-44	
MARION TWP.	BEAVER	PA	750	020,600	353-64	
MARION TWP.	BERKS	PA	752	020,602	1-37	
MARION TWP.	CENTRE	PA	763	020,613	503-517	
MARION TWP.	GREENE	PA	783	444,751	469-89	
MARIPOSA CO.		CA	35	002,492	99-204	
MARKS CREEK DIST.	WAKE	NC	647	444,660	311-22	
MARLBORO	WINDHAM	VT	929	444,928	213-35	
MARLBORO CO.		SC	856	444,819	243-366	
MARLBORO TWP.	STARK	OH	730	444,723	827-77	
MARLBORO TWP.	MONTGOMERY	PA	799	444,767	663-90	
MARLBOROUGH	HARTFORD	CT	41	003,069	873-903	
MARLBOROUGH	MIDDLESEX	MA	324	443,543	869-939	
MARLBOROUGH	CHESHIRE	NH	427	014,940	303-327	
MARLBOROUGH	ULSTER	NY	607	444,323	519-78	
MARLBOROUGH DIST.	PRINCE GEORGES	MD	295	443,526	137-57,	179-86
MARLBOROUGH TWP.	MONMOUTH	NJ	456	443,655	469-505	
MARLBOROUGH TWP.	DELAWARE	OH	675	020,223	707-720	
MARLOW	CHESHIRE	NH	428	014,941	735-51	
MARLTON	BURLINGTON	NJ	444	016,531	977-86	
MARPLE TWP.	DELAWARE	PA	776	444,744	399-419	
MARQUETTE	MARQUETTE	MI	357	443,573	387-90	
MARQUETTE	MARQUETTE	WI	1002	444,989	192-97	
MARQUETTE CO.		MI	357	443,573	387-90	
MARQUETTE CO.		WI	1002	444,989	125-336	
MARRS HILL TWP.	WASHINGTON	AR	31	442,877	657-72	
MARRS TWP.	POSEY	IN	166	442,944	467-501	
MARS HILL PLANT.	AROOSTOOK	ME	248	009,718	234	
MARSEILLES TWP.	WYANDOT	OH	741	444,734	705-717	
MARSH DIST.	SURRY	NC	646	444,659	664-77	

CITY, COUNTY, TOWN, OR TOWNSHIP	COUNTY	STATE	NA NO. M432	GD NO.	PAGES
MARSH ISLAND	LINCOLN	ME	260	443,497	75
MARSHALL	CALHOUN	MI	348	014,810	243-310
MARSHALL	ONEIDA	NY	562	444,278	303-353
MARSHALL	HARRISON	TX	911	024,890	101-119
MARSHALL		AL	10	002,352	353-548
MARSHALL CO.		IL	120	442,908	161-284
MARSHALL CO.		IN	160	442,938	897-1026
MARSHALL CO.		IA	187	442,962	591-99
MARSHALL CO.		KY	212	442,980	859-983
MARSHALL CO.		MS	377	443,589	417-758
MARSHALL CO.		TN	890	444,846	1-303
MARSHALL CO.		VA	959	444,949	477-719
MARSHALL DIST.	CLARK	IL	100	007,673	325-56
MARSHALL PREC.	CLARK	IL	100	007,673	338-56
MARSHALL TWP.	PLATTE	MO	410	443,618	644-66, 671-90
MARSHALL TWP.	HIGHLAND	OH	694	444,687	657-85
MARSHALL'S ISLAND	HANCOCK	ME	254	443,491	334
MARSHFIELD	WASHINGTON	ME	273	443,510	89-95
MARSHFIELD	PLYMOUTH	MA	332	443,551	303-346
MARSHFIELD	WASHINGTON	VT	928	444,927	295-321
MARSHFIELD	ALLEGAN	MI	346	014,808	119-26
MARTIN		IN	160	442,938	1-152
MARTIN CO.		NC	636	444,649	769-886
MARTIN CO.		GA	76	007,072	117-22
MARTIN'S FORD DIST.	LUMPKIN	NH	429	443,633	309
MARTIN'S LOCATION	COOS	IN	179	442,957	603-6
MARTINSBURG	WASHINGTON	NY	523	017,099	201-264
MARTINSBURG	LEWIS	OH	678	444,671	234-37
MARTINSBURG	FAYETTE	OH	700	444,693	748-49
MARTINSBURG	KNOX	VA	936	029,711	661-706
MARTINSBURG	BERKELEY	PA	755	020,605	149-59
MARTINSBURG BOR.	BLAIR	IL	100	007,673	505-532
MARTINSVILLE	CLARK	IN	162	442,940	87-92
MARTINSVILLE	MORGAN	OH	703	444,696	757-80
MARY ANN TWP.	LICKING	NY	579	444,295	269-320
MARYLAND	OTSEGO	OH	736	444,729	72-86
MARYSVILLE	UNION	ME	248	009,718	321-23
MASARDIS	AROOSTOOK	IL	126	442,914	529-37
MASCOUTAH	ST. CLAIR	MA	304	014,698	847-49
MASHPEE	BARNSTABLE	IL	108	007,681	355-66
MASON	GRUNDY	ME	262	443,499	475-77
MASON	OXFORD	NH	433	443,637	587-625
MASON	HILLSBORO	IL	120	442,908	285-426
MASON CO.		KY	212	442,980	1-337
MASON CO.		MI	357	443,573	393-95
MASON CO.		VA	959	444,949	723-887
MASON CO.		MI	349	014,811	517-32
MASON TWP.	CASS	MO	406	443,614	604-8
MASON TWP.	MARION	OH	701	444,694	709-735
MASON TWP.	LAWRENCE	NY	494	017,070	177-214
MASONVILLE	DELAWARE	IL	120	442,908	427-524
MASSAC CO.		NY	591	444,307	708-778
MASSENA	ST. LAWRENCE	PA	787	444,755	209-286
MASTIC TWP.	LANCASTER	TX	912	444,915	789-811
MATAGORDA CO.		TX	909	024,888	484-86
MATAGORDA ISLAND	CALHOUN	PA	775	444,743	643-45
MATAMORAS BOR.	DAUPHIN	VA	960	444,950	1-94
MATHEWS CO.		CA	34	002,491	681-84, 689-92
MATHINIAS CREEK	EL DORADO				699-706

CITY, COUNTY, TOWN, OR TOWNSHIP	COUNTY	STATE	NA NO. M432	GD NO.	PAGES	
MATINICUS ISLES	LINCOLN	ME	259	443,496	245-51	
MATINICUS LIGHT	HANCOCK	ME	254	443,491	430	
MATTAMISCONTIS	PENOBSCOT	ME	266	443,503	573-74	
MATTAMUSKEET DIST.	HYDE	NC	634	444,647	683-740	
MATTISON TWP.	BRANCH	MI	347	014,809	825-36	
MAUCH CHUNK BOR.	CARBON	PA	762	020,612	685-745	
MAUCH CHUNK TWP.	CARBON	PA	762	020,612	595-683	
MAUMEE TWP.	ALLEN	IN	135	007,748	407-9	
MAURICE RIVER TWP.	CUMBERLAND	NJ	446	016,533	161-214	
MAURY CO.		TN	890	444,846	307-710	
MAWVILLE TWP.	PULASKI	AR	29	002,483	633-39	
MAXATAWNY TWP.	BERKS	PA	753	020,603	151-92	
MAXATAWNY TWP.	BERKS	PA	754	020,604	359-84	
MAXFIELD	PENOBSCOT	ME	266	443,503	562-66	
MAXVILLE	SPENCER	IN	172	442,950	179-80	
MAY DIST.	RUTHERFORD	TN	894	444,850	423-40	
MAYFIELD	SOMERSET	ME	269	443,506	467-72	
MAYFIELD	FULTON	NY	506	017,082	1-59	
MAYFIELD	CUYAHOGA	OH	673	020,221	687-714	
MAYFIELD TWP.	DE KALB	IL	104	007,677	597-610	
MAYSVILLE	MASON	KY	212	442,980	61-112,	207-244
MAYTOWN	LANCASTER	PA	788	444,756	149-64	
MEAD TWP.	BELMONT	OH	661	020,209	39-78	
MEAD TWP.	CRAWFORD	PA	770	444,738	295-346	
MEAD TWP.	WARREN	PA	832	444,800	735-38	
MEADE CO.		KY	213	442,981	339-478	
MEADOWS DIST.	STOKES	NC	645	444,658	293-303	
MEADVILLE BOR.	CRAWFORD	PA	770	444,738	233-94	
MECCA	TRUMBULL	OH	733	444,726	671-91	
MECHANIC TWP.	HOLMES	OH	696	444,689	315-54	
MECHANICS VILLAGE	JEFFERSON PAR.	LA	232	443,475	163-67	
MECHANICSBURG	SANGAMON	IL	127	442,915	595-99	
MECHANICSBURG	CHAMPAIGN	OH	665	020,213	475-92	
MECHANICSBURG	CUMBERLAND	PA	773	444,741	433-55	
MECHANICSTOWN	DAUPHIN	PA	774	444,742	241-44	
MECHANICSVILLE DIST.	RUTHERFORD	TN	894	444,850	389-407	
MECKLENBURG CO.		NC	637	444,650	1-204	
MECKLENBURG CO.		VA	960	444,950	97-292	
MEDDYBEMPS	WASHINGTON	ME	273	443,510	241-47	
MEDFIELD	NORFOLK	MA	331	443,550	699-721	
MEDFORD	MIDDLESEX	MA	323	443,542	807-896	
MEDFORD	BURLINGTON	NJ	444	016,531	903, 906-922	
MEDFORD TWP.	BURLINGTON	NJ	444	016,531	864-939	
MEDIA BOR.	DELAWARE	PA	776	444,744	191-98	
MEDINA	LENAWEE	MI	355	443,571	238-76	
MEDINA	DANE	WI	995	034,509	835-46	
MEDINA CO.		OH	709	444,702	307-910	
MEDINA CO.		TX	912	444,915	815-38	
MEDINA RIVER	BEXAR	TX	908	024,887	291-98	
MEDINA RIVER	MEDINA	TX	912	444,915	833-38	
MEDINA TOWN	MEDINA	OH	709	444,702	425-49	
MEDINA TWP.	WARREN	IN	178	442,956	125-39	
MEDINA TWP.	MEDINA	OH	709	444,702	399-423	
MEDLEY'S EL. DIST.	MONTGOMERY	MD	295	443,526	811-53	
MEDWAY	NORFOLK	MA	331	443,550	631-97	
MEEME	MANITOWOC	WI	1002	444,989	90-94	
MEHOOPANY TWP.	WYOMING	PA	838	444,806	135-53	
MEIGS CO.		OH	710	444,703	1-434	
MEIGS CO.		TN	890	444,846	713-820	

CITY, COUNTY, TOWN, OR TOWNSHIP	COUNTY	STATE	NA NO. M432	GD NO.	PAGES
MEIGS TWP.	ADAMS	OH	657	020,205	49-83
MEIGS TWP.	MUSKINGUM	OH	718	444,711	901-940
MEIGSVILLE TWP.	MORGAN	OH	715	444,708	623-58
MELENDEZ SET.	BENTON	FL	58	006,714	53-55
MELROSE	ADAMS	IL	97	007,670	313-49
MELROSE	MIDDLESEX	MA	324	443,543	558-88
MELROSE PREC.	CLARK	IL	100	007,673	489-504
MELTONSVILLE DIST.	ANSON	NC	619	018,105	432-49
MEMPHIS	PICKENS	AL	13	442,864	10-12
MEMPHIS	SCOTLAND	MO	419	443,627	227-31
MEMPHIS, WARD 1	SHELBY	TN	895	444,851	1-34
MEMPHIS, WARD 2	SHELBY	TN	895	444,851	35-57
MEMPHIS, WARD 3	SHELBY	TN	895	444,851	58-78
MEMPHIS, WARD 4	SHELBY	TN	895	444,851	79-96
MEMPHIS, WARD 5	SHELBY	TN	895	444,851	97-123
MEMPHIS, WARD 6	SHELBY	TN	895	444,851	124-56
MENALLEN TWP.	ADAMS	PA	743	020,593	85-124
MENALLEN TWP.	FAYETTE	PA	779	444,747	255-88
MENARD CO.		IL	120	442,908	525-676
MENDHAM TWP.	MORRIS	NJ	458	443,657	219-60
MENDOCINO CO.		CA	35	002,492	207-8
MENDON	WORCESTER	MA	345	443,564	593-624
MENDON	MONROE	NY	529	017,105	460-537
MENDON	RUTLAND	VT	927	444,926	225-36
MENDON TWP.	CLAYTON	IA	182	007,791	345-53
MENDOTA	DAKOTA	MN	367	014,834	17-20
MENNO TWP.	MIFFLIN	PA	797	444,765	445-70
MENOMINEE	WAUKESHA	WI	1009	444,996	909-940
MENOMINEE PREC.	JO DAVIESS	IL	111	007,684	443-59
MENTOR TWP.	LAKE	OH	701	444,694	519-56
MENTZ	CAYUGA	NY	481	017,057	159-289
MEQUON	WASHINGTON	WI	1008	444,995	401-450
MERAMEC TWP.	ST. LOUIS	MO	414	443,622	745-78
MERCER	SOMERSET	ME	269	443,506	171-98, 237
MERCER BOR.	MERCER	PA	796	444,764	179-202
MERCER CO.		IL	120	442,908	677-808
MERCER CO.		KY	213	442,981	479-938
MERCER CO.		MO	406	443,614	745-810
MERCER CO.		NJ	454	443,653	1-673
MERCER CO.		OH	710	444,703	435-621
MERCER CO.		PA	796	444,764	129-927
MERCER CO.		VA	960	444,950	295-391
MERCER TWP.	BUTLER	PA	760	020,610	643-73
MERCERSBURG	FRANKLIN	PA	781	444,749	17-44
MEREDITH	BELKNAP	NH	425	014,938	17-100
MEREDITH	DELAWARE	NY	494	017,070	217-56
MERIDEN	NEW HAVEN	CT	46	003,074	65-151
MERIDEN	LA SALLE	IL	115	007,688	504-5, 565-66, 603-7
MERIDIAN TWP.	INGHAM	MI	351	443,567	143-51
MERIWETHER CO.		GA	77	442,886	609-811
MERRIMACK	HILLSBORO	NH	434	443,638	297-326
MERRIMACK CO.		NH	435	443,639	1-441
MERRIMACK CO.		NH	436	443,640	1-552
MERTON	WAUKESHA	WI	1009	444,996	786-809
MESOPOTAMIA	TRUMBULL	OH	733	444,726	497-519
METAL TWP.	FRANKLIN	PA	782	444,750	651-80
METAMORA	LAPEER	MI	354	443,570	720-39
METAMORA TWP.	FRANKLIN	IN	146	442,924	472, 529-51

CITY, COUNTY, TOWN, OR TOWNSHIP	COUNTY	STATE	NA NO. M432	GD NO.	PAGES
METHUEN	ESSEX	MA	314	014,708	491-552
METOMEN	FOND DU LAC	WI	997	444,984	665-82
METROPOLIS CITY	MASSAC	IL	120	442,908	427-37
MEXICO	OXFORD	ME	263	443,500	461-72
MEXICO	OSWEGO	NY	577	444,293	143-243
MEXICO	JUNIATA	PA	786	444,754	476-78
MEXICO VILLAGE	JUNIATA	PA	786	444,754	469
MIAMI CO.		IN	160	442,938	153-436
MIAMI CO.		OH	711	444,704	623-859, 1-382
MIAMI TWP.	CASS	IN	137	007,750	989-1005
MIAMI TWP.	CLERMONT	OH	667	020,215	213-77
MIAMI TWP.	GREENE	OH	683	444,676	703-747
MIAMI TWP.	HAMILTON	OH	686	444,679	535-66, 599-604
MIAMI TWP.	LOGAN	OH	704	444,697	151-78
MIAMI TWP.	MONTGOMERY	OH	713	444,706	45-125
MIAMISBURG	MONTGOMERY	OH	713	444,706	101-127
MICHIGAN	CLINTON	IN	139	007,752	862-65
MICHIGAN CITY	LA PORTE	IN	157	442,935	569-94
MICHIGAN TWP.	CLINTON	IN	139	007,752	841-61
MICHIGAN TWP.	LA PORTE	IN	157	442,935	563-67
MIDDLE PAXTON TWP.	DAUPHIN	PA	775	444,743	489-517
MIDDLE SMITHFIELD TWP.	MONROE	PA	798	444,766	259-94
MIDDLE TERRITORY	HENDRICKS	IN	150	442,928	262-68
MIDDLE TWP.	FRANKLIN	AR	26	002,480	255-68
MIDDLE TWP.	HENDRICKS	IN	150	442,928	84-100, 281-304
MIDDLE TWP.	CAPE MAY	NJ	446	016,533	75-120
MIDDLE WOODBURY TWP.	BEDFORD	PA	751	020,601	449-89
MIDDLEBOROUGH	PLYMOUTH	MA	333	443,552	389-516
MIDDLEBURG	SHIAWASSEE	MI	363	443,579	187-90
MIDDLEBURG	SCHOHARIE	NY	595	444,311	131-201
MIDDLEBURG TWP.	CUYAHOGA	OH	673	020,221	355-90
MIDDLEBURG TWP.	TIOGA	PA	830	444,798	329-55
MIDDLEBURY	NEW HAVEN	CT	45	003,073	141-59
MIDDLEBURY	WYOMING	NY	617	444,333	443-86
MIDDLEBURY	ADDISON	VT	920	027,446	253-336
MIDDLEBURY TWP.	ELKHART	IN	144	007,757	133-60
MIDDLEBURY TWP.	KNOX	OH	700	444,693	1-28
MIDDLECREEK TWP.	UNION	PA	831	444,799	19-33
MIDDLEFIELD	HAMPSHIRE	MA	320	443,539	1-18
MIDDLEFIELD	OTSEGO	NY	579	444,295	191-267
MIDDLEFIELD TWP.	GEAUGA	OH	682	444,675	239-60
MIDDLESEX	YATES	NY	618	444,334	55-87
MIDDLESEX	WASHINGTON	VT	928	444,927	499-531
MIDDLESEX CO.		CT	44	003,072	349-1013
MIDDLESEX CO.		MA	322	443,541	1-651
MIDDLESEX CO.		MA	323	443,542	655-1008, 1-332
MIDDLESEX CO.		MA	324	443,543	333-1001
MIDDLESEX CO.		MA	325	443,544	1-667
MIDDLESEX CO.		MA	326	443,545	669-894, 1-391
MIDDLESEX CO.		MA	327	443,546	395-1048
MIDDLESEX CO.		NJ	455	443,654	1-690
MIDDLESEX CO.		VA	961	444,951	395-444
MIDDLESEX TWP.	BUTLER	PA	760	020,610	101-157
MIDDLETON	ESSEX	MA	315	443,534	701-720
MIDDLETON	STRAFFORD	NH	439	443,643	197-99, 201-8
MIDDLETON	STRAFFORD	NH	440	443,644	401
MIDDLETON	MARION	OH	708	444,701	34-37
MIDDLETON DIST.	RUTHERFORD	TN	894	444,850	459-76
MIDDLETON TWP.	COLUMBIANA	OH	669	020,217	347-85

119

CITY, COUNTY, TOWN, OR TOWNSHIP	COUNTY	STATE	NA NO. M432	GD NO.	PAGES
MIDDLETON TWP.	WOOD	OH	741	444,734	335-42
MIDDLETON TWP.	DANE	WI	995	034,509	931-38
MIDDLETOWN	MIDDLESEX	CT	44	003,072	687-785
MIDDLETOWN	NEW CASTLE	DE	54	006,438	349-57
MIDDLETOWN	HENRY	IN	151	442,929	627-31
MIDDLETOWN	CHARLES	MD	290	443,521	457, 460, 498-502, 505-525, 528, 530-33, 578 581-82
MIDDLETOWN	DELAWARE	NY	495	017,071	851-926
MIDDLETOWN	BUTLER	OH	663	020,211	869-94
MIDDLETOWN	GUERNSEY	OH	684	444,677	481-87
MIDDLETOWN	NEWPORT	RI	842	022,265	615-37
MIDDLETOWN	RUTLAND	VT	927	444,926	679-99
MIDDLETOWN	FREDERICK	VA	945	444,935	644-52
MIDDLETOWN	MARQUETTE	WI	1002	444,989	156-64
MIDDLETOWN BOR.	DAUPHIN	PA	774	444,742	289-312
MIDDLETOWN CITY	MIDDLESEX	CT	44	003,072	913-1013
MIDDLETOWN EL. DIST.	FREDERICK	MD	293	443,524	621-710
MIDDLETOWN TWP.	MONMOUTH	NJ	457	443,656	597-674
MIDDLETOWN TWP.	BUCKS	PA	758	020,608	611-64
MIDDLETOWN TWP.	DELAWARE	PA	776	444,744	353-97
MIDDLETOWN TWP.	SUSQUEHANNA	PA	829	444,797	277-304
MIDLAND CO.		MI	357	443,573	493-94
MIDLAND TWP.	MIDLAND	MI	357	443,573	493-94
MIDWAY	MADISON	OH	706	444,699	455-56
MIFFLIN	IOWA	WI	999	444,986	741-56
MIFFLIN CO.		PA	797	444,765	337-737
MIFFLIN TWP.	ASHLAND	OH	658	020,206	289-310
MIFFLIN TWP.	FRANKLIN	OH	680	444,673	153-79
MIFFLIN TWP.	PIKE	OH	721	444,714	787-800
MIFFLIN TWP.	RICHLAND	OH	724	444,717	469-95
MIFFLIN TWP.	WYANDOT	OH	741	444,734	531-44
MIFFLIN TWP.	ALLEGHENY	PA	748	020,598	375-439
MIFFLIN TWP.	COLUMBIA	PA	769	444,737	495-519
MIFFLIN TWP.	CUMBERLAND	PA	773	444,741	617-54
MIFFLIN TWP.	DAUPHIN	PA	775	444,743	801-831
MIFFLIN TWP.	LYCOMING	PA	795	444,763	577-603
MIFFLINBURG BOR.	UNION	PA	831	444,799	549-68
MIFFLINTOWN	JUNIATA	PA	786	444,754	535-45
MILAM CO.		TX	913	444,916	1-59
MILAM DIST.	MILAM	TX	913	444,916	1-59
MILAN	COOS	NH	429	443,633	47-58
MILAN	DUTCHESS	NY	496	017,072	561-602
MILAN TWP.	ALLEN	IN	135	007,748	397-405
MILAN TWP.	MONROE	MI	358	443,574	761-76
MILAN TWP.	ERIE	OH	676	338,044	123-87
MILBRIDGE	WASHINGTON	ME	272	443,509	263-90
MILBURN	BALLARD	KY	190	007,843	552-53
MILES TWP.	CENTRE	PA	763	020,613	60, 73-103
MILESBURG BOR.	CENTRE	PA	763	020,613	61-72
MILFORD	NEW HAVEN	CT	46	003,074	757-815
MILFORD	LA GRANGE	IN	157	442,935	57-77
MILFORD	PENOBSCOT	ME	266	443,503	602-618
MILFORD	WORCESTER	MA	344	443,563	1-116
MILFORD	HILLSBORO	NH	434	443,638	329-80
MILFORD	OTSEGO	NY	580	444,296	199-252
MILFORD	JEFFERSON	WI	1000	444,987	37-54
MILFORD CENTRE	UNION	OH	736	444,729	177-82

CITY, COUNTY, TOWN, OR TOWNSHIP	COUNTY	STATE	NA NO. M432	GD NO.	PAGES
MILFORD HUN.	KENT	DE	52	006,436	165-304
MILFORD TWP.	OAKLAND	MI	360	443,576	533-67
MILFORD TWP.	BUTLER	OH	663	020,211	378-426
MILFORD TWP.	DEFIANCE	OH	674	020,222	154-70
MILFORD TWP.	KNOX	OH	700	444,693	163-94
MILFORD TWP.	BUCKS	PA	759	020,609	261-321
MILFORD TWP.	JUNIATA	PA	786	444,754	385, 389-420
MILFORD TWP.	PIKE	PA	825	444,793	11-30
MILFORD TWP.	SOMERSET	PA	828	444,796	451-500
MILL CREEK	UNION	OH	736	444,729	283-301
MILL CREEK	PENDLETON	VA	968	444,958	32
MILL CREEK HUN.	NEW CASTLE	DE	54	006,438	689-768
MILL CREEK PREC.	CLARK	IL	100	007,673	388-96
MILL CREEK PREC.	JO DAVIESS	IL	111	007,684	287-313
MILL CREEK TWP.	ASHLEY	AR	25	002,479	61-66
MILL CREEK TWP.	FRANKLIN	AR	26	002,480	281-87
MILL CREEK TWP.	MORGAN	MO	408	443,616	507-521
MILL CREEK TWP.	COSHOCTON	OH	670	020,218	435-55
MILL CREEK TWP.	HAMILTON	OH	685	444,678	1-150
MILL CREEK TWP.	WILLIAMS	OH	741	444,734	55-64
MILL CREEK TWP.	ERIE	PA	778	444,746	507-580
MILL CREEK TWP.	LEBANON	PA	791	444,759	51-81
MILL CREEK TWP.	MERCER	PA	796	444,764	525-45
MILL HALL BOR.	CLINTON	PA	768	444,736	35-46
MILL TWP.	GRANT	IN	147	442,925	288-314, 322-25
MILL TWP.	TUSCARAWAS	OH	735	444,728	583-620
MILLBURY	WORCESTER	MA	344	443,563	117-92
MILLEDGEVILLE CITY	BALDWIN	GA	61	007,057	179-207
MILLER CO.		MO	406	443,614	811-97
MILLER TWP.	DEARBORN	IN	141	007,754	583-610
MILLER TWP.	GENTRY	MO	399	443,607	397-400, 404-410, 437-44
MILLER TWP.	MARION	MO	406	443,614	581-603
MILLER TWP.	SCOTLAND	MO	419	443,627	257-72
MILLER TWP.	KNOX	OH	700	444,693	669-95
MILLERSBURG	MERCER	IL	120	442,908	749-51
MILLERSBURG DIST.	RUTHERFORD	TN	894	444,850	633-54
MILLERSPORT	FAIRFIELD	OH	677	444,670	415-17
MILLERSTOWN	LEBANON	PA	791	444,759	513-31
MILLERSTOWN BOR.	PERRY	PA	805	444,773	1215-25
MILLERSVILLE	LANCASTER	PA	787	444,755	373-85
MILLGROVE TWP.	STEUBEN	IN	173	442,951	268-80
MILLSBORO	SUSSEX	DE	55	442,884	340-45
MILLSBORO	WASHINGTON	PA	833	444,801	271-79
MILLSFIELD	COOS	NH	429	443,633	307
MILLSTONE TWP.	MONMOUTH	NJ	457	443,656	555-96
MILLVILLE PREC.	JO DAVIESS	IL	111	007,684	242-86
MILLVILLE TWP.	CLAYTON	IA	182	007,791	265-71
MILLVILLE TWP.	CUMBERLAND	NJ	446	016,533	271-326
MILLWOOD	GUERNSEY	OH	684	444,677	701-6
MILLWOOD	KNOX	OH	700	444,693	819-24
MILLWOOD TWP.	GUERNSEY	OH	684	444,677	681-722
MILO	PISCATAQUIS	ME	267	443,504	649-71
MILO	YATES	NY	618	444,334	347-461
MILTON	SUSSEX	DE	55	442,884	62-79
MILTON	DU PAGE	IL	105	007,678	117-40
MILTON	WAYNE	IN	180	442,958	575-94
MILTON	NORFOLK	MA	331	443,550	407-460
MILTON	STRAFFORD	NH	439	443,643	209-247

CITY, COUNTY, TOWN, OR TOWNSHIP	COUNTY	STATE	NA NO. M432	GD NO.	PAGES
MILTON	SARATOGA	NY	593	444,309	879-980
MILTON	CASWELL	NC	623	018,109	379-90
MILTON	MIAMI	OH	711	444,704	338-46
MILTON	CHITTENDEN	VT	923	444,922	367-425
MILTON	ROCK	WI	1005	444,992	659-83
MILTON BEAT	AUTAUGA	AL	1	002,343	140-54
MILTON BOR.	NORTHUMBERLAND	PA	804	444,772	152-91
MILTON DIST.	RUTHERFORD	TN	894	444,850	529-44
MILTON PLANTATION	OXFORD	ME	263	443,500	321-24
MILTON TWP.	JEFFERSON	IN	154	442,932	383-420
MILTON TWP.	CASS	MI	349	014,811	481-95
MILTON TWP.	ASHLAND	OH	658	020,206	33-68
MILTON TWP.	JACKSON	OH	698	444,691	621-56
MILTON TWP.	MAHONING	OH	707	444,700	1162-88
MILTON TWP.	WAYNE	OH	739	444,732	265-98
MILTON TWP.	WOOD	OH	741	444,734	259-64
MILTONSBURG	MONROE	OH	712	444,705	452-56
MILWAUKEE	CLACKAMAS	OR	742	020,298	31-33
MILWAUKEE CO.		WI	1003	444,990	337-1088
MILWAUKEE, DIST. 18	MILWAUKEE	WI	1003	444,990	1055-88
MILWAUKEE, WARD 1	MILWAUKEE	WI	1003	444,990	337-480
MILWAUKEE, WARD 2	MILWAUKEE	WI	1003	444,990	481-594
MILWAUKEE, WARD 3	MILWAUKEE	WI	1003	444,990	597-694
MILWAUKEE, WARD 4	MILWAUKEE	WI	1003	444,990	695-753
MILWAUKEE, WARD 5	MILWAUKEE	WI	1003	444,990	755-816
MINA	CHAUTAUQUA	NY	485	017,061	583-606
MINDEN	CLAIBORNE PAR.	LA	230	009,697	249-57
MINDEN	MONTGOMERY	NY	533	017,109	415-525
MINDON TWP.	ST. JOSEPH	MI	362	443,578	735-55
MINE CREEK TWP.	HEMPSTEAD	AR	26	002,480	513-33
MINERAL	BUREAU	IL	99	007,672	556-60
MINERAL POINT	IOWA	WI	999	444,986	614-75
MINERAL SPRINGS	STEWART	GA	82	442,891	240-53
MINERSVILLE	SCHUYLKILL	PA	826	444,794	493-506
MINERSVILLE BOR.	SCHUYLKILL	PA	826	444,794	507-563
MINERVA	ESSEX	NY	504	017,080	599-612
MINISINK	ORANGE	NY	574	444,290	429-548
MINOT	CUMBERLAND	ME	250	009,720	69-110
MINSTER	AUGLAIZE	OH	660	020,208	463-73
MISHAWAKA	ST. JOSEPH	IN	171	442,949	198-231
MISPILLION HUN.	KENT	DE	52	006,436	165-304
MISSION	LA SALLE	IL	115	007,688	638-57
MISSION ESPADA	BEXAR	TX	908	024,887	319-21
MISSION SALADO	BEXAR	TX	908	024,887	321
MISSION SAN JOSE	BEXAR	TX	908	024,887	313-14
MISSION SAN JUAN	BEXAR	TX	908	024,887	315-18
MISSISSINAWA TWP.	DARKE	OH	674	020,222	519-30
MISSISSINEWA TWP.	WESTMORELAND	PA	837	444,805	477-97
MISSISSIPPI BAR	SACRAMENTO	CA	35	002,492	408, 411, 415-1
MISSISSIPPI CO.		AR	28	002,482	673-712
MISSISSIPPI CO.		MO	406	443,614	899-955
MISSISSIPPI RIVER	JEFFERSON PAR.	LA	232	443,475	79-86, 136-62
MISSISSIPPI TWP.	DESHA	AR	26	002,480	146-50
MISSISSIPPI TWP.	PIKE	MO	409	443,617	482-85
MISSOURI CANYON	EL DORADO	CA	34	002,491	912-13
MISSOURI TWP.	CLARK	AR	25	002,479	444-53
MISSOURI TWP.	HEMPSTEAD	AR	26	002,480	481-90
MISSOURI TWP.	OUACHITA	AR	28	002,482	133-44
MISSOURI TWP.	PIKE	AR	29	002,483	387-94

CITY, COUNTY, TOWN, OR TOWNSHIP	COUNTY	STATE	NA NO. M432	GD NO.	PAGES
MITCHELL TWP.	POINSETT	AR	29	002,483	399-417
MITCHELTREE TWP.	MARTIN	IN	160	442,938	49-71
MITCHIE PREC.	MONROE	IL	121	442,909	67-79
MOBILE	MOBILE	AL	11	002,353	551-877
MOBILE CO.		AL	11	002,353	551-986
MOCUSSAN GAP DIST.	STEWART	GA	82	442,891	105-125
MOHAWK	MONTGOMERY	NY	533	017,109	704-780
MOHICAN TWP.	ASHLAND	OH	658	020,206	113-56
MOIRA	FRANKLIN	NY	505	017,081	181-212
MOLUNKUS PLANTATION	AROOSTOOK	ME	248	009,718	1-5
MOMENCE	WILL	IL	133	442,921	189-202
MONAGHAN TWP.	YORK	PA	840	444,808	615-39
MONDAY CREEK TWP.	PERRY	OH	719	444,712	571-97
MONEY CREEK	MC LEON	IL	117	007,690	109-116, 118
MONGUAGON TWP.	WAYNE	MI	366	443,582	925-48
MONHEGON ISLAND	LINCOLN	ME	259	443,496	327-28
MONHEGON PLANTATION	LINCOLN	ME	259	443,496	329
MONITEAU CO.		MO	407	443,615	1-130
MONKTON	ADDISON	VT	920	027,446	531-60
MONMOUTH	KENNEBEC	ME	257	443,494	107-151
MONMOUTH CO.		NJ	456	443,655	1-505
MONMOUTH CO.		NJ	457	443,656	509-736
MONMOUTH TWP.	JACKSON	IA	184	007,793	659-64, 667-69
MONOMA TWP.	CLAYTON	IA	182	007,791	355-62
MONONGAHELA BOR.	WASHINGTON	PA	834	444,802	490-513
MONONGALIA CO.		VA	961	444,951	447-738
MONONGEHELA TWP.	GREENE	PA	783	444,751	279-306
MONROE	FAIRFIELD	CT	37	003,065	671-705
MONROE	QUACHITA PAR.	LA	238	443,481	525-30
MONROE	WALDO	ME	270	443,507	177-215
MONROE	FRANKLIN	MA	317	443,536	543-49
MONROE	ORANGE	NY	573	444,289	535-636
MONROE	UNION	NC	647	444,660	1-4
MONROE	ASHTABULA	OH	659	020,207	571-608
MONROE	BUTLER	OH	663	020,211	931-36
MONROE	BRADFORD	PA	757	020,607	431-65
MONROE	GREEN	WI	999	444,986	427-54
MONROE CO.		AL	11	002,353	1-136
MONROE CO.		AR	28	002,482	720-63
MONROE CO.		FL	59	006,715	281-337
MONROE CO.		GA	78	442,887	1-163
MONROE CO.		IL	121	442,909	1-182
MONROE CO.		IN	161	442,939	437-738
MONROE CO.		IA	187	442,962	603-671
MONROE CO.		KY	213	442,981	739-903
MONROE CO.		MI	358	443,574	497-864
MONROE CO.		MS	378	443,590	1-226
MONROE CO.		MO	407	443,615	131-334
MONROE CO.		NY	528	017,104	277-888
MONROE CO.		NY	529	017,105	1-646
MONROE CO.		NY	530	017,106	1-449
MONROE CO.		NY	531	017,107	450-892
MONROE CO.		OH	712	444,705	383-1084
MONROE CO.		PA	798	444,766	1-336
MONROE CO.		TN	891	444,847	1-258
MONROE CO.		VA	961	444,951	741-964
MONROE PREC.	SALINE	IL	127	442,915	37-54
MONROE TWP.	LA FAYETTE	AR	27	002,481	339
MONROE TWP.	MISSISSIPPI	AR	28	002,482	673-83

CITY, COUNTY, TOWN, OR TOWNSHIP	COUNTY	STATE	NA NO. M432	GD NO.	PAGES	
MONROE TWP.	SEVIER	AR	30	442,876	398-405	
MONROE TWP.	OGLE	IL	123	442,911	155-64,	193
MONROE TWP.	ADAMS	IN	135	007,748	94-102	
MONROE TWP.	ALLEN	IN	135	007,748	345-54	
MONROE TWP.	CLARK	IN	138	007,751	139-78	
MONROE TWP.	DELAWARE	IN	143	007,756	679-96	
MONROE TWP.	GRANT	IN	147	442,925	283-87,	393-406
MONROE TWP.	HOWARD	IN	151	442,929	785-808	
MONROE TWP.	JEFFERSON	IN	154	442,932	553-78	
MONROE TWP.	MADISON	IN	158	442,936	18-47	
MONROE TWP.	MORGAN	IN	162	442,940	237-71	
MONROE TWP.	PIKE	IN	165	442,943	158-90	
MONROE TWP.	PULASKI	IN	166	442,944	651-63	
MONROE TWP.	PUTNAM	IN	167	442,945	715-44	
MONROE TWP.	RANDOLPH	IN	168	442,946	29-46	
MONROE TWP.	WASHINGTON	IN	179	442,957	765-800	
MONROE TWP.	JOHNSON	IA	185	442,960	351-57	
MONROE TWP.	MONROE	MI	358	443,574	524-46,	625
MONROE TWP.	MIDDLESEX	NJ	455	443,654	243-314	
MONROE TWP.	ADAMS	OH	657	020,205	123-52	
MONROE TWP.	ALLEN	OH	657	020,205	737-59	
MONROE TWP.	CARROLL	OH	664	020,212	54-80	
MONROE TWP.	CLERMONT	OH	667	020,215	1-44	
MONROE TWP.	COSHOCTON	OH	670	020,218	349-67	
MONROE TWP.	DARKE	OH	674	020,222	785-806	
MONROE TWP.	GUERNSEY	OH	684	444,677	819-46	
MONROE TWP.	HARRISON	OH	693	444,686	591-618	
MONROE TWP.	HOLMES	OH	696	444,689	255-78	
MONROE TWP.	KNOX	OH	700	444,693	565-98	
MONROE TWP.	LICKING	OH	702	444,695	377-411	
MONROE TWP.	LOGAN	OH	704	444,697	1-35	
MONROE TWP.	MADISON	OH	706	444,699	573-86	
MONROE TWP.	MIAMI	OH	711	444,704	233-82	
MONROE TWP.	MUSKINGUM	OH	718	444,711	597-620	
MONROE TWP.	PERRY	OH	719	444,712	493-527	
MONROE TWP.	PICKAWAY	OH	720	444,713	183-222	
MONROE TWP.	PREBLE	OH	723	444,716	765-96	
MONROE TWP.	RICHLAND	OH	724	444,717	637-78	
MONROE TWP.	BEDFORD	PA	751	020,601	255-83	
MONROE TWP.	CLARION	PA	767	444,735	88, 96-126	
MONROE TWP.	CUMBERLAND	PA	773	444,741	457-500	
MONROE TWP.	WYOMING	PA	838	444,806	203-217	
MONROE, WARD 1	MONROE	MI	358	443,574	691-722	
MONROE, WARD 2	MONROE	MI	358	443,574	723-47	
MONROE, WARD 3	MONROE	MI	358	443,574	749-60	
MONROEVILLE	JEFFERSON	OH	699	444,692	902-3	
MONSON	PISCATAQUIS	ME	267	443,504	429-44	
MONSON	HAMPDEN	MA	318	443,537	125-92	
MONT ROSE	LEE	IA	186	442,961	779-90	
MONT ROSE TWP.	LEE	IA	186	442,961	791-820	
MONTAGUE	FRANKLIN	MA	317	443,536	579-614	
MONTAGUE TWP.	SUSSEX	NJ	464	443,663	53-77	
MONTCALM CO.		MI	358	443,574	668-90	
MONTCALM TWP.	MONTCALM	MI	358	443,574	879-82	
MONTEREY	MONTEREY	CA	35	002,492	211-34	
MONTEREY	BERKSHIRE	MA	306	014,700	311-29	
MONTEREY	ALLEGAN	MI	346	014,808	69-74	
MONTEREY CO.		CA	35	002,492	211-56	
MONTEREY TWP.	PUTNAM	OH	723	444,716	161-63	

CITY, COUNTY, TOWN, OR TOWNSHIP	COUNTY	STATE	NA NO. M432	GD NO.	PAGES
MONTFORD COVE	RUTHERFORD	NC	644	444,657	558-61, 651-56
MONTGOMERY	HAMPDEN	MA	318	443,537	463-74
MONTGOMERY	SOMERSET	NJ	463	443,662	755-94
MONTGOMERY	ORANGE	NY	573	444,289	381-474
MONTGOMERY	FRANKLIN	VT	924	444,923	469-93
MONTGOMERY CO.		AL	12	002,354	139-389
MONTGOMERY CO.		AR	28	002,482	765-817
MONTGOMERY CO.		GA	78	442,887	165-203
MONTGOMERY CO		IL	121	442,909	185-334
MONTGOMERY CO.		IN	161	442,939	739-1170
MONTGOMERY CO.		KY	214	442,982	1-169
MONTGOMERY CO.		MD	295	443,526	629-889
MONTGOMERY CO.		MO	407	443,615	335-441
MONTGOMERY CO.		NY	532	017,108	1-412
MONTGOMERY CO.		NY	533	017,109	415-780
MONTGOMERY CO.		NC	637	444,650	205-327
MONTGOMERY CO.		OH	713	444,706	1-547
MONTGOMERY CO.		OH	714	444,707	547-934
MONTGOMERY CO.		PA	799	444,767	1-690
MONTGOMERY CO.		PA	800	444,768	691-870, 1-576
MONTGOMERY CO.		TN	891	444,847	262-549
MONTGOMERY CO.		TX	913	444,916	63-97
MONTGOMERY CO.		VA	962	444,952	1-165
MONTGOMERY TWP.	DESHA	AR	26	002,480	144-45
MONTGOMERY TWP.	MONROE	AR	28	002,482	739-44
MONTGOMERY TWP.	GIBSON	IN	147	442,925	87-144
MONTGOMERY TWP.	JENNINGS	IN	155	442,933	744-82
MONTGOMERY TWP.	OWEN	IN	164	442,942	31-55
MONTGOMERY TWP.	ASHLAND	OH	658	020,206	845-54, 877-920
MONTGOMERY TWP.	FRANKLIN	OH	679	444,672	807-841
MONTGOMERY TWP.	MARION	OH	708	444,701	80-94
MONTGOMERY TWP.	WOOD	OH	741	444,734	397-418
MONTGOMERY TWP.	FRANKLIN	PA	781	444,749	17-122
MONTGOMERY TWP.	INDIANA	PA	785	444,753	113-30
MONTGOMERY TWP.	MONTGOMERY	PA	800	444,768	181-204
MONTGOMERY, WARD 1	MONTGOMERY	AL	12	002,354	231-53
MONTGOMERY, WARD 2	MONTGOMERY	AL	12	002,354	254-74
MONTGOMERY, WARD 3	MONTGOMERY	AL	12	002,354	275-300
MONTICELLO	JEFFERSON	FL	59	006,715	1-5
MONTICELLO	PLATT	IL	124	442,912	29-32
MONTICELLO	AROOSTOOK	ME	248	009,718	181-86
MONTICELLO	LAFAYETTE	WI	1001	444,988	942-46
MONTICELLO TWP.	JONES	IA	185	442,960	406-411
MONTOUR CO.		PA	801	444,769	577-916
MONTOUR TWP.	COLUMBIA	PA	769	444,737	695-704
MONTOURSVILLE TWP.	LYCOMING	PA	795	444,763	957-60, 962
MONTPELIER	WASHINGTON	VT	928	444,927	323-77
MONTPELIER TWP.	MUSCATINE	IA	187	442,962	761-69
MONTROSE BOR.	SUSQUEHANNA	PA	829	444,797	347-69
MONTROSE TWP.	GENESEE	MI	350	443,566	463-64
MONTROSE TWP.	DANE	WI	995	034,509	913-21
MONTVILLE	NEW LONDON	CT	48	442,880	421-64
MONTVILLE	WALDO	ME	271	443,508	509-516, 518-54
MONTVILLE	MEDINA	OH	709	444,702	599-624
MONTVILLE TWP.	GEAUGA	OH	682	444,675	399-415
MONYOCK DIST.	CURRITUCK	NC	627	444,640	325-36
MOOERS	CLINTON	NY	490	017,066	769-849
MOON TWP.	ALLEGHENY	PA	748	020,598	654-87
MOON TWP.	BEAVER	PA	750	020,600	434-55

CITY, COUNTY, TOWN, OR TOWNSHIP	COUNTY	STATE	NA NO. M432	GD NO.	PAGES
MOONEY TWP.	PHILLIPS	AR	29	002,483	265-71
MOORE CO.		NC	638	444,651	329-504
MOORE TWP.	NORTHAMPTON	PA	803	444,771	765-827
MOOREFIELD	HARRISON	OH	693	444,686	647-53
MOOREFIELD	HARDY	VA	950	444,940	1-8
MOOREFIELD TWP.	CLARK	OH	666	020,214	501-531
MOOREFIELD TWP.	HARRISON	OH	693	444,686	647-78
MOORES HILL	DEARBORN	IN	141	007,754	902-6
MOORESVILLE	MORGAN	IN	162	442,940	211-23
MOOSE HEAD LAKE	PISCATAQUIS	ME	267	443,504	519
MOQUINO	VALENCIA	NM	470	443,668	470-74
MORAL TWP.	SHELBY	IN	172	442,950	570-99
MORAVIA	CAYUGA	NY	483	017,059	209-253
MOREAU	SARATOGA	NY	592	444,308	239-82
MOREAU TWP.	MORGAN	MO	408	443,616	443-69
MOREDOCK PREC.	MONROE	IL	121	442,909	35-40, 42-43, 45-51
MOREHOUSE	HAMILTON	NY	511	017,087	44-50
MOREHOUSE PARISH		LA	233	443,476	769-814
MORELAND TWP.	LYCOMING	PA	795	444,763	914-30
MORELAND TWP.	MONTGOMERY	PA	800	444,768	723-80
MORELAND TWP.	PHILADELPHIA	PA	808	444,776	311-22
MORETOWN	WASHINGTON	VT	928	444,927	535-66
MORGAN	ORLEANS	VT	925	444,924	297-308
MORGAN		AL	12	002,354	393-552
MORGAN CO.		GA	78	442,887	205-291
MORGAN CO.		IL	122	442,910	335-718
MORGAN CO.		IN	162	442,940	1-367
MORGAN CO.		KY	214	442,982	171-348
MORGAN CO.		MO	408	443,616	443-542
MORGAN CO.		OH	715	444,708	1-699
MORGAN CO.		TN	891	444,847	551-633
MORGAN CO.		VA	962	444,952	169-252
MORGAN TWP.	OWEN	IN	164	442,942	57-80
MORGAN TWP.	PORTER	IN	165	442,943	231-40
MORGAN TWP.	ASHTABULA	OH	659	020,207	865-86
MORGAN TWP.	BUTLER	OH	663	020,211	941-81
MORGAN TWP.	GALLIA	OH	681	444,674	795-821
MORGAN TWP.	KNOX	OH	700	444,693	697-717
MORGAN TWP.	MORGAN	OH	715	444,708	453-508
MORGAN TWP.	SCIOTO	OH	727	444,720	201-8
MORGAN TWP.	GREENE	PA	783	444,751	341-69
MORGANTON	BURKE	NC	622	018,108	687-93
MORGANTOWN	MORGAN	IN	162	442,940	123-26
MORIAH	ESSEX	NY	503	017,079	1-73
MORMON BAR	SUTTER	CA	36	442,879	63
MORMON ISLAND	SACRAMENTO	CA	35	002,492	402, 425-29
MORO TWP.	BRADLEY	AR	25	002,479	183-84
MORO TWP.	DALLAS	AR	26	002,480	1-7
MORRIS	GRUNDY	IL	108	007,681	301-315
MORRIS	OTSEGO	NY	580	444,296	497-548
MORRIS		NJ	458	443,657	1-463
MORRIS CO.		NJ	459	443,658	465-737
MORRIS CO.		NJ	458	443,657	97-218
MORRIS TWP.	MORRIS	OH	700	444,693	57-81
MORRIS TWP.	KNOX	PA	768	444,736	798-812
MORRIS TWP.	CLEARFIELD	PA	783	444,751	703-732
MORRIS TWP.	GREENE	PA	784	444,752	189-208
MORRIS TWP.	HUNTINGDON	PA	830	444,798	507-513
MORRIS TWP.	TIOGA				

CITY, COUNTY, TOWN, OR TOWNSHIP	COUNTY	STATE	NA NO. M432	GD NO.	PAGES
MORRIS TWP.	WASHINGTON	PA	834	444,802	791-831
MORRISTOWN	SHELBY	IN	172	442,950	744-47
MORRISTOWN	BURLINGTON	NJ	443	016,530	191-208
MORRISTOWN	ST. LAWRENCE	NY	589	444,305	47-102
MORRISTOWN	BELMONT	OH	661	020,209	904-914
MORRISVILLE BOR.	LAMOILLE	VT	925	444,924	313-47
MORROW	BUCKS	PA	758	020,608	313-26
MORROW CO.	WARREN	OH	737	444,730	185-204
		OH	716	444,709	701-1068, 1-136
MORVEN DIST.	ANSON	NC	619	018,105	339-46
MOSCOW	MUSCATINE	IA	187	442,962	793-805
MOSCOW	SOMERSET	ME	269	443,506	492-506
MOSCOW TWP.	HILLSDALE	MI	351	443,567	891-914
MOSQUITO CANYON	EL DORADO	CA	34	002,491	975-78
MOSS TWP.	LA FAYETTE	AR	27	002,481	345-49
MOTTVILLE TWP.	ST. JOSEPH	MI	362	443,578	563-77
MOULTON TWP.	AUGLAIZE	OH	660	020,208	573-83
MOULTONBOROUGH	CARROLL	NH	426	014,939	401-442
MOULTRIE CO.		IL	122	442,910	719-98
MOUND TWP.	WARREN	IN	178	442,956	19-38
MOUNDSVILLE	MARSHALL	VA	959	444,949	477-87
MT. AIRY DIST.	SURRY	NC	646	444,659	588-604
MOUNT CARMEL	WABASH	IL	130	442,918	755-80
MOUNT CARROLL	CARROLL	IL	99	007,672	701-712
MOUNT DESERT	HANCOCK	ME	255	443,492	725-43
MOUNT DESERT ROCK	HANCOCK	ME	255	443,492	785
MT. EPHRIAM	GUERNSEY	OH	684	444,677	723-26
MT. GILEAD	MORROW	OH	716	444,709	1017-32
MOUNT HOLLY	BURLINGTON	NJ	444	016,531	787-854
MOUNT HOLLY	RUTLAND	VT	927	444,926	723-59
MT. HOPE	ORANGE	NY	574	444,290	645-80
MOUNT JOY TWP.	ADAMS	PA	743	020,593	473-500
MOUNT JOY TWP.	LANCASTER	PA	788	444,756	1-63
MOUNT MORRIS	LIVINGSTON	NY	524	017,100	129-236
MOUNT MORRIS TWP.	OGLE	IL	123	442,911	31-32, 35-48
MOUNT MORRIS VILLAGE	OGLE	IL	123	442,911	23-30, 33-34
MT. PLEASANT	HENRY	IA	184	007,793	351-69
MOUNT PLEASANT	WESTCHESTER	NY	614	444,330	635-714
MOUNT PLEASANT	WAYNE	PA	835	444,803	23-59
MT. PLEASANT	MAURY	TN	890	444,846	431-34
MT. PLEASANT	GREEN	WI	999	444,986	505-518
MT. PLEASANT	RACINE	WI	1004	444,991	179-204
MT. PLEASANT BOR.	WESTMORELAND	PA	836	444,804	125-37
MOUNT PLEASANT TWP.	DELAWARE	IN	143	007,756	717-37
MT. PLEASANT TWP.	SCOTLAND	MO	419	443,627	236-37, 296-315
MT. PLEASANT TWP.	JEFFERSON	OH	699	444,692	769-813
MT. PLEASANT TWP.	ADAMS	PA	743	020,593	573-611
MOUNT PLEASANT TWP.	COLUMBIA	PA	769	444,737	478-94
MOUNT PLEASANT TWP.	WASHINGTON	PA	833	444,801	185-214
MT. PLEASANT TWP.	WESTMORELAND	PA	836	444,804	63-124
MOUNT PULASKI	LOGAN	IL	116	007,689	351-59
MT. STERLING	BROWN	IL	98	007,671	191-203
MT. STERLING	MADISON	OH	706	444,699	445-47
MT. TABOR	MONROE	IN	161	442,939	533-35
MOUNT TABOR	RUTLAND	VT	927	444,926	629-36
MOUNT VERNON	JEFFERSON	IL	110	007,683	795-801
MT. VERNON	POSEY	IN	166	442,944	335-62
MOUNT VERNON	KENNEBEC	ME	257	443,494	739-76
MOUNT VERNON	HILLSBORO	NH	434	443,638	277-94

127

CITY, COUNTY, TOWN, OR TOWNSHIP	COUNTY	STATE	NA NO. M432	GD NO.	PAGES
MT. VERNON, WARD 1	KNOX	OH	700	444,693	457-73
MT. VERNON, WARD 2	KNOX	OH	700	444,693	475-88
MT. VERNON, WARD 3	KNOX	OH	700	444,693	441-55
MT. VERNON, WARD 4	KNOX	OH	700	444,693	489-506
MT. VERNON, WARD 5	KNOX	OH	700	444,693	411-40
MOUNT WASHINGTON	BERKSHIRE	MA	306	014,700	453-61
MOUNTAIN	FENTRESS	TN	877	444,833	807-812
MOUNTAIN CREEK	RUTHERFORD	NC	644	444,657	554-57, 645-50, 663, 666-67
MOUNTAIN TWP.	CRAWFORD	AR	25	002,479	649-61
MOUNTAIN TWP.	MONTGOMERY	AR	28	002,482	765-75
MOUNTAIN TWP.	SCOTT	AR	30	442,876	282-88
MOUNTAIN TWP.	WASHINGTON	AR	31	442,877	727-46
MOUNTAINS, THE	COMAL	TX	910	024,889	128
MOUTH ST. CROIX	ST. CROIX	WI	1006	444,993	7, 13, 15-16
MOYAMENSING, WARD 1	PHILADELPHIA	PA	809	444,777	323-462
MOYAMENSING, WARD 2	PHILADELPHIA	PA	809	444,777	463-656
MOYAMENSING, WARD 3	PHILADELPHIA	PA	809	444,777	657-783
MOYAMENSING, WARD 4	PHILADELPHIA	PA	809	444,777	785-895
MOYAMENSING, WARD 5	PHILADELPHIA	PA	809	444,777	897-968
MUD CREEK BEAT	JEFFERSON	AL	7	002,349	305-324
MUD SPRINGS	EL DORADO	CA	34	002,491	726-37
MUDDY BAYOU TWP.	CONWAY	AR	25	002,479	499-503
MUDDY CREEK TWP.	BUTLER	PA	760	020,610	505-532
MUDDY PREC.	COLES	IL	101	007,674	157-75
MUDDY PREC.	JASPER	IL	110	007,683	568-71
MUHLENBERG CO.		KY	214	442,982	349-546
MUHLENBERG TWP.	PICKAWAY	OH	720	444,713	327-41
MUKWONAGO	WAUKESHA	WI	1009	444,996	602-628
MULBERRY GROVE	BOND	IL	98	007,671	793-94
MULBERRY P.O. BEAT	AUTAUGA	AL	1	002,343	1-6
MULBERRY TWP.	FRANKLIN	AR	26	002,480	241-50
MULBERRY TWP.	JOHNSON	AR	27	002,481	257-64
MULLICA TWP.	ATLANTIC	NJ	442	016,529	169-90
MUNCIE CENTRE TWP.	DELAWARE	IN	143	007,756	663-78
MUNCY BOR.	LYCOMING	PA	795	444,763	963-84
MUNCY CREEK TWP.	LYCOMING	PA	795	444,763	815-44
MUNCY TWP.	LYCOMING	PA	795	444,763	845-69
MUNDY TWP.	GENESEE	MI	350	443,566	501-519
MUNSON TWP.	GEAUGA	OH	682	444,675	347-75
MURDERKILL HUN.	KENT	DE	52	006,436	405-540
MURFREESBORO	RUTHERFORD	TN	894	444,850	687-715
MURPHY	CHEROKEE	NC	625	444,638	1-4
MURPHY DIST.	RUTHERFORD	TN	894	444,850	408-422
MURRAY	ORLEANS	NY	575	444,291	609-668, 713
MURRAY CO.		GA	78	442,887	293-590
MUSCATINE	MUSCATINE	IA	187	442,962	675-735
MUSCATINE CO.		IA	187	442,962	675-818
MUSCLE RIDGE PLANT.	LINCOLN	ME	259	443,496	326-27
MUSCOGEE CO.		GA	79	442,888	591-848
MUSCONGUS ISLAND	LINCOLN	ME	260	443,497	73-75
MUSKEGO	WAUKESHA	WI	1009	444,996	649-75
MUSKEGON	OTTAWA	MI	361	443,577	61-72
MUSKINGUM CO.		OH	717	444,710	137-541
MUSKINGUM CO.		OH	718	444,711	543-976, 1-26
MUSKINGUM TWP.	MUSKINGUM	OH	717	444,710	247-82
MYATT TWP.	LAWRENCE	AR	27	002,481	487-95
MYERSTOWN	LEBANON	PA	791	444,759	90-110
MYSTIC	NEW LONDON	CT	49	442,881	735-37

CITY, COUNTY, TOWN, OR TOWNSHIP	COUNTY	STATE	NA NO. M432	GD NO.	PAGES		
NAAUSAY	KENDALL	IL	113	007,686	503-516		
NACOGDOCHES	NACOGDOCHES	TX	913	444,916	101-8		
NACOGDOCHES CO.		TX	913	444,916	101-192		
NANKIN TWP.	WAYNE	MI	366	443,582	691-729		
NANSEMOND CO.		VA	962	444,952	255-435		
NANTAHALA	MACON	NC	636	444,649	757-58		
NANTICOKE	BROOME	NY	478	017,054	581-94		
NANTICOKE HUN.	SUSSEX	DE	55	442,884	186-222		
NANTUCKET	NANTUCKET	MA	328	443,547	585-786		
NANTUCKET CO.		MA	328	443,547	585-786		
NAPA	NAPA	CA	35	002,492	259-62		
NAPA CO.		CA	35	002,492	259-68		
NAPA VALLEY	NAPA	CA	35	002,492	263-68		
NAPERVILLE	DU PAGE	IL	105	007,678	28-66		
NAPIER TWP.	BEDFORD	PA	751	020,601	75-134		
NAPLES	SCOTT	IL	128	442,916	59-72		
NAPLES	CUMBERLAND	ME	249	009,719	215-39		
NAPLES	ONTARIO	NY	571	444,287	1-57		
NAPOLEON	JACKSON	MI	352	443,568	875-904		
NAPOLEON TWP.	DESHA	AR	26	002,480	109-112		
NAPOLEON TWP.	HENRY	OH	693	444,686	1-14		
NAPOLI	CATTARAUGUS	NY	479	017,055	109-141		
NAPP OF READ'S DIST.	GRANVILLE	NC	631	444,644	339-51		
NASH CO.		NC	638	444,651	505-662		
NASHUA	HILLSBORO	NH	434	443,638	475-615		
NASHUA TWP.	OGLE	IL	123	442,911	111-20		
NASHVILLE	HILLSBORO	NH	434	443,638	381-455		
NASHVILLE	DAVIDSON	TN	875	024,566	173-341		
NASHVILLE	JACKSON	TN	885	444,841	317-36		
NASSAU	RENSSELAER	NY	586	444,302	733-810		
NASSAU CO.		FL	59	006,715	341-69		
NATCHEZ	ADAMS	MS	368	014,847	1-72		
NATCHITOCHES	NATCHITOCHES	LA	233	443,476	130-48		
NATCHITOCHES PARISH		LA	233	443,476	1-150		
NATICK	MIDDLESEX	MA	323	443,542	655-720		
NATTAWAY PARISH	SOUTHAMPTON	VA	977	444,967	567-670		
NAUGATUCK	NEW HAVEN	CT	45	003,073	161-99		
NAUVOO	HANCOCK	IL	109	007,682	784-811		
NAVARRO DIST.	ELLIS	TX	910	024,889	259-78,	184,	279
NAVARRO DIST.	TARRANT	TX	910	024,889	171-84,	279	
NAVARRO CO.		TX	913	444,916	195-241		
NAZARETH	NORTHAMPTON	PA	802	444,770	418-27		
NEARREN TWP.	MARION	MO	406	443,614	672-702		
NEAVE TWP.	DARKE	OH	674	020,222	633-56		
NEEDHAM	NORFOLK	MA	330	443,549	565-611		
NEENAH	WINNEBAGO	WI	1009	444,996	943-76		
NEGRO BAR	SACRAMENTO	CA	35	002,492	417-24		
NEGRO HEEL DIST.	HARRIS	GA	73	007,069	252-66		
NEKIMI	WINNEBAGO	WI	1009	444,996	1120-42		
NELSON	CHESHIRE	NH	428	014,941	563-81		
NELSON	MADISON	NY	527	017,103	597-646		
NELSON CO.		KY	215	442,983	547-780		
NELSON CO.		VA	963	444,953	439-610		
NELSON TWP.	PORTAGE	OH	722	444,715	175-208		
NELSONVILLE	PUTNAM	NY	581	444,297	229-43		
NEOSHO TWP.	NEWTON	MO	408	443,616	641-63,	722,	

CITY, COUNTY, TOWN, OR TOWNSHIP	COUNTY	STATE	NA NO. M432	GD NO.	PAGES
					734-40
NEPEUSKUN	WINNEBAGO	WI	1009	444,996	1110-19
NESCOPECK	LUZERNE	PA	794	444,762	105-126
NESHANNOCK TWP.	LAWRENCE	PA	790	444,758	367-439
NESHOBA CO.		MS	378	443,590	227-308
NETHER PROVIDENCE	DELAWARE	PA	776	444,744	1-36
NETTLE CREEK	GRUNDY	IL	108	007,681	330-37
NETTLE CREEK TWP.	RANDOLPH	IN	168	442,946	49-79
NEVADA CITY	YUBA	CA	36	442,879	555-78, 583-61
					623-30
NEVERSINK	SULLIVAN	NY	603	444,319	453-507
NEVINS TWP.	VIGO	IN	177	442,955	239-58
NEW ALBANY	FLOYD	IN	145	442,923	593-691, 767-8
NEW ALBANY	FRANKLIN	OH	680	444,673	215-18
NEW ALBANY	MAHONING	OH	707	444,700	593-96
NEW ALBANY PREC.	COLES	IL	101	007,674	1-19
NEW ALBANY TWP.	FLOYD	IN	145	442,923	692-718, 863-7
NEW ALBION	CATTARAUGUS	NY	479	017,055	32-36, 38-71
NEW ASHFORD	BERKSHIRE	MA	305	014,699	281-85
NEW ATHENS TWP.	HARRISON	OH	693	444,686	423-30
NEW BALTIMORE	GREENE	NY	509	017,085	335-91
NEW BALTIMORE	HAMILTON	OH	686	444,679	643-46
NEW BARBADOES TWP.	BERGEN	NJ	442	016,529	303-356, 403
NEW BEDFORD	BRISTOL	MA	309	014,703	425-812
NEW BERLIN	CHENANGO	NY	487	017,063	285-346
NEW BERLIN	WAUKESHA	WI	1009	444,996	675-706
NEW BERLIN BOR.	UNION	PA	831	444,799	1-18
NEW BERN	CRAVEN	NC	626	444,639	549-614
NEW BOSTON	HILLSBORO	NH	432	443,636	333-69
NEW BRAINTREE	WORCESTER	MA	343	443,562	293-313
NEW BRAUNFELS	COMAL	TX	910	024,889	99-127
NEW BREMEN	LEWIS	NY	523	017,099	561-96
NEW BREMEN	AUGLAIZE	OH	660	020,208	474-81
NEW BRIGHTON TWP.	BEAVER	PA	750	020,600	39-71
NEW BRITAIN	HARTFORD	CT	40	003,068	29-75
NEW BRITAIN TWP.	BUCKS	PA	758	020,608	579-610
NEW BUFFALO BOR.	PERRY	PA	805	444,773	1195-98
NEW BUFFALO TWP.	SAUK	WI	1006	444,993	99-103
NEW CANAAN	FAIRFIELD	CT	38	003,066	661-723
NEW CARLISLE	CLARK	OH	666	020,214	209-225
NEW CASTLE	NEW CASTLE	DE	54	006,438	551-80
NEW CASTLE	LINCOLN	ME	260	443,497	779-826
NEW CASTLE	ROCKINGHAM	NH	437	443,641	233-54
NEW CASTLE	WESTCHESTER	NY	614	444,330	121-63
NEW CASTLE	SCHUYLKILL	PA	827	444,795	309-313
NEW CASTLE BOR.	LAWRENCE	PA	790	444,758	443-81
NEW CASTLE CO.		DE	53	006,437	543-801, 1-33
NEW CASTLE CO.		DE	54	006,438	337-768
NEW CASTLE HUN.	NEW CASTLE	DE	54	006,438	581-624
NEW CASTLE TWP.	SCHUYLKILL	PA	827	444,795	249-348
NEW CHESTER	ADAMS	PA	743	020,593	645-47
NEW CUMBERLAND	TUSCARAWAS	OH	735	444,728	577-81
NEW CUMBERLAND	HANCOCK	VA	949	444,939	634-38
NEW CUMBERLAND BOR.	CUMBERLAND	PA	773	444,741	765-72
NEW DESIGN PREC.	MONROE	IL	121	442,909	60, 131-63
NEW DIGGINGS	LAFAYETTE	WI	1001	444,988	857-98
NEW DIST.	LUMPKIN	GA	76	007,072	171-76
NEW DURHAM	STRAFFORD	NH	440	443,644	581-605
NEW DURHAM TWP.	LA PORTE	IN	157	442,935	615-34

CITY, COUNTY, TOWN, OR TOWNSHIP	COUNTY	STATE	NA NO. M432	GD NO.	PAGES
NEW ENGLAND COMPANY	SUTTER	CA	36	442,879	48
NEW FAIRFIELD	FAIRFIELD	CT	37	003,065	107-129
NEW FRANKFORT	SCOTT	IN	171	442,949	421-26
NEW GARDEN	CHESTER	PA	764	020,614	407-440
NEW GARDEN TWP.	WAYNE	IN	180	442,958	535-73
NEW GERMANTOWN BOR.	PERRY	PA	805	444,773	841-42
NEW GLARUS	GREEN	WI	999	444,986	603-613
NEW GLOUCESTER	CUMBERLAND	ME	250	009,720	113-56
NEW GOTTINGEN	GUERNSEY	OH	684	444,677	627-28
NEW HAMPTON	BELKNAP	NH	425	014,938	169-207
NEW HANOVER CO.		NC	638	444,651	665-892
NEW HANOVER TWP.	BURLINGTON	NJ	443	016,530	515-71
NEW HANOVER TWP.	MONTGOMERY	PA	799	444,767	337-75
NEW HARTFORD	LITCHFIELD	CT	42	003,070	217-82
NEW HARTFORD	ONEIDA	NY	562	444,278	457-572
NEW HAVEN	SHIAWASSEE	MI	363	443,579	113-16
NEW HAVEN	OSWEGO	NY	577	444,293	55-142
NEW HAVEN	HAMILTON	OH	686	444,679	639-42
NEW HAVEN	ADDISON	VT	920	027,446	337-76
NEW HAVEN CITY	NEW HAVEN	CT	47	003,075	209-693
NEW HAVEN CO.		CT	45	003,073	1-538
NEW HAVEN CO.		CT	46	003,074	539-852, 1-208
NEW HAVEN CO.		CT	47	003,075	209-749
NEW HAVEN (FAIR HAVEN)	NEW HAVEN	CT	47	003,075	697-728
NEW HAVEN PREC.	GALLATIN	IL	107	007,680	691-93
NEW HAVEN TWP.	HURON	OH	697	444,690	355-88
NEW HAVEN (WESTVILLE)	NEW HAVEN	CT	47	003,075	729-49
NEW HOLLAND	LANCASTER	PA	789	444,757	387-402
NEW HOPE BOR.	BUCKS	PA	758	020,608	393-420
NEW HUDSON	ALLEGANY	NY	476	017,052	657-92
NEW IPSWICH	HILLSBORO	NH	433	443,637	541-85
NEW KENT CO.		VA	963	444,953	613-76
NEW LEBANON	COLUMBIA	NY	492	017,068	1-58
NEW LENOX	WILL	IL	133	442,921	165-79
NEW LIGHT DIST.	WAKE	NC	647	444,660	251-63
NEW LIMERICK	AROOSTOOK	ME	248	009,718	90-94
NEW LISBON	OTSEGO	NY	579	444,295	557-600
NEW LONDON	NEW LONDON	CT	49	442,881	161-376
NEW LONDON	MERRIMACK	NH	436	443,640	211-33
NEW LONDON CO.		CT	48	442,880	1-646
NEW LONDON CO.		CT	49	442,881	647-836, 1-430
NEW LONDON TWP.	HENRY	IA	184	007,793	317-49
NEW LONDON TWP.	HURON	OH	697	444,690	671-702
NEW LONDON TWP.	CHESTER	PA	764	020,614	199-250
NEW LYNNE TWP.	ASHTABULA	OH	659	020,207	591-1005
NEW MADRID CO.		MO	408	443,616	543-639
NEW MANCHESTER	HANCOCK	VA	949	444,939	597-601
NEW MARKET	FREDERICK	MD	293	443,524	475-555
NEW MARKET	ROCKINGHAM	NH	438	443,642	303-348
NEW MARKET	YORK	PA	840	444,808	743-46
NEW MARKET TWP.	HIGHLAND	OH	694	444,687	417-56
NEW MARLBOROUGH	BERKSHIRE	MA	306	014,700	529-72
NEW MARTINSVILLE	WETZEL	VA	981	444,971	73, 75-77, 79
NEW MILFORD	LITCHFIELD	CT	43	003,071	239-348
NEW MILFORD	WINNEBAGO	IL	134	442,922	696-709
NEW MILFORD TWP.	SUSQUEHANNA	PA	829	444,797	399-433
NEW ORLEANS, WARD 1 (1ST MUNICIPALITY)	ORLEANS PAR.	LA	235	443,478	1-88
NEW ORLEANS, WARD 2	ORLEANS PAR.	LA	235	443,478	89-168

131

CITY, COUNTY, TOWN, OR TOWNSHIP	COUNTY	STATE	NA NO. M432	GD NO.	PAGES
(1ST MUNICIPALITY)					
NEW ORLEANS, WARD 3	ORLEANS PAR.	LA	235	443,478	169-232
(1ST MUNICIPALITY)					
NEW ORLEANS, WARD 4	ORLEANS PAR.	LA	235	443,478	233-340
(1ST MUNICIPALITY)					
NEW ORLEANS, WARD 5	ORLEANS PAR.	LA	236	443,479	341-480
(1ST MUNICIPALITY)					
NEW ORLEANS, WARD 6	ORLEANS PAR.	LA	236	443,479	481-697
(1ST MUNICIPALITY)					
NEW ORLEANS, WARD 7	ORLEANS PAR.	LA	236	443,479	699-802
(1ST MUNICIPALITY)					
NEW ORLEANS, WARD 1	ORLEANS PAR.	LA	237	443,480	1-104
(2ND MUNICIPALITY)					
NEW ORLEANS, WARD 2	ORLEANS PAR.	LA	237	443,480	105-190
(2ND MUNICIPALITY)					
NEW ORLEANS, WARD 3	ORLEANS PAR.	LA	237	443,480	191-406
(2ND MUNICIPALITY)					
NEW ORLEANS, WARD 4	ORLEANS PAR.	LA	237	443,480	407-542
(2ND MUNICIPALITY)					
NEW ORLEANS, WARD 1	ORLEANS PAR.	LA	238	443,481	1-204
(3RD MUNICIPALITY)					
NEW ORLEANS, WARD 2	ORLEANS PAR.	LA	238	443,481	205-292, 417-2
(3RD MUNICIPALITY)					
NEW ORLEANS, WARD 3	ORLEANS PAR.	LA	238	443,481	293-412, 421-2
(3RD MUNICIPALITY)					
NEW ORLEANS, WARD 4	ORLEANS PAR.	LA	238	443,481	413-16, 425-7
(3RD MUNICIPALITY)					
NEW PHILADELPHIA	TUSCARAWAS	OH	735	444,728	443-78
NEW PLATZ	ULSTER	NY	608	444,324	617-84
NEW PORT	WAKULLA	FL	59	006,715	493-96
NEW PORT DIST.	WAKULLA	FL	59	006,715	500
NEW PORTLAND	SOMERSET	ME	269	443,506	389-423
NEW PROVIDENCE TWP.	ESSEX	NJ	449	443,648	493-522
NEW ROCHELLE	WESTCHESTER	NY	615	444,331	319-78
NEW SALEM	FRANKLIN	MA	316	443,535	153-82
NEW SALEM	FAIRFIELD	OH	677	444,670	426-30
NEW SCOTLAND	ALBANY	NY	474	017,050	557-639
NEW SEWICKLEY TWP.	BEAVER	PA	750	020,600	611-61
NEW SHARON	FRANKLIN	ME	253	009,723	207-248
NEW SHOREHAM	NEWPORT	RI	842	022,265	1-32
NEW TRIER	COOK	IL	103	007,676	134-44
NEW UTRECHT	KINGS	NY	521	017,097	57-107
NEW VINEYARD	FRANKLIN	ME	253	009,723	160-75
NEW WASHINGTON	CLARK	IN	138	007,751	128-35
NEW WINDSOR	ORANGE	NY	573	444,289	475-533
NEW YORK DIV.	SUMTER	AL	15	442,866	533-36, 585-5 592
NEW YORK CITY, WARD 1	NEW YORK	NY	534	017,110	1-340
NEW YORK CITY, WARD 1	NEW YORK	NY	535	017,111	341-471
NEW YORK CITY, WARD 2	NEW YORK	NY	535	017,111	473-631
NEW YORK CITY, WARD 3	NEW YORK	NY	535	017,111	633-881
NEW YORK CITY, WARD 3	NEW YORK	NY	536	017,112	1-556
NEW YORK CITY, WARD 4	NEW YORK	NY	537	017,113	1-541
NEW YORK CITY, WARD 5	NEW YORK	NY	538	017,114	1-590
NEW YORK CITY, WARD 6	NEW YORK	NY	539	017,115	1-370
NEW YORK CITY, WARD 7	NEW YORK	NY	540	017,116	371-780
NEW YORK CITY, WARD 7	NEW YORK	NY	541	338,153	1-400
NEW YORK CITY, WARD 8	NEW YORK	NY	542	444,258	401-825
NEW YORK CITY, WARD 8	NEW YORK	NY	543	444,259	1-497
NEW YORK CITY, WARD 9					

CITY, COUNTY, TOWN, OR TOWNSHIP	COUNTY	STATE	NA NO. M432	GD NO.	PAGES
NEW YORK CITY, WARD 9	NEW YORK	NY	544	444,260	498-971
NEW YORK CITY, WARD 10	NEW YORK	NY	545	444,261	1-558
NEW YORK CITY, WARD 11	NEW YORK	NY	546	444,262	1-500
NEW YORK CITY, WARD 11	NEW YORK	NY	547	444,263	501-1049
NEW YORK CITY, WARD 12	NEW YORK	NY	548	444,264	1-109
NEW YORK CITY, WARD 12	NEW YORK	NY	549	444,265	110-256
NEW YORK CITY, WARD 13	NEW YORK	NY	550	444,266	257-930
NEW YORK CITY, WARD 14	NEW YORK	NY	551	444,267	1-605
NEW YORK CITY, WARD 15	NEW YORK	NY	552	444,268	1-539
NEW YORK CITY, WARD 16	NEW YORK	NY	553	444,269	1-624
NEW YORK CITY, WARD 16	NEW YORK	NY	554	444,270	1-637
NEW YORK CITY, WARD 17	NEW YORK	NY	555	444,271	1-503
NEW YORK CITY, WARD 17	NEW YORK	NY	556	444,272	504-1047
NEW YORK CITY, WARD 18	NEW YORK	NY	557	444,273	1-353
NEW YORK CITY, WARD 18	NEW YORK	NY	558	444,274	354-756
NEW YORK CITY, WARD 19	NEW YORK	NY	559	444,275	1-436
NEW YORK CO.		NY	534-40	017,110	1-16
NEW YORK CO.		NY	542-59	444,258	1-75
NEWARK	ALLEGAN	MI	346	014,808	1-6
NEWARK	TIOGA	NY	604	444,320	327-75
NEWARK	WAYNE	NY	612	444,328	550-80
NEWARK	LICKING	OH	702	444,695	1-87
NEWARK	CALEDONIA	VT	922	027,448	515-25
NEWARK	ROCK	WI	1005	444,992	763-83
NEWARK, EAST WARD	ESSEX	NJ	447	443,646	225-371
NEWARK, NORTH WARD	ESSEX	NJ	447	443,646	1-224
NEWARK, SOUTH WARD	ESSEX	NJ	447	443,646	373-610
NEWARK TWP.	LICKING	OH	702	444,695	1-121
NEWARK, WARD 5	ESSEX	NJ	448	443,647	831-940
NEWARK, WEST WARD	ESSEX	NJ	448	443,647	611-830
NEWAYGO CO.		MI	359	443,575	1-13
NEWBERG TWP.	CASS	MI	349	014,811	701-711
NEWBERRY	LA GRANGE	IN	157	442,935	78-90
NEWBERRY	YORK	PA	840	444,808	675-77
NEWBERRY	NEWBERRY	SC	856	444,819	367-78
NEWBERRY CO.		SC	856	444,819	367-544
NEWBERRY TWP.	MIAMI	OH	711	444,704	767-821
NEWBERRY TWP.	YORK	PA	840	444,808	683-729
NEWBURG	PENOBSCOT	ME	265	443,502	731-64
NEWBURG	CUYAHOGA	OH	672	020,220	649-86
NEWBURGH	WARRICK	IN	179	442,957	247-59
NEWBURGH	ORANGE	NY	573	444,289	1-272
NEWBURGH	LEWIS	TN	887	444,843	777
NEWBURY	ESSEX	MA	313	014,707	587-690
NEWBURY	MERRIMACK	NH	436	443,640	301-318
NEWBURY	ORANGE	VT	926	444,925	197-268
NEWBURY TWP.	GEAUGA	OH	682	444,675	537-66
NEWBURYPORT	ESSEX	MA	313	014,707	491-583, 691-830
NEWCASTLE	HENRY	IN	151	442,929	717-32
NEWCASTLE TWP.	FULTON	IN	146	442,924	910-27
NEWCASTLE TWP.	COSHOCTON	OH	670	020,218	1-30
NEWCOMB	ESSEX	NY	504	017,080	592-98
NEWCOMERSTOWN	TUSCARAWAS	OH	735	444,728	691-702
NEWFANE	NIAGARA	NY	444	444,277	741-818
NEWFANE	WINDHAM	VT	929	444,928	53-84
NEWFIELD	YORK	ME	276	443,513	521-54
NEWFIELD	TOMPKINS	NY	606	444,322	571-662
NEWINGTON	ROCKINGHAM	NH	438	443,642	349-60
NEWLIN TWP.	CHESTER	PA	764	020,614	285-302

133

CITY, COUNTY, TOWN, OR TOWNSHIP	COUNTY	STATE	NA NO. M432	GD NO.	PAGES
NEWMANSTOWN	LEBANON	PA	791	444,759	59-63
NEWPORT	LAKE	IL	114	007,687	39-62
NEWPORT	PENOBSCOT	ME	265	443,502	25-54
NEWPORT	SULLIVAN	NH	441	443,645	57-105
NEWPORT	HERKIMER	NY	512	017,088	305-355
NEWPORT	LUZERNE	PA	794	444,762	65-85
NEWPORT	NEWPORT	RI	842	022,265	639-866
NEWPORT	ORLEANS	VT	925	444,924	255-72
NEWPORT BOR.	PERRY	PA	805	444,773	1080-92
NEWPORT CITY	CAMPBELL	KY	195	007,848	1-140
NEWPORT CO.		RI	842	022,265	579-866, 1-198
NEWPORT TWP.	JOHNSON	IA	185	442,960	279-86
NEWPORT TWP.	WASHINGTON	OH	738	444,731	929-62
NEWRY	OXFORD	ME	262	443,499	478-88
NEWSTEAD	ERIE	NY	499	017,075	417-86
NEWTON	MIDDLESEX	MA	326	443,545	1-128
NEWTON	CALHOUN	MI	348	014,810	451-64
NEWTON	ROCKINGHAM	NH	438	443,642	101-117
NEWTON	CATAWBA	NC	624	444,637	527-28
NEWTON	TRUMBULL	OH	733	444,726	275-314
NEWTON CO.		AR	28	002,482	1-41
NEWTON CO.		GA	79	442,888	849-1044
NEWTON CO.		MS	378	443,590	309-390
NEWTON CO.		MO	408	443,616	641-740
NEWTON CO.		TX	913	444,916	245-75
NEWTON HAMILTON	MIFFLIN	PA	797	444,765	713-21
NEWTON PREC.	JASPER	IL	110	007,683	525-51
NEWTON TWP.	JASPER	IN	152	442,930	507-516
NEWTON TWP.	TANEY	MO	420	443,628	698-703
NEWTON TWP.	CAMDEN	NJ	445	016,532	291-348
NEWTON TWP.	SUSSEX	NJ	464	443,663	209-287
NEWTON TWP.	LICKING	OH	703	444,696	875-907
NEWTON TWP.	MIAMI	OH	711	444,704	347-82
NEWTON TWP.	MUSKINGUM	OH	718	444,711	199-255
NEWTON TWP.	PIKE	OH	721	444,714	699-710
NEWTON TWP.	CUMBERLAND	PA	773	444,741	575-616
NEWTON TWP.	LUZERNE	PA	793	444,761	365-82
NEWTOWN	YUBA	CA	36	442,879	611-18
NEWTOWN	FAIRFIELD	CT	37	003,065	1-81
NEWTOWN	WORCESTER	MD	299	443,530	677-85
NEWTOWN	QUEENS	NY	583	444,299	105-280
NEWTOWN	MANITOWOC	WI	1002	444,989	82-89, 100-105
NEWTOWN BOR.	BUCKS	PA	758	020,608	43-56
NEWTOWN TWP.	BUCKS	PA	758	020,608	57-76
NEWTOWN TWP.	DELAWARE	PA	776	444,744	471-90
NEWVILLE BOR.	CUMBERLAND	PA	773	444,741	557-74
NEWVILLE TWP.	DE KALB	IN	142	007,755	401-410
NIAGARA	NIAGARA	NY	561	444,277	507-555
NIAGARA CO.		NY	560	444,276	1-506
NIAGARA CO.		NY	561	444,277	507-1028
NICHOLAS	SUTTER	CA	36	442,879	114-18
NICHOLAS CO.		KY	215	442,983	781-992
NICHOLAS CO.		VA	963	444,953	679-771
NICHOLS	TIOGA	NY	604	444,320	87-132
NICHOLS	CANNON	TN	872	024,563	860-63, 866-75
NICHOLSON TWP.	FAYETTE	PA	779	444,747	195-225
NICHOLSON TWP.	WYOMING	PA	838	444,806	523-70
NILE TWP.	SCIOTO	OH	727	444,720	141-65
NILES	COOK	IL	103	007,676	225-35

CITY, COUNTY, TOWN, OR TOWNSHIP	COUNTY	STATE	NA NO. M432	GD NO.	PAGES	
NILES	CAYUGA	NY	483	017,059	255-303	
NILES TWP.	DELAWARE	IN	143	007,756	827-49	
NIMISHILLEN TWP.	STARK	OH	730	444,723	927-88	
NINEVEH TWP.	BARTHOLOMEW	IN	136	007,749	715-32	
NINEVEH TWP.	JENNINGS	IN	155	442,933	263-302	
NIPPENOSE TWP.	LYCOMING	PA	795	444,763	683-91	
NISKAYUNA	SCHENECTADY	NY	594	444,310	171-90	
NOBLE	BRANCH	MI	347	014,809	837-47	
NOBLE CO.		IN	162	442,940	371-583	
NOBLE TWP.	CASS	IN	137	007,750	869-87	
NOBLE TWP.	JAY	IN	153	442,931	611-28	
NOBLE TWP.	LA PORTE	IN	157	442,935	339-62	
NOBLE TWP.	NOBLE	IN	162	442,940	463-77	
NOBLE TWP.	SHELBY	IN	172	442,950	539-70	
NOBLE TWP.	WABASH	IN	178	442,956	812-96,	1-2
NOBLE TWP.	AUGLAIZE	OH	660	020,208	555-61	
NOBLE TWP.	DEFIANCE	OH	674	020,222	73-87	
NOBLE TWP.	MORGAN	OH	715	444,708	1-42	
NOBLESBORO	LINCOLN	ME	260	443,497	889-922	
NOBLESVILLE	HAMILTON	IN	148	442,926	311-28	
NOBLESVILLE TWP.	HAMILTON	IN	148	442,926	199-240	
NOCKAMIXON TWP.	BUCKS	PA	759	020,609	489-548	
NODAWAY	ANDREW	MO	391	014,871	114-16	
NODAWAY CO.		MO	408	443,616	741-89	
NODOWAY TWP.	ANDREW	MO	391	014,871	57-113	
NORFOLK	LITCHFIELD	CT	42	003,070	285-327	
NORFOLK	ST. LAWRENCE	NY	591	444,307	283-324	
NORFOLK	NORFOLK	VA	964	444,954	1-240	
NORFOLK CO.		MA	329	443,548	1-584	
NORFOLK CO.		MA	330	443,549	1-611,	1-45
NORFOLK CO.		MA	331	443,550	47-721	
NORFOLK CO.		VA	964	444,954	1-542	
NORMAN	GRUNDY	IL	108	007,681	378-79	
NORRIDGEWOCK	SOMERSET	ME	268	443,505	299-342	
NORRISTOWN BOR. LOWER WARD	MONTGOMERY	PA	800	444,768	505-576	
NORRISTOWN BOR. UPPER WARD	MONTGOMERY	PA	800	444,768	435-504	
NORRITON TWP.	MONTGOMERY	PA	799	444,767	455-93	
NORTH ANNVILLE TWP.	LEBANON	PA	791	444,759	513-64	
NORTH ANSON	SOMERSET	ME	269	443,506	361-88	
NORTH BANKS DIST.	CURRITUCK	NC	627	444,640	418-30	
NORTH BEAVER TWP.	LAWRENCE	PA	790	444,758	87-144	
NORTH BEND	WASHINGTON	WI	1008	444,995	72-87	
NORTH BEND TWP.	STARKE	IN	172	442,950	230-33	
NORTH BERGEN	HUDSON	NJ	452	443,651	408-9	
NORTH BERGEN TWP.	HUDSON	NJ	452	443,651	387-472	
NORTH BERWICK	YORK	ME	276	443,513	669-706	
NORTH BLOOMFIELD TWP.	MORROW	OH	716	444,709	793-827	
NORTH BRANFORD	NEW HAVEN	CT	45	003,073	387-410	
NORTH BRIDGEWATER	PLYMOUTH	MA	332	443,551	571-664	
NORTH BROOKFIELD	WORCESTER	MA	343	443,562	1-47	
NORTH BROWN TWP.	VINTON	OH	736	444,729	661-73	
NORTH BRUNSWICK TWP.	MIDDLESEX	NJ	455	443,654	451-690	
NORTH BUFFALO	ARMSTRONG	PA	749	020,599	175-96	
NORTH BUTLER TWP.	BUTLER	PA	760	020,610	159-92	
NORTH CASTLE	WESTCHESTER	NY	615	444,331	105-157	
NORTH CHELSEA	SUFFOLK	MA	339	443,558	943-65	
NORTH CODORUS TWP.	YORK	PA	839	444,807	709-760	

135

CITY, COUNTY, TOWN, OR TOWNSHIP	COUNTY	STATE	NA NO. M432	GD NO.	PAGES
NORTH COVENTRY TWP.	CHESTER	PA	765	020,615	339-62
NORTH CREEK DIST.	BEAUFORT	NC	620	018,106	723-34
NORTH DANSVILLE	LIVINGSTON	NY	525	017,101	637-741
NORTH EAST	DUTCHESS	NY	496	017,072	603-640
NORTH EAST	ONSLOW	NC	639	444,652	193-201
NORTH EAST BOR.	ERIE	PA	777	444,745	217-26
NORTH EAST, TOWN OF	CECIL	MD	290	443,521	148-55
NORTH EAST TWP.	ORANGE	IN	163	442,941	815-44
NORTH EAST TWP.	ERIE	PA	777	444,745	227-83
NORTH ELBA	ESSEX	NY	503	017,079	354-58
NORTH FAYETTE TWP.	ALLEGHENY	PA	748	020,598	589-623
NORTH FORK PREC.	GALLATIN	IL	107	007,680	734-45
NORTH FORK TWP.	IZARD	AR	27	002,481	36-43
NORTH HAMPTON	ROCKINGHAM	NH	438	443,642	549-68
NORTH HAVEN	NEW HAVEN	CT	45	003,073	463-94
NORTH HAVEN	WALDO	ME	271	443,508	107-126
NORTH HEIDELBURG TWP.	BERKS	PA	752	020,602	333-53
NORTH HEMPSTEAD	QUEENS	NY	582	444,298	1-103
NORTH HERO	GRANDE ISLE	VT	924	444,923	38-55
NORTH HUDSON	ESSEX	NY	504	017,080	681-96
NORTH HUNTINGDON	WESTMORELAND	PA	836	444,804	691-752
NORTH KINGSTON	WASHINGTON	RI	847	444,813	589-662
NORTH LEBANON TWP.	LEBANON	PA	791	444,759	281-338
NORTH MADISON	JEFFERSON	IN	154	442,932	51-57, 151-66
NORTH MAHONING TWP.	INDIANA	PA	785	444,753	473-92
NORTH MANHEIM	SCHUYLKILL	PA	826	444,794	631-702
NORTH MIDDLETOWN TWP.	CUMBERLAND	PA	772	444,740	59-112
NORTH MILL CREEK	PENDLETON	VA	968	444,958	35-38
NORTH NORWICH	CHENANGO	NY	487	017,063	437-64
NORTH PENN	PHILADELPHIA	PA	820	444,788	1-64
NORTH PLAINS	IONIA	MI	352	443,568	315-22
NORTH PROVIDENCE	PROVIDENCE	RI	843	444,809	549-731
NORTH SALEM	WESTCHESTER	NY	614	444,330	603-634
NORTH SEWICKLEY TWP.	BEAVER	PA	750	020,600	311-35
NORTH SHENANGO TWP.	CRAWFORD	PA	771	444,739	921-40
NORTH SLIPPERY ROCK TWP.	LAWRENCE	PA	790	444,758	187-240
NORTH STONINGTON	NEW LONDON	CT	48	442,880	599-646
NORTH STRABANE TWP.	WASHINGTON	PA	833	444,801	57-85
NORTH TWP.	COOK	IL	103	007,676	7
NORTH TWP.	LAKE	IN	157	442,935	314-16
NORTH TWP.	HARRISON	OH	693	444,686	563-89
NORTH WHITEHALL TWP.	LEHIGH	PA	792	444,760	515-88
NORTH WOODBURY TWP.	BLAIR	PA	755	020,605	63, 105-148
NORTH YARMOUTH	CUMBERLAND	ME	249	009,719	505-532
NORTHAMPTON	HAMPSHIRE	MA	320	443,539	149-274
NORTHAMPTON	FULTON	NY	506	017,082	285-325
NORTHAMPTON CO.		NC	639	444,652	1-164
NORTHAMPTON CO.		PA	802	444,770	1-547
NORTHAMPTON CO.		PA	803	444,771	549-972
NORTHAMPTON CO.		VA	965	444,955	545-636
NORTHAMPTON TWP.	SAGINAW	MI	361	443,577	187-89
NORTHAMPTON TWP.	BURLINGTON	NJ	444	016,531	787-862
NORTHAMPTON TWP.	SUMMIT	OH	732	444,725	601-628
NORTHAMPTON TWP.	BUCKS	PA	759	020,609	159-202
NORTHAMPTON TWP.	LEHIGH	PA	792	444,760	685-706
NORTHBOROUGH	WORCESTER	MA	343	443,562	497-533
NORTHBRIDGE	WORCESTER	MA	343	443,564	309-362
NORTHEAST	ADAMS	IL	97	007,670	351-62
NORTHERN LIBERTIES, UNINCORP. PHI.		PA	823	444,791	967-1013

CITY, COUNTY, TOWN, OR TOWNSHIP	COUNTY	STATE	NA NO. M432	GO NO.	PAGES	
NORTHERN LIBERTIES, WARD 1	PHILA.	PA	810	444,778	1-137	
NORTHERN LIBERTIES, WARD 2	PHILA.	PA	810	444,778	139-220	
NORTHERN LIBERTIES, WARD 3	PHILA.	PA	810	444,778	221-385	
NORTHERN LIBERTIES, WARD 4	PHILA.	PA	810	444,778	387-506	
NORTHERN LIBERTIES, WARD 5	PHILA.	PA	811	444,779	507-705	
NORTHERN LIBERTIES, WARD 6	PHILA.	PA	811	444,779	707-890	
NORTHERN LIBERTIES, WARD 7	PHILA.	PA	811	444,779	891-1138	
NORTHFIELD	COOK	IL	103	007,676	145-68	
NORTHFIELD	WASHINGTON	ME	273	443,510	109-114	
NORTHFIELD	FRANKLIN	MA	317	443,536	653-96	
NORTHFIELD	WASHTENAW	MI	364	443,580	533-56,	677-80
NORTHFIELD	MERRIMACK	NH	436	443,640	179-210	
NORTHFIELD	RICHMOND	NY	587	444,303	273-368	
NORTHFIELD TWP.	WASHINGTON	VT	928	444,927	73-142	
NORTHFORK PREC.	SUMMIT	OH	732	444,725	663-98	
NORTHMORELAND TWP.	JASPER	IL	110	007,683	572-85	
NORTHPORT	WYOMING	PA	838	444,806	177-95	
NORTHUMBERLAND	WALDO	ME	271	443,508	453-82	
NORTHUMBERLAND	COOS	NH	429	443,633	235-45	
NORTHUMBERLAND BOR.	SARATOGA	NY	592	444,308	283-326	
NORTHUMBERLAND CO.	NORTHUMBERLAND	PA	804	444,772	201-226	
NORTHUMBERLAND CO.		PA	804	444,772	1-715	
NORTHVILLE		VA	965	444,955	637-726	
NORTHWEST TWP.	LA SALLE	IL	115	007,688	695-717	
NORTHWEST TWP.	ORANGE	IN	163	442,941	962-92	
NORTHWOOD	WILLIAMS	OH	741	444,734	101-9	
NORTON	ROCKINGHAM	NH	438	443,642	569-600	
NORTON TWP.	BRISTOL	MA	307	014,701	57-104	
NORWALK	SUMMIT	OH	732	444,725	49-81	
NORWALK TWP.	FAIRFIELD	CT	38	003,066	265-375	
NORWAY	HURON	OH	697	444,690	1-36, 65-106	
NORWAY	OXFORD	ME	263	443,500	89-136	
NORWAY	HERKIMER	NY	513	017,089	513-38	
NORWEGIAN TWP.	RACINE	WI	1004	444,991	280-97	
NORWICH	SCHUYLKILL	PA	827	444,795	793-856	
NORWICH	NEW LONDON	CT	48	442,880	153-397	
NORWICH	HAMPSHIRE	MA	320	443,539	101-118	
NORWICH	CHENANGO	NY	487	017,063	349-435	
NORWICH TWP.	WINDSOR	VT	930	444,929	223-70	
NORWICH TWP.	FRANKLIN	OH	680	444,673	69-94	
NORWICK TWP.	MC KEAN	PA	795	444,763	111-17	
NOTAPASSA SET.	HURON	OH	697	444,690	189-213	
NOTTAWA TWP.	HILLSBOROUGH	FL	58	006,714	522	
NOTTINGHAM	ST. JOSEPH	MI	362	443,578	707-734	
NOTTINGHAM DIST.	ROCKINGHAM	NH	437	443,641	441-71	
NOTTINGHAM TWP.	PRINCE GEORGES	MD	295	443,526	114-36	
NOTTINGHAM TWP.	WELLS	IN	181	442,959	715-28	
NOTTINGHAM TWP.	MERCER	NJ	454	443,653	567-673	
NOTTINGHAM TWP.	HARRISON	OH	693	444,686	773-804	
NOTTOWAY CO.	WASHINGTON	PA	833	444,801	431-54	
NOVI TWP.		VA	965	444,955	727-86	
NOXUBEE CO.	OAKLAND	MI	359	443,575	397-430	
NUECES CO.		MS	379	443,591	391-509	
NUNDA		TX	913	444,916	279-96	
NUTBUSH DIST.	LIVINGSTON	NY	524	017,100	53-127	
NUTBUSH DIST.	GRANVILLE	NC	631	444,644	415-23	
NUTBUSH DIST.	WARREN	NC	648	444,661	25-40	

CITY, COUNTY, TOWN, OR TOWNSHIP	COUNTY	STATE	NA NO. M432	GD NO.	PAGES
OAK CREEK	MILWAUKEE	WI	1003	444,990	853-82
OAK FLATS	TUOLUMNE	CA	36	442,879	215-16, 218-20
OAK GROVE BEAT	PERRY	AL	12	002,354	663-71
OAKFIELD	KENT	MI	353	443,569	617-26
OAKFIELD	GENESEE	NY	508	017,084	579-615
OAKFIELD	FOND DU LAC	WI	997	444,984	584-602
OAKHAM	WORCESTER	MA	341	443,560	741-68
OAKLAND	OAKLAND	MI	359	443,575	283-306
OAKLAND	FAIRFIELD	OH	677	444,670	951-53
OAKLAND	JEFFERSON	WI	1000	444,987	251-70
OAKLAND CO.		MI	359	443,575	17-497
OAKLAND CO.		MI	360	443,576	499-793
OAKLAND TWP.	VENANGO	PA	832	444,800	165-84
OBION CO		TN	891	444,847	637-793
OCALA	MARION	FL	59	006,715	227-31
OCCAHANNOCK NECK	NORTHAMPTON	VA	965	444,955	626-32
OCEAN CO.		NJ	460	443,659	1-243
OCEAN TWP.	MONMOUTH	NJ	456	443,655	50-51, 77-169
OCEANA CO.		MI	361	443,577	797-804
OCKLOCKNA DIST.	WAKULLA	FL	59	006,715	517-19
OCONOMOWOC	WAUKESHA	WI	1009	444,996	731-58
OCRACOKE DIST.	HYDE	NC	634	444,647	799-809
ODESSA	IONIA	MI	352	443,568	269-70
ODIN TWP.	CHICOT	AR	25	002,479	371-76
OGDEN	LENAWEE	MI	355	443,571	335-48
OGDEN	MONROE	NY	529	017,105	163-226
OGLE CO.		IL	123	442,911	1-250
OGLETHORPE	MACON	GA	76	007,072	319-21
OGLETHORPE CO.		GA	80	442,889	1-105
OHIO	BOONE	IL	98	007,671	173-88
OHIO	BUREAU	IL	99	007,672	430-34
OHIO	HERKIMER	NY	513	017,089	541-66
OHIO		IN	163	442,941	585-720
OHIO CO.		KY	215	442,983	1-208
OHIO CO.		VA	966	444,956	1-427
OHIO CO.		IN	136	007,749	659-65
OHIO TWP.	BARTHOLOMEW	IN	139	007,752	137-55
OHIO TWP.	CRAWFORD	IN	172	442,950	91-127
OHIO TWP.	SPENCER	IN	179	442,957	247-82
OHIO TWP.	WARRICK	OH	667	020,215	826-929
OHIO TWP.	CLERMONT	OH	681	444,674	735-47
OHIO TWP.	GALLIA	OH	712	444,705	801-840
OHIO TWP.	MONROE	PA	744	020,594	665-720
OHIO TWP.	ALLEGHENY	PA	750	020,600	271-310
OHIO TWP.	BEAVER	PA	771	444,739	507-526
OIL CREEK TWP.	CRAWFORD	IN	165	442,943	834-46
OIL TWP.	PERRY	IL	126	442,914	624, 629-36
OKAW, EAST OF	ST. CLAIR	IL	101	007,674	95-121
OKAW PREC.	COLES	IL	124	442,912	24-28
OKAW RIVER	PLATT	MS	379	443,591	510-614
OKTIBBEHA CO.		ME	254	443,491	335
OLD HARBOUR ISLAND	HANCOCK	VA	942	444,932	103-112
OLD POINT COMFORT	ELIZABETH	AR	25	002,479	23-27
OLD RIVER TWP.	ARKANSAS	AR	25	002,479	365-67
OLD RIVER TWP.	CHICOT	FL	58	006,714	517-18
OLD TAMPA BAY SET.	HILLSBOROUGH	AL	4	002,346	479-88
OLD TOWN BEAT	DALLAS	AL	12	002,354	743-66
OLD TOWN BEAT	PERRY	KY	216	442,984	209-333
OLDHAM CO.					

CITY, COUNTY, TOWN, OR TOWNSHIP	COUNTY	STATE	NA NO. M432	GD NO.	PAGES
OLD TOWN	MC LEON	IL	117	007,690	179-93, 201-2
OLD TOWN	PENOBSCOT	ME	266	443,503	429-502
OLEAN	CATTARAUGUS	NY	479	017,055	329-50
OLEANDER BEAT	MARSHALL	AL	10	002,352	506-525
OLENA	HENDERSON	IL	109	007,682	135
OLEY TWP.	BERKS	PA	753	020,603	1-44
OLIO	SHEBOYGAN	WI	1006	444,993	278-81
OLIVE	ULSTER	NY	607	444,323	403-468
OLIVE TWP.	ELKHART	IN	144	007,757	210-20
OLIVE TWP.	CLINTON	MI	349	014,811	113-18
OLIVE TWP.	MEIGS	OH	710	444,703	256-77
OLIVE TWP.	MORGAN	OH	715	444,708	509-556
OLIVER TWP.	ST. JOSEPH	IN	171	442,949	53-73
OLIVER TWP.	MIFFLIN	PA	797	444,765	637-78
OLIVER TWP.	PERRY	PA	805	444,773	1135-56
OLMSTEAD TWP.	CUYAHOGA	OH	673	020,221	391-419
ONEANTA	OTSEGO	NY	580	444,296	252-97
ONECO	STEPHENSON	IL	129	442,917	561-82
ONEIDA	EATON	MI	349	014,811	300-311
ONEIDA CO.		NY	562	444,278	1-572
ONEIDA CO.		NY	563	444,279	573-998
ONEIDA CO.		NY	564	444,280	1-644
ONEIDA CO.		NY	565	444,281	1-462
ONEIDA CO.		NY	566	444,282	463-772
ONONDAGA	ONONDAGA	NY	568	444,284	523-658
ONONDAGA CO.		NY	567	444,283	1-522
ONONDAGA CO.		NY	568	444,284	523-1010
ONONDAGA CO.		NY	569	444,285	1-531
ONONDAGA CO.		NY	570	444,286	533-1050
ONONDAGA TWP.	INGHAM	MI	351	443,567	223-43
ONSLOW CO.		NC	639	444,652	165-308
ONTARIO	WAYNE	NY	612	444,328	203-56
ONTARIO CO.		NY	571	444,287	1-554
ONTARIO CO.		NY	572	444,288	555-1067
ONTONAGON	ONTONAGON	MI	361	443,577	1-10
ONTONAGON CO.		MI	361	443,577	1-10
ONTWA TWP.	CASS	MI	349	014,811	497-516
OPHIR	LA SALLE	IL	115	007,688	567, 599-602
OPPENHEIM	FULTON	NY	506	017,082	405-460
ORANGE	NEW HAVEN	CT	46	003,074	817-52
ORANGE	FRANKLIN	MA	317	443,536	552, 697-736
ORANGE	IONIA	MI	352	443,568	259-68
ORANGE	GRAFTON	NH	430	443,634	193-203
ORANGE	STEUBEN	NY	598	444,314	251-99
ORANGE	CUYAHOGA	OH	673	020,221	751-78
ORANGE	ORANGE	VT	926	444,925	269-92
ORANGE	ORANGE	VA	967	444,957	479-85
ORANGE CO.		FL	59	006,715	371-77
ORANGE CO.		IN	163	442,941	721-992
ORANGE CO.		NY	573	444,289	1-688
ORANGE CO.		NY	574	444,290	1-680
ORANGE CO.		NC	639	444,652	309-594
ORANGE CO.		VT	926	444,925	1-677
ORANGE CO.		VA	967	444,957	431-529
ORANGE TWP.	FAYETTE	IN	144	007,757	509-536
ORANGE TWP.	NOBLE	IN	162	442,940	511-25
ORANGE TWP.	ESSEX	NJ	449	443,648	387-491
ORANGE TWP.	ASHLAND	OH	658	020,206	951, 954-94
ORANGE TWP.	CARROLL	OH	664	020,212	81-118

CITY, COUNTY, TOWN, OR TOWNSHIP	COUNTY	STATE	NA NO. M432	GD NO.	PAGES
ORANGE TWP.	DELAWARE	OH	675	020,223	436-63
ORANGE TWP.	HANCOCK	OH	692	444,685	975-92
ORANGE TWP.	MEIGS	OH	710	444,703	131-51
ORANGE TWP.	SHELBY	OH	729	444,722	449-71
ORANGE TWP.	COLUMBIA	PA	769	444,737	354-79
ORANGEBURG CO.		SC	857	444,820	545-742
ORANGETOWN	ROCKLAND	NY	588	444,304	369-483
ORANGEVILLE	BARRY	MI	346	014,808	158-66
ORANGEVILLE	WYOMING	NY	616	444,332	63-98
OREGON	LAPEER	MI	354	443,570	768-72
OREGON	DANE	WI	995	034,509	533-48
OREGON BAR	SUTTER	CA	36	442,879	46
OREGON CANYON	EL DORADO	CA	34	002,491	885-86, 888
OREGON CITY	CLACKAMAS	OR	742	020,298	23-26, 51-63
OREGON CO.		MO	408	443,616	791-924
OREGON DIST.	COBB	GA	66	007,062	439-52
OREGON TWP.	OGLE	IL	123	442,911	57-62
OREGON TWP.	SCHUYLER	IL	128	442,916	679-96
OREGON TWP.	STARKE	IN	172	442,950	234-36
OREGON TWP.	LUCAS	OH	706	444,699	165-74
OREGON TWP.	WAYNE	PA	835	444,803	99-107
OREGON VILLAGE	OGLE	IL	123	442,911	49-56
ORFORD	GRAFTON	NH	431	443,635	459-92
ORIENT PLANTATION	AROOSTOOK	ME	248	009,718	39-43
ORION	FULTON	IL	107	007,680	564-76
ORION	OAKLAND	MI	359	443,575	255-82
ORLAND	HANCOCK	ME	255	443,492	789-826
ORLAND TWP.	COOK	IL	103	007,676	85-96
ORLAND VILLAGE	STEUBEN	IN	173	442,951	272-75
ORLEANS	BARNSTABLE	MA	303	014,697	207-250
ORLEANS	JEFFERSON	NY	515	017,091	133-211
ORLEANS CO.		NY	575	444,291	1-713
ORLEANS CO.		VT	925	444,924	1-383
ORLEANS PARISH		LA	234	443,477	151-760
ORLEANS PARISH		LA	235-36	443,478-81	
ORLEANS TWP.	ORANGE	IN	163	442,941	845-78
ORLEANS TWP.	IONIA	MI	352	443,568	362-73
ORNEVILLE	PISCATAQUIS	ME	267	443,504	621-31
ORO CITY	SUTTER	CA	36	442,879	113-14
ORONO	PENOBSCOT	ME	264	443,501	455-521
ORRINGTON	PENOBSCOT	ME	264	443,501	409-454
ORTER ISLAND	LINCOLN	ME	259	443,496	324
ORWELL	OSWEGO	NY	578	444,294	387-414
ORWELL	BRADFORD	PA	757	020,607	253-82
ORWELL	ADDISON	VT	920	027,446	65-100
ORWELL TWP.	ASHTABULA	OH	659	020,207	939-58
ORWIGSBURG BOR.	SCHUYLKILL	PA	826	444,794	397-418
OSAGE CO.		MO	408	443,616	825-981
OSAGE TWP.	BENTON	AR	25	002,479	125-60
OSAGE TWP.	CARROLL	AR	25	002,479	274-88
OSAGE TWP.	NEWTON	AR	28	002,482	39-41
OSAGE TWP.	MORGAN	MO	408	443,616	498-506
OSBORNE MILL DIST.	HARRIS	GA	73	007,069	216-29
OSCEOLA	LEWIS	NY	523	017,099	597-606
OSCEOLA	ST. CROIX	WI	1006	444,993	12, 14
OSCEOLA TWP.	LIVINGSTON	MI	356	443,572	837-59
OSHTEMO	KALAMAZOO	MI	353	443,569	110-23
OSKALOOSA	MAHASKA	IA	187	442,962	309, 312, 322-2
OSNABURG TWP.	STARK	OH	730	444,723	657-94, 696-710

CITY, COUNTY, TOWN, OR TOWNSHIP	COUNTY	STATE	NA NO. M432	GD NO.	PAGES
OSOLO TWP.	ELKHART	IN	144	007,757	67-78
OSSIAN	ALLEGANY	NY	476	017,052	175-205
OSSINNING	WESTCHESTER	NY	614	444,330	1-120
OSSIPEE	CARROLL	NH	426	014,939	177-225
OSWAYO	POTTER	PA	825	444,793	279-84
OSWEGATCHIE	ST. LAWRENCE	NY	589	444,305	155-344
OSWEGO	KENDALL	IL	113	007,686	463-501
OSWEGO	KOSCIUSKO	IN	156	442,934	704-7
OSWEGO CO.		NY	576	444,292	1-506
OSWEGO CO.		NY	577	444,293	507-780, 1-243
OSWEGO CO.		NY	578	444,294	245-733
OSWEGO, WARD 1	OSWEGO	NY	576	444,292	153-295
OSWEGO, WARD 2	OSWEGO	NY	576	444,292	297-355
OSWEGO, WARD 3	OSWEGO	NY	576	444,292	357-426
OSWEGO, WARD 4	OSWEGO	NY	576	444,292	427-506
OTEGO	OTSEGO	NY	580	444,296	297-339
OTIS	HANCOCK	ME	255	443,492	840-42
OTIS	BERKSHIRE	MA	306	014,700	281-310
OTISCO	ONONDAGA	NY	567	444,283	343-85
OTISCO TWP.	IONIA	MI	352	443,568	415-39
OTISFIELD	CUMBERLAND	ME	249	009,719	301-330
OTSEGO	ALLEGAN	MI	346	014,808	75-94
OTSEGO	OTSEGO	NY	579	444,295	463-556
OTSEGO CO.		NY	579	444,295	1-600
OTSEGO CO.		NY	580	444,296	1-586
OTSEGO TWP.	STEUBEN	IN	173	442,951	349-62
OTSEGO TWP.	COLUMBIA	WI	994	034,508	279-88
OTSELIC	CHENANGO	NY	487	017,063	86-128
OTTAWA	LA SALLE	IL	115	007,688	355-416, 492-94, 538-40, 568, 690-94
OTTAWA	WAUKESHA	WI	1009	444,996	475-93
OTTAWA CO.		MI	361	443,577	13-153
OTTAWA CO.		OH	719	444,712	269-350
OTTAWA TWP.	OTTAWA	MI	361	443,577	129-39
OTTAWA TWP.	PUTNAM	OH	723	444,716	119-46
OTTER CREEK TWP.	RIPLEY	IN	169	442,947	703-721
OTTER CREEK TWP.	VIGO	IN	177	442,955	219-38
OTTER CREEK TWP.	JACKSON	IA	184	007,793	613-14, 631, 641-43
OTTO	CATTARAUGUS	NY	479	017,055	581-90, 609-654
OUACHITA CO.		AR	28	002,482	43-210
OUACHITA TWP.	BRADLEY	AR	25	002,479	192-98
OUIHA	MEDINA	TX	912	444,915	823-24
OVERTON CO.		TN	892	444,848	1-244
OVID	SENECA	NY	597	444,313	209-263
OVID TWP.	BRANCH	MI	347	014,809	651-67
OVID TWP.	CLINTON	MI	349	014,811	133-37
OWASCO	CAYUGA	NY	483	017,059	305-334
OWASSO	SHIAWASSEE	MI	363	443,579	117-26
OWEGO	TIOGA	NY	604	444,320	377-551
OWEN	WINNEBAGO	IL	134	442,922	817-29
OWEN CO.		IN	164	442,942	1-311
OWEN CO.		KY	216	442,984	335-553
OWEN TWP.	DALLAS	AR	26	002,480	59-63
OWEN TWP.	CLARK	IN	138	007,751	91-108
OWEN TWP.	CLINTON	IN	139	007,752	732-47
OWEN TWP.	JACKSON	IN	152	442,930	375-404
OWEN TWP.	WARWICK	IN	179	442,957	336-52

CITY, COUNTY, TOWN, OR TOWNSHIP	COUNTY	STATE	NA NO. M432	GD NO.	PAGES
OWENSBORO	DAVIESS	KY	198	442,966	691-709
OWENSVILLE	GIBSON	IN	147	442,925	133-38
OWSLEY CO.		KY	216	442,984	555-643
OXFORD	NEW HAVEN	CT	46	003,074	717-55
OXFORD	OXFORD	ME	263	443,500	137-66
OXFORD	WORCESTER	MA	345	443,564	533-89
OXFORD	CHENANGO	NY	488	017,064	761-838
OXFORD	GRANVILLE	NC	631	444,644	111-17
OXFORD	ADAMS	PA	743	020,593	367-71
OXFORD	CHESTER	PA	764	020,614	139-43
OXFORD BOR.		ME	262	443,499	1-546
OXFORD CO.		ME	263	443,500	1-472
OXFORD CO.	GRANVILLE	NC	631	444,644	199-218
OXFORD DIST.	OAKLAND	MI	360	443,576	701-725
OXFORD TWP.	WARREN	NJ	465	443,664	795-836
OXFORD TWP.	BUTLER	OH	663	020,211	793-867
OXFORD TWP.	COSHOCTON	OH	670	020,218	537-63
OXFORD TWP.	DELAWARE	OH	675	020,223	579-98
OXFORD TWP.	ERIE	OH	676	338,044	767-90
OXFORD TWP.	GUERNSEY	OH	684	444,677	469-526
OXFORD TWP.	TUSCARAWAS	OH	735	444,728	667-90
OXFORD TWP.	ADAMS	PA	743	020,593	363-85
OXFORD TWP.	PHILADELPHIA	PA	820	444,788	65-107
OXVILLE	SCOTT	IL	128	442,916	78-80
OYSTER BAY	QUEENS	NY	582	444,298	355-519
OZAN TWP.	HEMPSTEAD	AR	26	002,480	420-46
OZARK	FRANKLIN	AR	26	002,480	297-98
OZARK CO.		MO	409	443,617	1-55
OZARK TWP.	GREENE	MO	400	443,608	739-52
PACKER TWP.	CARBON	PA	762	020,612	587-93
PADUCAH	MC CRACKEN	KY	211	442,979	271-320
PAGE CO.		IA	188	442,963	1-15
PAGE CO.		VA	967	444,957	533-694
PAHAQUARRY TWP.	WARREN	NJ	465	443,664	1101-1112
PAINESVILLE	LAKE	OH	701	444,694	347-422
PAINT	CLARION	PA	767	444,735	422-36
PAINT TWP.	FAYETTE	OH	678	444,671	48-77
PAINT TWP.	HIGHLAND	OH	694	444,687	317-81
PAINT TWP.	HOLMES	OH	696	444,689	631-69
PAINT TWP.	ROSS	OH	725	444,718	757-83
PAINT TWP.	WAYNE	OH	739	444,732	65-104
PAINT TWP.	SOMERSET	PA	828	444,796	141-59
PAINTED POST	STEUBEN	NY	598	444,314	1-105
PALATINE	COOK	IL	103	007,676	191-207
PALATINE	MONTGOMERY	NY	533	017,109	571-638
PALERMO	WALDO	ME	271	443,508	517, 555-94
PALERMO	OSWEGO	NY	577	444,293	45-94
PALESTINE	ANDERSON	TX	908	024,887	1-4
PALESTINE	MARION	VA	958	444,948	278-86
PALESTINE TWP.	BRADLEY	AR	25	002,479	199-201
PALMER	HAMPDEN	MA	319	443,538	519-612
PALMYRA	SOMERSET	ME	268	443,505	1-40
PALMYRA	LENAWEE	MI	355	443,571	376-402
PALMYRA	MARION	MO	406	443,614	540-62
PALMYRA	WAYNE	NY	612	444,328	1-96
PALMYRA	LEBANON	PA	791	444,759	587-93

CITY, COUNTY, TOWN, OR TOWNSHIP	COUNTY	STATE	NA NO. M432	6D NO.	PAGES
PALMYRA	JEFFERSON	WI	1000	444,987	341-64
PALMYRA TWP.	LEE	IL	116	007,689	151-65
PALMYRA TWP.	PORTAGE	OH	722	444,715	405-432
PALMYRA TWP.	PIKE	PA	825	444,793	107-118
PALMYRA TWP.	WAYNE	PA	835	444,803	179-226
PALOS TWP.	COOK	IL	103	007,676	77-84, 120
PAMELIA	JEFFERSON	NY	514	017,090	457-518
PAMPAS TWP.	DE KALB	IL	104	007,677	729-53
PANHANDLE DIST.	STEWART	GA	82	442,891	77-92
PANOLA CO.		MS	379	443,591	615-735
PANOLA CO.		TX	913	444,916	299-364
PANTHER BRANCH DIST.	WAKE	NC	647	444,660	197-206
PANTHERSVILLE	DE KALB	GA	67	007,063	335, 339-65
PANTON	ADDISON	VT	920	027,446	517-30
PAOLI TWP.	ORANGE	IN	163	442,941	879-929
PARACLIFTA TWP.	SEVIER	AR	30	442,876	373-75
PARADISE TWP.	LANCASTER	PA	789	444,757	549-92
PARADISE TWP.	MONROE	PA	798	444,766	315-25
PARADISE TWP.	YORK	PA	839	444,807	789-846
PARDEE VILLAGE	COLUMBIA	WI	994	034,508	330-31
PARIS	BOURBON	KY	192	007,845	451-57
PARIS	OXFORD	ME	263	443,500	331-99
PARIS	KENT	MI	353	443,569	486-98
PARIS	ONEIDA	NY	562	444,278	355-456
PARIS	PORTAGE	OH	722	444,715	905-930
PARIS	KENOSHA	WI	1000	444,987	525-47
PARIS TWP.	STARK	OH	730	444,723	714-17, 724, 761-826
PARIS TWP.	UNION	OH	736	444,729	72-110
PARISH	OSWEGO	NY	577	444,293	1-43
PARISHVILLE	ST. LAWRENCE	NY	590	444,306	231-81
PARK TWP.	SCOTT	AR	30	442,876	269-74
PARK TWP.	ST. JOSEPH	MI	362	443,578	757-76
PARKE CO.		IN	164	442,942	313-681
PARKER TWP.	BUTLER	PA	760	020,610	716-34
PARKERS DIST.	PITT	NC	641	444,654	113-26
PARKERSBURG	WOOD	VA	981	444,971	375-403
PARKMAN	PISCATAQUIS	ME	267	443,504	375-405
PARKMAN TWP.	GEAUGA	OH	682	444,675	289-321
PARKVILLE	PLATTE	MO	410	443,618	840-47
PARLIN POND PLANT.	SOMERSET	ME	269	443,506	547
PARMA	JACKSON	MI	352	443,568	539-65
PARMA	MONROE	NY	529	017,105	91-162
PARMA TWP.	CUYAHOGA	OH	673	020,221	199-230
PARSONSFIELD	YORK	ME	276	443,513	707-762
PASQUOTANK CO.		NC	640	444,653	595-734
PASS CHRISTIAN	HARRISON	MS	372	443,584	157-71
PASSADUMKEAG	PENOBSCOT	ME	266	443,503	531-37
PASSAIC CO.		NJ	461	443,660	247-808
PASSYUNK	PHILADELPHIA	PA	820	444,788	109-147
PATERSON TWP.	PASSAIC	NJ	461	443,660	381-664
PATOKA	GIBSON	IN	147	442,925	164-66
PATOKA TWP.	CRAWFORD	IN	139	007,752	17-39
PATOKA TWP.	DUBOIS	IN	143	007,756	931-68
PATOKA TWP.	GIBSON	IN	147	442,925	1-23, 44-86
PATOKA TWP.	PIKE	IN	165	442,943	1-70, 81-82
PATRICK CO.		VA	967	444,957	697-870
PATRICKTOWN PLANT.	LINCOLN	ME	259	443,496	581-94
PATTEN	PENOBSCOT	ME	266	443,503	725-36

CITY, COUNTY, TOWN, OR TOWNSHIP	COUNTY	STATE	NA NO. M432	GD NO.	PAGES
PATTERSON	PUTNAM	NY	581	444,297	51-83
PATTERSON TWP.	DARKE	OH	674	020,222	511-18
PATTERSON TWP.	BEAVER	PA	750	020,600	165-70
PATTON TWP.	ALLEGHENY	PA	747	020,597	559-80
PATTON TWP.	CENTRE	PA	763	020,613	536-46
PAULDING	JASPER	MS	374	443,586	117-20
PAULDING CO.		GA	80	442,889	107-244
PAULDING CO.		OH	719	444,712	351-98
PAVIDAL	VALENCIA	NM	470	443,668	581-82, 584
PAVILION	KALAMAZOO	MI	353	443,569	215-26
PAVILION	GENESEE	NY	508	017,084	369-408
PAW CREEK DIST.	MECKLENBURG	NC	637	444,650	34-54
PAW PAW TWP.	DE KALB	IL	104	007,677	683-98
PAWLET	RUTLAND	VT	927	444,926	545-88
PAWLING	DUTCHESS	NY	496	017,072	437-78
PAWTUCKET	BRISTOL	MA	308	014,702	651-740
PAXTON	WORCESTER	MA	341	443,560	173-92
PAXTON TWP.	ROSS	OH	725	444,718	719-56
PAYNESVILLE DIV.	SUMTER	AL	15	442,866	533, 548-53
PAYSON	ADAMS	IL	97	007,670	363-98
PEACH BOTTOM TWP.	YORK	PA	839	444,807	363-98
PEACH CREEK	GONZALES	TX	910	024,889	649-55
PEACHAM	CALEDONIA	VT	922	027,448	1-33
PEASE CREEK SET.	HILLSBOROUGH	FL	58	006,714	503, 506-7
PEASE TWP.	BELMONT	OH	661	020,209	361-444
PEAVINE	WALKER	GA	85	442,894	793-816
PEBBLE TWP.	PIKE	OH	721	444,714	731-52
PECAN TWP.	MISSISSIPPI	AR	28	002,482	701-3
PEE PEE TWP.	PIKE	OH	721	444,714	665-98
PEEBLES TWP.	ALLEGHENY	PA	747	020,597	611-53, 726-32
PEKIN	TAZEWELL	IL	129	442,917	206-212, 217-49
PELHAM	HAMPSHIRE	MA	321	443,540	559-82
PELHAM	HILLSBORO	NH	434	443,638	177-203
PELHAM	WESTCHESTER	NY	615	444,331	379-92
PEMBERTON TWP.	BURLINGTON	NJ	444	016,531	573-644
PEMBINA CO.		MN	367	014,834	45-72
PEMBINA DIST.	PEMBINA	MN	367	014,834	45-72
PEMBROKE	WASHINGTON	ME	273	443,510	123-64
PEMBROKE	PLYMOUTH	MA	332	443,551	267-300
PEMBROKE	MERRIMACK	NH	436	443,640	63-104
PEMBROKE	GENESEE	NY	508	017,084	521-77
PENCADER HUN.	NEW CASTLE	DE	54	006,438	625-87
PENCE BEAT	DALLAS	AL	4	002,346	563-67, 626-27
PENDLETON	MADISON	IN	158	442,936	204-212
PENDLETON	NIAGARA	NY	560	444,276	455-506
PENDLETON CO.		KY	216	442,984	645-794
PENDLETON CO.		VA	968	444,958	1-132
PENFIELD TWP.	LORAIN	OH	705	444,698	1005-1020
PENN DISTRICT	PHILADELPHIA	PA	820	444,788	149-361
PENN FOREST	CARBON	PA	762	020,612	439-48
PENN TWP.	JAY	IN	153	442,931	671-90
PENN TWP.	ST. JOSEPH	IN	171	442,949	232-70
PENN TWP.	JEFFERSON	IA	185	442,960	89-109
PENN TWP.	JOHNSON	IA	185	442,960	341-50
PENN TWP.	CASS	MI	349	014,811	683-99
PENN TWP.	MORGAN	OH	715	444,708	259-91
PENN TWP.	BERKS	PA	752	020,602	107-142
PENN TWP.	CHESTER	PA	764	020,614	145-63
PENN TWP.	CLEARFIELD	PA	768	444,736	700-711

144

CITY, COUNTY, TOWN, OR TOWNSHIP	COUNTY	STATE	NA NO. M432	GD NO.	PAGES
PENN TWP.	HUNTINGDON	PA	784	444,752	567-86
PENN TWP.	LANCASTER	PA	789	444,757	593-638
PENN TWP.	LYCOMING	PA	795	444,763	900-913
PENN TWP.	PERRY	PA	805	444,773	1043-59
PENN TWP.	UNION	PA	831	444,799	87-155
PENNFIELD	CALHOUN	MI	348	014,810	337-51
PENNFIELD	MONROE	NY	528	017,104	753-828
PENNINGTON TWP.	BRADLEY	AR	25	002,479	202-221
PENNSBURY TWP.	CHESTER	PA	765	020,615	235-53
PENN. HOSPITAL FOR INSANE PHILA.		PA	824	444,792	85-92
PENO TWP.	PIKE	MO	409	443,617	514-41
PENOBSCOT	HANCOCK	ME	254	443,491	203-240
PENOBSCOT CO.		ME	264	443,501	1-624
PENOBSCOT CO.		ME	265	443,502	625-803, 1-427
PENOBSCOT CO.		ME	266	443,503	429-765
PENSACOLA	ESCAMBIA	FL	58	006,714	233-67
PEORIA	PEORIA	IL	123	442,911	253-374
PEORIA CO.		IL	123	442,911	253-672
PEPPERELL	MIDDLESEX	MA	322	443,541	496-537
PEQUANAC TWP.	MORRIS	NJ	459	443,658	529-627
PERALTA	VALENCIA	NM	470	443,668	505-518, 583
PERDINALES	GILLESPIE	TX	910	024,889	606
PERINTON	MONROE	NY	529	017,105	333-402
PERIQUAL	VALENCIA	NM	470	443,668	475
PERKINS	LINCOLN	ME	261	443,498	529-30
PERKINS DIST.	PITT	NC	641	444,654	129-38
PERKINS TWP.	ERIE	OH	676	338,044	189-217
PERKINSVILLE	MADISON	IN	158	442,936	189-91
PERKIOMEN TWP.	MONTGOMERY	PA	799	444,767	65-103
PERQUIMANS CO.		NC	640	444,653	735-832
PERRY	PIKE	IL	124	442,912	110-18
PERRY	WASHINGTON	ME	273	443,510	165-96
PERRY	SHIAWASSEE	MI	363	443,579	167-74
PERRY	WYOMING	NY	617	444,333	394, 519-86
PERRY	LAKE	OH	701	444,694	463-90
PERRY	GREENE	PA	783	444,751	395-420
PERRY CO.		AL	12	002,354	555-766
PERRY CO.		AR	28	002,482	211-34
PERRY CO.		IL	124	442,912	675-800
PERRY CO.		IN	165	442,943	683-867
PERRY CO.		KY	216	442,984	795-867
PERRY CO.		MS	379	443,591	737-77
PERRY CO.		MO	409	443,617	57-218
PERRY CO.		OH	719	444,712	399-900
PERRY CO.		PA	805	444,773	717-1225
PERRY CO.		TN	892	444,848	247-382
PERRY MILLS	PERRY	MO	409	443,617	115-19
PERRY TWP.	JOHNSON	AR	27	002,481	295-307
PERRY TWP.	ALLEN	IN	135	007,748	521-41
PERRY TWP.	CLAY	IN	138	007,751	529-45
PERRY TWP.	CLINTON	IN	139	007,752	637-58
PERRY TWP.	DELAWARE	IN	143	007,756	585-610
PERRY TWP.	LAWRENCE	IN	158	442,936	902-934
PERRY TWP.	MARION	IN	159	442,937	301-344
PERRY TWP.	MARTIN	IN	160	442,938	83-119
PERRY TWP.	MIAMI	IN	160	442,938	271-98
PERRY TWP.	MONROE	IN	161	442,939	605-629
PERRY TWP.	NOBLE	IN	162	442,940	371-97
PERRY TWP.	TIPPECANOE	IN	175	442,953	282-306

CITY, COUNTY, TOWN, OR TOWNSHIP	COUNTY	STATE	NA NO. M432	GD NO.	PAGES
PERRY TWP.	VANDERBURGH	IN	176	442,954	904-20
PERRY TWP.	WAYNE	IN	180	442,958	151-71
PERRY TWP.	DAVIS	IA	182	007,791	497-513
PERRY TWP.	JACKSON	IA	184	007,793	632-33, 635-36, 638, 670-71, 67 680, 727-28
PERRY TWP.	ALLEN	OH	657	020,205	583-604
PERRY TWP.	ASHLAND	OH	658	020,206	69-112
PERRY TWP.	BROWN	OH	662	020,210	595 659
PERRY TWP.	CARROLL	OH	664	020,212	119-49
PERRY TWP.	COLUMBIANA	OH	669	020,217	48-106
PERRY TWP.	COSHOCTON	OH	670	020,218	133-64
PERRY TWP.	FAYETTE	OH	678	444,671	211-37
PERRY TWP.	FRANKLIN	OH	680	444,673	461-88
PERRY TWP.	GALLIA	OH	681	444,674	87-115
PERRY TWP.	HOCKING	OH	695	444,688	107-137
PERRY TWP.	LAWRENCE	OH	701	444,694	737-58
PERRY TWP.	LICKING	OH	703	444,696	695-725
PERRY TWP.	LOGAN	OH	704	444,697	227-61
PERRY TWP.	MONROE	OH	712	444,705	1047-84
PERRY TWP.	MONTGOMERY	OH	714	444,707	889-934
PERRY TWP.	MORROW	OH	716	444,709	847-74
PERRY TWP.	MUSKINGUM	OH	718	444,711	711-35
PERRY TWP.	PICKAWAY	OH	720	444,713	299-326
PERRY TWP.	PIKE	OH	721	444,714	769-86
PERRY TWP.	PUTNAM	OH	723	444,716	153-59
PERRY TWP.	RICHLAND	OH	724	444,717	821-43
PERRY TWP.	SHELBY	OH	729	444,722	389-410
PERRY TWP.	STARK	OH	731	444,724	419-532
PERRY TWP.	TUSCARAWAS	OH	734	444,727	305-339
PERRY TWP.	WOOD	OH	741	444,734	375-96
PERRY TWP.	ARMSTRONG	PA	749	020,599	1-20
PERRY TWP.	BERKS	PA	754	020,604	535-68
PERRY TWP.	CLARION	PA	767	444,735	312-45
PERRY TWP.	FAYETTE	PA	780	444,748	503-533
PERRY TWP.	JEFFERSON	PA	786	444,754	209-49, 300-301
PERRY TWP.	LAWRENCE	PA	790	444,758	293-305
PERRY TWP.	UNION	PA	831	444,799	197-230
PERRY TWP.	DANE	WI	995	034,509	894-96
PERRY'S MILL	FRANKLIN	NC	630	444,643	716-23, 767, 774-80
PERRYSBURG	CATTARAUGUS	NY	479	017,055	535-80
PERRYSBURG	WOOD	OH	741	444,734	207-236
PERRYSBURG TWP.	WOOD	OH	741	444,734	237-50
PERRYSVILLE	VERMILLION	IN	177	442,955	91-109
PERRYSVILLE BOR.	JUNIATA	PA	786	444,754	389-95
PERRYVILLE BEAT	PERRY	AL	12	002,354	694-703
PERSIA	CATTARAUGUS	NY	480	017,056	655-702
PERSON CO.	PERQUIMANS	NC	640	444,653	835-975
PERTH	FULTON	NY	506	017,082	327-54
PERTH AMBOY	MIDDLESEX	NJ	455	443,654	197-242
PERU	EL DORADO	CA	34	002,491	889-92
PERU	OXFORD	ME	263	443,500	265-91
PERU	BERKSHIRE	MA	305	014,699	573-85
PERU	CLINTON	NY	489	017,065	259-346
PERU	BENNINGTON	VT	921	027,447	187-200
PERU TWP.	MIAMI	IN	160	442,938	153-202
PERU TWP.	HURON	OH	697	444,690	245-84
PERU TWP.	MORROW	OH	716	444,709	115-36

CITY, COUNTY, TOWN, OR TOWNSHIP	COUNTY	STATE	NA NO. M432	GD NO.	PAGES
PETERBOROUGH	HILLSBORO	NH	433	443,637	655-707
PETERS CREEK	STOKES	NC	645	444,658	133-62, 165
PETERS TWP.	FRANKLIN	PA	781	444,749	123-77
PETERS TWP.	WASHINGTON	PA	833	444,801	86-108
PETERSBURG	MENARD	IL	120	442,908	525-41
PETERSBURG	PIKE	IN	165	442,943	71-80
PETERSBURG	RENSSELAER	NY	586	444,302	347-92
PETERSBURG	ADAMS	PA	743	020,593	181-89
PETERSBURG	DINWIDDIE	VA	941	444,931	649-869
PETERSBURG	HARDY	VA	950	444,940	113-15
PETERSBURG BOR.	HUNTINGDON	PA	784	444,752	143-49
PETERSBURG BOR.	PERRY	PA	805	444,773	1063-79
PETERSHAM	WORCESTER	MA	343	443,562	611-47
PETERSVILLE DIST.	FREDERICK	MD	293	443,524	753-94
PETITE ANSE	ST. MARTIN	LA	240	443,483	353-63
PETITE FAUSSE POINTE	ST. MARTIN	LA	240	443,483	370
PETTIS CO.		MO	409	443,617	219-320
PETTIS TWP.	PLATTE	MO	410	443,618	848-907
PEWAUKEE	WAUKESHA	WI	1009	444,996	835-60
PHARSALIA	CHENANGO	NY	487	017,063	254-83
PHELPS	ONTARIO	NY	572	444,288	733-864
PHELPSTOWN	INGHAM	MI	351	443,567	168-77
PHILADELPHIA	JEFFERSON	NY	515	017,091	301-347
PHILADELPHIA ALMS HOUSE	PHILA.	PA	824	444,792	93-140
PHILADELPHIA, CEDAR WARD	PHILA.	PA	812	444,780	1-215
PHILADELPHIA, CHESTNUT WARD	PHILA	PA	813	444,781	903-961
PHILADELPHIA CO.		PA	806-824	444,774-92	
PHILADELPHIA DIST.	MECKLENBURG	NC	637	444,650	137-43, 149
PHILADELPHIA, DOCK WARD	PHILA.	PA	817	444,785	877-1013
PHILADELPHIA, HIGH STREET WARD	PHI.	PA	816	444,784	327-411
PHILADELPHIA, LOCUST WARD	PHILA.	PA	814	444,782	173-427
PHILADELPHIA, LOMBARD WARD	PHILA.	PA	812	444,780	381-528
PHILADELPHIA, LOWER DELAWARE W.	PHI.	PA	816	444,784	1-153
PHILADELPHIA, MIDDLE WARD	PHILA.	PA	814	444,782	1-172
PHILADELPHIA, NEW MARKET WARD	PHI.	PA	817	444,785	677-875
PHILADELPHIA, NORTH MULBERRY W.	PHI.	PA	815	444,783	637-931
PHILADELPHIA, NORTH WARD	PHILA.	PA	817	444,785	413-676
PHILADELPHIA, PINE WARD	PHILA.	PA	813	444,781	529-675
PHILADELPHIA, SOUTH MULBERRY W.	PHI.	PA	814	444,782	429-635
PHILADELPHIA, SOUTH WARD	PHILA.	PA	812	444,780	217-379
PHILADELPHIA, SPRUCE WARD	PHILA.	PA	813	444,781	677-840
PHILADELPHIA, UPPER DELAWARE W.	PHI.	PA	816	444,784	155-326
PHILADELPHIA, WALNUT WARD	PHILA.	PA	813	444,781	841-901
PHILLIPS	FRANKLIN	ME	253	009,723	269-308
PHILLIPS CO.		AR	29	002,483	235-353
PHILLIPSBURG BOR.	BEAVER	PA	750	020,600	519-30
PHILLIPSTON	WORCESTER	MA	342	443,561	679-98
PHILLIPSTOWN	PUTNAM	NY	581	444,297	125-252
PHIPPSBURG	LINCOLN	ME	260	443,497	171-213
PHOENIX	OSWEGO	NY	577	444,293	564-84
PHOENIXVILLE BOR.	CHESTER	PA	765	020,615	155-218
PICKAWAY CO.		OH	720	444,713	1-522
PICKAWAY TWP.	PICKAWAY	OH	720	444,713	489-522
PICKENS CO.		AL	13	442,864	1-266
PICKENS CO.		SC	857	444,820	743-1059
PICKENSVILLE	PICKENS	AL	13	442,864	13-16
PICKERINGS ISLAND	HANCOCK	ME	254	443,491	424
PICKERINGTON	FAIRFIELD	OH	677	444,670	275-79
PIERMONT	GRAFTON	NH	431	443,635	373-95

CITY, COUNTY, TOWN, OR TOWNSHIP	COUNTY	STATE	NA NO. M432	GD NO.	PAGES	
PIERPONT	ASHTABULA	OH	659	020,207	689-712	
PIERREPONT	ST. LAWRENCE	NY	590	444,306	761-96	
PIERSON TWP.	VIGO	IN	177	442,955	383-96	
PIGEON ROOST TWP.	PRAIRIE	AR	29	002,483	611-16	
PIGEON TWP.	VANDERBURGH	IN	176	442,954	727-856	
PIGEON TWP.	WARRICK	IN	179	442,957	353-70	
PIGS EYE	RAMSEY	MN	367	014,834	111	
PIKE	WYOMING	NY	617	444,333	733-80	
PIKE	BRADFORD	PA	757	020,607	283-320	
PIKE	POTTER	PA	825	444,793	236-40	
PIKE	KENOSHA	WI	1000	444,987	549-65	
PIKE CO.		AL	13	442,864	269-558	
PIKE CO.		AR	29	002,483	355-98	
PIKE CO.		GA	80	442,889	245-454	
PIKE CO.		IL	124	442,912	45-495	
PIKE CO.		IN	165	442,943	1-191	
PIKE CO.		KY	217	442,985	869-995	
PIKE CO.		MS	380	443,592	1-104	
PIKE CO.		MO	409	443,617	321-567	
PIKE CO.		OH	721	444,714	523-800	
PIKE CO.		PA	825	444,793	1-153	
PIKE TWP.	JAY	IN	153	442,931	575-93	
PIKE TWP.	MARION	IN	159	442,937	846-92	
PIKE TWP.	WARREN	IN	178	442,956	3-16	
PIKE TWP.	MUSCATINE	IA	187	442,962	785-91	
PIKE TWP.	STODDARD	MO	420	443,628	577-78,	583-605
PIKE TWP.	BROWN	OH	662	020,210	723-47	
PIKE TWP.	CLARK	OH	666	020,214	243-80	
PIKE TWP.	COSHOCTON	OH	670	020,218	61-86	
PIKE TWP.	FULTON	OH	681	444,674	587-98	
PIKE TWP.	KNOX	OH	700	444,693	625-67	
PIKE TWP.	MADISON	OH	706	444,699	319-29	
PIKE TWP.	PERRY	OH	719	444,712	440-92	
PIKE TWP.	STARK	OH	731	444,724	383-417	
PIKE TWP.	BERKS	PA	754	020,604	897-918	
PIKE TWP.	CLEARFIELD	PA	768	444,736	569-98	
PIKETON	PIKE	OH	721	444,714	573-89	
PILESGROVE TWP.	SALEM	NJ	462	443,661	141-211	
PILOT DIST.	SURRY	NC	646	444,659	535-52	
PILOT HILL	EL DORADO	CA	34	002,491	938-47	
PINCHKNEY	LEWIS	NY	523	017,099	299-327	
PINCKNEYVILLE DIST.	GWINNETT	GA	71	007,067	275, 370-78, 453-55	
PINE BLUFF	JEFFERSON	AR	27	002,481	135-41	
PINE CREEK TWP.	OGLE	IL	123	442,911	1-22	
PINE CREEK TWP.	CLINTON	PA	768	444,736	193-212	
PINE CREEK TWP.	JEFFERSON	PA	786	444,754	295-313	
PINE FLAT BEAT	AUTAUGA	AL	1	002,343	78-95	
PINE FLAT BEAT	DALLAS	AL	4	002,346	469-78	
PINE GROVE	VAN BUREN	MI	363	443,579	341-42	
PINE GROVE	VENANGO	PA	832	444,800	147-64	
PINE GROVE BOR.	SCHUYLKILL	PA	826	444,794	851-66	
PINE GROVE TWP.	SCHUYLKILL	PA	826	444,794	867-914	
PINE GROVE TWP.	WARREN	PA	832	444,800	517-55	
PINE PLAINS	ALLEGAN	MI	346	014,808	15	
PINE PLAINS	DUTCHESS	NY	496	017,072	363-97	
PINE TWP.	WARREN	IN	178	442,956	87-109	
PINE TWP.	ALLEGHENY	PA	744	020,594	579-631	
PINE TWP.	ARMSTRONG	PA	749	020,599	315-69	

CITY, COUNTY, TOWN, OR TOWNSHIP	COUNTY	STATE	NA NO. M432	GD NO.	PAGES
PINE TWP.	CRAWFORD	PA	770	444,738	379-95
PINE TWP.	INDIANA	PA	785	444,753	635-67
PINETUCKY BEAT	PERRY	AL	12	002,354	575-84
PINEY FORK	LAWRENCE	AR	27	002,481	379-88
PINEY MOUNTAIN	RUTHERFORD	NC	644	444,657	641-44, 669-71
PINEY TWP.	JOHNSON	AR	27	002,481	288-94
PINEY TWP.	CLARION	PA	767	444,735	290-311
PIONEER TWP.	CEDAR CO.	IA	182	007,791	240-49
PIPE CREEK TWP.	MADISON	IN	158	442,936	48-84
PIPE CREEK TWP.	MIAMI	IN	160	442,938	407-418
PIQUA	MIAMI	OH	711	444,704	686-765
PISCATAQUIS CO.		ME	267	443,504	343-748
PISCATAWAY DIST.	PRINCE GEORGES	MD	295	443,526	207-241
PISCATAWAY TWP.	MIDDLESEX	NJ	455	443,654	125-96
PITCAIRN	ST. LAWRENCE	NY	589	444,305	501-513
PITCHER	CHENANGO	NY	487	017,063	158-92
PITT CO.		NC	641	444,654	1-163
PITT TWP.	WYANDOT	OH	741	444,734	455-76
PITT TWP.	ALLEGHENY	PA	748	020,598	1-49
PITTSBURG	COOS	NH	429	443,633	261-71
PITTSBURG TWP.	JOHNSON	AR	27	002,481	229-42
PITTSBURGH, WARD 1	ALLEGHENY	PA	745	020,595	1-101
PITTSBURGH, WARD 2	ALLEGHENY	PA	745	020,595	102-198
PITTSBURGH, WARD 3	ALLEGHENY	PA	745	020,595	199-411
PITTSBURGH, WARD 4	ALLEGHENY	PA	745	020,595	413-518
PITTSBURGH, WARD 5	ALLEGHENY	PA	746	020,596	519-714
PITTSBURGH, WARD 6	ALLEGHENY	PA	746	020,596	715-890
PITTSBURGH, WARD 7	ALLEGHENY	PA	746	020,596	891-954
PITTSBURGH, WARD 8	ALLEGHENY	PA	746	020,596	955-1072
PITTSBURGH, WARD 9	ALLEGHENY	PA	746	020,596	1073-1126
PITTSFIELD	PIKE	IL	124	442,912	263-78
PITTSFIELD	SOMERSET	ME	268	443,505	167-94
PITTSFIELD	BERKSHIRE	MA	305	014,699	433-572
PITTSFIELD	WASHTENAW	MI	364	443,580	961-90
PITTSFIELD	MERRIMACK	NH	435	443,639	347-90
PITTSFIELD	OTSEGO	NY	580	444,296	549-86
PITTSFIELD	RUTLAND	VT	927	444,926	269-81
PITTSFIELD	BROWN	WI	994	034,508	21-25
PITTSFIELD TWP.	LORAIN	OH	705	444,698	533-58
PITTSFIELD TWP.	WARREN	PA	832	444,800	633-50
PITTSFORD	MONROE	NY	529	017,105	405-459
PITTSFORD	RUTLAND	VT	927	444,926	105-153
PITTSFORD TWP.	HILLSDALE	MI	351	443,567	713-42
PITTSGROVE TWP.	SALEM	NJ	462	443,661	447-74
PITTSTON	KENNEBEC	ME	258	443,495	277-344
PITTSTON	LUZERNE	PA	794	444,762	265-360
PITTSTOWN	RENSSELAER	NY	585	444,301	781-869
PITTSYLVANIA CO.		VA	968	444,958	133-520
PLACENTIA ISLAND	HANCOCK	ME	254	443,491	333
PLACERVILLE	EL DORADO	CA	34	002,491	524-26, 533-664
PLAIN TWP.	KOSCIUSKO	IN	156	442,934	678-98
PLAIN TWP.	FRANKLIN	OH	680	444,673	181-214
PLAIN TWP.	STARK	OH	731	444,724	55-105
PLAIN TWP.	WAYNE	OH	740	444,733	709-766
PLAIN TWP.	WOOD	OH	741	444,734	309-320
PLAINFIELD	WINDHAM	CT	51	442,883	573-638
PLAINFIELD	WILL	IL	133	442,921	57-83
PLAINFIELD	HENDRICKS	IN	150	442,928	203-7
PLAINFIELD	HAMPSHIRE	MA	320	443,539	395-414

Plainfield

CITY, COUNTY, TOWN, OR TOWNSHIP	COUNTY	STATE	NA NO. M432	GD NO.	PAGES	
PLAINFIELD	KENT	MI	353	443,569	457-72	
PLAINFIELD	SULLIVAN	NH	441	443,645	21-54	
PLAINFIELD	OTSEGO	NY	580	444,296	119-53	
PLAINFIELD	WASHINGTON	VT	928	444,927	145-64	
PLAINFIELD TWP.	ESSEX	NJ	450	443,649	715-72	
PLAINFIELD TWP.	NORTHAMPTON	PA	803	444,771	723-64	
PLAISTOW	ROCKINGHAM	NH	438	443,642	1-18	
PLANE TWP.	ST. FRANCIS	AR	30	442,876	92-93	
PLANTATION NO. 1 AND 2	HANCOCK	ME	255	443,492	876-78	
PLANTATION NO. 4	FRANKLIN	ME	253	009,723	1-4	
PLANTATION NO. 7	HANCOCK	ME	255	443,492	535-39	
PLANTERS TWP.	CHICOT	AR	25	002,479	349-55	
PLANTERS TWP.	PHILLIPS	AR	29	002,483	345-53	
PLANTERSVILLE	PERRY	AL	12	002,354	719-28	
PLAQUEMINE	IBERVILLE PAR.	LA	231	009,698	613-14	
PLAQUEMINES PARISH		LA	238	443,481	533-97	
PLATO	KANE	IL	112	007,685	115-34	
PLATT CO.		IL	124	442,912	2-40	
PLATTE CITY	PLATTE	MO	410	443,618	607-616	
PLATTE CO.		MO	410	443,618	569-907	
PLATTE TWP.	ANDREW	MO	391	014,871	131-63	
PLATTE TWP.	BUCHANAN	MO	393	014,873	275-97	
PLATTE TWP.	CLAY	MO	396	443,604	694-713	
PLATTEKILL	ULSTER	NY	607	444,323	469-518	
PLATTSBURGH	CLINTON	NY	489	017,065	491-624	
PLEASANT	FULTON	IL	107	007,680	159-81	
PLEASANT GROVE PREC.	JO DAVIESS	IL	111	007,684	232-41	
PLEASANT GROVE TWP.	DES MOINES	IA	183	007,792	715-36	
PLEASANT HILL	EL DORADO	CA	34	002,491	738-44	
PLEASANT HILL BEAT	DALLAS	AL	4	002,346	489-92,	496-99
PLEASANT MILLS	ADAMS	IN	135	007,748	154-57	
PLEASANT MOUNT BOR.	WAYNE	PA	835	444,803	1-5	
PLEASANT PRARIE	KENOSHA	WI	1000	444,987	567-89	
PLEASANT RIVER TWP.	LAWRENCE	IN	158	442,936	838-48,	881-901
PLEASANT SPRINGS	DANE	WI	995	034,509	685-702	
PLEASANT TWP.	ALLEN	IN	135	007,748	435-50	
PLEASANT TWP.	GRANT	IN	147	442,925	442-67	
PLEASANT TWP.	JOHNSON	IN	155	442,933	29-59	
PLEASANT TWP.	LA PORTE	IN	157	442,935	465-80	
PLEASANT TWP.	PORTER	IN	165	442,943	243-52	
PLEASANT TWP.	STEUBEN	IN	173	442,951	294-312	
PLEASANT TWP.	SWITZERLAND	IN	174	442,952	647-700	
PLEASANT TWP.	WABASH	IN	178	442,956	779-812	
PLEASANT TWP.	BROWN	OH	662	020,210	543-90	
PLEASANT TWP.	CLARK	OH	666	020,214	533-66	
PLEASANT TWP.	FAIRFIELD	OH	677	444,670	669-716	
PLEASANT TWP.	FRANKLIN	OH	680	444,673	95-121	
PLEASANT TWP.	HANCOCK	OH	692	444,685	825-38	
PLEASANT TWP.	HARDIN	OH	692	444,685	209-260	
PLEASANT TWP.	HENRY	OH	693	444,686	79-86	
PLEASANT TWP.	KNOX	OH	700	444,693	527-49	
PLEASANT TWP.	LOGAN	OH	704	444,697	131-50	
PLEASANT TWP.	MADISON	OH	706	444,699	425-54	
PLEASANT TWP.	MARION	OH	708	444,701	264-91	
PLEASANT TWP.	PUTNAM	OH	723	444,716	101-117	
PLEASANT TWP.	SENECA	OH	728	444,721	613-51	
PLEASANT TWP.	VAN WERT	OH	736	444,729	360-68	
PLEASANT TWP.	WARREN	PA	832	444,800	719-24	
PLEASANT UNITY	WESTMORELAND	PA	837	444,805	673-76	

CITY, COUNTY, TOWN, OR TOWNSHIP	COUNTY	STATE	NA NO. M432	GD NO.	PAGES
PLEASANT VALLEY	DUTCHESS	NY	496	017,072	1-54
PLEASANT VALLEY	MADISON	OH	706	444,699	569-72
PLEASANT VALLEY	POTTER	PA	825	444,793	192-93
PLEASANT VALLEY	MARQUETTE	WI	1002	444,989	210-28
PLEASANT VALLEY TWP.	JOHNSON	IA	185	442,960	287-93
PLEASANTVILLE	SHELBY	IN	172	442,950	580-83
PLOVER	PORTAGE	WI	1004	444,991	2-8, 18-21
PLUM BAYOU TWP.	JEFFERSON	AR	27	002,481	153-58
PLUM RIVER PREC.	JO DAVIESS	IL	111	007,684	328-44
PLUM TWP.	ALLEGHENY	PA	747	020,597	581-610
PLUM TWP.	VENANGO	PA	832	444,800	25-44
PLUMCREEK TWP.	ARMSTRONG	PA	749	020,599	673-725
PLUMSTEAD TWP.	OCEAN	NJ	460	443,659	205-243
PLUMSTEAD TWP.	BUCKS	PA	758	020,608	421-75
PLUNKETS CREEK TWP.	LYCOMING	PA	795	444,763	1017-21
PLUNKETS CREEK TWP.	SULLIVAN	PA	828	444,796	613-17
PLYMOUTH	LITCHFIELD	CT	43	003,071	645-707
PLYMOUTH	PENOBSCOT	ME	265	443,502	1-23
PLYMOUTH	PLYMOUTH	MA	333	443,552	215-358
PLYMOUTH	GRAFTON	NH	431	443,635	341-71
PLYMOUTH	CHENANGO	NY	487	017,063	49-85
PLYMOUTH	WASHINGTON	NC	648	444,661	201-213
PLYMOUTH	ASHTABULA	OH	659	020,207	523-40
PLYMOUTH	WINDSOR	VT	931	444,930	837-66
PLYMOUTH	ROCK	WI	1005	444,992	523-35
PLYMOUTH	SHEBOYGAN	WI	1006	444,993	297-305, 308-321
PLYMOUTH CO.		MA	332	443,551	1-664
PLYMOUTH CO.		MA	333	443,552	1-684
PLYMOUTH DIST.	WASHINGTON	NC	648	444,661	141-57, 197-99
PLYMOUTH GRANT	AROOSTOOK	ME	248	009,718	199-204
PLYMOUTH TWP.	WAYNE	MI	366	443,582	765-822
PLYMOUTH TWP.	RICHLAND	OH	724	444,717	347-86
PLYMOUTH TWP.	LUZERNE	PA	793	444,761	136-71
PLYMOUTH TWP.	MONTGOMERY	PA	800	444,768	21-55
PLYMPTON	PLYMOUTH	MA	333	443,552	89-111
POCAHONTAS	BOND	IL	98	007,671	812-14
POCAHONTAS CO.		VA	969	444,959	523-602
POCONO TWP.	MONROE	PA	798	444,766	129-51
POCOPSON TWP.	CHESTER	PA	765	020,615	219-33
POESTENKILL	RENSSELAER	NY	585	444,301	81-130
POINSETT CO.		AR	29	002,483	399-447
POINT PLEASANT	GUERNSEY	OH	684	444,677	593-95
POINT PREC.	CALHOUN	IL	99	007,672	647-66
POINT REMOVE TWP.	CONWAY	AR	25	002,479	479-85
POINT TWP.	POSEY	IN	166	442,944	455-66
POINT TWP.	NORTHUMBERLAND	PA	804	444,772	279-309
POINTE	ST. MARTIN	LA	240	443,483	294-99, 332-34, 337-39
POINTE COUPEE PARISH		LA	239	443,482	1-84
POKAGON TWP.	CASS	MI	349	014,811	637-61
POLAND	CUMBERLAND	ME	249	009,719	67-130
POLAND	CHAUTAUQUA	NY	484	017,060	591-618
POLAND TWP.	MAHONING	OH	707	444,700	807-858
POLECAT BEAT	PERRY	AL	12	002,354	605-613
POLK	WASHINGTON	WI	1008	444,995	353-62, 381-400
POLK CO.		AR	29	002,483	449-78
POLK CO.		IA	188	442,963	17-124
POLK CO.		MO	411	443,619	1-140
POLK CO.		OR	742	020,298	215-40

CITY, COUNTY, TOWN, OR TOWNSHIP	COUNTY	STATE	NA NO. M432	GD NO.	PAGES
POLK CO.		TN	892	444,848	385-530
POLK CO.		TX	914	444,917	367-403
POLK DIST.	RUTHERFORD	NC	644	444,657	461-504, 506-7
POLK TWP.	ARKANSAS	AR	25	002,479	43-47
POLK TWP.	DALLAS	AR	26	002,480	12-21
POLK TWP.	MONTGOMERY	AR	28	002,482	813-17
POLK TWP.	NEWTON	AR	28	002,482	13-15
POLK TWP.	MONROE	IN	161	442,939	725-35
POLK TWP.	JEFFERSON	IA	185	442,960	226-40
POLK TWP.	GREENE	MO	400	443,608	571-88
POLK TWP.	CRAWFORD	OH	671	020,219	739-72
POLK TWP.	MONROE	PA	798	444,766	154-70
POLKTON	OTTAWA	MI	361	443,577	45-51
POLLOCKSVILLE DIST.	JONES	NC	635	444,648	223-29
POMEROY	MEIGS	OH	710	444,703	217-55
POMFRET	WINDHAM	CT	51	442,883	755-58, 763-74, 782-94
POMFRET	CHAUTAUQUA	NY	485	017,061	373-477
POMFRET	WINDSOR	VT	931	444,930	745-81
POMFRET TOWN	WINDHAM	CT	51	442,883	751-54, 761-62, 775-81
POMPEY	ONONDAGA	NY	567	444,283	151-246
POMPTON TWP.	PASSAIC	NJ	461	443,660	247-88
POND ISLAND	HANCOCK	ME	254	443,491	333
POND ISLAND	LINCOLN	ME	260	443,497	75
PONTIAC	LIVINGSTON	IL	116	007,689	291
PONTIAC	OAKLAND	MI	359	443,575	157-225
PONTOTOC CO.		MS	380	443,592	105-408
POPE CO.		AR	29	002,483	479-580
POPE CO.		IL	125	442,913	497-592
POPLAR BRANCH DIST.	CURRITUCK	NC	627	444,640	390-406
POPLAR PLAINS	FLEMING	KY	199	442,967	666-69
POPLAR SPRING	ANNE ARUNDEL	MD	278	013,195	1012-13
POPLIN	ROCKINGHAM	NH	437	443,641	427-39
PORT BOLIVAR	GALVESTON	TX	910	024,889	562-63
PORT CARBON	SCHUYLKILL	PA	827	444,795	349-401
PORT CLINTON	OTTAWA	OH	719	444,712	309-315
PORT DEPOSIT	CECIL	MD	290	443,521	287-310
PORT GIBSON	CLAIBORNE	MS	370	014,849	203-217
PORT HOPE TWP.	COLUMBIA	WI	994	034,508	383-86, 396-98, 400-401
PORT HURON	ST. CLAIR	MI	362	443,578	399-416
PORT HURON VILLAGE	ST. CLAIR	MI	362	443,578	361-98
PORT JEFFERSON	SHELBY	OH	729	444,722	601-6
PORT PENN	NEW CASTLE	DE	54	006,438	359-65
PORT ROYAL	CAROLINE	VA	939	029,714	593-98
PORT WASHINGTON	TUSCARAWAS	OH	735	444,728	703-9
PORT WASHINGTON	WASHINGTON	WI	1008	444,995	1-12, 175-84, 363-80
PORTAGE	KALAMAZOO	MI	353	443,569	135-52
PORTAGE	LIVINGSTON	NY	524	017,100	241-99
PORTAGE	POTTER	PA	825	444,793	233
PORTAGE CO.		OH	722	444,715	801-950, 1-460
PORTAGE CO.		WI	1004	444,991	1-34
PORTAGE LAKE PLANT.	AROOSTOOK	ME	248	009,718	245-48
PORTAGE PRARIE TWP.	COLUMBIA	WI	994	034,508	441-55
PORTAGE TWP.	PORTER	IN	165	442,943	299-305
PORTAGE TWP.	ST. JOSEPH	IN	171	442,949	1-52
PORTAGE TWP.	HANCOCK	OH	692	444,685	77-92

CITY, COUNTY, TOWN, OR TOWNSHIP	COUNTY	STATE	NA NO. M432	GD NO.	PAGES	
PORTAGE TWP.	OTTAWA	OH	719	444,712	309-324	
PORTAGE TWP.	SUMMIT	OH	732	444,725	763-868	
PORTAGE TWP.	WOOD	OH	741	444,734	289-98	
PORTER	OXFORD	ME	262	443,499	103-131	
PORTER	VAN BUREN	MI	363	443,579	329-39	
PORTER	NIAGARA	NY	561	444,277	893-954	
PORTER	ROCK	WI	1005	444,992	584-604	
PORTER CO.		IN	165	442,943	193-334	
PORTER TWP.	PORTER	IN	165	442,943	253-72	
PORTER TWP.	CASS	MI	349	014,811	533-64	
PORTER TWP.	GREENE	MO	400	443,608	589-600	
PORTER TWP.	DELAWARE	OH	675	020,223	629-53	
PORTER TWP.	SCIOTO	OH	727	444,720	457-96	
PORTER TWP.	CLARION	PA	767	444,735	214-59	
PORTER TWP.	CLINTON	PA	768	444,736	47-71	
PORTER TWP.	HUNTINGDON	PA	784	444,752	55-81	
PORTER TWP.	JEFFERSON	PA	786	444,754	132-50	
PORTER TWP.	LYCOMING	PA	795	444,763	663-81	
PORTER TWP.	SCHUYLKILL	PA	826	444,794	739-46	
PORTERSVILLE BOR.	BUTLER	PA	760	020,610	533-38	
PORTLAND	MIDDLESEX	CT	44	003,072	652-53,	845-912
PORTLAND	JAY	IN	153	442,931	557-61	
PORTLAND	IONIA	MI	352	443,568	273-92	
PORTLAND	CHAUTAUQUA	NY	485	017,061	325-70	
PORTLAND	WASHINGTON	OR	742	020,298	249-69	
PORTLAND	DODGE	WI	996	034,510	221-33	
PORTLAND ACAD. GT.	AROOSTOOK	ME	248	009,718	161-62	
PORTLAND BEAT	DALLAS	AL	4	002,346	518-22	
PORTLAND TWP.	ERIE	OH	676	338,044	4-122	
PORTLAND, WARD 1	CUMBERLAND	ME	252	009,722	1-106	
PORTLAND, WARD 2	CUMBERLAND	ME	252	009,722	111-65	
PORTLAND, WARD 3	CUMBERLAND	ME	252	009,722	169-212	
PORTLAND, WARD 4	CUMBERLAND	ME	252	009,722	215-83	
PORTLAND, WARD 5	CUMBERLAND	ME	252	009,722	289-354	
PORTLAND, WARD 6	CUMBERLAND	ME	252	009,722	357-432	
PORTLAND, WARD 7	CUMBERLAND	ME	252	009,722	435-532	
PORTSMOUTH	ROCKINGHAM	NH	437	443,641	1-232	
PORTSMOUTH	CARTERET	NC	623	018,109	217-25	
PORTSMOUTH	SCIOTO	OH	727	444,720	353-448	
PORTSMOUTH	DAUPHIN	PA	774	444,742	345-65	
PORTSMOUTH	NEWPORT	RI	842	022,265	45-88	
PORTSMOUTH CITY	NORFOLK	VA	964	444,954	241-392	
PORTSMOUTH PARISH	NORFOLK	VA	964	444,954	505-542	
PORTVILLE	CATTARAUGUS	NY	479	017,055	237-54	
POSEY CO.		IN	166	442,944	335-649	
POSEY TWP.	CLAY	IN	138	007,751	485-514	
POSEY TWP.	FAYETTE	IN	144	007,757	479-506	
POSEY TWP.	FRANKLIN	IN	146	442,924	403-426	
POSEY TWP.	RUSH	IN	170	442,948	1127-47	
POSEY TWP.	SWITZERLAND	IN	174	442,952	877-935	
POSEY TWP.	WASHINGTON	IN	179	442,957	451-96	
POST OAK TWP.	JOHNSON	MO	403	443,611	77-97	
POTOSI	WASHINGTON	MO	421	443,629	327-33	
POTSDAM	ST. LAWRENCE	NY	590	444,306	1-128	
POTTAWATTAMIE CO.		IA	188	442,963	127-311	
POTTER	YATES	NY	618	444,334	1-53	
POTTER CO.		PA	825	444,793	155-311	
POTTER TWP.	CENTRE	PA	763	020,613	143-95	
POTTSGROVE TWP.	MONTGOMERY	PA	799	444,767	105-145	

CITY, COUNTY, TOWN, OR TOWNSHIP	COUNTY	STATE	NA NO. M432	GD NO.	PAGES
POTTSTOWN BOR., E. WARD	MONTGOMERY	PA	799	444,767	201-226
POTTSTOWN BOR., W. WARD	MONTGOMERY	PA	799	444,767	227-40
POTTSVILLE, N.E. WARD	SCHUYLKILL	PA	827	444,795	687-726
POTTSVILLE, N.W. WARD	SCHUYLKILL	PA	827	444,795	611-86
POTTSVILLE, SOUTH WARD	SCHUYLKILL	PA	827	444,795	727-92
POUGHKEEPSIE	DUTCHESS	NY	497	017,073	57-389
POUILLY DIST.	FRANKLIN	NC	630	444,643	708-715
POULTNEY	RUTLAND	VT	927	444,926	425-80
POUND RIDGE	WESTCHESTER	NY	614	444,330	283-318
POWDER SPRINGS DIST.	COBB	GA	66	007,062	333-56
POWELL TWP.	GREENE	AR	26	002,480	386-98
POWELLS	JEFFERSON	AL	7	002,349	399-413
POWELLS POINT DIST.	CURRITUCK	NC	627	444,640	407-417
POWESHIEK CO.		IA	188	442,963	315-29
POWHATAN CO.		VA	969	444,959	605-674
POWNAL	CUMBERLAND	ME	249	009,719	379-404
POWNAL	BENNINGTON	VT	921	027,447	269-310
PRAIRIE	HOT SPRINGS	AR	26	002,480	587-97
PRAIRIE CO.		AR	29	002,483	581-630
PRAIRIE CREEK TWP.	VIGO	IN	177	442,955	571-92
PRAIRIE DU CHIEU	CRAWFORD	WI	995	034,509	471-501, 528-30
PRAIRIE DU LONG PREC.	MONROE	IL	121	442,909	19-34
PRAIRIE DU ROCKER	RANDOLPH	IL	125	442,913	193-95, 200-204
PRAIRIE DU SAC TWP.	SAUK	WI	1006	444,993	70-84
PRAIRIE DU SAC VILLAGE	SAUK	WI	1006	444,993	66, 68-69
PRAIRIE RONDE	KALAMAZOO	MI	353	443,569	153-69
PRAIPIE SPRINGS TWP.	JACKSON	IA	184	007,793	565, 579-81
PRAIRIE TWP.	ARKANSAS	AR	25	002,479	29-36
PRAIRIE TWP.	CARROLL	AR	25	002,479	289-315
PRAIRIE TWP.	FRANKLIN	AR	26	002,480	269-79
PRAIRIE TWP.	MADISON	AR	27	002,481	497-516
PRAIRIE TWP.	NEWTON	AR	28	002,482	1-4
PRAIRIE TWP.	PRAIRIE	AR	29	002,483	581-95
PRAIRIE TWP.	WASHINGTON	AR	31	442,877	763-801
PRAIRIE TWP.	HENRY	IN	151	442,929	651-82
PRAIRIE TWP.	KOSCIUSKO	IN	156	442,934	595-617
PRAIRIE TWP.	TIPTON	IN	176	442,954	499-514
PRAIRIE TWP.	DAVIS	IA	182	007,791	606-614
PRAIRIE TWP.	CHARITON	MO	395	443,603	333-50
PRAIRIE TWP.	RANDOLPH	MO	411	443,619	496-537
PRAIRIE TWP.	TANEY	MO	420	443,628	748-51
PRAIRIE TWP.	FRANKLIN	OH	680	444,673	219-43
PRAIRIE TWP.	HOLMES	OH	696	444,689	279-313
PRAIRIEVILLE	BARRY	MI	346	014,808	129-42
PRATTSBURG	STEUBEN	NY	600	444,316	549-615
PRATTSVILLE	GREENE	NY	509	017,085	51-98
PRATTVILLE	AUTAUGA	AL	1	002,343	29-39
PREBLE	CORTLAND	NY	493	017,069	629-60
PREBLE CO.		OH	723	444,716	461-980
PREBLE TWP.	ADAMS	IN	135	007,748	53-66
PRESCOTT	HAMPSHIRE	MA	321	443,540	891-918
PRESTON	NEW LONDON	CT	49	442,881	1-44, 159
PRESTON	CHENANGO	NY	488	017,064	919-45
PRESTON	WAYNE	PA	835	444,803	61-81
PRESTON	GRAYSON	TX	910	024,889	719-20
PRESTON CO.		VA	969	444,959	677-952
PRESTON TWP.	PLATTE	MO	410	443,618	776-805
PRICE TWP.	MONROE	PA	798	444,766	327-35
PRIMROSE TWP.	DANE	WI	995	034,509	867-904

CITY, COUNTY, TOWN, OR TOWNSHIP	COUNTY	STATE	NA NO. M432	GD NO.	PAGES
PRINCE EDWARD CO.		VA	970	444,960	1-112
PRINCE GEORGE CO.		VA	970	444,960	115-90
PRINCE GEORGE WINYAN	GEORGETOWN	SC	853	444,816	593-628
PRINCE GEORGES CO.		MD	295	443,526	1-243
PRINCE WILLIAM CO.		VA	970	444,960	193-328
PRINCE WILLIAMS PAR.	BEAUFORT	SC	849	022,529	29-71
PRINCESS ANNE CO.		VA	971	444,961	331-439
PRINCESS ANNE DIST.	SOMERSET	MD	297	443,528	833-73
PRINCETON	BUREAU	IL	99	007,672	479-84
PRINCETON	WASHINGTON	ME	273	443,510	389-95
PRINCETON	WORCESTER	MA	341	443,560	769-800
PRINCETON TWP.	DALLAS	AR	26	002,480	76-91
PRINCETON TWP.	GIBSON	IN	147	442,925	24-43
PRINCETON TWP.	MERCER	NJ	454	443,653	1-72
PRINCETOWN	SCHENECTADY	NY	594	444,310	85-109
PROCTOR TWP.	CRITTENDEN	AR	25	002,479	738-44
PROMPTON BOR.	PAYNE	PA	835	444,803	475-82
PROSPECT	NEW HAVEN	CT	46	003,074	193-208
PROSPECT	WALDO	ME	271	443,508	159-217
PROSPECT BOR.	BUTLER	PA	760	020,610	485-91
PROSPECT TWP.	MARION	OH	708	444,701	25-33, 38-45
PROSPERITY DIST.	MECKLENBURG	NC	637	444,650	104-5
PROVIDENCE	SARATOGA	NY	593	444,309	761-94
PROVIDENCE BOR.	LUZERNE	PA	793	444,761	507-518
PROVIDENCE CO.		RI	843	444,809	199-872
PROVIDENCE CO.		RI	844	444,810	1-432
PROVIDENCE CO.		RI	845	444,811	433-984
PROVIDENCE CO.		RI	846	444,812	1-440
PROVIDENCE DIST.	MECKLENBURG	NC	637	444,650	148, 150-61
PROVIDENCE TWP.	LUCAS	OH	706	444,699	268-74
PROVIDENCE TWP.	LUZERNE	PA	793	444,761	519-626
PROVIDENCE, WARD 1	PROVIDENCE	RI	844	444,810	1-172
PROVIDENCE, WARD 2	PROVIDENCE	RI	844	444,810	173-270
PROVIDENCE, WARD 3	PROVIDENCE	RI	844	444,810	273-432
PROVIDENCE, WARD 4	PROVIDENCE	RI	845	444,811	433-560
PROVIDENCE, WARD 5	PROVIDENCE	RI	845	444,811	561-736
PROVIDENCE, WARD 6	PROVIDENCE	RI	845	444,811	737-984
PROVINCETOWN	BARNSTABLE	MA	303	014,697	1-76
PROVISO TWP.	COOK	IL	103	007,676	97-108
PULASKI	JACKSON	MI	352	443,568	495-513
PULASKI	GILES	TN	879	444,835	653-70
PULASKI	IOWA	WI	999	444,986	845-49
PULASKI CO.		AR	29	002,483	633-743
PULASKI CO.		GA	80	442,889	455-546
PULASKI CO.		IL	125	442,913	593-646
PULASKI CO.		IN	166	442,944	651-713
PULASKI CO.		KY	217	442,985	1-314
PULASKI CO.		MO	411	443,619	141-233
PULASKI CO.		VA	971	444,961	443-532
PULASKI TWP.	WILLIAMS	OH	741	444,734	168-86
PULASKI TWP.	LAWRENCE	PA	790	444,758	45-86
PULTENEY	STEUBEN	NY	600	444,316	651-94
PULTNEY TWP.	BELMONT	OH	661	020,209	445-96
PULVIDERA	VALENCIA	NM	470	443,668	665-73
PUNGO RIVER DIST.	BEAUFORT	NC	620	018,106	703-6
PUNXSUTAWNEY	JEFFERSON	PA	786	444,754	151-58, 160, 163
PURDY	MC NAIRY	TN	888	444,844	1-7
PURYEAR'S DIST.	CLARKE	GA	65	007,061	91-95
PUSHETA TWP.	AUGLAIZE	OH	660	020,208	653-76

CITY, COUNTY, TOWN, OR TOWNSHIP	COUNTY	STATE	NA NO. M432	GD NO.	PAGES	
PUTNAM	WASHINGTON	NY	610	444,326	117-34	
PUTNAM CO.		FL	59	006,715	381-92	
PUTNAM CO.		GA	81	442,890	547-626	
PUTNAM CO.		IL	125	442,913	647-741	
PUTNAM CO.		IN	167	442,945	715-1166	
PUTNAM CO.		MO	411	443,619	235-76	
PUTNAM CO.		NY	581	444,297	1-349	
PUTNAM CO.		OH	723	444,716	1-185	
PUTNAM CO.		VA	971	444,961	535-646	
PUTNAM TWP.	LIVINGSTON	MI	356	443,572	700-723	
PUTNAM VALLEY	PUTNAM	NY	581	444,297	85-124	
PUTNAM-SPRINGFIELD TWP.	MUSKINGUM	OH	718	444,711	44-74	
PUTNAMVILLE	PUTNAM	IN	167	442,945	1051-56	
PUTNEY	WINDHAM	VT	929	444,928	85-119	
PYATT TWP.	PULASKI	AR	29	002,483	739-43	
PYMATUNING TWP.	MERCER	PA	796	444,764	217-68	
QUACHITA PARISH		LA	238	443,481	477-532	
QUAKER GAP	STOKES	NC	645	444,658	163-64,	166-72
QUAKERTOWN VILLAGE	BUCKS	PA	759	020,609	599-604	
QUANTICO DIST.	SOMERSET	MD	297	443,528	1050-70	
QUEEN ANNE DIST.	PRINCE GEORGES	MD	295	443,526	158-73,	242-43
QUEEN ANNES CO.		MD	296	443,527	245-596	
QUEENS CO.		NY	582	444,298	355-622,	1-103
QUEENS CO.		NY	583	444,299	105-619	
QUEENSBURY	WARREN	NY	609	444,325	47-173	
QUEMAHONING TWP.	SOMERSET	PA	828	444,796	267-87	
QUINCY	NORFOLK	MA	331	443,550	463-582	
QUINCY	BRANCH	MI	347	014,809	611-37	
QUINCY	LOGAN	OH	704	444,697	170-78	
QUINCY, MIDDLE WARD	ADAMS	IL	97	007,670	460-75	
QUINCY, NORTH WARD	ADAMS	IL	97	007,670	399-458	
QUINCY, SOUTH WARD	ADAMS	IL	97	007,670	477-519	
QUINCY TWP.	FRANKLIN	PA	782	444,750	803-870	
QUINCY, WARD 2	ADAMS	IL	97	007,670	521-55	
QUINCY, WARD 3	ADAMS	IL	97	007,670	557-72	
RABUN CO.		GA	81	442,890	627-82	
RACCOON TWP.	GALLIA	OH	681	444,674	823-58	
RACCOON TWP.	BEAVER	PA	750	020,600	393-417	
RACINE CITY	RACINE	WI	1004	444,991	35-76,	78-156
RACINE CO.		WI	1004	444,991	35-398	
RACINE TOWN	RACINE	WI	1004	444,991	77,	159-78
RADFORDSVILLE BEAT	PERRY	AL	12	002,354	684-93	
RADNER TWP.	DELAWARE	OH	675	020,223	677-705	
RADNOR TWP.	DELAWARE	PA	776	444,744	437-69	
RAGLAND DIST.	GRANVILLE	NC	631	444,644	183-98	
RAHWAY TWP.	ESSEX	NJ	450	443,649	773-852	
RAIN TWP.	INDIANA	PA	785	444,753	363-91	
RAISIN TWP.	LENAWEE	MI	355	443,571	477-507	
RAISINVILLE	MONROE	MI	358	443,574	667-90	
RALEIGH	SMITH	MS	381	443,593	691	
RALEIGH	WAKE	NC	647	444,660	511-75	
RALEIGH CO.		VA	972	444,962	1-42	
RALEIGH PREC.	SALINE	IL	127	442,915	83-108	

CITY, COUNTY, TOWN, OR TOWNSHIP	COUNTY	STATE	NA NO. M432	GD NO.	PAGES
RALLS CO.		MO	411	443,619	279-394
RAMAPO	ROCKLAND	NY	588	444,304	701-777
RAMSEY CO.		MN	367	014,834	75-131
RANAH DIST.	MECKLENBURG	NC	637	444,650	78-85
RANDALLS DIST.	COBB	GA	66	007,062	385-400
RANDOLPH	NORFOLK	MA	329	443,548	341-453
RANDOLPH	COOS	NH	429	443,633	93-95
RANDOLPH	CATTARAUGUS	NY	479	017,055	177-215
RANDOLPH	PORTAGE	OH	722	444,715	861-904
RANDOLPH	ORANGE	VT	926	444,925	425-88
RANDOLPH CO.		AL	14	442,865	563-820
RANDOLPH CO.		AR	30	442,876	1-73
RANDOLPH CO.		GA	81	442,890	683-876
RANDOLPH CO.		IL	125	442,913	1-266
RANDOLPH CO.		IN	168	442,946	1-376
RANDOLPH CO.		MO	411	443,619	395-566
RANDOLPH CO.		NC	641	444,654	165-503
RANDOLPH CO.		VA	972	444,962	45-166
RANDOLPH GROVE	MC LEON	IL	117	007,690	151-78
RANDOLPH TWP.	TIPPECANOE	IN	175	442,953	446-72
RANDOLPH TWP.	MORRIS	NJ	458	443,657	1-63
RANDOLPH TWP.	MONTGOMERY	OH	714	444,707	757-802
RANDOLPH TWP.	CRAWFORD	PA	771	444,739	591-620
RANDOLPH TWP.	COLUMBIA	WI	994	034,508	426-40
RANGE TWP.	MADISON	OH	706	444,699	455-80
RANKIN CO.		MS	380	443,592	409-504
RANSOM TWP.	HILLSDALE	MI	351	443,567	683-96
RANSOM TWP.	LUZERNE	PA	793	444,761	339-58
RAPHO TWP.	LANCASTER	PA	787	444,755	699-774
RAPIDES PARISH		LA	239	443,482	85-209
RAPPAHANNOCK CO.		VA	972	444,962	169-310
RARITAN TWP.	HUNTERDON	NJ	453	443,652	95-168
RARITAN TWP.	MONMOUTH	NJ	456	443,655	369-468
RATTLESNAKE BAR	SUTTER	CA	36	442,879	58-62
RAVENNA	OTTAWA	MI	361	443,577	52-53
RAVENNA TWP.	PORTAGE	OH	722	444,715	29-56, 241-66
RAVENSWOOD	JACKSON	VA	953	444,943	523-28
RAY	MACOMB	MI	357	443,573	125-56
RAY CO.		MO	412	443,620	567-778
RAY TWP.	FRANKLIN	IN	146	442,924	641-71
RAY TWP.	MORGAN	IN	162	442,940	131-60
RAYMOND	CUMBERLAND	ME	249	009,719	269-97
RAYMOND	ROCKINGHAM	NH	437	443,641	377-406
RAYMOND	RACINE	WI	1004	444,991	231-55
RAYMOND CAPE	CUMBERLAND	ME	249	009,719	298-99
RAYNHAM	BRISTOL	MA	307	014,701	249-85
READFIELD	KENNEBEC	ME	257	443,494	777-824
READING	MIDDLESEX	MA	324	443,543	425-99
READING	STEUBEN	NY	598	444,314	347-82
READING	WINDSOR	VT	931	444,930	867-94
READING, NORTH EAST WARD	BERKS	PA	752	020,602	355-433
READING, NORTH WEST WARD	BERKS	PA	752	020,602	434-98
READING, SOUTH EAST WARD	BERKS	PA	752	020,602	499-574
READING, SOUTH WEST WARD	BERKS	PA	752	020,602	574-660
READING, SPRUCE WARD	BERKS	PA	752	020,602	661-732
READING TWP.	HILLSDALE	MI	351	443,567	785-808
READING TWP.	PERRY	OH	719	444,712	671-736
READING TWP.	ADAMS	PA	743	020,593	441-71
READINGTON	HUNTERDON	NJ	453	443,652	584-650

Readsboro

CITY, COUNTY, TOWN, OR TOWNSHIP	COUNTY	STATE	NA NO. M432	GD NO.	PAGES
READSBORO	BENNINGTON	VT	921	027,447	342-61
RECOVERY TWP.	MERCER	OH	710	444,703	608-921
RED FORK TWP.	DESHA	AR	26	002,480	130-36
RED HOOK	DUTCHESS	NY	496	017,072	285-62
RED RIVER CO.		TX	914	444,917	407-466
RED RIVER TWP.	LA FAYETTE	AR	27	002,481	336-38
RED RIVER TWP.	VAN BUREN	AR	31	442,877	624-30
RED RIVER TWP.	WHITE	AR	31	442,877	940-44
RED ROCK	RAMSEY	MN	367	014,834	111
REDBANK TWP.	ARMSTRONG	PA	749	020,599	529-86
REDBANK TWP.	CLARION	PA	767	444,735	260-89
REDDING	FAIRFIELD	CT	37	003,065	365-406
REDDING TWP.	JACKSON	IN	152	442,930	249-80
REDFIELD	OSWEGO	NY	578	444,294	293-310
REDFORD	WAYNE	MI	366	443,582	541-79
REDHILL BEAT	MARSHALL	AL	10	002,352	496-505
REDLAND TWP.	HEMPSTEAD	AR	26	002,480	491-501
REDLION HUN.	NEW CASTLE	DE	54	006,438	497-549
REDSTONE TWP.	FAYETTE	PA	780	444,748	661-92
REED	WILL	IL	133	442,921	85-89
REED PLANTATION	AROOSTOOK	ME	248	009,718	5-7
REED TWP.	SENECA	OH	728	444,721	97-134
REED TWP.	DAUPHIN	PA	774	444,742	195-204
REEDS CREEK	LAWRENCE	AR	27	002,481	412-24
REEDS CREEK	PENDLETON	VA	968	444,958	41-43
REEVE TWP.	DAVIESS	IN	140	007,753	387-411
REFUGIO CO.		TX	914	444,917	469-75
REHOBOTH	BRISTOL	MA	307	014,701	599-649
REHOBOTH HUN.	SUSSEX	DE	55	442,884	85-127
REILY TWP.	BUTLER	OH	663	020,211	337-77
REMSEN	ONEIDA	NY	566	444,282	651-708
RENAULT PREC.	MONROE	IL	121	442,909	1-18
RENSSELAER CO.		NY	584	444,300	1-690
RENSSELAER CO.		NY	585	444,301	691-869, 1-206
RENSSELAER CO.		NY	586	444,302	207-895
RENSSELAERVILLE	ALBANY	NY	473	017,049	687-773
REPUBLICAN TWP.	JEFFERSON	IN	154	442,932	304-310, 313, 326-28, 331-36, 339-47, 471-79
RESERVE TWP.	ALLEGHENY	PA	744	020,594	455-82
REYNOLDS CO.		MO	412	443,620	779-822
REYNOLDSBURGH	FRANKLIN	OH	679	444,672	319-32
RHEA CO.		TN	893	444,849	533-639
RHINEBECK	DUTCHESS	NY	497	017,073	505-574
RICE	CATTARAUGUS	NY	479	017,055	353-75
RICE	SANDUSKY	OH	726	444,719	996-1007
RICH HILL TWP.	MUSKINGUM	OH	718	444,711	941-76
RICH HILL TWP.	GREENE	PA	783	444,751	571-622
RICH TWP.	COOK	IL	103	007,676	45-48
RICHFIELD	ADAMS	IL	97	007,670	574-92
RICHFIELD	OTSEGO	NY	580	444,296	82-117
RICHFIELD	WASHINGTON	WI	1008	444,995	301-327
RICHFIELD TWP.	GENESEE	MI	350	443,566	627-38
RICHFIELD TWP.	HENRY	OH	693	444,686	59-62
RICHFIELD TWP.	LUCAS	OH	706	444,699	275-84
RICHFIELD TWP.	SUMMIT	OH	732	444,725	699-729
RICHFORD	TIOGA	NY	604	444,320	553-82
RICHFORD	FRANKLIN	VT	924	444,923	439-65
RICHLAND	KALAMAZOO	MI	353	443,569	313-31

CITY, COUNTY, TOWN, OR TOWNSHIP	COUNTY	STATE	NA NO. M432	GD NO.	PAGES
RICHLAND	OSWEGO	NY	578	444,294	443-540
RICHLAND	CLARION	PA	767	444,735	347-79
RICHLAND CO.		IL	125	442,913	267-362
RICHLAND CO.		OH	724	444,717	187-946
RICHLAND CO.		SC	858	444,821	1-175
RICHLAND CO.		WI	1004	444,991	401-422
RICHLAND DIST.	CLAY	IL	100	007,673	559-662
RICHLAND DIST.	RICHLAND	IL	125	442,913	267-362
RICHLAND DIST.	SHELBY	IL	128	442,916	337-57
RICHLAND PREC.	CLARK	IL	100	007,673	397-418
RICHLAND TWP.	CRAWFORD	AR	25	002,479	635-47
RICHLAND TWP.	DESHA	AR	26	002,480	118-22
RICHLAND TWP.	JEFFERSON	AR	27	002,481	159-67
RICHLAND TWP.	MADISON	AR	27	002,481	531-48
RICHLAND TWP.	NEWTON	AR	28	002,482	11-12
RICHLAND TWP.	PHILLIPS	AR	29	002,483	299-312
RICHLAND TWP.	ST. FRANCIS	AR	30	442,876	76-78, 83-91
RICHLAND TWP.	SEARCY	AR	30	442,876	329-31
RICHLAND TWP.	WASHINGTON	AR	31	442,877	673-84
RICHLAND TWP.	DE KALB	IN	142	007,755	473-88
RICHLAND TWP.	FOUNTAIN	IN	145	442,923	201-242
RICHLAND TWP.	FULTON	IN	146	442,924	939-56
RICHLAND TWP.	GRANT	IN	147	442,925	421-41
RICHLAND TWP.	GREENE	IN	148	442,926	617-26, 634-53
RICHLAND TWP.	JAY	IN	153	442,931	709-717
RICHLAND TWP.	MADISON	IN	158	442,936	102-121
RICHLAND TWP.	MIAMI	IN	160	442,938	213-40
RICHLAND TWP.	MONROE	IN	161	442,939	481-90, 492, 503
RICHLAND TWP.	STEUBEN	IN	173	442,951	335-45
RICHLAND TWP.	JACKSON	IA	184	007,793	563-64, 566-70, 582-83
RICHLAND TWP.	JONES	IA	185	442,960	412-21
RICHLAND TWP.	GASCONADE	MO	399	443,607	385-88
RICHLAND TWP.	MORGAN	MO	408	443,616	477-97
RICHLAND TWP.	ALLEN	OH	657	020,205	713-36
RICHLAND TWP.	BELMONT	OH	661	020,209	236-315
RICHLAND TWP.	CLINTON	OH	668	020,216	629-77
RICHLAND TWP.	DARKE	OH	674	020,222	941-59
RICHLAND TWP.	DEFIANCE	OH	674	020,222	44-61
RICHLAND TWP.	FAIRFIELD	OH	677	444,670	769-811
RICHLAND TWP.	GUERNSEY	OH	684	444,677	245-81
RICHLAND TWP.	HOLMES	OH	696	444,689	497-529
RICHLAND TWP.	LOGAN	OH	704	444,697	197-26
RICHLAND TWP.	MARION	OH	708	444,701	235-62
RICHLAND TWP.	VINTON	OH	736	444,729	529-58
RICHLAND TWP.	WYANDOT	OH	741	444,734	439-53
RICHLAND TWP.	BUCKS	PA	759	020,609	605-646
RICHLAND TWP.	CAMBRIA	PA	761	020,611	283-313
RICHLAND TWP.	VENANGO	PA	832	444,800	227-50
RICHMOND	MC HENRY	IL	117	007,690	887-912
RICHMOND	MADISON	KY	211	442,979	499-503
RICHMOND	LINCOLN	ME	261	443,498	531-80
RICHMOND	BERKSHIRE	MA	306	014,700	41-62
RICHMOND	MACOMB	MI	357	443,573	1-24
RICHMOND	CHESHIRE	NH	428	014,941	387-414
RICHMOND	ONTARIO	NY	571	444,287	155-99
RICHMOND	STOKES	NC	645	444,658	212-40
RICHMOND	ASHTABULA	OH	659	020,207	737-53
RICHMOND	WASHINGTON	RI	847	444,813	481-524

CITY, COUNTY, TOWN, OR TOWNSHIP	COUNTY	STATE	NA NO. M432	GD NO.	PAGES
RICHMOND	FORT BEND	TX	910	024,889	449-52
RICHMOND	CHITTENDEN	VT	923	444,922	119-53
RICHMOND	HENRICO	VA	951	444,941	477-900
RICHMOND	WALWORTH	WI	1007	444,994	693-710
RICHMOND CO.		GA	81	442,890	877-1077
RICHMOND CO.		NY	587	444,303	1-368
RICHMOND CO.		NC	642	444,655	505-626
RICHMOND CO.		VA	972	444,962	315-414
RICHMOND DIST.	PHILADELPHIA	PA	820	444,788	363-502
RICHMOND TWP.	HURON	OH	697	444,690	127-41
RICHMOND TWP.	BERKS	PA	753	020,603	209-258
RICHMOND TWP.	CRAWFORD	PA	771	444,739	699-726
RICHMOND TWP.	TIOGA	PA	830	444,798	357-86
RICHMONDVILLE	SCHOHARIE	NY	596	444,312	563-602
RICHWOOD	UNION	OH	736	444,729	31-34
RICHWOODS TWP.	IZARD	AR	27	002,481	1-8
RICHWOODS TWP.	LAWRENCE	AR	27	002,481	389-96
RICHWOODS TWP.	PRAIRIE	AR	29	002,483	627-30
RICHWOODS TWP.	WASHINGTON	MO	421	443,629	288-306
RIDGE PRAIRIE DIST.	ST. CLAIR	IL	126	442,914	913-93, 1006-8
RIDGE TWP.	VAN WERT	OH	736	444,729	403-412
RIDGE TWP.	WYANDOT	OH	741	444,734	545-56
RIDGEBURY TWP.	BRADFORD	PA	757	020,607	787-826
RIDGEFIELD	FAIRFIELD	CT	37	003,065	309-362
RIDGEFIELD TWP.	HURON	OH	697	444,690	38-64, 107-125, 217-18
RIDGEVILLE DIST.	WASHINGTON	MD	298	443,529	545-46, 553-56
RIDGEVILLE TWP.	COOK	IL	103	007,676	123-33
RIDGEVILLE TWP.	HENRY	OH	693	444,686	39-42
RIDGEVILLE TWP.	LORAIN	OH	705	444,698	775-803
RIDGEWAY	ORLEANS	NY	575	444,291	359-473
RIDGEWAY	IOWA	WI	999	444,986	809-825
RIDGEWAY TWP.	LENAWEE	MI	355	443,571	461-76
RIDGEWAY TWP.	ELK	PA	776	444,744	669-74
RIDLEY TWP.	DELAWARE	PA	776	444,744	273-306
RIGOTT	STEPHENSON	IL	129	442,917	749-64
RIGA	LENAWEE	MI	355	443,571	349-53
RIGA	MONROE	NY	528	017,104	389-412, 423-4
RILEY	MC HENRY	IL	117	007,690	663-74
RILEY	ST. CLAIR	MI	362	443,578	435-42
RILEY TWP.	YELL	AR	31	442,877	1014-18
RILEY TWP.	VIGO	IN	177	442,955	297-320
RILEY TWP.	CLINTON	MI	349	014,811	63-67
RILEY TWP.	PUTNAM	OH	723	444,716	165-85
RILEY TWP.	SANDUSKY	OH	726	444,719	828-42
RINDGE	CHESHIRE	NH	428	014,941	503-533
RINGGOLD	EL DORADO	CA	34	002,491	527-32
RINGGOLD	WALKER	GA	85	442,894	755-60
RINGGOLD TWP.	JEFFERSON	PA	786	444,754	116-31
RIO ARRIBA CO.		NM	467	016,603	193-448
RIO GRANDE VALLEY	CAMERON	TX	909	024,888	507-709
RIO GRANDE VALLEY	STARR	TX	909	024,888	507-709
RIO GRANDE VALLEY	WEBB	TX	909	024,888	507-709
RIPLEY	BROWN	IL	98	007,671	326-30
RIPLEY	SOMERSET	ME	268	443,505	239-54
RIPLEY	CHAUTAUQUA	NY	485	017,061	205-246
RIPLEY	JACKSON	VA	953	444,943	517-22
RIPLEY CO.		IN	169	442,947	377-746
RIPLEY CO.		MO	412	443,620	823-88

CITY, COUNTY, TOWN, OR TOWNSHIP	COUNTY	STATE	NA NO. M432	GD NO.	PAGES
RIPLEY TWP.	MONTGOMERY	IN	161	442,939	1111-39
RIPLEY TWP.	RUSH	IN	170	442,948	1059-1104
RIPLEY TWP.	HOLMES	OH	696	444,689	599-630
RIPLEY TWP.	HURON	OH	697	444,690	421-50
RIPTON	ADDISON	VT	920	027,446	377-90
RISING SUN	OHIO	IN	163	442,941	585-626
RITCHIE CO.		VA	973	444,963	417-509
RITCHILTOWN	OHIO	VA	966	444,956	122-47
RIVER BEAT	DALLAS	AL	4	002,346	493-95, 500-501
RIVER SET.	HILLSBOROUGH	FL	58	006,714	519-20
RIVERHEAD	SUFFOLK	NY	602	444,318	499-559
RIVES	JACKSON	MI	352	443,568	777-89
ROANE CO.		TN	893	444,849	643-897
ROANE TWP.	LA FAYETTE	AR	27	002,481	333-34, 341, 377-78
ROANOKE CO.		VA	973	444,963	513-655
ROANOKE ISLAND DIST.	CURRITUCK	NC	627	444,640	431-42
ROARING CREEK TWP.	MONTOUR	PA	801	444,769	849-97
ROARING RUN	PENDLETON	VA	968	444,958	63
ROARINGCREEK TWP.	COLUMBIA	PA	769	444,737	551-63
ROARK TWP.	GASCONADE	MO	399	443,607	295-318
ROBB TWP.	POSEY	IN	166	442,944	503, 559-89
ROBBINSTON	WASHINGTON	ME	273	443,510	197-221
ROBERSON CREEK	RUTHERFORD	NC	644	444,657	568-72, 673-76, 681
ROBERTSON CO.		TN	894	444,850	1-294
ROBERTSON CO.		TX	914	444,917	479-94
ROBERTSON'S DIST.	LUMPKIN	GA	76	007,072	125
ROBESON CO.		NC	642	444,655	627-830
ROBESON TWP.	ALLEGHENY	PA	748	020,598	513-59
ROBESON TWP.	BERKS	PA	754	020,604	801-858
ROBINSON TWP.	POSEY	IN	166	442,944	503, 611-49
ROBINSON TWP.	GREENE	MO	400	443,608	543-70
ROBINSON'S DIST.	LUMPKIN	GA	76	007,072	126-38
ROBISON TWP.	WASHINGTON	PA	833	444,801	36-56
ROC ROE TWP.	MONROE	AR	28	002,482	720-25
ROCHESTER	PLYMOUTH	MA	333	443,552	517-607
ROCHESTER	STRAFFORD	NH	440	443,644	653-724
ROCHESTER	ULSTER	NY	608	444,324	685-761
ROCHESTER	WINDSOR	VT	930	444,929	1-36
ROCHESTER	RACINE	WI	1004	444,991	339-78
ROCHESTER BOR.	BEAVER	PA	750	020,600	1-37
ROCHESTER TWP.	FULTON	IN	146	442,924	825-60
ROCHESTER TWP.	CEDAR CO.	IA	182	007,791	176-200
ROCHESTER TWP.	ANDREW	MO	391	014,871	197-233
ROCHESTER TWP.	LORAIN	OH	705	444,698	601-622
ROCHESTER, WARD 1	MONROE	NY	530	017,106	1-73
ROCHESTER, WARD 2	MONROE	NY	530	017,106	75-161
ROCHESTER, WARD 3	MONROE	NY	530	017,106	162-268
ROCHESTER, WARD 4	MONROE	NY	530	017,106	269-356
ROCHESTER, WARD 5	MONROE	NY	530	017,106	357-449
ROCHESTER, WARD 6	MONROE	NY	531	017,107	450-624
ROCHESTER, WARD 7	MONROE	NY	531	017,107	627-709
ROCHESTER, WARD 8	MONROE	NY	531	017,107	710-79
ROCHESTER, WARD 9	MONROE	NY	531	017,107	780-892
ROCK	ROCK	WI	1005	444,992	508-521
ROCK CO.		WI	1005	444,992	425-925
ROCK CREEK	CARROLL	IN	137	007,750	696-726
ROCK CREEK TWP.	BARTHOLOMEW	IN	136	007,749	761-80

CITY, COUNTY, TOWN, OR TOWNSHIP	COUNTY	STATE	NA NO. M432	GD NO.	PAGES
ROCK CREEK TWP.	WELLS	IN	181	442,959	699-714
ROCK GROVE	STEPHENSON	IL	129	442,917	583-600
ROCK ISLAND CO.		IL	126	442,914	363-528
ROCK ISLAND, LOW. WARD	ROCK ISLAND	IL	126	442,914	408-410, 435-46
ROCK ISLAND, MID. WARD	ROCK ISLAND	IL	126	442,914	423-34
ROCK ISLAND, UP. WARD	ROCK ISLAND	IL	126	442,914	411-22
ROCK RUN	STEPHENSON	IL	129	442,917	708-731
ROCK SPRINGS	SUTTER	CA	36	442,879	46
ROCKAWAY TWP.	MORRIS	NJ	459	443,658	629-704
ROCKBRIDGE CO.		VA	973	444,963	659-946
ROCKBRIDGE DIST.	GWINNETT	GA	71	007,067	277-90
ROCKCASTLE CO.		KY	217	442,985	315-420
ROCKDALE TWP.	CRAWFORD	PA	771	444,739	767-92
ROCKFORD	WINNEBAGO	IL	134	442,922	830-80
ROCKFORD DIST.	SURRY	NC	646	444,659	701-2, 704, 707 715
ROCKHILL	BUCKS	PA	759	020,609	323-81
ROCKINGHAM	WINDHAM	VT	929	444,928	641-708
ROCKINGHAM		VA	974	444,964	2-432
ROCKINGHAM CO.		NH	437	443,641	1-602
ROCKINGHAM CO.		NH	438	443,642	1-649
ROCKINGHAM CO.		NC	643	444,656	1-219
ROCKINGHAM DIST.	RICHMOND	NC	642	444,655	567-87
ROCKLAND	LINCOLN	ME	259	443,496	121-241
ROCKLAND	SULLIVAN	NY	603	444,319	425-52
ROCKLAND		NY	586	444,304	369-777
ROCKLAND CO.					
ROCKLAND TWP.	BERKS	PA	754	020,604	447-79
ROCKLAND TWP.	VENANGO	PA	832	444,800	113-46
ROCKPORT	SPENCER	IN	172	442,950	129-40
ROCKPORT	ESSEX	MA	315	443,534	295-372
ROCKPORT TWP.	CUYAHOGA	OH	673	020,221	450-84
ROCKTON	WINNEBAGO	IL	134	442,922	792-816
ROCKVILLE	WILL	IL	133	442,921	151-63
ROCKVILLE EL. DIST.	MONTGOMERY	MD	295	443,526	747-810
ROCKY BAYOU TWP.	IZARD	AR	27	002,481	23-30
ROCKY BAYOU TWP.	IZARD	AR	28	002,482	713-18
ROCKY HILL	HARTFORD	CT	40	003,068	1-26
ROCKY MOUNT DIST.	LOWNDES	AL	8	002,350	351-79
RODMAN	JEFFERSON	NY	516	017,092	873-915
RODNEY	JEFFERSON	MS	374	443,586	163-67
ROLLIN TWP.	LENAWEE	MI	355	443,571	509-534
ROLLINSFORD	STRAFFORD	NH	440	443,644	369-70, 372-40 402-413
ROME	KENNEBEC	ME	256	443,493	259-78
ROME	ONEIDA	NY	565	444,281	1-189
ROME	BRADFORD	PA	756	020,606	221-52
ROME TWP.	JONES	IA	185	442,960	375-88
ROME TWP.	LENAWEE	MI	355	443,571	535-71
ROME TWP.	ASHTABULA	OH	659	020,207	921-38
ROME TWP.	ATHENS	OH	660	020,208	189-220
ROME TWP.	LAWRENCE	OH	701	444,694	815-42
ROME TWP.	CRAWFORD	PA	771	444,739	527-49
ROMULUS	SENECA	NY	597	444,313	159-207
ROMULUS TWP.	WAYNE	MI	366	443,582	833-46
RONALD TWP.	IONIA	MI	352	443,568	375-85
ROOT	MONTGOMERY	NY	533	017,109	639-704
ROOT TWP.	ADAMS	IN	135	007,748	25-52
ROOTSTOWN TWP.	PORTAGE	OH	722	444,715	267-98
ROSCOE	WINNEBAGO	IL	134	442,922	767-91

CITY, COUNTY, TOWN, OR TOWNSHIP	COUNTY	STATE	NA NO. M432	GD NO.	PAGES
ROSCOE'S BEAT	DALLAS	AL	4	002,346	574-87
ROSE	WAYNE	NY	613	444,329	929-82
ROSE HILL	JOHNSON	MO	403	443,611	114
ROSE TWP.	OAKLAND	MI	360	443,576	749-70
ROSE TWP.	CARROLL	OH	664	020,212	405-441
ROSE TWP.	JEFFERSON	PA	786	444,754	313-29
ROSENDALE	ULSTER	NY	607	444,323	251-308
ROSENDALE	FOND DU LAC	WI	997	444,984	706-722
ROSEVILLE TWP.	FRANKLIN	AR	26	002,480	296
ROSS	KALAMAZOO	MI	353	443,569	295-311
ROSS	STANLEY	NC	645	444,658	103-113
ROSS CO.		OH	725	444,718	1-793
ROSS TWP.	CLINTON	IN	139	007,752	702-727
ROSS TWP.	LAKE	IN	157	442,935	278-95
ROSS TWP.	BUTLER	OH	663	020,211	753-92
ROSS TWP.	GREENE	OH	683	444,676	749-82
ROSS TWP.	JEFFERSON	OH	699	444,692	921-48
ROSS TWP.	ALLEGHENY	PA	744	020,594	419-54
ROSS TWP.	LUZERNE	PA	793	444,761	196-213
ROSS TWP.	MONROE	PA	798	444,766	67-101
ROSSIE	ST. LAWRENCE	NY	569	444,305	413-48
ROSSVILLE	CLINTON	IN	139	007,752	728-31
ROSSVILLE	MIAMI	OH	711	444,704	623-25
ROSSVILLE	YORK	PA	840	444,808	783-84
ROSTRAVER TWP.	WESTMORELAND	PA	837	444,805	595-644
ROSWELL DIST.	COBB	GA	66	007,062	206-245
ROTTERDAM	SCHENECTADY	NY	594	444,310	111-70
ROUGH AND READY	YUBA	CA	36	442,879	531-46
ROULETT	POTTER	PA	825	444,793	186-91
ROUND GROVE TWP.	MARION	MO	406	443,614	722-44
ROUND POND TWP.	INDEPENDENCE	AR	26	002,480	719-28
ROUND PRAIRIE TWP.	JEFFERSON	IA	185	442,960	16-35
ROUNDHEAD	HARDIN	OH	692	444,685	397-400
ROUNDHEAD TWP.	HARDIN	OH	692	444,685	397-414
ROWAN CO.		NC	643	444,656	221-459
ROWE	FRANKLIN	MA	317	443,536	505-520
ROWLEY	ESSEX	MA	314	014,708	81-106
ROXANA	EATON	MI	349	014,811	312-20
ROXBOROUGH	PHILADELPHIA	PA	820	444,788	503-567
ROXBURY	LITCHFIELD	CT	43	003,071	211-37
ROXBURY	OXFORD	ME	262	443,499	411-16
ROXBURY	NORFOLK	MA	330	443,549	1-440
ROXBURY	CHESHIRE	NH	428	014,941	583-89
ROXBURY	DELAWARE	NY	495	017,071	779-850
ROXBURY	WASHINGTON	VT	928	444,927	165-88
ROXBURY TWP.	MORRIS	NJ	458	443,657	407-463
ROXBURY TWP.	WASHINGTON	OH	738	444,731	827-53
ROYAL OAK TWP.	DANE	WI	995	034,509	861-67
ROYAL TWP.	OAKLAND	MI	359	443,575	471-97
ROYALSTON	WHITE	AR	31	442,877	883-87
ROYALTON	WORCESTER	MA	340	443,559	517-53
ROYALTON	NIAGARA	NY	560	444,276	359-454
ROYALTON	FAIRFIELD	OH	677	444,670	497-502
ROYALTON	FULTON	OH	681	444,674	561-74
ROYALTON TWP.	WINDSOR	VT	930	444,929	177-221
ROYERSFORD VILLA	CUYAHOGA	OH	673	020,221	295-324
RUBICON	MONTGOMERY	PA	799	444,767	149-50
RUDDELL TWP.	DODGE	WI	996	034,510	355-74
	INDEPENDENCE	AR	26	002,480	751-75

CITY, COUNTY, TOWN, OR TOWNSHIP	COUNTY	STATE	NA NO. M432	GD NO.	PAGES
RUGGLES TWP.	ASHLAND	OH	658	020,206	952-53, 995-102
RUHFORD	ALLEGANY	NY	476	017,052	693-736
RUMFORD	OXFORD	ME	262	443,499	422-54
RUMLEY TWP.	HARRISON	OH	693	444,686	532-58
RUMNEY	GRAFTON	NH	431	443,635	313-39
RUPERT	BENNINGTON	VT	921	027,447	117-43
RUSCOMBMANOR TWP.	BERKS	PA	754	020,604	417-46
RUSH	SHIAWASSEE	MI	363	443,579	115-16
RUSH	MONROE	NY	529	017,105	599-646
RUSH CO.		IN	170	442,948	747-1147
RUSH CREEK TWP.	FAIRFIELD	OH	677	444,670	829-58
RUSH CREEK TWP.	LOGAN	OH	704	444,697	447-82
RUSH ISLAND	CADDO PARISH	LA	230	009,697	691-94
RUSH TWP.	BUCHANAN	MO	393	014,873	247-60
RUSH TWP.	CHAMPAIGN	OH	665	020,213	493-530
RUSH TWP.	TUSCARAWAS	OH	734	444,727	239-72
RUSH TWP.	CENTRE	PA	763	020,613	569-77
RUSH TWP.	DAUPHIN	PA	775	444,743	665-72
RUSH TWP.	NORTHUMBERLAND	PA	804	444,772	409-436
RUSH TWP.	SCHUYLKILL	PA	826	444,794	29-44
RUSH TWP.	SUSQUEHANNA	PA	829	444,797	125-52
RUSHFORD	WINNEBAGO	WI	1009	444,996	1097-1109
RUSHVILLE CORP.	SCHUYLER	IL	128	442,916	603-632
RUSHVILLE TWP.	SCHUYLER	IL	128	442,916	633-65
RUSK	CHEROKEE	TX	909	024,888	863-70
RUSK CO.		TX	914	444,917	497-642
RUSK DIST.	RUSK	TX	914	444,917	497-642
RUSSELL	HAMPDEN	MA	318	443,537	475-90
RUSSELL	ST. LAWRENCE	NY	590	444,306	797-842
RUSSELL CO.		AL	14	442,865	1-204
RUSSELL CO.		KY	217	442,985	421-539
RUSSELL CO.		VA	975	444,965	435-696
RUSSELL TWP.	PUTNAM	IN	167	442,945	836-68
RUSSELL TWP.	GEAUGA	OH	682	444,675	213-38
RUSSELLS DIST.	MUSCOGEE	GA	79	442,888	703-721
RUSSELLVILLE	LOGAN	KY	211	442,979	1, 123-34, 263
RUSSIA	HERKIMER	NY	512	017,088	101-156
RUSSIA TWP.	LORAIN	OH	705	444,698	483-532
RUSSIAVILLE	CLINTON	IN	139	007,752	789-90
RUTHERFORD CO.		NC	644	444,657	461-716
RUTHERFORD CO.		TN	894	444,850	297-715
RUTHERFORD TWP.	MARTIN	IN	160	442,938	121-35
RUTHERFORDTON	RUTHERFORD	NC	644	444,657	706-712, 714
RUTLAND	KANE	IL	112	007,685	59-79
RUTLAND	LA SALLE	IL	115	007,688	608-622
RUTLAND	WORCESTER	MA	341	443,560	801-830
RUTLAND	BARRY	MI	346	014,808	199-203
RUTLAND	JEFFERSON	NY	516	017,092	917-71
RUTLAND	TIOGA	PA	830	444,798	91-114
RUTLAND	RUTLAND	VT	927	444,926	13-101
RUTLAND	DANE	WI	995	034,509	549-67
RUTLAND CO.		VT	927	444,926	1-830
RUTLAND TWP.	MEIGS	OH	710	444,703	175-216
RYE	ROCKINGHAM	NH	438	443,642	361-91
RYE	WESTCHESTER	NY	615	444,331	159-220
RYE TWP.	PERRY	PA	805	444,773	727-43
RYEGATE	CALEDONIA	VT	922	027,448	35-73

CITY, COUNTY, TOWN, OR TOWNSHIP	COUNTY	STATE	NA NO. M432	GD NO.	PAGES
SABINAL	VALENCIA	NM	470	443,668	575-80, 674-88
SABINE CO.		TX	914	444,917	645-82
SABINE DIST.	SABINE	TX	914	444,917	645-82
SABINE PARISH		LA	239	443,482	211-90
SABULA	JACKSON	IA	184	007,793	689-90, 695-96
SACO	YORK	ME	275	443,512	585-723
SACRAMENTO	SACRAMENTO	CA	35	002,492	271-390, 431-81
SACRAMENTO CO.		CA	35	002,492	271-490
SADDLE RIVER	BERGEN	NJ	442	016,529	385-404
SADSBURY TWP.	CHESTER	PA	766	020,616	603-669
SADSBURY TWP.	CRAWFORD	PA	771	444,739	439-60
SADSBURY TWP.	LANCASTER	PA	789	444,757	1-37
SAFE HARBOR	LANCASTER	PA	787	444,755	367-71, 532-52
SAGINAW CO.		MI	361	443,577	157-219
SAGINAW TWP.	SAGINAW	MI	361	443,577	166-86
ST. ALBANS	SOMERSET	ME	268	443,505	255-97
ST. ALBANS	FRANKLIN	VT	924	444,923	135-220
ST. ALBANS TWP.	LICKING	OH	702	444,695	339, 341-75
ST. ANDREWS PARISH	CHARLESTON	SC	850	022,530	743-51
ST. ANTHONY	RAMSEY	MN	367	014,834	117-29
ST. ANTHONY PREC.	RAMSEY	MN	367	014,834	113-15
ST. ARMAND	ESSEX	NY	503	017,079	349-53
ST. AUGUSTINE	ST. JOHNS	FL	59	006,715	395-426
ST. BARTHOLOMEWS PAR.	COLLETON	SC	851	444,814	365-468
ST. BERNARD PARISH		LA	239	443,482	291-326
ST. BRIDES PARISH	NORFOLK	VA	964	444,954	405-479
ST. CHARLES	KANE	IL	112	007,685	209-259
ST. CHARLES	ST. CHARLES	MO	413	443,621	1-36
ST. CHARLES CO.		MO	413	443,621	1-227
ST. CHARLES PARISH		LA	239	443,482	327-51
ST. CLAIR	ST. CLAIR	MI	362	443,578	221-62
ST. CLAIR BOR.	SCHUYLKILL	PA	827	444,795	249-96
ST. CLAIR CO.		AL	14	442,865	207-339
ST. CLAIR CO.		IL	126	442,914	529-1008
ST. CLAIR CO.		MI	362	443,578	221-479
ST. CLAIR CO.		MO	413	443,621	229-302
ST. CLAIR TWP.	BUTLER	OH	663	020,211	239-300
ST. CLAIR TWP.	COLUMBIANA	OH	669	020,217	425-58
ST. CLAIR TWP.	BEDFORD	PA	751	020,601	319-65
ST. CLAIRSVILLE	BELMONT	OH	661	020,209	211-35
ST. CROIX CO.		WI	1006	444,993	1-16
ST. CROIX PREC.	WASHINGTON	MN	367	014,834	170-76
ST. DENNIS PARISH	CHARLESTON	SC	850	022,530	769-73
ST. FRANCIS	PHILLIPS	AR	29	002,483	241-56
ST. FRANCIS CO.		AR	30	442,876	75-165
ST. FRANCIS TWP.	CRITTENDEN	AR	25	002,479	752-53
ST. FRANCIS TWP.	GREENE	AR	26	002,480	399-409
ST. FRANCISVILLE WEST FELICIANA PAR.		LA	231	009,698	518-23
ST. FRANCOIS CO.		MO	413	443,621	303-405
ST. GEORGE	LINCOLN	ME	259	443,496	67-120
ST. GEORGE	CHITTENDEN	VT	923	444,922	85-88
ST. GEORGE PARISH	ACCOMACK	VA	932	029,707	155-311
ST. GEORGES HUN.	NEW CASTLE	DE	54	006,438	366-422
ST. GEORGES PARISH	COLLETON	SC	851	444,814	469-515
ST. HELEN PARISH	BEAUFORT	SC	849	022,529	1-28
ST. HELENA PARISH		LA	239	443,482	353-409
ST. JAMES GOOSE CREEK PAR.	CHAR.	SC	850	022,530	831-75
ST. JAMES PARISH		LA	239	443,482	411-91

CITY, COUNTY, TOWN, OR TOWNSHIP	COUNTY	STATE	NA NO. M432	GD NO.	PAGES
ST. JAMES SANTEE PAR.	CHARLESTON	SC	850	022,530	733-49
ST. JOHN THE BAPTIST PARISH		LA	239	443,482	493-560
ST. JOHN TWP.	LAKE	IN	157	442,935	296-307
ST. JOHNS BAR DIST.	DUVAL	FL	58	006,714	229-32
ST. JOHNS BERKLEY PAR.	CHARLESTON	SC	850	022,530	791-811
ST. JOHNS COLLETON PAR.	CHARLESTON	SC	850	022,530	775-90
ST. JOHNS CO.		FL	59	006,715	395-432
ST. JOHNSBURY	CALEDONIA	VT	922	027,448	89-154
ST. JOHNSVILLE	MONTGOMERY	NY	533	017,109	527-69
ST. JOSEPH CO.		IN	171	442,949	1-280
ST. JOSEPH CO.		MI	362	443,578	483-804
ST. JOSEPH ISLAND	REFUGIO	TX	914	444,917	469
ST. JOSEPH TWP.	ALLEN	IN	135	007,748	563-80
ST. JOSEPH TWP.	WILLIAMS	OH	741	444,734	152-66
ST. LANDRY PARISH		LA	240	443,483	1-272
ST. LAWRENCE CO.		NY	589	444,305	1-581
ST. LAWRENCE CO.		NY	590	444,306	583-842, 1-281
ST. LAWRENCE CO.		NY	591	444,307	283-842
ST. LOUIS CO.		MO	414	443,622	527-1091
ST. LOUIS CO.		MO	415-18	443,623-26	
ST. LOUIS TWP. (SO. HALF) ST. LOU.	MO	414	443,622	625-88
ST. LOUIS, WARD 1	ST. LOUIS	MO	415	443,623	1-324
ST. LOUIS, WARD 2	ST. LOUIS	MO	415	443,623	325-553
ST. LOUIS, WARD 3	ST. LOUIS	MO	416	443,624	555-839
ST. LOUIS, WARD 4	ST. LOUIS	MO	417	443,625	1-334
ST. LOUIS, WARD 5	ST. LOUIS	MO	417	443,625	335-632
ST. LOUIS, WARD 6	ST. LOUIS	MO	418	443,626	633-956
ST. LOUISVILLE	LICKING	OH	703	444,696	905-7
ST. LUCIE CO.		FL	59	006,715	435-37
ST. LUKES PARISH	BEAUFORT	SC	849	022,529	73-109
ST. LUKES PARISH	SOUTHAMPTON	VA	977	444,967	485-566
ST. MARCAS	HAYS	TX	911	024,890	239-45
ST. MARIE PREC.	JASPER	IL	110	007,683	552-61
ST. MARKS, PORT OF	WAKULLA	FL	59	006,715	497-99
ST. MARTIN PARISH		LA	240	443,483	273-397
ST. MARTINVILLE	ST. MARTIN	LA	240	443,483	382-97
ST. MARY PARISH		LA	240	443,483	398-495
ST. MARYS	AUGLAIZE	OH	660	020,208	501-521
ST. MARY'S CO.		MD	296	443,527	507-697
ST. MARYS DIST.	WAKE	NC	647	444,660	207-230, 341
ST. MARYS TWP.	ADAMS	IN	135	007,748	138-53
ST. MARYS TWP.	AUGLAIZE	OH	660	020,208	501-537
ST. MATTHEWS DIST.	WAKE	NC	647	444,660	231-49
ST. MICHAELS	TALBOT	MD	297	443,528	157-75
ST. MICHAELS	CHARLESTON	SC	850	022,530	165-732
ST. MICHAELS DIST.	TALBOT	MD	297	443,528	176-238
ST. OMER	DECATUR	IN	142	007,755	223-28
ST. PAUL	RAMSEY	MN	367	014,834	80-110
ST. PAULS PARISH	COLLETON	SC	851	444,814	517-39
ST. PETER RIVER	DAKOTA	MN	367	014,834	13-14
ST. PETERS PARISH	BEAUFORT	SC	849	022,529	111-63
ST. PHILLIPS PARISH	CHARLESTON	SC	850	022,530	165-732
ST. STEPHENS PARISH	CHARLESTON	SC	850	022,530	813-29
ST. STEPHENS PARISH	KING AND QUEEN	VA	954	444,944	297-305, 308-1▸ 316-26, 333, 33 36, 339-43, 35▸ 57, 365-83, 40▸
ST. TAMMANY PARISH		LA	241	443,484	497-590
ST. THOMAS PARISH	CHARLESTON	SC	850	022,530	769-73

CITY, COUNTY, TOWN, OR TOWNSHIP	COUNTY	STATE	NA NO. M432	GD NO.	PAGES
ST. THOMAS TWP.	FRANKLIN	PA	782	444,750	553-99
STE. GENEVIEVE	STE. GENEVIEVE	MO	413	443,621	407-424
STE. GENEVIEVE CO.		MO	413	443,621	407-525
STE. GENEVIEVE TWP.	STE. GENEVIEVE	MO	413	443,621	427-57
SALADO CREEK	BEXAR	TX	908	024,887	322-27
SALADO MISSION	BEXAR	TX	908	024,887	321
SALEM	NEW LONDON	CT	48	442,880	401-419
SALEM	WASHINGTON	IN	179	442,957	607-636
SALEM	FRANKLIN	ME	253	009,723	493-503
SALEM	WASHTENAW	MI	364	443,580	499-531
SALEM	ROCKINGHAM	NH	438	443,642	205-243
SALEM	SALEM	NJ	462	443,661	213-85
SALEM	WASHINGTON	NY	611	444,327	495-564
SALEM	FORSYTH	NC	630	444,643	427-46
SALEM	ORLEANS	VT	925	444,924	373-83
SALEM	KENOSHA	WI	1000	444,987	591-617
SALEM CO.		NJ	462	443,661	1-474
SALEM DIST.	CLARKE	GA	65	007,061	129-32
SALEM TWP.	CARROLL	IL	99	007,672	739-45
SALEM TWP.	DELAWARE	IN	143	007,756	697-715
SALEM TWP.	PULASKI	IN	166	442,944	684-87
SALEM TWP.	STEUBEN	IN	173	442,951	381-94
SALEM TWP.	HENRY	IA	184	007,793	455-89
SALEM TWP.	AUGLAIZE	OH	660	020,208	562-72
SALEM TWP.	CHAMPAIGN	OH	665	020,213	531-71
SALEM TWP.	COLUMBIANA	OH	669	020,217	1-47
SALEM TWP.	HIGHLAND	OH	694	444,687	585-604
SALEM TWP.	JEFFERSON	OH	699	444,692	221-73
SALEM TWP.	MEIGS	OH	710	444,703	1-34
SALEM TWP.	MONROE	OH	712	444,705	1007-1046
SALEM TWP.	MUSKINGUM	OH	718	444,711	543-69
SALEM TWP.	OTTAWA	OH	719	444,712	288-92
SALEM TWP.	SHELBY	OH	729	444,722	607-636
SALEM TWP.	TUSCARAWAS	OH	735	444,728	710-49
SALEM TWP.	WARREN	OH	737	444,730	185-268
SALEM TWP.	WASHINGTON	OH	738	444,731	641-70
SALEM TWP.	WYANDOT	OH	741	444,734	513-30
SALEM TWP.	LUZERNE	PA	793	444,761	246-73
SALEM TWP.	MERCER	PA	796	444,764	694-747
SALEM TWP.	WAYNE	PA	835	444,803	301-335
SALEM TWP.	WESTMORELAND	PA	836	444,804	753-803
SALEM, WARD 1	ESSEX	MA	312	014,706	1-118
SALEM, WARD 2	ESSEX	MA	312	014,706	119-218
SALEM, WARD 3	ESSEX	MA	312	014,706	219-368
SALEM, WARD 4	ESSEX	MA	312	014,706	371-489
SALESVILLE	GUERNSEY	OH	684	444,677	721-22
SALINA	ONONDAGA	NY	570	444,286	533-83
SALINE	WASHTENAW	MI	364	443,580	709-747
SALINE CO.		AR	30	442,876	167-252
SALINE CO.		IL	127	442,915	1-134
SALINE CO.		MO	419	443,627	1-148
SALINE PREC.	SALINE	IL	127	442,915	55-82
SALINE TWP.	DALLAS	AR	26	002,480	42-47
SALINE TWP.	HEMPSTEAD	AR	26	002,480	502-512
SALINE TWP.	HOT SPRINGS	AR	26	002,480	547-53, 557-58, 580-81, 619-22
SALINE TWP.	SEVIER	AR	30	442,876	428-34
SALINE TWP.	STE. GENEVIEVE	MO	413	443,621	475-91
SALINE TWP.	JEFFERSON	OH	699	444,692	949-74

CITY, COUNTY, TOWN, OR TOWNSHIP	COUNTY	STATE	NA NO. M432	GD NO.	PAGES
SALINEVILLE TOWN	COLUMBIANA	OH	669	020,217	257-62
SALISBURY	LITCHFIELD	CT	42	003,070	1-74
SALISBURY	LA SALLE	IL	115	007,688	417-46, 456, 461-62, 548, 579-81, 658-
SALISBURY	ESSEX	MA	313	014,707	1-75
SALISBURY	MERRIMACK	NH	436	443,640	439-68
SALISBURY	HERKIMER	NY	513	017,089	657-707
SALISBURY	ROWAN	NC	643	444,656	268-93
SALISBURY	ADDISON	VT	920	027,446	393-417
SALISBURY DIST.	SOMERSET	MD	297	443,528	973-1010
SALISBURY PREC.	COLES	IL	101	007,674	123-56
SALISBURY TWP.	MEIGS	OH	710	444,703	217-55, 328-395-424
SALISBURY TWP.	LANCASTER	PA	789	444,757	39-127
SALISBURY TWP.	LEHIGH	PA	792	444,760	1-43
SALMON FALLS	EL DORADO	CA	34	002,491	765-69
SALT CREEK TWP.	DECATUR	IN	142	007,755	103-21
SALT CREEK TWP.	FRANKLIN	IN	146	442,924	475-99
SALT CREEK TWP.	JACKSON	IN	152	442,930	221-48
SALT CREEK TWP.	MONROE	IN	161	442,939	713-23
SALT CREEK TWP	DAVIS	IA	182	007,791	461-78
SALT CREEK TWP.	HOCKING	OH	695	444,688	139-66
SALT CREEK TWP.	HOLMES	OH	696	444,689	455-95
SALT CREEK TWP.	MUSKINGUM	OH	718	444,711	771-99
SALT CREEK TWP.	PICKAWAY	OH	720	444,713	443-88
SALT CREEK TWP.	WAYNE	OH	739	444,732	161-200
SALT LAKE CO.		UT	919	025,540	137-222
SALT LAKE CO., GREAT		UT	919	025,540	47-136
SALT LICK TWP.	PERRY	OH	719	444,712	599-640
SALT RIVER TWP.	KNOX	MO	403	443,611	198-211
SALT RIVER TWP.	PIKE	MO	409	443,617	542-47
SALT RIVER TWP.	RANDOLPH	MO	411	443,619	550-66
SALT ROCK TWP.	MARION	OH	708	444,701	103-112
SALT SPRING TWP.	RANDOLPH	MO	411	443,619	424-28, 430-9
SALTLICK TWP.	FAYETTE	PA	780	444,748	901-922
SALTSBURG BOR.	INDIANA	PA	785	444,753	621-33
SALUDA REGIMENT	ABBEVILLE	SC	848	022,528	261-411
SALUDA TWP.	JEFFERSON	IN	154	442,932	348-82
SAMFORD'S DIST.	LUMPKIN	GA	76	007,072	89-97
SAMPSON CO.		NC	644	444,657	717-930
SAN ANTONIO	VALENCIA	NM	470	443,668	646-51
SAN ANTONIO	BEXAR	TX	908	024,887	199-276
SAN ANTONIO RIVER	BEXAR	TX	908	024,887	299-308
SAN ANTONITO	VALENCIA	NM	470	443,668	652-53
SAN AUGUSTINE CO.		TX	914	444,917	686-736
SAN AUGUSTINE DIST.	SAN AUGUSTINE	TX	914	444,917	686-735
SAN DIEGO CO.		CA	35	002,492	543-61
SAN FRANCISCO CO.		CA	DESTROYED BY FIRE		
SAN JOAQUIN CO.		CA	35	002,492	565-652
SAN JOSE MISSION	BEXAR	TX	908	024,887	313-14
SAN JUAN MISSION	BEXAR	TX	908	024,887	315-18
SAN LUIS OBISOP CO.		CA	35	002,492	655-62
SAN MIGUEL	SAN MIGUEL	NM	469	443,667	97-146
SAN MIGUEL CO.		NM	469	443,667	1-178
SAN PATRICIO CO.		TX	914	444,917	739-43
SAN PEDRO	VALENCIA	NM	470	443,668	624-27
SAND CREEK DIST.	SHELBY	IL	128	442,916	192-207
SAND CREEK TWP.	BARTHOLOMEW	IN	136	007,749	733-60

CITY, COUNTY, TOWN, OR TOWNSHIP	COUNTY	STATE	NA NO. M432	GD NO.	PAGES
SAND CREEK TWP.	DECATUR	IN	142	007,755	279-324
SAND CREEK TWP.	JENNINGS	IN	155	442,933	622-38
SAND LAKE	RENSSELAER	NY	586	444,302	671-731
SANDBORNTON	BELKNAP	NH	425	014,938	101-165
SANDERS DIST.	RUTHERFORD	TN	894	444,850	308-318
SANDERS FORKE	CANNON	TN	872	024,563	876-95
SANDGATE	BENNINGTON	VT	921	027,447	203-223
SANDISFIELD	BERKSHIRE	MA	306	014,700	573-612
SANDOWN	ROCKINGHAM	NH	437	443,641	409-422
SANDSTOWN	JACKSON	MI	352	443,568	567-87
SANDUSKY	SANDUSKY	OH	726	444,719	977-96
SANDUSKY CITY	ERIE	OH	676	338,044	1-3
SANDUSKY CO.		OH	726	444,719	785-1008, 1-121
SANDUSKY TWP.	CRAWFORD	OH	671	020,219	773-94
SANDUSKY TWP.	RICHLAND	OH	724	444,717	777-91
SANDUSKY TWP.	SANDUSKY	OH	726	444,719	785-827
SANDWICH	BARNSTABLE	MA	304	014,698	683-786
SANDWICH	CARROLL	NH	426	014,939	445-506
SANDY CREEK	OSWEGO	NY	578	444,294	311-69
SANDY CREEK	VENANGO	PA	832	444,800	203-226
SANDY CREEK DIST.	CLARKE	GA	65	007,061	79-83
SANDY CREEK DIST.	WARREN	NC	648	444,661	1-21
SANDY CREEK TWP.	MERCER	PA	796	444,764	561-629
SANDY LAKE TWP.	MERCER	PA	796	444,764	499-525
SANDY POINT DIST.	ANSON	NC	619	018,105	361-79
SANDY RUN	RUTHERFORD	NC	644	444,657	625-40
SANDY TWP.	STARK	OH	731	444,724	259-89
SANDY TWP.	TUSCARAWAS	OH	735	444,728	521-46
SANDYSTON TWP.	SUSSEX	NJ	464	443,663	21-52
SANDYVILLE	TUSCARAWAS	OH	735	444,728	546-51
SANFORD	YORK	ME	276	443,513	229-85
SANFORD	BROOME	NY	477	017,053	337-96
SANGAMON	MC LEON	IL	117	007,690	248
SANGAMON CO.		IL	127	442,915	137-602
SANGERFIELD	ONEIDA	NY	562	444,278	57-113
SANGERVILLE	PISCATAQUIS	ME	267	443,504	343-73
SANILAC	SANILAC	MI	363	443,579	1-8
SANILAC CO.		MI	363	443,579	1-51
SANPETE CO.		UT	919	025,540	223-32
SANTA ANNA	SANTA ANNA	NM	468	443,666	464-66
SANTA ANNA CO.		NM	468	443,666	451-566
SANTA BARBARA CO.		CA	35	002,492	493-521
SANTA BARBARA DIST.	SAN LUIS OBISPO	CA	35	002,492	655-62
SANTA BARBARA DIST.	SANTA BARBARA	CA	35	002,492	493-521
SANTA CLARA CO.		CA	LOST		
SANTA CRUZ	SANTA CRUZ	CA	35	002,492	525-29, 536
SANTA CRUZ CO.		CA	35	002,492	525-40
SANTA ROSA CO.		FL	59	006,715	441-91
SANTE FE	SANTA FE	NM	468	443,666	633-749
SANTE FE CO.		NM	468	443,666	569-756
SARANAC	CLINTON	NY	489	017,065	45-106
SARATOGA	GRUNDY	IL	108	007,681	325-29
SARATOGA	SARATOGA	NY	592	444,308	475-558
SARATOGA CO.		NY	592	444,308	1-558
SARATOGA CO.		NY	593	444,309	559-1105
SARATOGA SPRINGS	SARATOGA	NY	592	444,308	363-474
SARCOXIE TWP.	JASPER	MO	402	443,610	717-40
SARDINIA	ERIE	NY	500	017,076	193-234
SARDIS	MONROE	OH	712	444,705	828-31

CITY, COUNTY, TOWN, OR TOWNSHIP	COUNTY	STATE	NA NO. M432	GD NO.	PAGES
SARDIS DIST.	MECKLENBURG	NC	637	444,650	162-85
SAUCON TWP.	NORTHAMPTON	PA	802	444,770	65-132
SAUGERTIES	ULSTER	NY	608	444,324	159-350
SAUGUS	ESSEX	MA	310	014,704	389-425
SAUK CO.		WI	1006	444,993	19-123
SAUK PRAIRIE VILLAGE	SAUK	WI	1006	444,993	67
SAUK RAPIDS DIST.	BENTON	MN	367	014,834	1-10
SAUKVILLE	WASHINGTON	WI	1008	444,995	128-47
SAULT DE ST. MARIE	CHIPPEWA	MI	349	014,811	1-22
SAURATOWN	STOKES	NC	645	444,658	279-92
SAVAGE	ANNE ARUNDEL	MD	278	013,195	867-70, 872-74, 876
SAVAGE FACTORY	ANNE ARUNDEL	MD	278	013,195	866, 871
SAVANNA	CARROLL	IL	99	007,672	713-22
SAVANNA TWP.	CARROLL	IL	99	007,672	723-28
SAVANNAH·	ANDREW	MO	391	014,871	117-29
SAVANNAH	WAYNE	NY	613	444,329	983-1023
SAVANNAH	MACON	NC	636	444,649	682-83, 724-27, 754-55
SAVANNAH	HARDIN	TN	882	444,838	385-90
SAVANNAH DIST.	LUMPKIN	GA	76	007,072	29-39
SAVANNAH RIVER REG.	ABBEVILLE	SC	848	022,528	1-260
SAVILLE TWP.	PERRY	PA	805	444,773	745-80
SAVOY	BERKSHIRE	MA	305	014,699	175-98
SAYBROOK	MIDDLESEX	CT	44	003,072	473-75, 477-562
SAYBROOK	ASHTABULA	OH	659	020,207	609-641
SCARBOROUGH	CUMBERLAND	ME	251	009,721	701-744
SCARSDALE	WESTCHESTER	NY	615	444,331	251-59
SCHAEFFERSTOWN	LEBANON	PA	791	444,759	37-50
SCHAGHTICOKE	RENSSELAER	NY	585	444,301	1-80
SCHAUMBURG	COOK	IL	103	007,676	253-64
SCHELLSBURG	BEDFORD	PA	751	020,601	75-83
SCHENECTADY CO.		NY	594	444,310	1-488
SCHENECTADY, WARD 1	SCHENECTADY	NY	594	444,310	191-226
SCHENECTADY, WARD 2	SCHENECTADY	NY	594	444,310	227-70
SCHENECTADY, WARD 3	SCHENECTADY	NY	594	444,310	271-316
SCHENECTADY, WARD 4	SCHENECTADY	NY	594	444,310	317-405
SCHODACK	RENSSELAER	NY	586	444,302	811-95
SCHOHARIE	SCHOHARIE	NY	595	444,311	202-264
SCHOHARIE CO.		NY	595	444,311	1-404
SCHOHARIE CO.		NY	596	444,312	405-808
SCHOOLCRAFT	KALAMAZOO	MI	353	443,569	171-97
SCHOOLCRAFT CO.		MI	363	443,579	55
SCHROEPPLE	OSWEGO	NY	577	444,293	507-556, 558-65
SCHROON	ESSEX	NY	504	017,080	541-89
SCHUYLER	HERKIMER	NY	512	017,088	57-97
SCHUYLER CO.		IL	128	442,916	603-868
SCHUYLER CO.		MO	419	443,627	149-225
SCHUYLER FALLS	CLINTON	NY	489	017,065	206-256
SCHUYLKILL CO.		PA	826	444,794	313-944, 1-54
SCHUYLKILL CO.		PA	827	444,795	57-856
SCHUYLKILL HAVEN BOR.	SCHUYLKILL	PA	826	444,794	421-72
SCHUYLKILL TWP.	CHESTER	PA	765	020,615	255-88
SCHUYLKILL TWP.	SCHUYLKILL	PA	827	444,795	567-608
SCIO	WASHTENAW	MI	364	443,580	647-75, 1041-48, 1051-54
SCIO	ALLEGANY	NY	475	017,051	181-226
SCIOTA	SHIAWASSEE	MI	363	443,579	182-86
SCIOTO	PICKAWAY	OH	720	444,713	121-53

CITY, COUNTY, TOWN, OR TOWNSHIP	COUNTY	STATE	NA NO. M432	GD NO.	PAGES
SCIOTO CO.		OH	727	444,720	123-579
SCIOTO TWP.	DELAWARE	OH	675	020,223	527-53
SCIOTO TWP.	JACKSON	OH	698	444,691	691-723
SCIOTO TWP.	ROSS	OH	725	444,718	1-208
SCIOTOVILLE	SCIOTO	OH	727	444,720	458-63
SCIPIO	CAYUGA	NY	483	017,059	335-86
SCIPIO TWP.	ALLEN	IN	135	007,748	411-15
SCIPIO TWP.	LA PORTE	IN	157	442,935	595-614
SCIPIO TWP.	HILLSDALE	MI	351	443,567	869-89
SCIPIO TWP.	MEIGS	OH	710	444,703	35-68
SCIPIO TWP.	SENECA	OH	728	444,721	41-96
SCITUATE	PLYMOUTH	MA	332	443,551	103-154
SCITUATE	PROVIDENCE	RI	846	444,812	49-159
SCOTLAND	OSWEGO	NY	577	444,293	557
SCOTLAND CO.		MO	419	443,627	227-315
SCOTT	CORTLAND	NY	493	017,069	505-535
SCOTT	WAYNE	PA	835	444,803	83-97
SCOTT	SHEBOYGAN	WI	1006	444,993	276-86
SCOTT CO.		AR	30	442,876	253-323
SCOTT CO.		IL	128	442,916	1-190
SCOTT CO.		IN	171	442,949	283-429
SCOTT CO.		IA	188	442,963	333-475
SCOTT CO.		KY	218	442,986	791-1007
SCOTT CO.		MS	381	443,593	505-572
SCOTT CO.		MO	419	443,627	317-83
SCOTT CO.		TN	895	444,851	719-63
SCOTT CO.		VA	975	444,965	699-926
SCOTT TWP.	MISSISSIPPI	AR	28	002,482	698-700
SCOTT TWP.	OGLE	IL	123	442,911	165-68
SCOTT TWP.	KOSCIUSKO	IN	156	442,934	618-24
SCOTT TWP.	MONTGOMERY	IN	161	442,939	1035-63
SCOTT TWP.	STEUBEN	IN	173	442,951	312-23
SCOTT TWP.	VANDERBURGH	IN	176	442,954	961-88
SCOTT TWP.	JOHNSON	IA	185	442,960	273-77
SCOTT TWP.	ADAMS	OH	657	020,205	435-65
SCOTT TWP.	BROWN	OH	662	020,210	661-85
SCOTT TWP.	MARION	OH	708	444,701	185-202
SCOTT TWP.	SANDUSKY	OH	726	444,719	103-121
SCOTT TWP.	LUZERNE	PA	793	444,761	383-413
SCOTT TWP.	COLUMBIA	WI	994	034,508	415-25
SCOTTSVILLE	BIBB	AL	2	002,344	44-49
SCOTTSVILLE	ALBEMARLE	VA	932	029,707	589-99
SCOTTVILLE	MACOUPIN	IL	116	442,906	412-13
SCOTTVILLE	ALLEN	KY	190	007,843	200-4
SCREVEN CO.		GA	82	442,891	1-76
SCRIBA	OSWEGO	NY	577	444,293	714-80
SCRUBGRASS TWP.	VENANGO	PA	832	444,800	251-78
SCULL SHOALS DIST.	CLARKE	GA	65	007,061	151-61
SEABROOK	ROCKINGHAM	NH	438	443,642	41-71
SEAL TWP.	PIKE	OH	721	444,714	573-627
SEARCY CO.		AR	30	442,876	325-71
SEARCY TWP.	PHILLIPS	AR	29	002,483	235-41
SEARSBURG	BENNINGTON	VT	921	027,447	311-15
SEARSMONT	WALDO	ME	271	443,508	275-315
SEARSPORT	WALDO	ME	271	443,508	219-71
SEAVILLE	HANCOCK	ME	255	443,492	711-14
SEBAGO	CUMBERLAND	ME	249	009,719	191-211
SEBASTICOOK	KENNEBEC	ME	258	443,495	549-79
SEBEC	PISCATAQUIS	ME	267	443,504	673-702

CITY, COUNTY, TOWN, OR TOWNSHIP	COUNTY	STATE	NA NO. M432	GD NO.	PAGES
SEBEWA	IONIA	MI	352	443,569	245-51
SECOND COLLEGE GRANT	COOS	NH	429	443,633	97
SEDGWICK	HANCOCK	ME	254	443,491	275-304
SEEKONK	BRISTOL	MA	308	014,702	741-94
SEJEQUE	VALENCIA	NM	470	443,668	756-68
SELFS BEAT	JEFFERSON	AL	7	002,349	388-98
SELMA BEAT	DALLAS	AL	4	002,346	603-5, 615-18, 634
SELMA TOWN	DALLAS	AL	4	002,346	588-95, 606-613
SEMINOLE	CHATTOOGA	GA	64	007,060	750-69
SEMPLETOWN	MADISON	IL	119	442,907	748-53
SEMPRONIUS	CAYUGA	NY	483	017,059	81-111
SENACA	MC HENRY	IL	117	007,690	699-718
SENECA	LENAWEE	MI	355	443,571	277-302
SENECA	ONTARIO	NY	572	444,288	865-1067
SENECA	PENDLETON	VA	968	444,958	63-68
SENECA CO.		NY	597	444,313	1-619
SENECA CO.		OH	728	444,721	581-949, 1-300
SENECA FALLS	SENECA	NY	597	444,313	517-619
SENECA TWP.	GUERNSEY	OH	684	444,677	723-58
SENECA TWP.	MONROE	OH	712	444,705	499-550
SENECA TWP.	SENECA	OH	728	444,721	1-40
SENECAVILLE	GUERNSEY	OH	684	444,677	245-56
SENNETT	CAYUGA	NY	482	017,058	715-70
SEPTEMBER	BARRY	MI	346	014,808	189
SERENA	LA SALLE	IL	115	007,688	777-86
SERGEANT TWP.	MC KEAN	PA	795	444,763	31-35
SEVEN MILE	BUTLER	OH	663	020,211	715-17
SEVERE BEAT	PERRY	AL	12	002,354	673-83
SEVIER CO.		AR	30	442,876	373-447
SEVIER CO.		TN	895	444,851	767-923
SEWARD	WINNEBAGO	IL	134	442,922	593-600
SEWARD	SCHOHARIE	NY	596	444,312	647-99
SEWICKLEY TWP.	WESTMORELAND	PA	837	444,805	553-93
SEYMOUR	NEW HAVEN	CT	46	003,074	673-713
SHABEONA TWP.	DE KALB	IL	104	007,677	699-707
SHACKLEFORD BANKS	CARTERET	NC	623	018,109	339-46
SHADE TWP.	SOMERSET	PA	828	444,796	201-231
SHAFTSBURY	BENNINGTON	VT	921	027,447	1-46
SHAKER VILLAGE	HARTFORD	CT	39	003,067	82-86
SHAKERTOWN	MONTGOMERY	OH	713	444,706	161-62
SHALER TWP.	ALLEGHENY	PA	747	020,597	167-214
SHALERSVILLE TWP.	PORTAGE	OH	722	444,715	211-39
SHALLOTTE DIST.	BRUNSWICK	NC	621	018,107	349-63
SHALLOW FORD DIST.	DE KALB	GA	67	007,063	230-39
SHAMOKIN TWP.	NORTHUMBERLAND	PA	804	444,772	661-715
SHANDAKEN	ULSTER	NY	608	444,324	391-446
SHANESVILLE	TUSCARAWAS	OH	734	444,727	433-42
SHANNON CO.		MO	420	443,628	385-411
SHAPLEIGH	YORK	ME	276	443,513	289-321
SHARON	LITCHFIELD	CT	43	003,071	52-122
SHARON	NORFOLK	MA	331	443,550	95-121
SHARON	WASHTENAW	MI	364	443,580	779-99
SHARON	HILLSBORO	NH	433	443,637	711-16
SHARON	SCHOHARIE	NY	596	444,312	701-763
SHARON	MEDINA	OH	709	444,702	625-61
SHARON	POTTER	PA	825	444,793	267-78
SHARON	WINDSOR	VT	930	444,929	69-98
SHARON	WALWORTH	WI	1007	444,994	551-78

CITY, COUNTY, TOWN, OR TOWNSHIP	COUNTY	STATE	NA NO. M432	GD NO.	PAGES
SHARON BOR.	MERCER	PA	796	444,764	485-98
SHARON DIST.	MECKLENBURG	NC	637	444,650	122-26, 144-47
SHARON TWP.	FRANKLIN	OH	680	444,673	33-68
SHARON TWP.	RICHLAND	OH	724	444,717	679-725
SHARPSBURG	BATH	KY	191	007,844	207-211
SHARPSBURG BOR.	ALLEGHENY	PA	744	020,594	505-534
SHASTA	SHASTA	CA	35	002,492	665-69
SHASTA CITY	SHASTA	CA	36	442,879	140, 665-69
SHASTA CO.		CA	35	002,492	665-74
SHASTA CO.		CA	36	442,879	140, 495-97, 665-74
SHAWANGUNK	ULSTER	NY	607	444,323	579-678
SHAWNEE TWP.	FOUNTAIN	IN	145	442,923	173-99
SHAWNEE TWP.	ALLEN	OH	657	020,205	673-90
SHAWNEETOWN PREC.	GALLATIN	IL	107	007,680	746-87
SHAWSWICK TWP.	LAWRENCE	IN	158	442,936	744-835, 849-53, 880, 935-39
SHEBOYGAN	SHEBOYGAN	WI	1006	444,993	178-80, 206-248, 255-67, 287
SHEBOYGAN CO.		WI	1006	444,993	127-326
SHEBOYGAN FALLS TWP.	SHEBOYGAN	WI	1006	444,993	127-52
SHEFFIELD	BERKSHIRE	MA	306	014,700	463-528
SHEFFIELD	ASHTABULA	OH	659	020,207	501-521
SHEFFIELD	CALEDONIA	VT	922	027,448	489-508
SHEFFIELD TWP.	TIPPECANOE	IN	175	442,953	307-343
SHEFFIELD TWP.	LORAIN	OH	705	444,698	753-74
SHEFFIELD TWP.	WARREN	PA	832	444,800	727-34
SHELBURNE	FRANKLIN	MA	317	443,536	425-54
SHELBURNE	COOS	NH	429	443,633	189-200
SHELBURNE	CHITTENDEN	VT	923	444,922	89-118
SHELBY	MACOMB	MI	357	443,573	285-320
SHELBY	SHELBY	MO	420	443,628	419
SHELBY	ORLEANS	NY	575	444,291	474-552
SHELBY CO.		AL	14	442,865	343-514
SHELBY CO.		IL	128	442,916	192-382
SHELBY CO.		IN	172	442,950	433-813
SHELBY CO.		KY	218	442,986	541-790
SHELBY CO.		MO	420	443,628	413-503
SHELBY CO.		OH	729	444,722	301-656
SHELBY CO.		TN	895	444,851	1-415
SHELBY CO.		TX	915	444,918	1-79
SHELBY TWP.	JEFFERSON	IN	154	442,932	421-59, 463-64
SHELBY TWP.	RIPLEY	IN	169	442,947	645-701
SHELBY TWP.	TIPPECANOE	IN	175	442,953	1-18
SHELBYVILLE	SHELBY	IL	128	442,916	239-48
SHELBYVILLE	SHELBY	MO	420	443,628	413-18, 420
SHELBYVILLE CORPIN	SHELBY	IN	172	442,950	695-719
SHELDON	WYOMING	NY	616	444,332	1-61
SHELDON	FRANKLIN	VT	924	444,923	565-608
SHELL POINT DIST.	WAKULLA	FL	59	006,715	502-3, 508-516
SHELTER ISLAND	SUFFOLK	NY	602	444,318	883-92
SHELTON TWP.	WARRICK	IN	179	442,957	323-35
SHENANDOAH CO.		VA	976	444,966	1-307
SHENANGO TWP.	LAWRENCE	PA	790	444,758	307-365
SHENANGO TWP.	MERCER	PA	796	444,764	447-84
SHEPHERDSTOWN	BELMONT	OH	661	020,209	967-68
SHEPHERDSTOWN	JEFFERSON	VA	953	444,943	612-43
SHERBURNE	WILL	IL	133	442,921	347-57
SHERBURNE	MIDDLESEX	MA	322	443,541	627-51

CITY, COUNTY, TOWN, OR TOWNSHIP	COUNTY	STATE	NA NO. M432	GD NO.	PAGES
SHERBURNE	CHENANGO	NY	487	017,063	465-527
SHERBURNE	RUTLAND	VT	927	444,926	255-68
SHERIDAN	CALHOUN	MI	348	014,810	1-24
SHERIDAN	CHAUTAUQUA	NY	484	017,060	1-52
SHERMAN	FAIRFIELD	CT	37	003,065	83-106
SHERMAN	CHAUTAUQUA	NY	484	017,060	541-71
SHERMAN	GRAYSON	TX	910	024,889	721
SHERMAN TWP.	ST. JOSEPH	MI	362	443,578	697-705
SHERMAN TWP.	HURON	OH	697	444,690	215-16, 219-44
SHERWOOD TWP.	BRANCH	MI	347	014,809	551-67
SHESHEQUIN	BRADFORD	PA	757	020,607	553-87
SHIAWASSEE	SHIAWASSEE	MI	363	443,579	59-78
SHIAWASSEE CO.		MI	363	443,579	59-190
SHIELDS	LAKE	IL	114	007,687	25-38
SHIELDS	DODGE	WI	996	034,510	235-49
SHIELDSBOROUGH	HANCOCK	MS	372	443,584	97-112
SHIPPEN TWP.	MC KEAN	PA	795	444,763	117-26
SHIPPEN TWP.	TIOGA	PA	830	444,798	461-68
SHIPPENSBURGH TWP.	CUMBERLAND	PA	772	444,740	387-432
SHIRLAND	WINNEBAGO	IL	134	442,922	649-57
SHIRLEY	PISCATAQUIS	ME	267	443,504	473-78
SHIRLEY	MIDDLESEX	MA	323	443,542	1-28
SHIRLEY TWP.	HUNTINGDON	PA	784	444,752	351-91
SHIRLEYSBURG BOR.	HUNTINGDON	PA	784	444,752	341-50
SHOAL CREEK DIST.	LUMPKIN	GA	76	007,072	81-86
SHOAL CREEK TWP.	NEWTON	MO	408	443,616	711-21
SHOAL TWP.	APPANOOSE	IA	182	007,791	44-47
SHOKOKEN	HENDERSON	IL	109	007,682	171
SHOREHAM	ADDISON	VT	920	027,446	153-91
SHORES REED DIST.	STOKES	NC	645	444,658	173-85, 241-42
SHORT CREEK BEAT	JEFFERSON	AL	7	002,349	325-35
SHORT CREEK TWP.	HARRISON	OH	693	444,686	881-923
SHREVEPORT	CADDO PARISH	LA	230	009,697	659-85
SHREVEPORT WARD	CADDO PARISH	LA	230	009,697	690, 705-6
SHREWSBURY	WORCESTER	MA	343	443,562	451-92
SHREWSBURY	RUTLAND	VT	927	444,926	763-93
SHREWSBURY BOR.	YORK	PA	839	444,807	399-410
SHREWSBURY TWP.	MONMOUTH	NJ	456	443,655	1-49, 52-76
SHREWSBURY TWP.	LYCOMING	PA	795	444,763	894-99
SHREWSBURY TWP.	SULLIVAN	PA	828	444,796	619-23
SHREWSBURY TWP.	YORK	PA	839	444,807	495-536
SHULLSBURG	LAFAYETTE	WI	1001	444,988	761-800, 815
SHUTESBURY	FRANKLIN	MA	316	443,535	185-206
SIDDONSBURG	YORK	PA	840	444,808	637-38
SIDNEY	KENNEBEC	ME	256	443,493	209-256
SIDNEY	DELAWARE	NY	494	017,070	133-76
SIDNEY	SHELBY	OH	729	444,722	547-78
SILOAM DIST.	SURRY	NC	646	444,659	678-84, 691-70C
SILVER CREEK	STEPHENSON	IL	129	442,917	733-48
SILVER CREEK TWP.	CLARK	IN	138	007,751	39-62
SILVER CREEK TWP.	CASS	MI	349	014,811	755-67
SILVER CREEK TWP.	RANDOLPH	MO	411	443,619	395-423
SILVER CREEK TWP.	GREENE	OH	683	444,676	783-844
SILVER CREEK VILLAGE	CHAUTAUQUA	NY	484	017,060	55-67
SILVER LAKE TWP.	SUSQUEHANNA	PA	829	444,797	209-238
SILVER SPRING TWP.	CUMBERLAND	PA	773	444,741	501-556
SIMMONS HAMMOCK SET.	HILLSBOROUGH	FL	58	006,714	495-98
SIMPSON CO.		KY	218	442,986	1-139
SIMPSON CO.		MS	381	443,593	573-649

CITY, COUNTY, TOWN, OR TOWNSHIP	COUNTY	STATE	NA NO. M432	GD NO.	PAGES
SIMS TWP.	GRANT	IN	147	442,925	407-420
SIMSBURY	HARTFORD	CT	39	003,067	369-437
SKANEATELES	ONONDAGA	NY	568	444,284	865-962
SKINNERSVILLE DIST.	WASHINGTON	NC	646	444,661	161-62, 189-96
SKOWHEGAN	SOMERSET	ME	268	443,505	81-122
SKULL CAMP DIST.	SURRY	NC	646	444,659	631-38
SLANO RIVERS	GILLESPIE	TX	910	024,889	625
SLATE CREEK	EL DORADO	CA	34	002,491	863
SLIPPERY ROCK TWP.	BUTLER	PA	760	020,610	599-634
SMACKOVER TWP.	OUACHITA	AR	28	002,482	123-31
SMITH CO.		MS	381	443,593	651-724
SMITH CO.		TN	896	444,852	419-758
SMITH CO.		TX	915	444,918	83-168
SMITH DIST.	ANSON	NC	619	018,105	380-90
SMITH ISLANDS	NORTHAMPTON	VA	965	444,955	545
SMITH TWP.	BRADLEY	AR	25	002,479	227-39
SMITH TWP.	DALLAS	AR	26	002,480	92-108
SMITH TWP.	DREW	AR	26	002,480	193-208
SMITH TWP.	ST. FRANCIS	AR	30	442,876	97-103, 156-60
SMITH TWP.	GREENE	IN	148	442,926	787-94
SMITH TWP.	POSEY	IN	166	442,944	503, 591-610
SMITH TWP.	GENTRY	MO	399	443,607	457-60
SMITH TWP.	BELMONT	OH	661	020,209	497-541
SMITH TWP.	MAHONING	OH	707	444,700	631-68
SMITH TWP.	WASHINGTON	PA	833	444,801	1-35
SMITHFIELD	SOMERSET	ME	269	443,506	147-67
SMITHFIELD	MADISON	NY	526	017,102	505-544
SMITHFIELD	JOHNSTON	NC	635	444,648	1-7
SMITHFIELD	PROVIDENCE	RI	843	444,809	733-872
SMITHFIELD	PROVIDENCE	RI	846	444,812	161-295
SMITHFIELD	ISLE OF WIGHT	VA	952	444,942	227-37
SMITHFIELD	JEFFERSON	VA	953	444,943	728-36
SMITHFIELD TWP.	DE KALB	IN	142	007,755	441-56
SMITHFIELD TWP.	JEFFERSON	OH	699	444,692	319-64
SMITHFIELD TWP.	BRADFORD	PA	756	020,606	675-722
SMITHFIELD TWP.	MONROE	PA	798	444,766	227-58
SMITHS	STANLEY	NC	645	444,658	87-102
SMITHS BAR	SUTTER	CA	36	442,879	51-52
SMITH'S CREEK	PENDLETON	VA	968	444,958	46-47
SMITHSBURG	WASHINGTON	MD	298	443,529	489-97
SMITHTOWN	SUFFOLK	NY	601	444,317	243-89
SMITHVILLE	CHENANGO	NY	488	017,064	947-89
SMITHVILLE DIST.	BRUNSWICK	NC	621	018,107	317-35
SMOKE HOLES	PENDLETON	VA	968	444,958	38-40
SMOKY CREEK DIST.	CALDWELL	NC	623	018,109	30
SMOKY MOUNTAINS	MACON	NC	636	444,649	693-94
SMYRNA	AROOSTOOK	ME	248	009,718	171-75
SMYRNA	CHENANGO	NY	487	017,063	1-48
SMYRNA	CARTERET	NC	623	018,109	248-57
SMYRNA	HARRISON	OH	693	444,686	690-92
SMYRNA TWP.	JEFFERSON	IN	154	442,932	271-82, 284, 295-303, 465-70
SMYTH CO.		VA	976	444,966	311-480
SNAKE RIVER PREC.	RAMSEY	MN	367	014,834	131
SNI-A-BAR TWP.	JACKSON	MO	402	443,610	658-86
SNOW CREEK DIST.	STOKES	NC	645	444,658	243-78
SNOW HILL	WORCESTER	MD	299	443,530	597-609
SNOWDEN TWP.	ALLEGHENY	PA	748	020,598	481-512
SNOWSHOE TWP.	CENTRE	PA	763	020,613	547-57

CITY, COUNTY, TOWN, OR TOWNSHIP	COUNTY	STATE	NA NO. M432	GD NO.	PAGES
SNYDER TWP.	BLAIR	PA	755	020,605	81-104
SNYDER TWP.	JEFFERSON	PA	786	444,754	38-45
SOAP CREEK TWP.	DAVIS	IA	182	007,791	528-40
SOCORRO	VALENCIA	NM	470	443,668	628-40
SODUS	WAYNE	NY	612	444,328	317-426
SOLANO CO.		CA	36	442,879	1-15
SOLEBURY TWP.	BUCKS	PA	758	020,608	327-91
SOLON	SOMERSET	ME	269	443,506	66-101
SOLON	CORTLAND	NY	493	017,069	341-68
SOLON	CUYAHOGA	OH	673	020,221	815-42
SOMERS	TOLLAND	CT	50	442,882	145-80
SOMERS	WESTCHESTER	NY	614	444,330	561-602
SOMERS TWP.	PREBLE	OH	723	444,716	556-605
SOMERSET	PULASKI	KY	217	442,985	1-7
SOMERSET	BRISTOL	MA	308	014,702	833-60
SOMERSET	NIAGARA	NY	561	444,277	689-740
SOMERSET	PERRY	OH	719	444,712	641-70
SOMERSET	WINDHAM	VT	929	444,928	481-88
SOMERSET BOR.	SOMERSET	PA	828	444,796	1-21
SOMERSET CO.		ME	268	443,505	1-342
SOMERSET CO.		ME	269	443,506	1-568
SOMERSET CO.		MD	297	443,528	699-1108
SOMERSET CO.		NJ	463	443,662	477-952
SOMERSET CO.		PA	828	444,796	1-604
SOMERSET TWP.	HILLSDALE	MI	351	443,567	977-98
SOMERSET TWP.	BELMONT	OH	661	020,209	785-840
SOMERSET TWP.	SOMERSET	PA	828	444,796	43-103
SOMERSET TWP.	WASHINGTON	PA	833	444,801	395-430
SOMERSWORTH	STRAFFORD	NH	439	443,643	200, 249-366
SOMERSWORTH	STRAFFORD	NH	440	443,644	371
SOMERVILLE	MORGAN	AL	12	002,354	475-552
SOMERVILLE	MIDDLESEX	MA	324	443,543	705-789
SOMONAUK TWP.	DE KALB	IL	104	007,677	665-82
SONOMA	SONOMA	CA	36	442,879	27-31
SONOMA CO.		CA	36	442,879	19-33
SONORA	HANCOCK	IL	109	007,682	822-31
SONORA TWP.	TUOLUMNE	CA	36	442,879	359-62
SOPCHOPPY DIST.	WAKULLA	FL	59	006,715	520-22
SOUTH AMBOY	MIDDLESEX	NJ	455	443,654	397-450
SOUTH ANNVILLE TWP.	LEBANON	PA	791	444,759	565-93
SOUTH BEAVER TWP.	BEAVER	PA	750	020,600	243-69
SOUTH BERWICK	YORK	ME	276	443,513	607-668
SOUTH BLOOMFIELD	MORROW	OH	716	444,709	1033-68
SOUTH BRISTOL	ONTARIO	NY	571	444,287	101-127
SOUTH BROWN TWP.	VINTON	OH	736	444,729	478-93
SOUTH BRUNSWICK TWP.	MIDDLESEX	NJ	455	443,654	315-95
SOUTH BUFFALO	ARMSTRONG	PA	749	020,599	197-227
SOUTH BUTLER TWP.	BUTLER	PA	760	020,610	411-41
SOUTH CHARLESTON	CLARK	OH	666	020,214	293-303
SOUTH CHICAGO	COOK	IL	102	007,675	233-56
SOUTH CODORUS TWP.	YORK	PA	839	444,807	761-88
SOUTH COVENTRY	CHESTER	PA	765	020,615	289-305
SOUTH CREEK DIST.	BEAUFORT	NC	620	018,106	850-52, 859-74
SOUTH CREEK TWP.	BRADFORD	PA	757	020,607	769-86
SOUTH EASTON BOR.	NORTHAMPTON	PA	802	444,770	365-400
SOUTH FAYETTE TWP.	ALLEGHENY	PA	748	020,598	561-87
SOUTH FORK TWP.	CLARK	AR	25	002,479	416-21
SOUTH FORK TWP.	FULTON	AR	26	002,480	305-9
SOUTH FORK TWP.	JACKSON	IA	184	007,793	653, 709-717, 7

CITY, COUNTY, TOWN, OR TOWNSHIP	COUNTY	STATE	NA NO. M432	GD NO.	PAGES
SOUTH GROVE TWP.	DE KALB	IL	104	007,677	611-14
SOUTH HADLEY	HAMPSHIRE	MA	321	443,540	611-70
SOUTH HAMPTON	ROCKINGHAM	NH	438	443,642	73-84
SOUTH HANOVER	JEFFERSON	IN	154	442,932	315-24
SOUTH HANOVER TWP.	DAUPHIN	PA	774	444,742	205-223
SOUTH HAVEN	VAN BUREN	MI	363	443,579	343-48
SOUTH HERO	GRANDE ISLE	VT	924	444,923	1-17
SOUTH HUNTINGTON TWP.	WESTMORELAND	PA	837	444,805	519-51
SOUTH KINGSTON	WASHINGTON	RI	847	444,813	665-754
SOUTH LEBANON TWP.	LEBANON	PA	791	444,759	151-228
SOUTH MAHONING TWP.	INDIANA	PA	785	444,753	393-420
SOUTH MANHEIM	SCHUYLKILL	PA	826	444,794	473-92
SOUTH MIDDLETON TWP.	CUMBERLAND	PA	772	444,740	265-318
SOUTH MILFORD	SUSSEX	DE	55	442,884	163-71
SOUTH MILL CREEK	PENDLETON	VA	968	444,958	33
SOUTH NASHVILLE	DAVIDSON	TN	875	024,566	479-503
SOUTH NEWMARKET	ROCKINGHAM	NH	438	443,642	245-57
SOUTH OTTAWA	LA SALLE	IL	115	007,688	407-8, 492-94, 497-99
SOUTH PITTSBURGH	ALLEGHENY	PA	748	020,598	187-231
SOUTH READING	MIDDLESEX	MA	324	443,543	500-557
SOUTH RIVER TWP.	MARION	MO	406	443,614	658-71
SOUTH SCITUATE	PLYMOUTH	MA	332	443,551	155-97
SOUTH SHENANGO TWP.	CRAWFORD	PA	771	444,739	461-500
SOUTH SLIPPERY ROCK TWP.	LAWRENCE	PA	790	444,758	243-74
SOUTH STRABANE TWP.	WASHINGTON	PA	834	444,802	599-632
SOUTH THOMASTON	LINCOLN	ME	259	443,496	253-87
SOUTH UNION	LOGAN	KY	211	442,979	137-42
SOUTH VALLEY	CATTARAUGUS	NY	479	017,055	17-30, 37
SOUTH WHITEHALL TWP.	LEHIGH	PA	792	444,760	441-514
SOUTH WINDSOR	HARTFORD	CT	39	003,067	245-84
SOUTH WOODBURY	BEDFORD	PA	751	020,601	421-48
SOUTHAMPTON	HAMPSHIRE	MA	320	443,539	121-46
SOUTHAMPTON	SUFFOLK	NY	602	444,318	675-829
SOUTHAMPTON CO.		VA	977	444,967	485-670
SOUTHAMPTON TWP.	BURLINGTON	NJ	444	016,531	645-733
SOUTHAMPTON TWP.	BEDFORD	PA	751	020,601	285-317
SOUTHAMPTON TWP.	BUCKS	PA	759	020,609	203-36
SOUTHAMPTON TWP.	CUMBERLAND	PA	772	444,740	345-86
SOUTHAMPTON TWP.	FRANKLIN	PA	782	444,750	681-723
SOUTHBOROUGH	WORCESTER	MA	344	443,563	711-43
SOUTHBRIDGE	WORCESTER	MA	345	443,564	465-532
SOUTHBURY	NEW HAVEN	CT	46	003,074	635-70
SOUTHEAST	PUTNAM	NY	581	444,297	1-50
SOUTHEAST TWP.	ORANGE	IN	163	442,941	741-76
SOUTHFIELD	RICHMOND	NY	587	444,303	131-32, 134-99
SOUTHFIELD TWP.	OAKLAND	MI	359	443,575	431-70
SOUTHHAMPTON TWP.	SOMERSET	PA	828	444,796	403-434
SOUTHINGTON	HARTFORD	CT	40	003,068	139-91
SOUTHINGTON TWP.	TRUMBULL	OH	733	444,726	441-64
SOUTHOLD	SUFFOLK	NY	602	444,318	561-673
SOUTHPORT	LINCOLN	ME	260	443,497	137-50
SOUTHPORT	CHEMUNG	NY	486	017,062	625-700
SOUTHPORT	KENOSHA	WI	1000	444,987	619-27
SOUTHWARK, WARD 1	PHILADELPHIA	PA	821	444,789	1-186
SOUTHWARK, WARD 2	PHILADELPHIA	PA	821	444,789	187-375
SOUTHWARK, WARD 3	PHILADELPHIA	PA	821	444,789	377-518
SOUTHWARK, WARD 4	PHILADELPHIA	PA	821	444,789	377
SOUTHWARK, WARD 4	PHILADELPHIA	PA	822	444,790	519-707

CITY, COUNTY, TOWN, OR TOWNSHIP	COUNTY	STATE	NA NO. M432	GD NO.	PAGES
SOUTHWARK, WARD 5	PHILADELPHIA	PA	822	444,790	708-864
SOUTHWARK, WARD 6	PHILADELPHIA	PA	822	444,790	865-965
SOUTHWEST TWP.	WARREN	PA	832	444,800	682-91
SOUTHWICK	HAMPDEN	MA	318	443,537	263-89
SOUTHWORK PARISH	SURRY	VA	978	444,968	117-98
SPADRA TWP.	JOHNSON	AR	27	002,481	308-332
SPAFFORD	ONONDAGA	NY	568	444,284	819-64
SPANISH CANYON	EL DORADO	CA	34	002,491	804-8, 810-11
SPARTA	RANDOLPH	IL	125	442,913	26-37
SPARTA	KENT	MI	353	443,569	447-54
SPARTA	LIVINGSTON	NY	525	017,101	597-634
SPARTA	MORROW	OH	716	444,709	1065-68
SPARTA TWP.	DEARBORN	IN	141	007,754	887-901, 907-93
SPARTA TWP.	NOBLE	IN	162	442,940	431-45
SPARTA TWP.	SUSSEX	NJ	464	443,663	321-66
SPARTA TWP.	CRAWFORD	PA	771	444,739	551-72
SPARTANBURG	SPARTANBURG	SC	858	444,821	177-87
SPARTANBURG CO.		SC	858	444,821	177-615
SPAULDING DIST.	PRINCE GEORGES	MD	295	443,526	174-78, 187-206
SPENCER	WORCESTER	MA	343	443,562	49-102
SPENCER	TIOGA	NY	604	444,320	201-244
SPENCER	MEDINA	OH	709	444,702	847-78
SPENCER CO.		IN	172	442,950	1-223
SPENCER CO.		KY	219	442,987	141-254
SPENCER TWP.	JENNINGS	IN	155	442,933	708, 797, 802, 822-54
SPENCER TWP.	PIKE	MO	409	443,617	548-67
SPENCER TWP.	ALLEN	OH	657	020,205	705-712
SPENCER TWP.	GUERNSEY	OH	684	444,677	283-330
SPENCER TWP.	HAMILTON	OH	686	444,679	489-528
SPENCER TWP.	LUCAS	OH	706	444,699	293-99
SPERRY TWP.	CLAYTON	IA	182	007,791	307-311
SPICE VALLEY TWP.	LAWRENCE	IN	158	442,936	721-43
SPICELAND TWP.	HENRY	IN	151	442,929	501-533
SPOTSYLVANIA CO.		VA	977	444,967	673-851
SPRIGG TWP.	ADAMS	OH	657	020,205	153-227
SPRING ARBOR	JACKSON	MI	352	443,568	443-69
SPRING CREEK	DAUPHIN	PA	774	444,742	245-48
SPRING CREEK TWP.	PHILLIPS	AR	29	002,483	313-21
SPRING CREEK TWP.	YELL	AR	31	442,877	972-83
SPRING CREEK TWP.	MIAMI	OH	711	444,704	623-61
SPRING CREEK TWP.	ELK	PA	776	444,744	685-87
SPRING CREEK TWP.	WARREN	PA	832	444,800	617-31
SPRING GARDEN DIST., WARD 1 PHILA.		PA	818	444,786	569-724
SPRING GARDEN DIST., WARD 2 PHILA.		PA	818	444,786	725-89
SPRING GARDEN DIST., WARD 3 PHILA.		PA	818	444,786	893-1054, 1-138
SPRING GARDEN DIST., WARD 4 PHILA.		PA	819	444,787	137-311
SPRING GARDEN DIST., WARD 5 PHILA.		PA	819	444,787	312-516
SPRING GARDEN DIST., WARD 6 PHILA.		PA	819	444,787	517-725
SPRING GARDEN DIST., WARD 7 PHILA.		PA	819	444,787	727-930
SPRING GARDEN TWP.	YORK	PA	840	444,808	305-366
SPRING GROVE	GREEN	WI	999	444,986	473-89
SPRING HILL	MAURY	TN	890	444,846	426-28
SPRING HILL TWP.	DREW	AR	26	002,480	183-92
SPRING HILL TWP.	HEMPSTEAD	AR	26	002,480	539-44
SPRING LAKE TWP.	OTTAWA	MI	361	443,577	141-53
SPRING PRAIRIE	WALWORTH	WI	1007	444,994	361-94
SPRING RIVER TWP.	LAWRENCE	AR	27	002,481	455-74
SPRING ROCK TWP.	CLINTON	IA	182	007,791	412-14

CITY, COUNTY, TOWN, OR TOWNSHIP	COUNTY	STATE	NA NO. M432	GD NO.	PAGES
SPRING TWP.	CENTRE	PA	763	020,613	385-440
SPRING TWP.	CRAWFORD	PA	770	444,738	1-44
SPRING TWP.	PERRY	PA	805	444,773	925-55
SPRING VALLEY	ROCK	WI	1005	444,992	551-68
SPRING WELLS TWP.	WAYNE	MI	366	443,582	893-923
SPRINGBORO	WARREN	OH	737	444,730	871-81
SPRINGDALE TWP.	DANE	WI	995	034,509	905-912
SPRINGFIELD	SANGAMON	IL	127	442,915	137-250
SPRINGFIELD	LA GRANGE	IN	157	442,935	127-45
SPRINGFIELD	PENOBSCOT	ME	266	443,503	641-54
SPRINGFIELD	HAMPDEN	MA	319	443,538	1-279
SPRINGFIELD	GREENE	MO	400	443,608	533-42
SPRINGFIELD	SULLIVAN	NH	441	443,645	257-87
SPRINGFIELD	OTSEGO	NY	579	444,295	108-166
SPRINGFIELD	CLARK	OH	666	020,214	317-444
SPRINGFIELD	SUMMIT	OH	732	444,725	127-30
SPRINGFIELD	LIMESTONE	TX	912	444,915	767, 774
SPRINGFIELD	WINDSOR	VT	931	444,930	895-960
SPRINGFIELD, PUTNAM-	TWP. MUSKINGUM	OH	718	444,711	44-74
SPRINGFIELD TWP.	ALLEN	IN	135	007,748	417-33
SPRINGFIELD TWP.	FRANKLIN	IN	146	442,924	715-58
SPRINGFIELD TWP.	LA PORTE	IN	157	442,935	409-419
SPRINGFIELD TWP.	CEDAR CO.	IA	182	007,791	250-56
SPRINGFIELD TWP.	OAKLAND	MI	360	443,576	597-619
SPRINGFIELD TWP.	HENRY	MO	401	443,609	29-42
SPRINGFIELD TWP.	BURLINGTON	NJ	443	016,530	435-78
SPRINGFIELD TWP.	ESSEX	NJ	450	443,649	523-73
SPRINGFIELD TWP.	CLARK	OH	666	020,214	445-500
SPRINGFIELD TWP.	GALLIA	OH	681	444,674	859-88
SPRINGFIELD TWP.	HAMILTON	OH	685	444,678	191-278
SPRINGFIELD TWP.	JEFFERSON	OH	699	444,692	859-90
SPRINGFIELD TWP.	LUCAS	OH	706	444,699	213-30
SPRINGFIELD TWP.	MAHONING	OH	707	444,700	747-806
SPRINGFIELD TWP.	MUSKINGUM	OH	718	444,711	1-43
SPRINGFIELD TWP.	RICHLAND	OH	724	444,717	727-76
SPRINGFIELD TWP.	ROSS	OH	725	444,718	527-55
SPRINGFIELD TWP.	SUMMIT	OH	732	444,725	123-68
SPRINGFIELD TWP.	WILLIAMS	OH	741	444,734	188-206
SPRINGFIELD TWP.	BRADFORD	PA	756	020,606	723-68
SPRINGFIELD TWP.	BUCKS	PA	759	020,609	411-64
SPRINGFIELD TWP.	DELAWARE	PA	776	444,744	307-331
SPRINGFIELD TWP.	ERIE	PA	778	444,746	852-97
SPRINGFIELD TWP.	FAYETTE	PA	780	444,748	923-48
SPRINGFIELD TWP.	HUNTINGDON	PA	784	444,752	471-85
SPRINGFIELD TWP.	MERCER	PA	796	444,764	365-95
SPRINGFIELD TWP.	MONTGOMERY	PA	800	444,768	57-75
SPRINGFIELD TWP.	YORK	PA	840	444,808	517-50
SPRINGFIELD TWP.	DANE	WI	995	034,509	854-60
SPRINGHILL	BRADFORD	PA	757	020,607	625-45
SPRINGHILL TWP.	FAYETTE	PA	779	444,747	153-93
SPRINGPORT	JACKSON	MI	352	443,568	589-607
SPRINGPORT	CAYUGA	NY	483	017,059	419-67
SPRINGVALE	FOND DU LAC	WI	997	444,984	692-705
SPRINGVALE TWP.	COLUMBIA	WI	994	034,508	456-68
SPRINGVILLE TWP.	SUSQUEHANNA	PA	829	444,797	1-28
SPRINGWATER	LIVINGSTON	NY	525	017,101	461-525
SPRUCE MT.	PENDLETON	VA	968	444,958	66
SQUAW GROVE TWP.	DE KALB	IL	104	007,677	719-27
SQUAW MOUNTAIN	PISCATAQUIS	ME	267	443,504	513-14

CITY, COUNTY, TOWN, OR TOWNSHIP	COUNTY	STATE	NA NO. M432	GD NO.	PAGES
STAFFORD	TOLLAND	CT	50	442,882	73-144
STAFFORD	GENESEE	NY	507	017,083	173-219
STAFFORD CO.		VA	978	444,968	1-113
STAFFORD TWP.	DE KALB	IN	142	007,755	529-38
STAFFORD TWP.	GREENE	IN	148	442,926	751-62
STAFFORD TWP.	OCEAN	NJ	460	443,659	71-103
STAMFORD	FAIRFIELD	CT	38	003,066	544, 550-53, 75, 577-658
STAMFORD	DELAWARE	NY	494	017,070	355-98
STAMFORD	BENNINGTON	VT	921	027,447	317-36
STAMFORD TOWN	FAIRFIELD	CT	38	003,066	539-43, 545-4 554, 576
STAMPERS CREEK TWP.	ORANGE	IN	163	442,941	721-39
STANCILES DIST.	PITT	NC	641	444,654	21-29
STANDING STONE	BRADFORD	PA	757	020,607	647-66
STANDISH	CUMBERLAND	ME	249	009,719	133-88
STANFORD	DUTCHESS	NY	497	017,073	391-442
STANLEY CO.		NC	645	444,653	1-132
STARK	COOS	NH	429	443,633	273-82
STARK	HERKIMER	NY	513	017,089	617-56
STARK CO.		IL	129	442,917	383-472
STARK CO.		OH	730	444,723	657-1092
STARK CO.		OH	731	444,724	1-532
STARK TWP.	MONROE	OH	712	444,705	597-628
STARKE CO.		IN	172	442,950	225-40
STARKEY	YATES	NY	618	444,334	283-346
STARKS	SOMERSET	ME	269	443,506	199-235
STARKSBORO	ADDISON	VT	920	027,446	483-516
STARR CO.		TX	909	024,888	507-709
STARR TWP.	HOCKING	OH	695	444,688	765-90
STATESVILLE	IREDELL	NC	634	444,647	936-40
STAUNTON	MACOUPIN	IL	118	442,906	651-53
STAUNTON	FAYETTE	OH	678	444,671	285-87
STAUNTON TWP.	MIAMI	OH	711	444,704	37-72
STEEL CREEK	MECKLENBURG	NC	637	444,650	1-33
STEELE TWP.	DAVIESS	IN	140	007,753	255-67
STEELVILLE VILLAGE	CHESTER	PA	766	020,616	672-73
STEILACOOM	LEWIS	OR	742	020,298	114-15
STEPHENSBURG	FREDERICK	VA	945	444,935	661-89
STEPHENSON CO.		IL	129	442,917	473-764
STEPHENTOWN	RENSSELAER	NY	586	444,302	439-501
STERLING	WINDHAM	CT	51	442,883	403-427
STERLING	WORCESTER	MA	343	443,562	359-402
STERLING	MACOMB	MI	357	443,573	321-41
STERLING	CAYUGA	NY	481	017,057	351-418
STERLING	LAMOILLE	VT	925	444,924	237-42
STERLING TWP.	CRAWFORD	IN	139	007,752	41-62
STERLING TWP.	BROWN	OH	662	020,210	809-832
STERLING TWP.	WAYNE	PA	835	444,803	227-57
STETSON	PENOBSCOT	ME	265	443,502	75-95
STEUBEN	WASHINGTON	ME	272	443,509	1-27
STEUBEN	ONEIDA	NY	565	444,281	191-233
STEUBEN CO.		IN	173	442,951	241-394
STEUBEN CO.		NY	598	444,314	1-471
STEUBEN CO.		NY	599	444,315	473-780, 1-240
STEUBEN CO.		NY	600	444,316	241-780
STEUBEN TWP.	STEUBEN	IN	173	442,951	365-80
STEUBEN TWP.	WARREN	IN	178	442,956	39-56
STEUBENVILLE	JEFFERSON	OH	699	444,692	1-147

CITY, COUNTY, TOWN, OR TOWNSHIP	COUNTY	STATE	NA NO. M432	GD NO.	PAGES
STEUBENVILLE TWP.	JEFFERSON	OH	699	444,692	149-74
STEVENS POINT	PORTAGE	WI	1004	444,991	22-34
STEWARDSON	POTTER	PA	825	444,793	184-85
STEWART CO.		GA	82	442,891	77-287
STEWART CO.		TN	896	444,852	761-931
STEWARTS CREEK DIST.	SURRY	NC	646	444,659	605-611
STEWARTSTOWN	COOS	NH	429	443,633	59-76
STEWARTSVILLE DIST.	RICHMOND	NC	642	444,655	505-518
STILLWATER	SARATOGA	NY	592	444,308	167-237
STILLWATER PREC.	WASHINGTON	MN	367	014,834	154-69
STILLWATER TWP.	SUSSEX	NJ	464	443,663	143-84
STOCK TWP.	HARRISON	OH	693	444,686	619-40
STOCKBRIDGE	BERKSHIRE	MA	306	014,700	141-87
STOCKBRIDGE	INGHAM	MI	351	443,567	48-63
STOCKBRIDGE	MADISON	NY	526	017,102	275-324
STOCKBRIDGE	WINDSOR	VT	930	444,929	37-68
STOCKHOLM	ST. LAWRENCE	NY	590	444,306	143-230
STOCKPORT	COLUMBIA	NY	491	017,067	1-42
STOCKTON	CHAUTAUQUA	NY	485	017,061	479-518
STOCKTON DIST.	SAN JOAQUIN	CA	35	002,492	565-68
STOCKTON DIV.	SAN JOAQUIN	CA	35	002,492	569-652
STOCKTON TWP.	GREENE	IN	148	442,926	707-730
STODDARD	CHESHIRE	NH	428	014,941	639-65
STODDARD CO.		MO	420	443,628	505-605
STOKES CO.		NC	645	444,658	133-318
STOKES TWP.	LOGAN	OH	704	444,697	119-30
STOKES TWP.	MADISON	OH	706	444,699	481-96
STONE FORT PREC.	SALINE	IL	127	442,915	17-36
STONE MOUNTAIN DIST.	DE KALB	GA	67	007,063	189-200
STONEHAM	OXFORD	ME	262	443,499	285-96
STONEHAM	MIDDLESEX	MA	324	443,543	589-638
STONELICK TWP.	CLERMONT	OH	667	020,215	169-212
STONES DIST.	DE KALB	GA	67	007,063	313-34
STONEYCREEK TWP.	SOMERSET	PA	828	444,796	233-66
STONINGTON	NEW LONDON	CT	48	442,880	465-521, 563-79, 593-97
STONINGTON BOROUGH	NEW LONDON	CT	48	442,880	522-62, 581-91
STONY CREEK	MADISON	IN	158	442,936	173-78
STONY CREEK TWP.	HENRY	IN	151	442,929	409-433
STONY CREEK TWP.	RANDOLPH	IN	168	442,946	1-28
STORRS TWP.	HAMILTON	OH	685	444,678	151-90
STOUGHTON	NORFOLK	MA	329	443,548	193-276
STOUGHTON VILLAGE	DANE	WI	995	034,509	569-70
STOUT'S GROVE	MC LEON	IL	117	007,690	76-95
STOW	OXFORD	ME	262	443,499	270-81
STOW	MIDDLESEX	MA	324	443,543	793-827
STOW CREEK TWP.	CUMBERLAND	NJ	446	016,533	553-79
STOW TWP.	SUMMIT	OH	732	444,725	905-946
STOWE	LAMOILLE	VT	925	444,924	269-311
STOYSTOWN BOR.	SOMERSET	PA	828	444,796	511-58
STRABAN TWP.	ADAMS	PA	743	020,593	613-52
STRAFFORD	STRAFFORD	NH	440	443,644	533-78
STRAFFORD	ORANGE	VT	926	444,925	141-77
STRAFFORD CO.		NH	439	443,643	1-366
STRAFFORD CO.		NH	440	443,644	369-724
STRAITS	CARTERET	NC	623	018,109	258-71
STRASBURG	TUSCARAWAS	OH	735	444,728	755-56
STRASBURG BOR.	LANCASTER	PA	789	444,757	129-51
STRASBURG TWP.	LANCASTER	PA	789	444,757	153-94

CITY, COUNTY, TOWN, OR TOWNSHIP	COUNTY	STATE	NA NO. M432	GD NO.	PAGES
STRATFORD	FAIRFIELD	CT	37	003,065	589-638
STRATFORD	COOS	NH	429	443,633	247-60
STRATFORD	FULTON	NY	506	017,082	477-96
STRATHAM	ROCKINGHAM	NH	438	443,642	259-79
STRATTON	WINDHAM	VT	929	444,928	529-35
STRATTON MAJOR PAR.	KING AND QUEEN	VA	954	444,944	306-7, 312-15, 327-32, 334, 337 38, 344-51, 358-64
STRAWBERRY TWP.	LAWRENCE	AR	27	002,481	440-54
STREETSBORO TWP.	PORTAGE	OH	722	444,715	57-84
STRINGTOWN	ST. LOUIS	MO	414	443,622	576-78
STRONG	FRANKLIN	ME	253	009,723	469-92
STRONGSVILLE TWP.	CUYAHOGA	OH	673	020,221	325-53
STROUD TWP.	MONROE	PA	798	444,766	193-226
STROUDSBURG BOR.	MONROE	PA	798	444,766	173-92
STUMP SOUND	ONSLOW	NC	639	444,652	219-34
STURBRIDGE	WORCESTER	MA	345	443,564	413-63
STURGIS TWP.	ST. JOSEPH	MI	362	443,578	521-40
STUYVESANT	COLUMBIA	NY	492	017,068	785-828
SUAMICO	BROWN	WI	994	034,508	16-20, 35
SUDBURY	MIDDLESEX	MA	324	443,543	829-66
SUDBURY	RUTLAND	VT	927	444,926	315-31
SUFFIELD	HARTFORD	CT	39	003,067	173-244
SUFFIELD	PORTAGE	OH	722	444,715	827-60
SUFFOLK CO.		MA	334-38	443,553-57	
SUFFOLK CO.		MA	339	443,558	463-965
SUFFOLK CO.		NY	601	444,317	1-497
SUFFOLK CO.		NY	602	444,318	499-892
SUGAR CREEK	MECKLENBURG	NC	637	444,650	90-103
SUGAR CREEK	PUTNAM	OH	723	444,716	47-60
SUGAR CREEK	STARK	OH	731	444,724	291-332
SUGAR CREEK	TUSCARAWAS	OH	734	444,727	407-432
SUGAR CREEK	WALWORTH	WI	1007	444,994	711-30, 756-65
SUGAR CREEK TWP.	BENTON	AR	25	002,479	161-74
SUGAR CREEK TWP.	CLINTON	IN	139	007,752	810-21
SUGAR CREEK TWP.	HANCOCK	IN	149	442,927	457-76
SUGAR CREEK TWP.	MONTGOMERY	IN	161	442,939	873-89, 921, 927
SUGAR CREEK TWP.	PARKE	IN	164	442,942	455-87
SUGAR CREEK TWP.	SHELBY	IN	172	442,950	463-80
SUGAR CREEK TWP.	VIGO	IN	177	442,955	397-426
SUGAR CREEK TWP.	RANDOLPH	MO	411	443,619	451-73
SUGAR CREEK TWP.	ALLEN	OH	657	020,205	629-46
SUGAR CREEK TWP.	GREENE	OH	683	444,676	171-244
SUGAR CREEK TWP.	WAYNE	OH	739	444,732	105-160
SUGAR CREEK TWP.	ARMSTRONG	PA	749	020,599	21-61
SUGAR CREEK TWP.	VENANGO	PA	832	444,800	303-324
SUGAR GROVE	KANE	IL	112	007,685	355-72
SUGAR GROVE TWP.	WARREN	PA	832	444,800	453-89
SUGER HILL DIST.	GWINNETT	GA	71	007,067	382-96, 401-2, 404
SUGAR LOAF TWP.	CARROLL	AR	25	002,479	268-73
SUGAR LOAF TWP.	CRAWFORD	AR	25	002,479	539-60
SUGARLOAF	VAN BUREN	AR	31	442,877	618-23
SUGARLOAF TWP.	COLUMBIA	PA	769	444,737	407-438
SUGARLOAF TWP.	LUZERNE	PA	794	444,762	1003-1029
SULLIVAN	HANCOCK	ME	255	443,492	476-95
SULLIVAN	CHESHIRE	NH	428	014,941	591-602
SULLIVAN	MADISON	NY	526	017,102	1-114

CITY, COUNTY, TOWN, OR TOWNSHIP	COUNTY	STATE	NA NO. M432	GD NO.	PAGES
SULLIVAN	JEFFERSON	WI	1000	444,987	365-86
SULLIVAN CO.		IN	173	442,951	395-646
SULLIVAN CO.		MO	420	443,628	607-675
SULLIVAN CO.		NH	441	443,645	1-487
SULLIVAN CO.		NY	603	444,319	1-606
SULLIVAN CO.		PA	828	444,796	607-703
SULLIVAN CO.		TN	897	444,853	1-255
SULLIVAN TWP.	ASHLAND	OH	658	020,206	923-50
SULLIVAN TWP.	TIOGA	PA	830	444,798	49-90
SULLIVANS CREEK	TUOLUMNE	CA	36	442,879	247, 250
SULPHUR DIST.	RUTHERFORD	TN	894	444,850	332-48
SULPHUR FORK	LA FAYETTE	AR	27	002,481	335
SULPHUR SPRING TWP.	MONTGOMERY	AR	28	002,482	789-802
SULPHUR SPRING TWP.	POLK	AR	29	002,483	449-53
SULPHUR SPRINGS MISSION	BEXAR	TX	908	024,887	328
SUMMER GROVE WARD	CADDO PARISH	LA	230	009,697	657, 687-89
SUMMERFIELD	MONROE	MI	358	443,574	557-68
SUMMERFIELD	MONROE	OH	712	444,705	507-510
SUMMERFIELD BEAT	DALLAS	AL	4	002,346	635-47
SUMMERFORD	MADISON	OH	706	444,699	347-50
SUMMERFORD TWP.	MADISON	OH	706	444,699	331-50
SUMMERHILL	CAYUGA	NY	483	017,059	1-28
SUMMERHILL BOR.	CAMBRIA	PA	761	020,611	173-208
SUMMERHILL TWP.	CRAWFORD	PA	770	444,738	51-52, 141-68
SUMMERS DIST.	CALDWELL	NC	623	018,109	31-45
SUMMERSETT PREC.	SALINE	IL	127	442,915	1-16
SUMMERVILLE	CHATTOOGA	GA	64	007,060	709-713
SUMMERVILLE DIST.	CHATTOOGA	GA	64	007,060	714-35
SUMMIT	SCHOHARIE	NY	596	444,312	603-646
SUMMIT	WAUKESHA	WI	1009	444,996	707-730
SUMMIT BOR.	CAMBRIA	PA	761	020,611	163-72
SUMMIT CO.		OH	732	444,725	533-1006, 1-200
SUMMIT TWP.	CRAWFORD	PA	770	444,738	397-422
SUMMIT TWP.	SOMERSET	PA	828	444,796	527-50
SUMNER	OXFORD	ME	263	443,500	293-320
SUMNER CO.		TN	897	444,853	257-616
SUMPTER TWP.	WAYNE	MI	366	443,582	882-92
SUMTER CO.		AL	15	442,866	517-696
SUMTER CO.		GA	82	442,891	289-444
SUMTER CO.		SC	859	444,822	641-857
SUMTERVILLE	SUMTER	AL	15	442,866	543-45, 555-64, 567-68, 582
SUMTERVILLE	SUMTER	SC	859	444,822	843-55
SUN PRARIE	DANE	WI	995	034,509	797-808
SUNBURY BOR.	NORTHUMBERLAND	PA	804	444,772	509-538
SUNDERLAND	FRANKLIN	MA	317	443,536	761-79
SUNDERLAND	BENNINGTON	VT	921	027,447	49-60
SUNDFISH TWP.	PIKE	OH	721	444,714	721-29
SUNFIELD	EATON	MI	349	014,811	332-34
SUNFLOWER CO.		MS	381	443,593	725-33
SUNSBURY TWP.	MONROE	OH	712	444,705	412-51
SUPERIOR	WASHTENAW	MI	364	443,580	471-97
SUPERIOR TWP.	WILLIAMS	OH	741	444,734	71-88
SURROUNDED HILL TWP.	MONROE	AR	28	002,482	726-29
SURRY	HANCOCK	ME	254	443,491	93-121
SURRY	CHESHIRE	NH	427	014,940	121-34
SURRY CO.		NC	646	444,659	319-715
SURRY CO.		VA	978	444,968	117-98
SUSQUEHANNA	SUSQUEHANNA	PA	829	444,797	451-62

Susquehanna Co.

CITY, COUNTY, TOWN, OR TOWNSHIP	COUNTY	STATE	NA NO. M432	GD NO.	PAGES	
TALIAFERRO CO.		GA	83	442,892	633-83	
TALLADEGA CO.		AL	15	442,866	697-975	
TALLADEGA DIST.	TALLADEGA	AL	15	442,866	697-975	
TALLADEGA TWP.	JEFFERSON	AR	27	002,481	174-82	
TALLAHATCHIE CO.		MS	381	443,593	735-85	
TALLAPOOSA CO.		AL	15	442,866	1-273	
TALLMADGE	OTTAWA	MI	361	443,577	13-25	
TALLMADGE TWP.	SUMMIT	OH	732	444,725	947-1006	
TAMA CO.		IA	188	442,963	479	
TAMAQUA BOR., EAST WARD	SCHUYLKILL	PA	827	444,795	449-75	
TAMAQUA BOR., NORTH WARD	SCHUYLKILL	PA	827	444,795	425-45	
TAMAQUA BOR., SOUTH WARD	SCHUYLKILL	PA	827	444,795	477-503	
TAMPA	HILLSBOROUGH	FL	58	006,714	481-94,	508-9
TAMWORTH	CARROLL	NH	426	014,939	239-81	
TANEY CO.		MO	420	443,628	677-778	
TANEYTOWN	CARROLL	MD	289	443,520	479-85	
TANTON	EDGECOMB	NC	629	444,642	183-90	
TAOS CO.		NM	469	443,667	181-407	
TAPPAHANNOCK	ESSEX	VA	942	444,932	211-14	
TAR RIVER	GRANVILLE	NC	631	444,644	319-35	
TARENTUM BOR.	ALLEGHENY	PA	747	020,597	93-105	
TARLTON	PICKAWAY	OH	720	444,713	475-83	
TARRANT CO.		TX	910	024,889	171-84,	279-80
TATE TWP.	CLERMONT	OH	667	020,215	679-748	
TATTNALL CO.		GA	83	442,892	683-742	
TAUNTON	BRISTOL	MA	307	014,701	287-535	
TAYCHEEDAH	FOND DU LAC	WI	997	444,984	535-53	
TAYLOR	WAYNE	MI	366	443,582	825-31	
TAYLOR	CORTLAND	NY	493	017,069	369-96	
TAYLOR CO.		IA	188	442,963	481-85	
TAYLOR CO.		KY	219	442,987	255-388	
TAYLOR CO.		VA	978	444,968	295-424	
TAYLOR CREEK TWP.	HARDIN	OH	692	444,685	287-300	
TAYLOR TWP.	OUACHITA	AR	28	002,482	193-200	
TAYLOR TWP.	OGLE	IL	123	442,911	121-27	
TAYLOR TWP.	GREENE	IN	146	442,926	811-42	
TAYLOR TWP.	HOWARD	IN	151	442,929	825-39	
TAYLOR TWP.	OWEN	IN	164	442,942	151-64	
TAYLOR TWP.	APPANOOSE	IA	182	007,791	86-91	
TAYLOR TWP.	GREENE	MO	400	443,608	665-72,	686-97
TAYLOR TWP.	UNION	OH	736	444,729	159-68	
TAYLOR TWP.	CENTRE	PA	763	020,613	559-67	
TAYLOR TWP.	FULTON	PA	783	444,751	169-81	
TAYLORS BAY TWP.	JACKSON	AR	27	002,481	71-82	
TAYLOR'S RIDGE VALLEY	WALKER	GA	85	442,894	775-91,	817-26
TAYLORSVILLE	JOHNSON	TN	886	444,842	23-25	
TAYMOUTH TWP.	SAGINAW	MI	361	443,577	190-91	
TAZEWELL CO.		IL	129	442,917	1-288	
TAZEWELL CO.		VA	979	444,969	427-639	
TEBO TWP.	HENRY	MO	401	443,609	1-28	
TECUMSEH	LENAWEE	MI	355	443,571	105-170	
TEKONSHA	CALHOUN	MI	348	014,810	413-30	
TELFAIR CO.		GA	83	442,892	743-94	
TELL TWP.	HUNTINGDON	PA	784	444,752	509-533	
TEMPLE	FRANKLIN	ME	253	009,723	409-429	
TEMPLE	HILLSBORO	NH	433	443,637	719-32	
TEMPLETON	WORCESTER	MA	340	443,559	557-608	
TENNESSEE VALLEY	MACON	NC	636	444,649	629-81,	702-723, 728-36, 756,

CITY, COUNTY, TOWN, OR TOWNSHIP	COUNTY	STATE	NA NO. M432	GD NO.	PAGES
					759-64, 768
TENSAS PARISH		LA	241	443,484	591-612
TERRE NOIRE TWP.	CLARK	AR	25	002,479	432-37
TERREBONNE PARISH		LA	241	443,484	613-94
TETE DES MORTS TWP.	JACKSON	IA	184	007,793	575, 600-606, 610-12
TEWKSBURY	MIDDLESEX	MA	324	443,543	33-57
TEWKSBURY	HUNTERDON	NJ	453	443,652	527-82
TEXAS	KALAMAZOO	MI	353	443,569	125-34
TEXAS CO.		MO	421	443,629	1-56
TEXAS JUDICIAL DIST.	FORT BEND	TX	910	024,889	453-72
TEXAS TWP.	ST. FRANCIS	AR	30	442,876	133-38
TEXAS TWP.	CRAWFORD	OH	671	020,219	35-48
TEXAS TWP.	PAYNE	PA	835	444,803	413-74
THE FORKS	SOMERSET	ME	269	443,506	549-53
THERESA	JEFFERSON	NY	515	017,091	77-132
THERESA	DODGE	WI	996	034,510	439-57
THETFORD	GENESEE	MI	350	443,566	424-31
THETFORD	ORANGE	VT	926	444,925	45-92
THIBODAUX	LAFOURCHE PAR.	LA	232	443,475	587-608
THIRD CREEK TWP.	GASCONADE	MO	399	443,607	343-56
THOMAS BIGGS RANCH	VALENCIA	NM	470	443,668	654
THOMAS CO.		GA	83	442,892	1-118
THOMASTON	LINCOLN	ME	259	443,496	1-65
THOMASVILLE DIST.	DUVAL	FL	58	006,714	225-28
THOMPSON	WINDHAM	CT	51	442,883	223-333
THOMPSON	SULLIVAN	NY	603	444,319	65-142
THOMPSON DIST.	SURRY	NC	646	444,659	639-51
THOMPSON TWP.	PIKE	AR	29	002,483	364-73, 382-83, 395-97
THOMPSON TWP.	DELAWARE	OH	675	020,223	724-41
THOMPSON TWP.	GEAUGA	OH	682	444,675	567-95
THOMPSON TWP.	SENECA	OH	728	444,721	181-223
THOMPSON TWP.	FULTON	PA	783	444,751	125-40
THOMPSON TWP.	SUSQUEHANNA	PA	829	444,797	475-87
THORN TWP.	PERRY	OH	719	444,712	793-836
THORNAPPLE	BARRY	MI	346	014,808	185-88, 190-92
THORNBURY TWP.	CHESTER	PA	766	020,616	839-44
THORNBURY TWP.	DELAWARE	PA	776	444,744	213-33
THORNDIKE	WALDO	ME	270	443,507	1-25
THORNEY MEADOWS	PENDLETON	VA	968	444,958	21
THORNTON	GRAFTON	NH	431	443,635	531-55
THORNTON TWP.	COOK	IL	103	007,676	21-24, 26-29,
THURSTON	STEUBEN	NY	599	444,315	699-716
TICONDEROGA	ESSEX	NY	504	017,080	613-80
TIFFIN CITY	SENECA	OH	728	444,721	845-909
TIFFIN TWP.	ADAMS	OH	657	020,205	265-312
TIFFIN TWP.	DEFIANCE	OH	674	020,222	88-107
TILLIBAWASSEE TWP.	SAGINAW	MI	361	443,577	157-65
TIMBER RIDGE	PENDLETON	VA	968	444,958	73, 81
TIMBERLAKE'S DIST.	FRANKLIN	NC	630	444,643	666-83
TINICUM TWP.	BUCKS	PA	759	020,609	549-98
TINICUM TWP.	DELAWARE	PA	776	444,744	525-29
TINMOUTH	RUTLAND	VT	927	444,926	703-720
TIOGA	TIOGA	NY	604	444,320	133-200
TIOGA CO.		NY	604	444,320	1-608
TIOGA CO.		PA	830	444,798	1-598
TIOGA TWP.	TIOGA	PA	830	444,798	175-202
TIONESTA CREEK	VENANGO	PA	832	444,800	423-52

CITY, COUNTY, TOWN, OR TOWNSHIP	COUNTY	STATE	NA NO. M432	6D NO.	PAGES
TIONESTA TWP.	JEFFERSON	PA	786	444,754	4-6
TIPPAH CO.		MS	381	443,593	787-1166
TIPPECANOE	MIAMI	OH	711	444,704	237-48
TIPPECANOE CO.		IN	175	442,953	1-472
TIPPECANOE TWP.	CARROLL	IN	137	007,750	633-59
TIPPECANOE TWP.	KOSCIUSKO	IN	156	442,934	663-77
TIPPECANOE TWP.	PULASKI	IN	166	442,944	703-713
TIPPECANOE TWP.	TIPPECANOE	IN	175	442,953	49-78
TIPPECANOE TWP.	HENRY	IA	184	007,793	491-509
TIPTON	TIPTON	IN	176	442,954	473-77
TIPTON CO.		IN	176	442,954	473-558
TIPTON CO.		TN	897	444,853	619-730
TIPTON TWP.	CASS	IN	137	007,750	1039-61
TISBURY	DUKES	MA	309	014,703	837-80
TISHOMINGO CO.		MS	382	443,594	1-332
TITUS CO.		TX	915	444,918	187-262
TITUSVILLE BOR.	CRAWFORD	PA	771	444,739	501-6
TIVERTON TWP.	COSHOCTON	OH	670	020,218	87-107
TOBIN TWP.	PERRY	IN	165	442,943	778-819
TOBOYNE TWP.	PERRY	PA	805	444,773	845-61
TOBY TWP.	CLARION	PA	767	444,735	127-80
TOBYHANNA TWP.	MONROE	PA	798	444,766	295-308
TODD CO.		KY	219	442,987	389-576
TODD TWP.	CRAWFORD	OH	671	020,219	91-105
TODD TWP.	FULTON	PA	783	444,751	13-25
TODD TWP.	HUNTINGDON	PA	784	444,752	605-634
TOLEDO, WARD 1	LUCAS	OH	706	444,699	64-81
TOLEDO, WARD 2	LUCAS	OH	706	444,699	82-101
TOLEDO, WARD 3	LUCAS	OH	706	444,699	102-116
TOLEDO, WARD 4	LUCAS	OH	706	444,699	117-44
TOLLAND	TOLLAND	CT	50	442,882	1-35
TOLLAND	HAMPDEN	MA	318	443,537	523-37
TOLLAND CO.		CT	50	442,882	431-746, 1-181
TOM GROVE	MC LEON	IL	117	007,690	63-68
TOM TWP.	BENTON	MO	392	014,872	580-81, 591-99
TOMAHAWK TWP.	SEARCY	AR	30	442,876	335-41
TOME	VALENCIA	NM	470	443,668	525-38
TOMLINSON TWP.	SCOTT	AR	30	442,876	291-98
TOMPKINS	JACKSON	MI	352	443,568	609-624
TOMPKINS	DELAWARE	NY	495	017,071	603-678
TOMPKINS CO.		NY	605	444,321	1-402
TOMPKINS CO.		NY	606	444,322	403-946
TONAWANDA	ERIE	NY	500	017,076	237-86
TOOELE CO.		UT	919	025,540	233-37
TOPSFIELD	WASHINGTON	ME	273	443,510	397-403
TOPSFIELD	ESSEX	MA	315	443,534	721-48
TOPSHAM	LINCOLN	ME	261	443,498	685-732
TOPSHAM	ORANGE	VT	926	444,925	385-424
TORREON	VALENCIA	NM	470	443,668	741-45
TORRINGTON	LITCHFIELD	CT	42	003,070	425-76
TOWAMENSING TWP.	MONTGOMERY	PA	800	444,768	381-402
TOWANDA BOR.	BRADFORD	PA	756	020,606	1-30
TOWANDA TWP.	BRADFORD	PA	756	020,606	31-58
TOWN CREEK DIST.	BRUNSWICK	NC	621	018,107	301-315
TOWN DIST.	DE KALB	GA	67	007,063	261-74
TOWN DIST.	GWINNETT	GA	71	007,067	349, 356-60, 362-66, 463-76
TOWN DIST.	SHELBY	IL	128	442,916	223-38, 249-72
TOWN OF NORTH EAST	CECIL	MD	290	443,521	148-55

CITY, COUNTY, TOWN, OR TOWNSHIP	COUNTY	STATE	NA NO. M432	GD NO.	PAGES
TOWNSEND	MIDDLESEX	MA	323	443,542	125-71
TOWNSEND	SANDUSKY	OH	726	444,719	945-67
TOWNSEND TWP.	HURON	OH	697	444,690	757-88
TOWNSHAND	WINDHAM	VT	929	444,928	1-33
TOXAWAY	MACON	NC	636	444,649	743
TRACT HILLS	PENDLETON	VA	968	444,958	25-26
TRANTERS CREEK DIST.	BEAUFORT	NC	620	018,106	774-92
TRAPPE DIST.	SOMERSET	MD	297	443,528	934-71
TRAVIS CO.		TX	915	444,918	265-320
TREDYFFRIN TWP.	CHESTER	PA	764	020,614	687-728
TREMONT	TAZEWELL	IL	129	442,917	271-81
TREMONT	HANCOCK	ME	255	443,492	747-86
TREMONT TWP.	BUCHANAN	MO	393	014,873	117-37
TRENTON	WILL	IL	133	442,921	145-50
TRENTON	HANCOCK	ME	255	443,492	543-71
TRENTON	ONEIDA	NY	566	444,282	463-547
TRENTON	JONES	NC	635	444,648	246-47
TRENTON	GIBSON	TN	878	444,834	542-52
TRENTON	DODGE	WI	996	034,510	23-46
TRENTON	WASHINGTON	WI	1008	444,995	100-111
TRENTON DIST.	JONES	NC	635	444,648	248-51
TRENTON, EAST WARD	MERCER	NJ	454	443,653	305-398
TRENTON TWP.	HENRY	IA	184	007,793	393-416
TRENTON TWP.	DELAWARE	OH	675	020,223	292-321
TRENTON, WEST WARD	MERCER	NJ	454	443,653	399-459
TRESCOTT	WASHINGTON	ME	272	443,509	391-409
TRIADELPHIA	OHIO	VA	966	444,956	1-107
TRIANGLE	BROOME	NY	477	017,053	497-536
TRIGG CO.		KY	219	442,987	577-752
TRIMBLE CO.		KY	220	442,988	753-876
TRIMBLE DIST.	RUTHERFORD	TN	894	444,850	513-28
TRIMBLE TWP.	ATHENS	OH	660	020,208	391-412
TRINITY	CATAHOULA PAR.	LA	230	009,697	170-74
TRINITY CO.		CA	36	442,879	495, 123-39, 141-64
TRINITY RIVER	TRINITY	CA	36	442,879	130, 136-39
TRION DIST.	CHATTOOGA	GA	64	007,060	736-49
TRIPS BEAT	JEFFERSON	AL	7	002,349	374-87
TROUP CO.		GA	84	442,893	119-313
TROUPSBURG	STEUBEN	NY	599	444,315	517-60
TROWBRIDGE	ALLEGAN	MI	346	014,808	61-68
TROY	LA SALLE	IL	115	007,688	554, 556-64, 569-74
TROY	MADISON	IL	119	442,907	881-87
TROY	WILL	IL	133	442,921	273-81
TROY	PERRY	IN	165	442,943	720-59
TROY	WALDO	ME	270	443,507	435-70
TROY	OAKLAND	MI	359	443,575	17-51
TROY	CHESHIRE	NH	427	014,940	331-49
TROY	MIAMI	OH	711	444,704	152-99
TROY	ORLEANS	VT	925	444,924	207-230
TROY	WALWORTH	WI	1007	444,994	445-70
TROY BOR.	BRADFORD	PA	756	020,606	529-40
TROY ISLAND	PIKE	IL	124	442,912	487-94
TROY TWP.	MISSISSIPPI	AR	28	002,482	697
TROY TWP.	DE KALB	IN	142	007,755	391-400
TROY TWP.	FOUNTAIN	IN	145	442,923	84-110
TROY TWP.	ASHLAND	OH	658	020,206	761-83
TROY TWP.	ATHENS	OH	660	020,208	129-62

CITY, COUNTY, TOWN, OR TOWNSHIP	COUNTY	STATE	NA NO. M432	GD NO.	PAGES
TROY TWP.	DELAWARE	OH	675	020,223	555-78
TROY TWP.	GEAUGA	OH	682	444,675	261-88
TROY TWP.	MORROW	OH	716	444,709	829-46
TROY TWP.	RICHLAND	OH	724	444,717	909-946
TROY TWP.	WOOD	OH	741	444,734	423-37
TROY TWP.	BRADFORD	PA	756	020,606	541-75
TROY TWP.	CRAWFORD	PA	771	444,739	573-90
TROY, WARD 1	RENSSELAER	NY	584	444,300	1-94
TROY, WARD 2	RENSSELAER	NY	584	444,300	96-196
TROY, WARD 3	RENSSELAER	NY	584	444,300	197-263
TROY, WARD 4	RENSSELAER	NY	584	444,300	265-361
TROY, WARD 5	RENSSELAER	NY	584	444,300	363-406
TROY, WARD 6	RENSSELAER	NY	584	444,300	407-506
TROY, WARD 7	RENSSELAER	NY	584	444,300	507-624
TROY, WARD 8	RENSSELAER	NY	584	444,300	625-90
TRUMBULL	FAIRFIELD	CT	37	003,065	639-70
TRUMBULL CO.		OH	733	444,726	201-945
TRUMBULL TWP.	ASHTABULA	OH	659	020,207	845-64
TRURO	BARNSTABLE	MA	303	014,697	77-125
TRURO TWP.	FRANKLIN	OH	679	444,672	319-71
TRUXTON	CORTLAND	NY	493	017,069	253-339
TUCKAHOE DIST.	JONES	NC	635	444,648	258-69
TUCKASEGEE	MACON	NC	636	444,649	747-48
TUCKELATA	SAN MIGUEL	NM	469	443,667	147-78
TUCKER TWP.	CLARK	AR	25	002,479	381-87
TUFTONBOR	CARROLL	NH	426	014,939	283-314
TULIP TWP.	DALLAS	AR	26	002,480	48-58
TULLY	ONONDAGA	NY	567	444,283	305-342
TULLY TWP.	MARION	OH	708	444,701	113-30
TULLY TWP.	VAN WERT	OH	736	444,729	374-78
TULLYTOWN	BUCKS	PA	758	020,608	300-305
TULPEHOCKEN TWP.	BERKS	PA	752	020,602	63-106
TUNBRIDGE	ORANGE	VT	926	444,925	1-43
TUNICA CO.		MS	382	443,594	333-42
TUNKHANNOCK BOR.	WYOMING	PA	838	444,806	61-92
TUOLUMNE CO.		CA	36	442,879	167-366
TURBETT TWP.	JUNIATA	PA	786	444,754	437-39, 441-68, 470-72
TURBUT TWP.	NORTHUMBERLAND	PA	804	444,772	115-51
TURIN	LEWIS	NY	523	017,099	97-140
TURIN, WEST	LEWIS	NY	523	017,099	1-95
TURKEY CREEK TWP.	KOSCIUSKO	IN	156	442,934	648-62
TURKEY HILL	ST. CLAIR	IL	126	442,914	693-711
TURMAN TWP.	SULLIVAN	IN	173	442,951	611-45
TURNER	OXFORD	ME	263	443,500	1-62
TURNER DIST.	FAUQUIER	VA	943	444,933	533-655
TURTLE	ROCK	WI	1005	444,992	849-71
TURTLE CREEK	WARREN	OH	737	444,730	42-91, 269-349
TURTLE CREEK TWP.	SHELBY	OH	729	444,722	301-320
TUSCALOOSA CO.		AL	16	442,867	277-534
TUSCARAWAS CO.		OH	734	444,727	1-442
TUSCARAWAS CO.		OH	735	444,728	443-810
TUSCARAWAS TWP.	COSHOCTON	OH	670	020,218	235-74
TUSCARAWAS TWP.	STARK	OH	731	444,724	333-81
TUSCARORA TWP.	JUNIATA	PA	786	444,754	359, 361-62, 364-85, 386-88
TUSCOLA	TUSCOLA	MI	363	443,579	193-99
TUSCOLA CO.		MI	363	443,579	193-99
TUSCOLA TWP.	LIVINGSTON	MI	356	443,572	926-38

CITY, COUNTY, TOWN, OR TOWNSHIP	COUNTY	STATE	NA NO. M432	GD NO.	PAGES
TUTTLETOWN	TUOLUMNE	CA	36	442,879	248-49
TWELVE MILE PRAIRIE	ST. CLAIR	IL	126	442,914	712-33
TWIGGS CO.		GA	84	442,893	315-99
TWIN TWP.	DARKE	OH	674	020,222	807-841
TWIN TWP.	PREBLE	OH	723	444,716	847-92
TWIN TWP.	ROSS	OH	725	444,718	663-717
TWINSBURGH TWP.	SUMMIT	OH	732	444,725	731-61
TWO RIVERS	MANITOWOC	WI	1002	444,989	17-38
TYASKIN DIST.	SOMERSET	MD	297	443,528	1071-1108
TYLER CO.		TX	915	444,918	323-62
TYLER CO.		VA	979	444,969	643-775
TYMOCHTEE TWP.	WYANDOT	OH	741	444,734	659-704
TYNGSBOROUGH	MIDDLESEX	MA	322	443,541	474-93
TYRE	SENECA	NY	597	444,313	484-516
TYRINGHAM	BERKSHIRE	MA	306	014,700	231-50
TYRONE	STEUBEN	NY	598	444,314	301-346
TYRONE TWP.	LIVINGSTON	MI	356	443,572	884-904
TYRONE TWP.	ADAMS	PA	743	020,593	125-46
TYRONE TWP.	BLAIR	PA	755	020,605	55-62, 64-80
TYRONE TWP.	FAYETTE	PA	780	444,748	833-66
TYRONE TWP.	PERRY	PA	805	444,773	897-923
TYRONZA TWP.	CRITTENDEN	AR	25	002,479	754-56
TYRRELL CO.		NC	646	444,659	717-99
UHRICHSVILLE	TUSCARAWAS	OH	735	444,728	583-96
ULSTER CO.		NY	607	444,323	1-678
ULSTER CO.		NY	608	444,324	1-774
ULSTER TWP.	BRADFORD	PA	756	020,606	647-73
ULYSSES	TOMPKINS	NY	606	444,322	867-946
ULYSSES	POTTER	PA	825	444,793	194-210
UNADILLA	OTSEGO	NY	580	444,296	340-98
UNADILLA TWP.	LIVINGSTON	MI	356	443,572	724-48
UNDERHILL	CHITTENDEN	VT	923	444,922	239-77
UNGRANTED LANDS	GRAFTON	NH	431	443,635	494
UNION	WHITE	AR	31	442,877	888-93
UNION	FULTON	IL	107	007,680	397-418
UNION	LINCOLN	ME	259	443,496	491-538
UNION	WASHINGTON	MO	421	443,629	175-208
UNION	BROOME	NY	478	017,054	849-900
UNION	ROCK	WI	1005	444,992	605-629
UNION BEAT	DALLAS	AL	4	002,346	619-25
UNION BOR.	FAYETTE	PA	779	444,747	359-414
UNION CO.		AR	30	442,876	449-589
UNION CO.		GA	84	442,893	401-568
UNION CO.		IL	130	442,918	289-471
UNION CO.		IN	176	442,954	559-726
UNION CO.		KY	220	442,988	677-1038
UNION CO.		NC	647	444,660	1-196
UNION CO.		OH	736	444,729	1-301
UNION CO.		PA	831	444,799	1-640
UNION CO.		SC	859	444,822	1-228
UNION DEPOSITE	DAUPHIN	PA	774	444,742	221-23
UNION PARISH		LA	241	443,484	695-814
UNION TOWN	PERRY	AL	12	002,354	617-20
UNION TOWN	EL DORADO	CA	34	002,491	748-52
UNION TOWN	TRINITY	CA	36	442,879	123-27
UNION TOWN	MUSKINGUM	OH	718	444,711	259-67

CITY, COUNTY, TOWN, OR TOWNSHIP	COUNTY	STATE	NA NO. M432	GD NO.	PAGES
UNION TWP.	ASHLEY	AR	25	002,479	81-83
UNION TWP.	CONWAY	AR	25	002,479	531-38
UNION TWP.	FULTON	AR	26	002,480	311-19
UNION TWP.	GREENE	AR	26	002,480	349-59
UNION TWP.	INDEPENDENCE	AR	26	002,480	694-99
UNION TWP.	IZARD	AR	27	002,481	44-53
UNION TWP.	LAWRENCE	AR	27	002,481	475-86
UNION TWP.	NEWTON	AR	28	002,482	27-30
UNION TWP.	ST. FRANCIS	AR	30	442,876	128, 132, 142-49, 151, 154
UNION TWP.	VAN BUREN	AR	31	442,877	597-602
UNION TWP.	TOLLAND	CT	50	442,882	525-42
UNION TWP.	ADAMS	IN	135	007,748	108-118
UNION TWP.	BARTHOLOMEW	IN	136	007,749	699-713
UNION TWP.	CRAWFORD	IN	139	007,752	1-15
UNION TWP.	DE KALB	IN	142	007,755	489-507
UNION TWP.	DELAWARE	IN	143	007,756	781-807
UNION TWP.	ELKHART	IN	144	007,757	227-42
UNION TWP.	FULTON	IN	146	442,924	861-78
UNION TWP.	GRANT	IN	147	442,925	355-67
UNION TWP.	HANCOCK	IN	149	442,927	492-504
UNION TWP.	JOHNSON	IN	155	442,933	61-90
UNION TWP.	LA PORTE	IN	157	442,935	363-83
UNION TWP.	MADISON	IN	158	442,936	254-68
UNION TWP.	MIAMI	IN	160	442,938	299-320
UNION TWP.	MONTGOMERY	IN	161	442,939	739-872
UNION TWP.	PARKE	IN	164	442,942	489-516
UNION TWP.	PERRY	IN	165	442,943	847-66
UNION TWP.	PORTER	IN	165	442,943	287-98
UNION TWP.	RUSH	IN	170	442,948	1029-57
UNION TWP.	ST. JOSEPH	IN	171	442,949	134-49
UNION TWP.	SHELBY	IN	172	442,950	788-813
UNION TWP.	UNION	IN	176	442,954	658-85
UNION TWP.	VANDERBURGH	IN	176	442,954	989-1005
UNION TWP.	WELLS	IN	181	442,959	655-68
UNION TWP.	APPANOOSE	IA	182	007,791	92-97
UNION TWP.	CLINTON	IA	182	007,791	408-9
UNION TWP.	DAVIS	IA	182	007,791	479-96
UNION TWP.	DES MOINES	IA	183	007,792	869-95
UNION TWP.	JACKSON	IA	184	007,793	685-88, 691-94, 697-98
UNION TWP.	VAN BUREN	IA	189	442,964	765-88
UNION TWP.	BRANCH	MI	347	014,809	721-51
UNION TWP.	BENTON	MO	392	014,872	569-73
UNION TWP.	MARION	MO	406	443,614	703-721
UNION TWP.	RANDOLPH	MO	411	443,619	538-49
UNION TWP.	STE. GENEVIEVE	MO	413	443,621	493-512
UNION TWP.	CAMDEN	NJ	445	016,532	349-427
UNION TWP.	ESSEX	NJ	450	443,649	575-614
UNION TWP.	OCEAN	NJ	460	443,659	105-46
UNION TWP.	AUGLAIZE	OH	660	020,208	609-632
UNION TWP.	BELMONT	OH	661	020,209	891-946
UNION TWP.	BROWN	OH	662	020,210	1-105
UNION TWP.	BUTLER	OH	663	020,211	571-622
UNION TWP.	CARROLL	OH	664	020,212	32-51
UNION TWP.	CHAMPAIGN	OH	665	020,213	573-614
UNION TWP.	CLERMONT	OH	667	020,215	931-73
UNION TWP.	CLINTON	OH	668	020,216	679-765
UNION TWP.	FAYETTE	OH	678	444,671	123-80

CITY, COUNTY, TOWN, OR TOWNSHIP	COUNTY	STATE	NA NO. M432	GD NO.	PAGES
UNION TWP.	HANCOCK	OH	692	444,685	947-74
UNION TWP.	HIGHLAND	OH	694	444,687	383-416
UNION TWP.	KNOX	OH	700	444,693	819-48
UNION TWP.	LAWRENCE	OH	701	444,694	759-90
UNION TWP.	LICKING	OH	702	444,695	275-332
UNION TWP.	LOGAN	OH	704	444,697	83-102
UNION TWP.	MADISON	OH	706	444,699	351-90
UNION TWP.	MERCER	OH	710	444,703	529-46
UNION TWP.	MIAMI	OH	711	444,704	283-346
UNION TWP.	MONROE	OH	712	444,705	551-96
UNION TWP.	MORGAN	OH	715	444,708	377-420
UNION TWP.	MUSKINGUM	OH	718	444,711	865-900
UNION TWP.	PIKE	OH	721	444,714	545-58
UNION TWP.	PUTNAM	OH	723	444,716	25-37
UNION TWP.	ROSS	OH	725	444,718	209-272
UNION TWP.	SCIOTO	OH	727	444,720	185-200
UNION TWP.	TUSCARAWAS	OH	735	444,728	621-44
UNION TWP.	UNION	OH	736	444,729	177-207
UNION TWP.	VAN WERT	OH	736	444,729	372-73
UNION TWP.	WARREN	OH	737	444,730	1-41
UNION TWP.	WASHINGTON	OH	738	444,731	479-506
UNION TWP.	ADAMS	PA	743	020,593	529-51
UNION TWP.	BEDFORD	PA	751	020,601	491-520
UNION TWP.	BERKS	PA	754	020,604	569-608
UNION TWP.	CLEARFIELD	PA	768	444,736	865-71
UNION TWP.	ERIE	PA	777	444,745	75-100
UNION TWP.	FAYETTE	PA	779	444,747	289-357
UNION TWP.	HUNTINGDON	PA	784	444,752	393-408
UNION TWP.	JEFFERSON	PA	786	444,754	67-81
UNION TWP.	LEBANON	PA	791	444,759	431-68
UNION TWP.	LUZERNE	PA	793	444,761	214-45
UNION TWP.	MIFFLIN	PA	797	444,765	409-441
UNION TWP.	SCHUYLKILL	PA	826	444,794	1-26
UNION TWP.	TIOGA	PA	830	444,798	403-422
UNION TWP.	UNION	PA	831	444,799	423-57
UNION TWP.	WASHINGTON	PA	834	444,802	514-42
UNION VALE	DUTCHESS	NY	496	017,072	399-436
UNION VILLAGE	UNION	SC	859	444,822	73-78
UNIONTOWN	CARROLL	MD	289	443,520	467-76
UNIONTOWN	BELMONT	OH	661	020,209	970-74
UNIONTOWN	MONROE	VA	961	444,951	958-64
UNIONVILLE VILLAGE	CHESTER	PA	764	020,614	331-38
U.S. CUMBERLAND	ALLEGANY	MD	277	013,194	389-528
U.S. GLADE DIST.	ALLEGANY	MD	277	013,194	83-134
U.S. NAVY YARD	NORFOLK	VA	964	444,954	393-404
U.S.N. HOSPITAL PENSACOLA	ESCAMBIA	FL	58	006,714	283
U.S.N. YARD PENSACOLA	ESCAMBIA	FL	58	006,714	295-99
UNITY	WALDO	ME	270	443,507	491-530
UNITY	SULLIVAN	NH	441	443,645	465-87
UNITY TWP.	COLUMBIANA	OH	669	020,217	107-157
UNITY TWP.	WESTMORELAND	PA	837	444,805	645-745
UP RIVER DIST.	PERQUIMANS	NC	640	444,653	808-832
UPATOIE DIST.	MUSCOGEE	GA	79	442,888	723-35
UPPER ALLEN TWP.	CUMBERLAND	PA	772	444,740	1-30
UPPER ALLOWAYS CREEK	SALEM	NJ	462	443,661	287-347
UPPER ALTON	MADISON	IL	119	442,907	748-85
UPPER AUGUSTA TWP.	NORTHUMBERLAND	PA	804	444,772	375-407
UPPER BERN	BERKS	PA	752	020,602	225-66
UPPER CHICHESTER TWP.	DELAWARE	PA	776	444,744	49-61

CITY, COUNTY, TOWN, OR TOWNSHIP	COUNTY	STATE	NA NO. M432	GD NO.	PAGES	
UPPER DARBY TWP.	DELAWARE	PA	776	444,744	531-79	
UPPER DICKINSON TWP.	CUMBERLAND	PA	772	444,740	192-244	
UPPER DUBLIN TWP.	MONTGOMERY	PA	800	444,768	109-140	
UPPER FREEHOLD TWP.	MONMOUTH	NJ	457	443,656	675-736	
UPPER HANOVER TWP.	MONTGOMERY	PA	799	444,767	409-450	
UPPER HEIDELBERG	BERKS	PA	752	020,602	267-86	
UPPER LEACOCK TWP.	LANCASTER	PA	789	444,757	243-87	
UPPER MACUNGIE TWP.	LEHIGH	PA	792	444,760	171-219	
UPPER MAHANTONGO TWP.	SCHUYLKILL	PA	826	444,794	763-802	
UPPER MAHONOY TWP.	NORTHUMBERLAND	PA	804	444,772	618-48	
UPPER MAKEFIELD TWP.	BUCKS	PA	758	020,608	99-139	
UPPER MERION TWP.	MONTGOMERY	PA	800	444,768	781-870	
UPPER MILFORD TWP.	LEHIGH	PA	792	444,760	47-128	
UPPER MT. BETHEL TWP.	NORTHAMPTON	PA	803	444,771	905-972	
UPPER NAZARETH TWP.	NORTHAMPTON	PA	802	444,770	401-427	
UPPER OKAW PREC.	COLES	IL	101	007,674	95-110	
UPPER OXFORD TWP.	CHESTER	PA	764	020,614	79-104	
UPPER PAXTON TWP.	DAUPHIN	PA	775	444,743	853-93	
UPPER PENNS NECK	SALEM	NJ	462	443,661	349-406	
UPPER PITTSGROVE TWP.	SALEM	NJ	462	443,661	407-446	
UPPER PROVIDENCE TWP.	DELAWARE	PA	776	444,744	333-51	
UPPER PROVIDENCE TWP.	MONTGOMERY	PA	799	444,767	567-626	
UPPER REGIMENT	CHATHAM	NC	624	444,637	703-878	
UPPER RICHLANDS	ONSLOW	NC	639	444,652	165-76	
UPPER ST. CLAIR TWP.	ALLEGHENY	PA	748	020,598	441-79	
UPPER SALFORD	MONTGOMERY	PA	799	444,767	627-61	
UPPER SANDUSKY	WYANDOT	OH	741	444,734	628-46	
UPPER SAUCON	LEHIGH	PA	792	444,760	383-440	
UPPER SOUTHWEST	ONSLOW	NC	639	444,652	277-91	
UPPER SWATARA	DAUPHIN	PA	774	444,742	315-20,	322-44
UPPER TOWANENSING	CARBON	PA	762	020,612	785-824	
UPPER TWP.	CRAWFORD	AR	25	002,479	611-20	
UPPER TWP.	CAPE MAY	NJ	446	016,533	1-34	
UPPER TWP.	LAWRENCE	OH	701	444,694	897-956	
UPPER TULPEHOCKEN TWP.	BERKS	PA	752	020,602	175-224	
UPPER TURKEYFOOT TWP.	SOMERSET	PA	828	444,796	503-525	
UPSHUR CO.		TX	916	444,919	365-430	
UPSON CO.		GA	85	442,894	569-681	
UPTON	WORCESTER	MA	344	443,563	193-242	
URBANA	CHAMPAIGN	IL	99	007,672	188-92	
URBANA	STEUBEN	NY	600	444,316	695-744	
URBANA	CHAMPAIGN	OH	665	020,213	745-96	
URBANA TWP.	CHAMPAIGN	OH	665	020,213	827-61	
URSA	ADAMS	IL	97	007,670	593-655	
UTAH CO.		UT	919	025,540	239-93	
UTAH TERRITORY		UT	919	025,540	1-326	
UTICA	FULTON	IL	107	007,680	657-73	
UTICA	LA SALLE	IL	115	007,688	542-46,	584
UTICA	WINNEBAGO	WI	1009	444,996	1081-96	
UTICA TWP.	CLARK	IN	138	007,751	375-415	
UTICA, WARD 1	ONEIDA	NY	563	444,279	573-616	
UTICA, WARD 2	ONEIDA	NY	563	444,279	763-998	
UTICA, WARD 3	ONEIDA	NY	563	444,279	617-85	
UTICA, WARD 4	ONEIDA	NY	563	444,279	763-998	
UTICA, WARD 5	ONEIDA	NY	563	444,279	687-761	
UTICA, WARD 6	ONEIDA	NY	563	444,279	763-998	
UWCHLAN TWP.	CHESTER	PA	765	020,615	43-83	
UXBRIDGE	WORCESTER	MA	345	443,564	733-96	

CITY, COUNTY, TOWN, OR TOWNSHIP	COUNTY	STATE	NA NO. M432	GD NO.	PAGES	
VALENCIA	VALENCIA	NM	470	443,668	519-24	
VALENCIA CO.		NM	470	443,668	411-768	
VALLEY DIST.	RUTHERFORD	TN	894	444,850	575-89	
VALLEY PLAIN DIST.	HARRIS	GA	73	007,069	136-48	
VALLEY TWP.	MONTOUR	PA	801	444,769	681-99	
VAN BUREN	CRAWFORD	AR	25	002,479	707-716	
VAN BUREN	ONONDAGA	NY	570	444,286	817-909	
VAN BUREN	HANCOCK	OH	692	444,685	1-3	
VAN BUREN CO.		AR	31	442,877	591-656	
VAN BUREN CO.		IA	189	442,964	489-794	
VAN BUREN CO.		MI	363	443,579	203-352	
VAN BUREN CO.		TN	897	444,853	733-92	
VAN BUREN PLANTATION	AROOSTOOK	ME	248	009,718	265-89	
VAN BUREN TWP.	CRAWFORD	AR	25	002,479	691-706	
VAN BUREN TWP.	NEWTON	AR	28	002,482	31-37	
VAN BUREN TWP.	UNION	AR	30	442,876	489-504	
VAN BUREN TWP.	BROWN	IN	137	007,750	469-86	
VAN BUREN TWP.	CLAY	IN	138	007,751	583-604	
VAN BUREN TWP.	DAVIESS	IN	140	007,753	369-85	
VAN BUREN TWP.	FOUNTAIN	IN	145	442,923	141-72	
VAN BUREN TWP.	GRANT	IN	147	442,925	468-80	
VAN BUREN TWP.	KOSCIUSKO	IN	156	442,934	628-48	
VAN BUREN TWP.	MADISON	IN	158	442,936	1-10	
VAN BUREN TWP.	MONROE	IN	161	442,939	657-82	
VAN BUREN TWP.	PULASKI	IN	166	442,944	688-95	
VAN BUREN TWP.	SHELBY	IN	172	442,950	599-618	
VAN BUREN TWP.	JACKSON	IA	184	007,793	683-84,	699-703
VAN BUREN TWP.	VAN BUREN	IA	189	442,964	537-54	
VAN BUREN TWP.	WAYNE	MI	366	443,582	847-81	
VAN BUREN TWP.	JACKSON	MO	402	443,610	687-716	
VAN BUREN TWP.	NEWTON	MO	408	443,616	669-73,	676-86
VAN BUREN TWP.	DARKE	OH	674	020,222	909-927	
VAN BUREN TWP.	HANCOCK	OH	692	444,685	93-106	
VAN BUREN TWP.	MONTGOMERY	OH	713	444,706	129-62	
VAN BUREN TWP.	PUTNAM	OH	723	444,716	95-99	
VAN BUREN TWP.	SHELBY	OH	729	444,722	499-514	
VAN RENNSALAER	OTTAWA	OH	719	444,712	346-50	
VAN VORT TWP.	HUDSON	NJ	452	443,651	769-878	
VAN WERT CO.		OH	736	444,729	305-432	
VAN WERT TWP.	VAN WERT	OH	736	444,729	353-59	
VAN ZANDT CO.		TX	916	444,919	433-64	
VANDALIA	MONTGOMERY	OH	713	444,706	241-46	
VANDERBURGH CO.		IN	176	442,954	727-1005	
VANSVILLE DIST.	PRINCE GEORGES	MD	295	443,526	38-90	
VARICK	SENECA	NY	597	444,313	113-57	
VASSALBOROUGH	KENNEBEC	ME	256	443,493	437-520	
VAUGINE TWP.	JEFFERSON	AR	27	002,481	142-52	
VEALE TWP.	DAVIESS	IN	140	007,753	232-54	
VEASEY TWP.	DREW	AR	26	002,480	165-76	
VENANGO CO.		PA	832	444,800	1-452	
VENANGO TWP.	BUTLER	PA	760	020,610	680-715	
VENANGO TWP.	CRAWFORD	PA	771	444,739	727-65	
VENANGO TWP.	ERIE	PA	777	444,745	125-49	
VENICE	SHIAWASSEE	MI	363	443,579	95-99	
VENICE	CAYUGA	NY	483	017,059	31-79	
VENICE TWP.	SENECA	OH	728	444,721	135-80	
VERGENNES	KENT	MI	353	443,569	579-99	

CITY, COUNTY, TOWN, OR TOWNSHIP	COUNTY	STATE	NA NO. M432	GD NO.	PAGES
VERGENNES	ADDISON	VT	920	027,446	449-82
VERMILION CO.		IL	130	442,918	475-754
VERMILION PARISH		LA	241	443,484	815-72
VERMILION TWP.	ASHLAND	OH	658	020,206	785-844
VERMILION TWP.	ERIE	OH	676	338,044	867-903
VERMILLION	LA SALLE	IL	115	007,688	472-84
VERMILLION CO.		IN	177	442,955	1-218
VERMILLION TWP.	VERMILLION	IN	177	442,955	177-218
VERMONT	FULTON	IL	107	007,680	182-219
VERMONTVILLE	EATON	MI	349	014,811	335-42
VERNON	SUTTER	CA	36	442,879	119-20
VERNON	TOLLAND	CT	50	442,882	543-612
VERNON	LAKE	IL	114	007,687	189-212
VERNON	VAN BUREN	IA	189	442,964	489-509
VERNON	SHIAWASSEE	MI	363	443,579	79-94
VERNON	ONEIDA	NY	562	444,278	147-220
VERNON	TRUMBULL	OH	733	444,726	632-42
VERNON	WINDHAM	VT	929	444,928	193-212
VERNON	WAUKESHA	WI	1009	444,996	628-49
VERNON BEAT	AUTAUGA	AL	1	002,343	7, 11-16
VERNON TWP.	HANCOCK	IN	149	442,927	515-36
VERNON TWP.	JACKSON	IN	152	442,930	319-34
VERNON TWP.	JENNINGS	IN	155	442,933	663-707, 718-24, 727-36, 796, 798- 800, 855-63
VERNON TWP.	WASHINGTON	IN	179	442,957	407-450
VERNON TWP.	SUSSEX	NJ	464	443,663	79-141
VERNON TWP.	CLINTON	OH	668	020,216	401-436
VERNON TWP.	CRAWFORD	OH	671	020,219	661-92
VERNON TWP.	SCIOTO	OH	727	444,720	553-79
VERNON TWP.	CRAWFORD	PA	770	444,738	347-78
VERONA	ONEIDA	NY	564	444,280	245-379
VERONA	DANE	WI	995	034,509	922-30
VERSAILLES	BROWN	IL	98	007,671	256-58, 260-62
VERSAILLES	RIPLEY	IN	169	442,947	431-40
VERSAILLES DIST.	RUTHERFORD	TN	894	442,850	477-96
VERSAILLES TWP.	ALLEGHENY	PA	747	020,597	413-52
VERSHIRE	ORANGE	VT	926	444,925	93-118
VESTAL	BROOME	NY	478	017,054	901-949
VETERAN	CHEMUNG	NY	486	017,062	185-250
VEVAY	INGHAM	MI	351	443,567	82-100
VICKSBURG	WARREN	MS	382	443,594	343-403
VICTOR	ONTARIO	NY	572	444,288	677-732
VICTOR TWP.	CLINTON	MI	349	014,811	119-25
VICTORIA	KNOX	IL	113	007,686	858-60
VICTORIA	VICTORIA	TX	916	444,919	467-82, 492
VICTORIA CO.		TX	916	444,919	467-502
VICTORY	CAYUGA	NY	481	017,057	291-348
VICTORY	ESSEX	VT	923	444,922	819-22
VIEN RIVER	SOMERSET	ME	269	443,506	525-31, 555-59, 561-68
VIENNA	GRUNDY	IL	108	007,681	338-44
VIENNA	JOHNSON	IL	112	007,685	641-44
VIENNA	SCOTT	IN	171	442,949	324-26
VIENNA	KENNEBEC	ME	257	443,494	717-37
VIENNA	ONEIDA	NY	565	444,281	381-462
VIENNA	TRUMBULL	OH	733	444,726	717-40
VIENNA TWP.	SCOTT	IN	171	442,949	283-326
VIENNA TWP.	GENESEE	MI	350	443,566	453-62

CITY, COUNTY, TOWN, OR TOWNSHIP	COUNTY	STATE	NA NO. M432	GD NO.	PAGES
VIENNA TWP.	DANE	WI	995	034,509	786-91
VIGO CO.		IN	177	442,955	219-592
VILLAGE TWP.	JACKSON	AR	27	002,481	116-31
VILLAGE TWP.	VAN BUREN	IA	189	442,964	689-712
VILLEMONT TWP.	ARKANSAS	AR	25	002,479	11-14
VILLENOVA	CHAUTAUQUA	NY	464	017,060	177-213
VINALHAVEN	WALDO	ME	271	443,508	127-56
VINCENNES	KNOX	IN	156	442,934	459-510
VINEGAR HILL PREC.	JO DAVIESS	IL	111	007,684	425-42
VINEYARD TWP.	WASHINGTON	AR	31	442,877	839-54
VINLAND	WINNEBAGO	WI	1009	444,996	987-1002
VINSONS DIST.	CLARKE	GA	65	007,061	49-57
VINTON CO.		OH	736	444,729	435-673
VINTON TWP.	VINTON	OH	736	444,729	517-27
VIOLET TWP.	FAIRFIELD	OH	677	444,670	259-318
VIRGIL	KANE	IL	112	007,685	171-86
VIRGIL	CORTLAND	NY	493	017,069	761-62, 764-
VIRGINIA	CASS	IL	99	007,672	81-89
VIRGINIA TWP.	COSHOCTON	OH	670	020,218	205-234
VOLGA TWP.	CLAYTON	IA	182	007,791	295-99
VOLINIA TWP.	CASS	MI	349	014,811	721-36
VOLNEY	OSWEGO	NY	577	444,293	641-713
VOLUNTOWN	WINDHAM	CT	51	442,883	375-400
WABASH CO.		IL	130	442,918	755-870
WABASH CO.		IN	178	442,956	593-896, 1-2
WABASH DIST.	SHELBY	IL	128	442,916	367-80
WABASH PREC.	COLES	IL	101	007,674	77-94
WABASH PREC.	CUMBERLAND	IL	104	007,677	525-27
WABASH PREC	GALLATIN	IL	107	007,680	694-704
WABASH TWP.	ADAMS	IN	135	007,748	67-77
WABASH TWP.	FOUNTAIN	IN	145	442,923	53-83
WABASH TWP.	GIBSON	IN	147	442,925	203-210
WABASH TWP.	JAY	IN	153	442,931	629-37
WABASH TWP.	TIPPECANOE	IN	175	442,953	19-49
WABASH TWP.	DARKE	OH	674	020,222	531-38
WABASHA CO.		MN	367	014,834	135-40
WACCAMAW DIST.	BRUNSWICK	NC	621	018,107	365-73
WADDAMS	STEPHENSON	IL	129	442,917	611-38
WADESBORO	ANSON	NC	619	018,105	315-25
WADESBORO DIST.	ANSON	NC	619	018,105	326-38
WADSORTH	MEDINA	OH	709	444,702	515-54
WAHNAHTA CO.		MN	367	014,834	143-46
WAITSFIELD	WASHINGTON	VT	928	444,927	1-25
WAKE CO.		NC	647	444,660	197-575
WAKE FOREST DIST.	WAKE	NC	647	444,660	265-76
WAKEFIELD	CARROLL	NH	426	014,939	315-48
WAKEFIELD DIST.	SHELBY	IL	128	442,916	311-28, 358-6
WAKEMAN TWP.	HURON	OH	697	444,690	739-55
WAKESHMA	KALAMAZOO	MI	353	443,569	227-30
WAKULLA CO.		FL	59	006,715	493-522
WALDEN	CALEDONIA	VT	922	027,448	579-600
WALDO	WALDO	ME	271	443,508	353-72
WALDO CO.		ME	270	443,507	1-554
WALDO CO.		ME	271	443,508	1-621
WALDO TWP.	MARION	OH	708	444,701	1-24
WALDOBORO	LINCOLN	ME	259	443,496	389-489

CITY, COUNTY, TOWN, OR TOWNSHIP	COUNTY	STATE	NA NO. M432	GD NO.	PAGES
WALDRON	SCOTT	AR	30	442,876	255-56
WALDWICK	IOWA	WI	999	444,986	677-87
WALES	KENNEBEC	ME	257	443,494	91-105
WALES	HAMPDEN	MA	318	443,537	193-209
WALES	ST. CLAIR	MI	362	443,578	430-34
WALES	ERIE	NY	498	017,074	213-63
WALKER	KENT	MI	353	443,569	411-31
WALKER CO.		AL	16	442,867	538-657
WALKER CO		GA	85	442,894	683-955
WALKER CO.		TX	916	444,919	505-568
WALKER TWP.	CENTRE	PA	763	020,613	285-312
WALKER TWP.	HUNTINGDON	PA	784	444,752	313-40
WALKER TWP.	JUNIATA	PA	786	444,754	469, 473-75, 479-507
WALKINSVILLE DIST.	CLARKE	GA	65	007,061	117-28
WALLACE TWP.	INDEPENDENCE	AR	26	002,480	683-93
WALLINGFORD	NEW HAVEN	CT	46	003,074	1-62
WALLINGFORD	RUTLAND	VT	927	444,926	637-77
WALLKILL	ORANGE	NY	574	444,290	119-234
WALNUT	BUREAU	IL	99	007,672	435-36
WALNUT BOTTOM	PENDLETON	VA	968	444,958	30-31
WALNUT CREEK TWP.	HOLMES	OH	696	444,689	391-416
WALNUT TWP.	PHILLIPS	AR	29	002,483	257-63
WALNUT TWP.	MONTGOMERY	IN	161	442,939	977-1001
WALNUT TWP.	JEFFERSON	IA	185	442,960	71-88
WALNUT TWP.	FAIRFIELD	OH	677	444,670	389-439
WALNUT TWP.	GALLIA	OH	681	444,674	141-62
WALNUT TWP.	PICKAWAY	OH	720	444,713	25-68
WALPACK TWP.	SUSSEX	NJ	464	443,663	1-20
WALPOLE	NORFOLK	MA	331	443,550	47-93
WALPOLE	CHESHIRE	NH	428	014,941	667-715
WALTHAM	LA SALLE	IL	115	007,688	547, 551-53
WALTHAM	HANCOCK	ME	255	443,492	575-82
WALTHAM	MIDDLESEX	MA	325	443,544	561-667
WALTHAM	ADDISON	VT	920	027,446	441-47
WALTON	EATON	MI	349	014,811	184-95
WALTON	DELAWARE	NY	494	017,070	1-55
WALTON CO.		FL	59	006,715	525-58
WALTON CO.		GA	86	442,895	1-166
WALTZ TWP.	WABASH	IN	178	442,956	693-739
WALWORTH	WAYNE	NY	612	444,328	155-202
WALWORTH	WALWORTH	WI	1007	444,994	579-602
WALWORTH CO.		WI	1007	444,994	329-765
WANTAGE TWP.	SUSSEX	NJ	464	443,663	367-460
WAPAKONETA	AUGLAIZE	OH	660	020,208	693-704
WAPELLO CO.		IA	189	442,964	797-998
WAPELLO PREC.	JO DAVIESS	IL	111	007,684	388-95, 400-406
WAPELLO TWP.	LOUISA	IA	187	442,962	237-59
WAPPANOCCA TWP.	CRITTENDEN	AR	25	002,479	725-30
WAPSINONOC TWP.	MUSCATINE	IA	187	442,962	807-818
WAR EAGLE TWP	MADISON	AR	27	002,481	589-613
WAR EAGLE TWP.	VAN BUREN	AR	31	442,877	603-8
WARD TWP.	YELL	AR	31	442,877	966-68
WARD TWP.	RANDOLPH	IN	168	442,946	239-72
WARD TWP.	HOCKING	OH	695	444,688	889-908
WARDENSVILLE	HARDY	VA	950	444,940	82-84
WARDS GROVE PREC.	JO DAVIESS	IL	111	007,684	314-27
WARDSBORO	WINDHAM	VT	929	444,928	359-85
WARE	HAMPSHIRE	MA	321	443,540	724-815

CITY, COUNTY, TOWN, OR TOWNSHIP	COUNTY	STATE	NA NO. M432	GD NO.	PAGES
WARE CO.		GA	86	442,895	167-251
WAREHAM	PLYMOUTH	MA	333	443,552	609-684
WARMINSTER TWP.	BUCKS	PA	759	020,609	237-60
WARNER	MERRIMACK	NH	436	443,640	319-67
WARREN	BRADLEY	AR	25	002,479	175-82
WARREN	LITCHFIELD	CT	43	003,071	190-210
WARREN	HENDERSON	IL	109	007,682	131-32
WARREN	LAKE	IL	114	007,687	1-24
WARREN	HUNTINGTON	IN	152	442,930	125-29
WARREN	LINCOLN	ME	259	443,496	331-88
WARREN	WORCESTER	MA	341	443,560	97-740
WARREN	MACOMB	MI	357	443,573	343-59
WARREN	GRAFTON	NH	431	443,635	427-47
WARREN	HERKIMER	NY	513	017,089	64-104
WARREN	TRUMBULL	OH	733	444,726	741-811
WARREN	BRADFORD	PA	757	020,607	345-82
WARREN	BRISTOL	RI	841	022,264	133-207
WARREN	WASHINGTON	VT	928	444,927	29-51
WARREN BOR.	WARREN	PA	832	444,800	491-515
WARREN CO.		GA	86	442,895	253-404
WARREN CO.		IL	131	442,919	1-196
WARREN CO.		IN	178	442,956	3-188
WARREN CO.		IA	189	442,964	1001-1023
WARREN CO.		KY	220	442,988	1-260
WARREN CO.		MS	382	443,594	343-466
WARREN CO.		MO	421	443,629	57-174
WARREN CO.		NJ	465	443,664	565-1112
WARREN CO.		NY	609	444,325	1-416
WARREN CO.		NC	648	444,661	1-127
WARREN CO.		OH	737	444,730	677-942, 1-34
WARREN CO.		PA	832	444,800	453-800
WARREN CO.		TN	898	444,854	1-202
WARREN CO.		VA	980	444,970	1-116
WARREN DIST.	WARREN	NC	648	444,661	65-127
WARREN TWP.	CLINTON	IN	139	007,752	748-66
WARREN TWP.	MARION	IN	159	442,937	707-748
WARREN TWP.	PUTNAM	IN	167	442,945	1057-82
WARREN TWP.	ST. JOSEPH	IN	171	442,949	74-89
WARREN TWP.	WARREN	IN	178	442,956	141-68
WARREN TWP.	SOMERSET	NJ	463	443,662	703-754
WARREN TWP.	BELMONT	OH	661	020,209	719-84
WARREN TWP.	JEFFERSON	OH	699	444,692	365-410
WARREN TWP.	TUSCARAWAS	OH	735	444,728	553-76
WARREN TWP.	WASHINGTON	OH	738	444,731	733-68
WARREN TWP.	FRANKLIN	PA	781	444,749	1-15
WARRENSBURG	JOHNSON	MO	403	443,611	4-8
WARRENSBURG	WARREN	NY	609	444,325	205-249
WARRENSBURG TWP.	JOHNSON	MO	403	443,611	4-34
WARRENSVILLE	CUYAHOGA	OH	673	020,221	715-50
WARRENTON	MARSHALL	AL	10	002,352	481-95
WARRENTON	WARREN	MS	382	443,594	423-24
WARRENTON BEAT	DALLAS	AL	4	002,346	502-8, 514, 516-17
WARRENTON DIST.	WARREN	NC	648	444,661	41-63
WARRICK CO.		IN	179	442,957	189-405
WARRINGTON	ESCAMBIA	FL	58	006,714	284-94
WARRINGTON TWP.	BUCKS	PA	758	020,608	207-225
WARRINGTON TWP.	YORK	PA	840	444,808	783-821
WARRIORS-MARK TWP.	HUNTINGDON	PA	784	444,752	1-30

Washington Co.

CITY, COUNTY, TOWN, OR TOWNSHIP	COUNTY	STATE	NA NO. M432	GD NO.	PAGES
WARSAW	HANCOCK	IL	109	007,682	631
WARSAW	KOSCIUSKO	IN	156	442,934	597-94
WARSAW	CLAIBORNE PAR.	LA	230	009,697	259
WARSAW	WYOMING	NY	617	444,333	587-649
WARSAW DIV.	SUMTER	AL	15	442,866	644-59
WARSAW TWP.	JEFFERSON	PA	786	444,754	46-66
WARWICK	FRANKLIN	MA	317	443,536	627-52
WARWICK	ORANGE	NY	574	444,290	1-117
WARWICK	KENT	RI	841	022,264	211-394
WARWICK CO.		VA	980	444,970	119-34
WARWICK TWP.	TUSCARAWAS	OH	734	444,727	209-238
WARWICK TWP.	BUCKS	PA	758	020,608	227-56
WARWICK TWP.	CHESTER	PA	765	020,615	363-96
WARWICK TWP.	LANCASTER	PA	788	444,756	165-220
WASHBURN TWP.	SCOTT	AR	30	442,876	299-303, 307-310
WASHINGTON	HEMPSTEAD	AR	26	002,480	411-19
WASHINGTON	LITCHFIELD	CT	43	003,071	601-644
WASHINGTON		DC	57	006,703	481-516
WASHINGTON	WILKES	GA	87	442,896	665-72
WASHINGTON	TAZEWELL	IL	129	442,917	3-17
WASHINGTON	WAYNE	IN	180	442,958	240-46
WASHINGTON	VAN BUREN	IA	189	442,964	510-35
WASHINGTON	LINCOLN	ME	259	443,496	539-80
WASHINGTON	BERKSHIRE	MA	305	014,699	587-611
WASHINGTON	MACOMB	MI	357	443,573	247-83
WASHINGTON	SULLIVAN	NH	441	443,645	189-214
WASHINGTON	DUTCHESS	NY	497	017,073	729-98
WASHINGTON	FAYETTE	OH	678	444,671	123-36
WASHINGTON	GUERNSEY	OH	684	444,677	411-30
WASHINGTON	CLARION	PA	767	444,735	437-65
WASHINGTON	RHEA	TN	893	444,849	611-14
WASHINGTON	ORANGE	VT	926	444,925	645-77
WASHINGTON	BROWN	WI	994	034,508	162-66
WASHINGTON	GREEN	WI	999	444,986	581-88
WASHINGTON BEAT	AUTAUGA	AL	1	002,343	24-28
WASHINGTON BOR.	LANCASTER	PA	787	444,755	387-401
WASHINGTON BOR.	WASHINGTON	PA	834	444,802	673-732
WASHINGTON CO.		AL	16	442,867	661-90
WASHINGTON CO.		AR	31	442,877	657-880
WASHINGTON CO.		FL	59	006,715	561-95
WASHINGTON CO.		GA	87	442,896	405-548
WASHINGTON CO.		IL	131	442,919	199-364
WASHINGTON CO.		IN	179	442,957	407-828
WASHINGTON CO.		IA	189	442,964	1027-1146
WASHINGTON CO.		KY	221	442,989	261-478
WASHINGTON CO.		ME	272	443,509	1-468
WASHINGTON CO.		ME	273	443,510	1-535
WASHINGTON CO.		MD	298	443,529	241-608, 1-327
WASHINGTON CO.		MN	367	014,834	149-76
WASHINGTON CO.		MS	382	443,594	487-501
WASHINGTON CO.		MO	421	443,629	175-363
WASHINGTON CO.		NY	610	444,326	417-684, 1-344
WASHINGTON CO.		NY	611	444,327	347-830
WASHINGTON CO.		NC	648	444,661	129-214
WASHINGTON CO.		OH	738	444,731	351-1081
WASHINGTON CO.		OR	742	020,298	243-307
WASHINGTON CO.		PA	833	444,801	1-489
WASHINGTON CO.		PA	834	444,802	490-1099
WASHINGTON CO.		RI	847	444,813	441-848

CITY, COUNTY, TOWN, OR TOWNSHIP	COUNTY	STATE	NA NO. M432	GD NO.	PAGES
WASHINGTON CO.		TN	898	444,854	205-510
WASHINGTON CO.		TX	916	444,919	571-646
WASHINGTON CO.		VT	928	444,927	1-623
WASHINGTON CO.		VA	980	444,970	137-434
WASHINGTON CO.		WI	1008	444,995	1-467
WASHINGTON DIST.	BEAUFORT	NC	620	018,106	768-73, 831-.
WASHINGTON PARISH		LA	241	443,484	873-930
WASHINGTON PARISH	WESTMORELAND	VA	980	444,970	625-55
WASHINGTON TOWN	BEAUFORT	NC	620	018,106	671-98
WASHINGTON TWP.	CONWAY	AR	25	002,479	471-78
WASHINGTON TWP.	INDEPENDENCE	AR	26	002,480	741-50
WASHINGTON TWP.	LAWRENCE	AR	27	002,481	401-411
WASHINGTON TWP.	OUACHITA	AR	28	002,482	81-88
WASHINGTON TWP.	SEVIER	AR	30	442,876	440-47
WASHINGTON TWP.	YOLO	CA	36	442,879	381-88
WASHINGTON TWP.	ADAMS	IN	135	007,748	7-24
WASHINGTON TWP.	ALLEN	IN	135	007,748	285-316
WASHINGTON TWP.	BLACKFORD	IN	136	007,749	59-70
WASHINGTON TWP.	BROWN	IN	137	007,750	379-408
WASHINGTON TWP.	CARROLL	IN	137	007,750	696-726
WASHINGTON TWP.	CASS	IN	137	007,750	911-34
WASHINGTON TWP.	CLARK	IN	138	007,751	109-127, 136-
WASHINGTON TWP.	CLAY	IN	138	007,751	440-83
WASHINGTON TWP.	CLINTON	IN	139	007,752	659-77
WASHINGTON TWP.	DAVIESS	IN	140	007,753	169-231
WASHINGTON TWP.	DECATUR	IN	142	007,755	21-49, 327-74
WASHINGTON TWP.	DELAWARE	IN	143	007,756	744-61
WASHINGTON TWP.	ELKHART	IN	144	007,757	80-99
WASHINGTON TWP.	GIBSON	IN	147	442,925	167-85
WASHINGTON TWP.	GRANT	IN	147	442,925	481-504
WASHINGTON TWP.	GREENE	IN	148	442,926	763-74
WASHINGTON TWP.	HAMILTON	IN	148	442,926	1-46
WASHINGTON TWP.	HENDRICKS	IN	150	442,928	226-59
WASHINGTON TWP.	JACKSON	IN	152	442,930	297-317
WASHINGTON TWP.	KOSCIUSKO	IN	156	442,934	708-724
WASHINGTON TWP.	MARION	IN	159	442,937	797-845
WASHINGTON TWP.	MIAMI	IN	160	442,938	321-44
WASHINGTON TWP.	MONROE	IN	161	442,939	537-55
WASHINGTON TWP.	MORGAN	IN	162	442,940	33-92
WASHINGTON TWP.	NOBLE	IN	162	442,940	447-62
WASHINGTON TWP.	OWEN	IN	164	442,942	167-208
WASHINGTON TWP.	PARKE	IN	164	442,942	375-401
WASHINGTON TWP.	PIKE	IN	165	442,943	1-70, 81-82
WASHINGTON TWP.	PORTER	IN	165	442,943	219-30
WASHINGTON TWP.	PUTNAM	IN	167	442,945	1115-66
WASHINGTON TWP.	RANDOLPH	IN	168	442,946	81-118
WASHINGTON TWP.	RIPLEY	IN	169	442,947	615-43
WASHINGTON TWP.	RUSH	IN	170	442,948	1001-1028
WASHINGTON TWP.	SHELBY	IN	172	442,950	512-39
WASHINGTON TWP.	STARKE	IN	172	442,950	227-29
WASHINGTON TWP.	TIPPECANOE	IN	175	442,953	261-81
WASHINGTON TWP.	WABASH	IN	178	442,956	169-87
WASHINGTON TWP.	WASHINGTON	IN	179	442,957	637-88
WASHINGTON TWP.	WAYNE	IN	180	442,958	575-634
WASHINGTON TWP.	APPANOOSE	IA	182	007,791	77-85
WASHINGTON TWP.	JOHNSON	IA	185	442,960	253-62
WASHINGTON TWP.	JONES	IA	185	442,960	422-31
WASHINGTON TWP.	BUCHANAN	MO	393	014,873	1-97, 181-86
WASHINGTON TWP.	CLAY	MO	396	443,604	714-41

CITY, COUNTY, TOWN, OR TOWNSHIP	COUNTY	STATE	NA NO. M432	GD NO.	PAGES
WASHINGTON TWP.	JACKSON	MO	402	443,610	502-521
WASHINGTON TWP.	JOHNSON	MO	403	443,611	35-56
WASHINGTON TWP.	OSAGE	MO	408	443,616	955-81
WASHINGTON TWP.	TANEY	MO	420	443,628	721-28
WASHINGTON TWP.	BERGEN	NJ	442	016,529	507-552
WASHINGTON TWP.	BURLINGTON	NJ	444	016,531	1019-70
WASHINGTON TWP.	CAMDEN	NJ	445	016,532	429-80
WASHINGTON TWP.	MORRIS	NJ	459	443,658	465-527
WASHINGTON TWP.	WARREN	NJ	465	443,664	695-732
WASHINGTON TWP.	AUGLAIZE	OH	660	020,208	538-54
WASHINGTON TWP.	BELMONT	OH	661	020,209	1-38
WASHINGTON TWP.	BROWN	OH	662	020,210	751-79
WASHINGTON TWP.	CARROLL	OH	664	020,212	206-230
WASHINGTON TWP.	CLERMONT	OH	667	020,215	45-105
WASHINGTON TWP.	CLINTON	OH	668	020,216	527-58
WASHINGTON TWP.	COLUMBIANA	OH	669	020,217	257-86
WASHINGTON TWP.	COSHOCTON	OH	670	020,218	109-132
WASHINGTON TWP.	DARKE	OH	674	020,222	879-908
WASHINGTON TWP.	DEFIANCE	OH	674	020,222	120-30
WASHINGTON TWP.	FRANKLIN	OH	680	444,673	351-82
WASHINGTON TWP.	GUERNSEY	OH	684	444,677	1009-1032
WASHINGTON TWP.	HANCOCK	OH	692	444,685	839-70
WASHINGTON TWP.	HARDIN	OH	692	444,685	349-58
WASHINGTON TWP.	HARRISON	OH	693	444,686	841-72
WASHINGTON TWP.	HENRY	OH	693	444,686	25-37
WASHINGTON TWP.	HOCKING	OH	695	444,688	725-64
WASHINGTON TWP.	HOLMES	OH	696	444,689	562-97
WASHINGTON TWP.	JACKSON	OH	698	444,691	657-74
WASHINGTON TWP.	LAWRENCE	OH	701	444,694	671-86
WASHINGTON TWP.	LICKING	OH	703	444,696	807-839
WASHINGTON TWP.	LOGAN	OH	704	444,697	179-95
WASHINGTON TWP.	LUCAS	OH	706	444,699	175-94
WASHINGTON TWP.	MERCER	OH	710	444,703	586-95
WASHINGTON TWP.	MIAMI	OH	711	444,704	663-766
WASHINGTON TWP.	MONROE	OH	712	444,705	747-70
WASHINGTON TWP.	MONTGOMERY	OH	713	444,706	1-44
WASHINGTON TWP.	MORROW	OH	716	444,709	701-728
WASHINGTON TWP.	MUSKINGUM	OH	718	444,711	738-70
WASHINGTON TWP.	PAULDING	OH	719	444,712	389-92
WASHINGTON TWP.	PICKAWAY	OH	720	444,713	415-42
WASHINGTON TWP.	PREBLE	OH	723	444,716	461-533
WASHINGTON TWP.	RICHLAND	OH	724	444,717	423-68
WASHINGTON TWP.	SANDUSKY	OH	726	444,719	1008, 1-35
WASHINGTON TWP.	SCIOTO	OH	727	444,720	123-39
WASHINGTON TWP.	SHELBY	OH	729	444,722	515-45
WASHINGTON TWP.	STARK	OH	730	444,723	711-13, 718-23, 725-60
WASHINGTON TWP.	TUSCARAWAS	OH	734	444,727	341-68
WASHINGTON TWP.	UNION	OH	736	444,729	169-76
WASHINGTON TWP.	VAN WERT	OH	736	444,729	308, 315-23
WASHINGTON TWP.	WARREN	OH	737	444,730	905-942
WASHINGTON TWP.	WOOD	OH	741	444,734	321-32
WASHINGTON TWP.	BERKS	PA	753	020,603	45-72
WASHINGTON TWP.	BUTLER	PA	760	020,610	735-58
WASHINGTON TWP.	CAMBRIA	PA	761	020,611	122-62
WASHINGTON TWP.	DAUPHIN	PA	775	444,743	832-52
WASHINGTON TWP.	ERIE	PA	778	444,746	631-71
WASHINGTON TWP.	FAYETTE	PA	780	444,748	739-70
WASHINGTON TWP.	FRANKLIN	PA	781	444,749	263-323

CITY, COUNTY, TOWN, OR TOWNSHIP	COUNTY	STATE	NA NO. M432	GD NO.	PAGES
WASHINGTON TWP.	GREENE	PA	783	444,751	653-74
WASHINGTON TWP.	INDIANA	PA	785	444,753	421-47
WASHINGTON TWP.	JEFFERSON	PA	786	444,754	258-75
WASHINGTON TWP.	LEHIGH	PA	792	444,760	741-76
WASHINGTON TWP.	LYCOMING	PA	795	444,763	764-814
WASHINGTON TWP.	UNION	PA	831	444,799	231-60
WASHINGTON TWP.	WESTMORELAND	PA	836	444,804	805-854
WASHINGTON TWP.	WYOMING	PA	838	444,806	21-60
WASHINGTON TWP.	YORK	PA	840	444,808	823-54
WASHINGTON, WARD 1		DC	56	006,702	1-128
WASHINGTON, WARD 2		DC	56	006,702	129-285
WASHINGTON, WARD 3		DC	56	006,702	287-421
WASHINGTON, WARD 4		DC	56	006,702	423-630
WASHINGTON, WARD 5		DC	57	006,703	1-92
WASHINGTON, WARD 6		DC	57	006,703	93-180
WASHINGTON, WARD 7		DC	57	006,703	181-293
WASHINGTON, WEST OF 7TH ST. TUR.		DC	57	006,703	517-44
WASHTENAW CO.		MI	364	443,580	355-1057
WATAUGA	WATAUGA	NC	648	444,661	215-92
WATAUGA CO.		NC	648	444,661	215-93
WATERBORO	YORK	ME	276	443,513	409-456
WATERBURY	NEW HAVEN	CT	45	003,073	1-123
WATERBURY	WASHINGTON	VT	928	444,927	567-623
WATERFORD	NEW LONDON	CT	49	442,881	377-430
WATERFORD	FULTON	IL	107	007,680	339-46
WATERFORD	OXFORD	ME	262	443,499	297-381
WATERFORD	OAKLAND	MI	359	443,575	227-53
WATERFORD	SARATOGA	NY	592	444,308	1-64
WATERFORD	CALEDONIA	VT	922	027,448	217-50
WATERFORD BOR.	ERIE	PA	778	444,746	619-30
WATERFORD TWP.	CAMDEN	NJ	445	016,532	577-616
WATERFORD TWP.	WASHINGTON	OH	738	444,731	855-96
WATERFORD TWP.	ERIE	PA	778	444,746	581-618
WATERLOO	MONROE	IL	121	442,909	164-81
WATERLOO	JACKSON	MI	352	443,568	906-932
WATERLOO	SENECA	NY	597	444,313	356-446
WATERLOO	JEFFERSON	WI	1000	444,987	129-48
WATERLOO TWP.	FAYETTE	IN	144	007,757	458-78
WATERLOO TWP.	ATHENS	OH	660	020,208	365-89
WATERTOWN	LITCHFIELD	CT	43	003,071	761-98
WATERTOWN	MIDDLESEX	MA	326	443,545	669-734
WATERTOWN	JEFFERSON	NY	514	017,090	521-696
WATERTOWN	WASHINGTON	OH	738	444,731	699-732
WATERTOWN	JEFFERSON	WI	1000	444,987	57-88
WATERTOWN TWP.	CLINTON	MI	349	014,811	25-32
WATERTOWN VILLAGE	JEFFERSON	WI	1000	444,987	1-36
WATERVILLE	KENNEBEC	ME	258	443,495	179-274
WATERVILLE	GRAFTON	NH	431	443,635	493
WATERVILLE	LAMOILLE	VT	925	444,924	149-66
WATERVILLE TWP.	LUCAS	OH	706	444,699	231-67
WATERVLIET	ALBANY	NY	474	017,050	157-556
WATSON	ALLEGAN	MI	346	014,808	95-102
WATSON	LEWIS	NY	523	017,099	533-60
WATSON TWP.	LYCOMING	PA	795	444,763	735-41
WATTS TWP.	PERRY	PA	805	444,773	1183-94
WATTSBURG TWP.	ERIE	PA	777	444,745	19-24
WAUCONDA	LAKE	IL	114	007,687	101-119
WAUKEGAN	LAKE	IL	114	007,687	231-301
WAUKESHA	WAUKESHA	WI	1009	444,996	547-602

CITY, COUNTY, TOWN, OR TOWNSHIP	COUNTY	STATE	NA NO. M432	GD NO.	PAGES
WAUKESHA CO.		WI	1009	444,996	475-940
WAUPONSEE	GRUNDY	IL	108	007,681	349-54
WAUPUN	FOND DU LAC	WI	997	444,984	629-49
WAUSAW	MARATHON	WI	1002	444,989	109-121
WAUSHARA	DODGE	WI	996	034,510	1-21
WAUWATOSA	MILWAUKEE	WI	1003	444,990	959-1009
WAVERLY	PIKE	OH	721	444,714	667-83
WAVERLY	HUMPHREYS	TN	884	444,840	309-313
WAVERLY HALL DIST.	HARRIS	GA	73	007,069	118-21
WAVERLY TWP.	VAN BUREN	MI	363	443,579	349-52
WAWARSING	ULSTER	NY	608	444,324	1-158
WAWAYANDA	ORANGE	NY	574	444,290	429-87
WAYLAND	MIDDLESEX	MA	326	443,545	335-61
WAYLAND	ALLEGAN	MI	346	014,808	109-118
WAYLAND	STEUBEN	NY	600	444,316	281-330
WAYNE	DU PAGE	IL	105	007,678	202-222
WAYNE	STEPHENSON	IL	129	442,917	667-78
WAYNE	KENNEBEC	ME	257	443,494	1-34
WAYNE	STEUBEN	NY	600	444,316	617-49
WAYNE	ASHTABULA	OH	659	020,207	549-70
WAYNE	LAFAYETTE	WI	1001	444,988	661-68
WAYNE	WASHINGTON	WI	1008	444,995	13-28
WAYNE CO.		GA	87	442,896	549-75
WAYNE CO.		IL	131	442,919	365-528
WAYNE CO.		IN	180	442,958	1-634
WAYNE CO.		IA	189	442,964	1149-57
WAYNE CO.		KY	221	442,989	479-669
WAYNE CO.		MI	365	443,581	1-500
WAYNE CO.		MI	366	443,582	541-1077
WAYNE CO.		MS	382	443,594	502-538
WAYNE CO.		MO	421	443,629	365-464
WAYNE CO.		NY	612	444,328	1-593
WAYNE CO.		NY	613	444,329	595-1090
WAYNE CO.		NC	648	444,661	294-496
WAYNE CO.		OH	739	444,732	1-444
WAYNE CO.		OH	740	444,733	445-814
WAYNE CO.		PA	835	444,803	1-546
WAYNE CO.		TN	899	444,855	513-686
WAYNE CO.		VA	980	444,970	437-545
WAYNE TWP.	ALLEN	IN	135	007,748	158-284
WAYNE TWP.	BARTHOLOMEW	IN	136	007,749	679-97
WAYNE TWP.	FULTON	IN	146	442,924	895-909
WAYNE TWP.	HAMILTON	IN	148	442,926	135-59
WAYNE TWP.	HENRY	IN	151	442,929	535-86
WAYNE TWP.	JAY	IN	153	442,931	557-74
WAYNE TWP.	KOSCIUSKO	IN	156	442,934	815-33
WAYNE TWP.	MARION	IN	159	442,937	611-67
WAYNE TWP.	MONTGOMERY	IN	161	442,939	1140-69
WAYNE TWP.	NOBLE	IN	162	442,940	529-43
WAYNE TWP.	OWEN	IN	164	442,942	1-29
WAYNE TWP.	RANDOLPH	IN	168	442,946	189-216
WAYNE TWP.	TIPPECANOE	IN	175	442,953	408-445
WAYNE TWP.	WAYNE	IN	180	442,958	282-336, 437-500, 574
WAYNE TWP.	HENRY	IA	184	007,793	417-21
WAYNE TWP.	CASS	MI	349	014,811	737-53
WAYNE TWP.	BUCHANAN	MO	393	014,873	164-71
WAYNE TWP.	PASSAIC	NJ	461	443,660	289-316
WAYNE TWP.	ADAMS	OH	657	020,205	355-95

CITY, COUNTY, TOWN, OR TOWNSHIP	COUNTY	STATE	NA NO. M432	GD NO.	PAGES
WAYNE TWP.	AUGLAIZE	OH	660	020,208	593-608
WAYNE TWP.	BELMONT	OH	661	020,209	111-56
WAYNE TWP.	BUTLER	OH	663	020,211	715-50
WAYNE TWP.	CHAMPAIGN	OH	665	020,213	669-704
WAYNE TWP.	CLERMONT	OH	667	020,215	135-68
WAYNE TWP.	CLINTON	OH	668	020,216	767-801
WAYNE TWP.	COLUMBIANA	OH	669	020,217	487-510
WAYNE TWP.	DARKE	OH	674	020,222	605-632
WAYNE TWP.	FAYETTE	OH	678	444,671	181-210
WAYNE TWP.	JEFFERSON	OH	699	444,692	275-318
WAYNE TWP.	KNOX	OH	700	444,693	84-128
WAYNE TWP.	MONROE	OH	712	444,705	979-1006
WAYNE TWP.	MONTGOMERY	OH	713	444,706	201-227
WAYNE TWP.	MUSKINGUM	OH	718	444,711	802-836
WAYNE TWP.	PICKAWAY	OH	720	444,713	249-64
WAYNE TWP.	SCIOTO	OH	727	444,720	449-54
WAYNE TWP.	TUSCARAWAS	OH	735	444,728	751-810
WAYNE TWP.	WARREN	OH	737	444,730	677-774
WAYNE TWP.	WAYNE	OH	740	444,733	545-96
WAYNE TWP.	ARMSTRONG	PA	749	020,599	467-99
WAYNE TWP.	CLINTON	PA	768	444,736	213-22
WAYNE TWP.	CRAWFORD	PA	771	444,739	621-41
WAYNE TWP.	ERIE	PA	777	444,745	25-51
WAYNE TWP.	GREENE	PA	783	444,751	438-68
WAYNE TWP.	LAWRENCE	PA	790	444,758	275-92
WAYNE TWP.	MIFFLIN	PA	797	444,765	681-711
WAYNE TWP.	SCHUYLKILL	PA	826	444,794	803-849
WAYNESBORO	BURKE	GA	62	007,058	537-43
WAYNESBORO	FRANKLIN	PA	781	444,749	325-50
WAYNESFIELD TWP.	LUCAS	OH	706	444,699	1-57
WAYNESVILLE	DE WITT	IL	104	007,677	829-36
WAYNESVILLE	WARREN	OH	737	444,730	681-92
WAYNESVILLE DIST.	HOUSTON	GA	74	007,070	727-37
WEAKLEY CO.		TN	899	444,855	689-966
WEARE	HILLSBORO	NH	432	443,636	429-86
WEATHERSFIELD	WYOMING	NY	616	444,332	155-90
WEATHERSFIELD	TRUMBULL	OH	733	444,726	201-242
WEATHERSFIELD	WINDSOR	VT	931	444,930	399-443
WEAVERVILLE	EL DORADO	CA	34	002,491	501-523
WEAVERVILLE	TRINITY	CA	36	442,879	131-35
WEBB CO.		TX	909	024,888	507-709
WEBER CO.		UT	919	025,540	295-326
WEBSTER	LINCOLN	ME	261	443,498	859-85
WEBSTER	WORCESTER	MA	340	443,559	173-229
WEBSTER	WASHTENAW	MI	364	443,580	557-78, 1055-5
WEBSTER	MONROE	NY	528	017,104	829-88
WEBSTER TWP.	WOOD	OH	741	444,734	357-62
WEDOWEE BEAT	RANDOLPH	AL	14	442,865	563-66
WEISENBERG TWP.	LEHIGH	PA	792	444,760	129-70
WELBORN TWP.	CONWAY	AR	25	002,479	459-70
WELD	FRANKLIN	ME	253	009,723	5-28
WELLER TWP.	RICHLAND	OH	724	444,717	525-55
WELLFLEET	BARNSTABLE	MA	303	014,697	127-84
WELLINGTON	PISCATAQUIS	ME	267	443,504	407-421
WELLINGTON TWP.	LORAIN	OH	705	444,698	1085-1122
WELLS	YORK	ME	274	443,511	323-93
WELLS	HAMILTON	NY	511	017,087	1-12, 50
WELLS	RUTLAND	VT	927	444,926	525-44
WELLS CO.		IN	181	442,959	635-792

CITY, COUNTY, TOWN, OR TOWNSHIP	COUNTY	STATE	NA NO. M432	GD NO.	PAGES
WELLS TWP.	APPANOOSE	IA	182	007,791	70-76
WELLS TWP.	JEFFERSON	OH	699	444,692	815-58
WELLS TWP.	BRADFORD	PA	757	020,607	741-68
WELLS TWP.	FULTON	PA	783	444,751	183-92
WELLSBOROUGH	TIOGA	PA	830	444,798	387-402
WELLSVILLE	YORK	PA	840	444,808	815-16
WELLSVILLE TOWN	COLUMBIANA	OH	669	020,217	287-323
WENDELL	FRANKLIN	MA	317	443,536	553-76
WENDELL	SULLIVAN	NH	441	443,645	1-19
WENHAM	ESSEX	MA	314	014,708	593-616
WENLOCK	ESSEX	VT	923	444,922	841
WENTWORTH	GRAFTON	NH	431	443,635	397-425
WENTWORTH'S LOCATION	COOS	NH	429	443,633	327-28
WESLEY	WASHINGTON	ME	273	443,510	115-22
WESLEY TWP.	WASHINGTON	OH	738	444,731	789-826
WEST ALEXANDRIA	PREBLE	OH	723	444,716	882-87
WEST ALMOND	ALLEGANY	NY	476	017,052	17-40
WEST AMWELL TWP.	HUNTERDON	NJ	453	443,652	1-60
WEST ARMUCHY	WALKER	GA	85	442,894	745-54
WEST BATH	LINCOLN	ME	261	443,498	443-57
WEST BATON ROUGE PAR.		LA	229	009,696	445-90
WEST BEAVER TWP.	UNION	PA	831	444,799	262-90
WEST BELLEVILLE	ST. CLAIR	IL	126	442,914	906-912
WEST BEND	WASHINGTON	WI	1008	444,995	56-71
WEST BETHLEHEM	WASHINGTON	PA	833	444,801	310, 339-93
WEST BLOOMFIELD	OAKLAND	MI	359	443,575	93-119
WEST BLOOMFIELD	ONTARIO	NY	571	444,287	201-241
WEST BOYLSTON	WORCESTER	MA	343	443,562	403-446
WEST BRADFORD	CHESTER	PA	764	020,614	473-512
WEST BRANCH	POTTER	PA	825	444,793	241-43
WEST BRANDYWINE TWP.	CHESTER	PA	766	020,616	583-602
WEST BRIDGEWATER	PLYMOUTH	MA	332	443,551	535-69
WEST BROOK	MIDDLESEX	CT	44	003,072	349-77
WEST BROOKFIELD	WORCESTER	MA	341	443,560	141-72
WEST BROWNSVILLE	WASHINGTON	PA	833	444,801	280-91
WEST BRUNSWICK	SCHUYLKILL	PA	826	444,794	313-53
WEST BUFFALO TWP.	UNION	PA	831	444,799	379-402
WEST CALN TWP.	CHESTER	PA	766	020,616	519-54
WEST CAMBRIDGE	MIDDLESEX	MA	324	443,543	649-701
WEST CHESTER	CHESTER	PA	764	020,614	593-668
WEST CHICAGO	COOK	IL	102	007,675	913-24
WEST CHICKAMAUGA	WALKER	GA	85	442,894	877-909
WEST COCALICO TWP.	LANCASTER	PA	789	444,757	725-71
WEST CONNOQUENESSING	BUTLER	PA	760	020,610	193-225
WEST CREEK TWP.	LAKE	IN	157	442,935	240-51
WEST DEER TWP.	ALLEGHENY	PA	747	020,597	51-92
WEST DONEGAL TWP.	LANCASTER	PA	788	444,756	65-98
WEST EARL TWP.	LANCASTER	PA	789	444,757	453-92
WEST ELIZABETH BOR.	ALLEGHENY	PA	747	020,597	243-50
WEST FAIRLEE	ORANGE	VT	926	444,925	121-37
WEST FALLOWFIELD TWP.	CHESTER	PA	766	020,616	675-730
WEST FALLOWFIELD TWP.	CRAWFORD	PA	771	444,739	423-38
WEST FARMS	WESTCHESTER	NY	615	444,331	533-638
WEST FELICIANA PARISH		LA	231	009,698	509-570
WEST FINLEY	WASHINGTON	PA	834	444,802	895-923
WEST FORK TWP.	WASHINGTON	AR	31	442,877	747-61
WEST GENESEE TWP.	GENESEE	MI	350	443,566	555-60
WEST GOSHEN TWP.	CHESTER	PA	764	020,614	533-56
WEST GREENFIELD	LA GRANGE	IN	157	442,935	195-206

CITY, COUNTY, TOWN, OR TOWNSHIP	COUNTY	STATE	NA NO. M432	GD NO.	PAGES
WEST GREENVILLE	MERCER	PA	796	444,764	747-71
WEST GREENWICH	BRISTOL	RI	841	022,264	397-429
WEST HANOVER TWP.	DAUPHIN	PA	775	444,743	673-94
WEST HEMLOCK TWP.	MONTOUR	PA	801	444,769	841-45
WEST HEMPFIELD TWP.	LANCASTER	PA	788	444,756	323-87
WEST INDIAN TWP.	PENOBSCOT	ME	266	443,503	745-47
WEST JEFFERSON	MADISON	OH	706	444,699	529-39
WEST LACKAWANNOCK TWP.	MERCER	PA	796	444,764	419-46
WEST LAMPETER TWP.	LANCASTER	PA	788	444,756	437-78
WEST LIMA	LA GRANGE	IN	157	442,935	165-72
WEST MAHONING TWP.	INDIANA	PA	785	444,753	337-61
WEST MANCHESTER TWP	YORK	PA	840	444,808	551-84
WEST MARLBOROUGH TWP.	CHESTER	PA	764	020,614	303-330
WEST MIDDLETOWN BOR.	WASHINGTON	PA	834	444,802	1061-68
WEST MILFORD TWP.	PASSAIC	NJ	461	443,660	317-79
WEST MONROE	OSWEGO	NY	578	444,294	705-9, 711, 72
					723-33
WEST NANTMEAL TWP.	CHESTER	PA	765	020,615	397-440
WEST NEWBURY	ESSEX	MA	315	443,534	373-414
WEST NEWTON BOR.	WESTMORELAND	PA	837	444,805	499-517
WEST NOTTINGHAM	CHESTER	PA	764	020,614	1-3
WEST NOTTINGHAM TWP.	CHESTER	PA	764	020,614	4-18
WEST PENN TWP.	SCHUYLKILL	PA	827	444,795	506-565
WEST PENNSBORO	CUMBERLAND	PA	772	444,740	113-61
WEST PHILADELPHIA	PHILADELPHIA	PA	823	444,791	1035-1168
WEST PIKE RUN TWP.	WASHINGTON	PA	834	444,802	571-98
WEST PIKELAND TWP.	CHESTER	PA	765	020,615	19-39
WEST POINT	STEPHENSON	IL	129	442,917	639-44
WEST POINT	LEE	IA	186	442,961	987-98
WEST POINT TWP.	LEE	IA	186	442,961	999-1016
WEST POINT TWP.	COLUMBIA	WI	994	034,508	309-312, 317
WEST PROVIDENCE TWP.	BEDFORD	PA	751	020,601	195-229
WEST RIVER TWP.	RANDOLPH	IN	168	442,946	345-74
WEST SALEM TWP.	MERCER	PA	796	444,764	794-853
WEST SPARTA	LIVINGSTON	NY	525	017,101	745-83
WEST SPRINGFIELD	HAMPDEN	MA	318	443,537	291-362
WEST STOCKBRIDGE	BERKSHIRE	MA	306	014,700	189-229
WEST TOWN OF VICTORIA	VICTORIA	TX	916	444,919	493-94
WEST TROY VILLAGE	ALBANY	NY	474	017,050	157-338
WEST TURIN	LEWIS	NY	523	017,099	1-95
WEST TWP.	COLUMBIANA	OH	669	020,217	774-824
WEST TWP.	HUNTINGDON	PA	784	444,752	151-87
WEST UNION	STEUBEN	NY	599	444,315	633-56
WEST UNION	ADAMS	OH	657	020,205	272-82
WEST UNION	DODDRIDGE	VA	942	444,932	1-4
WEST VAN BUREN	LA GRANGE	IN	157	442,935	146-56
WEST VICTORIA	VICTORIA	TX	916	444,919	493-94
WEST VINCENT TWP.	CHESTER	PA	765	020,615	85-117
WEST WHITELAND	CHESTER	PA	766	020,616	847-74
WEST WINDSOR	WINDSOR	VT	931	444,930	489-512
WEST WINDSOR TWP.	MERCER	NJ	454	443,653	73-110
WESTAMPTON TWP.	BURLINGTON	NJ	443	016,530	479-514
WESTBOROUGH	WORCESTER	MA	344	443,563	751-807
WESTBROOK	CUMBERLAND	ME	250	009,720	611-724
WESTCHESTER	WESTCHESTER	NY	615	444,331	639-98
WESTCHESTER CO.		NY	614	444,330	1-714
WESTCHESTER CO.		NY	615	444,331	1-698
WESTCHESTER TWP.	PORTER	IN	165	442,943	313-21
WESTERLO	ALBANY	NY	473	017,049	85-153

CITY, COUNTY, TOWN, OR TOWNSHIP	COUNTY	STATE	NA NO. M432	GD NO.	PAGES
WESTERLY	WASHINGTON	RI	847	444,813	781-848
WESTERN	ONEIDA	NY	564	444,280	585-644
WESTFALL TWP.	PIKE	PA	825	444,793	55-68
WESTFIELD	BUREAU	IL	99	007,672	398-403
WESTFIELD	HAMILTON	IN	148	442,926	47-52
WESTFIELD	HAMPDEN	MA	318	443,537	363-462
WESTFIELD	CHAUTAUQUA	NY	465	017,061	249-322
WESTFIELD	RICHMOND	NY	587	444,303	201-271
WESTFIELD	TIOGA	PA	830	444,798	565-98
WESTFIELD	ORLEANS	VT	925	444,924	195-206
WESTFIELD DIST.	SURRY	NC	646	444,659	553-72
WESTFIELD TWP.	ESSEX	NJ	450	443,649	675-712
WESTFIELD TWP.	MEDINA	OH	709	444,702	371-98
WESTFIELD TWP.	MORROW	OH	716	444,709	1-34
WESTFIELD VILLAGE	SAUK	WI	1006	444,993	61-65
WESTFORD	MIDDLESEX	MA	323	443,542	89-124
WESTFORD	OTSEGO	NY	579	444,295	373-406
WESTFORD	CHITTENDEN	VT	923	444,922	331-65
WESTHAMPTON	HAMPSHIRE	MA	320	443,539	277-91
WESTHAVEN	RUTLAND	VT	927	444,926	505-523
WESTLAND TWP.	GUERNSEY	OH	684	444,677	923-50
WESTMINSTER	CARROLL	MD	289	443,520	527-46
WESTMINSTER	WORCESTER	MA	340	443,559	91-136
WESTMINSTER	WINDHAM	VT	929	444,928	537-78
WESTMORE	ORLEANS	VT	925	444,924	1-4
WESTMORELAND	CHESHIRE	NH	427	014,940	1-40
WESTMORELAND	ONEIDA	NY	564	444,280	165-243
WESTMORELAND		VA	980	444,970	549-655
WESTMORELAND CO.		PA	836	444,804	549-884, 1-325
WESTMORELAND CO.		PA	837	444,805	327-880
WESTON	FAIRFIELD	CT	38	003,066	125-36, 138-50
WESTON	AROOSTOOK	ME	248	009,718	28-35
WESTON	MIDDLESEX	MA	326	443,545	363-91
WESTON	PLATTE	MO	410	443,618	667-69
WESTON	WINDSOR	VT	931	444,930	447-69
WESTON TWP.	PLATTE	MO	410	443,618	569-606, 617-43
WESTON TWP.	WOOD	OH	741	444,734	343-56
WESTON VILLAGE	JO DAVIESS	IL	111	007,684	358-64
WESTPHALIA TWP.	CLINTON	MI	349	014,811	47-61
WESTPORT	FAIRFIELD	CT	38	003,066	137, 151-214
WESTPORT	DECATUR	IN	142	007,755	279-83
WESTPORT	LINCOLN	ME	260	443,497	151-70
WESTPORT	BRISTOL	MA	309	014,703	907-973
WESTPORT	ESSEX	NY	503	017,079	74-129
WESTPORT	DANE	WI	995	034,509	792-96
WESTTOWN TWP.	CHESTER	PA	766	020,616	811-29
WESTVILLE	FRANKLIN	NY	505	017,081	455-85
WETHERSFIELD	HARTFORD	CT	40	003,068	77-138
WETMORE ISLE PLANT.	HANCOCK	ME	254	443,491	81-90
WETUMPKA	AUTAUGA	AL	1	002,343	63-77
WETUMPKA CITY	COOSA	AL	4	002,346	1-9
WETZEL CO.		VA	981	444,971	1-104
WEYBRIDGE	ADDISON	VT	920	027,446	421-40
WEYMOUTH	NORFOLK	MA	329	443,548	457-584
WEYMOUTH TWP.	ATLANTIC	NJ	442	016,529	191-216
WHARTON	POTTER	PA	825	444,793	172-75, 177
WHARTON CO.		TX	916	444,919	647-59
WHARTON TWP.	FAYETTE	PA	779	444,747	1-43
WHARTON TWP.	POTTER	PA	825	444,793	176

CITY, COUNTY, TOWN, OR TOWNSHIP	COUNTY	STATE	NA NO. M432	GD NO.	PAGES
WHATELY	FRANKLIN	MA	316	443,535	125-51
WHEATFIELD	NIAGARA	NY	560	444,276	295-358
WHEATFIELD TWP.	INGHAM	MI	351	443,567	161-67
WHEATFIELD TWP.	INDIANA	PA	785	444,753	195-251
WHEATFIELD TWP.	PERRY	PA	805	444,773	1026-42
WHEATLAND	WILL	IL	133	442,921	91-108
WHEATLAND	MONROE	NY	528	017,104	441-512
WHEATLAND	KENOSHA	WI	1000	444,987	629-57
WHEATLAND TWP.	HILLSDALE	MI	351	443,567	943-75
WHEELER	STEUBEN	NY	600	444,316	745-80
WHEELERSBURG	SCIOTO	OH	727	444,720	465-76
WHEELING	COOK	IL	103	007,676	169-90
WHEELING TWP.	BELMONT	OH	661	020,209	947-64
WHEELING TWP.	GUERNSEY	OH	684	444,677	895-922
WHEELING, WARD 1	OHIO	VA	966	444,956	148-202
WHEELING, WARD 2	OHIO	VA	966	444,956	203-234
WHEELING, WARD 3	OHIO	VA	966	444,956	235-89
WHEELING, WARD 4	OHIO	VA	966	444,956	290-356
WHEELING, WARD 5	OHIO	VA	966	444,956	357-427
WHEELOCK	CALEDONIA	VT	922	027,448	555-75
WHETSTONE TWP.	CRAWFORD	OH	671	020,219	49-90
WHISKEY RUN TWP.	CRAWFORD	IN	139	007,752	79-101
WHIT PAIN TWP.	MONTGOMERY	PA	799	444,767	497-530
WHITAKERS DIST.	HARRIS	GA	73	007,069	202-215
WHITE CO.		AR	31	442,877	883-944
WHITE CO.		IL	132	442,920	529-741
WHITE CO.		IN	181	442,959	793-906
WHITE CO.		TN	900	444,856	1-248
WHITE CREEK	WASHINGTON	NY	611	444,327	567-638
WHITE DEER TWP.	UNION	PA	831	444,799	459-96
WHITE EYES TWP.	COSHOCTON	OH	670	020,218	459-85
WHITE HALL	GREENE	IL	108	007,681	295-300
WHITE LAKE	OAKLAND	MI	359	443,575	307-329
WHITE MARSH TWP.	MONTGOMERY	PA	799	444,767	241-98
WHITE OAK	CARTERET	NC	623	018,109	322-33
WHITE OAK	ONSLOW	NC	639	444,652	205-217
WHITE OAK DIST.	JONES	NC	635	444,648	230-37
WHITE OAK SPRINGS	LAFAYETTE	WI	1001	444,988	931-41
WHITE OAK TWP.	FRANKLIN	AR	26	002,480	217-40
WHITE OAK TWP.	JEFFERSON	AR	27	002,481	183-91
WHITE OAK TWP.	INGHAM	MI	351	443,567	193-205
WHITE OAK TWP.	HIGHLAND	OH	694	444,687	632-56
WHITE PIGEON TWP.	ST. JOSEPH	MI	362	443,578	541-61
WHITE PLAINS	WESTCHESTER	NY	615	444,331	261-94
WHITE POST TWP.	PULASKI	IN	166	442,944	680-83
WHITE RIVER	INDEPENDENCE	AR	26	002,480	660-82
WHITE RIVER TWP.	BENTON	AR	25	002,479	115-24
WHITE RIVER TWP.	IZARD	AR	27	002,481	31-35
WHITE RIVER TWP.	PRAIRIE	AR	29	002,483	623-26
WHITE RIVER TWP.	WASHINGTON	AR	31	442,877	701-716
WHITE RIVER TWP.	GIBSON	IN	147	442,925	145-66
WHITE RIVER TWP.	HAMILTON	IN	148	442,926	161-98
WHITE RIVER TWP.	JOHNSON	IN	155	442,933	93-129
WHITE RIVER TWP.	RANDOLPH	IN	168	442,946	119-72
WHITE ROCK TWP.	FRANKLIN	AR	26	002,480	251-54
WHITE ROCK TWP.	OGLE	IL	123	442,911	169-72
WHITE TWP.	ASHLEY	AR	25	002,479	49-60
WHITE TWP.	NEWTON	AR	28	002,482	5-10
WHITE TWP.	PIKE	AR	29	002,483	376-80

CITY, COUNTY, TOWN, OR TOWNSHIP	COUNTY	STATE	NA NO. M432	GD NO.	PAGES
WHITE TWP.	POLK	AR	29	002,483	454, 467-70, 475-78
WHITE TWP.	BENTON	MO	392	014,872	600-603, 639-53
WHITE TWP.	CAMBRIA	PA	761	020,611	1-16
WHITE TWP.	INDIANA	PA	785	444,753	25-55
WHITE WATER TWP.	FRANKLIN	IN	146	442,924	761-800
WHITEFIELD	LINCOLN	ME	259	443,496	595-646
WHITEFIELD	COOS	NH	429	443,633	213-33
WHITEFORD	MONROE	MI	358	443,574	593-609
WHITEHALL	WASHINGTON	NY	610	444,326	1-113
WHITEHALL BOR.	PHILADELPHIA	PA	808	444,776	45-56
WHITELEY	GREENE	PA	783	444,751	370-94
WHITESIDE CO.		IL	132	442,920	743-870
WHITESIDE SETTLEMENT	RUTHERFORD	NC	644	444,657	573-84, 685-94, 701
WHITESTOWN	ONEIDA	NY	564	444,280	1-163
WHITESTOWN	ADAMS	PA	743	020,593	180
WHITESVILLE DIST.	HARRIS	GA	73	007,069	238-51
WHITEWATER	WALWORTH	WI	1007	444,994	661-92
WHITEWATER TWP.	HAMILTON	OH	686	444,679	567-98
WHITING	WASHINGTON	ME	272	443,509	163-74
WHITING	ADDISON	VT	920	027,446	133-48
WHITINGHAM	WINDHAM	VT	929	444,928	157-90
WHITLEY CO.		IN	181	442,959	907-1028
WHITLEY CO.		KY	222	442,990	671-848
WHITNEYVILLE	WASHINGTON	ME	273	443,510	73-85
WICONISCO TWP.	DAUPHIN	PA	775	444,743	737-67
WILBRAHAM	HAMPDEN	MA	318	443,537	33-83
WILCOX CO.		AL	16	442,867	693-824
WILDCAT DIST.	CLARKE	GA	65	007,061	139-49
WILDCAT TWP.	TIPTON	IN	176	442,954	515-20
WILEY'S COVE TWP.	SEARCY	AR	30	442,876	358-71
WILKES CO.		GA	87	442,896	577-672
WILKES CO.		NC	649	444,662	499-761
WILKES-BARRE BOR.	LUZERNE	PA	794	444,762	759-89, 859-94
WILKES-BARRE TWP.	LUZERNE	PA	794	444,762	791-858, 955-58
WILKINS TWP.	ALLEGHENY	PA	747	020,597	487-558
WILKINSON CO.		GA	87	442,896	673-805
WILKINSON CO.		MS	382	443,594	539-627
WILKINSON CROSS RD. DIST.	RUTHER.	TN	894	444,850	377-88
WILKINSON TWP.	DESHA	AR	26	002,480	113-17
WILKSVILLE TWP.	VINTON	OH	736	444,729	573-97
WILL CO.		IL	133	442,921	1-419
WILLET	CORTLAND	NY	493	017,069	429-50
WILLIAM DIST.	WILLIAMSON	TX	916	444,919	663-96
WM. T. BURG CITY	JAMES CITY	VA	953	444,943	571-82
WILLIAM TWP.	KNOX	OH	700	444,693	195-222
WILLIAMS COLLEGE GT.	AROOSTOOK	ME	248	009,718	165-70
WILLIAMS CO.		OH	741	444,734	1-206
WILLIAMS TWP.	BENTON	MO	392	014,872	604-618
WILLIAMS TWP.	NORTHAMPTON	PA	802	444,770	1-64
WILLIAMSBURG	PISCATAQUIS	ME	267	443,504	713-15
WILLIAMSBURG	HAMPSHIRE	MA	320	443,539	293-329
WILLIAMSBURG	KINGS	NY	522	017,098	277-1010
WILLIAMSBURG	GUERNSEY	OH	684	444,677	359-67
WILLIAMSBURG	BLAIR	PA	755	020,605	37-54
WILLIAMSBURG CO.		SC	860	444,823	229-327
WILLIAMSBURG TWP.	WAYNE	IN	180	442,958	209-214
WILLIAMSBURG TWP.	CLERMONT	OH	667	020,215	634-78

CITY, COUNTY, TOWN, OR TOWNSHIP	COUNTY	STATE	NA NO. M432	GD NO.	PAGES
WILLIAMSFIELD	ASHTABULA	OH	659	020,207	713-36
WILLIAMSON	WAYNE	NY	612	444,328	259-315
WILLIAMSON CO.		IL	133	442,921	421-592
WILLIAMSON CO.		TN	900	444,856	251-620
WILLIAMSON CO.		TX	916	444,919	663-97
WILLIAMSON DIST.	RICHMOND	NC	642	444,655	541-52
WILLIAMSON DIST.	MILAM	TX	913	444,916	1-59
WILLIAMSON DIST.	WILLIAMSON	TX	916	444,919	663-96
WILLIAMSPORT	WARREN	IN	178	442,956	181-87
WILLIAMSPORT	WASHINGTON	MD	298	443,529	1-25
WILLIAMSPORT	MAURY	TN	890	444,846	484-87
WILLIAMSPORT BOR.	LYCOMING	PA	795	444,763	695-734
WILLIAMSTOWN	GRANT	KY	201	442,969	716-23
WILLIAMSTOWN	BERKSHIRE	MA	305	014,699	289-351
WILLIAMSTOWN	OSWEGO	NY	578	444,294	415-41
WILLIAMSTOWN	ORANGE	VT	926	444,925	529-63
WILLIAMSTOWN	DODGE	WI	996	034,510	459-80
WILLINGBORO TWP.	BURLINGTON	NJ	443	016,530	131-68
WILLINGTON	TOLLAND	CT	50	442,882	491-524
WILLISTON	CHITTENDEN	VT	923	444,922	1-40
WILLISTOWN TWP.	CHESTER	PA	764	020,614	557-92
WILLOUGHBY	LAKE	OH	701	444,694	295-346
WILLOW CREEK	LANCASTER	PA	787	444,755	585-89
WILLOW SPRINGS	LAFAYETTE	WI	1001	444,988	711-25
WILLS TWP.	LA PORTE	IN	157	442,935	433-48
WILLS TWP.	GUERNSEY	OH	684	444,677	411-68
WILLSBORO	ESSEX	NY	503	017,079	186-231
WILLSHIRE TWP.	VAN WERT	OH	736	444,729	325-50
WILMINGTON	NEW CASTLE	DE	53	006,437	1-335
WILMINGTON	WILL	IL	133	442,921	219-50
WILMINGTON	DEARBORN	IN	141	007,754	877-85
WILMINGTON	MIDDLESEX	MA	324	443,543	361-81
WILMINGTON	ESSEX	NY	503	017,079	320-48
WILMINGTON	NEW HANOVER	NC	638	444,651	789-892
WILMINGTON	CLINTON	OH	668	020,216	682-711
WILMINGTON	WINDHAM	VT	929	444,928	445-77
WILMINGTON TWP.	UNION	AR	30	442,876	541-52
WILMINGTON TWP.	DE KALB	IN	142	007,755	509-528
WILMINGTON TWP.	LAWRENCE	PA	790	444,758	483-518
WILMINGTON TWP.	MERCER	PA	796	444,764	203-216
WILMOT	MERRIMACK	NH	436	443,640	235-65
WILMOT	BRADFORD	PA	757	020,607	589-602
WILMURT	HERKIMER	NY	513	017,089	569-71
WILNA	JEFFERSON	NY	516	017,092	801-872, 751
WILSON	NIAGARA	NY	561	444,277	955-1028
WILSON	SHEBOYGAN	WI	1006	444,993	153-77, 272
WILSON CO.		TN	901	444,857	623-1110
WILTON	FAIRFIELD	CT	38	003,066	215-64
WILTON	WILL	IL	133	442,921	181-87
WILTON	FRANKLIN	ME	253	009,723	85-131
WILTON	HILLSBORO	NH	433	443,637	627-54
WILTON	SARATOGA	NY	592	444,308	327-62
WINCHENDON	WORCESTER	MA	340	443,559	609-667
WINCHESTER	LITCHFIELD	CT	42	003,070	369-423
WINCHESTER	SCOTT	IL	128	442,916	1-25
WINCHESTER	RANDOLPH	IN	168	442,946	173-85
WINCHESTER	MIDDLESEX	MA	325	443,544	429-61
WINCHESTER	CHESHIRE	NH	427	014,940	41-119
WINCHESTER	GUERNSEY	OH	684	444,677	789-93

CITY, COUNTY, TOWN, OR TOWNSHIP	COUNTY	STATE	NA NO. M432	GD NO.	PAGES
WINCHESTER	FREDERICK	VA	945	444,935	541-623
WINCHESTER TWP.	ADAMS	OH	657	020,205	313-53
WINDHAM	WINDHAM	CT	51	442,883	841-948
WINDHAM	CUMBERLAND	ME	251	009,721	299-355
WINDHAM	ROCKINGHAM	NH	438	443,642	121-40
WINDHAM	GREENE	NY	509	017,085	1-50
WINDHAM	PORTAGE	OH	722	444,715	931-50
WINDHAM	BRADFORD	PA	757	020,607	321-43
WINDHAM	WINDHAM	VT	929	444,928	709-728
WINDHAM CO.		CT	51	442,883	183-948
WINDHAM CO.		VT	929	444,928	1-728
WINDHAM TWP.	WYOMING	PA	838	444,806	101-115
WINDSOR	HARTFORD	CT	39	003,067	440-520
WINDSOR	KENNEBEC	ME	258	443,495	347-90
WINDSOR	BERKSHIRE	MA	305	014,699	379-400
WINDSOR	EATON	MI	349	014,811	279-84
WINDSOR	HILLSBORO	NH	434	443,638	1-4, 19
WINDSOR	BROOME	NY	477	017,053	397-459
WINDSOR	BERTIE	NC	621	018,107	141-44
WINDSOR	WINDSOR	VT	931	444,930	699-744
WINDSOR	DANE	WI	995	034,509	765-85
WINDSOR CO.		VT	930	444,929	1-396
WINDSOR CO.		VT	931	444,930	399-965
WINDSOR TWP.	ASHTABULA	OH	659	020,207	959-83
WINDSOR TWP.	LAWRENCE	OH	701	444,694	791-814
WINDSOR TWP.	MORGAN	OH	715	444,708	338-76
WINDSOR TWP.	BERKS	PA	754	020,604	507-534
WINDSOR TWP.	YORK	PA	840	444,808	221-63
WINFIELD	DU PAGE	IL	105	007,678	90-116
WINFIELD	HERKIMER	NY	512	017,088	269-304
WINFIELD TWP.	LAKE	IN	157	442,935	272-77
WING TWP.	LUCAS	OH	706	444,699	285-91
WINHALL	BENNINGTON	VT	921	027,447	61-79
WINNEBAGO	WINNEBAGO	WI	1009	444,996	1003-1041
WINNEBAGO CO.		IL	134	442,922	593-880
WINNEBAGO CO.		WI	1009	444,996	943-1190
WINNECONNA	WINNEBAGO	WI	1009	444,996	1143-90
WINNESHIEK CO.		IA	189	442,964	1161-74
WINSLOW	STEPHENSON	IL	129	442,917	601-610
WINSLOW	KENNEBEC	ME	258	443,495	459-501
WINSLOW TWP.	CAMDEN	NJ	445	016,532	481-518
WINSLOW TWP.	JEFFERSON	PA	786	444,754	206, 251-57, 275-77
WINSTON CO.		MS	382	443,594	629-752
WINTHROP	KENNEBEC	ME	257	443,494	35-87
WIOTA	LAFAYETTE	WI	1001	444,988	693-709
WIRT	ALLEGANY	NY	475	017,051	277-313
WIRT CO.		VA	981	444,971	107-186
WISCASSET	LINCOLN	ME	260	443,497	723-78
WOBURN	MIDDLESEX	MA	325	443,544	465-559
WOLCOTT	NEW HAVEN	CT	45	003,073	125-39
WOLCOTT	WAYNE	NY	613	444,329	1025-90
WOLCOTT	LAMOILLE	VT	925	444,924	245-66
WOLF CREEK TWP.	MERCER	PA	796	444,764	879-927
WOLF PIT DIST.	RICHMOND	NC	642	444,655	553-66
WOLF PITT	ONSLOW	NC	639	444,652	235-43
WOLF TWP.	LYCOMING	PA	795	444,763	870-93
WOLFBORO	CARROLL	NH	426	014,939	349-97
WOMELSDORF BOR.	BERKS	PA	752	020,602	39-62

CITY, COUNTY, TOWN, OR TOWNSHIP	COUNTY	STATE	NA NO. M432	GD NO.	PAGES	
WOOD CO.		OH	741	444,734	207-437	
WOOD CO.		VA	981	444,971	187-403	
WOOD TWP.	CLARK	IN	138	007,751	1-38	
WOODBERRY TWP.	BLAIR	PA	755	020,605	1-54	
WOODBRIDGE	NEW HAVEN	CT	45	003,073	517-38	
WOODBRIDGE TWP.	HILLSDALE	MI	351	443,567	663-72	
WOODBRIDGE TWP.	MIDDLESEX	NJ	455	443,654	1-124	
WOODBURN	MACOUPIN	IL	118	442,906	575-80	
WOODBURN	MORROW	OH	716	444,709	871-74	
WOODBURY	LITCHFIELD	CT	43	003,071	709-760	
WOODBURY	WASHINGTON	VT	928	444,927	471-96	
WOODBURY PREC.	CUMBERLAND	IL	104	007,677	528-40,	542-4
WOODCOCK TWP.	CRAWFORD	PA	771	444,739	643-98	
WOODEN BALL ROCK	HANCOCK	ME	254	443,491	430	
WOODFORD	BENNINGTON	VT	921	027,447	457-67	
WOODFORD CO.		IL	134	442,922	883-990	
WOODFORD CO.		KY	222	442,990	849-995	
WOODHULL	SHIAWASSEE	MI	363	443,579	175-81	
WOODHULL	STEUBEN	NY	599	444,315	473-516	
WOODLAND TWP.	CARROLL	IL	99	007,672	683-92	
WOODLAND TWP.	BARRY	MI	346	014,808	231-39	
WOODLAWN BEAT	DALLAS	AL	4	002,346	602, 628-33	
WOODS BEAT	JEFFERSON	AL	7	002,349	435-43	
WOODS PRECINCT	SUMTER	AL	15	442,866	677-88	
WOODSBORO DIST.	FREDERICK	MD	293	443,524	557-620	
WOODSFIELD	MONROE	OH	712	444,705	869-78	
WOODSTOCK	WINDHAM	CT	51	442,883	491-572	
WOODSTOCK	OXFORD	ME	263	443,500	403-427	
WOODSTOCK	LENAWEE	MI	355	443,571	27-50	
WOODSTOCK	GRAFTON	NH	431	443,635	449-58	
WOODSTOCK	ULSTER	NY	608	444,324	351-90	
WOODSTOCK	WINDSOR	VT	930	444,929	101-173	
WOODSTOCK TWP.	SCHUYLER	IL	128	442,916	781-97	
WOODSTOCK TWP.	CHAMPAIGN	OH	665	020,213	524-30	
WOODSVILLE	JEFFERSON	AR	27	002,481	192-96	
WOODVILLE	SANDUSKY	OH	726	444,719	45-76	
WOODVILLE BEAT	PERRY	AL	12	002,354	621-36	
WOODWARD TWP.	CLEARFIELD	PA	768	444,736	690-99	
WOODWARD TWP.	CLINTON	PA	768	444,736	135-46	
WOOLSEY	ESCAMBIA	FL	58	006,714	300-307	
WOOLWICH	LINCOLN	ME	261	443,498	459-94	
WOOLWICH TWP.	GLOUCESTER	NJ	451	443,650	275-352	
WOOSTER	SCOTT	IN	171	442,949	427-29	
WOOSTER	WAYNE	OH	740	444,733	445-512	
WOOSTER TWP.	WAYNE	OH	740	444,733	513-44	
WORCESTER	OTSEGO	NY	579	444,295	321-72	
WORCESTER	WASHINGTON	VT	928	444,927	451-67	
WORCESTER CO.		MD	299	443,530	329-700	
WORCESTER CO.		MA	340	443,559	1-667	
WORCESTER CO.		MA	341	443,560	669-830, 1-192	
WORCESTER CO.		MA	342	443,561	193-742	
WORCESTER CO.		MA	343	443,562	1-670	
WORCESTER CO.		MA	344	443,563	671-901, 1-242	
WORCESTER CO.		MA	345	443,564	245-796	
WORCESTER TWP.	MONTGOMERY	PA	799	444,767	531-66	
WORCESTER, WARD 1	WORCESTER	MA	342	443,561	193-236	
WORCESTER, WARD 2	WORCESTER	MA	342	443,561	237-93	
WORCESTER, WARD 3	WORCESTER	MA	342	443,561	297-353	
WORCESTER, WARD 4	WORCESTER	MA	342	443,561	361-402	

CITY, COUNTY, TOWN, OR TOWNSHIP	COUNTY	STATE	NA NO. M432	GD NO.	PAGES
WORCESTER, WARD 5	WORCESTER	MA	342	443,561	405-450
WORCESTER, WARD 6	WORCESTER	MA	342	443,561	453-516
WORCESTER, WARD 7	WORCESTER	MA	342	443,561	517-72
WORCESTER, WARD 8	WORCESTER	MA	342	443,561	573-618
WORTH	SANILAC	MI	363	443,579	37-51
WORTH	JEFFERSON	NY	516	017,092	705-712
WORTH TWP.	COOK	IL	103	007,676	9, 11-20, 53-54
WORTH TWP.	HANCOCK	IN	149	442,927	369-86
WORTH TWP.	CENTRE	PA	763	020,613	496-502
WORTH TWP.	MERCER	PA	796	444,764	853-77
WORTHINGTON	HAMPSHIRE	MA	320	443,539	45-72
WORTHINGTON	FRANKLIN	OH	680	444,673	57-68
WORTHINGTON TWP.	RICHLAND	OH	724	444,717	557-604
WRENTHAM	NORFOLK	MA	331	443,550	299-371
WRIGHT	OTTAWA	MI	361	443,577	26-38
WRIGHT	SCHOHARIE	NY	595	444,311	1-41
WRIGHT CO.		MO	421	443,629	465-543
WRIGHT TWP.	GREENE	IN	148	442,926	731-50
WRIGHT TWP.	HILLSDALE	MI	351	443,567	697-710
WRIGHT TWP.	GUERNSEY	OH	684	444,677	621-48
WRIGHTSTOWN TWP.	BUCKS	PA	758	020,608	77-97
WRIGHTSVILLE BOR.	YORK	PA	840	444,808	367-99
WYACONDAH TWP.	DAVIS	IA	182	007,791	580-88, 590-94
WYALUSING	BRADFORD	PA	757	020,607	667-98
WYANDOT CO.		OH	741	444,734	439-717
WYOCENA TWP.	COLUMBIA	WI	994	034,508	321-35
WYOCENA VILLAGE	COLUMBIA	WI	994	034,508	327-29
WYOMING	BATH	KY	191	007,844	107-9
WYOMING	KENT	MI	353	443,569	473-85
WYOMING	IOWA	WI	999	444,986	836-40
WYOMING CO.		NY	616	444,332	1-365
WYOMING CO.		NY	617	444,333	367-780
WYOMING CO.		PA	838	444,806	1-270
WYOMING CO.		VA	982	444,972	407-444
WYOMING TWP.	LEE	IL	116	007,689	271-90
WYSOX	BRADFORD	PA	757	020,607	525-52
WYSOX TWP.	CARROLL	IL	99	007,672	759-74
WYTHE CO.		VA	982	444,972	447-681
XENIA TWP.	GREENE	OH	683	444,676	1-169
YACHEY FALSE	LAFOURCHE PAR.	LA	232	443,475	568-71
YADKIN DIST	CALDWELL	NC	623	018,109	67-72, 102-111
YAHOOLA DIST.	LUMPKIN	GA	76	007,072	9-20
YALOBUSHA CO.		MS	382	443,594	753-960
YAMHILL CO.		OR	742	020,298	311-46
YANCEY CO.		NC	649	444,662	763-957
YANCEYVILLE	CASWELL	NC	623	018,109	347-54
YANKEE SPRINGS	BARRY	MI	346	014,808	178-84
YARMOUTH	CUMBERLAND	ME	249	009,719	453-504
YARMOUTH	BARNSTABLE	MA	304	014,698	505-566
YATES	ORLEANS	NY	575	444,291	553-608
YATES CO.		NY	618	444,334	1-499
YAZOO CO.		MS	382	443,594	961-1058
YELL CO.		AR	31	442,877	945-1018

CITY, COUNTY, TOWN, OR TOWNSHIP	COUNTY	STATE	NA NO. M432	GD NO.	PAGES
YELLOW CREEK	CHARITON	MO	395	443,603	387-98
YELLOW CREEK DIST.	LUMPKIN	GA	76	007,072	139-50
YELLOW CREEK TWP.	COLUMBIANA	OH	669	020,217	287-345
YELLOW SPRINGS	DELAWARE	IA	183	007,792	765-87
YEOPIM DIST.	PERQUIMANS	NC	640	444,653	735-49
YOLO CO.		CA	36	442,879	369-97
YONKERS	WESTCHESTER	NY	615	444,331	393-492
YORK	DU PAGE	IL	105	007,678	141-60
YORK	YORK	ME	274	443,511	399-470
YORK	WASHTENAW	MI	364	443,580	927-59
YORK	LIVINGSTON	NY	525	017,101	529-95
YORK	MEDINA	OH	709	444,702	817-45
YORK	SANDUSKY	OH	726	444,719	901-944
YORK	YORK	SC	860	444,823	329-532, 547-
YORK	DANE	WI	995	034,509	820-34
YORK	GREEN	WI	999	444,986	597-601
YORK BOR., NORTH WARD	YORK	PA	839	444,807	1-76
YORK BOR., SOUTH WARD	YORK	PA	839	444,807	77-174
YORK CO.		ME	274	443,511	1-516
YORK CO.		ME	275	443,512	517-723, 1-22
YORK CO.		ME	276	443,513	229-762
YORK CO.		PA	839	444,807	273-846, 1-21
YORK CO.		PA	840	444,808	221-876
YORK CO.		SC	860	444,823	329-604
YORK CO.		VA	982	444,972	685-739
YORK HAVEN	YORK	PA	840	444,808	679-82
YORK PREC.	CLARK	IL	100	007,673	468-88
YORK TWP.	DEARBORN	IN	141	007,754	761-84
YORK TWP.	ELKHART	IN	144	007,757	101-112
YORK TWP.	NOBLE	IN	162	442,940	399-412
YORK TWP.	STEUBEN	IN	173	442,951	324-35
YORK TWP.	SWITZERLAND	IN	174	442,952	937-75
YORK TWP.	ATHENS	OH	660	020,208	413-44
YORK TWP.	BELMONT	OH	661	020,209	79-110
YORK TWP.	DARKE	OH	674	020,222	929-40
YORK TWP.	FULTON	OH	681	444,674	631-50
YORK TWP.	MORGAN	OH	715	444,708	151-80
YORK TWP.	TUSCARAWAS	OH	734	444,727	1-33
YORK TWP.	UNION	OH	736	444,729	52-71
YORK TWP.	VAN WERT	OH	736	444,729	393-401
YORK TWP.	YORK	PA	839	444,807	175-219
YORKSHIRE	CATTARAUGUS	NY	480	017,056	900-947
YORKTOWN	TUOLUMNE	CA	36	442,879	187-94, 223
YORKTOWN	WESTCHESTER	NY	614	444,330	505-559
YORKVILLE	PICKENS	AL	13	442,864	1-2
YORKVILLE	YORK	SC	860	444,823	533-45
YORKVILLE	RACINE	WI	1004	444,991	256-79
YOUGHIOGHENY TWP.	FAYETTE	PA	780	444,748	949-57
YOUNG TWP.	INDIANA	PA	785	444,753	515-50
YOUNG TWP.	JEFFERSON	PA	786	444,754	151-93, 249,
YOUNGSTOWN BOR.	WESTMORELAND	PA	837	444,805	709-719
YOUNGSTOWN TWP.	MAHONING	OH	707	444,700	859-925
YOUNGSVILLE BOR.	WARREN	PA	832	444,800	667-75
YOUREO'S DIST.	RUTHERFORD	TN	894	444,850	591-612
YPSILANTI	WASHTENAW	MI	364	443,580	833-906
YUBA		CA	36	442,879	399-630
YUBA CITY	SUTTER	CA	36	442,879	105-112

CITY, COUNTY, TOWN, OR TOWNSHIP	COUNTY	STATE	NA NO. M432	GD NO.	PAGES
ZANE TWP.	LOGAN	OH	704	444,697	309-335
ZANESVILLE TWP.	MUSKINGUM	OH	717	444,710	351-541
ZANESVILLE TWP., WARD 1	MUSKINGUM	OH	717	444,710	351-96
ZANESVILLE TWP., WARD 2	MUSKINGUM	OH	717	444,710	397-441
ZANESVILLE TWP., WARD 3	MUSKINGUM	OH	717	444,710	443-86
ZANESVILLE TWP., WARD 4	MUSKINGUM	OH	717	444,710	487-541
ZELIENOPLE	BUTLER	PA	760	020,610	321-28
ZOAR	TUSCARAWAS	OH	734	444,727	400-405
ZODIAC	GILLESPIE	TX	910	024,889	629-32
ZODIAC MILLS	GILLESPIE	TX	910	024,889	603